Handbook of Oil Politics

Handbook of Oil Politics

Editor: Robert E. Looney

LONDON AND NEW YORK

First edition published 2012
by Routledge
2 Park Square, Milton Park, Abingdon, Oxfordshire OX14 4RN

Simultaneously published in the USA and Canada
by Routledge
711 Third Avenue, New York, NY 10017

First issued in paperback 2015

Routledge is an imprint of the Taylor & Francis Group, an informa business

© 2012 Routledge

The right of the editor to be identified as the author of the editorial material, and of the authors for their individual chapters, has been asserted in accordance with sections 77 and 78 of the Copyright, Designs and Patents Act 1988.

All rights reserved. No part of this book may be reprinted or reproduced or utilised in any form or by any electronic, mechanical, or other means, now known or hereafter invented, including photocopying and recording, or in any information storage or retrieval system, without permission in writing from the publishers.

Trademark notice: Product or corporate names may be trademarks or registered trademarks, and are used only for identification and explanation without intent to infringe.

Library of Congress Cataloging in Publication Data
Handbook of oil politics / editor, Robert E. Looney.
p. cm.
Includes bibliographical references and index.
ISBN 978-1-85743-583-2 (hb) – ISBN 978-0-203-85101-2 (ebook)
1. Petroleum industry and trade – Political aspects. I. Looney, Robert E.
HD9560.6.H27 2011
338.2'728 – dc22
2011014011

ISBN 13: 978-1-857-43808-6 (pbk)
ISBN 13: 978-1-85743-583-2 (hbk)

Typeset in Bembo
by Taylor & Francis Books

Editor Europa New Projects: Cathy Hartley

For Ginny
Thanks for the magical times we shared

Contents

List of Illustrations	x
Preface	xii
The Editor and Contributors	xiv
Abbreviations	xxiv

PART I
Politics of Oil Supply   1

1 Introduction   3
   Robert Looney

2 Key Issues Surrounding the Supply of Oil   10
   Paul Sullivan

3 The Changing Geopolitics of Oil   30
   Michael T. Klare

4 Politics of Oil Supply: National Oil Companies vs. International Oil Companies   45
   Jean-François Seznec

5 The Policy Implications of Peak Oil   60
   Laurel Graefe

6 Conflict and Instability   73
   Michael Ross

7 Co-operation Between Producers and Consumers   79
   Paul Stevens

8 Global Oil Markets: The Need for Reforms   90
   Giacomo Luciani

Contents

PART II
Political Responses — 107

9   Energy Security — 109
    Daniel Moran

10 Strategy, Foreign Policy and Climate Change: The Middle East in the Cross Hairs — 121
    James A. Russell

11 Do Governments Need to Go to War for Oil? — 135
    David R. Henderson

PART III
Oil and Political Power: Regional Dimensions — 147

12 Oil Rents and Political Power in Africa — 149
    Jessica Piombo

13 Oil Rents and Political Power in Latin America — 168
    Sidney Weintraub

14 Oil Rents, Political and Military Policies, and the Fallout: Implications for the MENA oil economies — 180
    Hossein Askari

15 Oil and Power in the Caspian Region — 191
    Richard Pomfret

16 Oil and Politics in Southeast Asia — 206
    Benjamin Smith

PART IV
Country Case Studies — 219

17 United States: The Politics of Alternative Energy — 221
    Alan Reynolds

18 Beyond the Oil Curse: Iraq's Wealthy State and Poor Society — 249
    Abbas Kadhim

19 Government Policy and Evolution of the Iranian Oil Industry — 262
    Farrokh Najmabadi

20	The Enduring Saudi Oil Power *Joseph A. Kéchichian*	284
21	Gas and Oil in Egypt's Development *Robert Springborg*	295
22	Oil and the Russian Economy *Philip Hanson*	312
23	An Oil Giant From the Emerging World: Petrobras *Flavia Carvalho*	325

PART V
Key Issues for the Future — 335

24	The Oil Curse: Causes, Consequences, and Policy Implications *Richard Auty*	337
25	Challenges in Global Oil Governance *Andreas Goldthau*	349
26	Sovereign Wealth Funds in the Gulf: Opportunities and Challenges *Gawdat Bahgat*	362
27	Oil, the Dollar, and the Stability of the International Financial System *Eckart Woertz*	375
28	China's Impact on Oil Markets *John Calabrese*	401
29	The Future of Oil in a Carbon Constrained World *Daniel J. A. Johansson, Fredrik Hedenus and Thomas Sterner*	415

Index — 435

Illustrations

Tables

10.1	Fresh water availability in Middle East/Gulf states	123
10.2	Historic and projected population in Middle East states	125
10.3	Gulf state ecological and carbon footprint per person, 2003	127
10.4	Middle East environmental vulnerability snapshot	128
11.1	Top 15 sources of US oil imports, August 2010	138
12.1	Top crude petroleum exporters in Africa	151
12.2	Petroleum refinery output in Africa	152
12.3	Oil dependence in African exporters, 2002	153
12.4	Governance in African oil exporters	158
12.5	Natural resources and governance in African countries, 2006	159
15.1	Production of crude oil and natural gas, Azerbaijan, Kazakhstan, Turkmenistan and Uzbekistan, 1985–2009	192
15.2	Demographic data, output and income, 1990–1 and 2007	193
15.3	Inward foreign direct investment, 1992–2008 (US$m.)	195
15.4	Growth in real GDP 1989–2008	197
16.1	Governance and political freedom scores, 2008	212
16.2	Oil and politics in Southeast Asia, 1990–2008	213
17.1	US crude oil imports	242
17.2	OPEC's real oil export revenues	243
17.3	US crude oil imports and average price per barrel of imported crude oil	244
19.1	Iranian oil and gas statistics (1973–78)	263
19.2	Gas Reinjection Programme in bcm/year	265
19.3	Iranian oil and gas statistics (1980–88)	267
19.4	Productivity of major Iranian oil fields	276
19.5	Petroleum product consumption (2001–09)	279
22.1	Russian government projections of production, domestic consumption, import and export of main fuels, annual totals in mn tons of standard fuel, 2008 actual 2030 projected	319
22.2	Scale of Russia's total fixed investment, equipment investment, equipment imports, and IFDI creating new capital, 2008, $bn	320
22.3	Sectoral composition of Russia's IFDI, 2009	320
23.1	Petrobras – corporate information, 2009	326
24.1	Share of rents in GDP 1994 and GDP growth 1985–97, by country natural resource endowment	338

24.2	GDP growth per head, MENA and other developing regions, 1961–2008	341
26.1	Portfolio overview by asset class	371
26.2	Portfolio overview by region	371
27.1	Total long-term and short-term US assets held by foreigners, US$m	387
27.2	Net liabilities to foreigners of US banking system, June 2009, US$m	388
27.3	Selected oil funds, assets, US$bn	388
27.4	Current account balances world 1980–2014, annual five year averages	396
29.1	The decline in demand for oil for three different CO_2 prices. In the calculations an untaxed world market price of oil of US$100 per barrel was assumed together with a long-run elasticity of -0.4	425

Figures

4.1	Possible money flows in Saudi oil transactions 2010	48
4.2	Generic oil money flows for NOCs/per 1 million b/d	51
8.1	Production cost of hydrocarbon reserves	93
10.1	Trends in Saudi grain production	124
13.1	Mexican total oil production, 1995–2010	169
13.2	Mexican imports of dry natural gas, 1995–2009	170
13.3	Venezuela oil production, 1995–2010	171
13.4	Bolivian exports of dry natural gas, 2000–09	173
13.5	Brazilian oil production, 2000–10	174
13.6	Natural gas imports in Argentina, 2000–09	176
13.7	Colombian total oil production, 1995–2010	177
16.1	Oil income and governance	216
22.1	Russia: GDP and the oil price 1998–2010	313
22.2	The development of Russian production and domestic consumption of oil, 2000–2009	314
22.3	The effects of a falling oil price? % change, year-on-year, 2009, Russia and other major oil-exporting nations	315
22.4	Energy efficiency: Russia and selected other nations, 2007	316
23.1	Petrobras: social capital composition, 2009	327
24.1	Low Rent Competitive Industrialization Development Model	340
24.2	High Rent Competitive Industrialization Development Model	340
27.1	OPEC net oil export revenues	382
27.2	Global imbalances 1980s and 1990s	383
27.3	Global imbalances in the 2000s	384
27.4	Current accounts of oil net exporters, 2010	385
29.1	Proven reserves and estimated additional recoverable resources of different fossil fuels, compared to cumulative emissions of CO_2 compatible with climate targets of 2 or 3°C above the pre-industrial level	420
29.2	A global energy supply scenario following an emissions path that limits cumulative carbon emissions to 550Gtons	421
29.3	Primary fossil fuel supply in baseline scenario compared to a stabilization of 550Gtons carbon of cumulative emissions.	422
29.4	Life-cycle CO_2-equivalent emissions for different liquid fuels	423

Preface

These days, one would have a difficult time picking up a newspaper, or watching a newscast that did not have a lead story dealing with some aspect of oil. From instability in the Middle East, to stock market crashes and concerns over the health of the world economy, to wars that seem to break out unexpectedly around the world, to discussions of global warming, and even speculation over the fate of mankind, oil is usually lurking somewhere in the background.

To many, oil markets and their linkages to a whole spectrum of events remain something of a mystery. Unfortunately, most of the easily obtained information on oil is deeply flawed. Whole web-conspiracy sites depict ruthless insiders and reckless dictators manipulating energy markets at will. The 29 essays in this volume, written by the leading experts in the field, attempt to set the record straight. While their assessments may lack the sensationalism of many popular pundits, serious readers will find their insights invaluable in the years to come in providing a framework for understanding many of the events of the day.

The volume is divided into sections. Part I provides a broad overview of the political dimensions underlying the supply of oil. Some of the key questions addressed include: is the world running out of oil? And if so, is the cause physical scarcity or political/policy failure? Why are many of the oil-producing countries in the developing world so unstable? Can oil markets be made to provide more stability to the world system? Part II examines some of the political responses to oil-related developments. Here, the key questions concern the role of the political process in the development of alternative sources of energy. The various means through which countries approach their energy security are assessed, as is the problem of climate change. The section ends with the provocative question, do governments really need to go to war for oil?

Oil production, energy markets, and the political environment produce distinct regional patterns. Part III examines oil and political power in Africa, Latin America, the Middle East and Southeast Asia. Part IV expands some of the main regional themes through a series of case studies on specific countries: Iraq, Iran, Saudi Arabia, Egypt, Russia and Brazil. A final section looks to the future: will the oil curse continue for many countries? How will the growth and expansion of China affect oil prices and availabilities? Will oil-based sovereign wealth funds contribute to global stability or will they create increased political tensions between consuming and producing countries? Will volatile oil markets undermine the US dollar as well as the global financial system? Perhaps appropriately, the volume ends with an assessment of the future of oil in a carbon constrained world.

All in all, the essays in this volume cover the whole spectrum of the politics of oil. Hopefully they will help shed light on this vital, yet still often misunderstood topic. The book does not represent any particular political or ideological position. Instead, each author has sought to objectively seek a deeper understanding as to the complexity and subtlety of forces that have all too often eluded policymakers around the world.

Clearly a book of this scope and sheer length could not have come to completion without the contributions of many individuals. In addition to the volume's many contributors, special thanks go to my colleagues at the Naval Postgraduate School – Bob Springborg, Daniel Moran, Jessica Piombo, James Russell and David Henderson, whose help and encouragement proved invaluable. Greta E. Marlatt of the Naval Postgraduate School Knox Library went far beyond the call of duty to keep me informed of the latest oil developments throughout the course of the manuscript – a task only she could perform. Most of all, thanks go to Cathy Hartley, Editor Europa New Projects who conceived of the original study, provided on-going guidance and most importantly provided good cheer and positive encouragement throughout.

Robert E. Looney
April 2011

The Editor and Contributors

Robert E. Looney is a Distinguished Professor at the Naval Postgraduate School, Monterey, California. He received his PhD in Economics from the University of California, Davis. He specializes in issues relating to economic development in the Middle East, East Asia, South Asia, and Latin America. He has published twenty-two books, including: *Economic Development in Saudi Arabia: Consequences of the Oil Price Decline* with a Foreword by Raymond Mikesell (Greenwich, CT: JAI Press, 1990); *The Economics of Third World Defense Expenditures* with a Foreword by Charles Wolf (Greenwich CT: JAI Press, 1995); *The Pakistani Economy: Economic Growth and Structural Reform* (Praeger Publishers, 1997); and *Iraq's Informal Economy: Reflections of War, Sanctions and Policy Failure* (Abu Dhabi: The Emirates Center for Strategic Studies and Research 2007); and as editor, *Handbook of US-Middle East Relations* (London: Routledge, 2009). He is currently working on a book assessing alternative futures for the Pakistani economy.

Dr Looney is on the board of editors of *International Journal on World Peace* and *Journal of Third World Studies*. In addition, he has over 250 articles appearing in numerous professional journals including: *World Economics, Journal of Development Economics, Middle East Policy, Middle Eastern Studies, Orient, OPEC Review, Middle East Journal, Economic Development and Cultural Change, Journal of Energy and Development, Development Policy Review, American-Arab Affairs, Iranian Studies, Challenge, World Development, Pakistan Development Review, Modern African Studies, Asian Survey, International Organization, Mediterranean Quarterly, South Asia, Economia Internationale, Journal of Economic Development, Journal of South Asian and Middle Eastern Studies, The National Interest* and *Contemporary South Asia*. As an international consultant, Dr Looney has provided advice and assistance to the governments of Iran, Saudi Arabia, Japan, Mexico, Panama and Jamaica as well as the World Bank, International Labor Office, Inter-American Development Bank, Stanford Research Institute, Rand Organization and the International Monetary Fund.

Hossein Askari is Iran Professor of International Business and International Affairs at the George Washington University. He served for two and a half years on the Executive Board of the International Monetary Fund (IMF) and was Special Adviser to the Minister of Finance of Saudi Arabia; he developed the idea for a special Quota increase for Saudi Arabia to have its own seat on the Board. During the mid-1980s he was director of the team that developed the first comprehensive domestic, regional and international energy models and plan for Saudi Arabia. He has written extensively on economic development in the Middle East, Islamic economics and finance, international trade and finance, agricultural economics, oil economics and on economic sanctions. During 1990–91 he was asked by the governments of Iran and Saudi

Arabia to act as an intermediary to restore diplomatic relations; and in 1992 he was asked by the Emir of Kuwait to mediate with Iran.

Richard Auty is Professor Emeritus of Economic Geography at Lancaster University. He has advised many multi- and bilateral agencies on economic development issues. His research interests include industrial policy, resource-driven development and the political economy of economic development. Recent books include: *Energy Wealth and Governance in the Caucasus and Central Asia* (London: Routledge, 2006), *Resource Abundance and Economic Development* (Oxford: Oxford University Press, 2004); *Sustainable Development in Mineral Economies* (Oxford: Oxford University Press, 1998); and *Patterns of Development: Resource Endowment, Development Policy and Economic Growth* (Edward Arnold, 1995).

Gawdat Bahgat is on the faculty of the National Defense University's Center for Strategic Studies, Near East and South Asia (NESA). Before joining NESA, Dr Bahgat was director of the Center for Middle Eastern Studies at Indiana University of Pennsylvania. For 20 years, he has taught political science and international relations in several universities. His areas of expertise include energy security, counter-terrorism, proliferation of weapons of mass destruction, International political economy, the Middle East, Caspian Sea/Central Asia, and US foreign policy.

Dr Bahgat is the author of six books and about 200 scholarly articles. His work has been translated into several foreign languages. Dr Bahgat has presented papers at conferences in Australia, Europe and the Middle East. He is a frequent contributor to media outlets including Voice of America and the *Wall Street Journal*. He holds a PhD in Political Science, Florida State University 1991, an MA in Middle Eastern Studies, American University in Cairo 1985, and a BA in Political Science, Cairo University, 1977. His most recent book, *Energy Security: An Interdisciplinary Approach*, was published by Wiley in 2011.

John Calabrese teaches US foreign policy at American University. He is also a Scholar in Residence at the Middle East Institute, General Series Editor of *MEI Viewpoints*, and Book Review Editor of the *Middle East Journal*. He earned his PhD in International Relations from the London School of Economics.

Flavia Carvalho, PhD in Innovation Studies and Development at UNU-MERIT (Netherlands) is a researcher at the Center of Innovation Studies at Fundação Dom Cabral, Belo Horizonte, Brazil. Research interests include innovation, internationalization and their influences on the development of nations. Current research project: Eco-innovations in Brazil.

Andreas Goldthau is Associate Professor at the Department of Public Policy of Central European University (CEU), an American graduate school based in Budapest, Hungary. He is also a Fellow with the Global Public Policy Institute (Berlin/Geneva), co-heading the Institute's Global Energy Governance programme. Having worked for thinks tanks such as the RAND Corporation before joining CEU, Dr Goldthau combines experience in both academia and applied policy research. His academic interests focus on energy security and on global governance issues related to oil and gas. Recent books authored or edited by Dr Goldthau comprise *Dynamics of Energy Governance in Europe and Russia* (Palgrave, 2011), *Global Energy Governance. The New Rules of the Game* (Brookings Press, 2010), *Imported Oil and National Security* (RAND, 2009) and *OPEC. Macht und Ohnmacht des Oelkartells* (Hanser, 2009). Dr Goldthau is a frequent contributor to the media on energy issues.

The Editor and Contributors

Laurel Graefe is a Senior Economic Policy Specialist in the research department at the Federal Reserve Bank of Atlanta. In this capacity, Ms Graefe directs inflation and energy market analysis for the research department and supports the Atlanta Fed's president and directors' assessment of macroeconomic conditions. Her work on inflation has been cited in numerous business publications, including the *Wall Street Journal* and *The Economist* online and she recently published a discussion of long-term energy supply dynamics in the Atlanta Fed's Economic Review, *The Peak Oil Debate*. Ms Graefe graduated from Agnes Scott College with a degree in economics.

Philip Hanson is an Emeritus Professor of Birmingham University and was formerly Director of its Centre for Russian and East European Studies. He is currently an associate fellow of the Russia and Eurasia programme at Chatham House. He learnt Russian in the British army, has a BA in Economics from Cambridge University and a PhD from Birmingham University. He has worked at the UK Treasury, the UK Foreign and Commonwealth Office, the UN Economic Commission for Europe and Radio Liberty, and been a visiting professor at the universities of Michigan, Harvard, Kyoto and Sodertoerns (Stockholm). His books include *Trade and Technology in Soviet-Western Relations* (1981), *Economic Change in Russian Regions* (co-edited with Michael Bradshaw, 2000) and *The Rise and Fall of the Soviet Economy* (2003). He has published many papers in academic journals and occasional opinion-piece articles (including in *The Times* and the *Financial Times*).

Fredrik Hedenus is an Assistant Professor at Physical Resource Theory, Department of Energy and Environment, Chalmers University of Technology. Hedenus has conducted research within the fields of energy system modeling, energy security and climate mitigation strategies. He has published more than a dozen journal articles, reports and book chapters on these topics. His present research focus is in technology assessment of energy technologies. He also teaches on sustainable development, energy system models and nuclear energy at the undergraduate as well as the graduate level.

David R. Henderson is a research fellow with the Hoover Institution. He is also an Associate Professor of Economics at the Naval Postgraduate School in Monterey, California. He is the editor of *The Fortune Encyclopedia of Economics* (Warner Books, 1993), a book that communicates to a general audience what and how economists think. The *Wall Street Journal* commented, "His brainchild is a tribute to the power of the short, declarative sentence." The encyclopedia went through three printings and was translated into Spanish. Henderson also writes frequently for the *Wall Street Journal* and *Fortune*, and was a monthly columnist with *Red Herring*, an information technology magazine.

Dr Henderson has been on the faculty of the Naval Postgraduate School since 1984 and a research fellow with Hoover since 1990. He was the John M. Olin Visiting Professor with the Center for the Study of American Business at Washington University in St Louis in 1994; a senior economist for energy and health policy with the President's Council of Economic Advisers from 1982–84; a visiting professor at the University of Santa Clara from 1980–81; a senior policy analyst with the Cato Institute from 1979–80; and an assistant professor at the University of Rochester's Graduate School of Management from 1975–79.

Daniel J. A. Johansson is an Assistant Professor at the Division of Physical Resource Theory, Department of Energy and Environment, Chalmers University of Technology. He has previously held positions as a Research Fellow at the Environmental Economics Unit, Department of Economics at the University of Gothenburg and as a Guest Research Scholar at the International Institute of Applied Systems Analysis (IIASA) in Austria. His main research interests are related to energy and climate change economics and policy. Within this field he does research about integrated energy economy climate modeling and climate change policies and its impact on long-term energy markets. He has published more than a dozen journal articles and book chapters on these topics. He teaches in various courses on climate, energy and economy related issues both at the undergraduate and graduate level.

Abbas Kadhim is an Assistant Professor of National Security Affairs at the Naval Postgraduate School in Monterey, California. He also holds Visiting Scholar status at Stanford University, a position he has held since 2005. Between 2003 and 2005 he taught courses on Islamic theology and ethics at the Graduate Theological Union in Berkeley, California. From 2001–5 he was an Instructor of Arabic language at the University of California, Berkeley. From 1999–2001 he taught Political Science at the Woodland Community College, Woodland, California. Professor Kadhim is a member of the editorial board of *History Compass*.

Among the awards he has received are the Dean's Normative Time Award (Fall 2004 and Spring 2005), University of California, Berkeley; Best Paper Published in an Academic Journal, awarded by the Center for Middle Eastern Studies, University of California, Berkeley for "The Mysterious Journey of Moses (Q. 18:60–82): Does It Refute or Confirm the Shi'i Doctrine of 'Ismah'?", *International Journal of Shi'i Studies* 2, No. 1 (Fall 2004): 97–119; Best Article Published in the Popular Press, awarded by the Center for Middle Eastern Studies, University of California, Berkeley for "Official US Reaction Compounds the Rage", an opinion-piece article on the Abu Ghraib Prison scandal, published by the *Los Angeles Times*, 9 May 2004; Graduate Division Summer Grant (Summer 2005), University of California, Berkeley; the Sultan bin Abdul Aziz Fellowship (Fall 2005 and Spring 2006), University of California, Berkeley; and he currently holds the 2009 Fellowship of The American Academic Research Institute in Iraq (TAARI).

Joseph A. Kéchichian is the CEO of Kéchichian & Associates, LLC, a consulting partnership that provides analysis on the Arabian/Persian Gulf region, specializing in the domestic and regional concerns of Bahrain, Iran, Iraq, Kuwait, Oman, Qatar, Saudi Arabia, the United Arab Emirates and the Yemen, as well as the Honorary Consul of the Sultanate of Oman in Los Angeles, California. Dr Kéchichian received his doctorate in Foreign Affairs from the University of Virginia in 1985, where he also taught (1986–88) and assumed the assistant deanship in international studies (1988–89). In the summer of 1989 he was a Hoover Fellow at Stanford University (under the US State Department Title VIII Program). Between 1990 and 1996, he was an Associate Political Scientist at the Santa Monica-based RAND Corporation, and a lecturer at the University of California in Los Angeles.

Between 1998 and 2001, Dr Kéchichian was a fellow at UCLA's Gustav E. von Grunebaum Center for Near Eastern Studies, where he held a Smith Richardson Foundation grant (1998–99) to compose *Succession in Saudi Arabia* (New York: Palgrave, 2001) and *Beirut and London: Dar Al Saqi*, 2002, 2003 (2nd edn – for the Arabic translation). He published *Political Participation and Stability in the Sultanate of Oman* (Dubai: Gulf Research Center, 2005), *Oman and the World: The Emergence of an Independent Foreign Policy* (Santa Monica: RAND, 1995), and edited *A Century in Thirty Years: Shaykh Zayed and the United Arab Emirates* (Washington, DC: The Middle East Policy Council 2000), as well as *Iran, Iraq, and the Arab Gulf States* (New York: Palgrave, 2001). In 2003 he co-authored (with R. Hrair Dekmejian) *The Just Prince: A Manual of Leadership* (London: Saqi Books), that includes a full translation of the *Sulwan al-Muta'* by

The Editor and Contributors

Muhammad Ibn Zafar al-Siqilli. In 2008 he published two new volumes, *Power and Succession in Arab Monarchies* (Boulder: Lynne Rienner) and *Faysal: Saudi Arabia's King for All Seasons* (Gainesville: University Press of Florida), and is currently composing a companion volume to the latter study, on the late Queen Effat Al Thunayan of Saudi Arabia. His book, *Political and Legal Reforms in Saudi Arabia*, is planned for publication in early 2012. A frequent traveller to the Gulf region, Dr Kéchichian is fluent in Arabic, Armenian, English, French, Italian and Turkish, and is learning Persian.

Michael T. Klare is the Five College Professor of Peace and World Security Studies (a joint appointment at Amherst College, Hampshire College, Mount Holyoke College, Smith College and the University of Massachusetts at Amherst), and Director of the Five College Program in Peace and World Security Studies (PAWSS), a position he has held since 1985. Before assuming his present post, he served as Director of the Program on Militarism and Disarmament at the Institute for Policy Studies in Washington, DC (1977–84).

Professor Klare has written widely on US defence policy, the arms trade and world security affairs. He is the author of: *Blood and Oil: The Dangers and Consequences of America's Growing Dependency on Imported Petroleum* (Metropolitan Books, 2004); *Resource Wars: The New Landscape of Global Conflict* (Metropolitan Books, 2001); *Rogue States and Nuclear Outlaws* (Hill and Wang, 1995); *American Arms Supermarket* (University of Texas Press, 1984); *Supplying Repression* (Field Foundation, 1978; 2nd ed., Institute for Policy Studies, 1981); and *War Without End: American Planning for the Next Vietnams* (Knopf, 1974). In addition, he is the editor or co-editor of *Light Weapons and Civil Conflict: Controlling the Tools of Violence* (Rowman and Littlefield, 1999); *World Security: Challenges for a New Century* (1st edition, 1991; 2nd edition, 1994; 3rd edition, 1998); *Peace and World Security Studies: A Curriculum Guide* (5th edition, 1989; 6th edition, 1994); *Lethal Commerce: The Global Trade in Small Arms and Light Weapons* (American Academy of Arts and Sciences, 1995); and *Low-Intensity Warfare* (Pantheon, 1988). Professor Klare is also the defence correspondent of *The Nation* and a Contributing Editor of *Current History*. He has contributed articles to the two aforementioned journals and to *Arms Control Today*, *Foreign Affairs*, *Foreign Policy*, *Harper's*, *International Security*, *Issues in Science and Technology*, *Journal of International Affairs*, *Le Monde Diplomatique*, *Mother Jones*, *Scientific American*, *Technology Review*, *Third World Quarterly*, and *World Policy Journal*.

Giacomo Luciani is the scientific director of the Master in International Energy, Paris School of International Affairs of Sciences-Po. He is a co-director of an Executive Master program in Oil and Gas Leadership at the Graduate Institute of International and Development Studies in Geneva, and a Princeton University Global Scholar, at Princeton's Woodrow Wilson School and Near Eastern Studies Department. He has been the Director of the Gulf Research Center Foundation (Geneva), Professorial Lecturer of Middle Eastern Studies at the SAIS Johns Hopkins University Bologna Centre and Visiting Professor, Graduate Institute of International and Development Studies (Geneva). Professor Luciani's career has been marked by repeated "trespassing" between academia, industry and government. He was an economist at the Bank of Italy (1972–74), founded and directed the Institute for Research on International Economics (IRECI) and worked for the Italian Institute of International Affairs (1977–86). From 1990 to 2000 he worked for ENI, the Italian Oil Company. He has taught at University of California, Los Angeles (1986–88), the Institut d'Etudes Politiques in Paris (1994–97), the Robert Schuman Centre of Advanced Studies at the European University Institute in Florence (2000–2006), and the College of Europe (2007–8). He has consulted for various international organizations, companies and Gulf governments. His research interests include political economy of the

Middle East and North Africa and geopolitics of energy. His work has focused primarily on the economic and political dynamics of rentier states and issues of development in the Gulf Co-operation Council countries.

Daniel Moran is Professor of International and Military History in the Department of National Security Affairs at the Naval Postgraduate School in Monterey, California. He was educated at Yale and Stanford Universities, and has been a member of the Institute for Advanced Study at Princeton, and professor of strategy at the Naval War College in Newport, Rhode Island. Professor Moran teaches and writes about strategic theory, American foreign relations, environmental and energy security, and the modern history of Europe and the Middle East. He is the author or editor of numerous books and articles in these fields, including most recently *Climate Change and National Security* (Georgetown University Press, 2011).

Farrokh Najmabadi is a former Iranian Minister of Mines and Industry and a former Deputy Chairman and Managing Director of the National Iranian Oil Company. After the Iranian Revolution he worked with the World Bank until 1995, when he retired.

Jessica Piombo is an Associate Professor in the Department of National Security Affairs at the Naval Postgraduate School, where she teaches courses on African politics, US Foreign Policy, comparative politics, and ethnic politics and conflicts. Piombo has been a visiting scholar at the Centre for Social Science Research and the African Studies Centre of the University of Cape Town, and the Center for African Studies at Stanford University. Her teaching and research specializes on political transitions, transitional regimes and post-conflict governance; institutional ways to channel and shape political identities; mechanisms to manage ethnic conflict; terrorism and countering terrorism in Africa; and the US military's role in reconstruction and stabilization. Dr Piombo is the author of *Institutions, Ethnicity and Political Mobilization in South Africa* (Palgrave Macmillan, 2009), editor of *Interim Governments: Institutional Bridges to Peace and Democracy?* (with Karen Guttieri, USIP Press, 2007) and editor of *Electoral Politics in South Africa: Assessing the First Democratic Decade* (with Lia Nijzink, Palgrave Macmillan, 2005). She has authored numerous articles, reports and book chapters on security, counter-terrorism and democratization in Africa. Piombo has conducted extensive research in South Africa, has monitored elections in South Africa and Nigeria (as part of the delegation of the International Republican Institute for the April 2007 elections), and conducted research in Ethiopia, Kenya and Djibouti.

Richard Pomfret is Professor of Economics at Adelaide University, and in 2010–11 Visiting Professor of Economics at the Johns Hopkins University School of Advanced International Studies in Bologna (Italy). He has also worked at universities in Canada, China, Germany and the USA. In 1993 he was seconded to the United Nations for a year, acting as adviser on macroeconomic policy to the Central Asian republics of the former Soviet Union. He has also acted as a consultant to the European Union, World Bank, UNDP, OECD and Asian Development Bank. He has published over one hundred articles and 17 books, including *The Central Asian Economies since Independence* (Princeton UP, 2006).

Alan Reynolds is an economist and Senior Fellow at the Cato Institute. He was formerly Director of Economic Research at the Hudson Institute and vice-president and chief economist at the First National Bank of Chicago. Reynolds served on President Reagan's transition team in 1981 (working on tax and budget policy), as Research Director with Jack Kemp's National Commission on Tax Reform and Economic Growth in 1996, and was commissioned to prepare one of the expert background papers for the National Commission on the Cost of Higher Education in 1997. Author of a textbook on *Income and Wealth* (2006), *The Microsoft Antitrust Appeal* (2001) and chapters in several anthologies, Reynolds' research has been published by such diverse groups as the OECD, the Joint Economic Committee, the Federal Reserve Banks of Atlanta and St Louis, the Philanthropy Roundtable and the Australian Stock Exchange. A former columnist with *Forbes* and Creators Syndicate, Reynolds has written for numerous publications including the *Energy Journal*, the *Georgetown Journal on Poverty Law and Policy*, the *Wall Street Journal*, *Fortune* and the *Harvard Business Review*.

Michael L. Ross is Professor of Political Science at the University of California, Los Angeles, and Director of the Center for Southeast Asian Studies, and the author of *The Oil Curse: how petroleum wealth shapes the development of nations* (Princeton University Press, 2012). He has served on advisory boards for the Revenue Watch Institute and the World Bank, and is a member of the Technical Group for the Natural Resource Charter. He has published widely on the political and economic problems of resource-rich countries. His article "Oil, Islam, and Women" received the 2009 Heinz Eulau Award from the American Political Science Association for the best article published in the *American Political Science Review*.

James A. Russell serves as Associate Professor in the Department of National Security Affairs at the Naval Postgraduate School, where he teaches courses on Middle East security affairs, terrorism and national security strategy. His articles and commentaries have appeared in a wide variety of media and scholarly outlets around the world. His commentaries have appeared in the *Philadelphia Inquirer* and the *San Jose Mercury News* and he has been interviewed as a subject matter expert on NPR's *All Things Considered* and *Newsweek*'s 'On Air' series. His latest articles are: 'Strategic Stability Reconsidered: Prospects for Escalation and Nuclear War in the Middle East', *IFRI Proliferation Papers*, Spring 2009; 'Illicit Procurement Networks and Nuclear Proliferation: Challenges for Intelligence, Detection, and Interdiction' (with Jack Boureston), *St. Anthony's International Review* 4, No. 2, Spring 2009. His latest book (edited with Daniel Moran) is *Energy Security and Global Politics: The Militarization of Resource Management* (New York: Routledge, 2009).

From 1988–2001, Mr Russell held a variety of positions in the Office of the Assistant Secretary Defense for International Security Affairs, Near East South Asia, Department of Defense. During this period he travelled extensively in the Persian Gulf and Middle East working on US security policy. He holds a Master's in Public and International Affairs from the University of Pittsburgh and a PhD in War Studies from the University of London.

Jean-François Seznec is Visiting Associate Professor at Georgetown University's Center for Contemporary Arab Studies. His research centres on the influence of the Arab-Persian Gulf political and social variables on the financial and oil markets in the region. He is focusing on the industrialization of the Gulf and in particular the growth of the petrochemical industry. He is Senior Advisor to PFC Energy in Washington, DC. He holds an MIA from Columbia University (1973), an MA and PhD from Yale University (1994). He has published and lectured extensively on petrochemicals and energy-based industries in the Gulf and their importance in world trade. He is interviewed regularly on national TV, radio and newspapers, as well as by the foreign media.

Dr Seznec has 25 years' experience in international banking and finance of which ten years were spent in the Middle East, including two years in Riyadh at SIDF and six years in Bahrain covering Saudi Arabia. Dr Seznec is a founding member and Managing Partner of the Lafayette

Group LLC, a US-based private investment company. He uses his knowledge of business in the Middle East and the USA to further his analysis of the Arab-Persian Gulf.

Benjamin Smith (PhD University of Washington 2002) is Associate Professor at the University of Florida where he teaches undergraduate courses in comparative and Asian politics, ethnicity and nationalism, post-conflict peace-building and the politics of modernity, and graduate courses on ethnicity and nationalism and research design. His first book, *Hard Times in the Land of Plenty: Oil Politics in Iran and Indonesia*, was published in 2007 by Cornell University Press. Dr Smith's research has been published in *World Politics*, the *American Journal of Political Science*, *Studies in Comparative International Development*, the *Journal of International Affairs*, and other journals and edited volumes. From 2002 to 2004 he was an Academy Scholar at the Harvard Academy for International and Area Studies. Dr Smith's research focuses on separatist conflicts, regime change and democratization, and on the politics of resource wealth. Smith is currently working on a book exploring the long-term factors that shape the success of separatist movements, as well as several article-length projects on redistribution and democratic breakdown (with Dan Slater) and on the politics of oil wealth in South-East Asia and elsewhere.

Robert Springborg is a Professor in the Department of National Security Affairs of the Naval Postgraduate School, and Program Manager for the Middle East, Center for Civil-Military Relations. Until August 2008 he held the MBI Al Jaber Chair in Middle East Studies at the School of Oriental and African Studies in London, where he also served as Director of the London Middle East Institute. Prior to this he was Director of the American Research Center in Egypt. From 1973–99 he taught in Australia, where he was University Professor of Middle East Politics at Macquarie University. He has also taught at the University of California, Berkeley, at the University of Pennsylvania and elsewhere.

Professor Springborg's publications include: *Mubarak's Egypt: Fragmentation of the Political Order*; *Family Power and Politics in Egypt*; *Legislative Politics in the Arab World* (co-authored with Abdo Baaklini and Guilain Denoeux); *Globalization and the Politics of Development in the Middle East* (co-authored with Clement M. Henry); *Oil and Democracy in Iraq*; *Development Models in Muslim Contexts: Chinese, 'Islamic' and Neo-Liberal Alternatives*; and several editions of *Politics in the Middle East* (co-authored with James A. Bill). He co-edited a volume on popular culture and political identity in the Gulf that appeared in 2008. He has published in the leading Middle East journals and was the founder and regular editorialist for the *Middle East* in London, a monthly journal that commenced publication in 2003. He has worked as a consultant on Middle East governance and politics for the United States Agency for International Development, the US State Department, the UNDP, and various United Kingdom government departments, including the Foreign and Commonwealth Office, the Ministry of Defence and the Department for International Development.

Thomas Sterner is a Professor of Environmental Economics at the University of Gothenburg in Sweden and a University Fellow of Resources for the Future, Washington DC. He is the Past President of the European Association of Environmental and Resource Economists (2010–11). He teaches various advanced economics courses both at the undergraduate and graduate levels in Gothenburg and in other universities. He has advised more than 20 PhD students and built up a research group consisting of four full professors and a total of more than a dozen senior researchers in Gothenburg. His primary research areas include issues concerning environment, resources, poverty and development. Much of his work is focused on the design of policy instruments to deal with climate change and other environmental threats to the ecosystems on which we depend. He has published more than a dozen books and over 60 journal articles.

Paul Stevens holds an Emeritus Chair at the Centre for Energy, Petroleum and Mineral Law and Policy (CEPMLP). He is currently a Senior Research Fellow (Energy) at Chatham House (The Royal Institute for International affairs) in London. At CEPMLP he held the position of Professor of Petroleum Policy, a chair created by BP and had been at the Centre since 1993, where he was the tutor responsible for the MSc course in Energy. He was educated as an economist and as a specialist on the Middle East at Cambridge and the School of Oriental and African Studies, London. Between 1979 and 1993 he taught at the American University of Beirut interspersed with two years as an oil consultant. Between 1979 and 1993 he was at the University of Surrey where he was a founder member of the Surrey Energy Economics Centre and joint creator of the Third World Energy Policy Studies Group. Professor Stevens has worked as a consultant for many companies and governments including work as an expert witness in the US-Iranian Claims Tribunal at the International Court in The Hague (1984–92).

Paul Sullivan has been a Professor of Economics at the National Defense University (NDU) since July 1999. He is an Adjunct Professor of Security Studies and Science, Technology and International Affairs at Georgetown University, where he teaches classes on global energy and security, energy security in the Middle East, and natural resources and conflict in Africa and the Middle East. Dr Sullivan is the Vice-President, Programs, for the United Nations Association, National Capitol Area, where he is a strategic leader and adviser for the many programmes and committees run by UNA-NCA. He was an adviser to the Sudan project at the United States Institute of Peace from March 2009 – July 2010.

Professor Sullivan was Senior Fellow at the East West Institute during 2007. He has also been involved in the energy work at UNCTAD with a focus on Africa. He has advised senior US officials on many issues at a high level. He is regularly invited to high level conferences, such as the Global Creative Leadership Summit and energy and environment conferences in the European Union, China and others. For six years before his time at NDU, Dr Sullivan was at the American University in Cairo, Egypt, where he taught classes and did research on the economics, economic history and political economy of the Middle East. He was also a columnist for the *Middle East Times* while in Cairo.

Sidney Weintraub holds the William E. Simon Chair in Political Economy at the Center for Strategic and International Studies. He is Professor Emeritus at the Lyndon B. Johnson School of Public Affairs of the University of Texas at Austin, where he was Dean Rusk Professor from 1976–94, and he also teaches at Johns Hopkins School of Advanced International Studies. A member of the US Foreign Service from 1949 to 1975, Dr Weintraub held the post of deputy assistant secretary of state for international finance and development from 1969 to 1974 and assistant administrator of the US Agency for International Development in 1975. He was also a senior fellow at the Brookings Institution.

Dr Weintraub recently published, with co-author Duncan Wood, *Cooperative Mexican–U.S. Antinarcotics Efforts* (CSIS, 2010). His latest book, *Unequal Partners: the United States and Mexico*, was published by the University of Pittsburgh Press in March 2010. Other recent books are *Energy Cooperation in the Western Hemisphere: Benefits and Impediments* (CSIS, 2007), *Issues in International Political Economy: Constructive Irreverence* (CSIS, 2004), *Free Trade in the Americas: Economic and Political Issues for Governance and Firms* (Edward Elgar Publishing, 2004), *NAFTA's Impact on North America: The First Decade* (CSIS, 2004), *Financial Decision-Making in Mexico: To*

Bet a Nation (Pittsburgh, 2000) and *Development and Democracy in the Southern Cone: Imperatives for U.S. Policy in South America* (CSIS, 2000). Dr Weintraub has published numerous articles in newspapers and journals. He received his PhD in economics from the American University as well as an MA in economics from Yale University.

Eckart Woertz is a visiting fellow at Princeton University and a consultant on food security, energy and financial issues in the Middle East. Formerly he has been Director of Economic Studies at the Gulf Research Center in Dubai, United Arab Emirates (UAE) and has held senior positions in financial services companies in Germany and the UAE, among them Delbrück & Co, one of the oldest German private banks. He has consulted international and regional organizations such as UNCTAD, UNDP and the Saudi Ministry of Economy and Planning. Dr Woertz is a regular contributor and commentator to major international and regional newspapers and TV channels. *Arabian Business Magazine* voted him among the ten most influential expatriates in the Gulf region in 2009. Since 2008 food inflation in the Gulf and Gulf Co-operation Council agro-investments abroad have been among his special interests. He holds an MA in Middle Eastern Studies and a PhD in Economics from Friedrich-Alexander University, Erlangen-Nuremberg, where he conducted research on structural adjustment politics in Egypt.

Abbreviations

bbpd	billion barrels per day
bn	billion
CEO	Chief Executive Officer
Edn	edition
EU	European Union
GCC	Gulf Co-operation Council
GDP	Gross Domestic Product
GNP	Gross National Product
IOC	International Oil Company
m.	million
mbpd	million barrels per day
MENA	Middle East and North Africa
NGO(s)	Non-governmental Organization(s)
NOC	National Oil Company
OECD	Organisation for Economic Co-operation and Development
OPEC	Organization of the Petroleum Exporting Countries
PhD	Doctor of Philosophy
TV	television
UAE	United Arab Emirates
UN	United Nations
UNCTAD	United Nations Conference on Trade and Development
UNDP	United Nations Development Programme
US(A)	United States (of America)

Part I
Politics of Oil Supply

1
Introduction

Robert Looney

"Follow the money" is the advice routinely offered to detectives in low-budget thrillers. For anyone attempting to understand the ebbs and flows of international politics, I offer a variant of that old line: "Follow the oil".[1]

This book grew out of the need for a comprehensive examination of the interaction of politics and oil in all dimensions at both the national and international levels. Its chapters capture the diversity and complexity of the global oil system, as well as those of many key oil-consuming and producing countries.

The volume's various themes are intended to provide a deeper understanding of the forces that have led to a series of booms and busts in oil prices, instability in the global economic system, economic nationalism, growing concern over climate, and, most recently, regime change in the Middle East. The forces described in the chapters that follow will no doubt also serve as catalysts for many future developments as well.

The global energy dilemma that the world currently faces serves as the book's unifying focus. Can we have secure, reliable and affordable supplies of energy and, at the same time, manage the transition to a low-carbon energy system? What policies are needed to make this transition and what factors impede it? Do we, either nationally or internationally, have the political will to make the hard decisions required?

To this end, the volume is divided into five main sections. The chapters in the first section examine the problems surrounding the continued availability of oil at reasonable prices. Those unfamiliar with the workings of the oil industry may be surprised to learn that experts are less concerned over oil's physical availability than with a broad spectrum of uncertainties that surround the petroleum industry.

Paul Sullivan's excellent overview in Chapter 2 looks at these uncertainties, as well as at many of the themes in the chapters that follow. He points out that it is unclear how politics, political instability and war will affect future oil exploration and production. It is also impossible to predict how changing attitudes toward technologies, like transportation, that contribute to climate change will combine with increased energy demand by developing countries to affect the demand for oil and overall conditions in the petroleum industry. Sullivan suggests that such potential conflicts between oil producers, consumers, environmentalists and other concerned groups cannot be resolved simply through reliance on the market price incentives and disincentives of the past, but will require political action.

Michael Klare's discussion of the politics of oil in Chapter 3 expands the uncertainty theme. Klare notes that geopolitics and oil have been closely intertwined for a very long time. Given oil's strategic importance to the efficient functioning of modern economies and military organizations, it is not surprising that the geopolitical picture has often been dominated by the efforts of the major oil-consuming economies to gain and retain influence in the major oil regions. Similarly, because key oil suppliers are often located far from the major sites of consumption, control over oil transportation routes is another source of geopolitical contention. As long as oil remains a critical commodity, oil-related conflicts are likely to be part of the geopolitical equation.

It is often assumed that the increasing share of world oil produced by national oil companies (NOCs), as opposed to profit-maximizing private international oil companies, (IOCs) provides an additional source of uncertainty. This assumption is based on the fact the ultimate goals of the NOCs are to maximize long-term economic benefits to their respective countries, whereas the IOCs attempt to maximize short-term benefits to their shareholders. Jean-Francois Seznec, however, comes to a different conclusion in his detailed assessment of NOCs and IOCs in Chapter 4, arguing that the 10-year lead time from decision to refining requires the IOCs to similarly engage in long-term planning. Based on this, he concludes that it is not surprising that many NOCs, like Total, Sinopec, Rosneft and Lukoil, have moved to private portions in their shareholding and predicts that NOCs may increasingly come to be owned by the public at large.

One area of uncertainty that has captured the imagination is peak oil, which is the point at which the world's petroleum output can no longer increase and production begins to level off or decline. Popular commentators often use the concept as a jumping-off point for speculation that the world is facing a painful and even catastrophic adjustment period. While peak oil makes intuitive sense, Laural Graefe's examination (Chapter 5) suggests the concept itself is imprecise and sheds little light on future uncertainties. For example, on the supply side, how much will companies invest in capacity? How will extraction and refining technology advance? How many hurricanes or wars will occur in oil producing regions? Similar unknowns exist on the demand side. In the end, Graefe concludes that the time at which peak oil occurs is at least partially under our control and that, by acting with foresight, it is possible to accomplish a smooth transition to fewer hydrocarbons and increased usage of other forms of energy.

A very different form of uncertainty over future oil supplies comes from the instability associated with many of the oil-producing countries, especially those in the developing world. In Chapter 6, Michael Ross associates this instability with the oil curse, a combination of factors that includes overvalued exchange rates (the so-called Dutch Disease), wasted revenues during boom times, and the increased corruption which high oil revenues facilitate. These factors often combine to produce stagnating economies ruled by authoritarians with little interest in the public good that eventually degenerate into high levels of violence, instability and reduced levels of oil production. As Ross notes, however the situation isn't hopeless, pointing to Canada and Norway as examples of countries that overcame the oil curse to become reliable suppliers. Hopefully, such examples will provide inspiration and instruction to new leaders and regimes wishing to develop their economies.

One way to increase the certainty of future oil supplies and prices is through improved cooperation between the producers and consumers, which in the past has been marred by mistrust and deceit on both sides. Paul Stevens explores the outlook for a more constructive dialogue between the two groups in Chapter 7. As in seemingly all group situations, the call of "why can't everyone just get along" becomes more imperative than ever with increased instability in the producing countries and slack growth in the major consuming nations. Sadly, after exploring possible avenues of co-operation, Stevens finds it unlikely that much progress will be made. As he notes, " … the fundamental self-interest of the marketplace will always provide a cold dose of reality to dampen desire for dialogue or co-operation."

In Chapter 8, the final paper in this section, Giacomo Luciani examines the uncertainty factor stemming from the structural instability of crude oil prices – the result of a series of rigidities in supply, demand, costs and associated short-term factors. Luciani, however, finds room for optimism, pointing to the willingness of Gulf countries to assume the role of swing producers, coupled with the increased storage capacity of consuming countries. In addition, he cites a number of exciting new financial instruments that have a great potential for reducing oil market uncertainties.

All in all, the papers in this section document the dramatic changes taking place in the oil industry and associated institutions. Unfortunately, with so many degrees of freedom, scenarios ranging from the highly optimistic to the catastrophic are possible. The next section attempts to shed further light on future developments in the industry by focusing on political responses to many of the problems identified above. Are there adequate policies that can be put in place to dampen instability stemming from the oil markets? Will governments have the will and courage to confront problems before they spiral out of control? All political solutions are complicated by two increasingly pervasive forces: climate change and the need for increased security.

Energy security clearly means different things to different people and countries, but, as Dan Moran observes in Chapter 9, at its center lies a basic concern about access to energy resources. Security concerns began with Churchill's decision in the early 1900s to diversify suppliers to avoid over-dependence on Persian oil and grew dramatically in the early 1970s with the rise of OPEC and the oil embargo. While energy security has a nice political ring to it, Moran reminds us that energy security is not an absolute value, but rather exists in varying degrees. It cannot be achieved without some proportional sacrifice of other social goods. "Sound policies to sustain it must be based on realistic expectations of what is possible, a fair accounting and equitable distribution of the sacrifices involved." Viewed in this light, Alan Reynolds' assessment of US policymaking (Chapter 17) becomes even less reassuring.

As James Russell notes in Chapter 10, American presidents in the post World War II era have been reluctantly drawn into the maze of Middle Eastern politics and security. Future American foreign policy in the region will be further complicated by "the myriad and cumulative challenges from climate change." While the Middle Eastern countries are not among the major contributors to the factors underlying climate change, they will become its victims as climate change accelerates a series of already negative trends in the region. Such trends include decreased precipitation and resulting crop failures, as well as flooding in highly populated low-lying coastal areas. Clearly these changes will create even more instability in an already unsettled part of the world. As with several other authors in this volume Russell is skeptical the USA will be willing and able to provide the leadership necessary to reverse many of the forces leading to a warmer planet. "Only if and when this happens can the Middle Eastern states and the international community begin to start building policies that will address the systemic challenge posed by climate change in the region."

A popular notion, especially on many of the web's conspiracy sites, is that the USA deals with its energy security directly – by going to war and taking over oil fields in countries such as Iraq. As David Henderson notes in Chapter 11, even a sophisticated thinker like Alan Greenspan has argued from time to time that wars for oil make a certain amount of sense. Henderson refutes this argument by demonstrating that the case for "war for oil" is profoundly weak, whereas the case against it rests on sound economic analysis. In stark terms, our oil supply is secure, not because our government threatens to use force against those who would make it insecure, but because the world's oil suppliers want to make money.

The chapters in the section illustrate that there exists in the major oil-consuming countries a large body of sophisticated analysis capable of providing straightforward policy solutions to most of the world's energy problems, even those closely intertwined with climate and security considerations. Unfortunately, this analysis has little effect on actual policy-making. There is plenty of oil in the world, yet policy-makers fret over self-inflicted oil shortages while doing little to expand supply. The planet is rapidly warming, yet policymakers do not feel immediate pressure to take action and, instead, pursue policies that speed up the warming. Even countries that hate the West are willing to sell large volumes of oil on a regular basis, yet military action and a large defense presence in the Gulf is felt necessary for energy security.

The chapters in the next section demonstrate that policymaking in many of the producing countries, while admittedly focused on a different set of issues, has been even more flawed, inept and even self-destructive. There is something about oil that seems to prevent people from applying logic and common sense to the issues that arise from its continued production and use. Clearly, oil rents corrupt, but their corrosive effects often go much deeper.

Jessica Piombo (Chapter 12) notes that, based on generous human and natural resource endowments, Africans possess the means to become among the wealthiest people in the world. Instead, they tend to rank lowest in most economic and human development indicators, and their political systems are often among the most corrupt and authoritarian. The worst performance occurs in the countries with the largest mineral resource endowments, and of these, the petroleum-rich countries have the most dismal records in governance, inequality and human development. Plimbo's analysis clearly makes the link between oil and deprivation in sub-Saharan Africa. The causal mechanism is straightforward: regime concerns with maintaining control over oil rents undermine government accountability and increase authoritarian tendencies, while access to oil rents increases regime stability even as it attenuates the link between rulers and citizens.

Oil has created a somewhat different set of political and policy problems in Latin America. While oil rents have not been as detrimental to governance structures, Sidney Weintraub (Chapter 13) observes the region's policymakers have failed to design programmes to transform oil wealth into the basis for strong, dynamic economies. Most often short-term political gains have trumped sound energy policies that emphasize a long-term viewpoint. Policies lack coherence because they have alternated between market-friendly and nationalistic orientations. Instead, they have focused on increasing domestic political support by limiting exports to ensure a cheap domestic supply, providing generous subsidies to ensure cheap domestic energy, and expanding the state in production to increase government revenues. Weintraub warns that: "These policies will ultimately backfire, as the statist energy policies from the 1950s-1980s did, and their successors will be left with the cleanup."

Energy politics and resource policymaking have not fared much better in the oil-abundant countries of the Middle East. As Hossein Askari notes (Chapter 14), in the oil-exporting countries of the Persian Gulf, economic and social policies have been largely designed to support the royal families (Kuwait, Qatar, Saudi Arabia and UAE) or ruling elites (Iran, Iraq). As a result, corruption is commonplace. Askari charges that the current policy-making mix verges on criminality in that "viable institutions have not been nurtured because effective institutions would reduce the role and importance of ruling families and illegitimate governments and prevent them from capturing the oil rent that rightfully belongs to the citizenry." His solution, which is increasingly gaining acceptance, is the development of an oil fund that takes revenues away from the state and invests them on behalf of all generations of citizens. No doubt in the years to come many of the region's deposed rulers will look back and rue the day they did not take this sound advice.

Many of the mistakes of the Middle East resource experience have been replicated in Kazakhstan, Azerbaijan, and Turkmenistan, where poor governance and authoritarian political structures are the norm. Richard Pomfret (Chapter 15) notes that in all three countries power is concentrated in the hands of the president. As in the Middle East, oil rents strengthen the incumbent's position and free him from the need to seek the population's support in order to raise state revenue. Pomfret warns that in the Caspian Region " … the dependence of economic and political decisions on the wisdom and health of the leader may be a source of future instability."

The final chapter of this section sounds a more optimistic note. Benjamin Smith's (Chapter 16) empirical examination of Southeast Asian oil producers, both old and new, reveals a strikingly broad set of oil-influenced political trajectories. From Brunei's archetypical oil monarchy to Indonesia's uneasy transition out of major exporter status to Malaysia's surprising economic transformation, the older producers in Southeast Asia have put their oil wealth to a wide variety of political uses. Even more impressive, the region's new group of oil exporters—Cambodia, Timor-Leste and Vietnam—illustrate both how potentially transformative and how modest a sizeable oil sector can be.

Benjamin Smith's chapter provides an excellent transition to the next section of country case studies. While looking at broad regional patterns has some distinct benefits, Smith's sound advice is that we should be careful in making blunt assessments that assume uniform relationships across all oil-producers. The chapters in this section provide detailed accounts of the unique political decisions that inform energy policy in six key countries: The United States, Iraq, Iran, Saudi Arabia, Egypt, Russia and Brazil. Their experiences confirm Smith's assessment by illustrating how truly conditional the effects of resource wealth can be.

Alternative energy would seem to be the obvious solution to many of the world's oil problems. In Chapter 17, Alan Reynolds notes that US alternative energy proponents with two quite different policy goals—reducing energy dependence and improving climate stability—share a common presumption that US passenger cars and the fuels they use are the single largest cause of both problems. As a result, US policies have centered on a series of tax credits, subsidies, and mandates to reduce automobile gasoline consumption and emissions. Focusing on the campaign to mandate and subsidize ethanol and also to subsidize the producers and buyers of hybrid and/or electrical cars, Reynolds' painstaking analysis shows that these policies unfortunately have little merit as a cost-effective means of dealing with global warming or even the high volumes of imported oil. Instead, the evidence suggests that these policies were designed by energy interest groups to reward politically influential coalitions of industrial, financial and ideological interests. "In other words, realists would be well advised to not view valuable subsidies and mandates for alternative fuels and vehicles as a means to an end, but rather as the end itself."

In Chapter 18, Abbas Kadhim looks at the destructive effects of oil in Iraq. There, oil facilitated policies that ultimately depleted the country's infrastructure, exhausted its human capital and retarded its economic potential through wars, political oppression, and the prohibition of modern technology and the free flow of information. With the overthrow of Saddam Hussein, the country has the opportunity to make a new start, and there are indications that its leaders may this time use oil revenues to compensate for the missed opportunities of the past.

The misuse of oil revenues also underlies many of the problems confronting present day Iran. Rather than dwell on the standard litany of oil-enabled policy failures, Farrokh Najmabadi's (Chapter 19) fascinating account of the country's oil industry illustrates how rentier state environments impede wealth creation, even in industries critical to regime survival. He notes that, from a technical perspective, the country's oil industry could possibly double its rate of production in the medium-term. Unfortunately under the present regime such a scenario is highly unlikely. Najmabadi concludes that, even in the absence of today's political and ideological interference, unless Iran's oil and gas sector becomes more accountable and transparent the best it can do is muddle through.

Given its history, the role of its royal family and its enormous reserves of oil and gas, Saudi Arabia may be a very unique case. The kingdom has not abused its oil revenues as in Iraq, nor has it descended into the stagnation and inefficiencies so prevalent in Iran. While those countries have experienced falling rates of production and export over the years, Joseph Kéchichian (Chapter 20) documents the responsible way in which oil policy has enabled the country to stabilize oil markets. He concludes that the country's willingness and ability to expand production should ensure it an enduring role as a contributor to world supplies for the foreseeable future.

Because Egypt is not a major oil producer, certainly by MENA standards, its economy is not typically described as being driven or even heavily influenced by hydrocarbons. In recent years, however, the situation has changed. As Robert Springborg notes in Chapter 21, nearly three-quarters of the country's merchandise exports were comprised of oil and gas in 2007. Unfortunately, despite being a relatively new hydrocarbon producer, Egypt appears to have learned little from the failed oil policies of its neighbors. As a result, Egypt's hydrocarbon-based development strategy is not sustainable nor does it lay the foundation for an alternative mode. As Springborg characterizes it, the " … authoritarianism once associated with state capitalism was reinvented within what was nominally a privatizing economy, but which in reality was an economy whose commanding heights were controlled by regime cronies." After reading Springborg's analysis, the reader comes away with a much clearer understanding of the forces that eventually resulted in the overthrow of the Mubarak administration.

In Chapter 22, Philip Hanson observes that if Russia is a petro-state, it is a rather unusual one. Its economy is moderately developed and diversified. It exports metals, nuclear reactors, weapons systems and, in most recent years, grain, as well as hydrocarbons. It is clearly an exception among major oil exporters in that around 60% of its oil is produced by private firms. On the other hand, the country shares many negative traits of oil economies. Energy rents account for a large share of government revenues and exports and have enabled the regime to retain many of its authoritarian tendencies. While there is no national oil monopoly, the government exerts undue political pressure on Russian oil firms, and international oil companies are restricted. Given the government's opaque and informal involvement in the industry, Hanson is not optimistic about the future development of the country's vast hydrocarbon resources or the constructive use of the revenues they generate.

This section on country experiences ends on an optimistic note as Flavia Carvalho documents the creation and rise of the giant Brazilian oil company Petrobras in Chapter 23. Petrobras is a rare success story coming out of the import substitution process common throughout Latin America in the 1950s, 60s and 70s. Of particular relevance are the strategic and political motivations for setting up a strong national oil industry. Import substitution should be looked at as an investment in the future, and that is how the Brazilian government approached the development of Petrobras. In contrast to other oil-based developing countries, the Brazilian government has played a positive role by providing the resources and human capital necessary to foster technological excellence and efficiency. Petrobras demonstrates the potential of objective, farsighted policies and the proper use of oil rents to expand the productive capabilities of a hydrocarbon rich economy.

The papers in the final section of this volume revisit some of the main themes developed previously and speculate on how they may play out in the future. Will the oil curse continue to plague many hydrocarbon based economies (Richard Auty, Chapter 24)? What will the main challenges be in global oil governance (Andreas Goldthau, Chapter 25)? What does the future hold for sovereign wealth funds (Gawdat Bahgat, Chapter 26)? Will the dollar maintain its role in oil trading or will the international monetary system undergo a major transformation in the years to come (Eckart Woertz, Chapter 27)? How will China's rise impact oil markets (John Calabrese, Chapter 28)? Finally, Daniel Johansson, Fredrik Hedenus and Thomas Sterner (Chapter 29) take on the question of the day: what is the future of oil in a carbon-constrained world?

While various chapters in this volume clearly document past mistakes in the critical area of national energy policy-making, many chapters also offer hope for oil policy-making in the future. One can only hope that governments will have the wisdom to learn from past errors and the foresight to take a longer term approach in both their management and use of the world's remaining hydrocarbon resources.

Note

1 Gideon Rachman, "The Crude Realities of Diplomacy," *Financial Times*, September 8, 2008.

2
Key Issues Surrounding the Supply of Oil

Paul Sullivan

As the famous American baseball player Yogi Berra once said: "prediction is hard, especially about the future." Indeed, in the case of oil it is very hard to predict what the future will hold. Oil is an industry that involves geology, chemistry, biology, physics, and fluid dynamics, all sorts of types of engineering, economics, politics, sociology, diplomacy, environmental sciences and more. Each of these disciplines and fields will be part of the complexity of trying to understand what problems and opportunities there might be in expanded production of oil in the future.

It is important to first give a brief and rather simplified description of how oil is produced and why.[1] Oil first needs to be found. When the industry started the way to find oil was to smell it, look for "salt domes," look at what the other oil prospectors were doing and where, and drilling a hole in the ground, usually on land not at sea, and usually just straight vertically – and hope for the best. Now there are sonar-based 3-D imaging systems that can "take a picture" of the prospective oil finds to many thousands of feet underground and undersea. A prospector, usually a major oil company, a wildcatter or an oil services company, could have a mapping ship go in a lattice-like fashion across hundreds of square kilometers at sea, for example, capture the data for the images, and send the data to a data mapping center on land maybe thousands of miles away. This mapping center, usually in an oil service company, will then analyze the data, develop holograms of the oil prospect, and send these holograms to an oil company (or energy company which could be involved in dozens of types of energy sources) or to an exploration drill-ship at sea. Let's say it goes to the exploration drill-ship.[2] They would receive these data and then find the locations via GPS on the hologram lattice developed to start test drilling. The ship is normally leased from a company that specializes in such ships, rather than the oil company trying to find the oil, so that adds a bit of business complexity and complex logistical timing to the venture. The ship then places itself over a good prospective site and develops the test well. This could take weeks or months and could involve many other companies both on and off the ship. This ship is expensive and every day that passes the oil company could be fretting over losses to their balance sheets, especially if all of this is happening during a time of large price changes in the oil markets.

As the oil ship drills let's say it hits oil. Now instead of just drilling vertically this exploration ship can drill horizontally and can actually direct the drill in many different locations to find the best sources of the oil. As the drilling is happening the ship is constantly sending back data to various service companies and the main energy company or companies. (This could be a syndicated venture.) If the oil field is deemed profitable enough to set up a rig at sea then the decision is made to do that. However, sometimes it is not just a rig or an oil derrick, but a series of subsea extraction, monitoring and injection devices. There could be many more subsea devices than the lone oil rig seen from the surface.

When the exploration and production happens on land there are similar processes of mapping, judging, finding, testing and production that are similarly complex, but often less expensive than when this is done at sea, and this is especially the case if it is done in very deep or ultra deep waters. If the land is in Arctic areas, or other remote or challenging places without much surrounding infrastructure, then costs increase significantly over the simpler, more connected places.

The oil found could be in the typical ranges of what is commonly known as conventional oil. This is normally oil that has light to medium API gravity ratings[3] and is oil that could flow easily through the oil well structures on to either a FSPO,[4] a floating, storage, production and offloading vessel, or to a series of pipelines that will then send it on to a GOSP (a gas oil separation plant) onshore. If the oil is of a heavier variety then greater expenditure will be required and the costs of getting that oil out are subsequently higher.

There are many types of oil. This is another element of the complexity of future problems and opportunities in oil production. So far, the largest source of oil that the world has been using has been the conventional varieties that are found, tested for, and produced in the manner described above.[5]

Some of the more massive sources of oil that could be used in the future are called unconventional oils. These include tar sands. The biggest presently known resources of this are in Alberta in Canada. There are lesser fields in Russia, Madagascar, and some other places on earth, but, so far, nothing like the tar sands of Canada has been found anywhere else. Then there are the heavy and super heavy oils. The largest finds for this type of oil have been in the Orinoco Basin of Venezuela. When the International Energy Agency looks at future unconventional oils they usually focus on these two places as the most promising sources of unconventional oil.[6]

There are also oil shale and shale oils.[7] There are massive potential reserves of these sources of "oil," especially in the USA. Most oil is found in what are called source rocks, most of which have some oil shale in them, in the form of kerogen. This is "near oil." It does not have the same chemical properties as the oils that go into most refineries. It needs to be processed further before it can be used as a feedstock into these oil refineries. This would entail more energy use, more CO_2 and greenhouse gases production, and more cost than getting conventional oil out of the same source rock.

There are some other possible near substitutes to the end refined results of oil. These include the products derived from coal-to-liquids (CTL). This uses a very complex process called Fischer-Tropsch that converts coal, a fuel that is more globally dispersed than oil and exists in huge amounts in the USA, to usable liquid fuels for cars, trucks and airplanes. Its output is more expensive to produce than refined oil overall, but in the future it could be a significant source of substitute fuels to oil-based fuels in some parts of the world. Another possible source of fuels is gas-to-liquids (GTL). Qatar is one of the most important places currently producing fuel in this way. This method also uses the Fischer-Tropsch process, but uses the natural gas as a feed stock directly rather than the coal being converted to gas first. The costs for producing liquid fuels for cars and aircraft in this way could be decreasing, and this is something to look out for as a significant source of liquid fuels. Any hydrocarbon can be turned more or less into any other hydrocarbon with certain processes applied. One can even make diesel fuel out of turkey waste and other bio-waste. Diesel and other liquid fuels can be made out of algae, switch grass, corn, sugar cane, and even municipal waste (after gasifying it and then converting it into liquid fuels). However technically possible all of these options are, it is the economics that largely holds them back and means they are not in direct and significant competition with conventional liquid fuels from oil. However, all of this may change with some technological, or even economic or political breakthroughs.[8]

Unconventional oils generally cost more to extract and process into usable liquid fuels than conventional oil. For example, tar sands require a huge amount of energy in either way of getting them out of the ground. If it is in situ production steam needs to be sent into the ground to separate the oil from the sands and other materials to pipe it to the surface. This oil is more viscous than conventional oil so it may also need heating to move it along the pipelines to the next stage of processing this unconventional oil into something approaching conventional oil. Each of these stages produces more CO_2 than conventional oil production (about 15% more on average) and requires more water per barrel of oil than conventional oil production. The other method of getting this unconventional oil out is by strip mining of the lands above it. The tar sands are placed in giant dump trucks, which then bring this gooey mass to a processing and upgrading plant to separate the viscous oils from the sands and other materials in the truck. This separation takes a lot of energy and a lot of water. Then there is the upgrading of the oil which then goes on to refineries in Canada or just about anywhere in the world for processing into transport fuels and the thousands of other products that require oil for their manufacture. The costs of producing this sort of oil are greater than typical conventional oil field production and processing.

The increased costs for tar sands over conventional oil also apply to the heavy oils and especially to the shale oil. Methods of extracting shale oil in more economical ways are still in development. The methods being used now include "retorting" the kerogen. This involves superheating the material over long periods of time in order to separate out the kerogen from the source rock. Another method, of many others, is to freeze the rock and then heat it. These methods of extracting the kerogen from the source rock are expensive. They can also require a lot of water, and sometimes these sources of unconventional oils are not in places with a lot of water, such as Jordan. Extracting and processing of shale oil also produces more CO_2 than typical conventional oil production.[9]

Even so, the costs of producing oil vary considerably across geological basins, within geological basins, and across countries.[10] For example, it is considerably cheaper to get a barrel of oil out of the ground in Libya than in most places in California. Getting conventional oil out of the ground in Saudi Arabia is quite cheap compared to getting oil out of the ground and transported to the processing and other facilities in the Arctic or other new places of exploration. Finding, extracting and transporting oil from the remote Arctic could prove to be far more expensive than the same activities being done just "around the corner," in places like Norway and Russia, where the infrastructure for oil is already in place. Many have commented that the era of "cheap oil" is over. However, there is more to "cheap oil" than just the extraction and processing costs. It also entails the market, politics, geostrategic concerns and more.

Another thing to consider in all of this is that a barrel of oil from Libya is not exactly the same barrel of oil from even some places in Egypt. Libyan oil is very light, sweet crude, whereas that barrel in Egypt might be a heavier and sourer variety. These barrels cannot easily be substituted in some refineries and may be impossible to substitute in others. This is also important in the understanding of the limits to production of oil in the future. There is only so much light sweet crude available at any one time or known as proven reserves at any one time. The same could be said for heavier and sourer varieties. Saying that there are 1.7 billion barrels of crude oil reserves does not allow for potential reserves that could be out there. Such an understanding of reserves needs to be broken down into varieties of oil, and varieties of demands and uses for those oils, to judge the economic and other risks, and the potential investments and opportunities that could be available. The prices of some types of oils rise or fall faster than others at any particular moment, because different kinds of oils have different markets.[11]

There is an oddity about what most would consider high oil prices. For the industry high prices are a good thing, up to a point. Profits go up normally for the oil-producing states (about 80% of conventional oil reserves are owned by national oil companies) and for the integrated oil companies and others producing the oil, that is, if the costs of finding, extracting and processing grow at a lesser rate than the prices of the oil on the market. However, another important aspect of increasing oil prices is that they often spur investment in these complex and expensive exploration and production processes for not just conventional oil, but also for unconventional oil. Every time there is a spike in oil prices, such as the one in 2008, there is a call to arms about the peaking of oil. But in reality, there is almost always an increase in reserves and production, with a lag, of course, after such price hikes, unless the price hike is followed by a deep recession such as the one after the 2008 oil spikes. However, if for any reason the oil companies think the price of oil is about to increase for some extended time the "rig counts"[12] increase as the rotary rigs to drill exploration wells increase in use to try to take advantage of the increasing prices of oil.[13] Indeed, there will necessarily be a time when oil peaks, probably bounces about a plateau of production, and then starts its inexorable decline. However, there is no consensus amongst oil experts when this will happen. Oil, like any non-renewable resource, is by definition finite. The problem is we do not know what that finiteness is exactly. According to the IEA and to others, conventional oil has already peaked. The IEA claims this happened in 2006.[14] Whether this is true or not is debatable and is certainly being argued over between and amongst the peak oil optimists and pessimists. Whether conventional oil has peaked or not is an important question for many reasons. One of the most important is that the next steps in the oil choice chain bring us to the more expensive and more environmentally damaging unconventional oils. It also means that we will need to refit and change our refinery processes to make gasoline, diesel, heating oil, jet fuel and the like from the unconventional oils. These sorts of investments could be gigantic globally, and would need to be phased in over time to make this shift from conventional to unconventional oils at all economically or even politically and socially feasible.

There are other ways of getting more of this conventional oil out of the ground. At present, in most typical fields, usually no more than 20–35% of the oil that is in the field can be extracted by economically or even technically feasible methods. Therefore most of the conventional oil that has been found in the ground remains there. That is, a massive amount of conventional, and very valuable, oil is stranded in the ground. How is this so?

When a find is drilled for the first time and the field is open to the pipeline there are natural pressures in the well that drive the oil up the pipeline to the collection stations, processing stations, etc. This is often called the "champagne effect." Most oil fields, which often include water and natural gas in them, have significant built up pressures that are unleashed when the source rock is opened with the test wells and the oil, water, and gas rush through the drill pipe to the surface. This is simple physics. The drillers want to control that pressure in order to control the rate of extraction of the oil, gas, etc. However, as the field gets exploited over time it will lose this natural pressure and something will need to be done to increase that pressure to keep the oil and gas flowing. That something is normally called enhanced oil recovery (EOR)[15] and it can go in many stages depending on the market prices of the oil and the costs per barrel of oil out via EOR. At the earlier stages water is often injected into the well to increase pressures. Many wells do this, and it is quite similar to the process used for shale gas and tight gas, otherwise known as fracking. One longer term problem with this is that when more and more water is poured into the field the field's water cut goes up. That is, more and more water is extracted with the oil and the profitability of the field declines.

Also, particularly if there is no closely usable natural gas pipeline, natural gas is pumped back into the field to keep the pressure up and the oil flowing. There are also ways of heating or even firing up parts of the field to get the oil moving more easily, much like the in situ heating that happens with tar sands. Others have gone to even more extreme lengths, including injecting polymers, nitrogen and other gases, surfactants, and even microbes. The polymers and surfactant injections not only increase the pressure of the well, but also help the oil flow more smoothly by changing the nature of the surface of the oil in the source rocks. Microbes are sent down with nutrients to feed them. They grow in numbers. Then the microbes are used to help the flow characteristics of the oil after they die off and become the biological equivalent of surfactants. As a well gets older and the pressures and water cut change then different types of EOR can be used, at increasingly expensive levels, to extract even more out of the well than would otherwise have been possible. That way there is less stranded oil.

Enhanced oil recovery methods that we know of today could be much improved in the future. It is hard to tell. This is but one of the many technological uncertainties that the oil industry faces in the problems and opportunities of increased oil production.

Other technological uncertainties are included along the entire logistics-value chain of the industry from exploration to the ultimate use of the refined product in transport, industry, and more. We may find cheaper and more effective ways of finding the oil. We may find cheaper and more effective ways of getting it out of the ground. We may find cheaper and more effective ways of changing the unconventional oils to easily refined conventional oils. We may find cheaper and more effective ways of extracting the unconventional oils. We may also establish cheaper and more effective ways of refining the oil. If this is the case, then less oil will be needed to make the same amount of refined product at the end of that part of the value chain. However, given the physical limitations on such processes, as we know them now, there might not be much there to work with.

Some of the better ways to use that barrel of conventional and unconventional oil would be to change our transportation systems and methods. This could take some of the pressure off the pursuit of finding and producing more oil. It could also lead to a drop in the price of oil, and mean that a lot less oil is required than we might currently think.

The greatest use of oil at present is in transport, and most of that oil transport demand now occurs in the OECD. The single largest user of oil for transport is the USA. However, the fastest growth in demand for oil-based transport is in developing Asia, and most particularly in China. There are many ways to temper these increasing demands. One of them, now being developed rather rapidly in China, is electric transport. China sells millions of electric bicycles and electric motorbikes each year. The electric bicycle has been successful in the EU, but to a much lesser extent. Electric bicycles and electric motorbikes are being sold in relatively tiny numbers in the USA.

Replacing oil-based transport vehicles with electric power, including electric plug-in cars, could make a significant dent in the world's overall demand for oil. However, how much of a dent and when the dent will happen will be determined not only by the market for electric vehicles, but also by the market for oil. This is one of the many examples when economics and the linkages *across* markets become so important to the future production decisions in the oil industry. If the price of oil goes up dramatically, in real terms, and remains there, and if the overall lifetime costs of the electric transport vehicles decline, relative to the overall lifetime costs of the conventional internal combustion transport vehicle (and these costs would include battery costs, oil-based fuel costs, initial and lifetime capital expenditures, maintenance, etc.), then the movement to electric vehicles should be faster and the demand for oil-based fuels should be slower than would otherwise be the case. This could temper the oil investment needs of the future. The environmental costs of the electric vehicles could also be significantly lower than the internal combustion vehicles, especially if the sources of that electricity end up to be nuclear, solar, wind, and other non-hydrocarbon fuels.

Another competing vehicle worldwide is that run by compressed natural gas or CNG. Vehicles run on CNG are spreading slowly in the USA, but in some parts of the world are moving more quickly on to the markets. The new finds of shale gas, tight gas, methane hydrates, and even the newer methods of producing methane from agricultural and urban waste, could add to the sources of natural gas and, in some places, make CNG cars even less expensive to run. The further development of liquid natural gas markets worldwide could also help develop this alternative to oil-based transport. Then, of course, as discussed above, we have the possibilities of turning natural gas to liquid fuels that could be an alternative to oil-based fuels. There are many other types of alternative energies for transport, which include disparate sources such as cooking oil, hydrogen, many types of fuel cells, etc. The more alternative fuels there are, the less oil will be needed.

Another way of controlling the demand for oil-based transport fuels is to create lighter, more aerodynamically and mechanically efficient vehicles. For the average automobile as much as 75–85% of the fuel used is to move the weight of the vehicle. This could change with the use of carbon fibers and the like. Moreover, carbon fiber cars could be a lot safer than the usual steel-aluminum-plastics cars. Drive trains and braking systems are another source of inefficiency in the use of cars. If the braking systems were connected to batteries in an electric car the car could, in part produce its own energy. Another source of inefficiency in car transport is the way that we drive. Acceleration, followed by braking, followed by acceleration, wastes a great deal of energy. If some of these problems can be tackled and transport vehicles made more efficient, less oil will be needed.[16]

Of course, another source of inefficiency in the way we use cars is that we use them at all. Some of the most energy and environmentally efficient places, in terms of their use of energy, are the major cities of the developed world, such as London and New York.[17] Why is that? They have excellent public transport systems, which reduce the need for personal car transport. These transport systems also use less fuel per person per mile than if the same trips were made by personal gasoline-powered automobiles. As the world becomes more urbanized we might see a lot less oil being used per capita, all else being the equal. However, in developing Asia their growing cities are not as energy or environmentally efficient as the cities of the developed world, owing to the fast pace of their construction, which is very energy intensive normally. Moreover, many of these growing cities in the developing world do not have good public transport systems or must rely on public transport systems that are still mostly oil based, such as buses and minibuses. As the world becomes more urbanized, as is expected, as the world's population growth rates slow down, the demand for oil may also see some slowing down. But the fast growth of incomes and wealth, in Asia in particular, could mitigate that decline in oil demand, unless new transport methods are developed.

The future of transport is constrained by the imaginations of inventors, the availability of investment funds and government policies, as well as the tastes and needs of the markets for transport vehicles. All of these remain uncertain and as we go further into the future the foggier the story gets, in terms of how much we really need to invest in producing oil.

Oil is not a major source of electricity production in most developed countries. There are exceptions, but the countries that use oil for electricity production and for heating and other residential uses are mostly found in the developing world, and those electricity generating plants are normally quite inefficient. As much as 80% of all of the BTU content of the fuel used to produce electricity is lost in the generating station (as heat mostly), along the step-up and step-down processes, along the transmission and distribution lines and in other ways. By the time a typical house sees its lights go on about 90% of the potential use of the initial fuel put into the plant is lost. Also, most typical light bulbs produce more heat than light. So even more of the precious fossil fuels, whether oil, gas or coal, are lost to waste. This is also true for electric vehicles. A great deal of energy is lost before that electricity reaches the electric motorbike plugged in to the owner's house.[18]

There could be many disruptive technologies lurking out in the market place of ideas that could completely throw off the estimates for supply and demand for oil in the future. If we are looking at the 5–10 year range there are probably not many. However, if we are looking at the 10–20 year range that risk of disruptive technologies increases. If we are looking at 50–100 years all bets are off on how we might be transporting, heating, cooling, cooking and manufacturing in factories and farms. There is an increasing risk to disruptive technological invention and innovation as time moves on. In the future the industry will have to look into extracting more unconventional oil in more difficult, arduous and expensive places to operate in the world, such as in the Arctic, in ultra-deep water, and other hostile environments. Examples of the latter are some of the newer finds in sub-salt. Not long ago the methods of mapping oil and gas in such places were quite weak.[19] With new fidelity and more powerful imaging methods it is now becoming more likely we can establish a better sense of what lies beneath the previously most opaque areas of the world. New methods of EOR could also be developed.

Then there is the lurking, although seemingly distant promise of fusion energy. If this is achieved in economical ways to produce electricity for transport then, once again, all bets are off for the future of transport fuels. A new nuclear resurgence could also change this picture, especially in China, Russia and parts of the Middle East. These new nuclear facilities, combined with electric vehicles, (and there could be hundreds of millions of these in the coming decades in China) could begin to bring the electricity industry closer to the transport industry and start the slow delinking process between oil and transport, at least for some transport methods and in some places.

It is hard to judge what the tastes of the market will be over the next few decades. That is another source of uncertainty in this story of the future of oil production. If tastes change to smaller cars, towards public transport, towards more environmentalism, and towards more efficient use of oil at many levels then the demands of the market could help define the supplies of the future. It may even help define the type of oil that is taken out of the ground.

One of the most significant areas of uncertainty is in government policies. The fallout from the Deepwater Horizon disaster could be a case in point. This was an oil spill of epic proportions caused by, according to the final report of the oil commissions tasked to investigate the matter, management errors, other human error, and the use of the wrong cementing for the well, combined with the lax application of safety and other regulations by the Minerals and Mines Management Service (MMS). The MMS had been known more for its faults than for its successes for many years previously, but this was the last straw for the Obama Administration. A new, and presumably more effective and stricter organization was established to replace the MMS, the Bureau of Ocean Energy Management, Regulation and Enforcement (BOEMRE). The safety and other regulations for offshore oil drilling have been tightened up in the USA.

The EPA under the Obama Administration has also applied CO_2 to the Clean Air Act and has defined CO_2 as a dangerous substance. The rules, fines and regulations from the EPA could result in organization at the federal, state and local levels adding much more cost to oil production, and not just in deep water, after such a disaster in the Gulf of Mexico. This remains to be seen, but the industry is working in an increasingly uncertain regulatory environment after the Deep Water Horizon accident, both offshore and onshore.[20]

There have been significant oil spills in some parts of the world that have been virtually ignored by the international community, even if they have not been by the local populations who have suffered them.[21] Examples of this can be found in Nigeria, where the equivalent of an Exxon Valdez spill happens every year in the Niger Delta. As countries like Nigeria get wealthier, their people more educated and have more of a voice, it will not be so easy to ignore these spills and their effects and the oil companies and others will have to incorporate more of these and other environmental and social development costs into their balance sheets. As the politics of oil states change, so do the costs of oil exploration and production.

Carbon taxing and cap-and-trade are policy changes that could have great effects on the oil industry in many ways. Such laws will likely not be applied fully, if at all, in some oil producing countries, but they are already being applied in the EU and in other regions. The higher the policy-determined price of carbon and the lower the initial handout of carbon credits to oil producers, refineries and so forth, the more of a cost effect this will have on production in the industry. If a draconian carbon tax is applied in many countries then the oil industry will need to adjust. The results of refining, gasoline and diesel, for example, are some of the largest sources of CO_2 on earth, after they have been burned in the internal combustion engine. The effects of any carbon tax or quota-credit trading system on the transport and industrial sectors will affect the overall demand for oil through the demand for oil-based products. Tougher CAFÉ standards or other standards for energy efficiency or pollutants on the transport industry, including shipping, aircraft, trucks, etc. could also have significant effects on the oil industry's supply projections. As the developing world gets richer there could also be greater emphasis on environmental and health issues. If this is the case then projections for oil demand would need to be readjusted. If there is another Deepwater Horizon incident in the USA or another developing country then one might expect a greater public outcry against the industry, even though, prior to this spill, its safety record (especially since 1990) was quite good.

An effective environmental protocol on global warming and climate change globally could seriously affect the oil industry. So far no such agreement has been reached and the idea of building a global consensus in this area seems weaker now than in the 1990s when such ideas seem to be gathering momentum. The recent Copenhagen meetings did not produce much effect. The Cancun meetings reached some sort of agreement, but its effectiveness will be greatly affected by how the governments and other leadership organizations in the signatory countries react to the agreement. The Kyoto Protocols were not agreed to by the USA and Australia, for example, and likely would not have been passed by their legislatures even if the leadership had agreed to them in an international meeting.

The US Congress today is unlikely to pass any climate legislation or even any real solid energy legislation. It is not a fully functioning organization on these and many other issues. Also, many of the surviving and new members of the legislative branch of the USA do not think climate change is anthropogenic (man made) and that any legislation to slow down global warming would be for naught. Moreover, some politicians in the USA deny the very existence of global warming. This is in great contrast to the views of many in the EU, China, Japan, and in many developing countries, especially in the places that may be harder hit, according to some scientists, such as India, Bangladesh, Egypt, and many sub-Saharan and small island countries. The science of climate change does have some uncertainty to it and is quite complex. But the acceptance of the mere existence of the problem is debated by many of the powerful.[22]

How climate will turn out is really quite a great source of uncertainty at many levels for the future supply of oil. If, for example, there is a tipping point in the near term and the effects of climate change really start to take hold then many legislatures and leaders in the world will push for quick passage of new carbon taxes and laws to hinder the production and use of oil. This could have devastating effects on parts of the industry depending on how quickly this occurs. If global warming happens faster than expected by scientific consensus then areas will be opened up in the Arctic and other places that would otherwise have not been considered for oil exploration and production. Climate change could also have a vast impact on farming, the hydrological cycle and more and could shift the demand for oil greatly, and not just via legislation, but by being pushed by climate events and trends. The debates on climate change and oil's part in it are very complex. What they do indicate is that there is a potentially significant global threat from the use of hydrocarbons, alongside weather, political and other threats to the oil industry that could come about from climate change.

That, of course, can lead us into one of the most uncertain aspects of oil production in the future: local, regional and global politics. As we watch the astonishing events recently in North Africa and the Middle East we are reminded that oil is most often found in places where political instability and civil strife are not unusual. About 65% of the known commercially available proven reserves of oil in the world can be found in the countries in the Gulf region of the Middle East. OPEC owns 76% of the proven conventional oil reserves in the world.[23] And most of the proven conventional oil reserves are owned by national oil companies, the majority of which are to be found in the Gulf region.[24] Much of the rest can be found in potentially unstable places like Russia, the Caucasus, North Africa and West Africa. Conventional oil production in the USA has been mostly in decline since the early 1970s. Many other countries have faced peaked or peaking conventional oil production over the past decades, including the United Kingdom, Norway, Indonesia, Syria, Egypt, and Mexico.[25] Canada's conventional oil production has already peaked.[26] Its overall production of oil is increasing, but that is mostly from the tar sands of Alberta, or unconventional oil. Oil production in Venezuela has been in decline. It is hard to tell whether the overall decline is due to a peaking of its more conventional oil and difficulties getting more of its heavier and sourer unconventional oil streams moving forward, or simply bad management and poor investment strategies of the national oil company PDVSA.[27] It is likely to be a combination of all of those.

The USA imports about 51% of its oil. About 23% of US imports of oil are from Canada, about 11% form Venezuela, about 10% from Saudi Arabia, about 9% from Mexico and about 8% from Nigeria.[28]

The USA is lucky to have Canada nearby, given that this country is its greatest source of imports of oil, and 45% of those imports are from the tar sands of Alberta. Also, Canada has over 50% of all of the accessible oil not owned by the national oil companies. But Canadian conventional oil has peaked. The EU is lucky to have stable and well-run Norway, but how long can that last? Norway's oil reserves are far smaller than those in Saudi Arabia. Mexico, the number two source of imported oil into the USA for most of 2010, is having serious problems with drugs-related and other violence and there are concerns about this country's future political and social stability. PEMEX, its national oil company, is not investing enough in exploration and production, and its major field, Canterell seems to have peaked and to be on a rapid decline in production. The USA is constantly wary of potential instability in its number five source of imported oil, Venezuela, and its number three and four sources, depending on the season and the production cycles, Nigeria and Saudi Arabia. Nigeria has the MEND and other sources of political and social instability, and massive problems with corruption. Scholars and other observers have been talking about the fall of Saudi Arabia since it was started, but this year things may be pointing in more worrisome directions than before.

This is a source of concern for many in the country for energy, economic and national security needs. Even so, the EU is more vulnerable to problems with oil imports than the USA, and its oil import dependency is likely to increase to close to 90% by 2030. Indeed, the EU is lucky to have Norway, but its single largest source of oil is Russia, where 33% of its oil imports come from. Norway has also peaked in its production of conventional crude. The EU gets 45% of its oil imports from the Middle East and is, therefore, more vulnerable to the oil shocks that could be coming out of that region given the new revolutionary fervor developing there. With regard to the situation in Libya, the country that is the most vulnerable is Italy, which gets about 15% of its oil from that country. The southern EU countries are generally more vulnerable to the political instability of the Middle East and North Africa, although countries such as Germany are not immune.

China is also quite reliant on potentially unstable countries and places. In 2009, for example, of the close to 4.2m. b/d China imported 839,000 b/d were from Saudi Arabia, 644,000 b/d were from Angola, 463,000 b/d were from Iran, 306,000 b/d were from Russia, 244,000 b/d were from Sudan, 143,000 b/d from Iraq, and 127,000 b/d were from Libya. This may seem diversified, but a lot of Chinese oil comes from places that could be unstable or have some increased transportation risks in the future.[29] One could also say this about Indian imports of oil.[30] Most of its imports come from the GCC/Iran and West Africa. Japan imports more than 75% of its oil from the GCC with about 10% coming out of Iran.[31] South Korea gets close to 75% of its oil from the GCC/Iran.[32] Any increased instability in the GCC region, in Iran, Iraq, or, the worst of all scenarios, Saudi Arabia, then these three major Asian economies and powers are in deep energy trouble. Over the years the geostrategic bookends of the oil industry have moved from the Middle East and the USA/EU to the Middle East and Asia.

As the instability unfolds in the Middle East we are reminded about how vulnerable the entire globe is to the vagaries of political power, civil strife and revolution in the countries where the oil is found. Where the revolutionary fervor will spread is anyone's guess. What the end results of such revolutions will be on energy, economic and other policies in important oil states and states where important oil transport nodes are found, such as Egypt, are also uncertain.

The present and future instabilities in the Middle East and North Africa are not just a risk to conventional oil production, but also to oil transport, such as around the Bab Al Mandab near Yemen, which carries about 3m. b/d, the Suez Canal and Sumed pipeline, which carry 3–3.5m. b/d, and the Straits of Hormuz, which carry between 12m. and 15m. b/d, and more.[33] As Yemen descends into a failed state we can see that the Straits of Aden and the Bab Al Mandab could be bookended by mostly failed states, including Somalia. Piracy could be a severely increased problem in this area in the future as the rule of law may evaporate even further in Yemen. Terrorism may also be more prevalent as Yemen collapses.

Then there are the risks associated with some of the major oil facilities in the Middle East and elsewhere. Examples of these are the Al Basra Oil Terminal and the Khor Al Amiya Oil Terminal in Iraq. These two terminals carry about 95% of Iraq's oil exports. They cover a tiny geographic space, but are strategically of great importance. Then there is the Ab Qaiq facility in Saudi Arabia. In 2006 Al Qaeda got inside the first fences in an attempted attack on this vital facility that processes 6–7m. b/d from the most important oil fields in Saudi Arabia. There are many oil facilities, ports, pumping stations, processing facilities and other related infrastructure in the Middle East that are at risk, including in Saudi Arabia, Iraq, Iran and Kuwait. The same could be said for some of the facilities of West Africa and North Africa. The early 2011 situation in Libya may be a foreshadowing of troubles to come.

So what we are seeing is the peaking of conventional oil in many areas and potentially extreme increases in infrastructure, market, piracy and terrorism risks for the oil industry.

This can lead us into the following questions: where can new oil reserves, conventional and unconventional, be found? How much potential oil is out there? The answers to these questions are not as simple as one might think. Frankly, we don't know how much oil is in the world. We have many different levels of estimates of reserves, including proved, probable and possible.[34] Then we have the next level of estimates for how much oil could be out there by adding in contingent resources and prospective resources, which could be huge. And these are just the reserves and resources defined for conventional oil. Then we have the same levels of reserves and resources definitions for the unconventional oils. And these could be even greater than the conventional oils. If we add in the potentials for coal-to-liquids, gas-to-liquids, and anything-into-oil then the proven reserves blossom and the probable and possible reserves seem to go well into any reasonable time horizon. If we add up the global reserves and resource base of conventional and unconventional oils it could be as much, or even more, than 5 trillion barrels. At the global use of 30,000m. barrels a year recently and with a reasonable growth rate in that demand over the next 100 years we could have more than enough. Now consider how long we have to use these conventional and unconventional sources if we can get the demand for oil way down due to new transportation technologies and methods, more efficient refining, and overall better efficiency in our use of oil for its other applications in industry, commerce, and in producing things as the ultimate feedstock into petrochemicals, fertilizers, pesticides, plastics and more. We also have to consider the increasing costs of producing oil as we move into more difficult geographical, political and other areas, and as we move toward more unconventional resources and deeper into those unconventional resources.

There are many uncertainties facing the future of oil production. Each of these uncertainties included under the general titles of technological, economic, geological, political, environmental, and more need to be considered carefully if countries, companies and others are going to make the right decisions about what oil to produce, when, how, for what end purpose and at what costs.

The bottom lines to all of this are:

We really don't know how much oil or oil substitutes are out there, although it surely looks like it is massive.
It is unclear what the future of peak conventional oil reserves will trend towards, but many countries have already peaked and some others are likely to join that group.
We are unsure of the economics of oil exploration and production in the future.
We can be somewhat certain that the "cheap" oil has already been found and that the oil production in the future is likely to be from more expensive areas and more expensive processes, especially those applied to unconventional oils vs. conventional oils.
We are unsure of the possible trends in oil exploration and production technologies that could add to our proven oil reserves and to our overall oil resource base. There is still a lot of oil in

the ground that might be brought out with new technologies. Some reserves that look depleted could be reinvigorated with enhanced oil recovery techniques, but these seem to have significant limits and only account for about 3m. b/d today. We are unsure what they could account for in the future.

We are unsure about how future politics, political instability and war could affect oil exploration and production.

We are not sure of how disruptive technologies in the future from inside and outside the industry could affect oil exploration and production. The more potentially disruptive technologies that develop could be in transportation and in other uses of oil, such as industry and electricity production (in the developing world).

We are not sure what the future of climate change will bring and what policies, directed at the oil industry, such changes could bring.

We are sure it will take a long time to change from a mostly oil-based transportation system to something else, and if peak "cheap" oil and climate issues are to be serious problems for the future then we should get moving on this.

What we now know as unconventional oil will likely be renamed as conventional oil as this process of energy change unfolds.

There are some serious problems ahead for the production of oil, and these problems include the obvious technical and economic ones, but we also will have to face significant political and policy uncertainties.

Oil reserves and resources might need to be redefined in the context of scenarios related to all of the potential risks and uncertainties associated with future finds and future exploration and production, including the demand side of oil. Peak demand may actually determine peak oil before we really get into a bind. At least that is what one would hope.

If peak conventional oil is a reality then we really need to move on to unconventional oils much more quickly and also refit our refineries and other energy-economy systems for this transition in a more systematic and methodological way than seems to have been so far.

If global climate change is indeed a serious problem and a direct and serious threat to many economic, political, health, hydrological, farming and food, and other human and environmental systems, and it is caused by our use of fossil fuels, then we need fundamentally to rethink the direction of oil production in the future.

The future of oil will be very complex and changeable due to the changes that can happen in technologies, knowledge, geopolitics, economics, and, and this is very import, the often unpredictable nature of the systems within systems that the oil industry is connected with.

The key to the demand for oil in the future will be how the transportation industry changes.

If the politics of the areas where most of the oil is found change for the worse in a major way, then all bets are off on what the future of oil will look like.

Notes

1 See U.S., DOE, EIA, "Oil Market Basics", www.eia.doe.gov/pub/oil_gas/petroleum/analysis_publications/oil_market_basics/default.htm, UNEP, "Overview of the Oil and Gas Exploration and Production Process", *Environmental Management in Oil and Gas Exploration and Production, www.ogp.org.uk/pubs/254.pdf*, Petrostrategies, Learning Center, "Drilling Operations", www.petrostrategies.org/Learning_Center/drilling_operations.htm, Petrostrategies, Learning Center, "Exploration", www.petrostrategies.org/Learning_Center/exploration.htm, Petrostrategies, Learning Center, "Oil and Gas Value Chains", www.petrostrategies.org/Learning_Center/oil_and_gas_value_chains.htm, Petrostrategies, Learning Center, "Production", www.petrostrategies.org/Learning_Center/production.htm

2 See Professional Mariner, "Drill Ship Technologies Create Ultra-Deep Solutions", www.professionalmariner.com/ME2/dirmod.asp?sid=420C4D38DC9C4E3A903315CDDC65AD72&nm=Archives&type=Publishing&mod=Publications%3A%3AArticle&mid=8F3A7027421841978F18BE895F87F791&tier=4&id=CBFD6 4D555804D7DB9EFD24DACE91582 for an example of such a ship.

3 See www.oilprices.org/types-of-crude-oil.html

4 See for an example of an FPSO: Offshore-technology.com, "Skarv and Indun Fields, North Sea Northern, Norway", www.offshore-technology.com/projects/skarv/ and www.fspo.net

5 IEA, Statistics, *Oil Information*, 2010, International Energy Agency, Paris, IEA, *World Energy Outlook 2010*, International Energy Agency, Paris, World Energy Council, "Crude Oil and Natural Gas Liquids" *Survey of Energy Resources 2010*, pp. 41–150, www.worldenergy.org/documents/ser_2010_report_1.pdf

6 IEA, *World Energy Outlook 2010*, International Energy Agency, Paris, IEA, Energy Technology Network, "Unconventional Oil and Gas Production", IEA, Energy Technology Network, "Unconventional Oil and Gas Production", ETSAP, May 2010, www.etsap.org/E-techDS/PDF/P02-Uncon%20oil&gas-GS-gct.pdf, U.S., DOE, EIA, "Liquid Fuels", *International Energy Outlook 2010, www.eia.doe.gov/oiaf/ieo/liquid_fuels.html*, Engemann, Kristie, "Unconventional Oil Production: Stuck in a Rock and a Hard Place", July 2010, *The Regional Economist*, http://research.stlouisfed.org/publications/regional/10/07/oil.pdf

7 IEA, *World Energy Outlook 2010*, International Energy Agency, Paris, Engemann, Kristie, "Unconventional Oil Production: Stuck in a Rock and a Hard Place", July 2010, *The Regional Economist*, http://research.stlouisfed.org/publications/regional/10/07/oil.pdf, Esser, Robert, "The Oil Industry Growth Challenge: Expanding Production Capacity", Testimony to the U.S. House of Representatives, House Energy and Air Quality Subcommittee, 7 December 2005, Washington, DC, http://energycommerce.house.gov/108/Hearings/12072005hearing1733/Esser.pdf, IEA, Statistics, *C02 Emissions from Fuel Combustion 2009*, 2009, International Energy Agency, Paris, National Oil Shale Association, "Oil Shale Facts and Figures", www.oilshaleassoc.org/documents/Oil%20Shale%20Facts%20and%20Fiction%20Final.pdf, National Oil Shale Association, "Oil Shale Update", May 2010, www.oilshaleassoc.org/documents/FinalUpdateMay2010.pdf, U.S. DOE, Office of Deputy Assistant Secretary for Petroleum Reserves, Office of Naval Petroleum and Oil Shale Reserves, "Strategic Significance of America's Oil Shale Resource: Volume I: Assessment of Strategic Issues", http://fossil.energy.gov/programs/reserves/npr/publications/npr_strategic_significancev1.pdf, U.S., GAO, "Energy-Water Nexus: A Better Coordinate Understanding of Water Resources Could Help Mitigate the Impacts of Potential Oil Shale Development", October 2010, www.gao.gov/new.items/d1135.pdf

8 Lemley, Brad, "Anything into Oil", *Discover Magazine*, 2 April 2006, http://discovermagazine.com/2006/apr/anything-oil, National Petroleum Council, "Topic Paper #18, Coal to Liquids and Gas", www.npc.org/Study_Topic_Papers/18-TTG-Coals-to-Liquids.pdf, Shell.com, "Pearl GTL", www.shell.com/home/content/media/news_and_media_releases/archive/2009/pearl_qatar_update_05022009.html

9 IEA, *World Energy Outlook 2010*, International Energy Agency, Paris, Engemann, Kristie, "Unconventional Oil Production: Stuck in a Rock and a Hard Place", July 2010, *The Regional Economist*, http://research.stlouisfed.org/publications/regional/10/07/oil.pdf, Esser, Robert, "The Oil Industry Growth Challenge: Expanding Production Capacity", Testimony to the U.S. House of Representatives, House Energy and Air Quality Subcommittee, 7 December 2005, Washington, DC, http://energycommerce.house.gov/108/Hearings/12072005hearing1733/Esser.pdf, IEA, Statistics, *C02 Emissions from Fuel Combustion 2009*, 2009, International Energy Agency, Paris, National Oil Shale Association, "Oil Shale Facts and Figures", www.oilshaleassoc.org/documents/Oil%20Shale%20Facts%20and%20Fiction%20Final.pdf National Oil Shale Association, "Oil Shale Update", May 2010, www.oilshaleassoc.org/documents/FinalUpdateMay2010.pdf, U.S. DOE, Office of Deputy Assistant Secretary for Petroleum Reserves, Office of Naval Petroleum and Oil Shale Reserves, "Strategic Significance of America's Oil Shale Resource: Volume I: Assessment of Strategic Issues", http://fossil.energy.gov/programs/reserves/npr/publications/npr_strategic_significancev1.pdf, U.S., GAO, "Energy-Water Nexus: A Better Coordinated Understanding of Water Resources Could Help Mitigate the Impacts of Potential Oil Shale Development", October 2010, www.gao.gov/new.items/d1135.pdf,

10 See www.theoildrum.com/files/murphyfig_1.png

11 www.eia.doe.gov/ask/crude_types1.html and www.eia.doe.gov/pub/oil_gas/petroleum/analysis_publications/oil_market_basics/price_transactions.htm, http://oilprice.com/Energy/Crude-Oil/A-

Detailed-Guide-on-the-Many-Different-Types-of-Crude-Oil.html, www.api.org/aboutoilgas/upload/OilPrimer.pdf

12 See Baker Hughes, "North American Rig Counts", http://investor.shareholder.com/bhi/rig_counts/rc_index.cfm, Baker Hughes, "World Rig Count", http://investor.shareholder.com/bhi/rig_counts/rc_index.cfm, and www.wtrg.com/rotaryrigs.html

13 One of the negative things for the industry from sustained very high prices is that alternative energies and greater efficiency in oil use will be developed much faster and more effectively when the expectation is that prices for oil will be very high, and increasing, for the medium to long runs.

14 www.energybulletin.net/stories/2010-11-24/its-official-economy-set-starve.

15 Alvarado, Vladimir, and Menrique, Eduardo, "Enhanced Oil Recovery: An Update Review", *Energies*, Volume 3, 2020, pp. 1529–75, www.mdpi.com/1996–1073/3/9/1529/pdf, Falcone, Gioia, et al., "Can We Be More Efficient in Oil and Gas Exploitation?", *Journal of Physics and Natural Sciences*, Volume 1, Issue 2, www.scientificjournals.org/journals2007/articles/1319.pdf, Gao, Chang Hong, Zekri, Abdulrazag and El-Tarabily, Khaled, "Microbes enhance Oil Recovery through Various Mechanisms", *Oil and Gas Journal*, 17 August 2009, Vol. 10, No. 31., IEA, *World Energy Outlook 2010*, International Energy Agency, Paris, Kokal, Sunil and Al-Kaabi, Abdulaziz, "Enhanced Oil Recovery: Challenges and Opportunities", World Petroleum Council, 2010, www.world-petroleum.org/docs/docs/publications/2010yearbook/P64–69_Kokal-Al_Kaabi.pdf, Laharerre, Jean, "Comments on "Squeezing More Oil From the Ground"", www.peakoil.net/headline-news/comments-by-jean-laherr-re-on-squeezing-more-oil-from-the-ground-scientific-american, Maugeri, Leonardo, "Squeezing More Oil From The Ground", *Scientific American*, October 2010, www.scientificamerican.com/article.cfm?id= squeezing-more-oil-edit-this, Mollet, Paul, "Squeezing More Oil from Existing Fields", Shell.com, www.shell.com/home/content/innovation/feature_stories/2007/eor/

Moritis, Guntis, "CO_2 Miscible, Steam Dominate Enhanced Oil Recovery Processes", *Oil and Gas Journal*, 19 April 2010, Vol. 108, No. 14, Regtien, Jergen, "EOR: A Key Mechanism for Meeting Tomorrow's Energy Needs", www.world-petroleum.org/docs/docs/publications/2010yearbook/P70–72_Jeroen_Regtien.pdf, Sandrea, Ivan and Sandrea, Rafael, "Recovery Factors Leave EOR Plenty of Room for Growth", *Oil and Gas Journal*, 12 November 2007, Volume 105, no. 42, U.S., DOE, NETL, "Carbon Dioxide Enhanced Oil Recovery", www.netl.doe.gov/technologies/oil-gas/publications/EP/small_CO2_eor_primer.pdf, U.S. DOE NETL, "Optimizing Recovery of Domestic Petroleum Resources", www.fossil.energy.gov/programs/oilgas/publications/environment_otherpubs/Optimal_Recov_Petro_factsheet_2009.pdf

16 www.oilendgame.com/, www.energyquest.ca.gov/transportation/index.html, www.eia.doe.gov/cneaf/alternate/page/atftables/afv_atf.html, www.time.com/time/world/article/0,8599,1904334,00.html, www.brammo.com/, http://www.scribd.com/doc/17166410/Overview-of-the-Ebike-and-Electric-Bike-Market, www.energy.gov/news/documents/1_Million_Electric_Vehicle_Report_Final.pdf, http://www.worldcng.com/2011/01/24/study-global-natural-gas-vehicle-sales-to-hit-3–2m-annually-by-2016/, http://blogs.edmunds.com/greencaradvisor/2010/03/shell-ceo-predicts-electric-drive-cars-will-comprise-40-of-global-market-by-2050.html, https://flowcharts.llnl.gov/

17 Sullivan, Paul, "Energetic Cities", *World Policy Journal*, Winter 2011, www.mitpressjournals.org/doi/pdf/10.1162/wopj.2011.27.4.11

18 www.npc.org/Study_Topic_Papers/4-DTG-ElectricEfficiency.pdf, http://ert.rmi.org/research/cgu.html, http://ert.rmi.org/research/energy-efficiency.html, https://flowcharts.llnl.gov/

19 www.westerngeco.com/~/media/Files/WesternGeco/resources/papers/2010/eage2010k041.ashx, www.offshore-mag.com/index/article-display/4608969650/articles/offshore/e-technology/middle-east/2010/02/supercomputing-cluster.html, www.searchanddiscovery.net/documents/2010/40508krieger/ndx_krieger.pdf

20 National Commission on the BP Horizon Oil Spill and Offshore Drilling, Report to the President, "Deepwater: The Gulf Oil Disaster and the Future of Offshore Drilling", www.oilspillcommission.gov/final-report

21 www.npr.org/templates/story/story.php?storyId=128624211

22 Sulivan, Paul, "Written Testimony in Support of the Oral Testimony of Professor Paul Sullivan, National Defense University and Georgetown University for the Western Hemisphere Subcommittee of the Foreign Affairs Committee, US House of Representatives Regarding the Need for Canadian Oil As We Face Increasing Turmoil in the Middle East, Increasing Competition for Energy Resources, Peak Conventional Oil, and an Increasingly Complex Geostrategic Environment", *Before the Western Hemisphere Subcommittee of the Foreign Affairs Committee, U.S. House of Representatives, March 31, 2011,*

found at http://foreignaffairs.house.gov/112/sul033111.pdf and United States, House of Representatives, Foreign Affairs Committee, Hearing Before the Western Hemisphere Subcommittee, "Rising Oil Prices and Dependence on Hostile Regimes: The Urgent Case for Canadian Oil", Full Transcript of Hearing at: http://foreignaffairs.house.gov/112/65494.pdf

23 www.eia.gov/energy_in_brief/world_oil_market.cfm
24 www.eia.gov/energy_in_brief/world_oil_market.cfm, www.eia.gov/energy_in_brief/images/charts/TotalOilProduction_large.jpg
25 www.eia.doe.gov/countries/cab.cfm?fips=UK, www.eia.doe.gov/countries/cab.cfm?fips=NO, www.eia.doe.gov/countries/cab.cfm?fips=SY, www.eia.doe.gov/countries/cab.cfm?fips=ID, www.eia.doe.gov/countries/cab.cfm?fips=EG, www.eia.doe.gov/countries/cab.cfm?fips=MX
26 www.capp.ca/getdoc.aspx?DocId=173003
27 www.eia.doe.gov/countries/cab.cfm?fips=VE
28 www.eia.doe.gov/pub/oil_gas/petroleum/data_publications/company_level_imports/current/import.html. See also www.capp.ca/GetDoc.aspx?dt=PDF& docID = 186104
29 www.eia.doe.gov/cabs/China/Oil.html
30 www.eia.doe.gov/cabs/India/Oil.html
31 www.eia.doe.gov/cabs/Japan/Oil.html
32 www.eia.doe.gov/cabs/South_Korea/Oil.html
32 www.eia.doe.gov/cabs/World_Oil_Transit_Chokepoints/Full.html
34 See U.S., GAO, "Uncertainty About Future Oil Supply Makes It Important to Develop a Strategy for Addressing a Peak and Decline in Oil Production", February 2007, www.gao.gov/products/GAO-07-283, U.S. Geological Survey, "Assessment of Undiscovered Oil and Gas Resources of the Nile Delta Basin Province, Eastern Mediterranean", http://pubs.usgs.gov/fs/2010/3027/pdf/FS10–3027.pdf, U. S. Geological Survey, "Assessment of Undiscovered Petroleum Resources of the Barents Sea Shelf", http://pubs.usgs.gov/fs/2009/3037/pdf/FS09–3037.pdf, U.S. Geological Survey, "Circum-Arctic Resource Appraisal: Estimates of Undiscovered Oil and Gas North of the Arctic Circle", http://pubs.usgs.gov/fs/2008/3049/, U.S. Geological Survey, "Geology and Resources of Some World Oil-Shale Deposits", http://pubs.usgs.gov/sir/2005/5294/pdf/sir5294_508.pdf, U.S. Geological Survey, "Geology and Total Petroleum Systems of the Gulf of Guinea Province of West Africa", http://pubs.usgs.gov/bul/2207/C/pdf/b2207c_508.pdf,U.S. Geological Survey, "USGS Reassesses Potential World Petroleum Resources: Oil Estimates up, Gas Down", 22 March 2000, www.usgs.gov/newsroom/article.asp?ID=636, Whitney, Gene, et al., "U.S. Fossil Fuel Resources: Terminology, Reporting and Summary", Congressional Research Service, 28 October 2009, http://epw.senate.gov/public/index.cfm?FuseAction=Files.View&FileStore_id = f7bd7b77-ba50–48c2-a635–220d7cf8c519, Witze, Alexandra, "That's Oil, Folks. ... ", *Nature*, Vol. 445, No. 4, 4 January 2007, World Energy Council, "Crude Oil and Natural Gas Liquids", *Survey of Energy Resources 2010*, pp. 41–150, http://www.worldenergy.org/documents/ser_2010_report_1.pdf, U.S., DOE, EIA, "World Proved Oil Reserves by Geographic Region as of January 1, 2010", www.eia.doe.gov/oiaf/ieo/excel/figure_35data.xls, U.S., DOE, EIA, "World proved Reserves of Oil and Natural Gas, Most Recent Estimates", www.eia.doe.gov/international/reserves.html, www.worldenergy.org/documents/ser_2010 _report_1.pdf, United Nations, Economic Commission for Europe, "United Nations Framework Classification for Fossil Energy and Minerals Resource", www.unece.org/se/pdfs/UNFC/UNFCemr.pdf, Society of Petroleum Engineers, "SPE Petroleum Resources Management System Guide for Non-Technical Users", www.spe.org/industry/reserves/docs/PRMS_guide_non_tech.pdf, Sandrea, Rafael, "New Tool Determines Reserves of Mature Oil and Gas Fields", *Oil and Gas Journal*, Vol. 10, No. 12, 23 March 2009, Renzi, Anthony, "Restoring Confidence in Reported Oil and Gas Reserves", *Oil and Gas Financial Journal*, http://www.akingump.com/files/Publication/c8b00d54–10fa–4898–8ad5-b398a36f29a0/Presentation/PublicationAttachment/2537b075-b666–49f0–958f-b71d0e99bcfb/693.pdf, Maugeri, Leonardo, "The Crude Truth about Oil Reserves", *The Wall Street Journal*, 4 November 2009, http://online.wsj.com/article/SB10001424052748704107204574470700973579402.html, Maugeri, Leonardo, *Oil: The Mythology, History and Future of the World's Most Controversial Resource,* Westport, CT, Praeger, 2006, Kovarik, William, "Comparison of USGS and Oil Industry Reserve Estimates", www.radford.edu/wkovarik/oil/oiltable.xls, Laharerre, Jean, "Reserve Growth: Technological Progress or Bad Reporting and Bad Arithmetic?", www.peakoil.net/publications/reserve-growth-technological-progress-or-bad-reporting-and-bad-arithmetic, Graefe, Laurel, "The Peak Oil Debate", *Economic Review*, Federal Reserve Bank of Atlanta, Vol. 94, Number 2, 2009, www.frbatlanta.org/filelegacydocs/er0902_graefe.pdf, Fisher, Brent, "Review and Analysis of the Peak Oil Debate", Institute for Defense

Analysis, August 2008, www.dtic.mil/cgi-bin/GetTRDoc?Location=U2&doc=GetTRDoc.pdf&AD=ADA488967, Campbell, Colin, "Comment: Just How Much Oil Does the Middle East Have and Why Does it Matter?", *Oil and Gas Journal*, 4 April 2005, Vol, 103, Issue 13, CERA, "Why the "Peak Oil" Theory Falls Down: Myths, Legends, and the Future of Oil Resources", CERA, Cambridge, MA, 2006, www.cera.com/aspx/cda/client/report/reportpreview.aspx?CID=8437&KID=61, CERA, "The Future of Global Oil Supply", 2009, CERA, www.cera.com/aspx/cda/client/report/report.aspx?KID=5&CID=10720, Anderson, Miranda, "The Future of Oil: Energy Security, Climate Risks, and Market Opportunities", 7 June 2007, CERES, www.incr.com/Document.Doc?id=188, Auguilera, Roberto, et al., "Depletion and Future Availability of Petroleum Reserves", *The Energy Journal*, Vol. 30, No. 1, International Association of Energy Economists, www.peakoil.net/publications/depletion-and-the-future-availability-of-petroleum-resources, Ahlbrandt, Thomas, "The USGS World Oil and Gas Assessment", www.searchanddiscovery.net/documents/ahlbrandt/images/usgs.pdf, Aleklett, Kjell, "Peak Oil and the Evolving Strategies of Oi Importing and Exporting Countries", OECD, International Transport forum, Joint Transport Research Centre, www.internationaltransportforum.org/jtrc/discussionpapers/DiscussionPaper17.pdf

Bibliography:

Ahlbrandt, Thomas, "The USGS World Oil and Gas Assessment", www.searchanddiscovery.net/documents/ahlbrandt/images/usgs.pdf [No date]

Aleklett, Kjell, "Peak Oil and the Evolving Strategies of Oil Importing and Exporting Countries", OECD, International Transport forum, Joint Transport Research Centre, www.internationaltransportforum.org/jtrc/discussionpapers/DiscussionPaper17.pdf [No date]

Alvarado, Vladimir, and Menrique, Eduardo, "Enhanced Oil Recovery: An Update Review", *Energies*, Volume 3, 2020, pp. 1529–75, www.mdpi.com/1996–1073/3/9/1529/pdf

American Petroleum Institute, *Understanding today's Crude Oil and Product Markets*, http://www.api.org/aboutoilgas/upload/OilPrimer.pdf [No date]

Anderson, Miranda, "The Future of Oil: Energy Security, Climate Risks, and Market Opportunities", 7 June 2007, CERES, www.incr.com/Document.Doc?id=188 [No date]

Auguilera, Roberto, Eggert, Roderick, Lagos C.C., Gustavo, and Tilton, John, "Depletion and Future Availability of Petroleum Reserves", *The Energy Journal*, Vol. 30, No. 1, International Association of Energy Economists, www.peakoil.net/publications/depletion-and-the-future-availability-of-petroleum-resources [No date]

Baker Hughes, "North American Rig Counts", http://investor.shareholder.com/bhi/rig_counts/rc_index.cfm [No date]

——, "World Rig Count", http://investor.shareholder.com/bhi/rig_counts/rc_index.cfm [No date]

Bina, Cyrus, "The Globalization of Oil", *International Journal of Political Economy*, Vol. 35, No. 2, Summer 2006, pp. 4–34

Bradshaw, Michael J., "Global Energy Dilemmas: A Geographic Perspective", *The Geographical Journal*, Vol. 176, No. 4, December 2010, pp. 275–90

Campbell, Colin, "Comment: Just How Much Oil Does the Middle East Have and Why Does it Matter?" *Oil and Gas Journal*, 4 April 2005, Vol. 103, Issue 13

CERA, "Why the "Peak Oil" Theory Falls Down: Myths, Legends, and the Future of Oil Resources", CERA, Cambridge, MA, 2006, www.cera.com/aspx/cda/client/report/reportpreview.aspx?CID=8437&KID=61

——, "The Future of Global Oil Supply", 2009, CERA, www.cera.com/aspx/cda/client/report/report.aspx?KID=5&CID=10720

Coleman, Les, "Why Explore for Oil When it is Cheaper to Buy?" *Applied Economic Letters*, Vol. 12, 2005, pp. 493–97

Cordesman, Anthony and Al-Rodhan, Khalid, "The Changing Risks in Global Oil Supply and Demand: Crisis or Evolving Solutions?", 3 October 2005, CSIS, http://csis.org/files/media/csis/pubs/050930_globaloilrisks.pdf

Engemann, Kristie, "Unconventional Oil Production: Stuck in a Rock and a Hard Place", July 2010, *The Regional Economist*, http://research.stlouisfed.org/publications/regional/10/07/oil.pdf [No date]

Esser, Robert, "The Oil Industry Growth Challenge: Expanding Production Capacity", Testimony to the U.S. House of Representatives, House Energy and Air Quality Subcommittee, 7 December 2005, Washington, DC, http://energycommerce.house.gov/108/Hearings/12072005hearing1733/Esser.pdf

Falcone, Gioia, Harrison, Bob, and Teodoriu, Catalin, "Can We Be More Efficient in Oil and Gas Exploitation?", *Journal of Physics and Natural Sciences*, Volume 1, Issue 2, www.scientificjournals.org/journals2007/articles/1319.pdf [No date]

Fisher, Brent, "Review and Analysis of the Peak Oil Debate", Institute for Defense Analysis, August 2008, www.dtic.mil/cgi-bin/GetTRDoc?Location=U2&doc=GetTRDoc.pdf&AD=ADA488967 [No date]

Frogatt, Anthony, "Sustainable Energy Security: Strategic Risks and Opportunities for Business", *Lloyd's 360 Risk Insight*, www.chathamhouse.org.uk/publications/papers/view/-/id/891/ [No date]

FSPO.NET, "FSPO World Fleet", http://www.fpso.net/ [No date]

Gao, Chang Hong, Zekri, Abdulrazag and El-Tarabily, Khaled, "Microbes enhance Oil Recovery through Various Mechanisms", *Oil and Gas Journal*, 17 August 2009, Vol. 10, No. 31.

Geology.com, "Drilling to the Earth's Mantle May Now Be Possible", http://geology.com/press-release/drilling-to-mantle/ [No date]

Graefe, Laurel, "The Peak Oil Debate", *Economic Review*, Federal Reserve Bank of Atlanta, Vol. 94, Number 2, 2009, www.frbatlanta.org/filelegacydocs/er0902_graefe.pdf

Hamilton, James D., "Causes and Consequences of the Oil Shock of 2007–8", *Brookings Papers in Economic Activity*, Brookings Institution, www.brookings.edu/economics/bpea/~/media/Files/Programs/ES/BPEA/2009_spring_bpea_papers/2009_spring_bpea_hamilton.pdf

Heubscher, Robert, "The Future of Oil", Advisor Perspectives, 2010, www.advisorperspectives.com/newsletters10/The_Future_of_Oil.php

Hughes, Siobhan, "U.S. News: Offshore Drilling Curbed Again", *Wall Street Journal*, 2 December 2010, p. A.3

Holland, Stephen, "Modeling Peak Oil", *The Energy Journal*, Vol. 29, No. 2, 2008, IAEE

IEA, Energy Efficiency Series, *Transport Energy Efficiency*, September 2010, International Energy Agency, Paris

IEA, Energy Technology Network, "Unconventional Oil and Gas Production", ETSAP, May 2010, www.etsap.org/E-techDS/PDF/P02-Uncon%20oil&gas-GS-gct.pdf

IEA, Statistics, *CO_2 Emissions from Fuel Combustion 2009*, 2009, International Energy Agency, Paris

——— *Oil Information*, 2010, International Energy Agency, Paris

IEA, *World Energy Outlook*, 2010, International Energy Agency, Paris

IPAA, "2008 Oil and Natural Gas Briefing Book", The Independent Petroleum Association of America, www.ipaa.org/reports/docs/2008BriefingBook.pdf

———, "Profile of Independent Producers 2009", www.ipaa.org/news/docs/IPAAProfile2009.pdf

Kokal, Sunil and Al-Kaabi, Abdulaziz, "Enhanced Oil Recovery: Challenges and Opportunities", World Petroleum Council, 2010, www.world-petroleum.org/docs/docs/publications/2010yearbook/P64–69_Kokal-Al_Kaabi.pdf

Kovarik, William, "Comparison of USGS and Oil Industry Reserve Estimates", www.radford.edu/wkovarik/oil/oiltable.xls [No date]

Laharerre, Jean. "Reserve Growth: Technological Progress or Bad Reporting and Bad Arithmetic?", www.peakoil.net/publications/reserve-growth-technological-progress-or-bad-reporting-and-bad-arithmetic [No date]

Laharerre, Jean, "Comments on "Squeezing More Oil from the Ground"", www.peakoil.net/headline-news/comments-by-jean-laherr-re-on-squeezing-more-oil-from-the-ground-scientific-american [No date]

———, Personal correspondences and discussion during 2010. [No date]

Lemley, Brad, "Anything into Oil", *Discover Magazine*, 2 April 2006, http://discovermagazine.com/2006/apr/anything-oil

Maugeri, Leonardo, *Oil: The Mythology, History and Future of the World's Most Controversial Resource*, Westport, CT, Praeger, 2006

———, "Squeezing More Oil from the Ground", *Scientific American*, October 2010, www.scientificamerican.com/article.cfm?id=squeezing-more-oil-edit-this

———, "The Crude Truth about Oil Reserve", *The Wall Street Journal*, 4 November 2009, http://online.wsj.com/article/SB10001424052748704107204574470700973579402.html

———, "Three Cheers for Expensive Oil", Foreign Affairs, Volume 82, No. 2, March-April 2006

Mollet, Paul, "Squeezing More Oil from Existing Fields", Shell.com, www.shell.com/home/content/innovation/feature_stories/2007/eor/ [No date]

Moritis, Guntis, "CO_2 Miscible, Steam Dominate Enhanced Oil Recovery Processes", *Oil and Gas Journal*, 19 April 2010, Vol. 108, No. 14

Moyer, Michael, "How Much is Left?", *Scientific American*, September 2010, www.scientificamerican.com/article.cfm?id=interactive-how-much-is-left

Nakhle, Carole, "Can the North Sea Still Save Europe?", *OPEC Energy Review* June 2008, www.iaee.org/en/publications/proceedingsabstractpdf.aspx?id=516 or http://econpapers.repec.org/article/blaopecrv/v_3a32_3ay_3a2008_3ai_3a2_3ap_3a123-38.htm

National Commission on the BP Horizon Oil Spill and Offshore Drilling, Report to the President, "Deepwater: The Gulf Oil Disaster and the Future of Offshore Drilling", www.oilspillcommission.gov/final-report [No date]

National Oil Shale Association, "Oil Shale Facts and Figures", www.oilshaleassoc.org/documents/Oil%20Shale%20Facts%20and%20Fiction%20Final.pdf [No date]

——, "Oil Shale Update", May 2010, www.oilshaleassoc.org/documents/FinalUpdateMay2010.pdf

National Petroleum Council, "Topic Paper #18, Coal to Liquids and Gas", www.npc.org/Study_Topic_Papers/18-TTG-Coals-to-Liquids.pdf [No date]

Newman, Peter, "Beyond Peak Oil: Will Our Cities Collapse?", *Res Publica*, Vol. 15, No. 1, www.cappe.edu.au/docs/pdf/Res%20Publica%2015-1.pdf [No date]

Newman, Peter J. and Burk, Victor A., "Presenting the Full Picture: Oil & Gas: Reserves Measurement and Reporting in the 21st Century", Deloitte, 2010, www.deloitte.com/view/en_GB/uk/industries/eiu/publications/0b36f4021a001210VgnVCM100000ba42f00aRCRD.htm

Offshore-technology.com, "Skarv and Indun Fields, North Sea Northern, Norway", www.offshore-technology.com/projects/skarv/ [No date]

Oxford Analytica, "International Oil Predictions for 2030 Vary Widely", OxResearch Daily Brief Service, Oxford, 4 December 2009, p. 1

Petrostrategies, Learning Center, "Are we Running out of Oil and Gas?", www.petrostrategies.org/Learning_Center/are_we_running_out_of_oil_and_gas.htm [No date]

——, "Drilling Operations", www.petrostrategies.org/Learning_Center/drilling_operations.htm [No date]

——, "Exploration", www.petrostrategies.org/Learning_Center/exploration.htm [No date]

——, "International Situation", www.petrostrategies.org/Learning_Center/international_situation.htm [No date]

——, "Oil and Gas Top Ten Lists", www.petrostrategies.org/Learning_Center/oil_and_gas_top_ten_lists.htm [No date]

——, "Oil and Gas Value Chains", www.petrostrategies.org/Learning_Center/oil_and_gas_value_chains.htm [No date]

——, "Oil Transportation", www.petrostrategies.org/Learning_Center/oil_transportation.htm [No date]

——, "Production", www.petrostrategies.org/Learning_Center/production.htm [No date]

Radler, Marilyn, "Total Reserves, Production Climb on Mixed Results", *Oil and Gas Journal*, 6 December 2010, Vol. 108, No. 46

Regtien, Jergen, "EOR: A Key Mechanism for Meeting Tomorrow's Energy Needs", www.world-petroleum.org/docs/docs/publications/2010yearbook/P70-72_Jeroen_Regtien.pdf [No date]

Renzi, Anthony, "Restoring Confidence in Reported Oil and Gas Reserves", *Oil and Gas Financial Journal*, www.akingump.com/files/Publication/c8b00d54-10fa-4898-8ad5-b398a36f29a0/Presentation/PublicationAttachment/2537b075-b666-49f0-958f-b71d0e99bcfb/693.pdf [No date]

Robelius, Fredrik, "Giant Oil Fields – The Highway to Oil", 30 March 2007, http://uu.diva-portal.org/smash/record.jsf?pid=diva2:169774

Sandrea, Ivan and Sandrea, Rafael, "Recovery Factors Leave EOR Plenty of Room for Growth", *Oil and Gas Journal*, 12 November 2007, Volume 105, no. 42.

Sandrea, Rafael, "New Tool Determines Reserves of Mature Oil and Gas Fields", *Oil and Gas Journal*, Vol. 10, No. 12, 23 March 2009

Schindler, Jorg and Werner Zittel, "Crude Oil – The Supply Outlook", February 2008, Energy Watch Group, www.energywatchgroup.org/fileadmin/global/pdf/2008-02_EWG_Oil_Report_updated.pdf

Shell.com, "Pearl GTL", www.shell.com/home/content/media/news_and_media_releases/archive/2009/pearl_qatar_update_05022009.html [No date]

Society of Petroleum Engineers, "SPE Petroleum Resources Management System Guide for Non-Technical Users", www.spe.org/industry/reserves/docs/PRMS_guide_non_tech.pdf [No date]

Stevens, Paul, "Cycles and the International Oil Industry: Where Are We Today?", www.chathamhouse.org.uk/files/16916_stevens_wp2010.pdf [No date]

Standard and Poor's, Industry Surveys, "Oil and Gas Production and Marketing", August 29, 2010, Standard and Poor's, New York

Stephens, Paul and Mitchell, John V., "Resource Depletion, Dependence and Development: Can Theory Help?", June 2008, Chatham House, www.chathamhouse.org.uk/files/11795_rddd0608theory.pdf

Sullivan, Paul, "Energetic Cities", *World Policy Journal*, Winter 2011, www.mitpressjournals.org/doi/pdf/10.1162/wopj.2011.27.4.11

Sulivan, Paul, "Written Testimony in Support of the Oral Testimony of Professor Paul Sullivan, National Defense University and Georgetown University for the Western Hemisphere Subcommittee of the Foreign Affairs Committee, US House of Representatives Regarding the Need for Canadian Oil As We Face Increasing Turmoil in the Middle East, Increasing Competition for Energy Resources, Peak Conventional Oil, and an Increasingly Complex Geostrategic Environment", *Before the Western Hemisphere Subcommittee of the Foreign Affairs Committee, U.S. House of Representatives, March 31, 2011, found at* http://foreignaffairs.house.gov/112/sul033111.pdf

The Oil Depletion Analysis Centre, "Preparing for Peak Oil", www.odac-info.org/sites/default/files/Preparing_for_Peak_Oil_0.pdf [No date]

U.K, Industry Task Force on Peak Oil and Energy Security, "The Oil Crunch: A Wake-Up Call for the U.K. Economy", February 2010, http://peakoiltaskforce.net/wp-content/uploads/2010/02/final-report-uk-itpoes_report_the-oil-crunch_feb20101.pdf

United Nations, Economic Commission for Europe, "United Nations Framework Classification for Fossil Energy and Minerals Resource", www.unece.org/se/pdfs/UNFC/UNFCemr.pdf [No date]

United States, House of Representatives, Foreign Affairs Committee, Hearing Before the Western Hemisphere Subcommittee, "Rising Oil Prices and Dependence on Hostile Regimes: The Urgent Case for Canadian Oil", Full Transcript of Hearing at: http://foreignaffairs.house.gov/112/65494.pdf

UNEP, "Overview of the Oil and Gas Exploration and Production Process", *Environmental Management in Oil and Gas Exploration and Production*, www.ogp.org.uk/pubs/254.pdf [No date]

U.S., DOE, *Fossil Energy Study Guide: Oil*, http://fossil.energy.gov/education/energylessons/oil/HS_Oil_Studyguide_draft2.pdf [No date]

U.S., DOE, EIA, "Crude Oil Production and Crude Oil Well Productivity, 1954–2009", http://tonto.eia.doe.gov/aer/pdf/pages/sec5_6.pdf [No date]

U.S., DOE, EIA, "Liquid Fuels", *International Energy Outlook 2010*, www.eia.doe.gov/oiaf/ieo/liquid_fuels.html [No date]

U.S., DOE, EIA, "Oil Market Basics", www.eia.doe.gov/pub/oil_gas/petroleum/analysis_publications/oil_market_basics/default.htm [No date]

U.S., DOE, EIA, "Petroleum Supply Monthly", ftp://ftp.eia.doe.gov/pub/oil_gas/petroleum/data_publications/petroleum_supply_monthly/current/pdf/psmall.pdf [No date]

U.S., DOE, EIA, "U.S. Crude Oil, Natural Gas and Natural Gas Liquids Reserves", www.eia.doe.gov/natural_gas/data_publications/crude_oil_natural_gas_reserves/cr.html [No date]

U.S., DOE, EIA, "Use of Oil", www.eia.doe.gov/energyexplained/index.cfm?page=oil_use [No date]

U.S., DOE, EIA, "Who are the Major Players Supplying the World Oil Market?", www.eia.doe.gov/energy_in_brief/world_oil_market.cfm [No date]

U.S., DOE, EIA, "World Crude Oil Production, 1960–2009", www.eia.doe.gov/aer/txt/ptb1105.html [No date]

U.S., DOE, EIA, "World Proved Oil Reserves by Geographic Region as of January 1, 2010", www.eia.doe.gov/oiaf/ieo/excel/figure_35data.xls [No date]

U.S., DOE, EIA, "World proved Reserves of Oil and Natural Gas, Most Recent Estimates", www.eia.doe.gov/international/reserves.html [No date]

U.S., DOE, NETL, "Carbon Dioxide Enhanced Oil Recovery", www.netl.doe.gov/technologies/oil-gas/publications/EP/small_CO2_eor_primer.pdf [No date]

U.S. DOE NETL, "Optimizing Recovery of Domestic Petroleum Resources", www.fossil.energy.gov/programs/oilgas/publications/environment_otherpubs/Optimal_Recov_Petro_factsheet_2009.pdf [No date]

U.S., DOE, NETL, "Preferred Upstream Management Practices", www.netl.doe.gov/technologies/oil-gas/publications/brochures/Pump.pdf [No date]

U.S., DOE, NETL, "Ultra-Deepwater and Unconventional Natural Gas and Other Petroleum Resources Research Program", www.fossil.energy.gov/programs/oilgas/ultra_and_unconventional/index.html [No date]

U.S., DOE, NETL, "Unconventional Fossil Energy Resources Program", www.netl.doe.gov/publications/factsheets/program/Prog100.pdf [No date]

U.S. DOE, Office of Deputy Assistant Secretary for Petroleum Reserves, Office of Naval Petroleum and Oil Shale Reserves, "Strategic Significance of America's Oil Shale Resource: Volume I: Assessment of

Strategic Issues", http://fossil.energy.gov/programs/reserves/npr/publications/npr_strategic_significancev1.pdf [No date]

U.S., GAO, "Energy-Water Nexus: A Better Coordinate Understanding of Water Resources Could Help Mitigate the Impacts of Potential Oil Shale Development", October 2010, www.gao.gov/new.items/d1135.pdf

U.S., GAO, "Uncertainty about Future Oil Supply Makes It Important to Develop a Strategy for Addressing a Peak and Decline in Oil Production", February 2007, www.gao.gov/products/GAO-07-283

U.S. Geological Survey, "Assessment of Undiscovered Oil and Gas Resources of the Nile Delta Basin Province, Eastern Mediterranean", http://pubs.usgs.gov/fs/2010/3027/pdf/FS10–3027.pdf [No date]

U.S. Geological Survey, "Assessment of Undiscovered Petroleum Resources of the Barents Sea Shelf", http://pubs.usgs.gov/fs/2009/3037/pdf/FS09–3037.pdf [No date]

U.S. Geological Survey, "Circum-Arctic Resource Appraisal: Estimates of Undiscovered Oil and Gas North of the Arctic Circle", http://pubs.usgs.gov/fs/2008/3049/ [No date]

U.S. Geological Survey, "Geology and Resources of Some World Oil-Shale Deposits", http://pubs.usgs.gov/sir/2005/5294/pdf/sir5294_508.pdf [No date]

U.S. Geological Survey, "Geology and Total Petroleum Systems of the Gulf of Guinea Province of West Africa", http://pubs.usgs.gov/bul/2207/C/pdf/b2207c_508.pdf [No date]

U.S. Geological Survey, "USGS Reassesses Potential World Petroleum Resources: Oil Estimates up, Gas Down", 22 March 2000, www.usgs.gov/newsroom/article.asp?ID=636 [No date]

Whitney, Gene, Behrens, Carl and Glover, Carol, "U.S. Fossil Fuel Resources: Terminology, Reporting and Summary", Congressional Research Service, 28 October 2009, http://epw.senate.gov/public/index.cfm?FuseAction=Files.View&FileStore_id = f7bd7b77-ba50–48c2-a635–220d7cf8c519

Witze, Alexandra, "That's Oil, Folks. ... ", *Nature*, Vol. 445, No. 4, 4 January 2007

World Energy Council, "Crude Oil and Natural Gas Liquids" *Survey of Energy Resources 2010*, pp. 41–150, www.worldenergy.org/documents/ser_2010_report_1.pdf [No date]

3
The Changing Geopolitics of Oil

Michael T. Klare

Geopolitics and oil have been closely intertwined for a very long time. Geopolitics – or the efforts undertaken by a state to advance its political and economic interests abroad – has a natural affinity with petroleum because oil is essential for the functioning of modern economies and military organizations and because it is only found in certain areas of the world. For over a century, the governments of the major powers have considered it necessary to ensure an adequate supply of oil to meet national requirements and, in times of crisis and conflict, to deny such a supply to their adversaries. Given that many of the world's principal sources of petroleum lie outside the borders of the major powers, the leaders of these countries have long sought to exercise control over (or influence in) the oil-producing areas. This had led to a fierce struggle for dominance in these key regions – a phenomenon best described as the geopolitics of oil.[1]

In many respects, the geopolitics of oil has retained the features it exhibited when initially inserting itself into world politics before and during World War I. At that time, petroleum first became crucial to warfare – with the introduction of oil-powered tanks, airplanes, and warships – and so assured *access* to oil became a principal military objective. This, in turn, highlighted the strategic importance of oil-producing areas, and made their protection or conquest a major military objective. Ever since then, oil geopolitics has emphasized efforts by the major oil-consuming nations to gain and retain positions of influence in the major oil regions. Also, because many key sources of supply are located far from the homeland or major sites of conflict, oil geopolitics has also emphasized control over the *transit routes* used to transport oil, such as the vitally important Suez Canal.

These features of oil geopolitics continue to shape world affairs. The USA – now the world's leading consumer and importer of petroleum – has established an elaborate overseas military apparatus to ensure the safe transport of foreign oil to international markets and has used force on several occasions to eliminate threats to this flow.[2] As in the post-World War I era, the major powers continue to compete for influence in the major oil-producing regions, using the various instruments at their disposal.[3] Concern over the safety of transportation of oil routes also remains a major international concern, especially in light of the recent upsurge in piracy off the coast of Yemen and Somalia, which has sometimes targeted oil tankers.

But despite this continuity, some aspects of oil geopolitics have changed over the years. Most significant are the shifts in the geographic foci of this competition. Before and after World War I, the major pivots of oil geopolitics were Romania, the upper Persian Gulf (what is now Iran and Iraq), and the Baku area (in what is now Azerbaijan); later, the Dutch East Indies (now Indonesia) were added to the mix. These areas attracted substantial interest from the major powers in the interwar years (1918–39) and were key strategic targets during World War II. Some of these areas, such as the Gulf area and Azerbaijan, continue to attract geopolitical interest, while others, including Romania and Indonesia, have become less important as oil producers. At the same time, new producers have arisen and gained in prominence, including several in Africa and the Caspian Sea region. In addition, the depletion of many existing oil reservoirs combined with impressive advances in extractive technology have given increased impetus to drilling in areas once considered inaccessible, such as far-offshore waters and the Arctic – lending these areas added geopolitical significance as well. As a result of all this, the global map of oil geopolitics is undergoing a dramatic transformation.

The geopolitics of oil has also been altered by the emergence of powerful new players. Up until World War II, the key actors in this contest were the European powers and the USA, joined in the 1930s by Japan. After World War II, the Europeans declined in importance while the USA and the Soviet Union reigned supreme. But now a host of new players, including China and India, have come to the fore; and while the Soviet Union is no more, Russia has emerged as a major player in its own right. All of this, too, has transformed the map of oil geopolitics.

The origins of oil geopolitics

Many scholars believe that it was Winston Churchill who first comprehended the geopolitical significance of oil. In 1912, as First Lord of the Admiralty, Churchill ordered the conversion of British warships from coal to oil propulsion in the belief this would give them an advantage over Germany's coal-powered ships in the event of war. Because Great Britain at that time did not possess domestic oil reserves of its own – the North Sea fields were not discovered until much later – Churchill determined that London must obtain a secure overseas source of oil under direct British control. In particular, he sought to extend government control over the Anglo-Persian Oil Company (APOC, the forerunner of British Petroleum), which had secured a concession to promising reserves in southwestern Persia (now Iran). Through his prodding, Parliament voted in 1914 to nationalize APOC and bring the Persian concession under British government control. From that point onward, the protection of APOC's concession area and of British supply lines to the Persian Gulf (especially the Suez Canal) were viewed as matters of vital national security by the British government.[4]

As predicted by Churchill, oil-powered weapons played a significant role during World War I. If this was not evident at the start of the war, it was certainly so at the end, following the dramatic appearance of oil-powered tanks, aircraft, and submarines. This, in turn, made it vitally important for the major powers to gain ensured access to prolific supplies of petroleum. "Oil in the next war will replace coal in the present war," Sir Maurice Hankey, the secretary of Britain's War Cabinet, told Foreign Secretary Arthur Balfour at the time, and so control over foreign oil deposits "becomes a first-class war aim."[5] As the war drew to a close, Britain, along with the other victorious powers, sought to redraw the postwar political landscape in such a way as to enhance their access to overseas oil supplies. Much of this effort focused on the fate of the Ottoman Empire, which was thought to possess significant oil deposits in areas of Mesopotamia (later Iraq) that bordered APOC's existing fields in Persia. Both Britain and France sought control over these areas, whose postwar destiny was a major issue in Franco-British relations during this period. Finally, under the San Remo Agreement of 1920, Britain obtained control over Mesopotamia through a mandate from the League of Nations; France, in turn, was assured access to 25% of all oil produced in the territory.[6]

The strategic aspect of the international competition for sources of energy continued to play a significant role in international relations throughout the period between World Wars I and II. The major European powers – possessing few domestic oil reserves of their own – focused much of their geopolitical efforts on gaining or expanding a foothold in the oil-bearing areas of the Persian Gulf basin. Great Britain, in particular, sought to extend its sway over an ever-greater swath of this region. Meanwhile, Japan – a rising industrial power with a similar paucity of oil – harbored imperial ambitions over the Dutch East Indies, then the major producer in Asia. The need to secure overseas sources of oil played a significant role in the evolving war plans of Germany and Japan, both of which sought to invade and conquer foreign sources of supply in order to fuel their military forces and domestic industrial machines. In 1941, when full-scale combat broke out, both undertook military strikes with this purpose in mind: Germany invaded the Soviet Union with Baku as one of its primary objectives; Japan invaded the Dutch East Indies. Because Tokyo assumed that its invasion of the Dutch East Indies would provoke a US military response of some sort, it simultaneously attacked the US naval base at Pearl Harbor in Hawaii, thus ensuring American entry into the war.[7]

Up until this point, the USA had not participated in the strategic (as distinct from commercial) pursuit of overseas oil, as it possessed sufficient domestic reserves to satisfy its wartime military requirements and those of its principal allies. As World War II progressed, however, President Franklin D. Roosevelt and his senior advisers became deeply concerned that the heavy wartime extraction of domestic oil was rapidly depleting US reserves, and so erasing America's capacity to sustain another full-scale war on the scale of World War II. (At this time, American geologists were unaware of major deposits in Alaska and the deeper waters of the Gulf of Mexico, making it appear that US reserves were shrinking faster than, in fact, later proved to be the case.) Accordingly, Roosevelt ordered the State and Commerce Departments to seek a reliable foreign source of oil to supplement American reserves in the event of a major future conflict.[8]

After considering the various possibilities, government experts became convinced that the Kingdom of Saudi Arabia constituted the best candidate to serve in this capacity. Whereas most of the rest of the Gulf area was under British dominion – and that of Britain's state-controlled oil company, APOC – Saudi Arabia had largely escaped British control. In addition, the Saudi monarch, King Abdul Aziz ibn Saud, had granted a substantial oil concession to an American oil firm, the Standard Oil Company of California (Socal), giving the USA a significant presence in the country. Early geological studies had suggested, moreover, that the concession area harbored vast reserves of oil. On the basis of these considerations, Roosevelt decided in 1943 to anoint Saudi Arabia as America's chosen foreign supplier of oil and to be brought under American military protection. To cement this arrangement, Roosevelt met with Abdul Aziz on February 14, 1945 and forged an agreement with him under which the USA received privileged access to Saudi oil in return for a US pledge to protect the monarchy against all enemies, foreign and domestic.[9] From this point onward, it was American policy to prevent any hostile power from invading Saudi Arabia or otherwise impeding US access to the oil supplies of the Persian Gulf area.

With this Roosevelt-Abdul Aziz agreement in place, the USA proceeded to insert a permanent military presence in the Gulf region. This led, in 1946–47, to the establishment of an air base at Dhahran in Saudi Arabia and a naval base at Bahrain. The USA also began to provide Saudi Arabia with advanced weaponry and other forms of military assistance.[10] For much of this period, the Soviet Union was viewed as the major threat to American strategic interests in the

Gulf, and so US policy was aimed at preventing any Soviet inroads into the region. This outlook was responsible for one of the formative episodes of the early Cold War era, a clash between Moscow and Washington over Soviet efforts to establish a pro-Soviet state in northern Iran, the short-lived Autonomous Republic of Azerbaijan.[11] This clash and continuing US concern over Soviet inroads in the Middle East provided the backdrop for several of the major US policy statements of the Cold War era, including the Truman Doctrine of 1947 and the Eisenhower Doctrine of 1957.[12]

But despite the perceived importance of ensuring access to Saudi Arabia and other Persian Gulf oil producers, American policymakers were largely content to allow Great Britain to shoulder responsibility for maintaining stability in the Gulf area during this period. Later, when London announced in 1968 that it would withdraw most British forces from "East of Suez" by the end of 1971, Washington again sought a friendly power to carry the burden of regional security – on this occasion choosing to rely on the Iranian regime of Shah Reza Mohammed Pahlavi, whom the Americans and British had helped install as absolute monarch through a CIA-orchestrated coup in 1953.[13] From 1971 to 1978, the Shah was the leading foreign recipient of US arms aid and technical support, including a wide array of advanced military equipment.[14] In early 1979, however, the Shah was driven from power by rebellious Shiite clergy, once again raising alarm in Washington over the safety of America's access to vital Persian Gulf oil supplies. Eleven months later, in December 1979, the security equation in the Gulf received a further jolt when the Soviet Union commenced its invasion and occupation of Afghanistan.

The "Carter Doctrine" and beyond

In the wake of these developments, then President Jimmy Carter and his top advisers determined that US interests in the Gulf had become too great to be entrusted into the hands of surrogates and so would have to come under the direct protection of American forces. This proposition, henceforth known as the Carter Doctrine, was spelled out in the president's January 1980 State of the Union address. To a degree unprecedented in modern American political discourse, Carter provided a geopolitical explanation for the expansion of American military power. "The region which is now threatened by Soviet troops in Afghanistan is of great strategic importance: it contains more than two-thirds of the world's exportable oil," he declared. "The Soviet effort to dominate Afghanistan has brought Soviet forces to within 300 miles of the Indian Ocean and close to the Straits of Hormuz, a waterway through which most of the world's oil must flow." As a result, "the Soviet Union is now attempting to consolidate a strategic position ... that poses a grave threat to the free movement of Middle East oil." America's response to this threat, he avowed, cannot be equivocal. "Let our position be absolutely clear: An attempt by any outside force to gain control of the Persian Gulf region will be regarded as an assault on the vital interests of the United States of America, and such an assault will be repelled by any means necessary, including military force."[15]

Because the USA did not, at that time, possess any forces earmarked for operations in the Persian Gulf area, President Carter established a new military organization to implement this policy, the Rapid Deployment Joint Task Force (RDJTF). He also announced plans to deploy additional warships in the Gulf and to acquire new bases in the surrounding region. Carter also began a policy of "pre-positioning" US military materiel in the Gulf area, thereby allowing for the rapid reinforcement of US forces already deployed there. These measures all received strong support from Carter's successor, Ronald Reagan, who elevated the RDJTF into a full-scale regional combat organization, the US Central Command (CENTCOM). In keeping with the strategic thinking of the time, CENTCOM was originally intended to repel a Soviet invasion of the Gulf area, but, over time, has been reconfigured to face threats emanating from states within the region, notably Iran and Iraq.[16]

Again and again, American officials have reaffirmed the basic precept embodied in Carter's January 1980 address. When Iranian naval forces began attacking Kuwaiti and Saudi oil tankers in the Persian Gulf itself during the Iran-Iraq War of 1980–88 – thus jeopardizing the flow of crude to American refineries – the administration of President Ronald Reagan threatened to employ military force to keep the oil flowing. "We would regard as especially serious any threat by either party to interfere with free navigation or act in any way that would restrict oil exports from the Gulf," Deputy Assistant Secretary of State Robert H. Pelletreau asserted in 1983.[17] When the Iranians failed to heed this and subsequent warnings, President Reagan authorized the "reflagging" of Kuwaiti tankers with the American ensign and ordered U.S. warships to escort them while traversing the Gulf. In this manner the United States became a *de facto* belligerent in that war, opposing Iran – and, by extension, aiding Iraq.[18]

American determination to ensure the safety of Persian Gulf oil supplies in accordance with the Carter Doctrine was next affirmed in 1990, when Iraqi forces invaded Kuwait and appeared to pose a threat to Saudi Arabia, the world's leading producer. In a nationally televised address on August 8 announcing his decision to employ military force in the Gulf, President George H. W. Bush cited America's energy needs as his primary impetus for intervention in the region. "Our country now imports nearly half the oil it consumes and could face a major threat to its economic independence," he declared. Hence, "the sovereign independence of Saudi Arabia is of vital interest to the United States."[19] Only later, when American forces were girding for combat with the Iraqis, did administration officials assert other justifications for war – the need to liberate Kuwait, to destroy Iraqi weapons of mass destruction (WMD), to bolster international sanctions against aggression, and so forth. The historical record makes it clear, however, that the President and his senior associates initially viewed the invasion of Kuwait through the lens of the Carter Doctrine: as a threat to Saudi Arabia and the safe flow of oil from the Gulf.[20]

Following the expulsion of Iraqi forces from Kuwait, the first President Bush considered – but eventually rejected – plans to invade Iraq and eliminate the threat posed by Saddam Hussein once and for all. Instead, he chose to weaken the regime (and hopefully spark a military coup) through a punishing system of economic sanctions – a policy subsequently embraced by his successor, President Bill Clinton. But despite painful consequences for ordinary Iraqis, the sanctions failed to achieve their intended goal of "regime change" in Baghdad – making US policy look increasingly ineffectual. It was on this basis (among others) that President George W. Bush eventually concluded that direct military action was needed to complete the task of regime change left unfinished at the conclusion of the first Gulf War.[21]

At present, American forces are in the process of withdrawing from Iraq. But the same geopolitical considerations that underlay the invasion of that country, as originally expressed in the Carter Doctrine, are now being extended to Iran – another country seen as posing a threat to the safe flow of Persian Gulf oil. Although Washington's chief argument with Tehran has been its suspected pursuit of nuclear weapons, US officials are also worried that the Iranians are prepared to impede oil shipping in the Gulf area in the event of any future confrontation with the USA.[22] To deter such action, the Bush Administration conducted highly conspicuous naval manoeuvres in the Gulf and issued stern warnings of likely US countermeasures. "With two carrier strike groups in the Gulf, we're sending clear messages to friends and adversaries alike," Vice-President Cheney declared during one such exercise, in May 2007. "We'll keep the sea lanes open. We'll stand with our friends in opposing extremism and strategic threats."[23]

President Obama has eschewed such harsh language and instead relied on a campaign of tough sanctions to pressure Tehran, but has not backed off from demands that the Iranians abandon their nuclear arms ambitions and ensure the safety of Persian Gulf oil supplies.

The extended Carter Doctrine

At present, US efforts to ensure access to overseas sources of oil remain centered on the Persian Gulf area. In recent years, however, this policy has been extended to other regions, including the Caspian Sea basin and West Africa. This is the result of dedicated efforts by Washington to "diversify" America's foreign sources of oil, thereby minimizing its reliance on any single area – such as the Gulf – that could be susceptible to periodic supply interruptions. A key US strategic goal, the Bush Administration affirmed in 2002, is "to strengthen [US] energy security and the shared prosperity of the global economy by working with our allies, trading partners, and energy producers to expand the sources and types of global energy supplied, especially in the Western Hemisphere, Africa, Central Asia, and the Caspian region."[24] And, as the USA has come to rely for more of its oil on areas outside the Persian Gulf area, it has begun to replicate in those areas the same sort of military measures adopted in the Gulf since Roosevelt's day to ensure the safe flow of petroleum.[25]

The first president to stress this approach was Bill Clinton, who crafted what might be termed an "extended Carter Doctrine" and applied it to the Caspian Sea region in the late 1990s.[26] Carter viewed the Caspian basin both as a promising new source of oil and as a welcome alternative to the ever-turbulent Middle East. At that time, the newly-independent states of Azerbaijan and Kazakhstan were eager to sell their petroleum riches to the West, but lacked an autonomous conduit for exports, as all existing pipelines from the Caspian Sea basin passed through Russia. (The Caspian itself is land-locked, so any petroleum exiting the region must travel by pipeline or rail cars.) Clinton agreed to assist in the construction of a new oil pipeline from Azerbaijan to Turkey via Georgia, bypassing Russia. Because this new conduit, the Baku-Tbilisi-Ceyhan (BTC) pipeline, passed through or near several areas of ethnic unrest, Clinton also agreed to help these states bolster their military capabilities.[27] Although never formally invoking the Carter Doctrine when announcing these actions, Clinton applied the same "national security" umbrella to Caspian Sea energy as Carter had done in the Gulf. Hence, in a 1997 White House meeting with Heydar Aliyev (then president of Azerbaijan), he affirmed that by facilitating Azerbaijan's oil exports, "we not only help Azerbaijan to prosper, we also help diversify our energy supply and strengthen our nation's security."[28]

Just as President Clinton extended the Carter Doctrine to the Caspian Sea basin, President George W. Bush extended it to Africa. As is true of the Caspian region, Africa is seen by American officials both as a valuable source of oil and as an alternative to reliance on the Persian Gulf.[29] Africa's potential role in satisfying US oil needs was first highlighted in the Bush Administration's National Energy Policy of May 2001: "Sub-Saharan Africa holds 7% of world oil reserves and comprises 11% of world oil production. ... West Africa is expected to be one of the fastest growing sources of oil and gas for the American market."[30] This obviously gave Africa a geopolitical significance it did not possess before. "African oil is of national strategic interest to us," Assistant Secretary of State Walter Kansteiner observed in 2002, "and it will increase and become more important as we go forward."[31] As in the Caspian, this perception of Africa's growing strategic importance has led to an increase in US military assistance.[32] As a further expression of Africa's increased importance, President Bush created a new military command organization for the region, the US Africa Command (AFRICOM), in February 2007. Although the establishment of AFRICOM was not explicitly tied to the protection of oil – as was the case for CENTCOM – it is evident from government statements that this is an underlying factor.[33]

Within Africa, particular emphasis has been placed on Nigeria – the leading sub-Saharan producer and one of America's principal foreign suppliers. "Nigeria is the fifth largest source of US oil imports, and disruption of supply from Nigeria would represent a major blow to US oil security strategy," the State Department noted in its Fiscal Year 2006 request for economic and military assistance to Nigeria. It is for this reason, the document asserts, that the USA should help bolster Nigeria's internal security forces and protect its vital oil installations – especially "in the vulnerable oil-producing Niger Delta region."[34] In addition to direct military assistance under various bilateral aid programs, Nigeria is a participant in several Pentagon-sponsored multinational programs that serve, under the rubric of the Global War on Terror, as supplemental conduits for US military support, including the African Contingency Operations Training and Assistance Program and the Trans-Saharan Counter-Terrorism Initiative. These programs were begun during the Bush Administration, but have been much expanded in the Obama Administration.[35]

Geopolitical initiatives by China and Russia

While it is the USA that has been most conspicuous in the pursuit of geopolitical advantage in oil-producing areas around the world, it is hardly alone; as has been true before, a number of other countries are competing for positions of influence in these areas. America's geopolitical competitors include some states, such as Russia, that have long sought positions of influence in these areas, along with others, including China, that are relative newcomers. China's emergence as a competitor is particularly striking. Until 1993, China was self-sufficient in oil and thus saw little need to establish overseas ties of the sort long nurtured by the USA with its leading suppliers. But as China's reliance on imported oil has grown, so, too, has its diplomatic and military intercourse with major foreign producers.

In 2009, according to BP's *Statistical Review of World Energy*, China consumed 8.6m. barrels of oil per day and produced 3.8 million b/d, forcing it to import 4.8m. b/d.[36] (By contrast, the USA imported approximately 11.5m. b/d in that year; Japan imported 4.3m. b/d.) China's import requirements are expected to grow in the years ahead, reflecting rising demand – much of it propelled by exploding automobile ownership – and stagnant production at home. In 2035, according to predictions by the US Department of Energy, China will remain number two in consumption after the USA (16.9 to 22.1 million b/d, respectively), but will overtake the USA to be the world's leading oil *importer*, requiring foreign supplies of 12.1m. b/d, compared to 10.7m. b/d for the USA. Because the number of foreign oil producers that can satisfy the import requirements of China and the USA are limited, these two countries are destined to be entwined in a desperate struggle for access and influence in the oil-producing regions.[37]

Chinese leaders appear to harbor little doubt about this geopolitical imperative, and so have been making vigorous efforts to establish close ties with favored producers in the major oil-producing regions. As part of this drive, Chinese President Hu Jintao, Premier Wen Jiabao, and other top officials have made numerous trips to Africa, the Persian Gulf, and the Caspian region to negotiate major oil purchases and to promote the involvement in joint ventures of state-controlled firms, including the China National Petroleum Corporation (CNPC), the China National Petrochemical Corporation (Sinopec), and the China National Offshore Oil Corporation (CNOOC).[38] In 1999, for example, China established a "strategic oil partnership" with Saudi Arabia, under which Sinopec is to co-operate with Saudi Aramco in developing oil and gas fields in the kingdom while Aramco would invest in refineries and petrochemical plants in China.[39] Similarly, in 2006, Hu Jintao met with then President Olusegun Obasanjo of Nigeria and negotiated a "strategic partnership" that included significant co-operation in the area of energy.[40] Chinese leaders have also sought to establish such relationships with Kazakhstan, Russia, and Venezuela, among other countries.[41]

Like the USA, China has also employed military means in its effort to cement ties with its foreign oil suppliers. The militarization of China's foreign energy ties is especially evident in Africa and Central Asia. China first became involved in the delivery of arms and military services to African oil providers in 1996, when it acquired a majority stake in the Greater Nile Petroleum Operation Company, Sudan's leading producer. At that time, Sudan faced a severe challenge from rebel forces in the south (where most of the country's oil fields were located) and desperately needed a fresh infusion of weapons for its army; when rebuffed by Western powers, the Khartoum regime turned to Beijing, which proved far more accommodating. Eager to ensure the safety of its recently-acquired oil assets in southern Sudan, China provided a wide array of modern arms, which were then used to drive the rebels out of the oil-producing region in what many observers termed a "scorched-earth campaign."[42] The Sudanese government reached a cease-fire agreement with the southern rebels in 2005, but has stepped up its efforts to suppress insurgents in the Darfur region – again reportedly using weapons supplied by China.[43]

As China has increased its reliance on other African suppliers, it has increased its military ties with them as well. Thus, when Chinese oil firms made their first significant bids for oil assets in Nigeria in 2005, Beijing agreed to provide the Nigerian government with jet aircraft and naval patrol boats.[44] The Chinese are also supplying arms and ammunition to a number of other African oil suppliers and, like the USA, are supplementing these deliveries with training programs, joint combat exercises, and intelligence-sharing activities.[45]

In the Caspian region and Central Asia, China has been reluctant to play an overly conspicuous role as an arms provider in its own right – no doubt being wary of giving any impression that it has imperial designs on the region – but has channelled such aid through the Shanghai Cooperation Organization (SCO), the regional organization it helped launch in 1996. Originally created to enhance counter-terrorism operations and border security in Central Asia, the SCO has evolved into a robust regional security organization with a decidedly anti-American cast.[46] At a 2005 SCO summit meeting, for example, member states called on the USA to vacate its military bases in the region.[47] As China has become more reliant on the Central Asian countries for supplies of oil and natural gas, it has increased the importance given to the SCO in its foreign policy and the resources devoted to the organization's growth. This has led to an accelerated tempo of joint military exercises and to the delivery – under SCO auspices – of Chinese arms to the Central Asian republics.[48]

Until now, China's efforts to protect its access to overseas sources of energy have been limited to the delivery of arms and military-support services. There is growing evidence, however, that China is expanding its capacity to employ military force in ensuring access to overseas supplies of oil and other vital resources. "China's reliance on foreign energy imports has affected its strategy and policy in significant ways," the US Department of Defense observed in the 2008 edition of its annual report, *The Military Power of the People's Republic of China*. At present, the report noted, China lacks the capacity to use force in ensuring access to its foreign sources of energy. However, "China's leaders may seek to close this gap" by acquiring a broad spectrum of "extended-range power projection" capabilities, including aircraft carriers and associated support vessels, long-range missiles, expeditionary forces, and overseas bases.[49] As if to confirm this assessment, the deputy commander of the East Sea Fleet, Rear Admiral Zhang

Huachen, told the Xinhua news agency in 2010 of China's expanding naval prospects. "With the expansion of the country's economic interests, the navy wants to better protect the country's transportation routes and the safety of our major sea lanes." To achieve this, "the Chinese Navy needs to develop along the lines of bigger vessels and with more comprehensive capabilities."[50]

Russia has also sought to expand its geopolitical presence in key oil-producing areas, especially the Caspian Sea basin. In its case, the motive is not to acquire energy for domestic use – Russia is self-sufficient in oil and natural gas – but rather to dominate the *transportation* of energy, in order to reap the attendant political and economic benefits. In the case of the Caspian Sea states, these countries were once part of the Soviet Union – and the Russian empire before that – so Russian leaders believe that they possess a natural right to exercise some degree of dominion over them. On top of that, the Russians seek to control the flow of oil and natural gas from the Caspian basin to Europe, thereby pocketing the lucrative transit fees involved and exercising a degree of influence over their needy customers in the West.[51] To achieve these goals, Moscow has used the same sort of intensive diplomacy and associated military instruments employed by Beijing and Washington in seeking influence in this region. Along with its participation in the Shanghai Cooperation Organization, Russia also works through the Collective Security Treaty Organization (CSTO) – a NATO-like entity composed of former Soviet republics – to provide arms and military aid to the Caspian Sea states. Using CSTO as an umbrella, Moscow also maintains military bases in some of these countries and engages in regular military exercises with their armed forces.[52]

How all this will play itself out in the years ahead cannot be foreseen. What can be said, however, is that the flow of arms, advisers, and other military capabilities into the oil-producing regions is accelerating as a result of the geopolitical struggle for advantage among China, Russia, and the USA, and that this brings with it an attendant risk of outside involvement in any local conflicts that might arise in these areas. For example, any future war between South Sudan and North Sudan over the division of their shared oil reservoirs could result in indirect involvement by the USA and China on opposite sides, with Washington supporting the South and Beijing the North. It is not hard to conjure up other comparable scenarios in the Caspian region, with Russia as an added participant. While the likelihood of any one of these particular scenarios unfolding may be low, history suggests that clashes of this sort become increasingly likely when states engage in intense geopolitical competition involving the transfer of arms and military personnel.

New geopolitical arenas

Although aspects of the competition have been altered, Africa, the Caspian Sea basin, and the Persian Gulf area have all experienced geopolitical competition before and, as the global thirst for petroleum grows, will do so again in the future. But now, as a result of developments in technology and growing international demand, this competition is extending to additional areas – many never exposed to such contestation before. Of particular note in this regard is the extension of oil drilling into deep-sea areas and the Arctic region. These areas were largely inaccessible to the oil companies until relatively recently, and so did not figure significantly in the realm of oil geopolitics; but now that they are coming within reach, these areas are attracting enormous interest. Because much of the world's remaining untapped oil and natural gas is believed to lie in such areas, and because many of them are blanketed by overlapping claims to sovereignty, they have become the subjects of geopolitical competition – in some cases accompanied by violence or the threat of violence.

Most of the world's major oil reservoirs were discovered 30, 40, 50, or more years ago, and are now facing systemic depletion. According to a comprehensive study by the International Energy Agency (IEA), crude oil output from all fields in operation in 2009 will decline from 68m. b/d in that year to a mere 16m. b/d in 2035, a drop of three-quarters. In order to sustain production and meet rising demand, the oil companies will have to find and develop new reservoirs – most of which are expected to be located offshore and in the Arctic region.[53] According to a March 2010 assessment by energy analyst John Westwood, offshore oil output will contribute 35% of global supplies in 2020, up from about 28% in 1995. More tellingly, the share of world oil provided by deep and ultra-deep wells will grow from only 3% in 2002 to a projected 10% in 2012. Westwood further predicts that after 2015, no further increase in output will occur in onshore and shallow coastal reservoirs, leaving deep-offshore fields as the *only* source of further worldwide production growth.[54]

Drilling in deep-offshore areas poses a host of technological and environmental challenges, as demonstrated by the April 2010 *Deepwater Horizon* disaster in the US Gulf of Mexico. But it also poses geological risks in areas where offshore borders are not fully demarcated. This is especially true in the Western Pacific and Southeast Asia, where the presence of many island chains complicates the task of determining maritime boundaries. The only international covenant that addresses this problem, the United Nations Convention on the Law of the Sea (UNCLOS), provides ambiguous criteria for determining the outer boundaries of coastal states, and there is no international court empowered (or equipped) to adjudicate such disputes. These distinctions did not matter much when states saw no value in these deep-offshore areas, but now that they hope to exploit the mammoth oil and natural gas deposits believed to be lying there, the location of offshore boundaries *do* matter – especially when a shift in such a boundary by 10 or 20 miles in either direction could mean the gain or loss of a multibillion-dollar gas field.[55]

The Western Pacific region harbors several such disputes, of which the most important and worrisome are those in the East and South China Seas. These are relatively large bodies of water separated from the Pacific proper by a string of islands: Japan and Taiwan in the north; the Philippines in the South. Both areas are believed to sit above large oil and natural gas deposits: the East China Sea is believed to sit atop a large natural gas field off eastern China; the South China Sea possesses valuable oil fields in areas off the Spratly Islands, situated between China, Malaysia, the Philippines and Vietnam. Because so many countries have advanced claims to all or part of these areas – China, Japan, and Taiwan in the East China Sea; Brunei, China, Indonesia, Malaysia, the Philippines, Taiwan, and Vietnam in the South China Sea – it has proven nearly impossible to establish firm offshore boundaries and award production licences to interested energy firms.[56] The problem has been compounded by Beijing's assertion that the greater part of *both* seas fall within its national territory and its stated unwillingness to compromise on these claims due to issues of national pride and sovereignty. To remove any uncertainty about their resolve in this matter, Chinese officials have regularly deployed naval forces in the disputed areas and, on occasion, employed force to seize and hold small islands also claimed by other countries.[57]

The East China Sea is believed to be especially rich in natural gas. A large field – called Chunxiao by the Chinese and Shirakaba by the Japanese – has been discovered in waters approximately midway between the two countries. But ownership of the field is contested: The Chinese claim that it lies on their outer continental shelf, and so is theirs alone to exploit; the Japanese say that it falls within their 200-nautical-mile exclusive economic zone, and so belongs to them. Both sides cite provisions of the United Nations Convention on the Law of the Sea to justify their claims; but because these provisions contradict one another, and because there is no formal process for resolving such disputes, each insists on an exclusive right to exploit the field. Complicating the dispute is the presence of powerful nationalistic sentiments on each side: many Chinese resent Japan's invasion and occupation of China during World War II and so oppose any territorial concessions to Tokyo; many Japanese are fearful of China's rise and so oppose any territorial concessions to Beijing.[58]

To demonstrate support for their respective claims in the East China Sea, both China and Japan have regularly deployed air and naval forces in the area, in some cases deploying in close proximity of one another. On at least one occasion this has led to a near confrontation – with crews of both sides aiming their weapons at each other or otherwise engaging in threatening manoeuvres.[59] Typically, this has led to an outpouring of nationalistic fervor in each country, resulting in mass demonstrations of anti-Chinese or anti-Japanese sentiment. In an effort to calm matters (and ensure the steady flow of bilateral trade), officials from the two countries have met on several occasions to find a solution to the impasse; at one meeting, in June 2008, they agreed to a formula whereby Japanese firms would participate in a Chinese drive to exploit the undersea field.[60] But neither side has surrendered its claim to the disputed area, and both continue to station warships in the general area; there is every risk, therefore, that some future incident at sea – accidental or otherwise – could lead to something far more serious.[61]

A similar scenario could easily unfold in that other disputed territory, the South China Sea. Here, too, large hydrocarbon deposits are believed to lie beneath a contested body of water. In this case, the protagonists are China, Taiwan, Vietnam, Malaysia, the Philippines, and Brunei – each of which claims all or part of the region. China, which says the entire area is part of its territorial waters, has placed small military garrisons on some of the small islands that dot the area and used military force to drive away ships belonging to the other claimants – in some cases, producing human casualties.[62] The Obama Administration has offered to support the other parties to this dispute in their efforts to reach a compromise solution with Beijing, but Chinese officials have warned the USA to stay out of the matter, saying it is an internal affair. Describing the South China Sea as one of China's "core interests," akin to Taiwan and Tibet, Chinese officials have warned that conflict could erupt if Washington does not stand aside.[63] This is another place, then, where a small incident could conceivably trigger something more dangerous.

Geopolitical competition is also spreading to the Arctic region, although it has not yet produced the same degree of friction as that witnessed in the East and South China Seas. As in the case of deep-offshore Asia, the Arctic has attracted such interest because it is believed to harbor large untapped reserves of oil and natural gas which are only now coming within the reach of oil-drilling technology. The region's hydrocarbon potential was first revealed in a 2008 study by the US Geological Survey (USGS). Although the area north of the Arctic Circle encompasses only about 6% of the earth's surface, the USGS noted, it is thought to harbor approximately 22% of the world's undiscovered hydrocarbon resources, including an estimated 1,689 trillion cubic feet of natural gas (30% of the world's undiscovered supply) and 90bn barrels of oil (13% of the undiscovered supply). As suggested by the USGS in a press release announcing the 2008 study, "the extensive Arctic continental shelves may constitute the geographically largest unexplored prospective area for petroleum remaining on Earth."[64]

Drilling in the Arctic, as in the deep waters of the Gulf of Mexico and the Atlantic, poses enormous technological and environmental challenges. Some of these – for example, the presence of thick sea ice during much of the year – could be lessened by the gradual warming of the earth's atmosphere as a result of climate change. But here, too, boundary disputes and competitive ambitions could prove an obstacle. The five Arctic nations – Canada, Denmark (representing Greenland), Norway, Russia, and the USA – have yet to agree on a regime for dividing the polar region, and all are parties to disputes over their respective offshore boundaries in various Arctic Ocean extensions, such as the Beaufort and Chukchi Seas.[65] Although all five of these countries have declared their intention to avoid the use of force in resolving these disputes, several have bolstered their military capabilities in the region and stated their intent to defend their Arctic interests by any means necessary. The Russians, for example, have created a new group of Arctic forces, and Canada has established a new base on Resolute Island, on Cornwallis Island in the Canadian Arctic Archipelago.[66] For now, the extraction of oil and gas from the Arctic is still at too low a level to spark any significant geopolitical contestation, but the risk of serious friction could increase as reservoirs elsewhere become depleted and Arctic production gains momentum.

Conclusions

So long as the world relies on oil for a substantial share of its energy supply, nations will compete for access to the available supply and the geopolitics of oil will play a conspicuous role in international politics. As in the past, this will entail competitive efforts by the leading oil-importing nations to secure positions of advantage in the oil-producing regions, often employing military means to achieve this objective. While much of this will resemble the oil geopolitics of earlier years, we will witness significant changes in the geographic foci of these endeavors as well as the identity of some key players. Advanced oil-drilling technologies will also extend the reach of geopolitics to entirely new realms, including the deep oceans and the Arctic. Whether these changes will increase or decrease the risk of conflict over contested supplies of oil cannot be foreseen, but the fact that the new players are employing the same military tools as their predecessors, and that contested offshore fields are being subjected to the same sort of militarized contestation once devoted to onshore fields, suggests that conflict has not disappeared from the geopolitical equation.

Notes

1 The best introduction to this theme is Daniel Yergin's magisterial study of the global struggle for oil, *The Prize: The Epic Quest for Oil, Money, and Power* (New York: Simon and Schuster, 1992).
2 For background and discussion of these events, see Michael T. Klare, *Blood and Oil: The Dangers and Consequences of America's Growing Dependency on Imported Petroleum* (New York: Metropolitan Books, 2004).
3 For background and discussion of these contests, see Michael T. Klare, *Rising Powers, Shrinking Planet: The New Geopolitics of Energy* (New York: Metropolitan Books, 2008).
4 For background on these developments, see Yergin, *The Prize*, pp. 153–64.
5 As quoted in ibid., p. 188.
6 Ibid., pp. 188–96.
7 Ibid., pp. 200–206, 292–301, 305–50.
8 See Aaron Dean Miller, *Search for Security* (Chapel Hill: University of North Carolina Press, 1980), pp. 54–57, 62–63, 74–77; and David S. Painter, *Oil and the American Century* (Baltimore: Johns Hopkins University Press, 1986), pp. 11–31, 34–35.
9 For background on these developments, see Miller, *Search for Security*, pp. 19–20, 49, 54–57, 62–63, 74–77, 128–31; Painter, *Oil and the American Century*, pp. 32–95; and Michael B. Stoff, *Oil, War, and American Security* (New Haven: Yale University Press, 1980), pp. 18–21, 35–39, 48–51, 57–88.
10 For background, see David E. Long, *The United States and Saudi Arabia* (Boulder, Colo.: Westview Press, 1985).
11 For background on this episode, see Michael A. Palmer, *Guardians of the Gulf* (New York: Free Press, 1992), pp. 29–35.
12 For background on these developments, see Klare, *Blood and Oil*, pp. 37–45; Palmer, *Guardians of the Gulf*, pp. 52–84; and Painter, *Oil and the American Century*, pp, 112–13.

13 For background on these events, see Stephen Kinzer, *All the Shah's Men* (Hoboken, N.J.: John Wiley, 2003).
14 For background and discussion, see Michael T. Klare, *American Arms Supermarket* (Austin: University of Texas Press, 1984), pp. 108–26.
15 Jimmy Carter, State of the Union Address, January 23, 1980, electronic document accessed at www.jimmycarterlibrary.org on March 31, 2007. For background, see Palmer, *Guardians of the Gulf*, pp. 101–11.
16 See Klare, *Blood and Oil*, pp. 1–7. See also Jay E. Hines, *History of U.S. Central Command*, US Central Command, electronic document retrieved at www.centcom.mil on November 21, 2003.
17 Statement before the Subcommittee on Near Eastern and South Asian Affairs of the House Foreign Affairs Committee, Washington, D.C., September 26, 1983, as cited in Palmer, *Guardians of the Gulf*, p. 118.
18 For background on these events, see Palmer, *Guardians of the Gulf*, pp. 118–27.
19 As quoted in *The New York Times*, August 9, 1990.
20 For background, see Bob Woodward, *The Commanders* (New York: Simon and Schuster, 1991), pp. 225–26, 230, 236–37.
21 For background and discussion see Klare, *Blood and Oil*, pp. 94–101. See also Bob Woodward, *Plan of Attack* (New York: Simon and Schuster, 2004).
22 For an assessment of US security concerns regarding Iran, see Kenneth Katzman, *Iran: U.S. Concerns and Policy Responses*, CRS Brief for Congress (Washington, D.C.: Library of Congress, Congressional Research Service, September 25, 2007).
23 As quoted in David E. Sanger, "Cheney on Carrier, Warns Iran to Keep Sea Lanes Open," *New York Times*, May 12, 2007.
24 The White House, *The National Security Strategy of the United States*, Washington, D.C., September 2002.
25 For discussion, see Klare, *Blood and Oil*, pp. 64–66.
26 The author first discussed this concept in Klare, *Blood and Oil*, p. 132.
27 The author first discussed these efforts in Klare, *Resource Wars*, pp. 81–108
28 "Visit of President Heydar Aliyev of Azerbaijan," statement by the press secretary, the White House, August 1, 1997, electronic document accessed at www.whitehouse.gov on March 2, 1998. For background on these developments, see Michael T. Klare, *Resource Wars: The New Landscape of Global Conflict* (New York: Metropolitan Books, 2001), pp. 1–5, 81–92.
29 The author first advanced this argument in Klare, *Blood and Oil*, pp. 143–45.
30 National Energy Policy Development Group, *National Energy Policy* (Washington, D.C.: White House, May 17, 2001), chap. 8, p. 11.
31 Quoted in Mike Crawley, "With Mideast Uncertainty, U.S. Turns to Africa for Oil," *Christian Science Monitor*, May 23, 2002.
32 Annual appropriations for military aid to Africa are tabulated in US Department of State (DoS), *Congressional Budget Justification*, vol. 2, *Foreign Operations* (by Fiscal Year). For discussion, see Michael Klare and Daniel Volman, "The African 'Oil Rush' and U.S. National Security," *Third World Quarterly*, vol. 27, no. 4 (2006), pp. 609–28.
33 For background, see Klare, *Rising Powers, Shrinking Planet*, pp. 173–74. See also Lauren Ploch, *Africa Command: U.S. Strategic Interests and the Role of the U.S. Military in Africa*, CRS Report for Congress (Washington, D.C.: Congressional Research Service, US Library of Congress, November 16, 2010), pp. 15–16.
34 DoS, *Congressional Budget Justification*, Fiscal Year 2007 (Washington, D.C.: DoS, 2006), p. 307.
35 For background on these multilateral programs, see Ploch, *Africa Command*, pp. 19–25. See also Daniel Volman, "Obama Moves Ahead with AFRICOM," electronic document retrieved at www.world-hunger.org on February 11, 2011.
36 BP, *Statistical Review of World Energy 2010* (London: BP, 2010), pp. 8, 11.
37 The author first made this argument in Klare, *Rising Powers, Shrinking Planet*.
38 For background and discussion, see Philip Andrews-Speed, Xuanli Liao, and Roland Dannreuther, *The Strategic Implications of China's Energy Needs*, Adelphi Paper no. 346 (Oxford: Oxford University Press and International Institute of Strategic Studies, 2002); and Erica Strecker Downs, *China's Quest for Energy Security* (Santa Monica: RAND Corporation, 2000).
39 Flynt Leverett and Jeffrey Bader, "Managing China-U.S. Energy Competition in the Middle East," *Washington Quarterly*, Winter 2005–6, p. 191.

40 Ministry of Foreign Affairs of the People's Republic of China, "Hu Jintao Talks with Nigerian President Obasanjo," April 27, 2006, electronic document retrieved at www.fmprc.gov.cn/eng on October 7, 2006.
41 For background, see Klare, *Rising Powers, Shrinking Planet*, pp. 76–77, 104–8, 132–37, 164–71.
42 For background and discussion, see Human Rights Watch (HRW), *Sudan, Oil, and Human Rights* (New York and Washington, D.C.: HRW, 2003).
43 See Eric Reeves, Prepared Statement, in US-China Economic and Security Review Commission (USCC), *China's Role in the World: Is China a Responsible Stakeholder?* Hearing, 109th Cong., 2nd Sess., August 3, 2006, electronic document retrieved at www.uscc.gov on May 12, 2007.
44 Dino Mahtani, "Nigeria Shifts to China Arms," *Financial Times*, February 28, 2006.
45 For background on Chinese arms transfers to Africa, see Amnesty International, "People's Republic of China: Sustaining Conflict and Human Rights Abuses, The Flow of Arms Accelerates," June 11, 2006, electronic document retrieved at www.amnesty.org on December 15, 2006. On Chinese training and advisory programs, see Susan Puska, "Resources, Security, and Influence: The Role of the Military in China's Africa Strategy," *China Brief*, Jamestown Foundation, May 30, 2007, pp. 2–6.
46 For background on the SCO, see Bates Gill and Matthew Oresman, *China's New Journey to the West* (Washington, D.C.: Center for Strategic and International Studies, 2003), pp. 5–8.
47 See C. J. Chivers, "Central Asians Call on U.S. to Set a Timetable for Closing Bases," *New York Times*, July 6, 2005.
48 Gill and Oresman, *China's New Journey to the West*, p. 20.
49 US Department of Defense (DoD), *Military Power of the People's Republic of China 2008* (Washington, D.C.: DoD, 2008), pp. 10, 13.
50 As quoted in Edward Wong, "Chinese Military Seeks to Extend Its Naval Power," *The New York Times*, April 23, 2010.
51 For background and discussion, see Klare, *Rising Powers, Shrinking Planet*, pp. 88–114, 128–32. See also Rosemarie Forsythe, *The Politics of Oil in the Caucasus and Central Asia*, Adelphi Paper no. 300 (Oxford: Oxford University Press and International Institute of Strategic Studies, 1996).
52 Klare, *Rising Powers, Shrinking Planet*, pp. 215–17.
53 International Energy Agency (IEA), *World Energy Outlook 2010* (Paris: IEA, 2010), pp. 118–22.
54 John Westwood, "Global Offshore Prospects," PowerPoint presentation to British Chamber of Commerce, Singapore, March 22, 2010, electronic document retrieved at www.dw-1.com on June 5, 2010.
55 For background on the problem of overlapping offshore territorial claims in Asia, see Mark J. Valencia, *China and the South China Sea Disputes*, Adelphi Paper no. 298 (Oxford: Oxford University Press and International Institute for Strategic Studies, 1995).
56 See: DoE/EIA, "East China Sea, Country Analysis Brief," Country Analysis Brief, March 2008, electronic document retrieved at www.eia.doe.gov/emeu/cabs/East_China_Sea/Full.html on June 21, 2010; and "South China Sea," Country Analysis Brief, March 2008, electronic document retrieved at www.eia.doe.gov/emeu/cabs/South_China_Sea/Full.html on June 21, 2010. See also Valencia, *China and the South China Sea Disputes*.
57 See: Stephanie Ho, "China Submits Maritime Claims to United Nations," Voice of America, May 13, 2009, electronic document retrieved at www.voanews.com on May 18, 2009; and James Manicom, "China's Claims to an Extended Continental Shelf in the East China Sea: Meaning and Implications," China Brief, Jamestown Foundation, *China Brief*, July 9, 2009, pp. 9–11.
58 For background, see Klare, *Rising Powers, Shrinking Planet*, pp. 221–26. See also: James Brooke, "Drawing the Line on Energy," *New York Times*, March 29, 2005; and Brooke, "For Japan and China, Strains from a Line in the Sea," *New York Times*, April 14, 2005
59 On incidents at sea, see also Mure Dickie and Kathrin Hille, "Japan Urges China Warships Probe," *Financial Times*, April 14, 2010. This article refers to an incident in the East China Sea in which a Chinese ship-based helicopter came within 300 feet of a Japanese destroyer.
60 Martin Fackler, "China and Japan Agree to End Offshore Gas Dispute," *New York Times*, June 18, 2008.
61 See Dickie and Hille, "Japan Urges China Warships Probe."
62 For background, see DoE/EIA, "South China Sea," March 2008. See also Valencia, *China and the South China Sea Disputes*.
63 See: Mark Lander, "Offering to Aid Talks, U.S. Challenges China on Disputed Islands," *New York Times*, July 24, 2010; and Andrew Jacobs, "Stay Out of Island Dispute, Chinese Warn the U.S.," *New York Times*, July 27, 2010.

64 US Geological Survey (USGS), "Circum-Arctic Resource Appraisal: Estimates of Undiscovered Oil and Gas North of the Arctic Circle," USGS Fact Sheet 2008–3049 (Washington, D.C.: USGS, 2008), p. 1.
65 For background, see McKenzie Funk, "Arctic Landgrab," *National Geographic*, May 2009, pp. 104–21; and Clifford Krauss, et al., "As Polar Ice Turns to Water, Dreams of Treasure Abound," *New York Times*, October 10, 2005.
66 On Russia's moves, see Roger McDermott, "Russia Planning Arctic Military Grouping," Eurasia Daily Monitor, Jamestown Foundation, April 15, 2009, electronic document retrieved at www.jamestown.org on April 24, 2009. On Canada's moves, see "PM Starts Fight for North," *The Star* (Toronto), August 10, 2007.

4

Politics of Oil Supply

National Oil Companies vs. International Oil Companies

Jean-François Seznec

Oil and gas supplies are produced by specialized firms that are usually described as National Oil Companies (NOCs), which are state owned and International Oil Companies (IOCs) that are owned by shareholders and the shares of which are traded on various stock markets. However, in the energy business, the concept of companies held in private hands versus state-owned companies can be misleading. The differences between the two are not always clear, some NOCs act as if they were large IOCs and some NOCs work very closely with the IOCs. This chapter equates "private" companies with the main IOCs, like ExxonMobil, Shell, ChevronTexaco, BP, Total, etc. It also equates the state-owned companies with the NOCs like Saudi Aramco, the National Iranian Oil Company (NIOC), PDVSA of Venezuela, or Kuwait Oil Company (KOC).

It would seem self evident that NOCs would be established and managed with the sole purpose of protecting the interest of the people of a given state. After all, oil and gas reserves are non-renewable and therefore their extractions impoverish the country daily. It thus becomes vital for a national oil or gas company to maximize the return on these resources, minimize the cost and keep the reserves going for as long as possible. Consequently, the yearly rate of return on investments should be of no importance but replaced by a long-term analysis of how the country has gained from the extraction and sale of the non-renewable assets and benefit the future generations. Unfortunately, such analysis by the NOCs seems to be more the exception than the rule.

Many countries take advantage of any new income from oil to buy arms, finance repression to remain in power; or even more often the money is siphoned out to Swiss accounts, bypassing the original aim of the NOC to create wealth for its own country.

For their part, the IOCs main concern is or should be to maximize the return to their shareholders, within the constraint of their understanding of their social responsibility. Thus, the primary goal of IOCs is to maximize their rate of return on investment (RoI). The stock markets of the world are the arbiters of whether the RoI is deemed to be high enough or too low. In order to maximize RoI, IOCs will have to focus not on whether their production will benefit the future generations of a given state, but whether their annual return will meet the expectations of the market. In all fairness to the IOCs, the process of maximizing returns is indeed complicated and not necessarily a short-term exercise. Indeed, most energy projects from prospection to extraction, to refining and marketing can easily take 10 years to come to proper fruition.

Hence, companies have to invest billions of dollars in highly risky prospection and extraction projects not really knowing if within the 10-year horizon of their decision, the prospective oil or gas will hit the market at a price able to match costs and shareholders' expectations.

This chapter will seek to show that in spite of the obvious differences between the goals and missions of the IOCs and NOCs, there are many different types of each and they place themselves in a continuum from the NOCs totally controlled by their government to NOCs totally independent from theirs to IOCs that are in fact dependent on their own state of origin to multinational firms with minimal obligations to their home country. By and large, the NOCs will seek to benefit their own country, and the IOCs will seek to benefit their shareholders, but neither will seek to benefit the world at large, despite the publicity campaigns of their public relations departments and consultants. Ultimately, it appears in this analysis that the NOCs have the capacity to become the main organizations in energy production as they control most of the world's reserves. However, to achieve a modicum of success in husbanding their reserves and production they must preserve their independence from their own state.

IOCs, on the other hand, have often been criticized, sometimes unfairly so, for trampling over people's and countries' rights, damaging the environment and for what could appear as callousness, because of their willingness to work with existing dictators, or lack of concern for local tribes and environments, all for the sake of maximizing their RoI. On the other hand the IOCs, by and large, do not own their oil and gas reserves in a strict sense; one way or another they are at the mercy of whoever controls the land where they operate. Hence, sometimes they work with some of the worst regimes to maintain their production levels. The whole issue of morality of such investments is difficult to gauge. IOCs are often caught between the requirement of the shareholders and their social responsibility in a given area. As could be expected, they sometimes will be viewed as morally excellent or morally abhorrent. In fact most companies will have to be mostly amoral and view their actions and investments as part of their doing business. Of course, just like the NOCs go from the most highly professional to the most highly incompetent, the IOCs will go from the most highly profitable and socially responsible, to the most greedy and socially irresponsible.

Furthermore, the distinctions between NOCs and IOCs are not always as clear-cut as it might appear at first. The IOCs are not "private." Many of them are corporations with sometimes millions of shareholders both individuals, pension funds, mutual funds and the like. The interest of these shareholders can sometimes be extremely powerful and be as important as the wealth of a nation is to a National Oil Company 100% owned by the state. To complicate matters, IOCs have operations, which cover numerous countries and their shareholders come from many different financial centers. Moreover, many companies are "mixed." They can have a large shareholding from the state and a large number of shareholders from the public at large. Are these companies NOCs or IOCs? The control is in the eye of the beholder (or of the shareholder in this case). Some companies fully state-owned, on the other hand, can only operate if they are well supported by foreign firms who provide the technical know-how and often the marketing. Hence, it seems that the NOCs can either become fully professional, like Saudi Aramco, or they will have to turn to the IOCs to catch up. On the other hand, as the IOCs lose their ability to find reserves, they may become more involved in some of the NOCs business and we could see a meshing of both interests in the long run. One could also speculate that even the NOCs from countries with large oil and gas reserves may begin to see decline in their easy oil and gas and could start eyeing investments abroad, thus becoming much closer to the IOCs who need to replace reserves every year. Hence, while IOCs may join forces with NOCs, we may see the latter become more like the former.

NOCs

There are as many types of NOCs as there are oil producing countries. Each one adapts and serves the needs of the country from which it emanates. However, one of the variables that seem to influence the management of the NOCs most is their level of independence from the state apparatus. Some NOCs appear to be very independent from day to day interference from their governments. Some even appear to be independent in making important strategic decisions with regards to production and investment levels. What perhaps appears to be a recurring pattern is that the most successful NOCs are the ones that are the most independent from their government.

Of course, the meaning of "successful" is charged. For the purpose of this paper, we will assume that "successful" means the ability to maintain oil and gas fields, provide stability to production, use "best practices" for exploration, exploitation, refining, and export of oil and gas. The NOC will also be deemed successful if it maintains environmentally acceptable operations, maximizes income for the country, minimizes foreign influence and does not become prey to corrupt practices. Of course for countries that have limited resources some of these criteria cancel each other out. It is difficult to provide "best practices" and be environmentally acceptable when production is small and funds are lacking. However, by and large, companies that follow best practices, in the long run will minimize accidents and maximize income.

The NOCs that appear to have the most operational freedom are the Saudi Aramco and Statoil of Norway. Both manage huge operations using very advanced technologies, on which they spend large amounts. Saudi Aramco has invested about $62bn on increasing capacity in its fields to 12mbpd[1] and Statoil has invested billions as well in limiting the decline of the North Sea fields, in which it works and which passed their peak some years ago.

Perhaps the most important factor in establishing independence by an NOC is its ability to retain some of the money it earns from the export of oil and gas to reinvest in its operations and to do so without having to revert to the government for approval of day to day expenses and basic investment in oil field maintenance, separation facilities, refineries or harbor development. Below (Figure 4.1) is a brief sketch of the flow of funds, likely to be observed at a very large NOC like Saudi Aramco. This chart does not claim to be representing the actual flow of money, nor does it show all the very intricate transactions that surround operations that gross about $200bn per year. It is merely a sketch of how funds circulate and at which moment in this flow, the NOC has the opportunity to keep a portion of the funds for its own use.

Figure 4.1 describes how funds flow from the moment of purchase of oil by Saudi Aramco's clients to the moment they are used either by the state or by Saudi Aramco. Saudi Aramco, like most of the exporting countries of the Gulf,[2] are very large, oil companies well capitalized and considered credit-worthy by Saudi Aramco. The Gulf NOCs do not sell to oil traders, mainly for ensuring maximum quality of credit. Most of the payments to Saudi Aramco on the sale of crude oil are made by use of irrevocable letters of credits, except for sale to the original founders of Aramco.[3] The payments are always in US dollars and paid by the openers of the letters of credit to one of the very large US banks in New York, most likely JPMorganChase or Citibank. The payments received are likely to be allocated by the New York bank per standing instruction from Saudi Aramco to accounts at the same bank in New York and in London. Enough funds are kept in New York to have cash on hand to pay for the purchases of Saudi Aramco and be available when any of the numerous letters of credit opened for the account of Saudi Aramco are negotiated by the sellers' banks and payments due hit the account. The balance of the money received from the oil purchase is then placed in Eurodollar accounts in London where they earn interest and are safe from any unlikely, but always possible, effort by the US Treasury to block the US dollar accounts of a depositor. Indeed, from the point of view of the Saudis or indeed from that of any

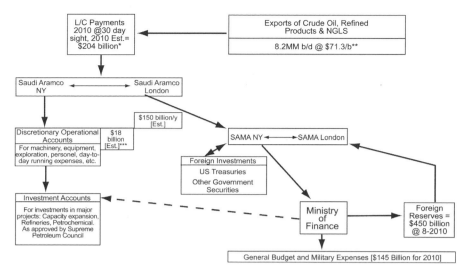

Figure 4.1 Possible money flows in Saudi oil transactions 2010
Notes:
* All buyers of Saudi Aramco have to provide irrevocable Letters of Credits for a major bank confirmed by an accepted Saudi bank payable at 30 day sight. The US companies that founded Aramco do not have to provide L/Cs
** Estimates from Jadwa Investments in Riyadh. Chart Book September 2010, p. 20
*** Estimates by the author based on and estimated cost of production of $4/b and expenses for overhead and investments of $2/b
Source: The Lafayette Group LLC 2008, 2009, 2010

recipient of large flows of money, keeping funds in Eurodollar accounts in London puts the funds under the regulations of England and less subject to political whimsy in Washington.

From time to time, Saudi Aramco will transfer funds to the accounts of the Saudi Arabian Monetary Agency (SAMA), probably, but not necessarily, in the same bank. SAMA in turn transfers funds from time to time, probably after the funds reach a certain pre-arranged level, to the Ministry of Finance for use under the budget. Amounts not needed by the ministry are placed in SAMA's investment account. SAMA is responsible for investing the balances and all the foreign reserves of the Kingdom, as well as the reserves of the various semi-independent agencies of the government, like the General Organization for Social Insurance (GOSI), or the Public Pension Authority (PPA). Just like Saudi Aramco, SAMA and the Ministry of Finance will keep balances in New York for payments of letters of credit opened for purchases by the government. The short-term balances will be invested in London Eurodollar accounts and in US Short-Term Treasuries. The Saudis do not technically have a Sovereign Wealth Fund in the sense that all the reserves are managed directly by SAMA and mostly kept in highly liquid and safe government instruments.

To an outsider, it seems that the major difference between the Saudis handling their money flows is that Saudi Aramco does not appear ever to have shortages of funds for its projects. It spends as needed on oil field maintenance and development. It does not lobby for more funds, as is the case for the Iranian or the Venezuelan oil authorities. In other words, Saudi Aramco seems to have its own funds to manage as it sees fit for the good of the company. In that sense, Saudi Aramco appears to be like any major IOC, such as ExxonMobil. This ability to use funds for proper management of the company, points to the strong likelihood that the Kingdom allows Saudi Aramco to maintain a substantial balance in its account. Saudi Aramco does not seem to have to go to the Ministry of Finance or to the council of ministers and plead for its budget. Indeed, Saudi Aramco seems to have enough leeway, i.e. cash, to invest not just in maintenance of the fields, and day-to-day expenses but also in major capital expenses like refineries, harbors, etc. Only when very large investments are needed for the development of new fields, or as was announced by Mr alFalih in October 2010, Saudi Aramco's President, a major effort to develop 280 tcf of non-traditional gas resources,[4] would the funds have to be approved outside Saudi Aramco. Even then, the method to obtain such approval seems to facilitate Saudi Aramco's work. Large investments requiring policy decisions would be coming from the Supreme Petroleum Council (SPC). The SPC is headed by the King and the Crown Prince, but, de facto is managed by the main ministers of the Kingdom (foreign affairs, defense, finance, oil, electricity, etc.). Hence, once the SPC makes a decision, any formal approval by the council of ministers, if needed, would be quasi-automatic.

In the past 20 years, Saudi Aramco has undertaken and brought on line some major projects. There are no records of Saudi Aramco announcing it would implement this or that project and not follow through with it. In other words, Saudi Aramco does not launch projects that are "subject to" funding or political decisions. Therefore, once a policy decision has been made by Saudi Aramco and accepted by the Supreme Oil Council, the company does not have to solicit funds. It is likely that Saudi Aramco can work from its internally generated funds, which are most likely to come directly from keeping a portion of the sales of oil. Technically speaking, Saudi Aramco's accounts would be credited by standing instruction to their bank, ordering a certain percentage of the payments under the oil letters of credit to remain in Saudi Aramco's accounts and the balance to be paid to SAMA. The net result of the format of the Saudi oil transactions is that Saudi Aramco can use its best judgment to manage the company and the oil production at all levels, without having to kowtow to the political, royal or military clans who may have different views on how to use the money.

In contrast, many NOCs seem to suffer from lack of investments in their oil fields. Iran today, in particular, appears to have minimal expenditures going into its oil and gas fields and industry in general. The lack of investments would explain why the country with the second largest gas reserves is a net importer of gas, why oil production declines slowly year after year, why the country's refineries are not modern enough to meet the demand for gasoline and why the new energy-based industries built to use natural gas are either unable to obtain gas feedstock or only partial quantities.

In Iraq, the mismanagement of the oil industry under Saddam Hussein has led Iraq into a downward spiral in its oil exports capacity. Since Saddam Hussein's downfall, the country has resumed exports but the fields have suffered greatly. The entire oil industry of Iraq requires enormous amounts of funds and technology to regain its past glory and to enable the entire country to benefit from its massive reserves. The realization of the problems has led the Minister of Oil, Mr Sharistani, to develop very successful rounds of bidding by the foreign companies, which will be reviewed below at more length.

The flow of funds from oil to the Kingdom of Saudi Arabia could be used as an example for many countries. Most countries with oil resources seem to have a greater need for funds than that which the oil delivers for them. Often their populations are very poor and very large, forcing the states to siphon all the money out of the NOC and to consider preservation of fields and modernization of oil infrastructure a luxury, which they cannot afford in the short term. Sometimes, the countries are under extreme stress, either internally or externally, and the priority becomes security, which leads them to spending money on their military and security apparatuses, such as in Chad and Sudan. Ultimately, Figure 4.2 on generic flows of funds for NOCs theorizes that the management of funds generated by the oil sales of the NOC is strongly centralized, usually in the hands of the various ministries of finance. Funds for investments (even in the investments absolutely required to maintain production) are decided upon by non-oil-related people, either in the ministries of finance, or the council of ministers and the inner workings of the leaders cabinets. Faced with major immediate demands on whatever funds can be raised now, many countries will resort to little or no investments in their oil industries.

One could argue that with so much money available to the Kingdom, it is easy for the Saudis to allow Saudi Aramco to manage itself as efficiently as any major IOC and run its budgets free of interference from the government. Indeed even if it keeps a relatively small percentage from oil sales for managing the operations and investments needed to use best practices and maximize returns on its assets, the amounts are staggering. If indeed the funds used by Saudi Aramco amount to between 7% and 10% of the total oil income, it still amounts to between $18bn to 20bn per year in 2010.

However, the Saudi financial structure is not as obviously favorable as it would appear or is indicated by the large surpluses of today. Indeed, from the early 1980s to 1999, the Kingdom had some decent cash flows but was incurring yearly budget deficits of $10–20bn per year. Fortunately, the country's financial authorities were and still are most professional. They managed to survive 20 years of budget deficit without having to resort to foreign borrowings by pushing their own local bank to purchase development bonds. The local borrowing of over $180bn by the Saudi government[5] in the 1980s and 1990s, created a fairly tense situation between the local banks, their merchant owners and the state. However, it allowed the Ministry of Finance to keep funding the industrial development of the Kingdom. Most important in the context of this chapter, the civil service managed to maintain Saudi Aramco's financial independence.

Unlike in many other oil states, the government did not resort to cutting the funding to Saudi Aramco, or force Saudi Aramco into re-opening the oil fields to foreign companies. When oil prices were down to the low teens in the late 1990s, the income of Saudi Arabia was around $35bn per year, eight times lower than in 2010 and deficits were mounting up. Hence, many in the Kingdom were clamoring to bring the IOCs back to expand production making Saudi Arabia sell huge amounts of oil, take market share away from other producers and ensure that the Saudis get as much cash as possible in a difficult world-wide glut. The efforts to bring back the IOCs culminated with a meeting in Washington organized by the then Ambassador, Prince Bandar bin Sultan, at which the then Crown Prince Abdullah bin AbdelAziz, asked the US IOCs to provide him with "suggestions" on how to maximize production. Of course, the IOCs were delighted to see an opening for them to have access to enormous reserves. However, as could be expected, the Saudi engineers and managers of Saudi Aramco and the Ministry of Petroleum and Minerals led by oil minister Ali al-Naimi, were adamant that they did not need the IOCs to improve the results of the Kingdom. One can assume that the oil experts in the Kingdom were arguing that bringing in the IOCs would deplete the reserves of the Kingdom too fast, flood the markets and thus decrease income even more. In the long term, they saw the Kingdom earning a bit more cash quickly, but ultimately impoverishing it irretrievably.

The stand taken by Ali al-Naimi and his colleague was indeed very courageous. He was taking on some of the strongest and most powerful princes, allied in their quest to bring back the American IOCs. Whether by sheer luck, or perhaps because of a very canny knowledge of the workings of OPEC, Ali al-Naimi was able to see a sudden rise in oil prices in 1999, which made Prince Bandar's meeting with the IOCs totally moot, as the Kingdom's revenues more than doubled that year and kept on increasing. At the same time, Saudi Aramco ran a very extensive public relations campaign to show how technically savvy they were. Indeed, until then, Saudi Aramco kept all its information quite secret, which ultimately could be interpreted as their seeking to hide a certain weakness. Very quickly they brought academics, engineers, bankers and journalists to their sites and research centers. They made very sophisticated presentations to all who would listen, particularly in the USA. Quite rapidly, the respect for Saudi Aramco spread to the governments and media abroad, as well as at home among both

Politics of Oil Supply

the general Saudi public and the princes. Hence the pressure to interfere with the company's management of the oil wealth declined. Saudi Aramco was able to demonstrate that it was as technologically advanced as any foreign IOC and therefore could protect the interests of the Kingdom better than ExxonMobil, Shell, or Total SA could. In fact, one could argue that Saudi Aramco by and large is managed like the best IOCs, but with the goal of developing the resources of the country for the long term, rather than creating short-term returns for the shareholders.

Few other NOCs can claim the same success in maintaining their independence and the professionalism of their companies. Certainly companies like Statoil of Norway and Petrobras of Brazil have shown their ability to maintain and develop their local energy industries. Both have become leaders in deep-sea technology, probably the most difficult frontier in the oil and gas industry. Like Saudi Aramco, they would be seen by the industry as managed like the best IOCs, with the ability to fund their efforts with minimal interference from their government, but with the aim of working for the long-term benefit of all the citizens of their countries.

However, the national oil companies of many other countries have not had the ability to manage their business, like a normal oil company would. Many NOCs have seen their companies decimated and their funding diverted, which ultimately led to a decline in oil production.

The graph below (Figure 4.2) shows how oil flows may work for a generic NOC. It does emphasize the financial links, which, if not formalized as is shown in Figure 4.1, show how NOCs can lose their ability to manage oil reserves.

Figure 4.2 summarizes the flow of funds of a NOC selling 1m. barrels of oil. This figure would seem to represent the pattern of very low investments in the oil industry for the sake of using funds for more urgent needs. The writer thinks that such a graph would apply to the likes of PDVSA and NIOC. In Figure 4.2, it is assumed that most of the funds are transferred directly to the Ministry of Finance, with only a minimum left for day-to-day expenses. Even these expenses may be subject to Ministry of Finance approvals. Should this graph be accurate, all

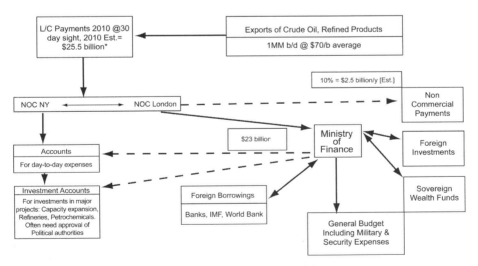

Figure 4.2 Generic oil money flows for NOCs/per 1 million b/d
Notes:
* Most buyers provide irrevocable Letters of Credits for a major bank confirmed by an accepted a local bank. These L/Cs have to be for the $ amount and oil volumes agreed by long term contract and are payable at 30 day sight [ie 30 days from the loading of the oil on the tanker].

Source: The Lafayette Group LLc 2008, 2009, 2010

investments must go through the Ministry of Finance; and hence they are at the mercy of governments. Needless to say, in many cases the governments find more important priorities than investing in machinery or engineering for the maintenance of oil or gas wells. It is very likely that the decline in production witnessed in Iran is directly related to its lack of investments in its own fields. There should be little doubt that the managers and engineers at NIOC are highly professional. They know what needs to be done to create long-term production, but their budgets are so restricted that they cannot save their own country as its money is used for "more important" causes defined on the basis of ideology, rather than common sense economics and business. The Iranian minister of oil himself complained a few years ago that without substantial investments in the upstream, Iran could become a net importer of oil.[6]

In fact, what is remarkable in countries like Iran or Iraq, when under extreme sanctions, is the fact that the personnel of the local NOCs have managed to maintain relatively high levels of production. This must demand daily miracles and extremely hard work, but in the long term without access to large sums of investments to get the right technology, these NOCs will lose the battle with slowly evolving geological formations and water penetration. They will be unable to compete against other countries and other sources of energy without massive investments in field management and technology from abroad, mostly from Western firms.

The Venezuelan oil company, PDVSA is an interesting case study. The control of operations was taken over by President Chavez and his associates to the great annoyance of the management and many of the employees of the company. After a brutal strike in 2003, some 19,500 of about 45,000 PDVSA employees were fired.[7] Today the number of employees has returned not only to normal but shows that PDVSA has become a haven of employment. From the 43,807 employees it had in 2005, the numbers have ballooned to 88,790 in 2009.[8] Since then the production of oil has remained pretty constant at 2,900mbpd, with limited ups and downs. Production did spike by 300mbpd in 2008, owing to an increase in very heavy bitumen oil from the Orinoco basin. It declined in 2009, but remained 100mbpd higher than the production level in 2007, at 3,170mbpd. It is interesting to note that PDVSA, unlike most other state controlled NOCs, publishes a 97-page long annual report with very detailed information on the fields, production, cost of productions and investment plans.

In the context of this paper, it is interesting to note that PDVSA intends to increase overall production, mainly through development of the extra-heavy reserves, by 1.3mbpd and plans to invest $252bn between 2010 and 2015. PDVSA "hopes"[9] to self-fund 78% of this amount, i.e. $196bn for six years, or $32bn per year. This could be an optimistic scenario. PDVSA gross income in 2009 was about $75bn per year, of which $24.7bn in 2009, $38bn in 2008 and $29.8bn in 2007[10] went to the state for taxes, social payments, dividends, etc. and about $48bn is used in production costs, overhead and inventory management. This leaves the company with only $2bn in cash, plus non-cash items, like depreciation of $5.7bn and other financial earnings of $5.8bn. In other words, PDVSA could be short of $18.5bn per year on its investment plan. The "hopes" of management to develop their industry and the needs of the country for employment and large funding from the country's main resources contradict each other.

Of course, it could be that the discrepancy between hopes and realities is exaggerated by the PDVSA to make sure the government knows and understands that it would not be PDVSA's fault if the increases in production cannot be obtained. Perhaps the writers of the annual report are aware that by showing that they need $252bn over 5 years, they will obtain less than a third of it, which would probably suffice to increase production by a planned 1.3mbpd. Indeed Saudi Aramco needed "only" $62bn to increase their net capacity by 3.5mbpd to 12mbpd.[11] However, both the Iranian case and the Venezuelan case show the main weakness of 100%-controlled NOCs. If the government interferes extensively with the management of the company, squeezes its financial ability to fund projects, maintenance and development of the oil fields as well as that of the downstream applications, and if it imposes large and inefficient numbers of employees on the company, it is then very likely that the NOC will fail in maintaining the value of the country's main assets. In other words, the governments will be tempted to slowly strangle the goose that lays the golden eggs. It is to the great credit of Saudi Aramco, that it focuses on efficiency, and it is a credit to the Saudi government that it lets Saudi Aramco manage the "golden goose" for the ultimate benefit of the country as a whole.

NOCs and IOCs working together

In between the likes of Saudi Aramco and of NIOC or PDVSA lie a large number of NOCs whose approaches to management and funding have features from both sides, but have adapted to their own needs. Many NOCs have the financial resources, but are lacking the technical and human resources to rival Saudi Aramco. These companies will control sales of oil and gas but will be working closely with IOCs for exploration and exploitation. For example, AbuDhabi National Oil Company (ADNOC) works very closely with ExxonMobil, Chevron and Occidental. In Qatar, the Qatar Petroleum Company (QPC) contracts the development of its oil and mainly its huge North Dome gas field to ExxonMobil, Total, Maersk, etc. The local populations of AbuDhabi and of Qatar are so small that they would be unable to develop enough engineering capacity on their own or be very limited in their ability to produce at the levels they are producing presently. Hence, it is vital for them to rely on trusted IOC, and oil field technology companies like Halliburton or Schlumberger. The priorities of the governments of the small states of the Gulf Cooperation Council are not to Qatar-ize or UAE-ize the work force of their oil companies but to create enough managers to ensure a local understanding and control of the flow of funds and then to use the flow of funds to invest in industries which they will be able to manage for the long term.

This system has led to some very interesting investment decisions in energy based industries. Perhaps the most interesting example of this industrial investment approach is Qatar's. The emirate decided to become the world leader in a few energy products, such as Liquid Natural Gas (LNG) and Gas To Liquids (GTL). Qatar is far from the main gas users of the world and cannot economically send its gas to Europe, India or China by pipeline as is being done between Canada and the USA, or between Russia and Western Europe. However, it needs to monetize its huge reserves of natural gas, which if left in the ground would be worthless. Export of gas can be done through transforming the natural gas into LNG or into GTL, which transforms methane into diesel fuel, ethylene, or a number of other fuels. Methane can also be transformed into ammonia and from ammonia into urea, a widely used fertilizer, as well as into a wide range of petrochemicals. On the other hand, it costs many billions of dollars to develop LNG trains, GTL plants, fertilizer plants and chemical complexes.

A great part of the cost of transforming natural gas into deliverable products is due to the very advanced technology required to successfully bring these products to market. Therefore, Qatar has relied heavily on the IOCs and other providers of advanced energy technology to become the largest world producer of LNG, producing 77m. tons by the beginning of 2011, and to become the world's largest producer of GTL when the new JV with Shell Oil starts full operations as expected in 2011.

Unlike what happened in Venezuela in the past few years, or what happened in the 1970s and 1980s in Iraq, Libya and Algeria, when local governments nationalized the assets of the IOCs, the relationship between NOCs and IOCs is not always confrontational. Many NOCs rely on and sign substantial service agreements with the IOCs to explore and exploit oil reserves on behalf of the NOCs. ADNOC and Qatar Petroleum Company were mentioned above as examples of such an approach. Countries with very little capital and technology will use production sharing agreements (PSAs). PSAs are especially important in the Gulf of Guinea and surrounding areas where most countries, except Nigeria, have very little resources and experience. Unfortunately, IOCs have to take all the risk and therefore require very large returns. In most cases the PSAs guarantee a certain return to the IOCs. The contract will ensure that the expenses incurred by the IOC are paid up front, as well as the agreed share of profits and the guaranteed return, all ahead of any money passed on to the local NOCs. The NOCs or their states usually get a signing bonus, and ultimately get some cash payments on a yearly basis for the duration of production. Altogether, the NOCs get very little for their country when compared to how much they would get if they had been a Saudi Aramco type of company. On the other hand, if they do not sign PSAs they will not be able to exploit their own reserves and ultimately will get nothing.

The Iraqi model

An interesting model has been developing in Iraq in the past three years. The central Iraqi oil company (SOMO), suffered a great deal under Saddam Hussein's rule, but managed to maintain a minimum amount of production. The sanctions made it very difficult for its production affiliates to obtain spare parts and technology, but through great feats of ingenuity managed to maintain almost 2mbpd. After the US invasion, the various Iraqi governments, prodded by the USA, attempted to increase production. The USA tried to push through a new oil law to stabilize the situation for foreign firms, and to create a comfortable environment for investment. However, the new draft law gave the biggest power over negotiations to the provincial governments, thereby providing them with greater funds and power to weaken the central government. This, of course, was greatly supported by the Kurdish provinces in the North, which assumed that the central government law would be passed and, thus in turn passed their own law defining the rules of engagement with IOCs. The vast majority of the Iraqi parliament, however, saw this law as a manoeuvre to weaken Iraq and instigate a de facto break-up of the country. They also saw that large oil companies with sales levels many times the GNP of medium size countries could negotiate much better deals for themselves in dealing with provincial governments, rather than negotiate with much more experienced and sophisticated central government experts. Hence, the federal law was never passed and is not likely to be passed in its present form any time soon. The absence of a definitive law, however, does not decrease the need for Iraq to improve its oil production. Iraq has 115bn barrels of reserves, second only to Saudi Arabia's 269bn barrels (or third if one accepts the Iranian stated reserves of 137.6bn barrels).[12] This figure developed under Saddam Hussein may be somewhat more than the reality, but is still very large. Iraq with proper management could produce as much, if not more, oil than Saudi Arabia for many years to come. Iraq needs money to develop and rebuild its economy and infrastructure now. Hence, it must increase production and sales as soon as possible. Consequently, to make up for the loss of technology and the brain drain it suffered for the past thirty years, the Iraqi government with the reluctant approval of the parliament agreed to bring back the IOCs, but not on regular PSA terms.

In 2009 the Ministry of Oil of Iraq, under the leadership of Ali Sharistani, decided to go through a round of bids for IOCs to propose service contracts (SCs) to develop the oil fields, which the ministry thought had potential for increased production. The bidding process was fairly long and subject to a lot of manoeuvring by the Iraqis and the IOCs, but suffice to say that it ended up quite favorably for the Iraqis when compared to PSAs negotiated by other countries. The bids were handled in a transparent manner (quite literally, as all the bids were actually placed in a large Lucite box in full view of live TV coverage) with each IOC or groups of IOCs proposing to develop existing fields according to formulas agreed by the Iraqi government.

For example, ExxonMobil in association with Shell won the bid to expand production from 0.27mbpd to 2.5mbpd in the West Qurna 1 field, for which they will be paid a fee of $1.90 per barrel. ExxonMobil and Shell will invest over $25bn in drilling 1,000 wells to increase production and spend a further $25bn to operate the field.[13] Furthermore, BP in joint venture with CNPC of China won the bid for the large Rumaila field to increase production from 1mbpd to 3.0mbpd for a fee, if successful, of $2.0 on the incremental production. BP's share of the venture is 38%, CNPC is 37% and SOMO, the Iraqi central oil company, 25%.[14] The SCs provided a reimbursement of the money spent to develop the fields, but did not guaranteed a rate of return on investment to the IOCs, which is the normal practice for PSAs. They also maximize the returns to the Iraqis especially if the market remains in the range of $70 per barrel to $80 per barrel. The IOCs for their part do not "own" the reserves and cannot pass them on their balance sheet, but it does give them access to substantial production, at less risk, if successful.

It is quite remarkable to see that, if the IOCs are successful in expanding the Iraqi oil production, Iraq will become the largest oil producer in the world at over 10mbpd within 15 years. Of course, it is less than sure that this will actually happen. After all, insecurity issues are still not resolved and the oil law, expected to stabilize relations between IOCs, the Kurdish territories and Iraq, is still languishing in the parliament. The insecurity and lack of stability are compounded by the fact that at the time of this writing Iraq has been without a government for 220 days, and the Kurdish separatists are still actively trying to undermine the control of oil resources by the central government. Nevertheless, the model established by Ali Sharistani is likely to be followed elsewhere and perhaps is the harbinger of a new model of relations between oil rich countries and the IOCs. It is a positive sign that in mid-October 2010, BP-CNPC announced that they had completed their first well, which would increase production of the Rumaila field by 100,000 bpd by November 2010.

"Mixed" ownership NOCs

An interesting NOC structure is that of companies often seen by most observers as being "national," but which in fact are owned by large numbers of shareholders and whose shares are traded on the world markets. These companies, theoretically at least should be mostly interested in maximizing the interest of their shareholders, not necessarily in maximizing the benefit to their country of origin. Some of the main Chinese and Russian companies follow this pattern. Sinopec and CNOOC have large, publicly-traded shareholdings, issue detailed annual reports, and are subject to detailed analysis by stock market experts. Information on these firms is widely available on the internet.

The main question, of course, is whether or not the structure of the ownership makes these NOCs less dependent on government influence. Certainly, it would seem that Chinese companies are mainly following China's strategic interest. For example, Chinese oil companies' involvement in Sudan or Angola is focused on meeting China's need for resources. From a purely capitalistic viewpoint, it could be argued that the interests of the shareholders of Sinopec are enhanced by the symbiotic relationship between the Chinese government and the company's expansion. However, there can be many instances, when strong government guidance could also force Sinopec, or any other such company to make investments or payments that are not in the interest of the shareholders. Whether, the voice of the shareholders could countermand governmental influence is not certain. On the other hand, should the governments take undue advantage of the company, it would make the NOCs' ability to raise funds on the international markets much more difficult. In other words, having NOCs de facto owned by bodies other than their home government does not guarantee their independence, but protects them from gross interference to a certain degree.

By and large, the Chinese companies such as Sinopec, CNOOC or CNPC, are usually considered to be national oil companies. Their shares are traded on the large stock markets of the world. Still, they work closely with the Chinese government and benefit from major diplomatic and state support in their ventures overseas. These companies, like Saudi Aramco, appear independent from state interference in their day-to-day operations. They are however responsible for supplying enough oil and oil products to the country to manage its enormous growth with declining local oil reserves. So in many ways Sinopec et al. have to act as IOCs in searching for oil worldwide and signing PSAs in as many countries as possible. They have signed agreements in Sudan, where they are now producing 0.48mbpd. They are also present in Angola, which has now become the largest supplier of oil to China, exporting over 1mbpd there. Furthermore, Chinese NOCs are trying to find oil in Iran and have signed huge contracts there for both oil and gas exploration, exploitation and gas production of LNG. To this day, however, they have not produced one barrel of oil or a cubic meter of gas in Iran. Eventually the Chinese companies will probably begin production in Iran, but in the meantime they are increasing purchases from Saudi Arabia, Qatar and Angola.

Another hybrid form of NOC can also be seen in Russia. Some of the main Russian oil companies like Lukoil or Rosneft are officially independent, but it is common knowledge that oil policy gets managed directly from the Kremlin. They have made interesting joint ventures with IOCs especially in difficult geological terrains like in Sakhalin with Shell and ExxonMobil. It seems, however, that the relations between the large IOCs and their Russian counterparts are often difficult. In 2008 BP and its Russian tycoon partners had substantial disagreements, which led the TNK-BP joint venture to force BP's appointed president out of the country. The relationship has improved somewhat lately, but as BP is reeling from its losses in the Gulf of Mexico debacle during 2010, the joint venture is now buying some of the assets of BP worldwide, such as BP's assets in Venezuela.[15] There is no doubt at this point that BP is no longer in the driver's seat and that the Russian owners have control of the joint venture.

Russia is the largest world producer of oil, and its NOCs are very large and quite sophisticated. Hence, their motivation in dealing with the IOCs is either to gain technology, which they will then use on their own, or to gain access to distribution of their exports of gas and oil. In these two areas, politics tend to dominate. Thus NOCs independence is quashed by national interest, whatever the shareholding structure may be.

Corruption issues

Another factor that may be affecting many NOCs of the world is corruption. It is, of course, extremely difficult to find precise information about this phenomenon. Also it is difficult to define where and how the corruption takes place. In some cases the buyers of oil could be paying an extra amount to various state employees to provide a long-term contract at a favorable price. This is rendered difficult now by various anti-corruption laws that were passed in Western countries criminalizing corruption. Another form of corruption can take place when concessions are provided by the government of any given country and take the form of signing bonuses, not all of them paid to the state.

In other cases, payments are not made by the buyers of oil, but take place between the time when the oil companies receive payments under letters of credit and transfer funds to their Ministry of Finance. As shown in Figure 4.2 above, the amount accounting for the corruption needs to be paid through standing instructions by the state sovereign or ministers to the bank requesting it to transfer a certain percentage of all payments from the NOCs to its ministry to a third party somewhere in a fiscal paradise with strong regulations on discretion. This timing allows the money to never show up in the accounts of the country. The country does not need to divulge the income of its NOC and will only show the income received by the Ministry of Finance (or the equivalent agency, which would normally receive funds from the NOC). It is probable that it is in this manner that many royal and/or ruling elites are able to fund their private treasuries for distribution to their clan members. The amount being diverted from the oil revenues before the latter enter the accounts of the state is certainly not clear. If the amounts were too high, most observers could figure out the discrepancies, if it were too low, the recipients could start showing great dissatisfaction with their given leader.

The IOCs

Just as the NOCs do not fit in a neat definitional mode, the IOCs also cover a very large spectrum of activities and state influence. Obviously companies like ExxonMobil, Chevron or Shell seek to maximize the returns to their shareholders and are less involved in maximizing benefits to their home country than PDVSA or KPC. In fact, it is interesting to note that until the spill of the Macondo well in the Gulf of Mexico in 2010, BP, a British-based firm, was the largest producer of crude oil in the USA. Furthermore, the very large IOCs, have operations, as well as shareholders, all over the world. Hence, they are mostly free of government interference in their home countries. They are not, however, totally free of government intervention. In 1987, BP, then called British Petroleum, placed over 10% of its capital to the Kuwait Investment Office (KIO). This created a major row in British politics and Prime Minister Margaret Thatcher demanded that the Kuwaitis decrease their shareholding for fear that the Kuwaiti investment could lead to the control of a major British company vital to the British economy.

IOCs are also subject to highly nationalistic pressures. In mid-2005, China's CNOOC made a $20bn offer to buy UNOCAL of California. CNOOC was mainly interested in the large oil reserves controlled by UNOCAL in the Far East. The board of UNOCAL was willing to accept the Chinese offer, but public clamor and political pressure quickly became intense and UNOCAL had to reject CNOOC's offer. UNOCAL eventually became absorbed by Chevron. Hence, BP and UNOCAL, nominally independent, publicly traded international oil companies were seen by their respective publics as being national oil companies, subject to national interest. One can well imagine that today an attempted takeover of Total would trigger a similar strong reaction from the French government, and ultimately the purchase of a substantial percentage ownership in an IOC like Chevron or ExxonMobil by, say, a large sovereign wealth fund would be met by strident opposition in the USA. Smaller IOCs like ENI of Italy or Repsol from Spain are closer and more dependent on their government support and in this manner are more similar to the Chinese or Russian firms.

Perhaps the IOCs that are the most independent from government interference or less reliant on government support, are the small independently owned and managed oil companies. Many of these firms are only active in North America, but a number are moving internationally. Firms like Amarada Hess, Hunt Oil, Marathon, or even non-Western firms like Dubai's Crescent Petroleum, which owns DanaGas, or DNO, also from Dubai, but part Norwegian, seem to act without regard for the diplomatic and political interests of their countries of origin. These "smaller" firms are only small compared to the behemoths like ExxonMobil, BP or Saudi Aramco, but their asset base can be substantial. Perhaps, small firms being of less importance to their base country can actually focus more on their shareholders than on political consideration. This is especially true of a company like Crescent Petroleum in Dubai, which has shareholders from Iraq and the Gulf, but is also active in the Kurdish areas against the wishes of the Iraqi government and of the Gulf States.

Conclusion

It appears that the major drawback of the NOCs lies in their propensity to become overwhelmed by government control. Some governments are under huge pressure to increase income rapidly without investing in necessary, but very expensive, technologies and maintenance programs to improve and maximize their upstream sector as well as their downstream sector. This is quite obvious in Iran and Venezuela, and had been the case in Iraq under Saddam Hussein. The governments of the countries mentioned want their oil companies to maximize income. Thus, in the OPEC meetings, they will usually ask for larger quotas and demand higher prices. However, even with higher quotas, they tend to be unable to increase production reliably, and when able, will not cut production when needed to maintain prices to maximize income. They will tend to freeload on the cuts made by the Saudis and other Gulf producers. The huge investments needed to maintain and develop the upstream and downstream in the countries of highly controlled NOCs just do not get made as the governments find higher priorities. The lack of investment, of course, slowly strangles the goose that had laid the golden eggs in the first place.

In contrast, the IOCs, like ExxonMobil, Chevron, Shell, BP or Total appear often to be more disciplined and better able to promote the proper management of the fields. They rely on the most advanced technology to extract the best of the geology and will develop technology to maximize their downstream activities. As a consequence, many of the NOCs have come to rely on the IOCs to develop the their resources. It is with some trepidation that many NOCs and their governments are watching to see if Iraq will be successful in increasing its production from 2.3mbpd to almost 10mbpd within the next 10 to 15 years through its very aggressive management of the production agreements signed with the major IOCs.

As we have seen some NOCs, like Saudi Aramco, Statoil or Petrobras, while being closely monitored by their governments have managed to keep their distance from overarching state interference. In fact some of these firms are as technologically advanced as the major IOCs and in some cases even more advanced than most IOCs. It seems indeed, that NOCs by and large should be the companies that will be more likely to succeed. They do control most of the world oil and gas reserves. If they could ensure a certain financial independence they would be able to increase their influence worldwide.

In cases where the NOCs do not have enough local crude oil reserves to draw from, they have started going international. This has been particularly the case of the Chinese companies who compete directly with the IOCs in Africa and Iraq and try to take advantage of the political tensions between the IOCs home countries and Iran.

In short, it seems that the NOCs and the IOCs are actually much closer than is often perceived. On the one hand, the management of technology, assets and finance of NOCs, like Saudi Aramco, Petrobras, Statoil, Sinopec and CNOOC are looking increasingly like the major IOCs. Moreover, they are more frequently going overseas, except Saudi Aramco, to develop resources there or merely sell their technology. They are also going extensively downstream beyond refining into petrochemicals, just like the IOCs.

Ultimately the goals of the NOCs and the IOCs may be different in that the NOCs are thinking more to maximize the long-term impact to their country, while the IOCs tend to seek maximization of income to their shareholders. However, in both cases, the result may end up being the same. The NOCs need to maximize income for the long run, while the IOCs require long-term thinking as they do have a ten-year lead time from decision to refining. Thus, it is not surprising that many NOCs are moving to privatize portions of their shareholding and like Total, Sinopec, Rosneft or Lukoil did some years back, may become increasingly owned by the public at large, both in their home country and internationally.

Notes

1 www.hartenergy.com/pr/20100318_RefinerAwards.pdf
2 In this chapter, the word "Gulf" will refer to the Gulf that lies between the Arabian Peninsula and Iran. Both sides of the Gulf are adamant and strident about the use of Arabian Gulf vs. Persian Gulf, both claiming that without any doubt they use the right nomenclature and in doing so are backed by history. The chapter will therefore use only the word "Gulf," thus avoiding taking side in the controversy, but probably insuring the ire of both parties.
3 After the various mergers in the oil industry in the past 30 years, there are only two left, ChevronTexaco and ExxonMobil.
4 *Saudi Gazette*, September 14, 2010.
5 PFC Energy, Saudi Arabia Country Report, Market Intelligence Service September 2002, Part 2, p. 18 and p. 22
6 PFC Energy in "National Iranian Oil Company" NOCs Strategy and Performance Profiles, Washington 2006, p. 47, quoted the then Minister of Oil Mr. Vaziri-Hamaneh, that due to lack of investments in the oil fields, Iran's production was declining by 500,000 per year and at the price of oil at that time estimated that Iran would have to pay out more than it takes in, by 2016.
7 From the Human Rights Watch Report, quoting Rafael Ramírez, President of PDVSA "We removed 19,500 enemies of the country from this business" referring to the employees fired after the 2002 strike. www.hrw.org/en/news/2010/09/22/cj-vezs-fix
8 PDVSA Annual Report, p. 41. The report can be found on PDVSA.com, "informes financieros."
9 "espera" in the Spanish text in the PDVSA Annual report, op. cit. p. 43.
10 PDVSA Annual Report 2009 p. 200.
11 *Oil and Gas Journal* 7/31/2010 and in *Saudi Gazette* March 19, 2010.
12 It was widely reported in the press that Iraq adjusted its reserves in September 2010 to 143bn barrels. Unsurprisingly, the Iranian oil ministry countered the Iraqi claim by announcing new reserves totaling 150.3bn barrels. Both of the claims appear highly unreliable due to their lack of any scientific justification.
13 Guardian.co.uk, ExxonMobil wins $50bn contract to develop West Quran oilfield. November 5, 2010.
14 bp.com/genericarticle.do?categoryId=2012968&contentId=7057650
15 Dow Jones Newswires 10–18–2010 "BP Agrees to Sell Assets to TNK-BP for $1.8billion"

5

The Policy Implications of Peak Oil[1]

Laurel Graefe

Introduction

For the past half century, a debate has raged over when "peak oil" will occur. Until recently, the debate had been largely academic in nature, with the public narrative only catching glimpses of a conversation that took place mainly between experts within the energy industry. But, as the price for crude oil became unusually volatile after the turn of the twenty-first century, the issue of peak production has received heightened attention among policy makers, and the tone has changed in the discussions among oil industry and energy watchdogs about the future of global oil supply. The world's energy supply still relies heavily on oil, and global energy demand is expected to rise steeply over the next 20 years, so understanding the factors affecting future oil supply has become more pressing.

While the debate about peak oil production is part of an important and valid discourse, some aspects of the dialogue are susceptible to emotional bias and selective interpretation of the data, with firm opinions falling on opposite ends of the spectrum. There is a notable absence of uniform standards for measuring and sharing estimates of oil resources and reserves, and no common framework of definitions with which simple comparisons can be made. Beyond that, discord about the effect of aboveground factors, which could greatly alter the future rate at which oil resources are depleted, adds to the uncertainty about future supply.

The world's energy supply is in a process of transition. As conventional oil is depleted (regardless of the exact timing of peak oil production) the world faces the challenge of adapting to a new model of energy supply. This chapter seeks to bring the peak oil debate into focus by reviewing sources of uncertainty in the oil supply outlook.

Define peak oil

The term "peak oil" is not about running out of oil; the world will likely have oil to pump for generations to come. Peak oil refers instead to the inevitable point at which the world's petroleum output can no longer increase, and production begins to level off or decline. At first glance this issue would not appear to be controversial. After all, it is largely a question of geology—how much oil is left? The disagreements center around uncertainty about basic aboveground factors. On the supply side, how much will oil companies invest in capacity? How will extraction and refining technology advance? Or how many hurricanes or wars will occur in oil-producing regions? On the demand side, how fast will global economic and population growth be? What impact will future environmental policies have on oil consumption and conservation? What role will renewable fuels play in replacing global dependence on hydrocarbon energy?

One may wonder what makes oil so special; why isn't oil treated just like other physical non-renewable commodities? You don't often hear of debates on the timing of the demise of gold, or diamonds, or zinc. So why the fuss about oil?

Countless numbers of popular books, papers, and blogs are fully committed to either proving or debunking the theory that world oil production either already has peaked or will peak soon. Peak oil is a centerpiece of some scientists' careers and it seems that a new organization or expert devoted to some aspect of the debate about peak oil emerges on a regular basis. Merely entering a discussion about peak oil can prove to be rather sticky, given the heated, often apocalyptic aspect of the debate. The sense that the peak oil argument tends to be fear-based often plays to people's emotions, adding more fervor to the dispute. Though the premise of much of the peak oil work is centered on the timing of peak production, or current supply fundamentals, the central underlying anxiety stems from a concern that there will be a painful, even catastrophic, adjustment period.

Political importance of peak oil

Despite the shortage of middle-of-the-road discourse, this topic should not be written off as fringe. Such a dismissal ignores the importance of how the prospect of peak oil will continue to shape global policy considerations.

Even with the increasing use of nonpetroleum resources such as natural gas and renewables, the world still relies heavily on crude oil for a considerable portion of its energy supply. Although global oil consumption decreased slightly in 2009, it still accounted for over one-third of total energy use, and is likely to remain an important component of the global energy mix for decades to come. In fact, in its *International Energy Outlook 2010*, the Energy Information Administration (EIA) projected that world energy demand will grow by nearly 50% between 2007 and 2035, with liquid fuels, a category consisting mostly of oil, remaining the world's largest single energy source (EIA 2010). Clearly then, having a better understanding of the future oil supply situation and the associated risks will remain a central policy issue for the short, medium, and long term.

As concern about the potential implications of peak oil production heightens, a call for a political response has become louder. Whether a strategy for limiting consumption before supply becomes a constraint, or a contingency plan for action in the case of a peak-induced global price or supply shock, political leaders have begun to entertain the notion that policy should incorporate the risk of peaking oil production.

Even if political entities choose not to endorse a specific projection for peaking oil supply, it is necessarily a scenario that should be taken into consideration when planning for future economic and environmental outcomes. An influential study published in response to a request from the US Department of Energy frames the political response to peak oil as an issue of risk management (Hirsch et al. 2005).[2] The argument is that the potential downside risks of being unprepared (social, economic, and political) once the world does indeed reach peak oil production are sufficiently dire to warrant significant political action to avoid such a scenario, even if such an outcome is considered unlikely.

Given that oil is not uniformly dispersed throughout the world (countries in the Middle East hold 63% of proved reserves, Central and South America 10%, Africa 10%, Eurasia 8%, North America 5%, and the rest of the world about 4%) reactions to the potential of peaking oil supply have been inherently heterogeneous. Though tactics vary on a country-by-country basis, planning for peak oil is often coupled with both climate change and energy security considerations. In general, net oil exporters will take much different approaches to planning for peak oil from net importers, which have tended to place more emphasis on conventional oil alternatives. Additionally, the energy intensity of an economy, and the local availability of substitutes also greatly influence how public policies incorporate the perception of peak oil.

However, policy makers are not passive observers in the peak oil discourse. Some even claim that a peak oil debate based purely on geology is irrelevant simply because global energy demand will peak before global supply does. Subscribers to this philosophy cite economic slack, efficiency advancements, and/or consumption cutbacks in response to environmental legislation as reasons why a peak in oil production will be driven by demand-side, rather than supply-side, constraints. So the peak oil/policy relationship is two-way. Not only does the prospect of peak production influence policy decisions, but also public policy inherently affects the use of oil and therefore the timing of any potential supply peak.[3]

Why there is a peak oil debate: sources of uncertainty

People have been calling for the beginning of the end of oil for about half the life of its industrial use.[4] In 1956, geologist M. King Hubbert predicted that the USA was near a national peak in petroleum output. Although his forecast was later proved to be accurate, at the time his proclamation spurred a remarkable backlash from critics determined to discredit Hubbert's predictions. Opponents criticized his methodology and claimed that his forecast was unrealistically dire, underestimating the potential for higher prices and improvements in production and exploration technology to increase measured supply.

Although the actors have changed, and technology and methods have evolved substantially since Hubbert's initial prediction, the basic premise of the two sides of the peak oil argument has transformed very little over the history of the debate. The pessimists argue that it is unrealistic to base forecasts on the assumption that some not-yet-realized technology or circumstances will establish access to today's inaccessible and inefficient resources. They maintain that production either has peaked or will soon peak, and painful shortages will ensue. And the resource optimists contend that easily accessible oil has been abundant for most of the industry's history, thus far providing little incentive for investment in new recovery or production techniques; technological advancements, and improved access will increase reserves over time.

The doomsayers, of course, must eventually be right, given the fact that the world's oil is an exhaustible resource and will ultimately run out, though they haven't been right so far. But the counterargument that oil production hasn't peaked yet, so it isn't going to, doesn't prove terribly convincing either.

Fortunately, most of the studies of peak oil recognize similar players and consider similar risks. Experts tend to agree that oil production, whether for an individual field, a country, or the world as a whole, more or less follows a bell curve. What is more ambiguous is the exact shape and asymmetry of the curve: Will production taper off slowly once production peaks, or will it undulate steadily for many years, or will it drop off steeply? The topic becomes even more divisive when an effort is made to pinpoint how far along the curve global production is today and the level at which the world will peak in the future.

The controversy arises as different studies cite seemingly similar dynamics and statistics only to reach opposing conclusions. The peak oil discussion would become much clearer if the terminology were more uniform; simple analytical mix-ups can lead to large discrepancies in estimates.[5] Most of the debate lies in the fuzzy nature of information at the margin.

Measuring remaining resources

A number of unknowns cloud the energy outlook and foster flexible interpretations of the supply data that are available. First, the world's oil resources are obscured deep below the earth's surface, making a definitive measure of total resources unattainable. Even the best estimates are susceptible to major revisions. Official measures of remaining resources rarely come in the form of one concrete number, but rather as a range of different estimates that are each assigned a probability. The US Geological Survey (USGS - a bureau of the US Department of the Interior), for example, estimates with 95% certainty that the world's undiscovered conventional petroleum is at least 0.4 trillion barrels, and with 5% certainty that undiscovered resources are at least 1.2 trillion barrels, with the mean estimate at 0.7 trillion barrels undiscovered (USGS 2000, table AR-1). These statistics are therefore open to interpretation and, depending on how they are analyzed, can be used on either side of the debate to prove a point. The same variation occurs in estimates of how much of the earth's oil resources will actually come into production; some analysts consider only "proved reserves," or those with a 95% probability of being produced, whereas others look at (higher) estimates of reserves with a lower probability of coming into production. Still others focus on entirely different indicators of the earth's remaining resources.[6]

Another factor that obscures the outlook for oil supply is that there is no internationally consistent method for collecting and sharing information on a country-by-country basis about national energy endowments. Though there is some momentum to move toward a global standardized methodology for reporting reserves and resources (United Nations Framework Classification for Fossil Energy and Mineral Resources), nearly every oil producing country currently uses a unique system for reporting and defining oil supply.

Reserve estimates

The ambiguity doesn't end with resource estimation, however. In fact, even the most optimistic forecaster is unlikely to argue that oil production will continue to rise until the world's entire resource endowment has been exhausted. The reality is that some oil resources are easier to get to than others. This is where reserve estimates come into play. Conversations about peak oil naturally center around assessments of how much of the earth's petroleum resource endowment is expected actually to be produced.

As is the case with resource estimates, there is no transparent or audited internationally agreed-upon procedure for calculating or reporting reserves. In some form or another, reserve estimates generally include some distinguishing mechanism to categorize remaining resources based on the likelihood of actually coming into production under given circumstances. There are three primary categories under which reserves are classified.

Proved reserves, commonly labeled 1P, consist of the petroleum that is "reasonably likely" to be producible using current technology at current prices, with current commercial terms and government consent. While "reasonably likely" can be interpreted in more than one way, the most common is reserves with a 95% probability of being produced, or "P95." Proved reserves are subdivided into "proved developed," which can be produced with no or minimal additional investment, and "proved undeveloped," which require additional capital investment (drilling new wells, installing gas compression, etc.) to bring the oil and gas to the surface. Proved reserves, then, tend to be the lowest estimates of reserves (and the figures often cited by peak oil pessimists who don't assume any improvement in "above ground" circumstances).

Probable reserves are those that are "reasonably probable" to be producible using current or likely technology at current prices, with current commercial terms and government consent. Probable reserves are usually considered to be at the median of the distribution function, or P50. They are also known as 2P, or proved plus probable reserves.

The most broadly encompassing estimate of reserves is *possible* reserves, or any reserves that have a chance to be developed under favorable circumstances, typically, those with a 5% certainty of being produced, or P5. In the industry, possible resources are often referred to as 3P, signifying proved plus probable plus possible reserves.

While these definitions are, in theory, relatively clear-cut, in practice it can be difficult to take an unbiased approach to applying this measurement framework. Notice how measures of proved reserves are directly associated with current prices, technology, and policy, making estimates highly susceptible to major revisions based on these aboveground, non-geological factors, which can vary significantly over a short period of time. Additionally, probable and possible reserve estimates, by definition, rely heavily on assumptions about future circumstances that tend to be difficult to predict, leaving even more room for guesswork. Confusion can also arise as some countries and companies often report only "reserves," without distinguishing which type (and therefore with how much certainty) is being reported.

The role of non-conventional resources

Within the classification of oil reserves, there is also an important distinction based on different physical and logistical characteristics. While some oil—conventional oil—tends to be relatively cheap and easy to produce, the earth contains a far greater quantity of nonconventional resources as well. Given the magnitude of some of the earth's nonconventional resources, including measures of non-conventional oil in calculations of peak oil supply can significantly alter outcomes. Though the terms conventional and non-conventional (or unconventional) are widely used, they lack a common framework of definitions and are thus not uniformly applied to resource estimates and forecasts. In general, whether a deposit is considered conventional is determined by the difficulty involved in extracting and producing the resource. There are two primary methods of classification, one economic and one geological.

In economic terms, *conventional* oil is oil that can be extracted and produced under existing (or foreseeable) technological and economic conditions. *Non-conventional* resources are those that are more difficult and expensive to put into production. Note that while this classification provides a valuable concept, it describes a moving target and involves a good deal of speculation about future economic circumstances and technological evolution, and therefore is too ambiguous to be applied to reported estimates.

A more precise, geological definition from the USGS differentiates between conventional and non-conventional oil on the basis of petroleum's density (API gravity) and resistance to flow (viscosity). According to Meyer and Attanasi (2003), the USGS defines conventional (light) oil as having an API gravity of at least 22° and a viscosity less than 100cP (a higher API gravity and lower viscosity indicate a less dense, thinner liquid).[7]

Non-conventional (heavy) oil is then loosely defined as any petroleum liquid oil having less than 22° API gravity. Non-conventional oil includes *extra-heavy oil,* with less than 10° API. Nearly all the world's discovered extra-heavy oil is located in Venezuela's Orinoco Oil Belt. *Oil sands,* also referred to as natural bitumen or tar sands, are a denser, thicker version of heavy oil, with a viscosity greater than 10,000 cP. At present, the only large-scale commercial oil sands production takes place in Canada's Alberta oil sands region, home to 70% of the world's total discovered bitumen resources.[8]

Other non-conventional oil resources. Some other resources are often categorized as non-conventional oil, depending on whether a study is defining oil by its physical attributes or its economic viability (Lepez 2007, 103–7; Schindler and Zittel 2008, 20–22).

Natural gas liquids (NGL), liquid components of natural gas, are often included in non-conventional oil estimates. NGLs are classified according to their vapor pressure and include condensate (low vapor pressure), natural gasoline (intermediate vapor pressure), and liquid petroleum gas (high vapor pressure). Propane, butane, pentane, hexane, and heptane are all NGLs.

Shale oil is created at heavy industrial installations that process kerogen (intermediate organic compounds found in certain types of sedimentary rock) at extremely high temperatures. Most of the world's shale oil (about 1.5 trillion barrels) is located in the western USA, notably Colorado and Utah (Dyni 2006). The World Energy Council estimates that the world's total shale oil resource is equivalent to about 2.8 trillion barrels of oil; however, little of that total is considered to be recoverable under current conditions given the high economic and environmental costs associated with oil shale production today (2009).

Deep-water petroleum is found beneath up to 500 meters of water; *ultradeep* oil is found at water depths as great as 2,000 meters. Although deep-water reservoirs tend to be geologically similar to those found in shallower areas or onshore, producing oil from such water depths presents extensive logistical and technological challenges.

Synthetic oil is liquid fuel created by chemically converting natural gas (gas-to-liquids), coal (coal-to-liquids), or biomass. The process is generally very expensive.

Polar oil resources are those located north of the Arctic Circle and south of the Antarctic Circle. Challenges are posed by the extreme climate and remote locations. In a 2008 assessment of oil resources in the Arctic Circle, the USGS (2008) estimated that the area holds some 90bn barrels of undiscovered oil.[9] The study notes that the majority of these resources are located offshore, adding that "the extensive Arctic continental shelves may constitute the geographically largest unexplored prospective area for petroleum remaining on earth."

Although the combined amount of non-conventional resources greatly exceeds the quantity of conventional oil reserves, non-conventionals still represent only a small fraction of global oil production. Conventional crude oil accounted for 67.9mbpd on average (or 84%) of the 81mbpd of total world liquids production in 2009. Natural gas liquids contributed 10.8mbpd (13%) in 2009, with non-conventionals (including extra-heavy oil, oil sands, shale oil, synthetic oil, and additives) comprising the remaining 2.3mbpd (just under 3%) (IEA 2010b, table 3.3).

Extracting and refining these non-conventional energy resources tends to be much more capital- and energy-intensive than for conventional oil, making them more expensive to produce than conventional sources. And given the relatively high environmental impact of extracting and processing non-conventional resources, legislation restricting or taxing their use often further increases production costs.

Still, despite their drawbacks, non-conventional resources will likely play an increasingly important marginal supply role in the future as reserves that are easier and cheaper to produce become depleted.[10] Technology has advanced substantially, and resources that were once dismissed as completely inefficient and cost-prohibitive, are now becoming real opportunities for new energy sources. The incentive for innovation and investment in more economically and environmentally efficient energy production methods (hydrocarbon-based or renewable) will continue to grow as the world exhausts conventional reserves.

The World Energy Council calculated that by the end of 2005, some 47% of the total reserves of conventional oil that had been discovered had already been consumed and that conventional oil output would peak within the following 10 to 20 years (2007, 42–43). Even if true, some would argue, the growing economic viability of non-conventionals would make a peak in what is today considered conventional irrelevant. In fact, much of the uncertainty regarding peak oil outcomes stems from experts' differing opinions about the ability of large-scale unconventional resource projects to produce at a rate necessary to both keep up with rising demand and replace conventional liquids production.

Aboveground factors

While estimates of the earth's total resource endowment are primarily concerned with physical belowground conditions, the future ability to extract oil and the path of future demand are equally determined by circumstances aboveground. Therefore, any attempt to calculate the long-run supply of oil must take into account much more than geology. Even if information about current resources and reserves were entirely transparent, estimates of a date for peak oil could still vary drastically, as expectations for aboveground circumstances differ.

The role of technology

As the descriptions of reserves demonstrate, a large gap exists between what is thought to be the earth's total petroleum resource endowment and the portion of those resources that are currently considered recoverable. Technological advancement plays an essential role in narrowing that gap as innovation allows more usable oil to be produced in a cost-effective manner.

For example, as oil is extracted, the pressure within the oil field diminishes and the water levels rise, contributing to a decline in the production rate. The decline can be delayed or reduced by injecting gas or water into the reservoir to increase the pressure or by heating the oil or injecting chemicals to reduce the viscosity of the oil. Today, these techniques of enhanced oil recovery (EOR) are commonly applied to aging fields to increase the amount of extractable oil (US Department of Energy 2008). The International Energy Agency estimates that EOR application to existing fields could as much as double current estimates of proved reserves (2010a).

Another major technological innovation for oil producers is the development of advanced drilling techniques that allow more precise well exploration and development. While standard vertical drills allow producers to access a reservoir only from directly above, *directional* or *horizontal* wells enable producers to reach underground reservoirs in a much more flexible, efficient manner (Feuillet-Midrier 2007, 89–90).

New technologies have also allowed for major advances in companies' ability to produce oil located beneath the ocean floor. Offshore extraction technologies have evolved in the past half-century from platforms reaching oil a few hundred feet below the water's surface and a few thousand feet below the ocean floor to today's major installations that are capable of drilling tens of thousands of feet. These advances have opened up new expanses of hydrocarbon reserves, including deep basins of deposits in the US Gulf of Mexico and the North Sea and off the coast of Brazil and West Africa.

Advancements in recovery and processing techniques, coupled with improvements in instruments geologists use to see what lies beneath the earth's crust, have made previously unreachable (and undiscovered) deposits viable for production, thus leading to increased measurements of recoverable reserves. Many disbelievers in the theory that oil is nearing peak production argue that oil reserves will continue to grow over time as technological evolution makes production of seemingly out-of-reach resources plausible. Maugeri (2009) points out that the world's 2.3 trillion barrels of proved reserves (1 trillion of which have already been consumed) account for only a segment of the earth's original petroleum deposits. He argues that the reason just a portion of the earth's original deposits are considered reserves is that easily accessible conventional oil has been abundant for most of the industry's history, providing little incentive for significant investment in innovation of non-conventional oil production techniques. However, Maugeri notes that, as the "easy" oil is used up, technological advancement will ensue, and reserves will grow as resources from undiscovered and mature fields and non-conventional sources become viable.

But it may not be entirely realistic to make predictions about future oil supply on the assumption that some yet-to-be-created technology will establish access to what today are considered to be inaccessible and inefficient resources. Besides, a growing scarcity of conventional oil and the accompanying high oil price could just as easily justify investment in renewable energy and conservation technology as advancements in oil recovery techniques.

The role of prices, and the prospect of peaking demand

The time at which peak oil production will occur is determined not only by the amount of resources that exist underground and the portion of those resources that can be extracted, but also by future oil demand, which will govern the speed at which the extractable resources are depleted. The pace of economic growth and the nature of globalization, environmental preferences and legislation, and the availability of close substitutes will all shape the level of future demand for oil. According to traditional economic thought, however, all of these aboveground factors will influence the oil supply/demand balance through one principal mechanism: prices.

Some economists would point out that, even in the absence of any major policy initiatives, society should naturally move away from conventional oil as it approaches peak because rising prices will make substitutes more economically attractive. Hotelling (1931) explained that a rising oil price in anticipation of future supply declines will allow time for a transition to an alternative or non-conventional source of energy (or more conservation) before a cut-back becomes physically necessary. According to Hotelling's rule, as long as information is transparent and markets are free to operate efficiently, since the price of oil includes the knowledge of future supply declines, preparation for peak oil will occur naturally because the market will establish an efficient allocation of oil over time. In other words, a rising oil price in anticipation of future supply shortages should allow time for a transition away from oil before cutbacks become physically necessary. This notion has generally been adopted as the conventional economic view of non-renewable resources.

However, as this chapter has described, information about the global oil market is far from being fully transparent. Current supply data are incomplete and often difficult to interpret, and the future paths of technological innovation and demand are difficult to foresee. Additionally, markets are not entirely free to incorporate expectations about the future. And in reality, political leaders do not necessarily act in the most economically efficient manner but instead implement taxes or subsidies or act to maximize short-term profits at the expense of long-term outcomes. OPEC, for example, functions as a cartel to deliberately influence market prices by colluding to withhold supply, thereby distorting market pricing. In addition, Morgan Stanley estimated in 2008 that one-half of the world's population received some form of fuel subsidy or price control. Although some of these policies were rolled back in attempts to shore up government fiscal positions during the price spike and subsequent economic collapse, government price intervention still cushions a significant percentage of global oil demand from market incentives.

Low energy prices, generally thought to encourage economic growth, can also have longer-term negative effects as they discourage efforts towards conservation and efficiency and impede future production projects.[11] Delayed investment spurred by soft energy prices could create an environment of lagging supply and price spikes.[12] This risk is particularly apparent in the case of non-conventional and alternative resources, which tend to be relatively expensive to produce.

Distortionary pricing discouraging investment is just one example of an aboveground issue that arguably can have just as much effect on the path of oil production as physical supply. Evolving technology, economic growth, fiscal regimes, geopolitics, and environmental preferences and regulations are all aboveground factors that will help determine the timing of peak oil production.

Looking ahead: investing in future supply and understanding options

The supply of energy as we have known it is in the process of transition. Today's "easy" conventional oil that the world relies upon as a primary energy source is being depleted, and, regardless of the exact timing of peak oil production (be it this year or fifty years down the road) the world faces the challenge of adapting to a new model of energy supply. Although the peak oil literature tends to concentrate heavily on the scenarios of peaking world oil production, the true underlying issue is a fear that the transition from conventional oil to substitutes will be expensive and chaotic, leaving insufficient time for supply substitution and adaptation.

This adaptation process, which involves using more renewable resources and conservation and developing new technology and processes better to locate hydrocarbon deposits and more efficiently extract and refine non-conventional sources, has already begun. But the road to the future energy balance, one with dwindling amounts of conventional oil, is far from mapped out.

It is possible that the world's vast endowments of hydrocarbon resources will be heavily relied upon to answer this growing call for substitutes for the conventional oil supply. However, there is also potential for an energy future largely diversified away from hydrocarbon use. Most likely, future energy supply will come from a combination of sources.

Appendix: Peak oil in practice

The relationship of prices and demand: a look at recent history.

During the five-year period from 2003 to 2007, global economic growth accelerated precipitously, led by the world's increasingly energy-intensive developing countries; this rapid growth placed significant pressure on the global oil balance and contributed to an unprecedented price spike. From January 2007 to July 2008, the price of crude oil nearly tripled, jolting businesses and consumers around the globe. The high prices were generally thought to be, at least in part, a result of tightening oil market fundamentals (energy demand outpacing supply); some, however, including OPEC, maintained that market fundamentals were healthy but that financial market speculation and movements in the dollar exchange rate were driving the run-up in prices (OPEC 2008).[13]

Regardless of the cause, the oil price spike had undeniable economic and social consequences across the globe. Hamilton (2009, 40) considers the 2007–8 oil price spike a critical factor that helped tip the USA into recession, finding that, "had there been no oil shock, we would have described the US economy in 2007:Q4–2008:Q3 as growing slowly, but not in recession." A wide range of estimates gauge the negative effect of a rising oil price on the global economy, with impacts on developing economies and oil-importing countries generally considered to be much greater than in developed countries.[14]

However, the price spike also had an upside: Consumers began to drive less and conserve more, while businesses and producers set out ambitious plans to invest in energy-saving technology and upgrade outdated equipment. Alternative (both non-conventional and renewable) sources of energy, which historically had been price prohibitive, emerged as attractive substitutes to $145 per barrel oil. World oil demand plummeted as record prices and a worldwide economic slowdown forced consumers to cut back on their energy use. But, just as talk of a new green era was entering the mainstream, the global economic recession caused crude prices to reverse much of the increase.

Government-controlled reserves (Resource Nationalism)

According to the EIA (2009), in 2007 some 88% of the world's proved reserves were owned by government-controlled oil companies, with over three-quarters of those reserves located in OPEC (Organization of the Petroleum Exporting Countries) countries, which are not subject to external auditing.[15] This situation, skeptics claim, is reason to be cautious about accepting official reserve data as fact.

The most prominent example of disagreement about remaining supply is doubtlessly the case of Saudi Arabia, which controls what are reportedly the world's largest conventional oil reserves. Some experts claim that the Saudis are intentionally overstating the country's reserves to encourage short-term demand and deter conservation and investment in alternative energy; such investment would accelerate if peak oil were thought to be approaching and would eventually decrease the overall value of the Saudis' reserves as the world diversifies away from oil.[16] After all, OPEC members have an unusual incentive to overstate their reserves because the cartel's export limits are based on member countries' reserve estimates. Many analysts point to a period in the late 1980s during which six of the 11 OPEC members reported large increases in reserve estimates, resulting in higher production quotas. If indeed OPEC reserve estimates are inflated, the world may actually be much closer to peak oil than the official numbers indicate.

On the other hand, there is also an argument that some of the world's oil exporters, including Saudi Arabia, are instead under-reporting reserves, taking advantage of expected high future returns on oil and saving for future generations. OPEC, however, maintains that its reported reserves are accurate, claiming that "availability is not an issue" and asserting that the "world's remaining resources of crude oil and natural gas liquids are clearly sufficient to meet demand increases for the foreseeable future" (OPEC 2008, 2).

Saudi oil production has been rather erratic over time largely because the oil-rich country has historically functioned as a price stabilizer, increasing output when prices spike and cutting back if prices fall below a comfort zone. However, in recent years, despite the Saudis' best efforts to influence the market, global prices have been exceptionally inelastic to supply announcements (to increase production when prices were at their peak and decrease when they dipped to lows in late 2008 and 2009). One could argue that OPEC's poor pricing power during the oil price spike and the subsequent drop in 2007 and 2008 was in part a reflection of market participants' distrust in the cartel's (Saudi Arabia's) ability to increase production enough to satisfy global oil demand.

Notes

1 Revised from an earlier piece published in *Economic Review* (2009).
2 The Hirsch report estimates that a mitigation program would need to be in place 20 years before peaking actually occurs in order to avoid a shortfall in global liquid fuels production.

3 Though this section focuses primarily on how perceptions of peak oil have influenced public policy, there is also a literature looking at how policies influence global oil supply, and what reactions governments might adopt when oil supply does actually peak. For instance, Matutinovic (2009) discusses the ways in which geopolitics influence oil supply—and thus the timing of peak oil—including political insecurity, resource nationalism, and resource pragmatism. And Friedrichs (2010) provides an overview of different reaction approaches that have been adopted in response to realized resource scarcity in the past that may be applied again in a peak oil situation.
4 Cambridge Energy Research Associates (CERA) (2006) calculates that the current era marks the fifth time that peak theorists have claimed the world is running out of oil, and each time advancements in technology and the opening of new frontier areas have disproved assertions of a decline.
5 Sweetnam (2008) identifies several steps that could remove some of the guesswork from analysis of future oil supply, including gaining a better understanding of future technology's impact on costs and maximum recovery factors, improving knowledge of the drivers of long-term oil demand, and developing an agreed-on terminology to more clearly distinguish substantive issues from those arising from inconsistent use of terms.
6 Bentley, Mannan, and Wheeler (2007) make a case for analyzing peak oil production using estimates of proved plus probable reserves (2P), instead of considering only proved reserves. CERA (2006) and Kovarik (2003) contend that scientists should be looking at estimates of total global resources, arguing that production capacity will rise well beyond today's measures of proved reserves, led by technological advancement, resource discovery, and increasing production of unconventional resources.
7 API gravity measures how heavy or light the liquid is. An API gravity greater than 10° indicates that the oil is light enough to float on water; petroleum with a gravity of less than 10° is heavier and will sink. Centipoise (cP) is the unit of measurement for viscosity, or resistance to flow. Water at 70°F has a viscosity of about one cP.
8 The volume of discovered original oil in place in Canada totals just under 1.7 trillion barrels. However, only about 11 percent of that (179bn barrels) was classified as technically recoverable in 2005 (Meyer and Attanasi 2007).
9 In addition to oil deposits, the study also identified 1,669 trillion cubic feet of natural gas and 44bn barrels of natural gas liquids located north of the Arctic Circle.
10 The International Energy Agency estimates that, given policies in place in 2010, non-conventional liquid fuel production (including NGLs) will average 20.6m. barrels per day in 2020, up 57% from 2009, and accounting for nearly 23% of total world liquids output (IEA 2010b, table 3.3).
11 CERA (2009) estimates that the decline in the price of oil could result in oil supply growth between 2009 and 2014 being half that anticipated when prices were at their peak (7.6mbpd of the total potential future net growth of 14.5mbpd are considered to be at risk).
12 Stevens (2008) expects insufficient investment by oil companies, rather than belowground physical supply factors, to be the likely driver behind an oil supply crunch.
13 Hamilton (2009, 42) finds that, while speculative investment and low interest rates may have played a role in the price increase, "some degree of significant oil price appreciation during 2007–8 was an inevitable consequence of booming demand and stagnant production."
14 For a review of estimates of the global economic implications of an increase in the price of oil, see Rogoff (2006).
15 Rogoff (2006) argues that investment in future oil production is greatly inhibited by the tendency of many oil-exporting countries to seek national control over oil production.
16 For example, Simmons (2005) claims that the Saudis have been deliberately overstating reserve capabilities for decades, maintaining that assessing the true quantity of reserves remaining in Saudi Arabia is the most significant issue in petroleum politics today. Petroleum geologist Colin Campbell (2004) asserts that OPEC countries are inflating their reported reserves for political reasons: to increase production quotas and/or make credit more accessible.

References

Bentley, R.W., S.A Mannan, and S.J. Wheeler. 2007. Assessing the date of the global oil peak: The need to use 2P reserves. *Energy Policy* 35, no 12:6364–82.
Cambridge Energy Research Associates (CERA). 2006. Peak oil theory—"World running out of oil soon"—is faulty; could distort policy and energy debate. Press release. November 14. www.cera.com/aspx/cda/public1/news/pressReleases/pressReleaseDetails.aspx?CID=8444 (accessed June 24, 2008).

———. 2009. 'Low oil prices putting supply growth at risk.' Press release. March 27. www.cera.com/aspx/cda/public1/news/pressReleases/pressReleaseDetails.aspx?CID=10189 (accessed April 20, 2009)

Campbell, Colin J. 2004. *The coming oil crisis*. Essex: Multi-Science Publishing Co. Ltd.

Dyni, John R. 2006. 'Geology and resources of some world oil-shale deposits.' USGS Scientific Investigations Report 2005–5294. June. http://pubs.usgs.gov/sir/2005/5294/ (accessed April 20, 2009)

Energy Information Administration (EIA). 2009. Who are the major players supplying the world oil market? *Energy in brief: What everyone should know about energy*. January 28. http://tonto.eia.doe.gov/energy_in_brief/world_oil_market.cfm (accessed February 2, 2009)

———2010. *International energy outlook 2010*. October 15. www.eia.gov/oiaf/ieo/index.html (accessed October 20, 2010)

Feuillet-Midrier, E. 2007. Oil and gas exploration and production. In *Oil and gas exploration and production: Reserves, costs, contracts*. Revised ed. Translated by Jonathan Pearse. Paris: Editions Technip.

Friedrichs, Jorg. 2010. 'Global energy crunch: How different parts of the world would react to a peak oil scenario.' *Energy Policy* 38 4562–69.

Fuel subsidies: crude measures. 2008. *The Economist*. May 29. www.economist.com/finance/displaystory.cfm?story_id=11453151 (accessed April 2, 2009)

Graefe, Laurel. 2009. The Peak Oil Debate. *Economic Review* vol. 94, no. 2. Federal Reserve Bank of Atlanta.

Hamilton, James D. 2009. 'Causes and Consequences of the Oil Shock of 2007–8.' NBER Working Paper No. w15002. May 2009.

Hirsch, Robert L., Roger Bezdek, Robert Wendling. 2005. 'Peaking of World Oil Production: impacts, mitigation, & risk management.' U.S. Department of Energy, National Energy Technology Laboratory. www.netl.doe.gov/publications/others/pdf/Oil_Peaking_NETL.pdf

Hotelling, Harold. 1931. The economics of exhaustible resources: The peculiar problems of mineral wealth. *Journal of Political Economy* 39, no. 2:137–75.

Hubbert, M. King, 1956. 'Nuclear Energy and the Fossil Fuels'. Paper presented at the Spring Meeting of the Southern District Division of Production, American Petroleum Institute Spring Meetings. www.hubbertpeak.com/hubbert/1956/1956.pdf (accessed June 2, 2009)

International Energy Agency (IEA). 2010a. 'Resources to Reserves 2010: oil, gas and coal technologies for the energy markets of the future.' www.iea.org/papers/2010/Flyer_RtoR2010.pdf (accessed October 2010)

International Energy Agency (IEA) and Organisation. 2010b. 'World Energy Outlook 2010.' Paris.

Kovarik, Bill. 2003. 'The oil reserve fallacy: Proven reserves are not a measure of future supply'. Radford University. www.runet.edu/~wkovarik/oil/ (accessed July 10, 2008)

Lepez, Vincent. 2007. Hydrocarbon reserves. In *Oil and gas exploration and production: reserves, costs, contracts*. Revised ed. Translated by Jonathan Pearse. Paris: Editions Technip.

Matutinovic, Igor. (2009) 'Oil and the political economy of energy'. *Energy Policy* 31, 4251–58.

Maugeri, Leonardo. 2009. 'Squeezing more oil out of the ground'. *Scientific American*. April 1. www.sciam.com/article.cfm?id=squeezing-more-oil-edit-this (accessed April 2, 2009)

McColl, David. 2009. 'The Eye of the Beholder: Oil Sands Calamity or Golden Opportunity?' Canadian Energy Research Institute.

Meyer, Richard F., and Emil D. Attanasi. 2003. 'Heavy oil and natural bitumen—strategic petroleum resources'. US Geological Survey. Fact Sheet 70–03, August. http://pubs.usgs.gov/fs/fs070–03/fs070–03.html (accessed October 10, 2009)

———2007, 'Natural bitumen and extra-heavy oil'. *2007 Survey of Energy Resources*, eds., J. Trinnaman and A. Clarke: World Energy Council, pp. 119–43.

Organization of the Petroleum Exporting Countries (OPEC). 2008. *World oil outlook 2008*. www.opec.org/library/World%20Oil%20Outlook/WorldOilOutlook08.htm (accessed April 13, 2009)

Rogoff, Kenneth. 2006. 'Oil and the global economy'. www.nes.ru/public-presentations/Papers/Oil%20and%20the%20Global%20Economy_Rogoff – v2.pdf (accessed June 11, 2009).Schindler, Jörg, and Werner Zittel. 2008. *Crude oil: The supply outlook*. Rev. ed. Energy Watch Group. February. www.energywatchgroup.org/Oil-report.32+M5d637b1e38d.0.html (accessed October 2008)

Simmons, Matthew R. 2005. *Twilight in the desert: The coming Saudi oil shock and the world economy*. Hoboken: John Wiley & Sons Inc.

Stevens, Paul. 2008. *The coming oil supply crunch*. Chatham House Report. August 7. www.chathamhouse.org.uk/publications/papers/view/-/id/652/ (accessed November 20, 2008).

Sweetnam, Glen. 2008. 'Long-term global oil scenarios: Looking beyond 2030'. Energy Information Administration. Presented at the EIA 2008 Energy Conference, Washington, D.C., April 7.

US Department of Energy. 2008. 'Enhanced oil recovery/CO2 injection'. February. www.fossil.energy.gov/programs/oilgas/eor/ (accessed April 14, 2009)

US Geological Survey (USGS). 2000. 'US Geological Survey World Petroleum Assessment 2000'—Description and Results. US Geological Survey Digital Data Series 60. http://pubs.usgs.gov/dds/dds-060/ (accessed February 15, 2009)

——. 2008. 'Circum-Arctic resource appraisal: Estimates of undiscovered oil and gas north of the Arctic Circle'. USGS Fact Sheet 2008–3049. http://pubs.usgs.gov/fs/2008/3049/fs2008–3049.pdf (accessed April 2, 2009)

World Energy Council. 2009. 'Survey of Energy Resources: Interim Update 2009'. www.worldenergy.org/documents/ser_interim_update_2009_final.pdf (accessed September 2010)

6
Conflict and Instability

Michael Ross

The world is far more peaceful today than it was 15 years ago. There were 17 major civil wars – with "major" meaning the kind that kill more than a thousand people a year – going on at the end of the Cold War; by 2006, there were just five. During that period, the number of smaller conflicts also fell, from 33 to 27.

Despite this trend, there has been no drop in the number of wars in countries that produce oil. The main reason is that oil wealth often wreaks havoc on a country's economy and politics, makes it easier for insurgents to fund their rebellions, and aggravates ethnic grievances. Today, with violence falling in general, oil-producing states make up a growing fraction of the world's conflict-ridden countries. They now host about one-third of the world's civil wars, both large and small, up from one-fifth in 1992. According to some, the US-led invasion of Iraq shows that oil breeds conflict between countries, but the more widespread problem is that it breeds conflict within them.

The number of conflicts based in oil-producing countries is likely to grow in the future as stratospheric prices of crude oil push more countries in the developing world to produce oil and gas. In 2001 the Bush Administration's energy task force hailed the emergence of new producers as a chance for the USA to diversify the sources of its energy imports and reduce its reliance on oil from the Persian Gulf. More than a dozen countries in Africa, the Caspian basin, and Southeast Asia have recently become, or will soon become, significant oil and gas exporters. Some of these countries, including Chad, East Timor, and Myanmar, have already suffered internal strife. Most of the rest are poor, undemocratic, and badly governed, which means that they are likely to experience violence as well. On top of that, record oil prices will yield the kind of economic windfalls that typically produce further unrest.

Oil is not unique; diamonds and other minerals produce similar problems. But as the world's most sought-after commodity, and with more countries dependent on it than on gold, copper, or any other resource, oil has an impact more pronounced and more widespread.

The curse

The oil booms of the 1970s brought great wealth, and later great anguish, to many petroleum-rich countries in the developing world. In the 1970s oil-producing states enjoyed fast economic growth. But in the following three decades, many suffered crushing debt, high unemployment, and sluggish or declining economies. At least one-half of the members of OPEC (the Organization of Petroleum Exporting Countries) were poorer in 2005 than they had been 30 years earlier. Oil-rich countries that once held great promise, such as Algeria and Nigeria, have unravelled as a result of decades of internal conflict.

These states were plagued by the so-called oil curse. One aspect of the problem is an economic syndrome known as Dutch disease, named after the troubles that beset the Netherlands in the 1960s after it discovered natural gas in the North Sea. The affliction hits when a country becomes a significant producer and exporter of natural resources. Rising resource exports push up the value of the country's currency, which makes its other exports, such as manufactured and agricultural goods, less competitive abroad. Export figures for those products then decline, depriving the country of the benefits of dynamic manufacturing and agricultural bases and leaving it dependent on its resource sector and so at the mercy of often volatile international markets. In Nigeria, for example, the oil boom of the early 1970s caused agricultural exports to drop from 11.2% of GDP in 1968 to 2.8% of GDP in 1972; the country has yet to recover.

Another facet of the oil curse is the sudden glut of revenues. Few oil-rich countries have the fiscal discipline to invest the windfalls prudently; most squander them on wasteful projects. The governments of Kazakhstan and Nigeria, for example, have spent their petroleum incomes on building new capital cities while failing to bring running water to the many villages throughout their countries that lack it. Well-governed states with highly educated populations and diverse economies, such as Canada and Norway, have avoided these ill effects. But many more oil-rich countries have low incomes and less effective governments and so are more susceptible to the oil curse.

Oil wealth also has political downsides, and those are often worse than the economic ones. Oil revenues tend to increase corruption, strengthen the hands of dictators, and weaken new democracies. The more money the governments of Iran, Russia, and Venezuela have received from oil and gas exports, the less accountable they have become to their own citizens and the easier it has been for them to suppress or buy off their opponents. A major boom in oil prices, such as the one that took the price of a barrel from less than US$10 in February 1999 to over $100 in March 2008, only heightens the danger.

Oil on fire

For new oil and gas producers, the gravest danger is the possibility of armed conflict. Among developing countries, an oil-producing country is twice as likely to suffer internal rebellion as a non-oil-producing one. The conflicts range in magnitude from low level secessionist struggles, such as those occurring in the Niger Delta and southern Thailand, to full-blown civil wars, such as in Algeria, Colombia, Sudan, and, of course, Iraq.

Oil wealth can trigger conflict in three ways. First, it can cause economic instability, which then leads to political instability. When people lose their jobs, they become more frustrated with their government and more vulnerable to being recruited by rebel armies that challenge the cash-starved government. A sudden drop in income can result in internal strife in any country, but because oil prices are unusually volatile, oil-producing countries tend to be battered by cycles of booms and busts. And the more dependent a government is on its oil revenues, the more likely it is to face turmoil when prices drop.

Second, oil wealth often helps support insurgencies. Rebellions in many countries fail when their instigators run out of funds. But raising money in petroleum-rich countries is relatively easy: insurgents can steal oil and sell it on the black market (as has happened in Iraq and

Nigeria), extort money from oil companies working in remote areas (as in Colombia and Sudan), or find business partners to fund them in exchange for future consideration in the event they seize power (as in Equatorial Guinea and the Republic of the Congo).

Third, oil wealth encourages separatism. Oil and gas are usually produced in self-contained economic enclaves that yield a lot of revenue for the central government but provide few jobs for local people, who also often bear the costs of petroleum development in the form of lost property rights and environmental damage. To reverse the imbalance, some locals seek autonomy from the central government, as have the people in the petroleum-rich regions of Bolivia, Indonesia, Iran, Iraq, Nigeria, and Sudan.

This is not to say that petroleum is the only source of such conflicts or that it inevitably breeds violence. In fact, almost one-half of all the states that have produced oil since 1970 have been conflict-free. Oil alone cannot create conflict, but it both exacerbates latent tensions and gives governments and their more militant opponents the means to fight them out. Governments that limit corruption and put their windfalls to good use rarely face unrest.

Unfortunately, oil production is now rising precisely in those countries where wise leadership is often in short supply. Most of the new energy-rich states are in Africa (Chad, Côte d'Ivoire, Mauritania, Namibia, and São Tome and Principe), the Caspian basin (Azerbaijan, Kazakhstan, and Turkmenistan), or Southeast Asia (Cambodia, East Timor, Myanmar, and Vietnam). Almost all are undemocratic. The majority are very poor and ill equipped to manage a sudden and large influx of revenues. And many also have limited petroleum reserves (just enough to yield large revenues for a decade or two) which means that if they succumb to civil war, they will squander whatever chance they had of using their oil windfalls to escape from poverty.

Diamonds in the rough

Since the early 1990s, the international community has developed an effective set of tools for ending insurrections. These include cutting off foreign aid to rebel groups, using diplomatic and economic sanctions to bring governments to the negotiating table, and deploying peacekeeping forces to monitor any agreements that might result from the pressure. Combined with the demise of the Soviet Union, such methods helped reduce the number of civil wars in non-oil-producing countries by over 85% between 1992 and 2006.

They have also been effective against insurgencies fuelled by diamond wealth. In 2000 six diamond-producing states in Africa were trapped in civil wars; by 2006, none was. Much of this success is the result of sanctions that the UN Security Council started to impose in 1998 against so-called conflict diamonds (diamonds sold by African insurgents or their intermediaries) and the adoption in 2002 of the Kimberley Process, an agreement by an unusual coalition of governments, non-governmental organizations, and major diamond traders to certify the clean origins of the diamonds they trade. After these measures were taken, rebels in Angola, Liberia, and Sierra Leone lost a key source of funding, and within a few years they were either defeated in battle or forced to sign peace agreements. In the mid-1990s conflict diamonds made up as much as 15% of the world's diamond trade. By 2006 the proportion had fallen to 1%.

See-through

Curtailing rebellions in oil-producing states will be harder. The world's thirst for oil immunizes petroleum-rich governments from the kind of pressures that might otherwise force them to the bargaining table. Since these governments' coffers are already overflowing, aid means little to them. They can readily buy friends in powerful places and therefore have little fear of sanctions from the UN Security Council. In any event, the growing appetite of oil importing countries for new supplies makes it easy for exporters to bypass such restrictions. The government of President Omar al-Bashir has used Sudan's oil sales to China to deflect diplomatic pressure from Western states asking it to stop the killings in Darfur. Myanmar's military government is following the same strategy: in exchange for Myanmar's selling its natural gas to China, Beijing is blocking tougher sanctions against the junta in the UN Security Council.

The best solution would be for rich countries to sharply reduce their consumption of oil and gas and help poor countries find a more sustainable path out of poverty than oil production. But the Western economies are so dependent on fossil fuels and the demand for oil and gas imports in China and India is growing so quickly that even the most aggressive push for alternatives would take decades to have any effect. In the meantime, a different approach is needed.

No single initiative will undo the oil curse and bring peace to oil-producing states, but four measures can help. The first would be to cut off funding to insurgents who profit from the oil trade. Oil-importing states could contribute by refusing to buy oil that comes from concessions sold by insurgents. Both the insurrection in the Republic of the Congo in 1997 and the 2004 coup attempt in Equatorial Guinea were financed by investors hoping to win oil contracts from the rebels once they controlled the government. A ban on oil stemming from these transactions, much like the ban on conflict diamonds, could help prevent such rebellions in the future.

A second way to limit the effects of the oil curse would be to encourage the governments of resource-rich states to be more transparent. Their national budgets are unusually opaque; this facilitates corruption and reduces public confidence in the state, two conditions that tend to breed conflict. The Extractive Industries Transparency Initiative, an effort launched by non-governmental organizations in 2002 and expanded by former British Prime Minister Tony Blair, encourages oil and mining companies to "publish what they pay" and governments to "disclose what they receive." This is a good idea, but it is not enough. Adherence to the EITI's reporting standards is voluntary, and although 24 countries have pledged to adopt them, none has fully complied yet. It is important that they do and that the effort to promote transparency be expanded. Oil-importing states, such as the USA, should insist, for example, that energy companies also "publish what they pump", that is, disclose from which countries their petroleum originates. This would give consumers the power to reward the most responsible companies. And that, in turn, would give companies an incentive to improve the conditions in oil-producing regions.

Another problem with the current standards is that even though exporting governments are pressured to disclose the revenues they collect, they are not expected to reveal how they spend the money. Oil revenues often vanish into the nooks of state-owned oil companies or into governments' off-budget accounts. According to the International Monetary Fund, between 1997 and 2002, the Angolan government accrued at least US$4.2bn in oil receipts that it could not account for; at the time, Angola had the fifth-highest infant mortality rate in the world.

One possible remedy would be for the EITI (or a similar effort) to develop guidelines for the transparent allocation of all revenues from extractive industries. In his recent book *The Bottom Billion*, the economist Paul Collier suggests creating a "natural resources charter" that would set international standards for the governance of natural-resource revenues. The charter would help citizens figure out if their governments are properly managing the wealth. International credit-rating agencies could also use it to assess governments' creditworthiness, which would give governments a financial incentive to abide by the charter.

A third way to help oil-exporting states cast off the oil curse would be to help them better manage the flow of their oil revenues. Since the earliest days of the oil business in the mid-nineteenth century, oil prices have alternately soared and crashed. There is no reason to think this will change. But neither is there any reason to assume that because oil prices are volatile a government's oil revenues must be too. In a typical oil contract, the oil company is guaranteed a steady income and the government gets to keep most of the profits but also must bear most of the risk of fluctuating prices. This setup is exactly backward. International oil companies are skilled at smoothing out their income flows, putting money aside in fat years to spend in lean ones, whereas governments are terrible at it. The terms of these contracts should be changed so that the oil companies bear more of the price risk than they do now and governments bear less.

Even with greater transparency and steadier revenues, many low income countries simply lack the capacity to translate oil wealth into roads, schools, and health clinics. For these, the best way to steer clear of the oil curse may be not to sell oil for cash at all but to trade it directly for the goods and services their people need. The governments of Angola and Nigeria are now experimenting with this type of barter: they have awarded oil contracts to Chinese companies in exchange for the construction of infrastructure. Western oil companies have been reluctant to make similar deals, pointing out that they know little about building railroads and have trouble competing against state-owned enterprises in this arena, such as the Chinese oil companies. But they could easily team up with reputable companies that could carry out the work. And why stop at infrastructure? By forming partnerships with experienced service providers, oil companies could pay back host countries by, say, conducting anti-malaria campaigns or building schools, irrigation projects, or microfinancing facilities. As more companies bid for such "oil-for-development" contracts, the terms of the contracts would become better for the governments. If inexperienced governments need help carrying out these auctions, the World Bank, or other international organizations, could provide technical assistance.

The power of pressure

One obstacle, of course, is that some leaders have little interest in better governance: they are too busy profiting from corruption and crushing their opponents. In order to buffer the people of these countries from the mismanagement of oil wealth by their leaders, a fourth set of measures is called for. Laggard governments should be pressed to respect human rights and negotiate with rebels who have legitimate grievances. The US Congress recently urged the State Department to consider withholding visas from corrupt officials who profit from the exploitation of their countries' natural resources. A visa ban might well be an effective tool: soon after Congress' call, the Cambodian government, one of the world's most corrupt, according to Transparency International, issued a bitter protest. The State Department should adopt the measure and enforce it broadly against leaders who are corrupt or ignore international human rights standards. And European governments should be encouraged to follow suit.

To avoid constraining measures from the West, some oil-producing governments have turned to national oil companies from China, India, and other developing states that do not concern themselves with their hosts' human rights practices. But pressure could also work against these companies, as many of them are publicly listed. Last January, the Dutch pension fund PGGM withdrew its US$54m. investment from the Chinese oil company PetroChina to protest against the operations of PetroChina's parent company in Sudan; it is now considering a similar move against the Indian oil and natural gas company ONGC. Other investors should follow this lead until even companies that have not cared about such issues in the past agree to push for transparency and better human rights standards in the countries where they operate.

Helping oil-rich countries avoid violent conflicts and, more broadly, escape the oil curse will not be easy. Many of their governments are indifferent to the incentives offered by diplomats and development specialists. On the other hand, if the main stakeholders (oil producers and energy companies, as well as international organizations, oil importers, and consumers) do not find better remedies, a whole new set of countries will suffer the same tragic fate as Angola, Nigeria, Sudan, and, yes, even Iraq.

Acknowledgment

This paper was originally published as "Blood Barrels: Why Oil Wealth Fuels Conflict", reprinted by permission of *Foreign Affairs*, May June 2008, Volume 87, Issue 3, copyright 2008 Council on Foreign Relations, Inc. (www.foreignaffairs.com). Appreciation is given to the Council on Foreign Relations to reprint this article in its entirety.

7

Co-operation Between Producers and Consumers

Paul Stevens

Introduction

The relationship between oil producers and oil consumers has had a history as long as the industry itself. Thus, producers create supply and consumers create demand. On this basis of course " ... the real dialogue is in the market between billions of consuming households and enterprises and a few hundred producing organizations, some of which have much more importance than others" (Mitchell, 2005 page 5). However, interactions on this basis are coloured and directed by the broader interactions between supply and demand. These take place in a context influenced by three cycles which characterize the international oil industry (Stevens, 2008): the political cycle which refers to the attitude to state intervention in the allocation of economic resources in an economy; the resource nationalist cycle which relates to the attitude to allowing foreign company involvement in the sector; and finally, the obsolescing bargain cycle which concerns the willingness and ability of the state to revise the fiscal terms inherent in the agreement. As a result of the role of these cycles, traditionally, "producer-consumer dialogue" as a subject for analysis and study has come to refer to relationships between oil producer and oil consumer (i.e. importing) governments.

In much of the literature on producer-consumer dialogue, two strands of thought are common. The first strand is that the producers tend to work through state-owned enterprises (i.e. national oil companies) over which they have direct control and the consumers tend to work through private companies over which they only have indirect control. The second strand is that attempts at dialogue were (and still are) driven by oil price volatility and the problem that the dialogue was supposed to address was seen as that of oil price instability.

However, while both these generalizations have some validity, in reality they can be overstated. The political cycle tended to determine how much was left to markets and how much to state intervention. In other words, the balance between state-owned enterprises and private companies changes. As will be seen, for much of the time, the problems with the dialogue arose because there was often a serious mismatch between the respective attitudes of producers and consumers, based largely upon fundamental differences in ideology reflected in the political cycle. Thus in the 1980s and 1990s as the so-called "Washington Consensus"[1] was gaining traction, the major consumer governments simply wanted to leave things to "market forces."

The concept of "dialogue" implied interfering with these "market forces," which was frowned upon, especially by successive US administrations. At the same time, producer governments were seeking greater intervention. The underlying approach of the majority of the OPEC members derived from what might be loosely described a "socialist" view of the world where state intervention ruled but where the rhetoric was of co-operation.[2] The problem with rhetoric is that if it is repeated often enough, people begin at the very least to pay lip service to the ideas. It is interesting to note in this context that as will be developed below, France, always a major player in the "dialogue," consistently found itself in the middle as a country that while being part of the Organization of Economic Co-operation and Development (OECD) did, with its indicative planning and general ideology, have a much greater belief in explicit government intervention in the economy that many of its comparator countries lacked.

As for the second generalization about the role of price, as will be developed below, while rising prices acted to encourage attempts at dialogue, at times the oil price volatility was so great (most obviously during the second oil shock of 1978–80) that ideas of multilateral co-operation and hence any form of "dialogue" were effectively ditched, not least between the consumer governments as they scrambled for supplies. Given this general context, what follows is a brief history of producer–consumer dialogue.

The early years: pre-1970s

In the early years before the oil shocks of the 1970s, the "consumers" were effectively represented by the major international oil companies; the so-called Seven Sisters. These companies, five American, one British and one Anglo-Dutch,[3] were seen by the producer countries (both governments and people) as representatives of the colonial powers, although in the case of the USA this view developed during the 1950s and 1960s as part of the so-called "Cold War." As such these companies were viewed with great suspicion, as were their host governments. As will be developed below this imperial/colonial legacy of suspicion continued to dog attempts at producer–consumer dialogue throughout the 1970s, 1980s and 1990s.

It was the producer governments who first presented a united front in the form of the Organization of Petroleum Exporting Countries (OPEC) created in 1960. This was a collective response to the actions of the consumers (as represented by the Majors) seeking to lower the posted price used to compute profits for taxation purposes. This inevitably led to a reduction in revenues for the producer governments. However, this was not per se an attempt by consumers to secure lower prices. Rather it was related to the legacy of trying to maintain what had been the traditional link between US domestic prices and the international price embodied in the Gulf Basing Point pricing system, developed as a consequence of the 1928 "As-Is" agreement. Final consumers saw relatively little benefit.[4] In the words that were common at the time "only fools and affiliates pay posted prices!"

The oil shocks of the 1970s

Between October and the end of December in 1973 the international price of crude oil quadrupled following decisions taken by OPEC.[5] This was in addition to the gradual increase in prices seen since the Tehran and Tripoli Agreements signed in 1971 between OPEC and the Majors. Central to the understanding of why this was a "shock" to the consumers and subsequent events was the position taken by the governments of the industrial consumers over the previous decade. Cheap oil had been a necessary condition for the "OECD Economic Miracle" which had seen the industrialized countries growing at unprecedented rates. Their governments had taken the position during the 1960s that the Majors had been doing an excellent job; oil was abundant and prices had been falling in real terms. Thus, in the 1960s when the political cycle had persuaded the necessity of heavy government intervention in most aspects of economic activity, the Majors were declared "off-limits" to government intervention. This was to create a major problem. When the dramatic increase in prices hit in the last quarter of 1973, the politicians in the OECD consuming countries inevitably asked their bureaucrats what was going on. They received the answer that the bureaucrats had no idea because they had been instructed that the industry be left alone. Thus, part of the "shock" for the OECD was that no one knew what on earth was going on. This was compounded because the academic economists to whom the bureaucrats turned for explanation could only come up with the ideas of Harold Hotelling from his 1931 article (Hotelling, 1931). This was because for the most part, they had no idea about the practicalities of the international oil industry.[6] Hotelling's views were of little relevance to the events.

It was in this context of bewildered uncertainty that the first efforts were made by the OECD governments to try and create some sort of dialogue with OPEC. Unfortunately, it began with an effort to create an organization, the International Energy Agency (IEA), that was explicitly intended act as a counterweight to OPEC. Thus, from the very start, the "dialogue" was seen as being confrontational. In January 1974, President Nixon proposed to the major consumer governments that a ministerial level conference should be held in Washington to formulate a "consumer action programme" in order to "develop a co-ordinated consumer position ... for producer-consumer relations" (Parra, 2004 page 190). The conference, held in February 1974 led to the creation of the IEA as part of the OECD with a secretariat based in Paris. In September 1974 the IEA members agreed on an international programme for oil stockpiling and a sharing programme in the event of any further disruptions to supply along the lines of the Arab Oil Embargo. Excluded from those among the OECD members was Norway who was about to become a significant oil exporter[7] and France who was desperately trying to distance itself from US influence in the world and pursue what it saw as its own interests.[8]

A major problem with the IEA that was to follow it for some considerable time (and any attempt at dialogue) was that its creation was perceived in the Arab world as the brainchild of Secretary of State Henry Kissinger. As a result of his role in developing "shuttle diplomacy" in the context of the Arab-Israeli conflict, the Arabs regarded him with deep suspicion. His outrageous duplicity was further reinforced by the position taken by Kissinger and the US administration during and after the Yom Kippur War of 1973.[9] The result was that the two sides, OPEC and the IEA, viewed each other with deep hostility. Thus OPEC saw itself as the champion of the Third World lined up against the forces of US-led imperialism.[10] This was not a situation conducive to any sort of genuine co-operative dialogue.

In October 1977, the IEA Ministers adopted 12 principles for energy policy. In essence the policy was aimed at picking winners (coal, nuclear and conservation) and designating losers (oil and gas in power generation) (Skinner, 2005). This was in the context where "oil prices were not market driven, but subject to a foreign cartel" (ibid. page 4). However, the 12th principle was to encourage "appropriate co-operation in energy" and in 1979, the IEA Ministers agreed to a dialogue and urged the creation of a better system for regular exchange of information on world energy supply and demand.[11]

Meanwhile, in an effort to try and sidestep the obvious antipathy between the IEA and OPEC there were further developments on dialogue trying to use the good offices of the United Nations. This received the grand title of the "North South Dialogue." In April and May 1974, at the formal request of the President of Algeria, Houari Boumedienne, the UN General Assembly met and adopted a "Declaration and Programme of Action" which was intended to establish a "New International Economic Order" to promote economic developments with "OPEC as a vanguard for the Third World" (Parra, 2004 page 191).

In September 1974 the European Economic Community Council of Ministers (that was beginning to feel marginalized by events) drew up a long-term energy strategy that included options for co-operation between oil consumers and producers. It then proceeded to open a Euro-Arab dialogue. In a stance that was to characterize much of producer-consumer dialogue for decades, this move was strongly opposed by the USA. In February 1975 in Dhaka, a conference proposed by President Giscard d'Estaing was held on the "Third World Strategy on Raw Materials and Economic Development" to consider energy and related issues.[12] This was intended to be a tripartite conference involving the industrialized countries, OPEC and the rest of the developing world. Representatives of the developing world wanted the conference to consider all raw materials. While this failed, a resolution was adopted expressing "solidarity" between the oil importing developing countries and OPEC.[13]

In March of the same year, at the OPEC Summit in Algiers a "solemn declaration" was passed with 14 points regarding OPEC's relations with the developing countries. This was effectively a wish list that was described accurately but unkindly as " ... a thoroughly unrealistic document" (Parra, 2004 page 192).

In December 1975, the First Plenary Conference on International Economic Co-operation (CIEC) was held in Paris co-chaired by Canada and Venezuela. Eight industrialized countries plus the President of the EEC representing all their members attended together with 19 developing countries and seven OPEC members. Four expert commissions were created for energy, raw materials, development and finance. The conference reconvened for the second plenary session in June 1977. Nothing emerged and the North South dialogue effectively disappeared.

All these efforts failed for a number of reasons. As already suggested, the USA was opposed to any sort of dialogue that even mentioned price on the grounds this would interfere with market forces. At the same time, the French took every opportunity to irritate the Americans by giving moral and verbal support to Third World and OPEC aspirations over commodity prices. Furthermore, many of the issues were already under discussion in the General Agreement on Tariffs and Trade (GATT) and the United Nations Conference on Trade and Development (UNCTAD) and there was a sense amongst some of the OECD participants that a producer-consumer dialogue was just duplicating effort for no good reason. Also, in this atmosphere there was increasing support for the view that solutions to the problems faced by consumers, both in terms of high prices and security of oil supplies, lay in the development of bilateral rather than multilateral relations. This took the form of a number of barter deals between oil exporters and importers to try and offset the damage done to the importers' balance of payments. There were also many efforts by consumer governments to improve relations with individual OPEC members by using their aid policy and, or, their foreign policy stances on a number of issues. Probably the most extreme example of this was Japan. The government moved to make significant changes in its foreign policy to assuage Arab feelings in the hope of securing crude supplies (Koyama, 2001).[14]

The final source of failure in these early attempts at producer-consumer dialogue was what can only be described an idealistic unreality. In the words of one observer "both sides displayed an extraordinary lack of realism" (Parra, 2004 page 193).

Even amongst the consumers there was a failure to manage the crisis presented by the second oil shock. As already alluded to, the competition for crude supplies between Japan and the USA was intensified as both governments encouraged their companies to fight for crude supplies. The IEA's emergency sharing mechanism was not invoked despite the fact that a number of countries experienced the trigger-level of loss of imports which would justify its introduction. This gave rise to a view that is prevalent today that in the event of real emergency and threat to physical oil supplies, the IEA's scheme would be dropped in a frantic free for all.[15]

If the consumers could not agree amongst themselves there was little hope for any fruitful producer-consumer dialogue. The oil price shock of 1986 that dramatically reduced international crude prices effectively killed the prospects for producer-consumer dialogue for the time being. Quite simply, the consumers lost interest, very much reflecting the role of prices as a driver of attempts to talk.

A revival of interest

The invasion by Iraq of Kuwait in August 1990 triggered a revival of producer-consumer dialogue and yet again it was the threat of price shocks that encouraged the revival of dialogue. Following the invasion the oil price (Brent) rose from an average of US$15.05 in June 1990 to $32.88 in November 1990. However, the price spike was short lived mainly because Saudi Arabia was able to deploy its existing spare producing capacity to good effect. Misunderstanding this key role of Saudi Arabia, there was a widespread view among many within the OECD, especially in the USA, that it was the triumph of market forces that had rescued the day. Thus, it was perceived that the doomsday scenario[16] of severe constraints on oil exporters from the Persian Gulf had been managed because markets had been allowed to function. It was seen, based upon this fundamental error of analysis, that co-operation between producers and consumers was not a necessary condition to manage supply disruptions and price volatility. All that was needed was to leave things to the market. The absolutely key role of Saudi Arabia and its spare capacity was ignored.

However, the events of 1990–91 had frightened a number of consumer governments. In June 1991, following the liberation of Kuwait, a meeting was convened in Paris chaired by France and Venezuela. This consisted of ministers from both the exporting and importing countries. The focus was on oil and gas (Mitchell, 2005). However, the meeting was strongly opposed by the USA (Skinner, 2005) who in the event sent only a Deputy Assistant Secretary of State, which in diplomatic circles was about as close to a snub as can be imagined. This meeting, which has met on alternate years ever since, became known as the International Energy Forum (IEF) and, as will be seen below, eventually led to a new chapter in producer-consumer dialogue.

Meanwhile, oil prices throughout the post 1991 period remained relatively low and stable averaging around US$17 per barrel, eventually culminating in the oil price collapse of 1998–99. Thus, price as a driver of co-operation had yet again faded into the background for the consumers. Nevertheless, during the price collapse of 1998, OPEC sought help and support from a number of non-OPEC producers, mainly Mexico, Norway, Oman and Russia. This help was forthcoming, although Norway and Russia subsequently reneged on their commitments to help. In the event, it was co-operation between Saudi Arabia and Iran which saved the day and paved the way to price recovery.

However, the events of 1998–99 had disturbed the producers, and the idea of co-operation with consumers gained a certain amount of traction. In 2000 Saudi Arabia offered to host a secretariat for the IEF in Riyadh. This secretariat was to limit its efforts to technical activities such as organizing conferences and seminars together with gathering information. The underlying political dialogue was to be performed by ministers. In 2003 Ambassador Arne Walther of Norway was appointed the first Secretary-General of the organization. In 2007 Noe van Hulst from the Netherlands who had previously been the Director of Long-Term Co-operation and Policy Analysis at the IEA replaced him.

Robert Mabro had effectively outlined the function of the IEF in the context of the market in 1991:

> ... the role of the market needs to be supplemented by another mechanism in two areas: one that improves the flow of economic information necessary for good investment decisions and one that provides indicators to the market about a level around which prices can fluctuate freely up and down in response to short term economic forces
>
> *(Mabro, 1991 Executive summary).*

To this end, one of the initiatives was the Joint Oil Data Initiative (JODI). The trigger for JODI was a widely held belief that a lack of transparency of oil market data was a major contributory factor to oil price volatility. It began in 2001 as the Joint Oil Data Exercise. Initially this was the product of co-operation between six pioneer organizations, the Asia Pacific Economic Co-operation (APEC), the Statistical Office of the European Communities (Eurostat), the International Energy Agency (IEA), the Latin-American Energy Organization (OLADE), the Organization of Petroleum Exporting Countries (OPEC) and the United Nations (through the UN Statistics Division). It was established as a permanent mechanism in 2003, renamed as JODI with the IEF Secretariat taking responsibility for co-ordinating the project in January 2005 and managing the JODI World Database. The JODI partner organizations covering some 90 countries submit monthly data to the IEF Secretariat on production, refining, trade, demand and stocks of seven product categories: crude oil, LPG, gasoline, kerosene, diesel oil, fuel oil and total oil.

There have been some efforts to extend JODI's remit to considering estimates of oil reserves but this is unsurprisingly proving to be controversial given the strategic sensitivities of such data.

At the same time, the agenda for the dialogue was starting to become wider and very specific. On September 25th 2005, an OPEC Communiqué stated, " ... dialogue must address all the issues of interest to the parties." It then proceeded to list 14 specific agenda items.[17] This was beginning to look a little like the wish list of the 1970s, described earlier as "thoroughly unrealistic."

As these events unfolded, two issues began to emerge which were to influence producer-consumer relations in a very negative way by creating sources of conflict. These were the role of consumer government taxation and the rise of the "paper markets."

In the aftermath of the second oil shock of 1979–81, the main industrialized countries met at two key G7 summits in Venice and Tokyo. Of central importance was how to counter the growing threat to their economies from rising oil prices. A major problem was that the obvious solution of increasing final prices increased the likelihood of countries acting to protect their competitive export positions. However, if all agreed to behave in the same way and increase energy prices, this problem could be solved. It was therefore resolved at these summits that each of the G7 would begin to increase final energy prices.[18] In most cases for oil products, this was achieved by imposing sales taxes of various sorts onto the pump price.

As the 1980s progressed, the imperative to increase sales taxes at the pump came from another source. Oil products are ideal targets for tax collectors. They have a very large tax base that means a large potential pool of revenue. They have a very inelastic demand that allows very high tax rates to be imposed without reducing consumption levels. Thus the potential gross revenue is huge. Then, because of the limited number of outlets, tax collection costs are relatively very low increasing net revenue. Oil products became an increasingly important source of revenues for many governments. There was one further advantage of raising revenue from oil products. Politicians could impose such high taxes pretending to be concerned about the environment. They could hide their revenue greed behind a cloak of green respectability.

This propensity to impose taxes on oil products became a major source of concern to OPEC. There were two main issues. The first was that OPEC saw the taxes as being unfair. They pointed out that the proportion of the final product barrel going to the producer government for the crude oil was very much lower than that going to the consumer governments from sales taxes. In reality this argument was very poor economics. The money accruing to the producer governments from the sale of crude was value added and a net addition to their GDP. The money accruing to the consumer governments from the sales taxes was merely a transfer payment from the citizens of the country to their government. The two are not comparable.

The second issue arising from the sales tax policy of the consuming governments, which had much greater validity than the first argument, was that such high levels of sales taxes were a restraint on trade. In 1985 Saudi Arabia made a fundamental change in its oil policy. It was no longer willing to defend the relatively high prices of oil by absorbing the cheating by other OPEC members on the quota system. Instead it decided to pursue a policy of greater price moderation in an effort to reverse the damage done to oil demand by the oil price shocks of the 1970s. Thus they moved away from administered prices. A key part of this policy was to maintain the cushion of spare capacity (some 2 to 2.5mbpd) to avoid a price spike in the event of another geopolitical outage. However, throughout the 1990s this strategy was consistently being undermined as the lower prices of crude oil failed to translate into lower oil product prices because of the growing levels of sales tax acting as a wedge between producers and final consumers. This issue of ever increasing sales taxes began to aggravate poor relations between producers and consumers as, from the producers' perspective, it was seen as part of a grand conspiratorial strategy to damage the vital strategic interests of the oil exporters.[19] It also persuaded many of the producers that if there was money on the table from selling and taxing oil products why should it not accrue to them. It seemed to legitimize much higher crude prices.

The second issue that began to create a major source of discord between producers and consumers in the oil market context was the growing importance of "paper markets."[20] Up to the time of the second oil shock there had been no paper markets for oil.[21] The explanation for this gap is simple. Such paper markets had been developed to hedge the price risk faced by producers and consumers of the commodity.[22] Until 1986, because the international price of crude was an administered price, it was seen that there was little or no price risk. However, that did not prevent the development in the first half of the 1980s of "forward markets," mainly for North Sea crude. These were unregulated markets where paper contracts to deliver crude oil at Sullom Voe[23] within a fairly short period, usually three weeks, were bought and sold. However, there was growing unease with these forward markets due to a lack of control and regulation and questions over the reliability of some of the players.

An important consequence of the oil price collapse of 1986 and its aftermath was that administered prices were dropped as the basis for pricing crude and replaced by market prices reflecting (at first) market movements in spot prices. As a result price risks began to mount. In 1987 the New York Metal Exchange (NYMEX) began trading in contracts for West Texas Intermediate (WTI). A year later the International Petroleum Exchange (IPE) opened in London trading in Brent.[24]

This is not the place to describe these developments and their consequences in detail, but one major consequence for producer-consumer relations concerns the fact that these "paper markets" began to impact upon oil price levels and their volatility. While the impact is uncertain and extremely controversial (Stevens, 2008a) it meant that many began to perceive that oil prices were now being driven by the whims of Wall Street rather than the physical "wet barrel" markets where real people traded real barrels of crude oil.

Thus whenever crude prices began to rise, the consumer governments blamed OPEC for failing to supply the market with enough crude. In response, OPEC blamed the "speculators" on the paper markets for increasing the price.[25] This conflict became greatly aggravated in 2008. In August 2007 the OPEC basket averaged US$68.71 per barrel. At the start of 2008 it was $88.35 and by June had reached $128.33. As the price increased, President Bush, Prime Minister Gordon Brown, and other leaders of the industrialized countries, began to make speeches about the need for OPEC to increase production to mute the rise in prices. They claimed in effect that the price rise was because of crude oil shortages. In response, the OPEC producers argued that the rising price had nothing to do with crude oil shortages but was the result of speculation and the lack of investment in refining.

Eventually, Saudi Arabia under great pressure from the USA announced it would host a meeting of the IEF in Jeddah in June. The purpose of the meeting was unclear.[26] However, the outcome was that Saudi Arabia offered to put another 500,000 b/d onto the market. This was effectively a sop to the consumer countries. In the event, while they offered the crude, they did so at existing price levels. Given the crude on offer was heavy sour crude, not surprisingly there were no takers which allowed Saudi Arabia a rather dubious "I told you so" moment in the debate over the causes of higher prices. The meeting also announced that there would be a follow-up meeting in London in the December to review "progress."

However, before the London meeting could take place, the oil market underwent a major trauma. In September, Lehman Brothers was declared bankrupt and the already fragile global financial system went into melt-down. The result was a collapse in oil prices driven by falling oil demand and by December the OPEC basket averaged $38.60 compared to the peak in July of $131.22. Yet again the imperative of prices as a driver of the producer–consumer dialogue, at least from the perspective of the consumers, weakened.

The next major event for the IEF was the 12th ministerial meeting in Cancun in March 2010. This represented a number of steps forward in consolidating and developing the IEF's role. The meeting agreed that the IEF should continue on the following objectives:

1. Aim to narrow the differences among producing and consuming countries, both developed and developing.
2. Working together to promote transparency of data, stability of markets and predictability of energy policy.
3. Facilitating high quality analysis and wider collection, compilation and dissemination of data in order to focus debate more effectively.
4. Identifying principles and guidelines to enhance energy market stability and sustainability.

They also agreed to share analysis on i) present and future market trends, ii) links between physical markets, financial markets and regulation, and iii) enhancing transparency even further through collecting data on natural gas and annual investment plans on energy production. It was also agreed that an IEF Charter would be created.

Despite the apparent success of the Cancun Summit, the future of the IEF remains in question. The underlying divisions between producers and consumers concerning price, remain. The Secretariat has great difficulty in persuading staff to go and work in Riyadh and therefore those that are there are over-burdened with work. JODI continues but is based upon a fundamental misconception that more and better information will reduce price volatility. Given that much of the volatility is the result of "herd behaviour" it is unlikely that better information will help to smooth prices. Furthermore, historically, real price volatility stems largely from geopolitical events that no amount of "better information" will pacify or neutralize. There are also a large number of competing bodies that already discuss the sorts of issues covered by the IEF. These range from the World Trade Organization (WTO), GATT, The Agreement on Trade Related Investment Measures (TRIMs) and the Energy Charter Treaty. There are also a large number of regional organizations discussing these issues such as the North American Free Trade Area (NAFTA), the European Economic Area, the Association of South East Asian Nations (Asean) and its various mutant offshoots, the Gulf Co-operation Council (GCC), the Southern Common Market in Latin America (Mercosur) and the Latin American Free Trade Area (LAFTA) to mention just a few. There are also a wide variety of other mechanisms to manage oil price volatility for both producers and consumers (Skinner, 2005). These range from the use of paper markets to hedge price risk, oil stabilization funds, rebates and payments to the poor, reduced consumer taxes and a fund for poor countries.[27]

While the oil price remains important in national and international economies, so too will producer-consumer relations. Extreme price volatility in either direction will revive interest and provide a driving force for meetings and discussions. Sadly, however, the fundamental self-interest of the market place will always provide a cold dose of reality to dampen desire for dialogue and co-operation.

Notes

1. The Washington Consensus refers (disparagingly) to the revival of neo-classical economic thinking in the 1980s and 1990s espousing the virtues of market forces being promoted by the International Monetary Fund (IMF) and the World Bank Group
2. Of course a number of OPEC members, most obviously those in what is now called the Gulf Cooperation Council espoused the joys of free markets and found Marxian concepts of "socialism" an anathema. However, these were (and are) essentially tribal societies and it can be argued as such did espouse the benefits of co-operation as opposed to the cut-throat competition of capitalism which appeared to emerge from the concepts of Adam Smith.
3. Conventionally the French company CFP was also included. They were collectively referred to as "the Majors."
4. This needs some qualification since the international prices of crude did fall in real terms during the 1960s as the control mechanisms exercised by the Majors came under strain. As will be developed below this was the crucial ingredient that fuelled the "OECD economic miracle."
5. Before 1970, the price was an administered price determined by the representatives of the majors. Between 1970 and October 1973, OPEC joined the deliberations over price determination. This period might be viewed as a form of "producer-consumer dialogue." After October 1973, OPEC unilaterally took over the setting of the administered price.
6. At the time, very few academic economists had the first idea about the international oil industry. The exceptions were a small handful that included Edith Penrose, Maurice Adelman and Robert Mabro.
7. In 1974, Norway produced only 35,000 barrels per day but by 1978 this had risen to 356,000 barrels per day (BP, 2010).
8. In the period between 1973 and 1978, France was leading in the attempt to develop bilateral relations with the OPEC countries. At the same time in 1975, it had made the strategic decision to reduce its dependence upon imported oil by developing a nuclear option to produce electricity.
9. At the time, it was widely rumoured that Kissinger had advocated invading Saudi Arabia as the "solution" to the problems created by the Arab Oil Embargo. Subsequently released documents and research confirm that this was actually true!
10. Indeed, OPEC was extremely concerned that the developing countries that had been seriously hurt by the higher oil prices would turn against them and destroy the image of Third World solidarity. They tried to reduce the risk of that by creating a fund for economic aid for importers. In late 1975, they converted this into the OPEC Development Fund that began operations in late 1975 with resources of $800m.

11 In 1977, the OECD (not the IEA) produced the first World Energy Outlook. This consisted of 106 pages as compared to 731 pages in the 2010 World Energy Outlook.
12 This was part of the French strategy to take a leading role in relations with the Third World and at the same time (frankly) to irritate the Americans.
13 This then encouraged OPEC later in the year to create the OPEC Development Fund–see footnote 10.
14 It is interesting to note that despite all its efforts and gyrations, when the second oil shock hit, Japan saw absolutely no benefit for all its efforts and Japanese companies found themselves fighting tooth and nail with American companies to secure spot sales of crude oil. It was this competition which greatly aggravated the rise in oil prices seen between 1979 and 1980 (Mitchell, 1982).
15 Interestingly the US Strategic Petroleum Reserve (SPR) was also not used in the emergency. The SPR had been created in 1975 as part of the Energy Policy and Conservation Act. Construction of the infrastructure began in June 1977 and filling began in July. It is not entirely clear why the SPR was not used during the crisis but this author has heard the story that as the system was being created for the SPR, they had only got as far as the capability to fill the salt caverns that formed the basis of the storage. Apparently there was no infrastructure in 1979 actually to withdraw crude from storage for use above ground.
16 A doomsday scenario is a possible future that while having a low probability of occurrence would have very serious consequences. The cessation of Gulf exports of crude as a result of wars and other disruptions, for example the closure of the Straits of Hormuz had long occupied the minds of strategic planners in the West.
17 These included: demand security; downstream product taxation; consumers' anti-oil policies; downstream integration; strategic petroleum reserves; the Kyoto protocol; sharing the burden of spare capacity; price bands; the Asian Premium; other trade related issues such as dual pricing and US restrictions of ethanol trade; reserve transparency; aid to poor developing countries; and finally political issues such as Israel-Palestine.
18 Given the sensitive nature of this discussion and the subsequent decision there is little by way of formal record.
19 It has been suggested to the author that an important motivation for Saudi Arabia's negotiating and eventually joining the WTO in December 2005 was that this would allow it to raise the issue of oil product taxes as a restraint of trade.
20 By "paper markets", this chapter is referring to markets where promises to deliver or take delivery that are committed to paper are exchanged. They are often more commonly referred to as "futures markets" but this is somewhat misleading because this implies markets regulated by the financial authorities, as is the case for NYMEX in New York and the ICE in London. There are however an increasing number of paper transactions, often referred to as "over the counter trades" which fall outside these institutional contexts.
21 In 1978 there was only a very small futures market for gasoil in Chicago.
22 The first such market was created in Kyoto in 1710 for rice – the Dojima Rice Exchange.
23 This is the loading terminal for Brent on the Shetland Islands.
24 In 2001 the IPE was taken over by the Intercontinental Exchange (ICE).
25 OPEC also argued that there was a refinery story behind crude oil price movements. Thus they argued there had been insufficient investment in upgrading capacity. That put great pressure on the demand for light sweet crude oils thereby increasing their prices above a "norm." This had long been a source of irritation within OPEC since the nature of their crude exports was that of heavy sour crude. In June 2005 they changed the composition of the OPEC basket price from one of predominantly light sweet crudes to one of predominantly heavy sour crudes to better represent what they were receiving financially in the oil markets.
26 During the meeting apparently the most commonly heard comment from the other OPEC participants was "why on earth are we here?"
27 There have also been suggestions that the major oil producers should be made part of the IEA's Emergency Sharing Scheme to encourage them to carry spare capacity or offset outages. Thus in the event of shortage, the producers would get first bite to supply at higher prices while the consumers held back their stocks (Stevens, 2008a).

Bibliography

BP (2010) 'Statistical Review of World Energy'. BP London
Hotelling, H. (1931) 'The Economics of Exhaustible Resources' *Journal of Political Economy*, Volume 39, no. 2, April 1931, pp. 137–175.

Koyama, K. (2001) 'Japan's Energy Strategy Towards the Middle East'. Phd University of Dundee Scotland.
Mabro, R. (1991) 'A dialogue between the producers and consumers: The why and the how'. SP2 *The Oxford Institute for Energy Studies*. Oxford.
Mitchell, J.V. (1982) 'Anatomy of an Oil Crisis'. *Energie Wirtschaft*, Vol 2, June.
Mitchell, J. (2005) 'Producer-Consumer Dialogue: What can energy ministers say to each other?' Chatham House Report November. Chatham House, London.
Parra, F. (2004) *Oil Politics: A modern history of petroleum*. I.B.Taurus, London.
Skinner, R. (2005) 'Energy Security and Producer – Consumer Dialogue: Avoiding a Maginot Mentality. Background Paper for Government of Canada Energy Symposium Energizing Supply: Oil and gas Investment in Uncertain Times.' October 28th, 2005 Sheraton Hotel, Ottawa, Canada.
Stevens, P. (2008) 'Oil Wars: Resource nationalism and the Middle East'. P. Andrews-Speed (ed.) *International Competition for Resources: The role of law, the state and of markets*. Volume to celebrate the Thirtieth Anniversary of CEPMLP, Dundee University Press Dundee. 2008.
——(2008a) 'The Coming Oil Supply Crunch'. Chatham House Report. Chatham House, London.

8
Global Oil Markets: The Need for Reforms

Giacomo Luciani[1]

Structural causes of oil price instability

Crude oil prices are structurally unstable. This is a characteristic that oil has in common with multiple other raw materials and manufactured products, whose supply is rigid relative to price in the short term. In the case of oil, not only supply, but also demand, is rigid in the short term. Whenever unilateral or bilateral rigidity prevails, prices will tend to swing widely.

The cause of rigidity of supply may be either that production can simply not be modified in the short run; or that capacity additions tend to take place in large increments (this being the norm in most heavy industries, where scale economies are important: oil refining, petrochemicals, metal smelting etc.).

A further cause of rigidity is in the structure of costs. If production requires large upfront investment, it is likely that indirect or sunk costs will dominate over direct costs in the total cost structure of the industry. In this case, whenever additional capacity is created, it will tend to be used to spread the indirect cost on a larger production base. Oil exploration and production definitely belong to the category of industries in which sunk costs dominate. Hence, when a new field is discovered or new capacity is added, it will tend to be used to the maximum level which is compatible with the preservation of the long-term value of the field.

It is only in some OPEC countries, notably Saudi Arabia and the other Arab Gulf producers, that large-scale investments are made to create capacity, which is then deliberately kept on stand-by rather than used: this is because these countries are pursuing the objective of being able to condition other producing countries' behavior through their potential influence on prices. In other words, this behavior is already part of an effort to counteract the structural instability of prices, not a manifestation of the spontaneous tendency of the market.

The effectiveness of OPEC's quota policy (or more precisely of the Saudi and some other OPEC members' policy to invest in capacity and keep it fallow) is however dubious, as in the end what matters is the sentiment of the market. At times of intense demand the "swing producers" may increase their production, which means that their unused capacity will decline: the market may take this decline as a reason for expecting higher prices, just as well as it might take the increased production as reason for expecting lower prices. The opposite may be the case when prices are weak and quotas are lowered. So, swing producers run the risk of obtaining exactly the opposite outcome than was intended.

It is said sometimes that the source of oil price instability is the fact that OPEC countries maintain prices at artificially high levels through production quotas: in this view, uncertainty concerning quota policies breeds instability. This is, however, certainly not the case, because price instability existed well before OPEC, and is found in all markets in which supply is rigid in the short term, even if these markets are highly competitive. The destruction of OPEC's quota system may well lead to lower average prices, but it would not lead to greater stability. In fact, by driving out of the market a lot of marginal sources (offshore, non-conventional oil) maximization of OPEC output may very well increase instability.

Demand, too, is rigid relative to price changes in the short run. There are several causes of this, some structural, some man-made. Among the former the key one is that the consumption of energy is largely determined by the characteristics of our cities, houses, vehicles and appliances. Do we live close to or far from our workplace? Do we have access to public transportation to commute? Do we live in apartments or individual homes? How large? How well insulated? What kind of car do we drive? How efficient are the appliances we purchase? And so on. All of these are questions, the answer to which depends on decisions made in the past under different price conditions, none of which is likely to be rapidly revised when prices change. The final consumer will need to be convinced that the change in prices is here to stay before he considers changing such important aspects of his lifestyle. Eventually, change will occur, but it is likely to be slow and very gradual.

Another reason for the limited reaction of demand to prices changes is that in the past 30–40 years the proportion of energy expenditure in the average family budget has constantly declined. It is only in 2008 that prices rose to the point that the average family was spending on energy as much as it did in 1980 in proportion to its total income.[2] Final consumers will keep spending on energy because by and large they can afford to do so. The level of affluence in the industrial countries is such that families enjoy greater discretionary power in their spending patterns, and can devote more to energy if prices increase.

Among man-made reasons for price rigidity we should mention all those mechanisms which insulate the final consumer from the direct impact of price changes. These may be high excise taxes on hydrocarbon fuels in many OECD countries (not the USA!) or subsidies in many developing countries for which the end result is the same.

Demand does react to prices in the longer run. This is important because once the pattern of energy consumption has changed it is unlikely to revert to what it was earlier. For this reason we sometime hear about "demand destruction": demand is destroyed because once the consumer has bitten the bullet and opted for energy conservation he is unlikely to increase his consumption in a mirror fashion if prices decrease. High prices will destroy a share of the pre-existing demand.

The delayed response of demand to price changes will not necessarily lead to price stability. It will, in contrast, lead to even greater uncertainty, as investors and governments will not know exactly what to expect on the demand side.

It is indeed rather extraordinary how badly we understand global oil demand. We have sophisticated models to forecast demand in different sectors and countries, yet we are constantly faced with surprises.[3] The International Energy Agency adjusts its demand forecasts for the current year several times during the year and not by a small margin. So, when it comes to the more distant future uncertainty is very high.

Price instability is a problem because it becomes impossible to predict future prices. If we do not understand thoroughly the extent to which demand will react to prices and the timing of the reaction, forecasting prices becomes very difficult.

That the oil market is characterized by bilateral price rigidity does not, of course, mean that prices have no influence at all on demand and supply, but the influence they have is retarded and not necessarily straightforward.

Furthermore, given short-term supply and demand, prices may be undetermined within a broad margin. Existing supply and demand will seriously react only if prices reach very high or very low levels. Given a prevailing price discovery mechanism, the mechanism will generate a specific price; but the same balance or imbalance between demand and supply would prevail even with higher or lower prices. So, the so-called market fundamentals, demand and supply, will normally validate whatever price has come to prevail. This price may be influenced by factors that are totally unrelated to oil fundamentals (for example, the value of the dollar relative to other currencies) and change accordingly; fundamentals will not "resist" this change. For the best part of 2007 and the first half of 2008 oil prices kept rising higher and higher, and it was then said that the market was testing where the upper limit that demand would tolerate would be.[4] This rather mythical "tipping point," beyond which demand would finally collapse, was never truly found: prices collapsed because the financial crisis intervened.

Consequences of oil price instability and the relevant definition of volatility

When we speak of price instability or volatility, it is necessary to define exactly what is meant. Volatility exists for intraday trading, indeed within the hour or the minute, as well as for longer periods. Which type of volatility interests us?

The best approach to a useful definition of volatility is to focus on its consequences. Why are we concerned with volatility? The key problem is that volatility may lead to the impossibility of forming a sufficiently stable expectation about future prices to guide investment decisions. The latter may be corporate decisions concerning large-scale projects or individual consumer decisions concerning which car to buy next: all have implications for several years

Thus, not all volatility constitutes a problem. Acute volatility which would occur around an identifiable trend line would not be as much of a problem: investors would still be able to form expectations concerning the future of prices and factor in the volatility as a random element of risk which could be addressed with the appropriate financial techniques. The problem arises when the pattern of price changes is such that no stable trend or underlying rule is detectable.

In forming our expectations about future prices we can only look at past experience and attempt to extrapolate into the future. If prices swing widely, no stable trend line can be identified. No attempt to endogenize prices into econometric models has ever succeeded, leaving us totally in the dark about where future prices may be.[5] We may, with difficulty, predict future fundamentals but, as mentioned above, each demand and supply equilibrium is compatible with a whole range of prices, not just one. Where will the price "stick" within the range?

A confirmation of the growing uncertainty concerning future prices comes from the work of the Energy Intelligence Administration of the United States. Their International Energy Outlook, published yearly, normally contains three scenarios for future energy supply and demand: a reference, a high oil price and a low oil price scenario. Prices are exogenously assumed and differentiate the scenarios. The gap between the high and low oil prices which are used to establish the scenarios has progressively widened over time: in 2005, based on the fact that the previous year prices had averaged about US$35 per barrel, the high price assumption was $50 per barrel for 2025, and the low price assumption was $20 per barrel already before 2010, remaining stable until 2025; in 2010 the high price scenario assumption is prices growing rapidly to $186 per barrel by 2020, then decelerating up to $210 per barrel in 2035; and the low price scenario assumes prices rapidly declining to $52 per barrel in 2015 and remaining stable for the next 20 years. Therefore, the price in the first scenario is 400% of the price in the second by the end of the period: it is hard to imagine two more radically divergent hypotheses, a clear indication that there is extreme uncertainty about the future of oil prices. Furthermore, the low hypothesis in 2010 equals what only five years earlier was taken to be the high price hypothesis, to be reached in 2025. What if the expectations that we had five years ago turn out to be more appropriate than those of today? Can we exclude this? Hardly so. At any moment in time we have a tendency to extrapolate into the future the most recent trend (the best information about future prices is today's price) and yet it is evident that reality does not conform to this expectation.

Attempts at defining a long-term equilibrium price

Repeated attempts have been made at defining long-term equilibrium prices for crude oil, but with limited success.

We have information on the cost of producing oil (although there might be multiple definitions of this cost) and may attempt to construct a long-term supply curve, i.e. a curve which tells us how much oil may be commercially produced for each level of prices.

This is summarized in Figure 8.1, originally introduced by the International Energy Agency and subsequently widely utilized in different versions.[6]

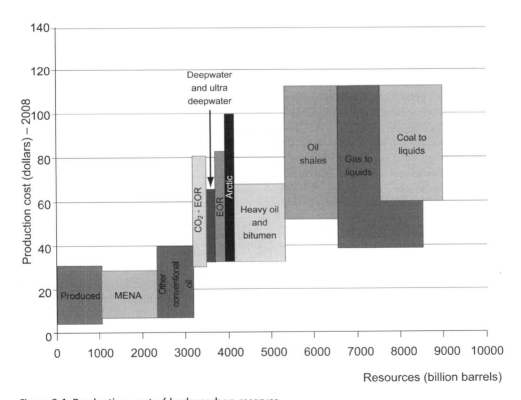

Figure 8.1 Production cost of hydrocarbon reserves

The chart is not properly a long-term supply schedule: it tells us which reserves are commercially exploitable at any given level of prices, but says nothing about the pace at which they will be exploited. Thus, we cannot easily pass from the knowledge that all conventional oil is commercially viable at US$40 per barrel or less, to an expected level of production at $40 per barrel. Competitive markets would ensure that the lowest cost oil is produced first, and higher cost resources are only exploited when lower cost ones are exhausted. If this were the case, and in the absence of policy constraints to production or investment, a level of production sufficient to satisfy demand might be compatible with prices at or below $40 per barrel.

However, it is argued that the world cannot rely exclusively on low cost conventional oil, and a plurality of other resources should be developed for comfort and security of supply. Hence the idea arises that prices ought to be somewhat higher than $60 per barrel, lest the world depends too much on OPEC. This then becomes a politically desirable level of prices, which is said to be potentially stable. But will it actually be stable? There is absolutely no solid ground for expecting this much: at any moment in time capacity may be insufficient or redundant, causing prices to rise or fall.

All that we can say is that a level of prices somewhat above $60 per barrel would be compatible with diversification of sources and meeting demand. But could prices fall below or rise above for extended periods of time with little consequence for supply and demand (both rigid to prices)? Surely so.

All discussion about long-term equilibrium points to prices that would be desirable on the basis of more or less complex considerations: in some cases issues of fairness or producing countries' budget or investment requirements are also considered[7] on the basis that producers will not tolerate a price they consider to be unfair. At any moment in time, however, prices can seriously diverge from any desirable level. From the point of view of investors, the conclusion that eventually prices may tend to converge towards a desirable level is of little comfort, if this convergence comes about only very slowly and in the meantime the project is a financial disaster.

The vast majority of energy investment projects have very long gestation periods, easily exceeding five years. The discussion of long-term fundamentals, if it gives us any guidance at all, does so for an unspecified "long term," which by definition is longer than the gestation period of individual projects, since it is through the implementation of investment projects that prices may be expected to converge to what we believe is their long-term equilibrium point. But from the point of view of investors, returns in the early years of operation of a project are crucial to determine financial viability. Thus, information concerning long-term equilibrium prices is of limited comfort when a final investment decision has to be made for any specific project. Investment becomes an act of faith.

Price makers and price takers before Brent

It is because of the structural reasons discussed so far that the oil industry has tended to have well defined price makers and price takers. Depending on the specific historical period under observation, either one or a group of companies or a group of governments have "made" prices, which the rest of the investors' universe has tended to accept. As at any moment in time fundamentals will be compatible with a range of prices, not just a single point in the curve, a price maker only needs to point to any price that falls within the broad acceptable range to see it validated by fundamentals.

In the golden age of the oil industry, price making power was enjoyed by the seven or eight "sisters," with the support of institutions such as the Texas Railroad Commission, the US Treasury Department, the British government and more, all of which tended to implement policies which supported the sisters rather than rocking the boat. Price stability was in the interest of all, and it required some "management" of competition.

Oil was traded then, primarily physically and bilaterally, but the market was neither transparent nor a level field. The sisters traded at preferential prices between themselves, to compensate for their internal imbalances (some were long, some were short of crude) and eliminate the incentive to compete with each other. Sales to outsiders were at less favorable prices, to ensure that they could not become a threat to the sisters' market dominance.

The success of this lightly camouflaged cartel was facilitated by rapidly growing demand for oil, which resulted not only from energy demand growing rapidly, but also from oil being priced sufficiently low progressively to displace coal.

Nevertheless, the position of the companies was constantly threatened by newcomers, attracted by the high rates of return, notwithstanding the fact that oil prices were relatively low. Newcomers enjoyed a protected position because the sisters were able to manage the market and guarantee that the marginal producer would be able to achieve a profit rate above zero. Today it is OPEC that performs essentially the same service for the benefit of the international oil companies (IOCs).

This state of affairs, however, could not last forever. As the share of oil grew and that of coal shrank, the outlook for growing oil demand worsened. The pace of new entries into the industry quickened in the 1950s and 1960s, and the sisters found it impossible to defend prices. As the latter eroded, producing countries' governments reacted by forming OPEC. By the end of the 1960s margins had thinned and the sisters were expressing concerns that prices were untenably low.

Then control shifted from companies to governments, and OPEC became the price maker. This, however, should be qualified, because in fact OPEC simply attempted to ratchet up and consolidate price increases, which were largely determined by "the market". As this continued to be non-transparent and insufficiently liquid, at any political crisis (the Yom Kippur war, the Iranian Revolution, the onset of the Iraq-Iran war) some refiners found themselves cut off from their customary sources and went scrambling to find alternatives; as the market was segmented, these were difficult to find, and prices were jacked up. Then what were in essence prices on fringe, non-representative transactions were taken by OPEC as being the new equilibrium price, which they manifestly were not.

OPEC therefore turned out to be a poor price maker, and by 1985 completely lost this role: Saudi Arabia broke ranks and eventually opted for reference pricing. This proves that playing the role of price maker is not necessarily an easy task, and one which requires a good deal of flexibility and pragmatism.

Yet the failure of OPEC as price setter was not due exclusively to the organization's inability to stand up to the task: important structural causes contributed to it.

Firstly, the industry's vertically integrated structure was destroyed in the 1970s. The sisters lost control of reserves in almost all leading producing countries: while in 1970 they still controlled three-quarters of global production, by the end of the decade their share was less than one-quarter. The rest was now in the hands of national oil companies (NOCs) which had only very limited integration downstream into refining and marketing. The industry therefore became disintegrated, meaning that the dominant share of crude produced was sold at arm's length, while previously it had been traded between units of the same company. As long as crude oil was exchanged within the same company, the role of prices posted by the companies was essentially to determine their tax liabilities in the exporting vs the importing country. But when crude is sold at arm's length between two financially independent entities, price makes all the difference, and equilibrium, in what amounts to a bilateral oligopoly, becomes unstable.

All the more so since the temporary increase in prices creates an opportunity for appropriating a rent; the latter will swing from exporter to importer depending on their respective bargaining power. At the same time, higher prices also encouraged new entrants, as had happened in previous decades: and it so happened that just at that time new provinces were rapidly expanding their production thanks to recent discoveries: the North Sea, first and foremost, but also Alaska, Mexico and the Soviet Union.

The emergence of an effective price maker therefore depends on several circumstances, including the degree of vertical integration and the cost of overcoming barriers to entry: both are well established generalizations in the literature on oligopolistic markets. Today, the industry remains predominantly disintegrated, as the NOCs have not pursued (or have been prevented from pursuing) vigorous integration downstream in the markets of the importing countries. However, barriers to entry are much more significant, because the pace of new discoveries has slowed, and incumbent IOCs struggle to replenish their proved reserves, let alone manage to expand them. Smaller discoveries may or may not mean that we are heading towards a global plateau in oil production, but in the shorter term certainly mean that new oil is not coming to the market.

The Brent market: from physical to financial

As OPEC was unable to defend the prices that it had attempted to consolidate, the price making function shifted to two markets: Brent in the United Kingdom and WTI in the USA. We should, however, more appropriately speak of price discovery function, rather than price making, as neither market has a clear price leader.

The market for WTI had existed for a long time, while the market for Brent emerged with the increase in North Sea oil production. Several circumstances facilitated the emergence of the Brent market: the fact that this was crude produced in an industrial country with a very pro-market government, the fact that Brent is a seaborne crude, hence potentially exportable everywhere in the world and the fact that several producers were independently operating in the North Sea and potentially competing with each other.

It is an interesting historical question exactly why WTI and Brent became benchmarks for setting the price of all other crude oils in the so-called reference pricing system, and I believe that it would be difficult to argue that there was any kind of historical necessity. Simply, as the industry needs a price discovery mechanism, and no other one was available, these two emerged. Surely, the preference of the former sisters, which were the major producers of oil in the British North Sea and controlled the logistics, was an important facilitating factor.

Both Brent and WTI were originally physical markets. Oil was traded bilaterally and over the counter, and transactions could only be observed through the work of reporting services. Futures and options linked to Brent were only launched by the IPE (today's ICE) in 1988 and 1989, respectively. Previous attempts had failed. The reason that they then succeeded is precisely because, in the meantime, Brent had become a benchmark.

So what is "reference pricing"? Reference pricing means that the price of a crude which is not freely traded is tied by some formula to the price of another crude which is freely traded. The crucial point of this definition is that the vast majority of crude oil which is exchanged internationally is not freely traded. Limitations are in some cases imposed by the exporter, who only allows lifters that intend to refine the crude oil and sell the products; these undertake not to sell on a cargo to some other potential refiner or buyer, and the seller imposes limitations on destination, also in order to benefit from price discrimination depending on the destination. In other cases it is allowed to sell on cargoes to other buyers, but exchanges occur only between a limited number of players, for large deals and over the counter, hence are not easily observed. In fact, multiple other markets for crude oil exist, but they have slowly lost importance; transactions have increasingly been carried out at a differential to Brent or WTI rather than at fixed prices. Markets such as that for Alaska North Slope (ANS), Ural blend or Dubai have mimicked Brent and WTI.

The process whereby a benchmark emerges is fairly straightforward, and it is self-perpetuating, in the sense that once a benchmark has emerged it will be difficult for an alternative benchmark to become accepted. A benchmark emerges because a specific market displays greater liquidity, and parties trading in other markets become reluctant to accept prices that greatly diverge from those of the more liquid market, on the assumption that they would in any case have the alternative of trading in the benchmark. In other words, even if I am buying Ural blend rather than Brent, I am not willing to pay a price for Ural which is unrelated to that of Brent because I assume that I would in any case have the alternative of buying Brent. However, this assumption is not well founded: it has never been so, and it is even less so today now that the production of Brent (and other North Sea crude oil that have progressively been added to Brent to preserve its credibility) is rapidly declining.

However, the fact that at some point the physical Brent market has emerged as one of two key benchmarks has facilitated the launching of the paper market (futures and options) because whoever wished to hedge his position and manage his risk could efficiently do so on the Brent paper market even if he was not trading in Brent, because the price of the crude that he was trading in was tied to Brent. Hence, the fact that the physical market initially became a benchmark facilitated the birth of a paper market; today it is the existence of a vast paper market that is the main reason why Brent remains a benchmark.

Originally, paper contracts were constructed to converge to the physical price. They were in essence bets on the future level of physical prices. But over time as liquidity on the paper side of the market increased and on the physical side decreased, it is now the price of physical contracts which converges to the price of paper. No physical trader will enter into a contract at a price which substantially diverges from that signalled by the paper market, because the accepted price is that which everybody believes is prevailing. Demand and supply play only a minor role in shaping market beliefs and expectations, and the price of paper barrels dominates that of physical barrels.

This is not to say that the price of paper barrels is totally independent of fundamentals: obviously if this price were pushed out of the range of prices that are compatible with existing demand and supply, then fundamentals would react, but even more important would be the expectation, founded or unfounded, that fundamentals would react. As we have seen, the very existence of a "tipping point" is questionable, as neither demand nor supply has ever tipped. We just presume that there must be one.

Thus, as trading in paper has progressively grown over trading in physical barrels (a process that has continued incrementally from 1988 to 2003) paper trading has become the main price discovery mechanism, but the market was nevertheless broadly reflecting if not of fundamentals, at least of expectations about fundamentals. However, beginning around 2003 or 2004 the market appears to have known a radical transformation, as commodities in general and oil in particular have become an asset class on a par with equities, bonds and currencies, and trading in derivatives has become more important in all of the above.[8] This transformation led to the formation of an extraordinary oil price bubble. The bursting of the financial bubble, and consequently also of the oil price bubble, in the summer of 2008 opened the door to a period of greater stability, but it is not at all clear whether this was just a parenthesis or another fundamental turning point.

Consequences of "financialisation" and the quest for sanity

What is the problem with oil futures becoming an asset class and attracting increasing attention from individual investors, hedge funds, index funds and the like? The problem is that financial markets increasingly have characteristics which are incompatible with the role of oil as a physical commodity.

Notwithstanding all hypotheses concerning the rationality of markets and of individual investors, financial markets are prone to creating bubbles and alternating booms and busts. Rationality would require trading on the basis of the intrinsic value of an asset, that is buying an asset when its price is deemed to be low relative to its intrinsic value (the asset is underpriced) and selling when it is deemed to be high (the asset is overpriced). If we speak about stocks or bonds, the measure of under- or overpricing is the expected return (dividend, interest coupon) on the asset. In the case of commodities, which per se generate no return, the measure of under- or overpricing is the expectation of the future price of the commodity as determined in physical markets by the equilibrium of demand and supply. But if, as for oil, it is the paper market that discovers the price of the physical commodity, the reasoning becomes circular: investors will view the asset as overpriced if they expect the price to decline, and underpriced if they expect the price to increase. This means that they will sell if they expect others to sell and vice versa will buy if they expect others to buy. This tends to generate waves of buying or selling: while a lower limit to prices necessarily exists, an upper limit is much more difficult to identify.

For all financial markets, be they equities, bonds or commodities, it has been demonstrated that momentum trading brings greater rewards than value trading.[9] Momentum trading (that is trading in accordance with the recent tendency of the market) is based purely on past information and totally ignores information about the future; it tends to amplify the structural oscillations of the market (which, in the case of oil, already tend to be wide) and generates better profits if oscillations are wide. If the market is uncertain and registers small oscillations with no clear direction (in this case it is sometimes said that the market is rangebound) momentum trading may generate poor returns or even losses.

Momentum trading can be encapsulated in mathematical algorithms, and is therefore easily used for automatic, computer-based trading. This has been a growing phenomenon, opening the door to flash trading, which is becoming increasingly important as well as controversial, owing to the fact that very short-term volatility is increased if a lot of flash trading takes place.

Momentum rules are conceived to react to turning points in the market after they have occurred. They may react very promptly or with some delay, depending on the specific rule retained, but they always follow. It is of course possible to design trading rules that attempt to anticipate turning points, although it is not clear that they would yield better returns. A rule anticipating turning points must be built on some assumption of minimum or maximum boundary for the price, some notion of a tipping point. This is easier to have when prices are in a downward rather than in an upward spiral. It is likely that expectations concerning where the turning point might be will be influenced by considerations concerning fundamentals, and in this sense the market will always display some reactivity to fundamentals, although this manifestly does not prevent some very wide swings. This is not surprising, because after all we have argued that oil prices are structurally unstable and at any moment in time the prevailing price is arbitrarily determined within a range whose boundaries are not precisely defined.

What the transformation of oil into a financial asset does, therefore, is to create a phenomenon of resonance, amplification of the structural instability of oil prices into wider and wider swings fuelled by momentum trading. The mathematical expression for resonance tells us that this is contained within certain boundaries by a damper.[10] If the damper were zero, oscillations would become infinite, i.e. explosive. In the oil market, the damper is the market's view of where the boundaries are, although it should be stressed that this view is purely subjective, in the sense that we have never witnessed supply decline significantly because prices had gone too low, nor demand because prices had gone too high. We have never observed a physical tipping point.

Furthermore, the volatility of prices, and especially the evidence of wide swings, attracts additional liquidity. At any moment in time, investors or professional traders can choose their playground, i.e. which asset they will be trading. As the key for maximizing profits is in the price swings, investors will move from the more sedate to the more unstable markets. Hence, money moves in and out of a specific market depending on its observed pattern, and as it does so it also amplifies or reduces the swings. Hence we also have self-reinforcing expectations of volatility/stability: the former attracts liquidity which will enhance volatility, the latter will lead to liquidity being drained away, which will enhance stability.

In short: financialisation is not the cause of instability, the latter is structural to the oil industry, but it amplifies oscillations and undermines confidence in any concept of long-term equilibrium price. Yet, financialisation is inevitable, because physical traders need to contain their risk through hedging, and it is investors (speculators) that make hedging possible. As we cannot either limit the number of investors or the liquidity that they will direct towards this market, speculation leads progressively to financialisation, which in the end magnifies oscillations, hence the demand for hedging. This will create bubbles, which will inevitably burst. For some time thereafter the market will be less prone to wide swings and liquidity will be drained to other markets. There are storms and periods of calm.

Anchors and storms

Because expectations play such a central role in the behaviour of the market and the price discovery process, it has been suggested that the key to stable oil prices is in influencing expectations and providing the market with an "anchor" in the form of a central price that the market will come to accept as the equilibrium price at least for some time.[11]

This eminently declaratory recipe assumes that an entity exists with sufficient voice and credibility that the market will believe. The message may or may not be reinforced by the availability of some tool to punish whoever may be tempted to challenge it.

Following the crazy swing of 2008, several voices were heard asserting that the right price would be in the region of US$75 dollars per barrel.[12] A rare almost complete convergence of opinion between exporting and importing countries was observed, reinforced by the opinion of some leading experts which argued that such price has multiple advantages.[13] The Saudi Minister of Petroleum has not lost an opportunity to repeat the mantra that prices in the $70–80 per barrel range are just perfect.[14]

In fact, prices in the latter part of 2009 and 2010 have kept within a relatively narrow trading range centered on that magic number. The reduced volatility has led to liquidity moving towards other markets (notably currencies) and some important traders have disappeared[15] or decided to size their operations down.[16]

So, the anchor appears to be working, but this might be not because of its strength and ability to resist the pull of the ship, but simply because we are now in a period of calm, and nothing has happened to encourage investors to challenge the centrality of $75 per barrel. Yet a new storm is possible at any moment, and could easily be sparked by instability in the currency markets: a weak dollar immediately translates into higher oil prices, and a minor upward trend can be set in motion which would progressively lead to a bubble. The 2008 episode was fully four years in the making: the most convincing starting date that one can find for it is 2004, with the combination of unexpected growth in Chinese demand and clear evidence that the demise of the Saddam regime would not have led to a rapid increase in Iraqi demand anytime soon. So, we may conceive of a scenario of dollar weakness, persistent high growth in China and other emerging countries, inflationary fears in the OECD and loss of enthusiasm for renewable sources of energy, in some combination: a new, long upward trend in prices would then almost certainly appear. But, just as easily, prices may hedge down from the magic level, in response to continuing sluggish growth, an objectively well supplied market, renewed expectation of a rapid increase in Iraqi production and abundant spare capacity. It is probably the very ambiguity of the current situation that keeps prices in an uneasy balance: as soon as expectations would conform in one direction, and price movements become unidirectional, a new storm may erupt.[17]

If so, will the anchor hold? Well, it has very little force to keep the ship in place, as there is no clear tool to resist a new swing if one is set off. If prices were to decline, can we expect OPEC to step in and cut production? As long as the decline in prices is minor, maybe OPEC will succeed in maintaining discipline. But beyond a certain point member governments will find meeting their budget obligations increasingly difficult, and some will start cheating on their quotas. Non-OPEC members that also have important expenditure commitments, such as Russia, will move in the opposite direction, that is they will pump more to preserve revenue. The market will smell blood and even more forcefully bid prices down. We know what comes next, because we witnessed it already twice: Saudi Arabia will either threaten or implement a price war, and prices will collapse. When this happened in 1986, following a period when they were relatively high, prices settled at a considerably lower level for no less than 15 years. When it happened again in 1999, coming out of a period of low prices, the decline could be stemmed. A new wave of downward speculation starting from the current level is more likely to inaugurate a protracted episode of lower prices. In the opposite direction, there is nothing to prevent a repeat of the 2007–08 episode, possibly reaching even wilder highs. After all, the upward trend in 2008 was interrupted by the financial crisis, the collapse of Lehman and the brutal drainage of liquidity that ensued. It could have gone on longer; it could even have consolidated a higher level of stable prices, at or above $100 per barrel, for a relatively long period. Fundamentals would have validated what investors might have brought about.

Obviously, OPEC would not intervene in a rising market. Saudi Arabia might declare that it is ready to increase production and satisfy any request to lift its oil, but would not actively flood the market to bring prices down. In addition, governments of importing countries would not lightly resort to drastic measures to reduce demand in the short term (such as some form of rationing), because in the end consumers would be willing to pay and, as long as oil exporters either adjust expenditure to the higher income or invest in OECD government bonds, the net outcome does not need to be deflationary. In fact, in the event of a deflationary effect the OECD governments would in all likelihood react with expansionary monetary and fiscal policy, further ensuring that demand does not decline.

The relative stability of the post-2008 period is therefore precarious and may be quickly reversed. We may be living in a lull between storms: a good opportunity to reinforce the anchoring.

Reinforcing the anchor

We can think of several ways in which the anchor may be reinforced. These should preferably not be considered in isolation from each other, but as a package of mutually reinforcing measures and tools. The underlying idea is that the feedback from fundamentals to expectations must be reinforced: this is the damper that may prevent resonance from becoming catastrophic.

Increase physical trading

A first step in the right direction would be to increase the volumes of crude oil that are available for physical trading in transparent and well supplied exchanges. This can be attempted either in the proximity of plural producers (e.g. in the Arabian/Persian Gulf) or in the proximity of major logistical and refining hubs. Oil exchanges supported by abundant storage facilities should be set up to trade in standard parcels of various quality crudes, presumably through regular auctions, or through a futures contract which is physically deliverable, although the latter is more difficult. This would allow crude sellers and buyers to deal on a fixed price basis rather than on a differential to a benchmark, although they obviously would also have to be aware of what is happening to the benchmark. The ultimate objective of establishing such physical markets would be to reinforce the price signal coming from fundamentals and facilitate the feedback from physical demand and supply to prices.

The establishment of such markets would require the co-operation or at least the acceptance of producers, who would allow secondary trading of their crude. Although, as mentioned earlier, many of the most important producers impose limitations to the trading of their crude oil, this is not true of all of them. It may be possible to encourage some producers to take the lead or simply make this development possible.

Physical oil exchanges may be conceived of in traditional hubs such as Singapore or the Caribbean, or in new hubs. Examples of these worth noting are the Turkish port of Ceyhan, where several pipelines are expected to converge to load crude oil from various producing countries and companies into tankers, and the European ports of Rotterdam and Trieste, where crude oil from various origins is received to be fed into multiple inland logistical distribution networks. The system of oil pipelines carrying crude oil to various refineries in the European Union could also be developed into a trading platform.

These markets would not be as hugely liquid as today's benchmarks, but would, so to speak, have their feet more firmly on the ground. One of these may even succeed in launching its own futures trading activity, progressively offering an alternative to current benchmarks.

Increased vertical integration

The process of vertical disintegration has been identified as one of the causes of increasing instability in oil prices. Moving in the opposite direction, that is, re-establishing vertical integration in the industry, would help to contain instability.

This may happen either through companies of the importing countries acquiring greater access to upstream resources in producing countries and relying less on arm's length purchases of crude oil, or through oil companies of the producing countries integrating downstream into refining and distribution in some of the markets of their clients.

Both processes are visibly underway, although the heirs of the seven sisters are not in the forefront. The companies of the two pre-eminent emerging importers, China and India, are seeking access to upstream resources pretty much globally. Some of the companies of the producing countries are integrating downstream, by refining more of their oil at home, and investing internationally in refineries in their key foreign markets.

The process is slowed down by the perception that the producing countries' NOCs would not be allowed to take over companies from the importing countries. Ever since the UK Monopolies and Mergers Commission was instrumental in forcing the Kuwait Investment Office to sell the bulk of the participation in the equity of BP[18] (that it had acquired picking up shares in a bear market when the British government decided to divest its participation) it has been clear that there are certain red lines that the NOCs will not be allowed to cross. This negatively impacts security of supply and price stability.

Importing countries should stop protecting the independence of their NOCs through various non-competitive tools, such as a golden share, and move in the direction of allowing some presence of the oil companies of producing countries in their markets.

The promotion of co-operative international storage

The International Energy Agency and several governments of countries that are not members of this organization have established mechanisms to create strategic storage to be used in the event of a serious physical shortfall of oil supplies. The experience of 30 years of managing such strategic storage facilities is that the physical shortage conditions that would trigger their use never occur; prices are impacted first. However, strategic storage is assumed not to be a tool for market intervention, that is, not to be used to keep prices down if they tend to increase beyond a point, although in certain documents and legislative acts market disturbances or excessive price increases are mentioned as possible triggers.[19] In short, strategic storage is helplessly mired in definitional ambiguity, and essentially useless.

Clearly the stability of the oil market would gain out of expanding commercial storage availability. Greater storage availability would allow better physical arbitrage of short-term imbalances between demand and supply, and improved management of prices. Storage however is expensive and oil stored in the producing countries may not be viewed as being fundamentally different from oil that is left in the ground.

A possible co-operative approach to commercial storage would be for the importing countries to invest in storage facilities either in the importing countries themselves, or in a transit country in strategic locations. The storage facilities would be available for exporting countries to deposit their oil at times when the market might be oversupplied, and draw it down at times when oil is scarce. The decision to deposit or draw down would be entirely in the hands of the owner of the oil, who is the depositor, or a party that has acquired the deposit from the owner. Tradable certificates of deposit would be issued by the storage facility. Deposited oil and/or certificates issued against it would be accepted as collateral for loans from official agencies of the importing countries, such as the European Investment Bank, or commercial banks willing to enter in this trade.

The ability to deposit oil and receive a loan for it would encourage exporters to make more oil available. Oil deposited in storage would have a depressing effect on prices, but not as direct as oil on the market which cannot find a buyer; and oil from storage would flow to the market more promptly in case of rising prices. In short, this would be a way to increase the elasticity of supply, hence the feedback to price changes from the supply side.

The provision of demand security / TOP contracts

Availability of excess capacity in the major producing countries is an essential contributor to price stability. If excess capacity is not available, investors will bet that prices can only rise, hence push them higher; and in case of weak prices the major producers lack the clout to impose discipline and stem the decline.

Saudi Arabia has an official policy of maintaining an unused capacity cushion of at least 2mbpd, and in fact maintains much more than that. However, this costs billions of dollars in investment which has essentially no return. It is therefore not surprising that major exporters, which are expected to invest and establish capacity ahead of demand, would clamor for demand security as the other side of the coin of the supply security which is demanded by importers. It is hardly acceptable that they be expected to maintain large unused capacity in slack markets while smaller or non-OPEC producers (notably Russia) may increase exports at will, while benefitting from the higher prices that are made possible by OPEC discipline.

The simple way out of this dilemma is to borrow a page from the gas trade and offer oil for sale on a take or pay (TOP) basis. This may sound strange because TOP contracts are out of fashion with the "free market at all costs", but in fact they remain popular in the gas industry and an essential tool for stability. Transforming current evergreen arrangements into TOP contracts simply means that the buyer accepts an obligation to lift certain minimum volumes at some agreed formula prices. Presumably TOP buyers could receive a modest discount in exchange for their commitment, and formula prices used in TOP contracts might be based on lags and longer moving averages, as is the case for gas, thus smoothing out the oscillations of benchmark prices. This approach may not be very popular with the IOCs of the OECD countries, but things appear to be moving in this direction in relations between the Gulf producers and some of the major East Asian importers, notably China, which are more concerned about security of supply than price minimization in the short term.

The imposition of advance notice of final consumer price changes

A last tool which may be used to encourage greater price stability is imposing an obligation of significant advance notice to companies operating in the retail market before they are allowed to change prices to final consumers. The rationale for this approach is that these companies are in a position to hedge their supplies, while retail final customers normally are not. If retailers can change their prices to the final customer overnight, they have little interest in hedging. In fact, it is well known that the oligopolistic nature of the retail fuels market allows retailers to pass price increases on to the final customer very promptly, while price decreases are passed on at a much more leisurely pace. There is hardly any real price competition at the retail level.

Requiring retailers to announce price changes several months in advance would not only encourage them to hedge, and allow final consumers to plan ahead their response (for example, by bringing forward or postponing purchases), but also encourage competition, because the cost of falling out of step with the competition would be potentially higher. The latter effect would be further enhanced if, in addition to the requirement for advance notice, limitations were added to the frequency at which adjustments could be made.

Retailers are, in most cases, part of vertically integrated structures or sufficiently large buyers that they can exercise some market power and resist excessive price increases. It is important to align interests in such a way that retailers will be encouraged to defend the interests of the final consumers, and for that it is necessary to limit their ability to pass on price increases to consumers. While consumers have little voice and will not generate a feedback signal to resist excessive price increases, retailers and large consumers can do so.

The role of the Gulf producers

In the context of a concerted international effort to increase oil price stability and credibility, the Gulf producers have a crucial role to play. Simply because they are the most important producers and have the lowest budget constraints, they are naturally in the position of being price leaders. Theirs are the marginal barrels, even if they refuse to play the role of swing producers.

Some movement in the direction sketched above has taken place already. With respect to enhancing the role of physically traded oil, the launch of the Oman future contract on the DME has been a fundamentally important step. The contract has attracted steadily increasing liquidity, and is being used as a tool to receive delivery of physical barrels. It may still be too small to generate a signal that can influence other markets, but eventually this will happen.

There are several scenarios for the future of the Oman contract and physical trading in the Gulf. One possibility is that some of the major producers shift to the Oman contract as their benchmark, dropping the essentially useless Oman/Dubai assessed by Platts (which has no life of its own). This would certainly attract considerable liquidity into the Oman futures contract. Another possibility is that other Gulf major oil producers might set up their own forward and futures markets for physical delivery of their crude. A detailed description of how this might be implemented, based on the parallel with the market of government bonds, has been proposed in another paper of mine.[20]

Interest in vertical integration into the final markets of the OECD countries has been apparent for some time and should be encouraged; Kuwait acquired significant downstream assets in the 1970s, and PDVSA (Venezuela) acquired CITGO in the USA. Abu Dhabi has a significant participation in OMV (Austria) through its company IPIC. Saudi Aramco has been mostly absent from the European market but has entered in joint ventures in the USA and several Asian countries. After the KIO/BP episode no further attempts to acquire a major participation in an IOC have been registered, although it is not clear why mergers between IOCs, which lead to a progressive decline of competition in the industry, should be viewed positively, while acquisitions from NOCs of the producing countries should be taken as a threat.

Some agreements which provide for importing countries to make storage available to exporters are emerging in the Far East, and the same can be said of supply arrangements with an implicit or explicit lifting commitment similar to a TOP contract. The Gulf countries are in a position to push for much more of these, especially in the context of intensifying exchanges with the Far East. Doing the same with Europe or the USA might be more difficult owing to the popular and entirely irrational view that the USA should "wean" itself off dependence on Arabian oil. In the case of Europe, Gulf oil is being marginalized by the expected increase of Russian, Central Asian and North African exports, which may be increasing further because of rapidly growing Iraqi exports from Mediterranean loading terminals.

Thus, the game of oil price stabilization may turn out to be very much an Asian affair. The long established practice of discriminating by destination may come to be used less as a tool to extract a small extra rent from Far Eastern customers than as a tool to stabilize the Asian market and have global oil prices discovered there rather than in the volatile financial markets of New York or London.

Notes

1 Giacomo Luciani is a Princeton Global Scholar, Scientific Director of the Master in International Energy at the Paris School of International Affairs of Sciences-Po, and visiting Professor at the Graduate Institute for International Development Studies in Geneva.
2 See Bassam Fattouh "Global Demand Dynamics: Determinants and Policy Issues" paper presented at the Rahmania Annual Seminar, January 2010, page 8.
3 For example in 2004 one of the factors which started the upward trend in prices eventually culminating in 2008 was an unexpected increase in Chinese demand.
4 See Paul Horsnell "The Dynamics of Oil Price Determination" *Oxford Energy Forum*, November 2007, pages 13–15, where he introduces the notion that the market is like a toddler, "constantly in search of defining where the boundaries of behavior should be, and then constantly pushing towards those boundaries until it finds them and gets a reaction."
5 Different empirical "predictors" have proven valid at different times: volumes of oil in storage, production costs, the strength/weakness of the dollar, the S+P index, expectations of inflation … Some models have endogenously computed prices, but these are not meant to be reliable predictions of the level of prices at specific dates, more like broad tendencies or consistency requirements.
6 For example, Ali Aissaoui ("GCC Oil Price Preferences: At the Confluence of Global Energy Security and Local Fiscal Sustainability," *Energy Security in the Gulf: Challenges and Prospects* (ECSSR: 2010); proceedings of the ECSSR 15th Annual Energy Conference, Abu Dhabi, November 16–18, 2009) uses the chart to argue that "oil prices in the range of $60 to $80 per barrel should be appropriate to support energy investments worldwide." However, his main thesis is that the market is unable to discover an appropriate price and this should be reached through non-market considerations, and presumably enforced through an agreement between exporters and importers to maintain prices within a band.

7. E.g. again Ali Aissaoui, op. cit. Aissaoui proposes a complex calculation based on the permanent income hypothesis and multiple assumptions concerning the GCC's production profile, domestic consumption, population growth, as well as interest rates, to conclude that a price of $90 per barrel would reasonably satisfy the group's fiscal requirements. In this writer's opinion, Aissaoui's is an important result, and it is true that in the end the interests of oil producers must be taken into account, however many of his assumptions are debatable, and in any case it is not clear how the market would be influenced, so that the desired price is achieved.
8. Roger Diwan "Rahmaniah Occasional Paper 02" (same series as my "From Price Taker to Price Maker?"). "The financialisation of the oil market and the increasing impact of financial institutions in the pricing of crude oil" Rahmania Occasional Paper, no. 2, 2010.
9. For a recent and remarkably elegant discussion of this point see Andrew G. Haldane "Patience and Finance" Oxford China Business Forum, Beijing 2 September 2010, available from www.bankofengland.co.uk/publications/speeches/2010/speech445.pdf
10. Wikipedia has good articles on Resonance, Harmonic oscillator and Damping.
11. This is very elegantly explained by Bassam Fattouh in "Price Formation in Oil Markets: Some Lessons from 2009," OIES, Oxford Energy Comment March 2009.
12. This price was declared "fair" by King Abdullah of Saudi Arabia.
13. French President Nicolas Sarkozy and the British Prime Minister Gordon Brown essentially concurred, advocating a price that would ensure long-term supplies. Among analysts, Ali Aissaoui has published several Commentaries arguing in favor of $75 per barrel. The most complete presentation of his argument is in "GCC oil price preferences-at the Confluence of Global Energy Security and Local Fiscal Sustainability," a paper presented at the ECSSR 2009 Energy Security Conference.
14. The power of his statements was demonstrated by the reaction of the market when he changed his statement from $70–80 per barrel to $70–90 per barrel: see Reuters "Saudi's Naimi shifts up to $70-$90 price range" November 2, 2010.
15. Including of course Lehman Brothers. Among those that folded their commodity trading practice we count UBS, while City sold Phibro to Occidental.
16. "BP plans for trading arm shake-up," FT October 7, 2010.
17. In fact at the time of writing (November 2010) the upward trend story appears to be gaining ground in the market. See e.g. "Oil heats up as bulls target $100-a-barrel price" FT October 19, 2010.
18. The Monopolies and Mergers Commission (UK) "The Government of Kuwait and the British Petroleum Company plc – A report on the merger situation, presented to Parliament by the Secretary of State for Trade and Industry by Command of Her Majesty, October 1998" London 1988. Available from: www.competition-commission.org.uk/rep_pub/reports/1988/231kuwaitbp.htm
19. I have examined this point at length in "Strategic Oil stocks and security of supply", CEPS, Working Document #353, June 2011, Brussels.
20. G. Luciani "From Price Taker to Price Maker? Saudi Arabia and the World Oil Market" to be published in Haykel, Bernard Thomas Hegghammer and Stephane Lacroix (editors) *Complexity and Change in Saudi Arabia* Cambridge 2011.

References

Aissaoui, Ali "Shaping Long Term Oil Price Expectations for Investment: is it Workable? Is it Achievable?" APICORP Commentary Volume 3 No. 11–12 Nov.-Dec. 2008 www.apicorp-arabia.com/html/cms/media/pdf/research/Commentary03112008.pdf
——"What Is A Fair Price For Oil And What Makes $75 A Barrel Seem Fair?" APICORP Commentary Volume 3 No. 11–12 Nov.-Dec. 2008 Volume 4 No. 4 April 2009 www.apicorp-arabia.com/html/cms/media/pdf/research/Commentary_Vol_4_No_4_2009.pdf
——"GCC oil price preferences-At the Confluence of Global Energy Security and Local Fiscal Sustainability", a paper presented at the ECSSR 2009 Energy Security Conference.
Allsopp, Christopher and Bassam Fattouh "The Price Band and Oil Price Dynamics" OIES Comment July 2009 www.oxfordenergy.org/pdfs/comment_01_07_09.pdf
——"Oil prices: fundamentals or speculation?" presentation at the Bank of England, June 13th 2008.
Diwan, Roger "The financialisation of the oil market and the increasing impact of financial institutions in the pricing of crude oil" Rahmania Occasional Paper, no. 2, 2010.
Energy Charter Secretariat "Putting a Price on Energy – Pricing Mechanisms for Oil and Gas" 2007.

Fattouh, Bassam "The Drivers of Oil Prices: The Usefulness and Limitations of Non-Structural Model, the Demand–Supply Framework and Informal Approaches" OIES WPM 32 March 2007 www.oxfordenergy.org/pdfs/WPM32.pdf
———"The Dynamics of Crude Oil Price Differentials" OIES WPM 36 January 2008 www.oxfordenergy.org/pdfs/WPM36.pdf
———"Prospects of the DME Oman Crude Oil Futures Contract" OIES Monthly Comment March 2008 www.oxfordenergy.org/pdfs/comment_0308–1.pdf
———"Basis Variation and the Role of Inventories: Evidence from the Crude Oil Market" OIES WPM38 January 2009 www.oxfordenergy.org/pdfs/WPM38.pdf
———"Reinforcing Feedbacks, Time Spreads and Oil Prices" Oxford Energy Comment March 2009 www.mees.com/postedarticles/oped/v52n17–5OD02.htm
———"The Oil Market Through the Lens of the Latest Oil Price Cycle: Issues and Proposals" Presentation at the OIES conference on "Oil Price Volatility: Causes and Mitigation Strategies," October 9, 2009.
———"Global Demand Dynamics: Determinants and Policy Issues" paper presented at the Rahmania Annual Seminar, January 2010.
———"Price Formation in Oil Markets: Some Lessons from 2009" Oxford Energy Comment March 2010.
Haldane, Andrew G. "Patience and Finance" Oxford China Business Forum, Beijing 2 September 2010.
Horsnell, Paul "The Dynamics of Oil Price Determination" *Oxford Energy Forum* #71, November 2007.
Kilian, Lutz "Oil Price Volatility: Origins and Effects" WTO Staff Working Paper ERSD–2010–02: January 2010.
Luciani, Giacomo "From Price Taker to Price Maker? Saudi Arabia and the World Oil Market" to be published in Haykel, Bernard Thomas Hegghammer and Stephane Lacroix (editors) *Complexity and Change in Saudi Arabia*, Cambridge 2011.
———"Price and Revenue Volatility: What Policy Options and Role for the State" *Global Governance*, 17 (204), 213–228.
———"Functioning of the international oil markets and security implications" CEPS Working Document #351, May 2011.
———"Strategic Oil stocks and security of supply" CEPS Working Document #353, June 2011.
Mabro, Robert "The International Oil Price Regime: Origins, Rationale and Assessment" *JEL* XI, 1 June 2005, pages 3–20.
Monopolies and Mergers Commission (UK) "The Government of Kuwait and the British Petroleum Company plc – A report on the merger situation, presented to Parliament by the Secretary of State for Trade and Industry by Command of Her Majesty, October 1998" London 1988.
OIES Summary of Conference on "Oil Price Volatility: Causes and Mitigation Strategies" *Oxford Energy Forum* #79 of November 2009.
US Interagency Task Force on Commodity Markets, "Interim Report on Crude Oil," www.cftc.gov/stellent/groups/public/@newsroom/documents/file/itfinterimreportoncrudeoil0708.pdf [No date]

Part II
Political Responses

9
Energy Security

Daniel Moran

Energy security is a concept that resists concise definition. At its center lies a basic concern about access to energy resources, which first emerged as a distinctive problem of international politics in the 1970s, although harbingers of its significance had been apparent for decades before that. More recently, anxieties about access have been compounded by worries about the smooth functioning of global energy markets, which have become more integrated, extended, and complex as energy consumption has increased in absolute terms, especially among countries that did not consume much energy in the old days, but now do. Secure access to energy is no longer simply a matter of exercising geopolitical control over natural resources, if it ever was. It also requires the successful management of a range of financial and logistical relationships, whose breakdown will prove troubling even for states whose physical control of such resources is unchallenged.

Around this already daunting set of problems swirl others of even greater consequence. It is now widely accepted, first of all, that mankind's voracious appetite for fossil fuels has begun to alter the earth's climate. Even in the most optimistic scenarios, this remarkable development will require extensive modifications to the way much of humanity goes about its business. In the process, it is safe to assume that the environmental costs of consuming fossil fuels are gradually going to get priced into the energy markets, whose smooth functioning has become central to the idea of security. How this pricing-in will affect that smooth functioning is anyone's guess.

To all of which, finally, must be added a range of corrosive doubts about what life will be like in a world in which familiar forms of energy use may be dramatically curtailed, either because supplies of traditional fuels are running down, or because the social costs of consuming them have risen too high. It is through such anxieties that energy security, in the narrow sense of access to resources, has become connected to what is now called "human security," which is security in the broadest sense imaginable. Even if energy security is best understood in terms of international politics and global markets—and this essay is constructed on the assumption that it is—any significant failure in this realm of policy will directly touch the lives of ordinary people in ways that few governments are going to be able to ignore for long.

The place of oil within this array of problems varies. Oil consumption plays only a modest role in the production of greenhouse gases, for instance. The human contribution to global climate change is being driven mainly by demand for electricity, in whose generation oil plays a minor part. If we step back to consider the larger economic patterns that explain why all that electricity is being generated, however, the picture becomes more complicated. Electricity is the key to the supply side of the world economy. Oil is the key to the demand side: it is the transportation fuel that connects producers of almost everything, from high-tech electronics to basic commodities, to the distant markets that support production at levels beyond what can be consumed locally. It is oil that has allowed for the increasing scale and diversity of consumption that is characteristic of modern life. If supplies of oil were to fail there would be far less reason for the turbines to turn, regardless of whether the fuel turning them is coal, uranium, or sunlight.

This head-bone-connected-to-the-toe-bone aspect of energy security is what makes the subject so unwieldy, analytically. It is disconcerting to consider, for example, that the relative abundance and cheapness of food today, compared to any period in the past, is largely owed to the abundance and cheapness of oil. Even the poorest among us eat better now than they used to, because of the economic advantages that more concentrated forms of agricultural production afford, once they can be supported by the aggregated demand of multiple markets. Cheap oil makes this possible. The rich, for their part, can eat vine-ripe tomatoes year round, grown thousands of miles away, and transported to the grocery store at a price that barely registers at checkout. From a policy perspective, this kind of realization mostly serves to illustrate the gravity of the issues at stake, while lending them a scale that can make them seem almost insurmountable.

One must be allowed to hope that this last impression is mistaken; though it is not the purpose of this chapter to make the case one way or another. Its aim instead is to highlight the problems that the production and consumption of oil pose for international politics, and to survey the policy responses those problems have inspired up to now, as well as some that may arise as present circumstances change. From a security perspective, oil is an imperfect stand-in for energy in general, being neither the most abundant nor the most heavily consumed of modern fuels. In the long run, successfully navigating the challenges posed by mankind's thirst for oil will not guarantee a secure abundance of energy. Failing to navigate them, however, may mean that there is no long run, at least none in which the comforts of modernity can propagate and survive in recognizable form.

Climbing Hubbert's Peak

Whatever challenges oil may present to international security, the one thing we know for sure is that they will not last forever. Like coal and natural gas, oil is a finite, non-renewable resource. All three will one day be entirely consumed, unless mankind loses interest in consuming them. In the case of oil, however, there are those who argue that that day may be approaching quickly enough to matter to current policy, a claim that cannot be made credibly for other fossil fuels.

The seed from which the "peak oil" problem sprang is an article written by M. King Hubbert in 1949.[1] Hubbert, a geologist, compared then-known estimates of fossil fuel reserves to then-anticipated rates of consumption, and concluded that, when an expanding human population sets about consuming a finite resource, there must be a point at which the supply of that resource begins to dwindle toward zero. At first Hubbert did not possess the data necessary to estimate when that point might be reached, which gave his early work a theoretical and speculative cast. A few years later, however, better evidence led him to propose that the peak of American oil production might arrive as early as the late 1960s, a prediction that proved surprisingly accurate.[2] Ever since, the amplitude and location of what has become known as Hubbert's Peak—the apex of the curve that describes the global production of oil—has been the subject of recurring public controversy, and a continuing search for scientific consensus.[3]

Politically, the public's perspective on peak matters as much as the scientific consensus. That consensus has driven Hubbert's Peak decades into the future, far enough that contemporary policy-makers may still (just barely) feel able to ignore it a while longer.[4] But that there will in the end be some kind of curve that describes the history of humanity's consumption of oil is beyond scientific dispute. The best that today's earth science can offer to policy is a faintly ticking clock of unknown accuracy. It cannot create more oil. Nor can it describe what the far side of Hubbert's Peak will look like.

This latter issue is the crucial one. Hubbert presented his work as a harbinger of disaster. He assumed that, once the peak of oil production had been reached, the curve describing it would plunge asymptotically downward, as unconstrained demand collided with diminishing supply. If so, then the advent of peak oil becomes a call for measures to prevent mankind from jumping off a cliff. Such measures might include taxes to depress oil consumption by manipulating prices upward; spending public money on the development of substitute fuels or more energy-efficient technologies; or campaigns of public education and social engineering, to prepare people for a world in which economic growth, and all the social and cultural aspirations it supports, will no longer be sustainable. Viewed in these terms, the security risks posed by humanity's demand for oil are mainly a consequence of unrestrained consumption, which must eventually give rise to intense, violent, and ultimately pointless competition for the last drops of a wasting asset that is destined to run out anyway.

Not everyone accepts this vision of the abyss. From the start, the concept of peak oil has been challenged on the grounds that it recapitulates the error of Thomas Malthus, the English clergyman who proposed in 1798 that starvation awaited most of mankind, since the production of food could not keep pace with the natural growth of population.[5] Malthus had not considered that unknown future technologies might overturn his grim calculus, as they have in fact done in the centuries since he wrote. Given the track record of human ingenuity in the industrial era, it is argued, something similar must surely be in the offing for the energy field. It would therefore be a mistake to adopt policies grounded in premature pessimism. Artificial constraints on oil consumption are more likely to incite conflict than avert it. Better to make a maximum effort to extract the oil that is there, at whatever cost to other competing social goods, rather than risk a crisis arising from local shortages. Asking people to stop consuming oil is literally asking for trouble. Allow them to continue as they are used to, however, and new science will eventually provide a new path. When it does, the other side of Hubbert's Peak will turn out to be a smooth slope leading to a new energy regime whose details we cannot foresee, any more than Malthus could have foreseen nitrogen-based fertilizers.[6]

These competing visions of what lies beyond Hubbert's Peak mark the central fault line of energy politics in the developed world. The policy prescriptions they support are contrastive, but not mutually exclusive: a maximum effort to expand oil production is not incompatible with efforts to artificially manage its price, for instance, in order to increase incentives for the development of replacement fuels.[7] It is, however, incompatible with a high regard for environmental protection, and also tends to undermine the process of psychological adaptation that is deemed essential by those who believe growth must slow as the oil runs out. There is clearly some risk that extreme efforts to maximize production will promote the illusion that Hubbert's Peak is not real; whereas the only serious argument is about how to manage oil consumption as we move toward the summit, so as to minimize the risks on the way down the other side. When it comes to oil, there can be no credible argument about security that claims current patterns of consumption can be extended indefinitely.

The concept of security, as applied to oil at any rate, is not about protecting the status quo, but about buying time in order to ease what is certain to be a profound social transformation from one energy regime to another. Legitimate disputes exist about how the time should be paid for—whether in the form of diminished expectations and artificially suppressed demand; unstinting investment in exploration, production, and research; or both. But the central problem remains the same: how to ensure that humanity's climb up Hubbard's Peak is not interrupted by actions that destabilize the international system to the point where it cannot recover the equilibrium required to get down the other side in one piece.

The oil weapon

There is little reason to think any important international actor would wish to impede humanity's transit of Hubbert's Peak. It is harder to say whether its looming presence will dissuade states from employing their position in global oil markets for strategic advantage, a practice that has proven dangerous in the past. Oil is inherently tempting as a source of coercive leverage internationally, because so much of it is produced far from where it is consumed. This long distance trade is a reflection of oil's high energy density: the amount of heat generated from burning a kilogram of oil is more than twice that of coal. Couple this with the fact that liquid oil is easy to transport, and the result is an almost laughably intricate web of international pipelines, encircled by a daisy-chain of supertankers wending their way through maritime choke points around the world.

The dependence of oil-consuming states on distant producers necessarily exposes them to whatever threats might be directed against this attenuated distribution system. The first systematic attempt to exploit that dependence came in the 1930s, following Italy's invasion of Abyssinia (modern Ethiopia). The USA, then the world's largest producer of oil, opposed this new outburst of European imperialism. It sought to organize American oil companies in a voluntary embargo calculated to limit Italian oil consumption to the level it had achieved prior to the onset of the war.

In practice this policy came to nothing, because the war ended in an Italian victory before the Roosevelt Administration could perform whatever arm-twisting was required to secure the co-operation of American oil companies. Some of its features are worth noting, however. It is obvious, first of all, that the strategic criticality of oil was recognized long before it had become a necessity of daily life. Ordinary Italians did not yet depend on oil to go about their business. The Italian armed forces did, however, and it was this that caused the USA to attempt to employ its dominant position in the oil market in lieu of some more direct form of intervention, for which the necessary domestic backing could not have been obtained precisely because the risks were so apparent. Part of the appeal of the oil weapon was that it seemed to offer significant leverage at minimal risk.

America's views on this matter contrasted sharply with those of Great Britain, the leading state of the League of Nations. Britain and its partners had organized an international embargo against the Italians, but one from which oil had been excluded. In Britain's judgment tampering with Italy's access to oil involved escalatory risks it was not prepared to accept. It also recognized that attempting to moderate that risk, as the Americans did, by imposing an embargo pegged to pre-war oil consumption would not work: Mussolini was certain to continue prosecuting his war anyway, while deflecting public outrage away from himself, and toward whatever foreign powers had put themselves between Italians and their oil. If oil was indeed going to be used as a weapon, it was best to think of it as a broadsword, not a stiletto.

Britain's wary outlook would be vindicated a few years later, when the USA embarked on a more determined effort to restrict the sale of American oil to Japan. In contrast to Italy, which had barely figured in American military planning, the USA had been contemplating war with Japan since the turn of the twentieth century. This may explain why, on this occasion, the risks of an oil embargo were well recognized in Washington. There is, indeed, some evidence that a comprehensive embargo was not intended. The policy seized upon by the Americans in the summer of 1941 was actually a freeze of Japanese dollar-denominated financial assets, a step chosen in explicit preference to an oil embargo, because it was believed that the latter would lead to war. Then as now, however, oil was priced in dollars, and once the dollars dried up, the oil did too—a consequence of which America's leaders may not have been sufficiently aware, but from which they were unwilling to retreat. Japan for its part judged America's actions as equivalent to an act of war, amply sufficient to justify the breathtaking wave of attacks that crashed over American and British forces throughout the Pacific a few months later.

Could something similar happen again? Only a fool would answer "No" unequivocally, if only because miscalculation and overconfidence are destined to remain permanent features of international life. Yet the conditions prevailing in 1941 would be difficult to recreate, and not simply because attitudes toward war have changed, now that the apocalyptic character of industrialized violence has been fully revealed. No oil-exporting state today, nor any combination of them, has the kind of generalized military and economic power the USA possessed on the eve of the Second World War. As the energy weapon has passed into less capable hands, its limitations as a source of international disorder have become more apparent.

In October 1973 the Arab members of the Organization of Petroleum Exporting Countries (OPEC), supported by Egypt, Syria, and Tunisia, announced an embargo of oil sales to the USA, in retaliation for its support of Israel during the Yom Kippur War. The aim of this action, which was extended to include other states considered too friendly to Israel, was to force the USA to adopt a more even-handed policy toward the Arab-Israeli conflict, as judged in Arab capitals. The embargo was linked to other measures calculated to make oil more profitable, including a 70% increase in crude prices, and progressively stepped-down limits on production. It was to achieve greater profitability that OPEC had been formed thirteen years earlier. Its efforts had achieved only modest success, however, by the time its Arab members sought to use their market leverage to alter the course of the military struggle between Israel and its neighbors.

The impact of the Arab embargo and associated price hikes was immediate and severe. Crude oil prices quadrupled in a matter of months, even as supply shortages sent governments around the world scrambling to impose rationing and other draconian measures to moderate demand. It is not easy to disaggregate the impact of the embargo from other contemporaneous changes in the world economy. Of these the most important was the collapse, two years before, of the Bretton Woods monetary system, which had served as an anchor for global currency values since the Second World War. The inflation of Western currencies that followed would have presented a strong motive for oil producing states to seek higher prices anyway. The Arab effort to link their pricing preferences to demands for political and diplomatic concessions by Israel and the USA thus includes some elements of ordinary opportunism, a means of jump-starting a secular price adjustment that was about to get under way more slowly no matter what. Nevertheless, it was an opportunity consciously seized as part of the military planning that preceded the Yom Kippur War.[8] For Israel's Arab opponents, aware of their conventional military limitations, and facing an adversary armed with nuclear weapons, oil was supposed to be their ace in the hole.

It did not prove to be, though the attempt to make it so would have far-reaching consequences. It was the oil crisis of 1973–74 that established "energy security" as a distinctive theme of modern politics.[9] Public and official opinion throughout the rich world was galvanized by the realization that access to such a critical resource had fallen disproportionately under the control of a small group of developing states with scant interest in business as usual. Energy insecurity had now been experienced first hand, and soon gave rise to a host of innovative policies designed to promote energy efficiency, expand exploration and drilling, and stimulate the development of alternative fuels. Fear of dependence on "foreign oil" remains a shibboleth of American politics to this day. This in itself is testimony to the psychological impact of the Arab embargo.

Its strategic impact, on the other hand, was negligible, at least in relation to the goals for which it was undertaken. There is no evidence that the Arab embargo altered the outcome of the Yom Kippur War. It may have hastened the subsequent negotiations, shepherded along by the USA in an atmosphere of rising public anger about gasoline prices, by which the belligerent armies were disentangled. It was the conclusion of this disentanglement, signified by the Israeli withdrawal from the west bank of the Suez Canal, that provided the occasion for the embargo to be called off in March 1974. But there was nothing about any of this that could have been mistaken for a shift in the strategic balance in the region. If anything, the embargo had drawn the USA and Israel closer together, whereas the point had been to drive them apart. The engineered price increases that accompanied the embargo did contribute to the souring of relations between Israel and much of Europe, which was and is far more reliant on Middle Eastern oil than the USA. But this was an entirely symbolic accomplishment, so long as co-operation between Washington and Tel Aviv remained intact.

The embargo also failed in its broader strategic purpose, which was to assert the right of the world's oil producers to play a role commensurate with the value of the resources they controlled. Here the realities of the global energy market, which were supposed to provide the Arab states with new strategic clout, cut against their ability to sustain a confrontation that, to say the least, had required a lot of nerve. It did not take long for nerves to fail. Saudi Arabia, whose security had been underwritten by the USA since the Second World War, came to question the wisdom of a measure that, if persisted in, might cast that relationship into doubt, and also threatened to reduce its relative share of world oil sales. By the start of 1974 Saudi's oil minister was already backing away from the production quotas and price increases that had been imposed with such fanfare only a few months before. Egypt, having recruited OPEC's Arab members to unsheathe the oil weapon on its behalf, eventually made peace with Israel on terms judged so treacherous that Egypt was expelled from the Arab League. In 1980 two of OPEC's own members, Iran and Iraq, went to war with each other for control of the oil fields around the Shatt-al-Arab.

The decision of OPEC's Arab members to step out onto the stage of strategic confrontation exposed the fissures and cross purposes of governments whose livelihoods depend on their ability to sell the same commodity to the same customers. Their successful collusion caused prices to rise, true enough, and the wealth of producer states along with it. At the same time, however, OPECs success in raising oil prices increased the opportunity costs of persisting in the production cuts that had given the embargo its strategic bite, while creating proportionally greater incentives for non-OPEC states to step up production and exploration. The leverage afforded by such price manipulation as OPEC was able to achieve did not compare to that applied by the USA against Japan, because the USA was able, on its own, to prevent Japan from obtaining the fuel required to prosecute its on-going war in China. It was the implacable finality of the asset freeze that made it an act of war from Tokyo's perspective. No one, including the Israelis, regarded the oil shock of 1973–74 as an act of war, because it became apparent almost immediately that its disruptive effects would be dissipated and absorbed in the marketplace, and would never reach the battlefield, nor even the negotiating table.

Like the American effort to coerce Japan in 1941, the Arab oil embargo turns out to be a story mainly of miscalculation; though the miscalculation in the Arab case is more complicated. The Roosevelt Administration misjudged Japan's willingness to use force in circumstances in which the risk of war was well recognized. It was a calamitous mistake, but conceptually a simple one. OPEC, on the other hand, failed to anticipate that the second-order effects of dramatically higher oil prices would prove unmanageable, owing to market efficiencies they underestimated for the simple reason that they had not previously been put to the test. The results remain instructive, and arguably reassuring, to this day. Within the framework of an efficient, integrated, and diversified global market, the energy weapon is not merely a unwieldy broadsword. It is a sword that has no handle. You can only use it if you are willing to grasp the blade.

Defending the market

The experience of the 1970s continues to shape thinking about energy security in two respects. First, it has strengthened confidence that market integration is conducive to peace and security. Second, it has focused attention on the problem of how to stabilize, modernize, and defend the Middle East. To recognize this is not to suggest that other features of the world oil market might not present cause for concern. The social fragility and political caprice of Middle Eastern politics are no less apparent in other important producer states like Venezuela and Nigeria, either of which might break down or act up in ways that would roil global markets for a time. Russia, which has lately become an important producer state, clearly represents a kind of wild card within the system: the only producer state with the undoubted capacity to turn oil wealth into other forms of power. Yet it also possesses a sufficient diversity of economic interests that, like the major consumer states, its strongest interest lies in the stability of the market overall. That is where any discussion of energy security as it relates to oil must focus, and it is that problem that has made the security of the Middle East and security of the world oil market virtually synonymous.

The proposition that expansion of trade discourages the use of force internationally is, needless to say, very old. It can be found in recognizable form in the work of early market theorists like Adam Smith and David Ricardo, and has underpinned much of American foreign policy since the birth of the republic.[10] Those who have embraced it have suffered recurring disappointment, most emphatically in the outbreak of the First World War, when the Great Powers of Europe all went to war against their best customers. Yet this setback and others have not discredited the idea that it is mainly through market relationships that the true costs of modern war can be revealed and, once revealed, avoided. If anything, energy stands out among military planners today as the only credible exception to this general rule, the last *casus belli* that might cause advanced societies to go to war with each other.[11]

The case for pessimism is strengthened to some extent by the fact that, in contrast to earlier times, the consumer side of the global energy market now includes important participants whose commitment to market principles is purely pragmatic. It is reasonable to wonder how far respect for the integrity of global markets will carry countries like China or Russia, whose internal social and economic practices are overwhelmingly governed by authoritarian (if not kleptocratic) values. No one can rule out the possibility that such values might assert themselves internationally, should the going get tough. Neither, however, should anyone automatically assume that they will. Although the developing world's ideological commitment to the ideal of the market falls below that of the mature economies of the West, its practical stake in the market's smooth functioning is equally high.

Even if we accept that oil scarcity may cause powerful states to subvert the markets on which they had previously relied, it remains difficult to devise any scenario in which this actually happens that does not involve some kind of crisis in the Middle East. Its criticality is owed to two factors. The first is the proportion of the world's proved oil reserves that are found there. The second is its propensity for political and social instability.

The question of what counts as oil reserves is contested, so that the Middle East's relative share is dependent in theory on how unconventional reserves, including extra heavy oil, oil shale, bituminous sands, biomass-based liquids, and so on, are accounted for; also on what degree of geological confidence one requires in estimating how much oil is in the ground. Proved reserves are conventionally defined as oil that presents "reasonable certainty [of recovery] under existing economic and operating conditions"; in essence, oil that comes out of a well without extraordinary assistance. Approximately 56% of all such oil is found in states bordering the Persian Gulf.[12]

Geologically, unconventional reserves outweigh proved reserves by a ratio of two or three to one—a fact of obvious significance in estimating the shape and location of Hubbert's Peak.[13] To the extent that energy security is a matter of ensuring market stability during the ascent, however, such reserves count for little, because of the difficulty and high cost of recovering them. As the oil crisis of 1973–74 illustrates, energy insecurity manifests itself first of all as a combination of supply shortages and high prices, effects that can only be moderated by oil that is brought to market quickly and cheaply. Most such oil, and nearly all of the world's excess production capacity, upon which the management of price depends, are in the Middle East.

From a security perspective such a concentration of market leverage in any single region would be worrisome. In the Middle East, however, we have a region prone to conflict of every sort, and also resistant to democratization and other modernizing reform.[14] Governance everywhere is in the hands of dynastic or military regimes of limited capacity. Few if any can claim to possess the consent of the governed, a fact that is manifest in the absence of orderly political dissent, and in the prominence of the disorderly variety, ranging from vernacular social violence to well-organized international terrorism; both of which are abetted by mutual subversion among regional governments, and the mutual resentments of Shi'i and Sunni Muslims. Despite having spent hundreds of billions of dollars on military equipment over the last thirty years, none of the oil-producing states of the Middle East possesses more than a rudimentary ability to defend itself. One of them, Iran, is apparently seeking to redress its conventional military incapacity by pursuing nuclear weapons. Its effort, if successful, will cast all existing security arrangements in the region into doubt.

These circumstances pose two kinds of risks to the world oil market. Inter-state violence or social unrest within the region may interfere with oil production on a scale sufficient to impact global supplies and prices. A number of such episodes have already occurred, including the Iranian Revolution of 1979, the Iran-Iraq War that began the following year, and Iraq's subsequent invasion of Kuwait in 1990. Energy infrastructure has also been a frequent target of terrorist attacks, though none have yet succeeded on a scale discernable in international markets. Rather like the oil shock of 1973–74, however, these events, while unnerving and unpleasant, can be viewed as reassuring in retrospect, because they testify to the resilience of the market in the face of major challenges on the supply side.

The second form of risk to which the market is exposed by the instability of the Middle East is more difficult to appraise. Because the region's oil producers are all consumers of security, it is possible that they will fall disproportionately under the sway of whoever is protecting them. It is difficult to predict the reactions of other major consumer states if this were to happen; but it would be nonsense to assume that they would be without recourse, if not militarily, then via the multiple avenues for influence afforded by the market itself.

For the last thirty years that protection has been supplied overwhelmingly by the USA. In January 1980 then-President Jimmy Carter declared in his State of the Union address that the USA regarded the uninterrupted export of Persian Gulf oil as a vital American interest, and that any threat to it would be "repelled by any means necessary, including military force." Carter's statement was conditioned by the regional instability of the preceding decade, culminating in the humiliating seizure of American diplomats as hostages in Iran, but its immediate impetus came from the Soviet invasion of Afghanistan a few months before. The USA saw this move as an attempt to "consolidate a strategic position ... that poses a grave threat to the free movement of Middle East oil." America's military commitment to the Middle East was thus rooted in the confrontational logic of the Cold War, rather than in any systemic concern for the region in relation to the larger world. Nevertheless, Carter had begun his address by declaring that "it has never been more clear that the state of our Union depends on the state of the world."[15] This general truth has weighed heavily on his successors, all of whom, as Michael Klare has observed, have sought to extend what became known as the Carter Doctrine to encompass an increasingly diverse range of threats to the Persian Gulf, while extending American protection to include the oil-producing states of Central Asia and Africa.[16]

The steps by which American engagement in the Gulf has unfolded are too familiar to require detailed discussion. The first occurred in the last years of the Iran-Iraq war, in the form of naval operations to protect neutral shipping against attack not from the Soviet Union, but from Iran. A few years later the USA took the lead in rolling back the Iraqi invasion of Kuwait. Afterward it sought to discourage similar adventurism by maintaining forward-deployed forces in Saudi Arabia and elsewhere in the Gulf, and by establishing the headquarters of its 5th Fleet in Bahrain. In 2003, in the aftermath of terrorist attacks on the Pentagon and the World Trade Center, it embarked on a war to overthrow the government in Iraq. This action was justified in part by the thought that the destruction of one of the Middle East's most detestable regimes would inspire democratic reform and curtail the spread of Islamic extremism. In 2009, contemplating the potential threat posed by a nuclear-armed Iran, America's Secretary of State, Hillary Clinton, declared that in such circumstances the USA would extend its "defense umbrella" throughout the region.[17]

These actions have been accompanied by vague mutterings, within and beyond the Arab world, that the real American purpose has been to seize control of the Gulf's oil reserves. This view has not gained much traction in the capitals of the major consuming states, because the USA has been scrupulous about forswearing special advantages for itself or for American oil companies, especially in its handling of the occupation of Iraq. Nevertheless, the underlying point is not trivial. It is not easy to distinguish between the use of force to defend the market, which is the true American interest in the region, and the use of force to corner the market, which is not in its interest, but might well be regarded by disinterested observers as within its power.

Given that the stability of the Middle East and, by extension, of the world oil market, is going to depend for the indefinite future on security provided by consumer states, that stability would be reinforced if some kind of institutional architecture were developed to ensure that the provision of military protection did not convey disproportionate economic advantages to whoever provides it. How this could be accomplished, given the enormous disparity of military power between the USA and other developed nations, is hard to say. Neither the theatrical multilateralism of the 1991 Gulf War, nor the threadbare coalition of the willing that was assembled around the US invasion of Iraq in 2003, seem likely to suffice. In the energy field, as in most areas of international life, the maintenance of good order depends on the co-operation of strong states, not the symbolic mobilization of weak ones. American leadership will be required to accomplish this, and it may now be emerging, as the true costs of its recent drift toward unilateralism have begun to pile up. If it does not, and if America's shadow in the Middle East continues to deepen, it is hard to believe its motives will not eventually come in for closer scrutiny.

It is also easy to see that America's efforts to shield the oil market have been hobbled by unexpected consequences and second-order effects similar to those that have unhinged earlier attempts to employ oil as a weapon. It is apparent, for instance, that the substantial American military presence left behind following the liberation of Kuwait contributed to the flourishing of Islamic radicalism, which produced the terrorist attacks of 2001. Those attacks in turn created the psychological conditions that made the invasion of Iraq in 2003 possible. While the outcome of the Iraq war is not yet known, the fact that it has dragged on so long and produced such a dispiriting spectacle of internecine violence, has done nothing to enhance America's overall standing in the world, or the attractions of the protection it has to offer.

It has also rekindled the embers of the Iranian Revolution, and with it the nuclear weapons program that had fallen into abeyance following the overthrow of the Shah. It has been revived at least in part as insurance that America's interest in "regime change" will not be extended to Teheran. Secretary Clinton's effort to alleviate concerns about Iran's nuclear ambitions with talk of defense umbrellas, while intended to be soothing, has proved to be unnerving instead. Many observers in the Gulf Arab states, and also in Israel, have wondered whether such a comment might not suggest the USA has abandoned hope of forestalling Iran. It has also raised doubts about whether the concept of extended deterrence makes any sense at all in a region where security co-operation remains vestigial, despite decades of expanding American involvement.[18]

What we see here is no straight-forward escalatory process, by which each violent act inspires a more violent response, but rather a progressive entanglement, brought about by the perverse incentives that so often attend even the successful use of force. America's frustrations are not symptomatic of bad faith, nor necessarily of strategic incompetence; though they do reflect a strategic vision that has been plagued by cross purposes. Since the 1980s the USA has been caught between its desire to stabilize a violent region, and to transform and modernize a backward one. The security of the Middle East, and of the global oil market, can doubtless be improved by either approach. But it might at least be recognized that it is difficult to transform a region and stabilize it at the same time; which recognition should, at a minimum, inspire modesty about what energy security means or, more precisely, about how much of it we can expect to achieve at acceptable cost in blood and treasure.

With respect to oil, moderate expectations are often in short supply. One economist has noted with dismay, for instance, that nine of the last 10 recessions in the USA have been preceded by rising oil prices.[19] Observations of this kind are useful in reminding the citizens of the developed world of how tightly their general welfare is bound to their consumption of a commodity whose supply is destined to diminish over time. Yet it would surely be a mistake to identify energy security with the absence of economic recessions, or with undesirable fluctuations in the price of oil.

Energy security, like national security, is not something that nations get to enjoy alone, at least not for long. With respect to oil, security is best understood as a characteristic of the system by which resources are produced and distributed, and of the market mechanisms by which that system must be regulated if it is to retain the confidence of producers and consumers. It is also worth recalling that security is not an absolute value, as applied to energy or anything else. It exists in varying degrees, and cannot be achieved at all without some proportional sacrifice of other social goods. Sound policies to sustain it must be based on realistic expectations of what is possible, a fair accounting and equitable distribution of the sacrifices involved, and a determined effort to broaden the ranks of those prepared to step up and defend a system on which the whole world depends.

Notes

1. M. King Hubbert, "Energy from Fossil Fuels," *Science* 109. 4 February 1949, pp. 103–9, www.eoearth.org/article/Energy_from_Fossil_Fuels_(historical).
2. M. King Hubbert, "Nuclear Energy and Fossil Fuels," Paper Presented to the American Petroleum Institute, San Antonio, Texas, 7–9 March 1956, www.energybulletin.net/node/13630. The accuracy of this prediction (US oil production peaked in 1970) has contributed to the special connection of Hubbert's work with oil. As the titles of his papers demonstrate, Hubbert wrote about all fossil fuels. Conceptually his approach can be applied to any non-renewable natural resource.
3. One of the most influential efforts to popularize Hubbert's ideas, and mobilize public opinion around them, is Matthew R. Simmons, "Revisiting *The Limits to Growth*: Could the Club of Rome Have Been Correct, After All?" October 2000, www.greatchange.org/ov-simmons,club_of_rome_revisted.html. Simmons, who was an investment banker, later claimed that the peak of global oil production probably occurred in 2005 (Barbara Lewis, "Oil Has Peaked, but Where's the Data?" *Reuters*, 14 February 2007, www.reuters.com/article/idUSL1325232620070214). *The Limits of Growth*, to which Simmons' paper refers, is a 1972 report by the Club of Rome that presented a path-breaking analysis of the impact of resource constraints on economic growth. For a survey of the scientific debate that Hubbert's work has inspired, see Moujahed Al-Husseini, "The Debate over Hubbert's Peak: A Review," *GeoArabia* 11/12, 2006, pp. 181–210.
4. Current estimates place peak global oil production in the years 2030–70, a range that reflects the variety of realistic assumptions that are possible about remaining reserves, resource substitution, and consumption patterns. See Guy Caruso, "When Will World Oil Production Peak?" Paper presented at the Tenth Annual Asia Oil and Gas Conference, Kuala Lumpur, Malaysia, 13 June 2005, www.eia.doe.gov/neic/speeches/caruso061305.pdf.
5. *An Essay on the Principle of Population*, London: J. Johnson, 1798. Subsequent editions, of which there were six during Malthus' lifetime, included revisions and responses to criticism, but never retracted the claim that "the power of population is indefinitely greater than the power in the earth to produce subsistence for man" (chapter 1).
6. For an analysis of the peak oil issue that envisions the far side of Hubbert's Peak as an "undulating plateau," see Peter Jackson, "The Future of Global Oil Supply: Understanding the Building Blocks," Cambridge Energy Research Associates Special Report, 4 November 2009, www.cera.com/aspx/cda/client/report/report.aspx?KID=5&CID=10720.
7. Some analysts are prepared to find virtue in both approaches. See for instance Joshua Busby, "Overcoming Political Barriers to Reform in Energy Policy," in Sharon Burke and Christine Parthemore, eds., *A Strategy for American Power: Energy, Climate and National Security* (Washington, DC: Center for a New American Security, 2008), pp. 35–66.
8. Daniel Yergin, *The Prize: The Epic Quest for Oil, Money, and Power*, New York: Simon and Schuster, 1991, p. 597.
9. Simon Langlois-Bertrand, *The Contemporary Concept of Energy Security*, Defence R& D Canada: Centre for Operational Research and Analysis, Ottawa, July 2010, pp. 3–5, summarizes a number of earlier studies that support this observation, including Yergin, *The Prize*, and Francisco Parra, *Oil Politics: A Modern History of Petroleum*, London: I. B. Taurus, 2005.
10. On the history of thinking about the relationship of free markets to peace, see Edmund Silberner, *The Problem of War in Nineteenth-Century Economic Thought*, translated by Alexander H. Krappe, Princeton, NJ: Princeton University Press, 1946. On the influence of such ideas on American foreign policy, see William H. Becker and Samuel F. Wells, Jr., eds, *Economics & World Power: An Assessment of American Diplomacy since 1789*, New York: Columbia University Press, 1984.
11. For contrasting views of this issue, see Michael T. Klare, *Resource Wars: The New Landscape of Global Conflict*, New York: Metropolitan Books, 2001; and Steve Yetiv, *Crude Awakenings: Global Oil Security and American Foreign Policy*, Ithaca, NY: Cornell University Press, 2004.
12. "World Proved Reserves of Oil and Natural Gas, Most Recent Estimates," United States Energy Information Administration, 3 March 2009, www.eia.doe.gov/emeu/international/reserves.html.
13. Hussein Alboudwarej et al., "Highlighting Heavy Oil," *Oilfield Review*, Summer 2006, www.slb.com/~/media/Files/resources/oilfield_review/ors06/sum06/heavy_oil.ashx.
14. The Middle East and North Africa is the only region on earth where the measures of political freedom and civil rights employed by Freedom House have declined since 1973. See its downloadable spreadsheet "Country Status by Region" at www.freedomhouse.org/template.cfm?page=439. The

Failed States Index compiled by the Fund for Peace judges most of the countries bordering the Persian Gulf to be either failed states, or in danger of failing. The exceptions are Bahrain, Oman, Qatar, and the United Arab Emirates. See "Failed States Index Scores 2010," at www.fundforpeace.org/web/index.php?option=com_content& task=view&id=452&Itemid=900.

15 Jimmy Carter, State of the Union Address, 23 January 1980, www.jimmycarterlibrary.gov/documents/speeches/su80jec.phtml.
16 Michael T. Klare, "Petroleum Anxiety and the Militarization of Energy Security," in Daniel Moran and James A. Russell, eds., *Energy Security and Global Politics: The Militarization of Resource Management*, New York: Routledge, 2009, especially pp. 47–50.
17 *New York Times*, 22 July 2009, www.nytimes.com/2009/07/23/world/asia/23diplo.html.
18 On the reactions inspired by Secretary Clinton's statement, and the problem of extended deterrence, see Bruno Tertrais et al., *Perspectives on Extended Deterrence,* Fondation pour la Recheche Stratégique, Paris, 2010, www.isn.ethz.ch/isn/Digital-Library/Publications/Detail/?ots591=0c54e3b3–1e9c-be1e-2c24-a6a8c7060233&lng=en&id=116457; and Daniel Moran, "Teheran's Umbrella: Extended Deterrence and the Challenge of Proliferation," Paper presented at the 7th Pan-European Conference on International Relations, Stockholm, September 2010, http://stockholm.sgir.eu/uploads/Teheran's%20Umbrella.pdf. The deterrence issue was anticipated by Kathleen J. McInnis, "Extended Deterrence: The U.S. Credibility Gap in the Middle East," *Washington Quarterly*, 2005, pp. 169–86, www.twq.com/05summer/docs/05summer_mcinnis.pdf.
19 Oil and the Macroeconomy, 24 August 2005, prepared for the Palgrave Dictionary of Economics, http://dss.ucsd.edu/~jhamilto/JDH_palgrave_oil.pdf. The Federal Reserve Bank of St. Louis has sought to apply this finding to other developed economies. See Kristie M. Engemann, Kevin L. Kliesen, and Michael T. Owywang, "Do Oil Shocks Drive Business Cycles? Some U.S. and International Evidence," Federal Reserve Bank of St. Louis Working Paper 2010–007C, December 2010, http://research.stlouisfed.org/wp/2010/2010–007.pdf.

10
Strategy, Foreign Policy and Climate Change
The Middle East in the cross hairs

James A. Russell

In 2007 the United Nations' Intergovernmental Panel on Climate Change, or IPCC, presented evidence suggesting that the stock of greenhouse gases in the atmosphere could triple by the end of the century, leading to a 50% chance of temperature rises of up to 5°C between now and the end of the century. Researchers believe that climate change is expected to accelerate a series of already negative trends in the Middle East and Persian Gulf:[1]

- Decreased precipitation and decreased river flows that are critical to regional populations. For example, some analysts believe that the Euphrates River could shrink by 30% and the Jordan River by 80% between now and the end of the century. Ground water aquifers are also being depleted at dangerous rates.
- Lower yields on major food crops that will only further politicize the issue of food security in an already overpopulated region that still maintains one of the highest population growth rates in the world.
- Rising sea levels that will affect populations in the eastern Mediterranean and the Nile Delta. Populations in the coastal areas of the Gulf region such as Abu Dhabi, Dubai and Doha will also be affected.
- Rising temperatures are generally believed to negatively affect economic growth, in part due to the increased mitigation and adaptation costs. The lesser developed states in the Middle East, such as Egypt, Jordan, and Syria will have less ability to cope with increased temperatures than the wealthier states of the Gulf.
- Hotter, drier climates will negatively affect human health throughout the region.
- Biodiversity throughout the region will be negatively affected by rising temperatures.
- Weather patterns that will become more erratic, with sandstorms and other disturbances that will make life more difficult for the region's inhabitants.

Environmental stresses in the region are of course not new, but these stresses promise to gather momentum over the next quarter-century and beyond. These stresses promise to overflow the in-boxes of decision-makers around the world as world leaders show little interest in seriously addressing climate change as a systemic challenge to global security and stability. Meanwhile, the Middle East staggers towards an environmental crisis. As visitors to and inhabitants of the contemporary Persian Gulf and Middle East can attest, the region's vast efforts to make its environment appear to be anything other than dusty and sand-colored have required extraordinary and expensive interventions by the region's governments to create an artificial and man-made world that allows its inhabitants to escape from the effects of the inhospitable physical environment. The tree-lined highways and flower-dotted promenades of today's modern cities throughout the Middle East and Persian Gulf are all testaments to efforts mounted over the last several decades to mitigate the impact of an environment that is hotter and drier than any place on earth. States have gone to extraordinary lengths in this quest, and the work continues unabated. For example, Saudi Arabia continues to hopefully seed clouds with calcium, chloride and silver iodide in an attempt to generate sorely needed rain over its arid landscape.[2]

As the world slowly and reluctantly wrenches its attention to the daunting challenges of addressing climate change and the specter of a future in which environmental issues may exert an increasing impact on regional security and stability,[3] the Middle East offers lessons on the problems and prospects of adapting to and mitigating the effects of an already hostile environment on its human inhabitants. While on the one hand the steel and glass towers of Dubai, Riyadh, Doha, and Beirut represent the envy of developing states around the world, their continued existence is inextricably intertwined with the planet's continued environmental and economic folly. These cities depend on the continued expansion of world petroleum markets, which are themselves dumping carbon emissions, largely from the developed world, into the atmosphere. These emissions must be controlled if the world is to address credibly the inexorable march of climate change. Hence the challenge of climate change is undeniably linked to the functioning of world petroleum markets on which the states of the Persian Gulf, in particular, depend for their environmental mitigation and adaptation efforts. If these mitigation and adaptation efforts fail or are compromised, societies throughout the Gulf and the wider Middle East will be negatively affected. Regional stability will surely be a casualty of this process.

This chapter addresses the challenge posed by climate change and environmental security to the Middle East, with particular focus on the states surrounding the Gulf, such as Iran, Iraq, Saudi Arabia and the smaller states of Bahrain, Kuwait, Qatar, the United Arab Emirates and Oman. Each of these states faces similar challenges. The Gulf states particularly depend upon oil markets to continue their economic growth. These markets have also provided these states with the means to delay political reforms while they maintain anachronistic forms of governments. After assessing the environmental challenges in the region, the chapter will address the degree to which climate impacts hypothesized for 2030 may lead to an appreciable additional factor in triggering disruptive social change and the likelihood of civil conflict. Lastly, it will address the foreign policy challenges for the USA and the region.

Environmental stress in the Middle East

That environmental stresses strike hard in the Persian Gulf states as they do throughout the wider Middle East is not in question. The Persian Gulf and the wider Middle East exist in what could only be described as one of the most hostile environments on the planet with burgeoning, youthful and largely unemployed populations. All statistical indicators suggest that the Persian Gulf is one of the hottest, most water-starved environments in the world. With the exception of Iraq and Iran, which have somewhat better access to fresh water than its neighbors, most states in the Gulf and the wider region suffer from acute fresh water scarcity (defined by the World Bank as access to less than 1,000 cubic meters a year). These scarcities promise to become more acute as the world's temperature increases and the demand for fresh water increases due to population growth. Domestic water demand is projected to double in the Gulf by 2025 and the demand for water required for industrial uses will increase threefold over the period.[4] As indicated below in Table 10.1, the baseline of renewable fresh water availability in today's Gulf is already an environmental crisis.[5]

The United Nations identifies fresh water scarcity as a critical risk factor in all societies, contributing to such systemic problems as poverty, unplanned urbanization, environmental degradation and the stresses on fragmented institutional governing structures where shortages are particularly acute.[6] In other words, water security is now deemed essential to the growth, development and stability of a society.[7] Water scarcity is perhaps the most serious of the direct environmental impacts in the Gulf that will be felt by increasing temperatures over the next 20 years. It is by any measure a systemic problem. The World Bank projects that per capita water availability throughout the Middle East and North Africa region will decline from today's average availability of 1,000 cubic meters per year to 500 cubic meters by 2050. In contrast, by 2050 when the world's population is expected to reach 9bn people, average per capita annual water availability will amount to 6,000 cubic meters per person.[8]

Total water demand is projected to increase in the Gulf Co-operation Council (GCC) states by 36% over the next decade.[9] In addition to systemic shortages, water scarcity in the Persian Gulf region in particular promises to gather momentum over the coming decades as a result of persistent mismanagement by the regional states of their limited renewable water resources. It is a disheartening picture. In 2007 the GCC countries extracted 19.5m. cubic meters of fresh water from underground aquifers, while the recharge of these aquifers accumulated at the rate of only 4.8m. cubic meters. The Gulf states currently extract 91% of their total water demand from these underground sources, with the remaining demand satisfied by desalinization and treated effluent.[10] This unsustainable practice has resulted in falling water tables, a deterioration in water quality and saline water intrusion into the declining aquifers.[11]

In some regional cities the depletion of ground aquifers is already a crisis. Researchers at the Center for Strategic and International Studies found that residents of Sana'a (with an estimated population of 1.7m. in 2010) in Yemen are resorting to oil drilling equipment to reach water to preserve existing wells. The water table in Sana'a is estimated to be falling at the rate of 4–6 meters per year and some believe the city will run out of groundwater by the year 2017.[12]

Table 10.1 Fresh water availability in Middle East/Gulf States

Country	Renewable Water Availability in 2005 in cubic meters per capita
Saudi Arabia	96
Yemen	198
Egypt	790
Bahrain	157
Jordan	160
Syria	1440
UAE	49
Qatar	86
Oman	340
Lebanon	1190
Kuwait	8
Iraq	2920
Iran	1970

There are few alternative sources to this water for Yemen's population, since building desalinated water plants is prohibitively expensive.

Jordan also faces a short-term water crisis due in part to a deliberate program to expand irrigated areas during the 1990s. Jordan invested heavily in expanding agricultural production during this period and now exports food valued at over US$500m. annually. This unsustainable increase in agriculture production has come at a serious long-term price. Not only does this hugely inefficient program deplete Jordan's underground aquifers, but it also creates a political problem for the regime since a wealthy, politically-connected elite controls much of the water for this agricultural production.[13]

The experiences in Yemen and Jordan are not anomalies. States throughout the Middle East have pursued a nonsensical and hugely inefficient policy of developing their own agriculture despite the inhospitable environment. A staggering 85% of the ground water in the GCC states is used for agricultural production of food that could be imported much more cheaply.[14] Moreover, the disproportionate investment of their limited fresh water assets in agriculture has been of negligible benefit to their economies, contributing on average less than 1% of GDP throughout the region.[15] Saudi Arabia's particularly egregious agriculture program illustrates the point. During the 1980s Saudi Arabia became the sixth largest wheat exporter in the world (with production reaching nearly 5m. tons in the early 1990s) courtesy of non-renewable ground water provided through inefficient irrigation systems.[16] In belated recognition of this folly, Saudi Arabia announced plans in early 2008 to reduce grain production annually by 12.5% and to halt all production by 2016.[17] Figure 10.1 below indicates trends in Saudi grain production.

Another egregious example of Saudi Arabia's fresh water folly is represented by the Al Safi Dairy Farm, identified in the *Guinness Book of World Records* as the largest integrated dairy farm in the world. The farm, located about 60 miles outside Riyadh, covers 14 square miles and supplies approximately one-third of the country's dairy needs. The farm's 29,000 cows produce an estimated 122,000 gallons of milk per day, with each cow needing up to 30 gallons of fresh water daily to drink and stay cool in temperatures that can reach as high as 115°F in the summer. Water for the entire operation is pumped from a depth of 6,000 feet underground. In

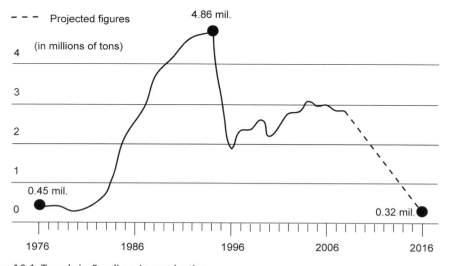

Figure 10.1 Trends in Saudi grain production

addition to cooling down the cows, the water is used to grow all the food for the farm's four-legged inhabitants.[18] Clearly, projects like this must become a casualty of the region's dwindling fresh water supplies.

As dire as this well known story of fresh water scarcity may be, however, all these states have taken dramatic steps to address chronic shortages by building desalinization plants. The region today boasts the most developed infrastructure for fresh water production in the world. Desalinated water is extremely expensive to produce, costing on average from $0.5-0.6 per cubic meter.[19] The Gulf states today operate over one-half of the world's estimated 10,400 desalination plants that produce over 35m. cubic meters of water per day around the world. Saudi Arabia's Saline Water Conversion Company (SWCC) is the largest desalinated water company in the world, producing approximately 3m. cubic meters per day and 5000 megawatts of power, representing 50% of the kingdom's drinking water supply and 20% of its power generation. In March 2006 SWCC Governor, Fehied al Shareef, indicated that the kingdom will need an additional 6m. cubic meters of water and 30,000 megawatts of power generation capacity to meet anticipated demand.[20]

The scale of the joint desalination/electrical power projects under consideration throughout the region is truly staggering. In August 2007, the French company Veolia Water Solutions and Technology announced it had launched an $805m. project to build a desalination plant in Fujairah in the United Arab Emirates that will produce 590,000 cubic meters of water per day upon completion in 2010. The same company also received a $1.4bn contract in June 2007 to build what will be the world's largest desalinization plant in Jubail, Saudi Arabia that will produce 800,000 cubic meters of water per day.[21] In December 2006, Saudi Arabia began studying a potential $5.3bn "Water Bank" project in Tihama that will add significant desalination capacity for the entire country.[22] Demand for desalinated water in the region is projected to grow at an annual rate of 6% and may require an investment of over $100bn in new capacity over the next decade to meet increased demand.[23]

The fresh water shortage is the Gulf states' critical environmental stress for the foreseeable future and becomes exacerbated by population growth and the economic growth that must sustain the region's burgeoning population. As indicated in Table 10.2 below, population in the Gulf state region is expected to grow from 117m. in 2000 to 219m. by 2050, an increase of over 85%.

Table 10.2 Historic and Projected Population in Middle East States[24]

Country	1950	2000	2050
Saudi Arabia	3.200	20.800	45.03
Iran	16.900	66.001	100.17
Iraq	5.300	25.020	61.90
Yemen	4.316	18.182	53.689
Kuwait	0.152	2.200	5.20
Egypt	21.514	70.174	129.533
Jordan	0.472	4.853	10.241
Syria	3.536	16.511	36.911
Oman	0.456	2.400	4.60
Qatar	0.025	0.617	1.30
Bahrain	0.116	0.650	1.17
Totals	55.987	227.408	449.744

Note: Population in millions

Regional economic growth to accommodate this increased population will for most of these states literally be fueled by the functioning of world petroleum markets. It is less clear where the water will come from. Without the revenues provided by these global markets, the Gulf states may face the prospect of economic stagnation and political uncertainty. Income from oil exports is a vital supporting component in the system of government practised by all regional regimes, a system of government that features no taxation and little representation. The future, however, appears bright for regional regimes as they seek to preserve their "rentier" governmental model of redistributing energy market proceeds. The US Energy Information Administration (EIA) forecasts that the world will need 40% more oil than it is using today by 2030, when global demand will increase from approximately 85mbpd in 2008 to between 118 and 120mbpd.[25] Developing Asia and the USA will drive the increase in demand. The USA is anticipated to need an additional 10mbpd by 2030, taking its consumption to between 28 and 30mbpd by 2030. Asia will be the Gulf's most important market over this period. Asian anticipated economic expansion will be enabled and fueled by increased production of gas and oil in the Gulf. Net oil imports in China and India combined are expected to increase from 5.4mbpd in 2006 to 19.1mbpd in 2030. Gulf producers must nearly double production to keep pace with anticipated growth in demand, and these producers will face particular pressure to increase production after 2020 when non-OPEC suppliers are projected to plateau. The EIA projects that Persian Gulf share of worldwide petroleum exports may reach 66% by 2025.[26]

The paradox of the Gulf states' situation is that their continued ability to adapt and mitigate the impact of environmental stresses for their growing population depends upon the functioning of markets that must somehow be artificially restrained if the world is to successfully regulate carbon emissions. This fundamental contradiction lies unaddressed by all the major energy market participants. Both suppliers and consumers of fossil fuels continue to believe that the future will be like the past. That the Gulf states are proceeding down the road of planning their future based on the premise of continued, unrestrained revenue growth is not in question. The recent past suggests their reasons for optimism. Revenues in the region delivered courtesy of the increase in oil prices have resulted in a veritable waterfall of cash into the coffers of these states. According to a recent Kuwaiti economic report, regional oil revenues surged from $364bn in 2007 to $636bn in 2008; aggregate oil revenues may have topped $1.3 trillion in 2008 and 2009.[27]

These revenues are required to allow the regional regimes to continue the environmental mitigation and adaptation efforts upon which their survival and prosperity depends. The future for economic growth and development looks bright in the Gulf states. The region today is among the fastest growing in the world. The Saudi American Bank forecast in June 2008 that GCC economies could expect growth rates of 14 and 15% in 2009 and 2010, with medium-term growth rates into the next decade of at least 8% annually.[28] Contrary to popular perception, while the current boom in the Gulf states is moved inexorably higher by energy markets, non-oil sector growth is an equally important factor in driving the growth in Gulf economies.[29] The GCC has taken steps to open its markets to outside investors over the last decade and is becoming steadily more competitive relative to other global states, according to World Bank figures. The region boasts an estimated $2 trillion in ongoing development projects: $1.3 trillion in construction projects and $266 billion in energy infrastructure represent the main components of these developing economies.[30]

Dubai, once regarded as a model of sustainable economic development, now confronts a landscape littered with half completed highrises after the economic tsunami of 2009 wreaked havoc on its aggressive development projects to position itself as the Monte Carlo of the Middle

Strategy, Foreign Policy and Climate Change

Table 10.3 Gulf State ecological and carbon footprint per person, 2003

Country	Ecological Footprint	Carbon Emissions
Saudi Arabia	4.60	3.43
Iran	2.40	1.52
Iraq	0.90	0.75
Kuwait	7.30	0.29
UAE	11.0	9.06
Qatar	N/A	N/A
Oman	N/A	N/A
Bahrain	N/A	N/A
MENA Avg	2.20	1.36
Global Avg	2.23	1.06

East. The Emirate of Abu Dhabi is pursuing a similar series of fantastical development projects. In early 2008 Abu Dhabi broke ground on a project called Masdar City, a $22bn project to build a 6-square kilometer carbon-free city.[31] Similar aggressive development is proceeding in Doha, fueled by export revenues from the North Dome natural gas field.[32] Other ambitious projects abound throughout the region. Three are plans, for example, to position the region as a leading producer of aluminum in global markets. A series of huge, environmentally unfriendly aluminum smelter projects are underway in Kuwait, Qatar, Oman, and the United Arab Emirates that will boost production to 1.8m. metric tons per year by 2010.[33]

Saudi Arabia has launched aggressive plans to build a series of new cities for its increasing population that will provide housing and jobs. The Saudi Arabian General Investment Authority has launched a massive development plan to build six new cities that it hopes will add $150bn to the nation's economy by 2020; housing for 4.3m. people and 1.3m. jobs. The King Abdullah Economic City, Knowledge Economic City in Medinah, Prince Abdulaziz bin Mousaed Economic City in Hail (500 miles north of Riyadh), Jizan Economic City, and Petro Rabigh represent the cornerstone of the regime's attempts to build an infrastructure that can absorb the bow wave of population growth that will be breaking over the kingdom during the next 30 years.[34]

Unsurprisingly, the rapid economic growth of the last five years has increased the environmental footprint of the region's populations. The World Wildlife Foundation has developed an index to measure the demand a country places on biosphere in terms of the area of biologically productive land and sea required to provide the resources and absorb the waste of the world's population.[35] The index references the number of global hectares used per person for resource consumption in each country (see Table 10.3 above)[36]. The ecological footprint of the region is significantly higher than global averages, particularly in countries like Saudi Arabia and the United Arab Emirates. The figures indicate that the United Arab Emirates boasts the world's largest ecological footprint on a per capita basis, in which each citizen is using a staggering 11.8 hectares for resource consumption and waste absorption.

Environmental vulnerability

The dire projections for the impact of declining access to fresh water are but one component in assessing the cumulative impact of climate change on regional states. Table 10.4 below summarizes the findings from the Center for International Science Information Network at Columbia University that assesses the aggregate vulnerabilities of selected Middle Eastern States over the next 20 years to climate change.

Table 10.4 Middle East environmental vulnerability snapshot[37]

Country	Aggregate Vulnerability Score	Relative Temp. Vul.	Temp. Change	2000 Pop. w/access to annually less than 1000 m3	2030 Pop. w/access to less than 1000 m3	% change	Agricultural productivity impact
Egypt	0.90	Avg.	0.71	66.4	74.8	8.5	Positive
Iraq	1.06	Avg.	0.74	31.5	50.1	18.6	Very serious
Iran	0.96	Avg.	0.83	83.2	90.8	7.6	Serious
Saudi Arabia	0.78	Avg.	0.66	94.1	96.3	2.2	Moderate

Interestingly, the data above does not indicate a "serious" societal vulnerability to projected increases in the world's temperature. While the data shows that in Iran and Saudi Arabia there will be continued significant shortages of potable water, these shortages are not deemed threatening to the social fabric of the societies. Another of the environmental phenomena commonly associated with climate change is the prospect of rising sea levels. Of the four countries above, only Egypt is assessed to suffer significant impact of a rise of between 1 and 3 meters in sea levels. An estimated 10% of Egypt's population (6m. people) would be affected by a 1-meter rise in sea level, with that number increasing to 10m. people by a 3-meter rise.[38] While none of the Gulf states in the sample (Saudi Arabia, Iran and Iraq) are assessed to have significant coastal populations that might be affected by dramatic rises in sea levels that is not true elsewhere in the Gulf. The island nation of Bahrain could lose up to 15 kilometers of coastline with significant increases in sea levels.[39] Moreover, the aggressive development of man-made islands off the coast of Dubai and the land "reclamation" projects in Qatar and Bahrain certainly would become more problematic in the event of rises in sea levels. Low-lying areas in Egypt's Nile River delta, which are among the most agriculturally productive in the country, will also be submerged by significant rises in sea levels.

Regional stability and climate change

Climate change in and of itself does not significantly affect the Middle East, since the region is already one of the hottest, driest places on the planet. Limitations of the physical environment have always proven to be a powerful and systemic factor shaping these societies. As the Gulf societies have moved from agrarian to industrial economies and moved from rural to urban populations, the region's ruling elites have devised sophisticated and expensive means to mitigate and adapt to the systemic limitations imposed upon them by a hostile environment. The environmental adaptive capacities throughout the Gulf states today are the most advanced in the world, although Iraq and Iran have some catching up to do relative to the states of the Arabian Peninsula. Saudi Arabia, for example, has constructed an elaborate adaptive infrastructure at a cost of billions of dollars that has enabled the kingdom to cope with environmental extremes. There is an admitted air of unreality to these measures, that have been taken without regard to cost or common sense. To survive, regional regimes must continue to fund expensive and environmentally unfriendly programs to continue the process. Assuming that these societies can continue their unfettered investments in fresh water development, power generation, housing and economic development these efforts can continue as long as petroleum markets provide revenues that will allow them to do so. Continuing down this path may mitigate the prospect of internal instability. All the Gulf states thus find themselves in a series of difficult contradictions. They all rely on revenues from fossil fuels, which must be limited if the world is to successfully address CO_2 emissions.

The Al Saud is frankly ahead of the rest of the world in its thinking on the impact of climate change and the politics of climate change on its national interests. This is in part due to the fact that Saudi Arabia is already one of the most environmentally inhospitable parts of the planet, and the regime has spent much of the last 50 years investing in arguably the world's best developed climate-related adaptation and mitigation infrastructure. An American football metaphor illustrates the Al Saud's approach. At a time when the rest of the world still has yet to arrange a huddle to call plays, the Al Saud is already positioned in a prevent defense on the issue of climate change (a strategy to prevent the "hail mary" touchdown pass with the recognition that the defense is prepared to give up the short pass and the run up the middle).

This approach to the politics of climate change has earned them the ire of environmental groups, who, in 2006 rated Saudi Arabia as the worst country in the world at addressing climate change.[40] At the December 2007 United Nations conference on climate change held in Bali, environmental groups labeled Saudi Arabia as the "fossil of the day" for its reluctance to support the global climate change talks.[41] The Saudi approach to the issue seems encapsulated, on the one hand, by King Abdullah's announcement in November 2007 that the kingdom would spend $300m. to support climate change research, and, on the other, by the simultaneous announcement that Prince Alaweel bin Abdulaziz al Saud was spending $300m. for an Airbus 380 flying palace.

Saudi Arabia, the USA, and China have united over the last eight years to water down findings of the Intergovernmental Panel on Climate Change.[42] The Saudi approach to the issue has been perhaps best articulated by Saudi oil minister Ali bin Abrahim al-Naimi, who, in objecting to attempts in the industrialized world to restrain gasoline demand through higher taxes, told the United Nations General Assembly in September 2007 that "Those industrialized nations are imposing more high taxes which are ... providing direct and indirect aid for the industries of coal and nuclear energy which are the most polluting sources of climate and the global environment ... This affects growth rates in the world for demanding oil in the coming period and contributes to the negative impact on the march of development in our country." Naimi added that "The call for moving away from fossil fuel consumption as a way to address climate change is not a viable alternative. I can assure you that through the use of technology solutions the world can continue to rely on oil."[43]

The Al-Saud family fears not the impact of climate change on their own physical environs that will change little if the world continues to heat up, but they do foresee disaster in the politics and policies of climate change as the international community starts to grapple with the problem. The Saudi and Gulf state nightmare is global agreement on a system of market distorting forces that produce two outcomes: (1) a reduced demand for energy; (2) demands that energy producers shoulder the costs for states that lack the resources to implement climate-related adaptation and mitigation measures.

This is a strategy to hold off for as long as possible a system of global carbon taxes and/or mechanisms to spread the costs of adaptation and mitigation to climate change. The Al Saud and their colleagues around the region look upon this outcome as inevitable, but the longer they can avoid dipping into their own pockets as part of the market distorting measures, the better off they will be in building up their own environmental adaptation and mitigation efforts. The Al Saud is motivated by economic self-interest in this matter and, more broadly, by the recognition that the kingdom depends upon increasing amounts of cash to cope with the traditional sources of instability that confront it: population growth, urbanization, unemployment, lack of fresh water, and disruptive social movements that could spring from Saudi urban centers, to name but a few.

The Al Saud and the other Gulf state ruling families have ruled their country and paid close attention to a series of domestic stakeholders in cementing their hold on their respective countries. In Saudi Arabia, these stakeholders include the extended royal family; the religious establishment; the merchants of the Hijaz; the new caste of dissident religious clerics that wield influence in the Nejd; Shias in the eastern provinces, which are still second class citizens in the kingdom; tribal and clan leaders throughout the peninsula that have been indirectly integrated into the familial structure via marriage. Each of these stakeholders benefits in various ways from the system of economic and political patronage that characterizes the internal system of governance in the kingdom.

Internally, each family in the Gulf states has constructed an elaborate system of political patronage and wealth redistribution in the form of free education, cheap gas and electricity and government jobs for a mostly underemployed male population. Continued economic growth built on the continued expansion of world demand for energy provides the means for them to continue this "rentier" system that keeps their friends happy and co-opts and buys off potential internal opponents.

The Saudis and the Gulf state partners greatly fear the impact that climate change could have on the orderly functioning of global markets for petroleum and they fear that the politics of the issue may result in market distorting forces. Both issues could lead to a drop in revenue and mitigate the regime's ability to address traditional risk sources.

Second order effects of climate change

The stresses stem not from the environment per se, but from the regime's ability to continue the process of adaptation and mitigation to an already stressed environment. If the regimes can't continue to produce this artificial construct, the basis of the internal "rents" system becomes unglued since domestic constituencies can no longer be bought off and co-opted. In such a scenario, the regional regimes devolve down to Mukhabarat (police states), the consequences of which could be catastrophic for the regimes over the long term. In Saudi Arabia, the most serious near term political threat that could be energized by market disrupting forces are the dissident populist clerics that are operating outside the confines of the government sanctioned religious establishment. This group is highly xenophobic, virulently anti-Shia, and virulently anti-Western.

This analysis suggests that regional security will not be seriously threatened by climate change per se in the period to 2030, assuming that climate change or other factors lead to no systemic changes in international energy markets. Climate change impacts are not forecast to gather forceful momentum until the second half of the 21st century. The Al Saud and other regional regimes above all seek to ensure the security of the family and their continued political and economic ascendance. As previously indicated, we can expect all the Gulf state regime leaders to act with alacrity in managing threats to the state that stem from market distorting forces. As long as the world demand for energy continues on its inexorable path, regional regimes are provided with the means to stave off stresses to the state stemming from environmental and climate-related forces.

Here, however, it is worth noting that the climate models do not account for disruptive, cascading events that can dramatically alter orderly political and economic interaction between and among global actors. In other words, the cumulative impact of climate change may produce unanticipated incremental changes that can materialize into much more serious problems. Surprises happen. Climate change will affect economic development around the world and will make it more difficult for various states, particularly in Asia, to sustain a predictable path of economic development. The continued economic expansion in Asia is vitally important to Saudi Arabia as a source for its oil exports.

The analysis here is that the latent reserves of social and political resilience are proportionate to latent reserves of oil and natural gas. If the oil runs out or if markets fundamentally change due either to a sustained global economic slowdown or to successful energy demand mitigation efforts around the world, it is doubtful that today's residents of the Gulf will willingly and peacefully return to the Bedouin-type existence of their ancestors (a way of life that coped with the extreme environment before oil was discovered). The Saudis hope this will never happen, and their hope seems justified. The US Geologic Survey estimates that the kingdom may have as much as 1 trillion barrels in recoverable reserves of all kinds of oil. No amount of demand mitigation measures will dry up the world's thirst for oil.

It is unlikely that Saudi Arabia, for example, will ever be a preferred destination for migrants or refugees of any kind, unless they are perhaps Muslim religious refugees fleeing persecution. This is not necessarily the case in the more socially relaxed Gulf states such as Bahrain, Qatar and the United Arab Emirates. In the United Arab Emirates and Qatar, for example, foreign nationals already outnumber the host nation nationals. Saudi vulnerability stems from the functions of international energy markets and the faith, or lack thereof, in these markets. This is a phenomenon that could be described as the "militarization of energy security," a situation in which states lose confidence in markets to deliver mean reversion in energy pricing. Alternatively, states judge that successively higher cost plateaus in energy pricing are unacceptable, weighting the cost-benefit calculus on the use of force towards using force. Such a scenario is not difficult to imagine if "peak oil" becomes a reality or if the world's advanced states decide that successively increasing prices of oil are politically and economically unacceptable. In such an environment, the Gulf states, and most particularly Saudi Arabia, become subjected to intimidation and coercion by advanced states. I argue here that the potential of armed aggression directed at Saudi Arabia stems not from climate-related issues but from a loss of confidence in international energy markets.

Foreign policy implications

All states in the Middle East face profound environmental stresses over the coming decades. But it must be stated that the regional regimes are reasonably experienced at dealing with these stresses with their elaborate and expensive mitigation and adaptation efforts. For example, the region is heavily investing in new fresh water capacity to address its shortfalls and prepare for the population growth that is expected over the next several decades. Unlike the oil wealth explosion of the early 1980s, this time the regional states are heavily investing in development projects at home to build their infrastructures to ensure some form of sustainable development.

Despite these prudent steps, however, the regional regimes all remain vulnerable to fluctuations in global energy markets. A sudden drop in global demand for energy or a sustained drop in energy prices will negatively affect their ability to continue their mitigation and adaptation efforts. The global politics of climate change threaten to change the dynamics of international energy markets in ways that redound to the disadvantage of the Gulf state producers. They will thus continue to publicly embrace "green" development policies at home while joining together with other states to forestall a global system that will limit emissions and, hence, demand for energy. Moreover, they will seek to avoid schemes that distribute their wealth to the lesser developed world to pay for the climate-related mitigation and adaptation efforts that they themselves have build their modern societies around. Any global system that comprehensively addresses climate change will have to incorporate the needs and interests of the energy producing states in the Gulf.

As previously noted, regional regimes will seek to mitigate developments in global politics that distort the functioning of international energy markets. To do this, the regimes must engage with a variety of international actors around the world, both states and international organizations. This engagement is necessary to pursue their strategy of forestalling the development of market distorting forces and delaying being placed in the position of paying for adaptation and mitigation costs elsewhere. They are amenable to Western interests as a function of maintaining good customer relations with a group of countries that also possess not insignificant military capacities that are useful to the kingdom. The Saudis have assiduously avoided offending their erstwhile protector (the USA) and they have in parallel built close political relationships with established European states both as a counter to US hegemony and another source of protection against external threats. There is no reason to suggest that the Al Saud will alter and/or change this approach over the forecast period, unless revolution from within topples the House of Al Saud, replacing it with some kind of populist Islamic figure.

For the USA, the long-range challenges of climate change in the region are significant. When layered upon an already unstable region, environmental stresses promise to add another complicating factor to US policy makers in this strategically vital region. Unfortunately, the USA shows no inclination to think and plan strategically on these or any other foreign policy issues. The collapse of the 2009 United Nations Climate Change Conference in Copenhagen illustrated the inability of the US to take a leadership position on climate change. The lack of leadership on climate change and other global issues stems from many sources. First and perhaps most important is America's fractious domestic politics, which has seen the breakdown of the centrist political consensus that drove foreign and domestic policy for most of the post-World War II era. The polarization of American domestic politics has burst apart this centrist coalition and its realist-oriented foreign policy and has yet to be replaced by anything else with political and strategic coherence. Neither the Obama nor the Bush Administrations conducted a foreign policy based on sound realist strategic principles and both appeared strategically and intellectually confused about how to define, further, and protect America's global interests and objectives.

Seizing a global leadership position on climate change issues is symptomatic of the strategic fog shrouding US global strategy and policy that is felt acutely in the Middle East. The situation calls for strong and purposeful US global leadership that can be used as the basis to initiate policies that will start slowing the dumping of carbon into the atmosphere. The oil exporting states of the Middle East must play a central role in addressing this problem and their needs and interests must somehow be figured into the global solution. That is less likely to happen without strong US leadership that has to date been lacking. The world must hope that the USA awakes from its strategic and intellectual torpor to seize the mantle of leadership on climate change that the world wants and needs. Only if and when this happens can the Middle Eastern states and the international community begin to start building policies that will address the systemic challenge posed by climate change throughout the region.

Notes

* The views in this paper are those of the author and do not represent the views and positions of the Naval Postgraduate School.

1 List drawn from Mostafa K. Tolba and Najib W. Saab, Eds., *Arab Environment Climate Change: Impact of Climate Change on Arab Countries* (Beirut: Arab Forum for Environment and Development, 2009); Jeannie Sowers and Erika Weinthal, "Climate Change Adaptation in the Middle East and North

Africa," Working Paper No. 2, The Dubai Initiative, September 2010; Oli Brown and Alec Crawford, "Rising Temperatures, Rising Tensions: Climate Change and the Risk of Violent Conflict in the Middle East," International Institute for Sustainable Development, Winnipeg, Manitoba, Canada, 2009.
2 As reported by Samir Al Saadi, "Kingdom to Carry Out Another Cloud Seeding Experiment," *Arab News,* June 3, 2008 at www.arabnews.com/?page=1&section=0&article=110547&d=3&m=6&y=2008
3 Nermina Biberovic, "Water and Agriculture Issues in the Gulf," Gulf Research Center, Dubai.
4 United Nations Education, Scientific and Cultural Organization, *The State of the Resource,* 132–35, at www.unesco.org/water/wwap/wwdr/wwdr2/pdf/wwdr2_ch_4.pdf
5 *Water Hazard Risks,* United Nations-Water Series, Vol. 1, January 2005, at www.unwater.org/downloads/unwaterseries.pdf
6 See Synthesis of the Fourth World Water Forum, Mexico City, September 2006 at www.worldwatercouncil.org/fileadmin/wwc/World_Water_Forum/WWF4/synthesis_sept06.pdf
7 *Making the Most of Scarcity: Accountability for Better Water Management Results in the Middle East and North Africa,* The World Bank (Washington, DC: 2007) 5; online at http://web.worldbank.org/WBSITE/EXTERNAL/COUNTRIES/MENAEXT/0,contentMDK:21244687~pagePK:146736~piPK:146830~theSitePK:256299,00.html
8 / 9 As exhaustively detailed in Mohamed A. Dawoud, "Water Scarcity in the GCC Countries," Research Paper, Gulf Research Center, Dubai, 2007.
10 Ibid.
11 Jon B. Alterman and Michael Dziuban, "Clear Gold: Water as a Strategic Resource in the Middle East," Center for Strategic and International Studies, Washington, DC, December 2010.
12 Ibid.
13 Ibid.
14 Mohamed Bazza, "Policies for Water Management and Food Security Under Water Scarcity Conditions: The Case of the GCC Countries," paper presented at the 7th Gulf Water Conference organized by the Water Science and Technology Association, Kuwait 19–23 November 2005.
15 *Making the Most of Scarcity,* World Bank, op. cit. 12.
16 Andrew England, "Water Fears Lead Saudis to End Grain Output," *Financial Times,* February 27 2008; online at www.ft.com/cms/s/f02c1e94-e4d6-11dc-a495-0000779fd2ac,Authorised=false.html?_i_location=http%3A%2F%2Fwww.ft.com%2Fcms%2Fs%2F0%2Ff02c1e94-e4d6-11dc-a495-0000779fd2ac.html%3Fnclick_check%3D1&_i_referer=&nclick_check = 1
17 As posted in Marianne Lavelle, "Beyond the Barrel," May 21, 2008, *US News & World Report*; online at www.usnews.com/blogs/beyond-the-barrel/2008/05/21/forget-saudi-peak-oil-worry-about-peak-grain.html
18 Details drawn from Craig Smith, "Al Kharj Journal: Milk Flows From Desert at Unique Saudi Farm," *New York Times,* December 31, 2002; online at http://query.nytimes.com/gst/fullpage.html?res=9A07E2DC153FF932A05751C1A9649C8B63
19 Phil Dickie, *Making Water,* World Wildlife Fund Freshwater Programme, World Wildlife Fund, June 2007.
20 Javid Hassan, "Kingdom Leads in Desalination, But Needs More to Meet Demand," Arab News, March 22, 2006; online at www.arabnews.com/?page=1&section=0&article=79565&d=22&m=3&y=2006
21 Details at "Veolia Awarded Huge Desalinization Contract in Saudi Arabia," posted at http://media.cleantech.com/1392/veolia-awarded-huge-desalination-contr
22 Mariam al Hakeem, "Saudis Consider $5.3 Billion Water Project," *Gulf News,* December 24, 2006; online at http://archive.gulfnews.com/articles/06/12/24/10091822.html
23 Meena Janardhan, "Water Day-Gulf: Forced to Look Beyond Desalinization Plants," Inter Press Service News Agency, March 21, 2007; online at http://ipsnews.net/news.asp?idnews=37013.
24 World Population Prospects: The 2006 Revision Population Database, The United Nations; online at http://esa.un.org/unpp/
25 International Energy Outlook 2008, Energy Information Administration, Department of Energy, Washington DC; online at www.eia.doe.gov/oiaf/ieo/highlights.html
26 Ibid.
27 John Isaac, "UAE Oil Income May Hit $110B," *Khaleej Times Online,* June 22, 2008 at www.khaleejtimes.com/DisplayArticle.asp?xfile=data/business/2008/June/business_June706.xml&section=business&col=
28 *GCC Economic Outlook,* Saudi American Bank (SAMBA), Riyadh, Saudi Arabia, June 2008; online at www.samba.com/GblDocs/GCC_Economic_Outlook1_jun2008_eng.pdf
29 Ibid.

30 Ibid. 9.
31 Abu Dhabi Masdar Initiative Breaks Ground on Carbon-Neutral City, PR Newswire, February 9, 2008.
32 For a summary of the largest of these regional projects see SAMBA report above, Appendix 1, Selected GCC Projects, May 2008, 18
33 "Gulf States Plan Higher Aluminum Output," *Engineering and Mining Journal*, September 2004; online at http://findarticles.com/p/articles/mi_qa5382/is_200409/ai_n21357315?tag=untagged
34 Jad Mouawad, "The Construction Site Called Saudi Arabia," *New York Times*, January 20, 2008 at www.nytimes.com/2008/01/20/business/worldbusiness/20saudi.html; Raid Qusti, "Saudi Arabia to Build Two More Economic Cities This Year," *Arab News*, April 27, 2009 at www.arabnews.com/?page=6&section=0&article=95554&d=29&m=4&y=2007
35 Living Planet Report 2006, World Wildlife Fund, 14. The WWF defines the footprint as follows: "The footprint of a country includes all the cropland, grazing land, forest, and fishing grounds required to produce the food, fibre and timber it consumes, to absorb the wastes emitted in generating its energy uses, and to provide space for its infrastructure. People consume resources and ecological services from all over the world, so their footprint is the sum of these areas, wherever they may be on the planet."
36 Living Planet Report 2006, World Wildlife Fund, 30.
37 Data drawn from model on anticipated climate change by year 2030 prepared by Dr. Marc Levy and the Center for International Earth Science Information Network at Columbia University.
38 CIESN data
39 Mohamed A. Raouf, "Climate Change Threats, Opportunities, and the GCC Countries," *The Middle East Institute Policy Brief No. 12*, April 2008.
40 "US, Saudi, China Rank Among Worst on Climate Change: Group," Agence France Presse, November 14, 2006. The report by the German environmental group Germanwatch rated Sweden as best, with the USA, China and Saudi Arabia at the bottom of the heap.
41 "Saudi Arabia Tops the Roll of Dishonour," One World Net, December 5, 2007 at http://uk.oneworld.net/article/view/155885/1/
42 As noted in "Billions Face Climate Change Risk," *BBC News* April 6, 2007 at http://news.bbc.co.uk/2/hi/science/nature/6532323.stm
43 Remarks as reported in Andrew Leonard, "Don't Cry for Saudi Arabia," *Salon.com*, September 27, 2007 at www.salon.com/tech/htww/2007/09/27/saudi_arabia_oil/

11

Do Governments Need to Go to War for Oil?

*David R. Henderson**

Introduction

In his book, *The Age of Turbulence*, Alan Greenspan wrote:

> I am saddened that it is politically inconvenient to acknowledge what everyone knows: the Iraq war is largely about oil.[1]

He made clear, in a later interview with broadcaster Charlie Rose, that he wasn't simply saying that many people's motive for the war was oil, but also that that motive made sense. Greenspan gave no evidence for his assertion. But in making it, he confirmed the views of many opponents of the war, and even some supporters, that the 2003 war on Iraq was, or at least should have been, about oil. He also joined a long list of prominent people who have made the case for war for oil ever since the Organization of Petroleum Exporting Countries (OPEC) formed an effective cartel that raised the world price from $3 per barrel to $11 per barrel in the fall of 1973.

Yet the case for "war for oil" is profoundly weak. The pragmatic case against war for oil, which rests on basic economic analysis, is fundamentally strong. This case rests on a few facts. First, no oil-producing country, no matter what it does to its oil supply, can cause people in another country to line up for gasoline. Second, an oil-producing country cannot impose a selective embargo on a target country because oil is sold in a world market. Third, the only way a country's government can hurt another country using the "oil weapon" is by cutting output; doing so will hurt all oil consumers (not just the target country), will help all oil producers, friend and foe alike, and will hurt the country that cuts its output.

"War for oil" threats

Before I make the case against war for oil, consider how long many people in the foreign policy establishment has taken as given the idea that the US government needs to use military force to keep the world supply of oil flowing.

In March 1975, *Harper's Magazine* published an article, "Seizing Arab Oil," authored by "Miles Ignotus." The author's name, explained *Harper's*, "is the pseudonym of a Washington-based professor and defense consultant with intimate links to high-level US policy makers." The author expressed frustration at the high price of oil and argued that no non-violent means of breaking the cartel's back would work. Even massive conservation, he argued, was unlikely to solve the problem. Moreover, he claimed, "there is absolutely no reason to expect major new discoveries." So what options were left, according to "Ignotus"? He wrote:

> The goal is not just to seize some oil (say, in accessible Nigeria or Venezuela) but to break OPEC. Thus, force must be used selectively to occupy large and concentrated oil reserves, which can be produced rapidly in order to end the artificial scarcity of oil and thus cut the price. Faced with armed consumers occupying vast oil fields whose full output can eventually bring the price down to 50 cents per barrel, most of the producers would see virtue in agreeing to a price four or five times as high, but still six times lower than present prices. This being the ultimate goal, there is one feasible target: Saudia Arabia.

Ignotus's article, though one of the most articulate, was far from the only call in the USA for a US invasion of a Middle East oil country. Of course, no such US invasion occurred in the 1970s. Nevertheless, Ignotus's kind of extreme thinking made respectable the idea that the US government should seriously consider invading countries in the Persian Gulf to drive down the price, or assure the supply, of oil.

On January 1, 1975, just two months before Ignotus's article appeared, Secretary of State Henry Kissinger had stated[2] that military force should not be used "in the case of a dispute over price," but should be considered "where there is some actual strangulation of the industrialized world." Kissinger did not say what he meant by "strangulation." In May of that year, Secretary of Defense James R. Schlesinger made further threatening noises.[3]

Indeed, in 1977 President Jimmy Carter issued an order for the US military to start a Rapid Deployment Force. The idea of such a force was to give the government the ability to quickly send a substantial invasion force to various parts of the world. After the fall of the Shah of Iran in 1979, the Rapid Deployment Force became focused on the Persian Gulf. In 1983, during the Reagan administration's tenure, this Rapid Deployment Force became known as the US Central Command (CENTCOM). The cost of this force, even in years of relative peace, has been high. Although the US government tends to hide the cost of various programs, making it hard for analysts, let alone average citizens, to know these costs, one analyst, Earl Ravenal, estimated that the fiscal year 1985 budget for CENTCOM at US$59bn,[4] $47 billion of which, he claimed, was for the Persian Gulf alone. At the time, that amounted to a full 1% of the USA's GDP. To put that $47bn in perspective, in today's dollars, it would be $94bn.

Finally, of course, the US government initiated the first Gulf war at least partly over oil. President George Bush, snr, stated that his military action in the Persian Gulf was partly about "access to energy resources that are key … to the entire world." Bush claimed that if Saddam Hussein had gotten greater control of oil reserves in the Middle East, he would have been able to threaten "our jobs" and "our way of life."[5] James A. Baker III, Secretary of State at the time, claimed that Saddam Hussein, by controlling much of the world's oil, "could strangle the global economic order, determining by that whether we all enter a recession, or even the darkness of a depression."[6] And the ever-present Henry Kissinger wrote[7] that an unchecked Saddam Hussein would be able to "cause a worldwide economic crisis."

Yet the advocates of war for oil have never confronted some basic economic realities. Economists are often criticized for their pessimism, but an understanding of how oil markets work leads, not to pessimism, but to optimism about a secure oil supply.

Do Governments Need to Go to War for Oil?

No price controls, no line-ups

When many Americans over the age of 50 worry about Middle East producers playing havoc with the world oil supply, they think back to the gasoline line-ups that we had in the USA in 1973 and 1979. But no cut in supply by a foreign producer can cause us to line up for gasoline. The organization responsible for that fiasco was the US government. President Nixon had imposed a freeze on all prices on August 15, 1971. He gradually relaxed controls on prices, but when OPEC raised the price in the fall of 1973, Nixon's price controls prevented the price of oil and gasoline from rising sufficiently. Whatever else economists may disagree on, one thing they agree on is that a price control that keeps the price below that which would have otherwise existed in a competitive market will cause a shortage. The reason is that at a price below the competitive price, consumers will demand more than otherwise and producers will supply less. President Ford and Congress altered the price controls and President Carter inherited them and kept them. Although Carter did, in 1980, sign legislation to phase out price controls, a tightening of world oil supplies in 1979 combined with the price controls to cause further shortages. The good news is that since then the US government and most governments around the world have refrained from imposing price controls. The result has been that people in those governments' countries have not had to queue for gasoline.

The impotence of selective embargoes: musical chairs with everyone seated

To say that a reduction in the supply of oil cannot cause a shortage is not to say that it cannot cause harm. In any country where the amount of oil consumed exceeds the amount produced, that is, any country that is a net importer of oil, a rise in the price will cause more harm, measured in dollars, to consumers than the gain in dollars that it provides to domestic producers. But the key is that the supply must fall. If the supply of oil does not fall, nothing important changes.

Imagine that the government of country A currently sells oil to people in country B and wishes to harm people in country B by refusing to sell to country B or by reducing sales to country B. What happens next depends crucially on whether government A cuts its own oil production or maintains its production. Assume that government A maintains its production. This means that government A must look around for people in other countries to sell the suddenly-freed-up oil to. To make the issue more concrete, consider the case of the USA. In August 2010, as Table 11.1 shows, the five most important exporters of oil to the USA, in order of importance, were Canada, Mexico, Saudi Arabia, Venezuela, and Nigeria. Total imports from these countries were 56% of US imports. Of these five, the one most likely to want to hurt the USA currently is Venezuela or, more accurately, Venezuela's government under Hugo Chávez. Interestingly, Chávez has done the exact opposite, actually subsidizing oil exports to favored groups in north-eastern parts of the USA.[8] But imagine the worst: imagine that Chávez wants to target the USA using the "oil weapon." So he cuts sales to the USA by about one-half, or 500,000 barrels per day. Then consumers in the USA get 500,000 barrels a day fewer than they wish to buy. They will look for other sources of oil. Where will they find them? Remember that Chávez needs to find people in other countries to sell this freed-up 500,000 barrels a day to. Let's say he ships the oil to buyers in China. Then those buyers in China will find that they want to buy 500,000 fewer barrels from their suppliers, say Iraq or Saudi Arabia. Presto! The American buyers' problems are solved because they can get their 500,000 barrels from Iraq or Saudi Arabia. In short, when the government of one country tries

Table 11.1 Top 15 Sources of US Oil Imports, August 2010 (mbpd)

Canada	2,483
Mexico	1,282
Saudi Arabia	1,132
Venezuela	1,022
Nigeria	985
Russia	786
Algeria	565
Angola	484
Colombia	372
Virgin Islands	339
Iraq	281
United Kingdom	266
Brazil	251
Kuwait	251
Ecuador	242
Total of All Imports	12,341

Source: US Energy Information Administration

to selectively target people in another country, but still wishes to maintain its output, it cannot succeed. The selective "oil weapon" is a dud. It's like a game of musical chairs with the same number of chairs as players. The game would be awfully boring, which is why it is not played that way. But in the case of international trade, boring is good.

There are three complications in this musical chairs story, none of which changes the bottom line. First, it is unlikely that the government of Venezuela, or of any country, would maintain output simply by selling the freed-up output to people in only one other country. It is also unlikely that people in the targeted country would get supplies from producers in only two other countries. But that complication doesn't change the conclusion. Second, one main reason for the particular pattern of oil exports and imports was probably transportation costs. An oil user in New Orleans is more likely to buy from Venezuela than from Iran because the cost of shipping from Venezuela is so much lower than the cost of shipping from Iran. It follows, therefore, that when a country's government disrupts this pattern by cutting off oil supplies to a nearby country, transportation costs rise. The higher transportation cost acts like an excise tax, the burden of which is typically shared by the buyers and sellers. The disrupting government would be hurt by having to accept a somewhat lower price from a more-distant buyer. The people in the disrupted country would be hurt by having to pay a somewhat higher transportation cost to get their oil. But the maximum hurt in either case would be no more than the difference in transport costs and this would be a small number, probably under $2 per barrel. For the hypothetical 500,000-barrel production cut, therefore, the maximum hurt to US consumers would be $1m. dollars per day or $365m. per year, a very small number. To put this in perspective, it is about $1.20 per year per US resident. The third complication relates to Venezuela specifically. Venezuela's crude oil is heavy and sour. Many refiners around the world can't handle Venezuela's oil, which means that Venezuela, in the short run, is stuck selling its oil to the USA.

The economics of a reduction in supply

Of course, a government of an oil-producing country can do substantial harm to the people of another country by cutting the amount of oil it produces and sells. I use the word "government" on purpose for two reasons. First, outside Canada, the USA, and Britain, almost all the world's oil is produced by governments. Second, restricting supply, to have a substantial effect, would have to be done by a government. The reason is that even the biggest private producer in an oil-producing country has too small an output relative to world output to have a substantial effect on the world oil price.

Any government that wants to hurt a particular country by reducing its oil supply faces three huge problems. First, an oil producer cannot single out particular countries or consumers to hurt. If one oil producer cuts supply, then, all other things equal, the world oil supply is lower than otherwise and the price will be higher. All oil consumers are hurt and their hurt is proportional to the amount of oil they use. Thus the "oil weapon" is an incredibly blunt tool that, when used, will hurt friend and foe alike. Second, the oil-producing country, by cutting output, will cause the world price of oil to rise, which will help other oil producing countries that don't reduce their supply. So, for example, if Iran's government chose to reduce its supply of oil to hurt the USA, it would also help its avowed enemy, Saudi Arabia. Not only is oil an incredibly blunt weapon, therefore, but also, when used, it strengthens some of one's foes.

Third and finally, to continue with the weapon analogy, the oil weapon blows up in its user's face. Specifically, any country that produces less than about 10% of the world supply will find that the price increase it gets will not compensate for the reduction in revenues due to lower production.

On this third point, consider the case of Saddam Hussein in 1990. When he took over Kuwait, he controlled oil production of 4.3mbpd in a 60mbpd market. His motive for taking over Kuwait was probably not, as Kissinger, Baker, and George H.W. Bush feared, to cut output and increase the price at all, but simply to have more oil to sell. A thief does not steal a television set to watch TV; instead he steals a TV to fence it. Similarly, an oil thief wants to steal oil to sell it.

Nevertheless, imagine that Saddam Hussein, wanting to hurt the USA, had cut output by 1mbpd. (You have to use your imagination here because Saddam was a US ally.) This would have been 23% of 4.3mbpd, but only 1.7% of world output. A reasonable estimate of the world's short-run elasticity of demand for oil is −0.1. What that means is that a 10% reduction in world output leads to a 10% increase in price. Therefore a 1.7% reduction in output would have caused a 17% increase in price, raising the world price from about $20 per barrel to about $23.40 per barrel. The harm to the USA, which had been importing about 8mbpd at the time, would have been $27m. per day (8mbpd x $3.40), or $9.9bn per year. At the time, this would have been less than 0.2% of US GDP. Note also that even with this $3.40 per barrel increase, Saddam Hussein's revenues would have been lower than had he not cut output at all. He would have brought in $77m. per day (3.3mbpd x $23.40) or $28.2bn a year, but had he not cut output, he would have brought in $86m. per day (4.3mbpd x $20), or $9m. per day more, which, on an annual basis is 4.3mbpd x $20, or $32.4bn. It's true that by producing less, Hussein would also have had lower costs. So let's bias the analysis in favor of his getting a gain from cutting output by assuming that the cost of oil production for the last 1mbpd was $5 per barrel, a number that virtually all observers would regard as being on the high side. Then his cut in output would have saved him $5m. per day. So he would have given up $9m. per day in revenue to save $5m. per day, which would not have been a good deal for him. In short, there is good reason to think that if Saddam Hussein had been as ruthless as he appeared to be, he would have wanted to cut output by less than 1mbpd, or maybe even not at all.

Of course, 1mbpd is less than 4.3mbpd. Therefore the estimated damage from the hypothetical 1mbpd cut in oil output by Saddam Hussein is well below the actual damage done to the USA by the United Nations' 1990–91 restrictions on output from Iraq and Kuwait, restrictions for which the US government was a key instigator.

Moreover, even these estimates of hurt are overstated. Why? Because producers in other countries do not sit passively by when the price of oil rises. When the price increases, producers produce more. This is for two main reasons. First, to the extent producers expect the price increase to be temporary, they will produce more quickly from existing reserves. Second, there are some sources of supply that weren't worth exploiting at the previous lower price but are worth exploiting at a higher price. This increased production from other producers moderates the price increase from a given producer's cut in output, further limiting the damage that can be done to countries, such as the USA, that are net importers of oil. It is interesting to note, in this context, that within months of the 1990 UN embargo, other producers, by increasing their output in response to the higher price, had made up for most of the supply lost.[9]

An aside on "dependence" on foreign oil

Many people worry about the fact that the US is dependent on foreign oil. But the basis for the worry is lacking. First, notice the use of the word "dependent." The image that creates is of a poor, helpless waif, US consumers in this case, seeking the good will of the powerful oil producing nations. When I hear the term "dependent," I think of the character in the musical, *Oliver*, saying meekly, "Please, sir, I want some more." But a little economics is needed here. Remember that international trade in oil is just that: trade. Both sides gain from trade. Both sides, therefore, are dependent on each other. As the above calculations show, if one side decides not to export to the other, that side loses too. Producers of oil "depend" on the dollars, euros, and yen that buy that oil. This fact is commonly recognized when the topic is US exports; many Americans worry that we don't export enough because they want our exporters to earn money from people in other countries. But somehow this simple fact gets lost when the topic is exporters of oil in the Middle East or Venezuela. "Dependence on foreign oil," because it is so one-sidedly misleading, is a term that belongs in the dustbin of history.

The resilience of modern economies to oil price increases

One important economic fact that many people remember from the 1970s is the presence of "stagflation," that is, the simultaneous occurrence of inflation and stagnation or slow growth. Even many economists at the time believed that a major cause of this stagnation was higher prices of oil and gasoline. Yet more recent research[10] by economists Rajeev Dhawan of Georgia State University and Karsten Jeske of the Federal Reserve Bank of Atlanta has shown this belief to be false. There is no doubt that a net importer of oil will suffer a loss when the price of an import rises. So, for example, if the USA imports 6mbpd, as it did in 1973, and the price of oil rises by $9, the loss to the US economy (assuming Americans do not own shares in any of the foreign companies that export to the US) is $54m. per day or about $19.7bn per year. In 1973, GDP was $1,383bn, which means that the price increase of oil should have made GDP $19.7bn, or 1.4%, less than otherwise. In an economy whose normal growth rate of real GDP was 2 to 3%, this 1.4% drop would not have been enough to cause a recession and stagflation. Why, then, did economic growth fall by substantially more than 1.4% in the early 1970s, putting the US economy into a deep recession?

The added cause, according to Dhawan and Jeskie, was price controls. Price controls on any good, imported or domestic, will cause not only a shortage, but also a misallocation. Without price controls, the goods go to their highest-valued uses. When price controls are in place, the good is allocated more randomly, either by line-ups, government fiat, or both. In the case of gasoline, it was both. Price controls on gasoline caused people to line up for it. That meant that it tended to go to those with the lowest value of time, such as students or retirees, rather than to those who valued the good most. In such a case, there are two economic losses: the loss in valuable time for all who line up and the loss due to misallocation of the good. When government steps in to allocate, as the federal government did in the 1970s, the good tends to go disproportionately to those with more political pull rather than to those who value it most. Also no central planners, however brilliant and well-intentioned they are, can know the highest-valued uses when there are literally millions of uses and users. So, for example, the federal government decided to allocate gasoline based on historical allocation. If 90% of the previous year's gasoline were available, the government required gasoline refineries to sell 90% of last year's sales to each location. This meant that expanding suburbs went without and that rural areas, where people had traveled a lot the previous year because they had been confident of getting supplies, got too much. Americans in short, got to experience a little Sovietization of the US economy. An analysis that omits the substantial costs of misallocation by waiting and misallocation by central planning is incomplete.

Certainly Dhawan's and Jeske's evidence is consistent with experience in the economies that have avoided price controls on oil. For example, despite huge price increases on oil since 2002, economic growth in the USA, which imports even a higher percentage of its oil than it did in the 1970s, remained strong. Oil prices increased from an average of $23.78 (inflation-adjusted to 2006) in 2002 to an average of $58.30 in 2006,[11] an increase of 145%. Yet during that same time, annual US economic growth averaged 3.2%, which is at the high end of the normal range of growth rates.

Other cases for war for oil

I have dealt with the main argument most people make for going to war over oil, namely to ensure the continued supply of oil rather than a reduction. But are there other grounds for war for oil? There appear to be four other cases.

The first is increased supply. In all of the analysis so far, I took as given that the amount of oil produced in a given country does not depend on who produces it. But that assumption flies in the face of so much of what we know about socialism versus free markets. Socialism is high-cost, uninnovative, and inefficient, whereas production by private firms tends to be innovative and efficient. And the simple fact is that about 90% of the world's oil is produced under socialism, that is, government ownership. As *The Economist* noted recently,[12] Exxon Mobil, which, in early August 2006, was the world's most valuable listed company, with a market capitalization of $412bn, was only 14th in the world when measured by the amount of oil left in reserves. The 13 "companies" above it were all government owned. Number one among these was Saudi Aramco, number two was the National Iranian Oil Company, and so on through the list that included Russia's Gazprom, Venezuela's PDVSA, and Nigeria's National Petroleum Corporation. The article noted just how inefficient government oil producers are and highlighted Venezuela's PDVSA as an example, partly due to actions taken by President Hugo Chávez since he came to power in 1999. So if the US government took over a socialist oil bureaucracy and sold it to a private for-profit firm, the supply of oil could increase due to increased efficiency.

But even one who agrees with the above facts about the inefficiency of government production would not then necessarily be driven to believe in war. The only legitimate case for war, in my view, is to repel a foreign invasion of the homeland or to prevent an imminent such invasion. But I state the case because it is certainly one that some people could make. Again, though, one would have to consider the costs of war to weigh against these benefits. The obvious costs of an invasion to establish privatization—the slogan isn't exactly ringing—are the substantial costs of arming, feeding, and supporting a substantial military. Moreover, there could be unintended consequences. People in the country invaded could well be upset about the invasion and could sabotage production so that the hoped-for output never emerges. Whether or not the US government's motive in invading Iraq had any connection to oil, that intervention seems to have led to sabotage of production and shipping of oil. The amount of oil produced in Iraq in 2004 and 2005, the two years after the US invasion, was below what it was when there were no UN sanctions restricting Iraqi supply. Indeed, the amount of oil produced in Iraq in those years was below even the amount produced during the last five years of sanctions, from 1998 to 2002. During those years, production averaged 2,328mbpd; in 2004 and 2005, by contrast, production was 2,011 and 1,878mbpd, respectively.[13]

The other case for war to increase supply is that war is a particularly violent antitrust action to break up an international monopoly, namely OPEC, and reduce market power, thus increasing output. This, in fact, was the case made by "Miles Ignotus" and others in the 1970s that was referenced earlier. But, as noted, no individual producing country with an annual output the size of Iraq's output would produce enough that it would have an incentive to withhold output. Taking over a country that produces as much as Iraq produces, therefore, would not lead to much of an increase in world output. War as an international antitrust action, therefore, would work only if directed against a number of producers. That would make the war even more expensive.

Cheap oil

Another argument for war for is for consumers to get cheaper oil. But as we shall see, this argument collapses to the previous argument, the argument for increased supply.

There are two ways to get oil cheap. One is to steal it. Think of the image of "armed consumers" that the above-mentioned "Miles Ignotus" wrote about. The first obvious point to make against such a case for war is that it is wrong. We teach our children not to steal. We do so, presumably, not just because we want our children not to steal but also because we want them to grow up to be adults who do not steal. How does it suddenly become right to steal when a number of adults get in control of a government?

Interestingly, the second, more-subtle, argument against stealing oil is that it would not benefit the majority of consumers in the country whose government stole it. The reason is that if the government stole it, it would likely hand it over to an oil company. The government could do so in two ways. Either it could sell the oil to the company at market rates, in which case neither the company nor the consumers the company sells to would benefit. Instead, the government would benefit. The other way is that the government could give the oil to the company or sell it at a below-market rate. In that case, the company would benefit, but consumers would not. Instead, the company would turn around and resell the oil at the world market price: the consumers in the company's country of headquarters would get no special deal. So not only is stealing wrong, but also it wouldn't even benefit consumers.

This brings us to the second way of getting oil cheap. For consumers to get cheaper oil as a result of their government's war for oil, the war would have to result in a lower world oil price. This would happen only if the war were to result in a higher world supply. Thus, the case for war to make oil cheap for consumers collapses into the case for war to increase supply.

Expensive oil

The third case for war for oil is that the purpose of making war on various countries is to make oil more expensive. This sounds absurd. Why would a government, especially of an oil-importing nation, want to make oil more expensive for its consumers? Yet, why should oil be different from other goods that government makes more expensive for its citizens? Governments often impose tariffs or limit imports using import quotas. The US federal government, for example, prevents US consumers from buying foreign sugar in excess of a tight quota, thus driving up the domestic price of sugar. To enforce these programs, as the very word "enforce" implies, governments stand ready to use force against their own producers and consumers. The famous pro-free-trade economist Henry George wrote, "What protection teaches us, is to do to ourselves in time of peace what enemies seek to do to us in time of war."[14] Governments, in short, already use force to prevent their own citizens from getting goods cheaply. Why, then, would those same governments, in their pursuit of high prices, hesitate to use force against foreigners?

Interestingly, it was a fan, not an enemy, of then President Bush, who revealed Bush's thinking about the problem with cheap energy. In his encomium to Bush, *The Right Man*, the economically literate David Frum wrote:

> I once made the mistake of suggesting to Bush that he use the phrase cheap energy to describe the aims of his energy policy. He gave me a sharp, squinting look, as if he were trying to decide whether I was the very stupidest person he had heard from all day or only one of the top five. Cheap energy, he answered, was how we had got into this mess. Every year from the early 1970s until the mid-1990s, American cars burned less and less oil per mile traveled. Then in about 1995 that progress stopped. Why? He answered his own question: Because of the gas-guzzling SUV. And what had made the SUV craze possible? This time I answered. "Um, cheap energy?" He nodded at me. Dismissed.[15]

In other words, early in his presidency, George W. Bush argued that cheap energy was the problem. Why would a man from an oil family, who himself was an oilman, and who lived most of his adult life in an oil-producing state, hesitate to use military force to "solve" the problem? I hasten to add that I don't think that expensive oil was his goal. But certainly we cannot immediately dismiss this motive.

The case against this argument for war for oil is easy. The reason is that such a war, if "successful," would carry two costs to the USA and no benefits. First, of course, are the substantial costs of a military invasion and occupation. Second are the net costs to the US economy of the higher price of oil. While such a war, if it increased the price, would help producers in Alaska, Texas, Oklahoma, New Mexico and other oil-producing states, the costs to consumers would be higher, in dollar terms, than the gains to producers. This conclusion is a well-established result in the economic literature on trade. But to establish it here, consider the following calculation. In 2002, the last full year before the March 2003 invasion of Iraq, domestic production of oil was 9mbpd, domestic consumption of oil was 20mbpd, and imports were 11mbpd. World prices in 2002 averaged about $23 per barrel. Imagine that the invasion reduces world supply and raises prices by $4 per barrel. Then domestic producers gain $4 per barrel on 9 mbd, or $36 million per day, while domestic consumers lose $4 per barrel on 20mbpd, or $80m. per day. Thus the loss to consumers exceeds, by a large margin, the gain to domestic producers. This leaves out two small effects of the price increase. First, producers will produce a little more because of the higher price and make some profit on this additional production. Second, consumers will cut back somewhat on consumption, making consumers' losses slightly lower. But these two effects are small, which means that the earlier conclusion that consumers' losses outweigh producers' gains holds up.

It is possible that in pointing to cheap energy as a problem, President Bush was concerned about the environmental costs of cheap energy. But then a solution that has a much lower cost than war is to impose a tax on energy so that the revenues from the tax can be used for something valuable. If the cost matters, then going to war to drive up the price of oil is low on the list of solutions.

In short, to make the case that the US government should declare war on oil-producing countries to drive up the price is to argue that the US government should spend taxpayers' money on war to cause US consumers to spend more money on oil. Think of the war for oil in this case as a particularly violent restriction on imports.

Benefiting particular oil firms

The fourth and final case that could be made for war for oil is that the war might be fought to benefit specific firms that produce oil, firms, let's say, that get to take over oil production in the invaded country. It's easy to see the attraction of such a war. A particular firm would bear the costs of the war only in proportion to its net income (through the corporate income tax) but could get benefits from the war out of all proportion to its net income. In other words, certain firms might lobby for the war because they can "privatize" the benefits but "socialize" the costs.

Certainly, this has happened historically. Various companies since World War I have lobbied the British and US governments to give them privileged access to oil in the Middle East. The economic case against such a war is easy. The costs of a war are large and the gains to the particular firms that benefit, while much greater than their pro rata share of the costs, are still tiny compared to the massive overall costs.

Conclusion

In 1776, Adam Smith wrote, in *The Wealth of Nations*, "It is not from the benevolence of the butcher, the brewer, or the baker that we expect our dinner but from their regard for their own self-interest." Similarly, it is not due to the benevolence of the world's oil suppliers that we get our oil but from their regard for their own interests. Our oil supply is secure, not because our government threatens to use force against those who would make it insecure, but because the world's oil suppliers want to make money.

Notes

* David R. Henderson is an associate professor of economics at the Graduate School of Business and Public Policy, Naval Postgraduate School, in Monterey, California and a research fellow with Stanford University's Hoover Institution. His e-mail address is davidrhenderson1950@gmail.com and he blogs at http://econlog.econlib.org/.

1 Alan Greenspan, *The Age of Turbulence*, New York: Penguin Press, 2007, p. 463.
2 "Kissinger on Oil, Food, and Trade," *Business Week*, 13 January 1975, p. 69.
3 "Now a Tougher U.S.: Interview with James R. Schlesinger, Secretary of Defense," *US News & World Report*, 26 May 1975, pp. 26–27.
4 Earl C. Ravenal, *Defining Defense: The 1985 Military Budget* (Washington D.C.: Cato Institute, 1984), p. 17, quoted in David Isenberg, "The Rapid Deployment Force: The Few, the Futile, the Expendable," Cato Policy Analysis, No. 44, 8 November 1984.

5 Both quotes are from President George Bush, "Against Aggression in the Persian Gulf," in US Department of State Bureau of Public Affairs Washington D.C. (15 August 1990), Current Policy No. 1293.
6 Quoted in Gerald F. Seib and Robert S. Greenberger, "Bush Wants U.S. to Forgive Egypt Debt; Prolonged Presence in Gulf Is Indicated," *Wall Street Journal*, 5 September 1990, p. A3.
7 Henry Kissinger, "America Has Crossed Its Rubicon in the Middle East," *Los Angeles Times Syndicate*, 19 August 1990.
8 See James Kirchik, "Chavez's Friend in Massachusetts," *The New Republic*, 1 September 2009, accessed on 4 November 2010 at www.tnr.com/print/article/politics/chavezs-friend-massachusetts.
9 *Economic Report of the President*, February 1991, p. 81.
10 Rajeev Dhawan and Karsten Jeske, "How Resilient Is the Modern Economy to Energy Price Shocks?", Federal Reserve Bank of Atlanta, *Economic Review*, Third Quarter, 2006, pp. 21–32.
11 These data were accessed from http://inflationdata.com/inflation/Inflation_Rate/Historical_Oil_Prices_Table.asp on 26 February 2007.
12 "Really Big Oil," *The Economist*, 12 August 2006, p. 11 and "Oil's Dark Secret," *The Economist*, 12 August 2006, p. 55.
13 These data are from www.eia.doe.gov/ipm/supply.html, Table 4.1a.
14 Henry George, *Protection or Free Trade*, New York: Doubleday, Page & Co, 1905, Chapter VI, accessed at www.econlib.org/library/YPDBooks/George/grgPFT6.html, VI.7, on 7 November 2010.
15 David Frum, *The Right Man*, New York: Random House, 2003, p. 65.

Part III
Oil and Political Power
Regional Dimensions

12
Oil Rents and Political Power in Africa

Jessica Piombo[1]

> "The lived experience of oil-exporting countries over the past several decades tells a story which differs radically from the promise of petroleum. When taken as a group, all 'rich' less developed countries dependent on oil exports have seen the living standards of their populations drop – and drop dramatically."[2]

Africa is a continent of contrast. There are extremes of wealth and poverty, of development and progress as well as underdevelopment and stagnation, and of stunning beauty next to desperate squalor. Based on generous human and natural resource endowments, Africans possess the means to become amongst the wealthiest people in the world, yet instead they tend to rank lowest in most economic and human development indicators, and their political systems tend to rank among the most corrupt and authoritarian in the world. The trends are worst in the countries with the largest mineral resource endowments, and of these, the petroleum-rich countries have the worst records in governance, inequality, and human development. Much of this is due to the ways that the competition for control over, access to and use of oil income has shaped politics (and from this, economics) in these countries. This chapter will analyze the politics of oil in sub-Saharan Africa, arguing that regime concerns with maintaining control over oil rents undermine government accountability and increase authoritarian tendencies, while access to oil rents increases regime stability at the same time as it attenuates the link between rulers and citizens.

Africa has suffered various forms of the "resource curse" over time.[3] Between the 16th and 19th centuries, the continent's human resources condemned whole regions to exploitation for labor as the international slave trade captured, enslaved and sent millions of Africans to the New World. In the 19th century, natural resource exploitation by imperial powers led to the creation of political and economic regimes designed to facilitate the expropriation of raw goods, rather than the development of internally dynamic systems that benefited residents in the colonial territories. Post-independence regimes have struggled with overcoming these legacies since the 1960s. In these struggles can be found the most recent manifestation of the resource curse: rapacious governments, fuelled by a reliance on the rents from exportable natural resources such as petroleum or copper, have faced little incentive to diversify their economies and develop accountable systems of good governance. As a result, the resources that could have served as engines of growth have, yet again, condemned many ordinary Africans to lives of exploitation and expropriation. In a handful of countries resources have also given rise to and/or have helped to extend brutal conflicts.

After briefly reviewing oil exploration and production in Africa since the 1950s, this chapter will review the main influence that oil has had in the politics of the largest of the oil exporters. The analysis will focus on the relationship between oil and political regimes, the quality of governance, policy processes, and the institutionalization of the state. The chapter will also review the economic impacts of oil and how the politics of oil affect state-society relations and, in some cases, the incidence and nature of conflict. Overall, the argument advanced here is that in a continent known for poor governance, personalized rule, and tendencies towards authoritarianism, the countries that could perform best (those with abundant oil reserves) in actuality tend to perform the worst on most governance and economic performance indicators.

Unlike the Middle East, where for decades, autocratic regimes were able to maintain power through the strategic distribution of oil proceeds, there is no pattern of oil and autocratic peace in Africa. A few countries have been able to build stable authoritarian regimes through the use and manipulation of oil proceeds, such as those found in Gabon, Cameroon, Algeria, Egypt and Libya. However a significant number of the sub-Saharan oil exporters, including Nigeria, Angola, the Republic of Congo (also referred to as Congo-Brazzaville), and Sudan, have all experienced conflict related to oil. Competition over access to and control over oil resources fuelled large-scale civil wars in Angola and the Republic of Congo, while secessionist or regionally-focused conflicts arose in the Niger Delta and the Cabinda region of Angola. Sudan's second civil war (beginning in 1983) was fuelled in part by the discovery of oil in the late 1970s, and ongoing tensions over the border between the north and south are tied to the location of oil fields. Sudan's oil deposits just happen to be located alongside, though mostly just south of, the border between the north and south.[4]

In order to trace the enduring influence of oil on politics, the chapter primarily considers countries in sub-Saharan Africa that have been exporting oil steadily for at least the past two decades. Countries that began oil exploration and export only in the late 2000s, such as Ghana and Chad, are not specifically included in the analysis.[5] The rationale is that oil has not been exploited long enough in these countries to analyze its impact. The chapter therefore focuses primarily on Angola, Cameroon, Equatorial Guinea, Gabon, Nigeria and Sudan, although other countries will be discussed as well.

African oil: a brief review

The African oil sector historically has been located offshore, where oil is derived from capital-intensive drilling platforms located in places where local strife rarely affects production. This only increased in the 1990s as the technology of oil extraction enabled "ultra-deep water" wells to become profitable. In Angola, for example, in mid-2001, onshore oil concessions contributed just 2% of national production.[6] In these countries, petroleum drilling forms an enclave economy: governments gain access to oil income with relatively low cost, focusing on capital intensive extraction, with economic activity occurring in a location that is geographically separate and therefore inaccessible to the local population. These countries tend to have higher levels of corruption than others in Africa, since it is relatively easy for governments to hide how much oil is being produced and how much income generated from the general population. In West Africa, many of the new discoveries are also located offshore, while the oil deposits in East Africa that are expected to be brought into production in the coming decades are located onshore. This is likely to affect the influence of the enclave economy and the protection from local contestation that offshore oil enjoys.

Table 12.1 Top Crude Petroleum Exporters in Africa (Thousands of Barrels Per Day)

	1999	2000	2001	2002	2003	2004	2005	2006	2007	2008	2009	World %
Algeria	1515	1578	1562	1680	1852	1946	2015	2003	2016	1993	1811	0.02
Angola	745	746	742	905	870	1103	1405	1421	1684	1875	1784	2.30%
Cameroon	95	88	81	72	67	89	82	87	82	84	73	0.10%
Chad	–	–	–	–	24	168	173	153	144	127	118	0.20%
Egypt	827	781	758	751	749	721	696	697	710	722	742	0.90%
Equatorial Guinea	100	91	177	200	244	346	376	364	376	350	307	0.40%
Gabon	340	327	301	295	240	235	234	235	230	235	229	0.30%
Libya	1425	1475	1427	1375	1485	1623	1745	1815	1820	1820	1652	2.00%
Nigeria	2066	2155	2274	2103	2238	2431	2499	2420	2305	2116	2061	2.60%
Republic of Congo	266	254	234	231	215	216	246	262	222	249	274	0.40%
Sudan	63	174	217	241	265	301	305	331	468	480	490	0.60%
Tunisia	84	78	71	74	68	71	73	70	97	89	86	0.10%
Other Africa	56	56	53	63	71	75	72	66	84	79	79	0.10%
Total Africa	7583	7804	7897	7990	8386	9324	9921	9925	10238	10219	9705	12.00%

Note: British Petroleum Global Energy Outlook 2010. Access at: www.bp.com/liveassets/bp_internet/globalbp/globalbp_uk_english/reports_and_publications/statistical_energy_review_2008/STAGING/local_assets/2010_downloads/oil_section_2010.pdf

As a proportion of the world's total, African oil accounts for 12% of crude oil exports.[7] Several countries have been exporting oil for decades; these are located on the west coast and include Nigeria, Angola, Cameroon, Gabon, the Republic of Congo, and Equatorial Guinea. Africa's five largest exporters have historically been Nigeria, Libya, Algeria, Egypt and Angola; if considering just sub-Saharan producers, the largest exporters are Nigeria, Angola, Gabon, Cameroon and Equatorial Guinea (Table 12.1 lists the main African oil exporters). Nigeria was the first sub-Saharan country to begin exporting oil in 1958 followed by Angola (1968) and then the Republic of Congo, Cameroon, Gabon and Equatorial Guinea (where oil was discovered in the 1960s but not extracted until 1991).[8] Two of these countries are members of OPEC: Nigeria (which joined in 1971) and Angola (2007). Gabon had been a member until 1996, when it withdrew on account of the high membership fee.

African petroleum sector activities are primarily upstream, and until the early 2000s a relatively small set of companies were involved in extraction. These were primarily Anglo-Dutch and British (Shell and British Petroleum) and French (Elf Aquitaine, now privatized as Total), followed by American companies (Shell Oil, Chevron/Chevron Texaco and Exxon-Mobil), and the Italian company Agip. Since the early 2000s, this club was joined by a host of smaller companies, particularly from the USA and China, as rising oil prices made the costly investments in exploiting the deepwater reserves, and the onshore reserves in conflict-prone countries more economically viable.[9]

Most African countries operate state-owned oil companies in addition to a host of local oil companies, and all licence exploration and extraction rights to the foreign companies rather than granting outright ownership. Examples are the Nigerian National Petroleum company, and Sonangol in Angola.[10] Downstream activities in terms of refinery output are relatively low compared to the volume of crude oil exports: in 2009, for example, sub-Saharan countries

Table 12.2 Petroleum refinery output in Africa (thousands of barrels per day)

	1999	2000	2001	2001	2003	2004	2005	2006	2007
Algeria	475	434	453	450	457	421	433	392	406
Angola	44	38	39	41	42	40	41	42	38
Cameroon	27	33	32	25	30	39	41	42	40
Cote d'Ivoire	89	64	67	64	53	81	72	81	70
Democratic Republic of Congo	1	1	1	0	0	0	0	0	0
Egypt	579	546	555	574	655	642	706	691	653
Gabon	18	16	13	16	15	16	16	16	15
Ghana	21	23	24	26	29	41	36	21	27
Kenya	36	42	36	33	35	36	34	34	33
Libya	318	317	323	351	357	333	368	359	325
Madagascar	4	7	7	7	7	7	8	0	0
Mauritania	21	21	0	0	0	0	0	0	0
Morocco	145	139	141	129	90	124	136	127	114
Nigeria	200	103	227	220	118	102	191	145	93
Republic of Congo	0	8	10	9	11	11	11	13	14
Senegal	17	19	18	19	24	24	21	8	17
Sierra Leone	5	5	0	5	5	5	6	5	4
Somalia	2	0	0	0	0	0	0	4	4
South Africa	551	553	557	590	657	691	750	626	523
Sudan	12	45	65	62	75	82	87	113	112
Tanzania	13	0	0	0	0	0	0	0	0
Tunisia	39	41	40	37	38	37	39	36	37
Zambia	5	1	9	10	10	11	12	12	13
Total Africa	2622	2454	2619	2669	2709	2742	3008	2766	2540

Note: U.S. Energy Information Administration (http://tonto.eia.doe.gov/cfapps/ipdbproject/iedindex3.cfm?tid=5&pid=54&aid=1&cid=regions&syid=2005&eyid=2009&unit=TBPD).

exported 227.1m. metric tons of crude petroleum, compared to just 5.6m. tons of product exports.[11] The major refineries are located in South Africa, Nigeria, Egypt and Algeria, though many other countries operate small refineries (see Table 12.2).[12] Among the sub-Saharan producers, downstream activities are particularly important for the economies of Cameroon and the Republic of Congo, and with the completion of the Chad to Cameroon oil pipeline in 2003, Cameroon has positioned itself to become a transshipment point.[13] While additional refineries are under development in Mozambique, Sudan, and Uganda, overall African oil sector activities are primarily focused on exportation of crude oil to refineries elsewhere.

Most of Africa's oil flows into the global market rather than serving domestic or regional customers. Crude exports flow in large part to the USA, Europe and China. In 2009, annual exports of oil from West, East and Southern Africa to the USA totalled 79.2m. metric tons (all from West Africa); to China, 53.9m. tons; and to Europe, 48.4m. tons (all but 0.1m. from West Africa). This trade accounted for 78% of sub-Saharan Africa's oil exports, and most of it was from West Africa as opposed to East or Southern (217.6m. tons as opposed to 15.1m.).[14] The African Development Bank estimates that by the mid-2000s, China was importing a quarter of its oil from Africa, while Nigeria and Angola respectively ranked the fifth and ninth largest suppliers of oil to America.[15] With this much of Africa's oil being exported beyond the continent and the global rise in oil prices, Africa is beginning to face an energy crisis of its own. For example, by the mid-2000s, energy supply in Nigeria was so unreliable that most moderately wealthy homes owned diesel generators, which had to be used at least once per day. In 2008, South Africa experienced rolling blackouts, which are common in many other countries as well. In Dakar, Senegal, state-owned utility companies could not afford to pay for fuel, leading to rolling power cuts in 2006 and 2007, and a near doubling of taxi fares between 2005 and 2007.[16]

Economic impacts of oil

Economically, the countries producing oil have become overwhelmingly dependent on the petroleum industry for government revenue. In Nigeria, Angola, the Republic of Congo and Equatorial Guinea, oil constitutes over 90% of exports and, between 60 and 90% of government revenue (see Table 12.3). Cameroon is slightly less dependent on oil than the others; this may be in part due to fears that the country's oil reserves are running out and a subsequent search for alternative sources of income. Additionally, most of growth in exports across the entire continent has been driven by oil: fossil fuels accounted for 65% of the total increase in export values in African countries between 2000 and 2005, while in the oil-exporting countries, since 1990 share of fuels in the total exports increased by about 12%, to almost 90%.[17] Given that oil is a non-renewable resource, that the oil industry employs few domestic laborers, and that oil profits accrue to the state rather than to entrepreneurs within the countries, the contraction of the economies and dominance of oil is problematic on multiple levels.

All of the long-standing oil exporters demonstrate the classic economic problems associated with the resource curse: economic growth has been lower than non-resource endowed African countries, income inequalities have become extreme, and non-oil sectors have contracted (particularly the agriculture and nascent manufacturing sectors). Most foreign direct investment (FDI) to the continent now goes to oil and gas projects in Angola, Algeria, Sudan, Nigeria and Gabon.[18] Since oil began to be exploited, agricultural and other sectors in most of these countries have contracted, and urbanization increased.[19] Concerned primarily with doling out the economic rents from the petroleum industry, the African governments that survive on oil revenues have rarely sought to diversify and resist the contraction around the oil economy.

This creates economies in which the majority of the population cannot become involved in the sole productive economic sector. Most labor is left in rural areas, but those are highly unproductive, as little improvements are devoted to the agricultural sectors. In contrast to the enrichment of the elite classes that are allied with the ruling regimes, the masses become even poorer as a result.

In Gabon, for example, a structural shift in the Gabonese economy has indeed occurred. According to the World Bank's African Indicators, per capita real value added in agriculture,

Table 12.3 Oil dependence in African exporters, 2002

Country	% GDP	% Exports	% Government Revenue
Angola	45	90	90
Cameroon	49	60	20
Congo-Brazzaville	67	94	80
Equatorial Guinea	86	90	61
Gabon	73	81	60
Nigeria	40	95	83

Note: Table from Ian Gary and Terry Lynn Karl, *Bottom of the Barrel: Africa's Oil Boom and the Poor* (Catholic Relief Services, 2003), p. 12. Accessed at http://crs.org/publications/showpdf.cfm?pdf_id=183. The authors drew the data for the table from the World Bank, IMF, CIA World Factbook 2002, US Department of State and the US Energy Information Association.

manufacturing, and industry declined at an average annual rate of about 2.5, 0.5 and 0.5%, respectively between 1981 and 2002. Meanwhile, the corresponding figure for services (essentially non-tradable) was an increase of over 1%. As a result, agriculture and fishing currently account for less than 6% of GDP, despite Gabon's signficant endowment in arable land and waters rich in fish. The decline in agriculture has coincided with an increase in Gabon's urbanisation ratio from around 30% in 1970 to over 80% currently.[20]

Similarly, in Angola, extreme dependence on this single commodity (oil) has left the country dangerously exposed to the ups and downs of the international oil market, sometimes with serious consequences for the rest of the economy, as in 1985–86 when the steep fall in oil prices triggered Angola's debt crisis. Perhaps even more important is the fact that, despite periodic falls in the oil price, the general trend of rising production and rising real oil revenues has tended to lull the country's rulers into a state of complacency about the decline of the non-oil sectors of the economy. To all intents and purposes, the state has lapsed into living off the revenue from oil. The oil revenue has basically been used to finance large military expenditures and sustain basic government operations, while providing some minimal services and subsidies for the country's largely unproductive but swollen urban enclaves and thus helping to maintain social peace in the cities. By contrast, very little public money has gone to investments in infrastructure and human capital, which are critical for development and economic diversification.[21]

In the Republic of Congo, only 2% of the country's arable land is farmed (yet 40% of the population is employed by the agricultural sector); oil provides 70% of the country's income, 80% of the government's annual budget, and between 90 and 95% of export revenues.[22]

As oil becomes increasingly dominant in the economies of these countries, it fails to provide broader benefits in terms of increased jobs or complementary industries. For example, the oil industries in both Gabon and Angola employ very few locals, and there are minimal linkages to the rest of the economy in either country.[23] Capital and financial services to support the petroleum industries are often imported from abroad. Therefore, not only do the fiscal impacts of the oil industry make economic diversification more difficult, the insular nature of the extraction process and the dominance of international companies means that developing oil industries rarely leads to ripple effects in the development of supporting economic sectors.

The African twist to this familiar story is that the personalized rule common to most African governments makes these resource-endowed regimes even less supportive of diversifying their economies than the leaders of other rentier states. The reason is that the personalized, patron-client networks that sustain rulers and which are funded by oil rents could be threatened were an independent business class to grow.[24] If there were a path to economic prosperity outside of being a part of the oil-dependent patronage network, the rulers' influence would decline. In this situation, the power holders become even less inclined to re-invest oil rents in society and to build diverse economies.

Finally, the result of all this is that the over-reliance on crude oil exports has meant that each of these countries has been severely affected by booms and busts in oil prices. During the oil booms, governments engaged in extravagant spending in poorly planned projects, increased the size of state bureaucracies as patronage-jobs were doled out, borrowed funds when oil incomes failed to cover costs, and experienced the inflationary pressures that are typical of "Dutch disease." Writing about the Republic of Congo, Ghazvinian speculates that: "It's also not understood why Congo-Brazzaville, like Gabon, has fallen prey to the ravages of the *rentier* mentality. Successive governments have proven more interested in prestige projects and radio stations than in roads and schools and hospitals. The current President, Denis Sassou-Nguesso, has been particularly fond of the trappings of sovereignty, playing host to such events as the African athletics championships or a festival of African film, and opening costly embassies in foreign capitals, all designed to show the world that Congo punches above its weight.[25] In Gabon, President Omar Bongo's "'spectacular mismanagement' of [the] country's oil boom has left it with 'little more than a handful of rusting factories, a choo-choo train [describing the Trans-Gabonais railway] and massive government debt'."[26]

In the bust years, the now-bloated bureaucracies resisted cutbacks, wasteful projects continued, agricultural sectors failed to rebound, credit ratings declined while deficits increased (leading to more inflation and damage to the economy), and poverty increased.[27]

Far from serving as the engine to drive economic development and national wealth, therefore, the discovery and exploitation of oil in Africa has led to a broad set of economic problems. In turn, these economic woes have contributed to and been increased by the politics of oil. Access to oil rents has enabled governments to separate themselves from society, linking only through elaborate networks of patronage that are financed through oil wealth. State institutions have withered, use of public resources for private gain increased, and governance decreased in all of these countries. Finally, a complex relationship between oil wealth and conflict has emerged in the sub-Saharan African oil exporters.

The impacts of oil on politics

Hodge's description of Angola is typical of how scholars of Gabon, Equatorial Guinea, Cameroon and Nigeria all describe the impact of oil in each of those countries. The political and economic impacts of the oil industry are closely related; access to oil rents has enabled these countries to develop an extreme form of the personalized, disconnected political regime that manifests in many sub-Saharan African countries.

In the largest sub-Saharan oil exporters, there are some general characteristics of how access to oil rents in an enclave economy has affected politics. First of all, fundamental aspects of state building were affected by the access to oil rents in an enclave economy, which led to a set of political regimes with similar characteristics. Most African states are poorly institutionalized, but in the oil-dependent regimes, there is an element of intentional de-institutionalization.[28] Because a strong, well-institutionalized state would curtail the ease with which oil rents are used for personal purposes, rulers in Africa's petro-states intentionally invert the state and stymie institutional development. Second, regimes have tended to be stable and authoritarian, though not conflict-free. Nigeria is alone in the sub-Saharan oil exporters in the degree of executive instability it has experienced over the years. The rest, despite challenges that escalated to civil war in Angola and the Republic of Congo, have enjoyed relatively stable executive administrations. Third, policy processes have reflected the personalized networks that sustain these regimes: rather than creating policies that foster broad social and economic development, policies and the provision of public goods and services are oriented towards rewarding those within the patronage network. As a result, these countries perform poorly on all indicators of governance, corruption, transparency, and political accountability (see Table 12.4). Being financed by oil revenue and less reliant on foreign assistance, these regimes are less influenced than other African countries by the governance and anti-corruption campaigns of international donors.

A second set of factors relates to oil and security concerns. These states also tend to prioritize the security apparatus, as the military is needed to keep resistance suppressed. As a result, these states tend to become less able to process conflicts over time. When conflict does break out, it tends to have characteristic hallmarks: fighting is for control over the central state and it is likely occur in short bouts, unless there are other resources, like diamonds, that can be used to finance

Oil and state building

It is almost a cliché to discuss the weakness of African states. Most authors who discuss "state building" in Africa begin with colonialism and describe the challenges that faced would-be state builders in the post-colonial era. In the standard accounts, African states have been unable to extend control over their territories because they inherited territories that were skewed towards extraction: capital cities were located close to the coasts, while populations tended to reside farther inland; public transport infrastructure was designed to link sites of resource extraction to points of export, rather than facilitating movement within the country. These two dynamics created governments physically distant from most of the governed, and a situation in which it was difficult to physically move around the country's territory. As a result, newly independent regimes were unable to extend control and expand the state apparatus into the rural hinterlands of their countries, resulting in an "uncaptured peasantry" that lived largely outside the reach of the modern state.[29] Politics therefore reflected an urban bias, since these were the citizens most closely tied to the national elites in capital cities, and a tension between state elites who wished to extend their control and the peasants determined to preserve their autonomy.

Authors who have studied economic influences on state building, and particularly those who have examined natural resources and state building, see a different dynamic at work. Unlike the classic theorists who describe a would-be nationalist elite that is unable to incorporate the entire territory into the ambit of state control, others argue that state elites have chosen not to seek to control the entire territory of the country. Instead, they focus their energies on gaining access to and control over commercial networks and the geographic areas where natural resources are located.[30] As part of this process, elites in these resource-rich countries intentionally subvert the development of strong, independent and capable bureaucratic institutions, because they threaten the use of state resources to finance the personalized networks that are critical to the survival of these rulers. State weakness is not accidental but intentional: it is the byproduct of the adaptive strategies of African leaders who attempt to build political systems that support the maintenance of power.

In the oil economies, these processes were made easier by the location of oil deposits and the nature of the oil industry. In West Africa, the offshore location and capital-intensive nature of the extraction technology limited the degree to which rulers needed to control both territories and populations in order to maintain control of and exploit the resource. Unlike diamond or timber resources, which require control over specific areas within the territory and some mobilization of labor to extract the resource, rulers in the West African petro-states focused on maintaining control over central governments, because that granted control of the oil contracts. In Angola, this meant that the ruling People's Movement for the Liberation of Angola (MPLA) has historically focused on retaining control over the capital city of Luanda and the Cabinda territory, the area adjacent to the most productive offshore oil fields.[31] In Nigeria, competition centered on obtaining or maintaining control over the seat of national power (first Lagos, then Abuja), and allowing state institutions that should have integrated this vast country to wither. In Sierra Leone and Liberia, in contrast, rival politicians competed for control of geographically distributed sites where diamonds and timber were located.[32]

The offshore drilling platforms are easily defended from domestic unrest, so that even when citizens mobilize against the regime, incumbents maintain access to a steady and reliable stream of income.

Oil and governance

Related to the nature of state building, and owing to many of the same mechanisms, the oil states have tended to have more closed governments that govern poorly. In terms of political openness, in 2011 none of the petro-states were ranked as free by Freedom House, and only one (Nigeria) rated as "partly free." The rest scored as "not free." In terms of government performance, the Failed States Index classifies these states as failing, their public services scores all lie on the extreme of poor performance, and most fall in the bottom quartile of the World Bank government effectiveness (see Table 12.4 for scores/rankings and sources).

Ruling elites in these countries are less inclined to allow political competition than rulers in other African countries. In large part, this is because once the economies contract, oil becomes the only game in town. Access to oil revenues only comes with possession of the central state. This is due to the nature of the oil industry, in which international oil companies negotiate contracts directly with governments, and the international legal regime, which specifies that only a country's sovereign ruler can gain access to oil rents.[33] Therefore, losing control of the state means being set adrift in an economic system with no opportunities outside the oil industry. In this scenario, control over the central state apparatus becomes even more important than in other economies, and controlling the central state for long periods of time becomes the primary goal of incumbents. In their pursuit of power maintenance, rulers close the political system, militarize society, and further personalize political networks. As part of this personalization, leaders further undermine state institutions as they populate them with political cronies who support the ruling elite.

While they close the political system, the ruling elite in these countries head off potential opposition by co-opting emerging rival politicians and enmeshing them in patron-client relationships.[34] This has been a pattern in Equatorial Guinea, Republic of Congo, Cameroon and Gabon. For the most part, the rulers have been able to effect these goals through manipulation, coercion and co-option. It is rare for them to hold on to power through violent repression, however. "Bongo may have had a poor head for development economics," Ghazvinian writes, "but there is no denying that he is one of the shrewdest and most skilled politicians in Africa, if not the world. Using a combination of strategic alliances with foreign leaders and an impressive ability to buy the loyalty of potential opposition figures at home, Bongo has managed to remain Gabon's president for nearly four decades, without resorting to brutality or violence."[35]

The rulers of these countries further attempt to buy social peace by influencing the media and the intellectual community, that is, societal opinion makers, to support the regime, and by providing some degree of public services to these and other influential communities. The most stable of the authoritarian oil regimes have been Equatorial Guinea, Cameroon, and Gabon; followed by the Republic of Congo (before the civil wars of the 1990s).

When they cannot co-opt resistance, these leaders attempt to repress it. The human rights records in each of these countries are relatively poor, and active resistance in the Niger Delta and Cabinda region of Angola have been dealt with harshly by regimes in each country. Respect for civil liberties, political and economic freedoms have been on the rise in Africa since the mid-1990s, yet the ones that show the most significant increases are those without oil or other valuable mineral resources.[36] When they can, leaders suppress electoral competition or entirely legislate it away. For example, Equatorial Guinea, Cameroon, Gabon, and the Republic of Congo were all *de jure* one party states for significant periods of time. When they could not prevent opposition parties from forming and contesting elections, the rulers undermine the electoral process by purchasing votes or buying the voices of public opinion makers. They sustained this repression by buying off political elites and reinforcing their tactics with military strength.

Table 12.4 Governance in African oil exporters

	Freedom House Rating (2011)[1]	Human Development Index Ranking[2] (out of 169)	HDI Empowerment and Governance Ranking	Failed States Index (2010)[3]	Failed States Index Public Service Score	World Bank Government Effectiveness Percentile Rank (2009)[4]	World Bank Regulatory Quality Percentile Rank (2009)	Corruption Perceptions Index (CPI) Rank (2010)[5]	CPI Score (2010)
Angola	Not Free	146	146	83.7	8	20.0	16.7	168	1.9
Cameroon	Not Free	131	105	95.4	7.8	23.3	26.2	146	2.2
Equatorial Guinea	Not Free	126	152	88.5	8.4	2.9	6.3	168	1.9
Gabon	Not Free	117	125	75.3	6.4	25.2	34.1	110	2.8
Nigeria	Partly Free	93	131	100.2	8.8	17.0	25.7	134	2.4
Republic of Congo	Not Free	142	112	92.5	8.6	3.8	7.1	154	2.1
Sudan	Not Free	154	144	111.8	9.9	7.8	12.2	172	1.6

Notes:
1 Freedom in the World 2011: The Authoritarian Challenge to Democracy, available at www.freedomhouse.org.
2 2010 Human Development Report, http://hdr.undp.org/en/media/HDR_2010_EN_Complete_reprint.pdf
3 Data derived from the 2010 Failed States Index, accessible at Failed States Index: www.foreignpolicy.com. Ratings are placed on a scale of 0 to 10, with 0 being the lowest intensity (most stable/best performing) and 10 being the highest intensity (least stable/worst performing). The total score is the sum of the 12 indicators and is on a scale of 0–120
4 World Bank Governance Indicators for 2009: info.worldbank.org/governance/wgi. These percentiles are from the top performing to the least performing countries; a percentage ranking of 20 means that 80% of countries surveyed performed better on that measure.
5 Corruption Perceptions Index from Transparency International: www.transparency.org/policy_research/surveys_indices/cpi/2010. Corruption perception scores range from 10 (very clean) to 0 (highly corrupt). The rank is out of 178 countries.

Oil and policy process

Part of the process by which the rulers attempt to maintain power involves manipulating public policy processes, both to help provide patronage and to provide a cloak for illicit activities. As discussed previously, part of the state inversion process involved the compromise of the integrity of state institutions in order to facilitate the maintenance of personalized networks of power. This same dynamic also affects the quality of governance when considered in terms of policy process and outcomes.

Political decision-making is centralized in these countries, and the bureaucracies are staffed with cronies of the regime. Public goods are provided primarily to the clients of the state, rather than to the society at large, further impacting on the quality of life for the average citizen in these countries. To give just one concrete example, "Under Obiang, Equatorial Guinea became a classic criminal state, with many top-level institutions involved in various illicit behaviors. ... Few oil rents have been invested in programs to improve the quality of life for the people, with spending on health care services averaging a mere 1.23% of GDP."[37]

This is part of the reason that oil proceeds distort economic development: the leaders direct resources to the communities that keep them in power. The mass of citizens are not within those networks, and therefore do not benefit from most of the goods that the government provides. There is little incentive to provide broad-based development because it could lead to the development of an independent entrepreneurial class that might demand reform.

Finally, the regimes seek to reduce transparency by cloaking the policy process (budget allocations, spending decisions, awards of government contracts, etc.) because transparency would undermine their ability to dispense patronage. The end result, as Hazel McFerson describes it, is that the combination of mineral resources and patrimonial regimes has made these regimes virtually synonymous with bribery. Public services are unevenly provided and of extremely poor quality; civil servants are so poorly paid (by design) that they have to resort to petty corruption in order to survive; the institutions intended to provide checks and balances within the system are badly under-resourced and totally lacking in independence; and the judicial and law enforcement systems function by bribes or as agents of the regime.[38]

Corruption

The above statement is borne out by comparing governance indicators across African countries with different resource endowments and different types of resources. Table 12.5 shows that governance indicators are not much worse in countries rich in resources as compared to those

Table 12.5 Natural resources and governance in African countries, 2006

	Voice and Accountability	Political Stability	Government Effectiveness	Regulatory Qualities	Rule of Law	Control of Corruption
Resource-rich countries	−0.8	−0.7	−0.8	−0.7	−0.9	−0.8
Oil-exporting countries	−1.3	−1.0	−1.0	−1.0	−1.1	−1.0
Mineral-exporting countries	−0.4	−0.3	−0.5	−0.5	−0.6	−0.5
Resource-scarce countries	−0.5	−0.4	−0.7	−0.7	−0.6	−0.5

Note: AfDB and the AU, *Oil and Gas in Africa*, p. 108 (AfDB is drawing on World Bank governance indicator analyses from 2007). The governance scores range from −2.5 to +2.5.

without, with the exception of the corruption indicators. Oil-rich countries, however, perform distinctly less well than mineral-rich countries on all the indicators, whether of the openness of the political system, the quality of government performance, or the measures of corruption. The data shows that the oil-producing countries score lowest in voice and accountability, political stability, government effectiveness, regulatory quality, rule of law, and control of corruption. The differences are stark.

Why is this? Easy access to oil rents acts as a substitute for quality governance, and the regimes undermine political openness in order to help retain control over the central state. When they do not have to rely on taxation to support government expenditure, and when they do not have to please international donors, these countries are more free to shirk their governance duties and manipulate the political system for their own ends. The key issue is that natural resource revenues tend to replace more stable and sustainable revenue streams, exacerbating problems of transparency and accountability. With sizeable resource revenues, the reliance on non-resource taxes and other government incomes decreases. This tends to free natural resource-exporting governments from the types of citizen demands for fiscal transparency and accountability that arise when people pay taxes directly to the government. Thus, natural resource export earnings actually sever important links between the people and their governments, links related to popular interests and control mechanisms. The larger the public purse, the less noticeable the leakage to interest groups. Rent seeking is greater in resource-rich countries because wealth is concentrated in the public sector (or possibly in a small number of companies). Therefore, the bulk of the rents created in these economies are channelled by bureaucrats, the majority of whom are members of the politically dominant groups.[39]

The ease of access to oil rents without any effort from the government is one aspect of the classic rentier phenomenon; governments earn revenue without engaging in any productive activities.

Not only does this substitution of oil rents for taxes sever the accountability link, it also reduces the need for governments to operate effectively or efficiently. The governments become less concerned with developing alternate revenue streams and regulating their own spending, leading to the cycles of overspending on inappropriate projects discussed previously. "Politically, the regimes need tight control in order to appropriate the resource revenue. Economically, they have no need to free up their economies to attract foreign investors, nor do they need foreign aid or have an interest in sound economic policies. This contrasts with resource-poor but well-managed countries (Lesotho, Namibia, Senegal, and others) which recognize the need to create an investment- and business-friendly environment to boost economic performance."[40] In effect, oil rents insulate the governments from social pressures, weaken the accountability link to citizens, and skew the distribution of public goods. These governments substitute popular legitimacy with purchased loyalty, and they undermine state institutions in order to guarantee the perpetuation of this system.

In contrast, countries without such revenues are either reliant on foreign aid or their own economies to generate revenue. In both cases, the resource-poor countries are more vulnerable to external and internal pressures to increase government efficiency, improve services, and reduce corruption and mismanagement. It must be acknowledged that for a limited time and under certain conditions, foreign aid can have the same effect as oil revenue: access to income with little effort, through channels that are largely hidden from the general public. Foreign aid, however, is more likely to be subject to political or other conditionalities than oil rents, and this is a critical difference. Foreign aid flows are fickle; they ebb and flow with international attention, donor whims and priorities. Additionally, while donors will impose political and economic conditionalities on aid recipients, they almost never pressure their national oil companies to stop doing business with governments that perform poorly or behave badly (obviously there are exceptions like the divestment campaigns for companies operating in South Africa in the 1980s and oil embargoes against Iraq in the 1990s). Overall, however, oil income is less subject to the laws of political supply and demand than foreign aid.

Oil and conflict

Despite these strong links between oil and authoritarianism, corruption, and the insulation of the state from societal pressures, the oil industry does not necessarily make the African petroleum exporters more peaceful than other countries.[41] Four of the largest oil exporters have both been relatively authoritarian and experienced significant conflicts that range from low-level insurgencies to outright civil wars: Nigeria, Republic of Congo, Angola and Sudan. There is no set pattern for the type of conflict that they experience. Oil rents triggered conflict in the Niger Delta and the Republic of Congo, while they facilitated and lengthened conflict in Angola and Sudan.

In Nigeria, the insurgency in the Niger Delta began in the 1990s as localized movement to protest environmental degradation in the mangrove swamps through which run the oil pipelines. Over time, the movement developed into a multi-ethnic insurgency that agitates for an increased share of oil revenue and compensation for environmental destruction. "Oil bunkering," the illegal siphoning of petroleum from the miles of pipes that crisscross the delta, helps to finance the insurgents (as does ransom from kidnapped oil industry workers). Political power in Nigeria has historically been centered in the executive, but it has been one of the least politically-stable countries, experiencing multiple rounds of coups, counter-coups, and short-lived civilian regimes. Nigeria is currently in its longest period of civilian rule (beginning in 1999), though because fiscal control is still centered at the national capital, the insurgency remains.[42]

In the Republic of Congo, a 28-year period of one-party rule under Dennis Sassou-Nguesso came to a close when multiparty elections were held in 1992. The elections were highly contested, as control over the country's patron-client network was at stake.[43] Congo-Brazzaville then experienced three short conflicts (1993, 1997, 1998 and 2002), as elites vied for political power and access to oil rents outside of the new political system. Each of these was short, and the goal was state capture, rather than a push for regional autonomy or asymmetric revenue sharing as experienced in Nigeria. This was because while ethnic and regional rivalries factored heavily in the conflicts, the combatants desired to control the state and its access to oil profits. The oil industry in the Republic of Congo is entirely offshore, and the enclave nature protected it from the fighting. It also meant, however, that fighting focused in the capital city, Brazzaville, rather than penetrating into rural areas.

In Angola, in contrast, a long-running civil war was tied more directly to regional and ethnic rivalries, rather than competition to control the state and the oil empire it would bequeath. In this case, oil revenue helped to fuel the war, enabling it to persist past the end of the Cold War and the attendant reduction in foreign patronage. Southern Africa's parallel case of civil war, Mozambique, negotiated an end to its civil war in 1992, in large part because the combatants had run out of means to fund their fight. The comparison between Mozambique and Angola is instructive, because without mineral resource of any kind, in Mozambique the rebel movement did not have the ability to re-engage in conflict when it lost elections in 1992. In Angola, however, both the government and opposition had access to commodities that could sustain their war machines (oil for the former and diamonds for the latter). In this case the negotiated settlement failed when Jonas Savimbi, the leader of the rebel União Nacional para a

Independência Total de Angola (UNITA, National Union for the Total Independence of Angola), refused to accept defeat in the transitional elections of 1992. Fuelled by access to diamond revenue, Savimbi re-launched the war rather than cede power to Eduard dos Santos and the Movimento Popular de Libertação de Angola (MPLA – People's Movement for the Liberation of Angola).

Unlike in the Republic of Congo, the Angolan civil war was not instigated by competition to control the access to oil revenue. Oil proceeds were critical, however, for example in enabling the MPLA government to wage a brutal, destructive and unpopular war. The MPLA enmeshed the Angolan military in a web of lucrative oil concessions, ensuring their loyalty and continued willingness to fight to support the MPLA regime. In a similar vein, access to diamond revenue helped the rebel UNITA to finance its war efforts. UNITA, however, had to rely on conscripted labor to extract the diamonds from the alluvial fields and diamond mines, rendering UNITA more vulnerable to population pressures, displacements and more reliant on coercion than the MPLA. The oil enclave economy was rarely affected by the conflict itself, while UNITA had to retain control over the diamond fields in order to maintain the ability to fight. This affected both the goals of the organizations and the patterns of the fighting. Finally, reflecting the fact that while the combatants did wish to rout each other and claim leadership of the whole country, after a while the MPLA and UNITA settled into a somewhat stable division of power and territory delineated by their resource bases. Once this happened in the mid-1980s, most of the fighting occurred in the borderlands between the territories where each held sway. When attacks ventured farther, UNITA would aim to take the capital city of Luanda, while the MPLA would hit out at both the rebel headquarters and the diamond fields.[44] Aside from the civil war, Angola also faces a secessionist movement in the far-northern Cabinda region, which is physically separated from the rest of Angola and is the location whose offshore oil fields generate approximately 70% of Angola's oil exports.

The last case of oil-related conflict in the countries surveyed in this chapter is the Sudanese civil war. Here, an extremely complex conflict between the northern and southern regions of the country began in the 1960s (the Anya Nya rebellion), died down by 1973, and erupted again in the early 1980s into a larger war that pitted a united south against the northern ruling regime. In the second phase of the war oil was a factor, though not the only one: while oil deposits had been discovered along the line demarcating the north and south in the 1970s, the conflict prevented the full development of an oil industry as few companies would risk the capital investment. What was critical to aspects of the conflict was that most of the oil deposits were located just south of the border between the north and south. Southern secessionism was revitalized by the knowledge of potential oil proceeds, even though actual development of the oil industry only began in 1999. Once exploited, the new oil industry further complicated an already complex conflict, and added an international dimension whereby self-interested third parties (companies and governments) aided the various sides in return for being granted lucrative oil concessions.[45]

Writing in 2002, as the final negotiations were beginning, the International Crisis Group assessed that the expansion of oil development had complicated the search for peace, raised the stakes of the war and given both sides an increased commitment to the battlefield. Any equitable peace deal would require oil revenue sharing. The government enjoyed a rapidly increasing defence budget since 1999 and improving relations with countries eager to develop lucrative oil contracts. Despite strong rhetorical support for religious fundamentalism, maintaining the unity of the country and keeping control of the oilfields was not its predominant objective. Oil rents did not directly impact the conflict, although they were part of the strategic calculations in why the north did not want to allow the south the right to choose to secede, and why the southern Sudanese were confident that they could be economically viable when they achieved independence. Once the conflict began its final phase of negotiations in the early 2000s, the process of oil development complicated the process.[46]

The relationship between oil and conflict in Sudan, therefore, represents a fourth distinct dynamic. While control over oil rent did not ignite this longstanding conflict, knowledge of the resource and the anticipated spoils helped to entrench the fighting and complicate the peace process.

Conclusion

Overall, the relationship of oil to politics and economics in African countries so far has not been a positive one for the average citizen or the quality of governance. The sub-Saharan African oil exporters demonstrate a set of state-society relations that are deeply affected by their governing regimes' reliance on oil rents. As described throughout this chapter, access to oil revenue in an enclave economy undermines the links between state and society. Without the need to tax, the governments have no obligation to citizens. They govern, therefore, in the interests of those within the patron-client networks and leave the rest behind. While this inevitably creates social unrest, most of the leaders are insulated from social pressure and discontent because of their close relationships with their military forces, who are part of the patronage networks, and because of the strategic use of oil revenue to co-opt opposition. This leads to a pattern of politics in which oil rents are distributed to specific groups and public goods provided on a selective basis, all in the effort to maintain political, and hence economic, power.

In these countries, control of the central state for long periods of time becomes the main and overriding goal of incumbents. This is because the nature of the extraction technology (capital intensive and requiring huge investments in exploration, platform development and pipeline construction) and the international political regime that requires contracts be made with representatives of sovereign states, concentrates oil revenues at the national tier and in the central government. The enclave economy associated with oil production further focuses attention on maintaining control of the state and makes it easier to maintain such control through corruption and state inversion.

The end result of these dynamics is to make the attainment and retention of political power the ultimate goal for the oil exporters. Once in power, leaders attempt to stay there, so that several of the regimes are characterized by extreme longevity in the executive and further manipulations of governance to maintain that power. These manipulations lead to trends towards authoritarianism, militarization, and the further personalization of office as strategies to retain power.

Over time, these states become less able to process conflicts. With the regimes heavily invested in maintaining the status quo, and with bureaucracies that have been sapped of all independent capacity, rulers lose their ability to process conflicts. When oil busts hit, and patronage resources are scrapped, these regimes become particularly vulnerable to popular uprisings. In these times, even those within the patronage networks may seek to realign them, and those outside of the networks are more likely to attempt to change the power regime altogether. In some ways, the Niger Delta is an example of a bottom-up challenge that successive regimes have been unable to quell. Over time, it has developed and evolved and become a much more significant challenge to the Nigerian state than it was in the early 1990s, when the movement was limited to a few mobilized, yet localized, ethnic groups demanding more rights (the Ogoni People's Movement, for example).

When conflicts break out, they are often centered around obtaining control of the central state. This means that conflicts where oil is a decisive factor will tend to be shorter than when other resources are present. If it becomes obvious that the insurgents cannot take the capital, they become more amenable to accepting concessions from the government (being bought off with oil rents) as the successive combatants in the Republic of Congo demonstrated. When oil is present with other resources, as in Angola, then the dynamic shifts entirely and conflicts are likely to rage for longer. In these situations, the various groups are less vulnerable to international sanctions and economic pressures, as long as they can export their saleable resource.

This also points to a difference in the politics of oil that is related to whether the resource is located onshore or offshore. Onshore oil is more difficult to hide from public scrutiny (not impossible, of course), and is more vulnerable to local conflict. In the future, many of the new oil fields that are under exploration are located onshore: within Uganda, the Democratic Republic of Congo, and Ethiopia, for example. It is possible that the extractive industries in these countries may be less cloaked from the public and therefore less inimical to good governance, transparency, and democracy. The failed attempt to prevent the misuse of oil revenue in Chad (see endnote 13) does not provide a positive example, however. It remains to be seen how the new oil states will develop.

Notes

1. The views expressed in this chapter are the author's own and do not reflect official positions of the United States Government.
2. Ian Gary and Terry Lynn Karl, *Bottom of the Barrel: Africa's Oil Boom and the Poor* (Catholic Relief Services, 2003), p. 17; accessed at http://crs.org/publications/showpdf.cfm?pdf_id=183.
3. For a definition of the term "resource curse," see Michael L. Ross, "The Political Economy of the Resource Curse," *World Politics* 51, no. 2 (January 1999): 297–322.
4. In July 2011, Southern Sudan became an independent country, splitting from the north. Because this chapter largely refers to events preceding this, it uses "Sudan" throughout.
5. In the coming decade, a significant number of newly-discovered oil deposits are expected to be brought into the production line. As new technologies for oil extraction and rising prices of oil make previously inaccessible, or economically unfeasible, deposits exploitable, many more African countries are expected to begin oil exports. These include discoveries in East Africa, where deposits are both onshore and offshore (Uganda, Democratic Republic of Congo, Ethiopia, Uganda, Kenya, Madagascar, and potentially even Somalia), West Africa (Ghana, Sao Tome and Principe, Mauritania). See Nick Wadhams, "Is East Africa the Next Frontier for Oil," *Time* March 10, 2010 (www.time.com/time/business/article/0,8599,1970726,00.html), and John Ghazvinian, *Untapped: The Scramble for Africa's Oil* (New York: Harcourt, Inc, 2007), particularly chapter four, "Instant Emirates."
6. Tony Hodges, *Angola: Anatomy of an Oil State* (2nd edn) (Bloomington, IN: Indiana University Press, 2010), p. 146.
7. BP Statistical Review of World Energy (2010): www.bp.com/statistical review (exact link to report: www.bp.com/liveassets/bp_internet/globalbp/globalbp_uk_english/reports_and_publications/statistical_energy_review_2008/STAGING/local_assets/2010_downloads/oil_section_2010.pdf).
8. For brief reviews of the oil sector in each of these countries, see "Oil and Gas in Africa," compiled by Mbendi Information Services: www.mbendi.com/indy/oilg/af/p0005.htm.
9. Nicholas Norbrook, "Who Owns Africa's Oil?" *The Africa Report* (February 1, 2010): www.theafricareport.com/special-reports/sector-reports/oil-a-gas/3286482-who-owns-africas-oil-.html.
10. In 2007 the NNPC was ranked the eighth-largest oil company (in terms of reserves and production) and Sonangol the 24th. See www.petrostrategies.org/Links/Worlds_Largest_Oil_and_Gas_Companies_Sites.htm; the website is drawing from data provided by the *Oil and Gas Journal*: "OGJ 200/100", *Oil & Gas Journal*, September 15, 2008.
11. BP Statistical Review of World Energy 2010, "Imports and exports 2009," p. 21.
12. African Development Bank and the African Union, *Oil and Gas in Africa* (Oxford: Oxford University Press, 2009), pp. 48–50.

13 The Chad to Cameroon oil pipeline was an innovative attempt to create a socially-responsible, conflict and corruption-free extraction industry in landlocked Chad, widely thought to have failed in its goal to prevent the Chadian government from using oil revenues to procure arms and maintain a corrupt and authoritarian government. For a variety of resources on the pipeline, see the case study prepared by J.Paul Martin at the University of Columbia: www.columbia.edu/itc/sipa/martin/chad-cam/maj_theme01.html#Aims.
14 BP Statistical Review of World Energy 2010, p. 20. Total exports for West, East and Southern Africa (in million metric tons) were 232.7; 217.6 MMT of this was from West Africa. North Africa sent 59% of its oil to Europe and 20.6% to the USA. Only 6% of North African oil went to China.
15 AfDB and the AU, *Oil and Gas in Africa*, p. 70.
16 AfDB and the AU, *Oil and Gas in Africa*, p. 73.
17 AfDB and the AU, *Oil and Gas in Africa*, p. 94.
18 AfDB and the AU, *Oil and Gas in Africa*, p. 97.
19 Nicholas Shaxson, "New Approaches to Volatility: Dealing with the 'Resource Curse' in sub-Saharan Africa," *International Affairs* 81, no. 2 (2005): 311–24.
20 Ludvig Söderling, "After the Oil: Challenges Ahead in Gabon," *Journal of African Economies* 15, no. 1 (July 2005): 117–48, 121.
21 Tony Hodges, *Angola: Anatomy of an Oil State* (2nd ed) (Bloomington, IN: Indiana University Press, 2010), pp. 141–42.
22 John Ghazvinian, *Untapped: The Scramble for Africa's Oil* (New York: Harcourt, Inc, 2007), p. 119. Ghazvinian is providing approximate values for "most years" in the Republic of Congo.
23 Hodges, p. 150; Soderling, p. 118.
22 Luc Désiré Omgba, "On the Duration of Political Power in Africa: The Role of Oil Rents," *Comparative Political Studies* 42, no. 3 (2009): 416–36.
25 Ghazvinian, *Untapped*, p. 119.
26 Ghazvinian, *Untapped*, p. 108.
27 Shaxson, "New Approaches to Volatility."
28 See Herbst for the modern "standard" on state building in Africa; Jackson and Rosberg are the original.
29 For a sample of the new and old classics on state building in Africa, see: Jeffrey Herbst, *States and Power in Africa: Comparative Lessons in Authority and Control* (Princeton, NJ: Princeton University Press, 2000); Gyoran Hyden, *Beyond Ujamaa in Tanzania: Underdevelopment and an Uncaptured Peasantry* (Berkeley, CA: University of California Press, 1980); Robert H. Jackson, and Carl G. Rosberg, *Personal Rule in Black Africa: Prince, Autocrat, Prophet, Tyrant* (Berkeley, CA: University of California Press, 1982).
30 Joshua Bernard Forrest, "State Inversion and Nonstate Politics," in *The African State at a Critical Juncture: Between Disintegration and Reconfiguration*, ed. Leonardo A. Villalon, and Phillip A. Huxtable (Boulder, CO: Lynne Rienner Publishers, 1998); William Reno, "War, Markets, and the Reconfiguration of West Africa's Weak States," *Comparative Politics* 29, no. 4. (July 1997): 493–510.
31 In 2001, the Cabinda oil fields accounted for 70 percent of Angola's crude oil production (Hodges). Cabinda, which is geographically dislocated from the rest of Angola, has a separatist movement that, unsurprisingly, demands either complete independence or increased autonomy and a greater share of the oil revenues stemming from the region.
32 William Reno. "War, Markets, and the Reconfiguration of West Africa's Weak States," *Comparative Politics* 29, no. 4. (July 1997): 493–510.
33 Pierre Englebert and James Ron, "Primary Commodities and War: Congo-Brazzaville's Ambivalent Resource Curse," *Comparative Politics* 37, no. 1 (October 2004): 61–81.
34 Luc Désiré Omgba, "On the Duration of Political Power in Africa: The Role of Oil Rents," *Comparative Political Studies* 42, no. 3 (2009): 416–36.
35 Ghazvinian, *Untapped*, p. 108.
36 Hazel M. McFerson, "Extractive Industries and African Democracy: Can the 'Resource Curse' be Exorcised?" *International Studies Perspectives* 11, no. 4 (November 2010): 335–53.
37 Brendan McSherry, "The Political Economy of Oil in Equatorial Guinea," *African Studies Quarterly* 8, no. 3 (Spring 2006): 23–45, 25.
38 McFerson, "Extractive Industries and African Democracy," 341.
39 AfDB and the AU, *Oil and Gas in Africa*, pp. 105–6.
40 McFerson, "Extractive Industries and African Democracy," 341.
41 For a concise review of the relationships between resources and conflict, see Philippe Le Billon, *Fuelling War: Natural Resources and Armed Conflicts* (New York, NY: Routledge, March 2006).

42 The Niger Delta crisis also has strong overtones of ethnic rivalries and a generational revolt of youth against their elders. See Caroline Ifeka, "Conflict, Complicity & Confusion: Unravelling Empowerment Struggles in Nigeria After the Return to 'Democracy'" *Review of African Political Economy* 27, no. 83 (March 2002): 115–123; and CEDCOMS, "Oil and Violent Conflicts in the Niger Delta," CECOMS Monograph Series, No. 1. Eds Charles Ukeje, Adetanwa Odebiyi, Amadu Sesay and Olabisi Aina (Ife-Ife, Nigeria: Center for Development and Conflict Management Studies, 2002).

43 Englebert and Ron, "Primary Commodities and War."

44 Philippe le Billon, "Angola's Political Economy of War: The Role of Oil and Diamonds, 1975–2000," *African Affairs* no. 100 (January 2001): 55–80. For a monograph on Angola, the conflict and oil, see Tony Hodges, *Angola: Anatomy of an Oil State*. For an accessible, concise account of Mozambique and its conflict cycle without resources, see Chris Alden, *Mozambique and the Construction of the New African State* (New York: Palgrave MacMillan: 2001).

45 See, for example, Dana Harman, "In Sudan, China Focuses on Oil Wells, Not Local Needs," *Christian Science Monitor* (June 25, 2007); accessed at www.csmonitor.com/2007/0625/p11s01-woaf.html (February 15, 2011); and Moira Herbst, "Oil for China, Guns for Darfur," *Bloomberg Business Week* March 14, 2008; accessed at www.businessweek.com/globalbiz/content/mar2008/gb20080314_430126.htm (February 14, 2011).

46 For more on the Sudanese civil war, see International Crisis Group, "God, Oil and Country: Changing the Logic of War in Sudan," Africa Report N°39, 28 January 2002. Available online at www.crisisgroup.org/home/index.cfm?id=1615&l=1 or www.crisisgroup.org/library/documents/report_archive/A400534_28012002.pdf.

References

African Development Bank and the African Union. *Oil and Gas in Africa*. Oxford: Oxford University Press, 2009.

Alden, Chris. *Mozambique and the Construction of the New African State*. New York: Palgrave MacMillan: 2001.

[No Author] 'BP Statistical Review of World Energy' (2010): www.bp.com/statistical review www.bp.com/liveassets/bp_internet/globalbp/globalbp_uk_english/reports_and_publications/statistical_energy_review_2008/STAGING/local_assets/2010_downloads/oil_section_2010.pdf).

CEDCOMS. "Oil and Violent Conflicts in the Niger Delta." CEDCOMS Monograph Series, No. 1. Eds Charles Ukeje, Adetanwa Odebiyi, Amadu Sesay and Olabisi Aina. Ife-Ife, Nigeria: Center for Development and Conflict Management Studies, 2002.

Englebert, Pierre and James Ron. "Primary Commodities and War: Congo-Brazzaville's Ambivalent Resource Curse." *Comparative Politics* 37, no. 1 (October 2004): 61–81.

Forrest, Joshua Bernard. "State Inversion and Nonstate Politics," in *The African State at a Critical Juncture: Between Disintegration and Reconfiguration*, ed. Leonardo A. Villalon, and Phillip A. Huxtable. Boulder, CO: Lynne Rienner Publishers, 1998.

Gary, Ian and Terry Lynn Karl. *Bottom of the Barrel: Africa's Oil Boom and the Poor*. Baltimore, MD: Catholic Relief Services, 2003; accessed at http://crs.org/publications/showpdf.cfm?pdf_id=183 (February 5, 2011).

Ghazvinian, John. *Untapped: The Scramble for Africa's Oil*. New York: Harcourt, Inc, 2007.

Harman, Dana. "In Sudan, China Focuses on Oil Wells, Not Local Needs," *Christian Science Monitor* (June 25, 2007); accessed at www.csmonitor.com/2007/0625/p11s01-woaf.html (February 15, 2011).

Herbst, Jeffrey. *States and Power in Africa: Comparative Lessons in Authority and Control*. Princeton, NJ: Princeton University Press, 2000.

Herbst, Moira. "Oil for China, Guns for Darfur." *Bloomberg Business Week* (March 14, 2008); accessed at www.businessweek.com/globalbiz/content/mar2008/gb20080314_430126.htm (February 14, 2011).

Hodges, Tony. *Angola: Anatomy of an Oil State* (2nd edn). Bloomington, IN: Indiana University Press, 2010.

Hyden, Gyoran. *Beyond Ujamaa in Tanzania: Underdevelopment and an Uncaptured Peasantry*. Berkeley, CA: University of California Press, 1980.

Ifeka, Caroline. "Conflict, Complicity & Confusion: Unravelling Empowerment Struggles in Nigeria After the Return to 'Democracy.'" *Review of African Political Economy* 27, no. 83 (March 2002): 115–123.

International Crisis Group. "God, Oil and Country: Changing the Logic of War in Sudan." Africa Report N°39, 28 January 2002. Available online at www.crisisgroup.org/home/index.cfm?id=1615&l=1.

Jackson, Robert H. and Carl G. Rosberg. *Personal Rule in Black Africa: Prince, Autocrat, Prophet, Tyrant*. Berkeley, CA: University of California Press, 1982.

Le Billon, Philippe. "Angola's Political Economy of War: The Role of Oil and Diamonds, 1975–2000," *African Affairs* no. 100 (January 2001): 55–80.

——. *Fuelling War: Natural Resources and Armed Conflicts*. New York: NY: Routledge, March 2006.

McFerson, Hazel M. "Extractive Industries and African Democracy: Can the 'Resource Curse' be Exorcised?" *International Studies Perspectives* 11, no. 4 (November 2010): 335–53.

McSherry, Brendan. "The Political Economy of Oil in Equatorial Guinea." *African Studies Quarterly* 8, no. 3 (Spring 2006): 23–45, 25.

Norbrook, Nicholas. "Who Owns Africa's Oil?" *The Africa Report* (February 1, 2010): www.theafricareport.com/special-reports/sector-reports/oil-a-gas/3286482-who-owns-africas-oil-.html.

Omgba, Luc Désiré. "On the Duration of Political Power in Africa: The Role of Oil Rents." *Comparative Political Studies* 42, no. 3 (2009): 416–36.

Reno, William. "War, Markets, and the Reconfiguration of West Africa's Weak States." *Comparative Politics* 29, no. 4 (July1997): 493–510.

Ross, Michael L. "The Political Economy of the Resource Curse." *World Politics* 51, no. 2 (January 1999): 297–322.

Shaxson, Nicholas. "New Approaches to Volatility: Dealing with the 'Resource Curse' in sub-Saharan Africa." *International Affairs* 81, no. 2 (2005): 311–24.

Söderling, Ludvig. "After the Oil: Challenges Ahead in Gabon." *Journal of African Economies* 15, no. 1 (July 2005): 117–48, 121.

Wadhams, Nick. "Is East Africa the Next Frontier for Oil?" *Time* (March 10, 2010); accessed at www.time.com/time/business/article/0,8599,1970726,00.html (February 8, 2011).

13
Oil Rents and Political Power in Latin America

Sidney Weintraub

While not often included in discussions of major oil-producing regions, Latin America is a significant contributor to world energy supplies and a major supplier to the US market.[1] From oil in Mexico and Venezuela to natural gas in Bolivia and Argentina, much of the region is blessed with abundant reserves. Despite these resources, policy concerning their development has perpetually been in flux. Alternating between market-friendly and nationalistic policies, the region has failed to develop any comprehensive, long-term view over the most effective way to utilize these resources. Instead, policy has often been short-sighted and geared towards increasing domestic political support. These policies often entail limiting exports to ensure a cheap domestic supply, generous subsidies to ensure cheap domestic energy, an expanded role of the state in production to increase government revenues, or some combination of the above. In short, political, not economic, decisions often determine how energy policy and revenues are handled.

This chapter will examine how current energy policy in Latin America is characterized by short-term decisions meant to increase political support. By neglecting long-term strategy, many governments have failed to maximize the benefits of their vast reserves of oil and natural gas. Colombia, however, appears to be moving against this trend and adopting a long-term view toward developing its oil reserves. The chapter will offer some thoughts on energy policy in the region and finding the balance between satisfying domestic needs and ensuring continuity in energy policy.

Mexico

Mexico is currently the second-largest oil producer in Latin America and seventh-largest in the world. However, exports have steadily dropped since reaching a high of 1.6mbpd in 2004, falling to 1.23mbpd in 2009.[2] Much of this decline can be attributed to the rapidly declining production of Mexico's Cantarell oil field. While discovered in the 1970s, it was not until Mexico's state-owned oil company Petróleos Mexicanos (Pemex) began injecting nitrogen into the oil field to maintain pressure in the 1990s that Cantarell production began to take off. Since production peaked in 2004, Pemex has been unable to develop any significant oil fields. Faced with declining production, some analysts have predicted that Mexico will become a net oil-importing country by 2020–25.[3]

This prediction ignores the likelihood that Mexico has untapped oil in the deep waters of the Gulf of Mexico. Pemex, however, lacks the experience and capital needed for deep water drilling. This is true for other countries that have sought to develop technically difficult oil reserves. Most have overcome this hurdle by bringing in international oil companies (IOCs) that have expertise in deep water drilling. This is not a realistic option under Mexican policy. Following the nationalization of Mexico's oil sector in 1938 by President Lázaro Cárdenas, Pemex received a monopoly on oil production. Political considerations are a deep part of Pemex's problems. Pemex currently finances roughly 40% of the Mexican government's budget. Tax collection is at the relatively low level of between 11 and 12% of GDP, and the government is unable to enact any comprehensive tax reform. The Mexican government therefore relies on Pemex revenue to fund general government operations. Privatization is an unlikely option for Pemex. If it were private the company could act as a normal company and retain its revenues for its own investment decisions. Given the government's dependence on oil revenues, this also seems unlikely in the short-term. With Pemex already obtaining many operating funds from borrowing, it cannot afford to take on more debt to finance its operations. This leads to the current situation, with declining production and a hope that staying the course will lead to an unforeseen discovery of oil down the road.[4]

Recent attempts have been made to address the shortcomings of Mexico's energy policy. In 2008, the government under President Calderón introduced several modest reforms, including changes to the administrative structure of Pemex, changes to the regulatory framework, and opening the possibility of service contracts with private companies.[5] While the legislation passed, the service contracts met with a lukewarm response and the reforms did not address the underlying causes of Pemex's problems. Attention is now turning to the 2012 presidential election. Security issues now dominate Mexican politics and it is unlikely any further action will be taken with respect to Pemex until late 2012, at the earliest.

There is recognition that Mexico will face an energy crisis if it continues on its current path. This can particularly be seen in the adaptation of natural gas as the key fuel for power generation. Mexico is a net importer of natural gas and despite potential gas reserves in the deep waters of the Gulf of Mexico, Pemex's inability to invest in development of these areas leaves

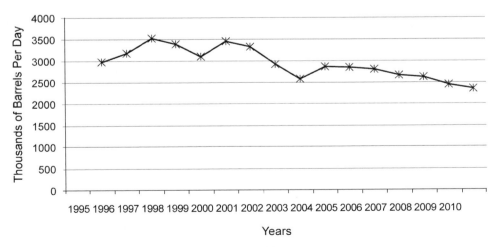

Figure 13.1 Mexican total oil production, 1995–2010
Source: Energy Information Administration

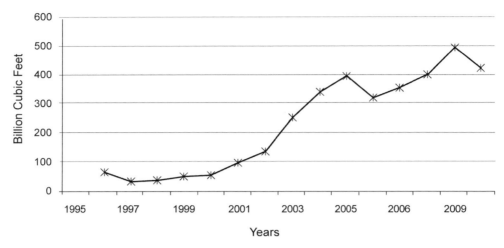

Figure 13.2 Mexican imports of dry natural gas, 1995–2009
Source: Energy Information Administration

them largely untapped. Mexico now has two terminals for processing liquefied natural gas (LNG), with several more under construction. Natural gas represents an opportunity to diversify Mexico's energy matrix. It also points to the inability of recent Mexican governments to tackle the problem of declining oil production.

Politics continue to paralyze Mexico's ability to maximize the benefits of its natural resources. Instead of recognizing the implication of falling production for Mexico's fiscal stability, policy-makers continue to appeal to nationalistic sentiment over state control of oil production and delay much needed reforms. In the absence of any political will-power to address this problem, it appears that only a fiscal crisis, as a result of declining oil exports, will spur reform.

Venezuela

Venezuela is the largest oil exporter in the Western Hemisphere, and the Venezuelan economy is dominated by the oil sector. According to the US Energy Information Administration (EIA), Venezuela exported 1.89mbpd in 2008, making it the eighth largest oil exporter in the world, although production and exports have been declining over much of the past decade.[6] Venezuela also sits on nearly 100bn barrels of proven oil reserves. In its Orinoco belt, which is in the early stages of production, Venezuela may have nearly 500bn barrels more to develop.[7] Venezuela's national oil company Petróleos de Venezuela, S.A (PdVSA), created with the nationalization of the oil industry in 1976, controls much of the oil sector in the country, a control that has tightened under the presidency of Hugo Chávez. While oil exports have long dominated Venezuela's economy, according to the EIA they currently account for one-half of government revenues and three-quarters of export earnings.[8]

The largest destination for Venezuela's exports is the USA. This presents somewhat of a problem for Chávez's "21st Century Socialism." While Chávez frequently rails against US foreign policy, particularly that of the George W. Bush Administration, his government remains dependent on the US market, a reality that escapes his anti-US tirades. Chávez has made some efforts at diversifying Venezuela's oil exports, particularly to China, where exports increased from 39,000 barrels per day in 2005 to 120,000 barrels per day in 2008. Chávez and Chinese President Hu Jintao have publicly stated their intention to increase oil exports from Venezuela, with the goal being 1mbpd by 2013, but for the foreseeable future, Venezuela will remain dependent on US demand for its oil.[9]

PdVSA productive capacity has greatly diminished during the Chávez presidency. Since assuming the presidency in 1999, Chávez has systematically used PdVSA as the engine of his domestic programs as well as a tool for his foreign policy goals.[10] Various legal changes have allowed the Chávez presidency to increase the government's oil rent. In 2001, royalties on oil production nearly doubled, climbing from 16.6% to 30%.[11] Nationalizations of various companies, including oil service companies in 2009, have allowed the Venezuelan government to increase its stake in the oil industry. Finally, the Chávez government has staffed PdVSA with those loyal to its agenda. Following a massive strike by PdVSA employees in 2002, where nearly half the workforce stopped working, PdVSA fired nearly 18,000 employees, losing many of its most competent workers. This firing allowed the Chávez government to staff PdVSA with staff friendlier to his agenda; PdVSA's payroll increased from 28,000 to 75,000.[12]

The amount of decreased production during Chávez's presidency is hard to verify given the reliability of PdVSA statistics. At a Woodrow Wilson Center conference on energy reform possibilities in Latin America, analyst Ana María Sanjuán of the Universidad Central de Venezuela noted that many estimates place the production decline at 25% over the last decade.[13] Recognizing this decline, and the need for foreign investment to develop the heavy oil of the Orinoco belt, the Venezuelan state welcomed foreign oil companies to bid on four blocks of the Orinoco belt, with preference for other national oil companies (NOCs) from China and Russia. Despite this bleak scenario presented, little reform of this path is expected under a Chávez presidency, where oil revenues have allowed the President to finance his domestic and international goals.

This puts Venezuela in a position similar to Mexico. While Venezuela continues to allow foreign investment in its oil sector, the increasing control of the state over the oil sector has diminished the ability of PdVSA to invest in its future and develop new oil fields. The Chávez presidency has instead relied on PdVSA, with the help of high oil prices for much of the past decade, to finance his many social and political goals. While this has brought him strong support domestically and internationally, it has brought into question the future of PdVSA and the Venezuelan oil sector. Given that the Venezuelan government receives one-half of its revenues

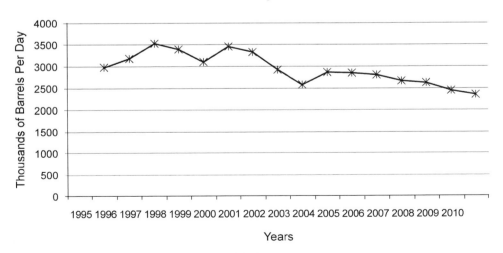

Figure 13.3 Venezuela oil production, 1995–2010
Source: Energy Information Administration.

from PdVSA, reform may only come after a crisis, such as a sustained drop in oil prices or continued decline of oil exports. By then, any gains made by the Venezuelan people under Chávez will likely have been erased.[14]

Bolivia

Bolivia has one of the largest natural gas reserves in the Western Hemisphere and the second largest reserves in South America after Venezuela.[15] Much of Bolivia's vast natural gas reserves have only recently been developed, as regulatory policies enacted in the 1990s allowed the Brazilian oil company Petrobras to join with Yacimientos Petrolíferos Fiscales Bolivianos (YPFB), the Bolivian NOC, to develop the San Alberto gas field, with exports destined for Brazil. As Bolivia continued to develop its natural gas reserves in the 1990s, it was poised to become the focal point of a natural gas hub connecting Bolivia with Brazil, Argentina, and Chile. Yet Bolivian plans to develop its natural gas industry floundered in the early 2000s as government plans to export natural gas through Chile were met with large protests, leading to the resignations of Presidents Gonzalez Sánchez de Lozada in 2003 and Carlos Mesa in 2005.[16]

Amidst the tumultuous gas protests in Bolivia, Evo Morales, a union leader, emerged as the head of the Movimiento al Socialismo (MAS) political party. Winning the election for president in 2005 following the resignation of Carlos Mesa, Morales embarked on a nationalistic path, reversing many of the economic and energy reforms that had been enacted in the 1990s. Most notably, Morales quickly followed through with his campaign promise to nationalize the industry, sending troops to occupy some 56 gas fields. This was followed with a decree that stated field operations must be turned over to YPFB, which was given control of setting prices. The decree also raised state taxes and royalties from 50 to 82% on most fields. The foreign companies were given 180 days to comply with the new demands or leave.[17]

The new Morales government justified the effective nationalization of the gas industry by pointing to the low price Bolivia was receiving for its exports. At the time of nationalization, Bolivia received $3.26 per million British thermal units (BTU) from Brazil, whereas the price for natural gas imports in Mexico was $7.65 per million BTU.[18] With natural gas prices rising sharply, it was perhaps not surprising that Morales wanted to increase the government's share of export revenue. Yet, for two reasons, the decision only proved effective in the short term.

First, the actions of the Morales government have sharply divided Bolivia. Much of Bolivia's natural gas production is centered in the east and south, which is one of the more prosperous regions of Bolivia due to natural gas revenue. The GASBOL pipeline runs from southern Bolivia to several points in Brazil, making it Bolivia's main avenue for gas exports. Following the nationalization of the industry, the eastern region struck back at the policies of Morales. This culminated in the May 2008 autonomy referendums held in four eastern provinces, in which these four provinces deemed themselves autonomous from the central government. While all four provinces passed the referendum, the Morales administration quickly deemed them illegal. With the resounding victory by Morales in his re-election bid in 2009, relations remain tense between the central government and the gas-producing provinces.[19]

Second, and more relevant to Bolivia's future as a gas-producing nation, have been the reactions of Brazil and Argentina, Bolivia's two largest export markets. Recognizing that Bolivia's actions would likely affect its exports, Brazil and Argentina have moved to decrease their dependence on Bolivian natural gas. Brazil, in particular, has moved aggressively to decrease its imports. With Petrobras holdings affected by the nationalization of the industry, Brazil has sought to develop its own natural gas industry. With the discoveries of natural gas associated with the pre-salt oil fields, and construction of two LNG regasification terminals, Brazil will

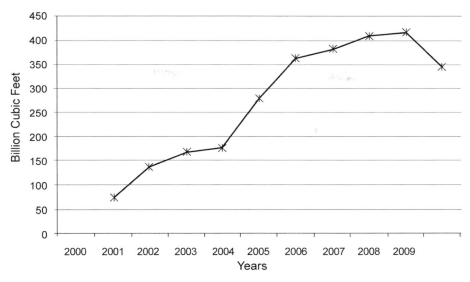

Figure 13.4 Bolivian exports of dry natural gas, 2000–09
Source: Energy Information Administration.

increasingly become self-sufficient in producing natural gas for its domestic market, especially given the relatively low amount used in its energy consumption.[20] Bolivia and Brazil signed a 20-year agreement on natural gas exports in 1999, but this expires at the end of the decade and it is doubtful an agreement of that sort will be renewed. This is particularly true as Bolivia has had difficulty ensuring it meets its contractual obligations, as rising domestic demand and declining production have given Bolivia decreasing supplies for exports.

If Brazil and Argentina wean themselves off Bolivian natural gas, Bolivia will have few markets to turn to. Unwilling to ship to Chile, and with other countries in South America possessing large natural gas reserves, natural gas production in Bolivia may face a crisis. This is due to the fact that, unlike oil, natural gas is a regional product, not a global one. Absent any regional demand, Bolivia could do little with its reserves. Bolivia could potentially transform its natural gas to LNG for shipment to international markets, but has not yet moved in this direction, lacking the facilities or the expertise to do so. With the Bolivian government and many of its programs dependent upon export revenues, this could prove disastrous, and reveal that the political and economic gains of the 2006 nationalization were not sustainable. Once again, Bolivia shows the recent trend in Latin America to focus on short-term political gains at the expense of a long-term vision to develop energy reserves and maximize their potential, which would ultimately prove more beneficial and sustainable to each county's population.

Brazil

Brazil presents an example of one Latin American nation that has generally adopted a successful energy policy and where recent oil discoveries may be pushing the government to increase state control of the oil sector in the hopes of capturing future revenue. Brazil's current energy policy largely began as a reaction to the oil shocks of the 1970s, such as the development of ethanol, and an increasing focus on self-sufficiency.[21] With ample hydroelectric resources and its advanced ethanol industry, petroleum has traditionally played a smaller role in Brazil's energy consumption than most other members of the OECD.[22] This has begun to change under Lula, as vast oil

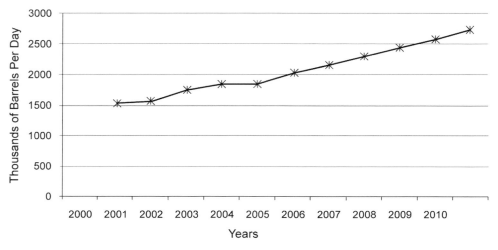

Figure 13.5 Brazilian oil production, 2000–10
Source: Energy Information Administration.

discoveries and associated natural gas have increased domestic production – and consumption – of both products.

Much of the recent rise in Brazil's oil and natural gas production can be attributed to major discoveries in 2007. These new pre-salt reserves, which are found at a depth between 5,000 to 7,000 meters and below 2,000 meters of salt, likely hold billions of barrels of oil, with the first five wells drilled having an estimated 1.5–2bn barrels of oil equivalent.[23] With a very high success rate of 87% for the 31 wells drilled in the pre-salt area, Brazil appears poised to become a major player in international oil markets. As Brazil exports expand from current production estimates of 2.4mbpd, the pre-salt reserves will allow Brazil to greatly increase this number.[24]

The euphoria over Brazil's recent discoveries appears to have taken hold of the Brazilian governments, first under the popular Luiz Inácio Lula da Silva and now under his successor, President Dilma Rousseff. Recognizing the potential revenue that could be generated from these discoveries, the Brazilian government has altered the regulatory environment for their development. These can broadly be characterized as a new production-sharing agreement, where Petrobras is the sole operator with a minimum 30% stake in any consortium; the creation of a new state company, Petro-Sal, which will represent the state in the daily operations of contracts regarding exploration and production; a new sovereign wealth fund that will provide funds for various government programs, ranging from poverty alleviation projects to cultural funds; and a fourth provision that allows the state to relinquish the rights to 5bn barrels of oil in exchange for stock in Petrobras.[25] These regulatory changes have profoundly changed how the pre-salt finds will be developed and utilized by Brazil, capturing a much greater share of income that will be generated than if Brazil had continued with the previous regulatory regime, which continues to govern previous finds in the pre-salt region.

The increased role of the Brazilian state and Petrobras in the oil sector has attracted much attention. While Petrobras is a well-respected international oil company, some question if it has the technological capacity to develop the pre-salt fields and would not have been better served to give a larger role to foreign oil companies that have more expertise in this area. The recent oil spill in the Gulf of Mexico has only heightened these concerns. Another worry is that, even with the creation of the sovereign wealth fund, future governments flush with oil revenues may not hesitate to increase spending, leading to worries of inflation or an overreliance on the oil sector. Development of the pre-salt region is in its infancy, and it is too early to be certain whether Brazil is truly following the trend of increased resource nationalism in Latin America. But its early efforts to increase the government take of oil revenues show that it is not immune to the temptation of increased political benefits over sound development of its energy resources.

Argentina

Possessing reserves between 15 and 16 trillion cubic feet (Tcf), Argentina has the third largest reservoir of natural gas in South America after Venezuela and Bolivia.[26] Beginning with the deregulation of the natural gas industry in 1989, including the privatization of the state company Yacimientos Petrolíferos del Estado (YPF) in 1993, investment into Argentina's natural gas sector steadily increased throughout the 1990s. With production climbing, Argentina emerged as a major factor in South American natural gas markets. Recognizing neighboring Chile's need for natural gas, the Argentine government signed a protocol on natural gas integration with Chile in 1995, with five gas pipelines constructed between the two countries since the agreement was signed.[27] As a result of Argentina's increasing production, natural gas emerged as Argentina's most-used fuel source, accounting for 51% of primary energy consumption by the mid-2000s.[28] Natural gas had become the dominant fuel in domestic consumption and an important source of revenue for the government.

Argentina's economic collapse in 2002, when GDP shrank nearly 11%, had a profound effect on its natural gas sector, most of it detrimental. Much of the change can be found in the economic emergency law of 2002, which converted end-user rates into Argentine pesos on a one-to-one basis, when the market exchange rate was closer to 3 Argentine pesos per US dollar and froze rates at 2001 levels. This did not technically freeze the price producers could charge, but the failure to pass price increases to domestic distributors and consumers, where 90% of Argentine production is directed, meant prices were frozen in practice.[29]

Frozen natural gas prices have dramatically altered natural gas production in Argentina. Low prices throughout the 2000s have led to stagnant investment in the sector from private companies. As production has stagnated, low prices have led to a surge in demand as the economy has boomed since 2002, with growth averaging 7.4% a year from 2003–10.[30] Demand has occasionally outstripped supply since 2004 and Buenos Aires has witnessed several blackouts. This has caused Argentina to renege on its agreement with Chile to ensure it is able to meet its domestic needs first. It has also forced Argentina to sign a natural gas agreement with Bolivia to increase natural gas imports to ensure adequate supply.

To address Argentina's chronic energy shortages, the answer would appear relatively straightforward: let end-user prices reflect the cost of production and shipment. Argentines, in fact, pay a mere 0.29 pesos per cubic meter, much less than neighboring Chileans, who pay 4.6 pesos, or Brazilians, who pay 8 pesos.[31] Yet, as a result of Argentine politics, this simple remedy is often ignored.[32]

Under former president Néstor Kirchner and current President Cristina Fernández de Kirchner, low energy prices have mainly acted as a subsidy to the middle class, one of the largest supporters of the current President. Despite the rapidly growing economy since 2003, many Argentines have also seen their purchasing power erode due to yearly inflation ranging from 20–25%. Unwilling to risk the ire of the middle class, the Kirchners instead opted to maintain current policy and import more expensive Bolivian natural gas. Although the Argentine government signalled it would decrease some energy subsidies as its summer approached in

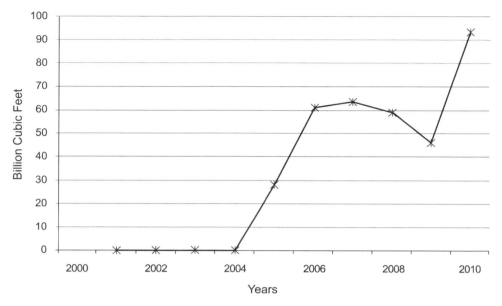

Figure 13.6 Natural gas imports in Argentina, 2000–09
Source: Energy Information Administration.

November 2010, much more reform is needed if Argentina is fully to exploit its potential with natural gas.

This makes Argentina but another example where domestic political concerns have trumped long-term energy policy. Argentina has the option of maintaining subsidies for Argentina's poor while removing them for the middle class. As Thomas O'Keefe has pointed out, the Argentine government purchases more expensive foreign natural gas with general tax funds while continuing to refuse passing on the cost of fuel to consumers, preferring to exercise control over the revenue flow from domestic natural gas.[33] With presidential elections in late 2011, it remains unlikely that this situation will be altered. Instead, the current policy will prevail, and natural gas production (and the revenues that could be generated from its export) will continue to be ignored in order to maintain political support for Cristina Fernández in her probable bid to be re-elected.

Colombia: bucking the regional trend

Given the increased resource nationalism in Latin America over much of the past decade, as many governments seek to extract a greater share of rising commodity prices, there has been little good news in sound, long-term energy policy. One country that has gone against this trend is Colombia, where recent regulatory reforms have led to increased production and exports. Colombia has 1.36bn barrels of proven oil reserves, the fifth-largest in South America.[34] Approximately one-half of Colombia's production is used for domestic consumption, with the rest destined for export, primarily to the USA.[35] After peaking in 1999, oil production stagnated in the early 2000s. However, several regulatory reforms enacted in 1999 have led to resurgence in production, which has quickly rebounded since 2007. These reforms focused on increasing foreign investment into Colombia's upstream oil sector, including the allowance of foreign oil companies to own 100% of oil ventures. Longer exploration licences were introduced as well, while Colombia's government sold many shares in the state-run oil company Ecopetrol to private investors while also forcing more competition upon Ecopetrol.[36]

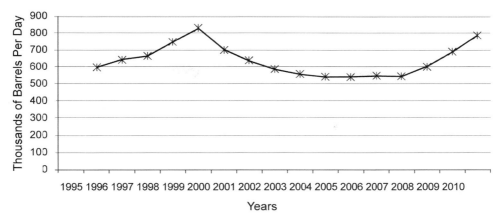

Figure 13.7 Colombian total oil production, 1995–2010
Source: Energy Information Administration.

While many Colombians had feared that their country would become a net oil importer by 2010, these reforms have led to a surge in investment and production. FDI increased fivefold between 2002 and 2010, rising from $2bn to $10bn.[37] In the oil sector, FDI flows reached $2.95bn in 2009 and were expected to increase to $3.5bn in 2010.[38] Combined with the dramatically improving security situation, which has led to a large decrease in attacks on oil infrastructure and personnel, Colombian oil production has steadily climbed back from its nadir in the mid-2000s. Output reached roughly 670,000 barrels per day in 2009, with expectations that production will nearly double to 1.2mbpd in 2012.[39] Due to Colombia's rapidly expanding oil production, many within the country worry about "Dutch Disease," as the Colombian peso has steadily appreciated amidst the recent global economic turmoil.

Thus, Colombia represents one example in Latin America where a well-planned, long-term energy policy has led to a rebirth of its oil industry. With high oil prices and demand from the USA, Colombia has developed a regulatory framework that has attracted the needed investment to exploit its resources. Under this framework, Colombia can now adopt a long-term vision towards how best to spend its oil revenues in such areas as reducing poverty and improving infrastructure. It is worth noting that it took a near crisis (the threat of once again becoming a net oil-importing nation and its fiscal implications) to spur change in Colombia's oil sector. In many of the countries previously discussed, it will likely take something similar to spur reforms similar in nature to Colombia's.

Conclusion

Latin America is not unique in how short-term political gains often trump sound energy policies that emphasize a long-term viewpoint. In the USA, for instance, the recent debate over corn ethanol has shown the importance of politics over policy. US-produced ethanol is mainly corn-based, while in many other countries ethanol is derived from sugar cane, a much more efficient process. Despite the lower costs of sugar ethanol and the fact that it is more environmentally sustainable, the USA maintains a 54 cent tariff on ethanol imports, mostly as a favor to the Corn Belt.[40] Numerous other examples could be given, but are not needed to show that many countries, whether developing or developed, often fall prey to policies enacted for maximum political benefit.

Wealthier countries such as the USA, however, can more easily afford the resource waste created by these policies. In Latin America, this is not the case. Bolivia, the poorest country in

Latin America with a per capita GDP of approximately $4,800, could benefit from the increased revenue a robust natural gas sector would likely bring. It could also build a sovereign wealth fund, similar to what Chile did with record copper revenues, allowing the Bolivian government leeway to operate during economic downturns. Instead, the Bolivian government, like many other oil and natural gas exporters in Latin America, has chosen to increase the role of the state in these sectors to satisfy domestic constituents. And these actions have brought short-term gains, political and economic. Many of the presidents that have presided over these recent state expansions have been re-elected and benefit from high public support, stemming from Latin America's robust growth rate for much of the last decade. These policies will ultimately backfire, as the statist energy policies from the 1950s–1980s did, and their successors will be left with the clean-up. In Venezuela, there are signs that this may be happening, as the country's economy remains mired in recession while the rest of the region records vigorous economic growth. Only when these countries are once again driven by crisis to reform their oil and natural gas policies will their populations benefit from the sustainable practices that bring long-term economic benefits, not the short-term vision that characterizes the region today.

Notes

1. Canada is the top oil supplier to the US market, with Mexico and Venezuela typically among the top five exporters. In 2009 the top five exporters, in order, were Canada, Mexico, Venezuela, Saudi Arabia, and Nigeria.
2. United States, Energy Information Administration, *Country Analysis Briefs: Mexico*, June 2010, pp. 3–4.
3. Duncan Wood, "The Outlook for Energy Reform in Latin America," *Woodrow Wilson Center Update on the Americas*, March 2010, pp. 2–3.
4. Sidney Weintraub, "Mexico's Oil, Gas, and Energy Policy Options," *Issues in International Political Economy*, August 2005, Num. 68.
5. Wood, "The Outlook for Energy Reform in Latin America," pp. 5–6.
6. United States, Energy Information Administration, *Country Analysis Briefs: Venezuela*, February 2010, p. 1.
7. A recent US geological survey estimated the amount of recoverable oil from the Orinoco belt to be 513bn barrels. If this estimate proves accurate, it would give Venezuela more oil reserves than Saudi Arabia.
8. EIA, *Venezuela I*, pp. 1–2.
9. Eric Watkins, "China, Venezuela Agree to Speed up Increased Oil Shipments," *Oil and Gas Journal*, Vol. 107, Iss. 15; p. 27.
10. Wood, "The Outlook for Energy Reform in Latin America," pp. 3–4.
11. Ibid.
12. Ibid.
13. Ibid.
14. While this section focused on Venezuela's oil production, Venezuela also has the second-largest natural gas reserves in the hemisphere, although the most recent EIA report states that 70% of natural gas production is consumed by the oil industry.
15. Although admittedly much smaller. The 2007 EIA Bolivia Country Analysis Brief placed Bolivia's reserves at 24 trillion cubic feet, compared to Venezuela's 152.4 trillion cubic feet.
16. The decision to use a Chilean seaport was met with strong resistance due to historical animosity between Chile and Bolivia. This animosity stems from the War of the Pacific, fought from 1878–84, in which Chile annexed Bolivian land rich in sulfur and nitrates. The subsequent boom in nitrates production, and the copper boom in northern Chile in the 20th century, still factors in Chilean-Bolivian relations, as well as Bolivia's loss of access to the Pacific Ocean.
17. Sidney Weintraub, "Bolivia's Natural Gas Nationalization," *Issues in International Political Economy*, May 2006, Num. 77.
18. Ibid.
19. The tensions between the regions are based on much more than the nationalization of the gas industry, but the nationalization played a prominent role in the 2008 referendums.

20 United States, Energy Information Administration, *Country Analysis Briefs: Brazil*, September 2009.
21 Ricardo Ubiraci Sennes and Thais Narciso, "Brazil as an International Energy Player," in Lael Brainard and Leonardo Martinez'Diaz (eds), *Brazil as an Economic Superpower?* Brookings Institution Press: Washington, DC, 2009, pp. 17–19.
22 Ibid.
23 Annette Hester, "Brazil: Trailblazing the Hydrocarbon Frontier" Working Paper, Center for Strategic and International Studies (CSIS), November 2009, p. 3.
24 EIA, *Brazil*, p. 3. Brazil's rapidly rising oil production allowed the nation to become a net oil exporter in 2009.
25 Hester, "Brazil: Trailblazing the Hydrocarbon Frontier," pp. 5–7.
26 United States, Energy Information Administration, *Country Analysis Briefs: Argentina*, February 2008, p. 4.
27 Thomas Andrew O' Keefe, "Argentina," in Sidney Weintraub et al., *Energy Cooperation in the Western Hemisphere: Benefits and Impediments*, Center for Strategic and International Studies: Washington, DC, 2007, p. 221.
28 EIA, *Argentina*, p. 4.
29 O'Keefe, "Argentina," p. 220.
30 Based on IMF figures, October 2010.
31 Jude Webber, "Argentines Brace for Energy Price Hikes," *beyondbrics*, September 28, 2010.
32 In fact, the Argentine government did allow for partial price increases for larger industrial and commercial users in 2004, but has largely been unwilling to follow suit with other consumers.
33 O'Keefe, "Argentina," p. 221.
34 United States, Energy Information Administration, *Country Analysis Briefs: Colombia*, p. 2.
35 Ibid.
36 Ibid.
37 Mac Margolis, "Colombia Becomes the New Star of the South," *Newsweek*, July 16, 2010, p. 1.
38 EIA, *Colombia*, p. 2.
39 Chris Kraul, "Colombia's Oil Production is Gushing," *Los Angeles Times*, May 12, 2010.
40 In truth, most Brazilian-produced ethanol is also consumed domestically, but the tariff has been a point of contention between the two countries.

14

Oil Rents, Political and Military Policies, and the Fallout

Implications for the MENA oil economies

Hossein Askari[1]

Editor's note: This chapter was written before the wave of popular uprisings beginning with those in Tunisia began sweeping through the MENA region. Through identifying many of the region's underlying institutional impediments to development and human progress it foretells many of the momentous events that will shape the region for years to come.

The fallout from economic rents associated with petroleum and gas depletion, or indeed with the depletion of any valuable exhaustible resource, has occupied academics for many years—the Dutch Disease, the curse of oil, corruption, conflicts, civil wars and foreign wars, underdevelopment, foreign interference, dictatorships, oppression and more. A quick glance at oil-rich countries does not convey a pretty picture of the presumed "blessings" of oil. The exceptions to what appear to be dismal results seem to be Canada, the USA, the United Kingdom and Norway—countries that were already developed and had good institutions when large oil and gas deposits were discovered. What are the lessons? What are the political and military fallouts? What can be done to diminish the negative and enhance the positive for oil-rich developing countries?

Oil and institutions

The nexus of oil and gas reserves and institutions, especially the rule of law, is at the heart of the question of whether oil reserves have a positive or negative effect on oil-rich countries. A glance at countries with significant reserves of oil reveals one undeniable fact. Countries that have benefited—achieved enhanced economic development and growth—from significant oil and gas reserves are countries that had good institutions and legal traditions before the discovery of oil and gas reserves. The reasoning behind this conclusion is intuitive, if not obvious. If countries have good institutions, including legal institutions and the rule of law, the discovery of reserves on public lands and offshore would either lead to the competitive leasing of these rights for development by the private sector or development by the state; and no matter whether public or private development the proceeds would be used to benefit all generations of citizens. That is, oil and gas reserves on public lands and offshore would be leased and exploited in a way that maximizes the public benefit for all generations. In the absence of good institutions, much of the oil revenue would be absconded or leases would be underpriced, robbing current and future generations of their birthright. Later, as the oil comes on line, good institutions would enable the state to collect royalties (if called for under lease arrangements) and to assess and collect taxes, while assessments would be low and royalties and taxes would go uncollected in the absence of effective institutions. Even with the availability of revenues from oil sales, lease payments, royalties and taxes, the associated benefit will depend on how productively the government uses the resources.

The quality of institutions may even have implications for oil that is discovered on private lands, in countries that uphold private ownership of exhaustible resources. Although the oil rents accrue to private citizens, private citizens are much more likely to invest the proceeds domestically if the quality of institutions is high, the economic and business environment is supportive, property rights are transparent and enforced and private sector assets are protected. Where the quality of institutions is poor, owners of oil reserves would be more likely to hide the proceeds in foreign bank accounts, with little benefit to the country where the oil was discovered (with more on this below).

In most countries, especially developing countries, exhaustible resources are the property of the state and, in turn, the heritage of current and future generations. The state has the responsibility to preserve equal benefits for all generations. Economists, most eloquently Robert Solow, have long recognized the special characteristics of exhaustible resources. That is, exhaustible resources are a part of society's stock of capital and their depletion should not be used to finance consumption. Instead, commensurate capital of another form should replace the depletion of exhaustible resources for the benefit of current and future generations. In the case of Islamic communities, where much of the world's oil resides, this must be done in such a way that all citizens—current and future generations, rulers and the ruled alike—benefit equally as required by Islam; just as societies must take care of the air and water for their own lives and for all who follow them, they must take care of their exhaustible resources for the benefit of all generations. Again, how effectively and efficiently this is done depends on the quality of institutions.

While it may appear from the above that the exploitation of oil reserves in countries that lack good institutions may afford little benefit, the fact is that oil may actually impact development and growth negatively, thus reducing development below that of comparable countries that do not have oil. This would confirm the notion of the "curse" of oil. Again, the reasons are intuitive and are supported by facts. The discovery of oil reserves in countries that are developing, that lack checks and balances and effective institutions, gives added incentive to those in power to solidify their position and to be repressive. Their goal would be to capture as much as possible of the income from oil for their own personal benefit. Given this goal, the last thing the ruling élite would want is to establish effective institutions. The rulers do not need a productive economy to generate output and revenues to finance their lavish lifestyle because oil does this and more. As a result, what might be considered the foundational basis of development—effective institutions—is turned upside down, because effective institutions would reduce the personal enrichment of rulers. Instead of nurturing effective institutions, the goal becomes the prevention of good institutions with all the attendant negative fallouts. Once again, we see the "curse" of oil.

Most, if not all, of the facets and the fallouts of the oil curse have been on display during the "Arab Spring" or "Arab Awakening" of early 2011 in the Middle East and North Africa that was sparked by the self-immolation of a vegetable vendor in Tunisia. These Muslim countries had been under oppressive rule. All of the countries with abundant oil reserves, all Arab with the exception of Iran, were under harsh unrepresentative rule; the ruling élites had benefited beyond belief from the exploitation of oil reserves with vast fortunes squirrelled away abroad, while the majority of the citizens lived under varied degrees of deprivation; economic performance had been below that of developing countries that did not have abundant oil reserves; military expenditures and arms imports as a percentage of GDP were high; and all of the countries were plagued by corrupt and ineffective institutions. The major demand of protestors in these countries could only be addressed with better institutions and representative governance.

Developing oil-rich countries have suffered, and continue to suffer, from inadequate and ineffective institutions. Institutions are essentially formal and operate under enforceable rules. Interactions become more predictable when they are subject to rules, thus effective institutions lead to fewer ambiguities in business and trade. Once rules are in place, they then allow co-ordination among individuals who now share a belief in those rules and their outcome. It is the ability of rules to reduce ambiguity in the behavior of others that allows co-ordination in human interaction and a subsequent emergence of collective action. More specifically, the institutional structure of a society is composed of constitutions, laws and rules that govern the society, its government, finances, economy and politics; written rules, codes and agreements govern contractual relations and exchange and trade relationships; and commonly-shared beliefs, social norms and codes govern human behavior. The clarity of rules, of social norms and enforcement characteristics are important to the degree of compliance exhibited by the members of a society. The higher the degree of rule compliance, the more stable the social order and the lower the transaction costs in the society. For example, social norms that prescribe trustworthiness and co-operation have a significant impact on encouraging collective action and co-ordination by inducing people to do the things they would not do without the relevant social norms. When countries with ineffective institutions discover oil, the prevention of adequate institutions and all that goes with it (as described above), becomes the all-important goal for those in power and those who hope to benefit from rent-seeking activities.

Economists know that ineffective institutional structures result in poor economic performance. The absence of good institutional structures usually reflects an entrenched belief system that cannot change because changes would pose a threat to existing political, religious or business leaders. Necessary changes in the institutional structure may be difficult to implement because social norms are often inflexible and their enforcement characteristics are slow to respond to attempts for change.

A major conclusion of economic research has been that without adequate institutional structure, policies to improve economic performance—such as creating an incentive structure for the private sector—would fail to lead to rapid and sustainable economic development and growth. Even a cursory glance across countries that are richly endowed with oil would confirm the sorry state of their institutional infrastructure. For the most part, it is corrupt families and governments, with little or no legitimacy, who rule these countries. Such rulers eschew effective institutions that promote the rule of law and encourage compliance, in favor of their own personal control of economic opportunities. As a result, the oil-rich developing countries exhibit about the highest degree of corruption (as revealed by most available corruption indicators), and thus economic and financial uncertainty, of any region in the world. As is to be expected, this corruption extacts a heavy price by reducing economic and political growth and development.

Politically-driven policies

The quest to maintain and consolidate power and to prevent the establishment of effective institutions in oil-rich developing countries has, in turn, led to the adoption of policies that undermine economic, political and social growth and development.

Short-sighted economic policies

The quest of rulers and their supporters to maximize personal gains from oil rents invariably leads to economic policies that support their short-term objectives, at the expense of sustained economic growth and development. To keep the population at large sufficiently satisfied not to instigate unrest, rulers and governments are motivated to maintain a high level of domestic expenditure even if economic absorption is limited, bottlenecks exist and waste is high. During the protest in 2011, perhaps the most vivid example of this practice was the announcement of an additional expenditure of over US$50bn by the government in Saudi Arabia to welcome King Abdullah home after medical recuperation abroad. This time-tested policy may be less effective in the aftermath of the unprecedented protests across the region.

Invariably, rapid and significant increases in government expenditures fuel inflation, with the price of non-tradable goods and services—housing, land, healthcare and the like—going up faster than that of tradables, which can be readily imported; this then results in an appreciation of the real exchange rate. Higher inflation with a fixed or managed exchange rate would result in an overvalued currency, adversely affecting the development of non-oil exports. Similarly, a rise in the price of non-tradables relative to tradables encourages investment in and production of non-tradables to the detriment of non-oil exports. The end result is what has been coined the "Dutch Disease." The policy response to counter the Dutch Disease and its adverse impact on the development of non-oil exports is to reduce domestic expenditures and to give production subsidies for non-oil exports in areas where the country enjoys a long-term comparative advantage.

Although the indicated policies to combat the Dutch Disease are clear, they may be politically difficult to adopt. Rulers and government officials are instead motivated to afford the citizenry some visible and direct benefits from the exploitation of oil. Thus they invariably increase domestic expenditures and give consumer subsidies for food products, gasoline, electricity and the like. In some countries in the Persian Gulf, consumer subsidies have at times amounted to more than 25% of GDP, encouraging waste at the expense of productive investment and sustained economic growth and development.

High level of military expenditures

In most, if not all, of the oil-rich economies of the Middle East and North Africa, rulers and governments enjoy very little, if any, legitimacy. They maintain power and clamp down on dissent through repressive use of security measures, the police and armed forces. The harsh treatment of protestors in the aftermath of the disputed presidential elections of 2009 in Iran and during the uprisings of 2011 in Libya and Bahrain are vivid examples of oppressive rule in these countries. Such forces contribute nothing to economic output and are a drain on depletable and limited resources. Moreover, because members of these security and armed forces enjoy enhanced access to oil rents and great wealth, they draw some of the most educated and talented individuals into the ranks of the security sector and the military.

An aggressive military in turn demands a high level of military expenditures and sophisticated arms imports. The Persian Gulf is arguably the most militarized region in the world and the biggest importer of arms; for instance, the Persian Gulf's per head arms imports, the highest in the world, have been about seven times the world average during the period between 1988 and 2005.[2] These expenditures are a reflection of the importance the rulers place on their military and of how much they rely on the military's support to stay in power. In addition, military expenditures, especially arms imports, afford the military and rulers a lucrative channel for collecting large bribes from suppliers of arms, bribes that are simply tagged onto the price. Sophisticated arms and a well-equipped military invariably promote internal repression and spark conflict in countries that lack effective domestic institutions. High levels of military expenditures and arms imports, and frequent conflicts and wars are an integral component of the Persian Gulf landscape, a region with about 65% of the world's oil and gas reserves.

Conflicts and wars can exact an unimaginable toll. For instance, the Iran-Iraq War is estimated to have had a combined cost of about $1.4 trillion for the two countries (and an even higher cost for the wider region), with a cost of $790bn for Iran and $555bn for Iraq (excluding the cost of human life to each country) or roughly 160% of each country's oil revenues over the period between 1975 and 2000.[3] Conflicts and wars are not restricted to those between countries in the region; Kuwait was liberated by a coalition of foreign forces as they deposed Saddam Hussein.

Conflict with oil-rich countries in the region

Oil-rich countries are not all equal. Some oil-rich countries, such as Nigeria, have low oil reserves-per-head ratios, while others, such as the United Arab Emirates and Qatar (natural gas), have ratios that are in the stratosphere. Among the major oil exporters in the Persian Gulf region, the ranking of the highest to the lowest oil/gas reserves-per-head ratios are: Qatar, the United Arab Emirates, Kuwait, Saudi Arabia, Iraq and Iran. The high per head reserve ratio countries present a "tempting target." Kuwait knows this only too well. Sadly, Kuwait was the first to be invaded, but it won't be the last. If Saddam Hussein had managed to occupy and absorb Kuwait into Iraq, the return on his military expenditures would have been impressive! Such easy targets are especially tempting for countries that have failed economically, have large external debts and are looking for a quick way to restore domestic confidence, prosperity and support.

Another source of future conflict, and one that apparently in part precipitated Saddam Hussein's invasion of Kuwait are oil and gas fields that straddle the border of two countries. The financial implications can be daunting. For example, although today Iran and Iraq enjoy good relations, a conflict could arise from the vast Majnoon oil field and others that may be discovered in the future that straddle their border.

Cognizant of these dangers, the weak and dictatorial rulers turn increasingly to foreign supporters for protection, leading to ever higher military expenditures, greater arms imports (for pre-positioning to be used by the military or their backers in case of conflict and as a form of payback for protection) and greater economic incentives (such as large contracts and gifts to influential companies and individuals in the countries that back their regime). This pattern is visible in the Persian Gulf. Many former senior US government officials, including even presidents, receive direct and indirect financial contributions from weak oil-rich developing countries.

Solicitation of foreign support

In their quest to hold a tight grip on power, illegitimate rulers, besides relying on their intelligence, police and military forces, also turn to foreign powers for support. The major powers are happy to support "friendly" dictators who sit atop vast oil and gas reserves. Illegitimate rulers are weaker, more malleable, more easily manipulated and more vulnerable than legitimate democratic governments with checks and balances. Weak rulers also afford the major powers a lucrative market for their exports, including the export of arms.

The nature of foreign support for oil-rich "friendly" dictators was clearly visible during the Arab uprisings in 2011. The USA and other Western powers backed the protestors in Tunisia, Egypt and Libya ("unfriendly" dictator), but were mute when it came to protests in the oil rich Persian Gulf countries of Kuwait, Saudi Arabia and Bahrain (supported by Saudi forces).

External financing

Everything being equal, oil wealth increases a country's borrowing capacity. Illegitimate rulers, especially those who want to secure more funds for themselves or for their cronies, or rulers who have run deficits, are likely to turn to external sources of funding when faced with lower oil revenues but still needing revenues to keep the lid on dissent. Bankers are invariably happy to lend them money, expecting higher oil prices, higher oil revenues and an excellent ability to service debt. However, if wasted, as has usually been the case, this borrowing becomes an added burden on the general citizenry and on future generations. In fact, illegitimate rulers, who are recognized by the major powers and who are allowed to borrow vast sums on behalf of their countries, end up wasting or stealing the proceeds with ominous implications for future generations.

Foreign interference and meddling

While we have mentioned the increased likelihood that illegitimate rulers will turn to the major powers for protection and support in order to hold onto power, we should also stress that this is a two-way street. Foreign powers have much more incentive to meddle in the affairs of an oil-rich country than in those of a non oil-rich country. But foreign meddling invariably has attendant costs for a country.

Given the prevailing global energy outlook, foreign powers increasingly view access to oil (and gas) reserves as a critically important area of competition, especially among the USA, the EU, China, Russia and India.[4] Imagine how the USA could cripple Chinese ambitions if it controlled access to all Persian Gulf oil and gas reserves? China's continued rapid economic growth would be undermined, the country would not be in a position to project global military power, and Chinese ambitions would be contained. But with competition for access to oil and gas reserves, there would be negative fallouts. The USA, acting in its own national interests, may have been persuaded that the "best" form of governance for its client states was authoritarian rule and maintenance of the status quo with continued suppression of the quest for effective institutions, including the rule of law and checks and balances. This approach has, in turn, undermined economic, social and political progress in oil-rich countries.

More pointedly, oil-rich countries could become the focus of rivalry among major powers, with each power supporting a different group and inciting instability and conflict. Again, economic, social and political progress in the target countries would suffer.

In the aftermath of the protests of 2011, however, things may have to be different. Yet at the time of writing in May of 2011, it appeared that the USA could not jettison its old ways, at least when it came to dealing with the rich oil monarchies of the Persian Gulf. Although the USA supported protestors all over the region, it was mute when it came to Saudi Arabia and the other member countries of the Gulf Co-operation Council. However, a continuation of the old US approach may be doomed if uprisings are successful in the rest of the region.

Prior to the protests of 2011, the possibility of effective institutions, democratic rule, sound economic policies and, in turn, economic, political and social development and growth, described above, may have been simply wild dreams in these countries. But in 2011, there is newfound hope for a turnaround.

The best option for a turnaround

To achieve a turnaround in their political, social and economic development, oil-rich countries would have to overcome a number of monumental hurdles and adopt all of the following: effective institutions, policies to dramatically reduce corruption, measures to remove the incentive for rulers and average citizens to engage in rent-seeking activities, consistent economic policies that maintain a constant capital stock associated with oil depletion, and policies that guarantee equal benefits from oil exploitation to current and future generations of citizens. These are not easy steps for humans with all the usual human frailties.

The depletion of oil should result in an increase in non-oil capital stock to compensate for the depletion of oil capital stock, maintaining a constant total capital stock. This would indicate a higher than normal savings rate. But there is more. The major oil-exporting countries must diversify their sources of economic output. They must encourage export diversification to stabilize government revenues, to diversify the government's sources of revenues, reduce the overbearing role of the public sector, and protect intergenerational equity in the depletion of oil and gas resources.

Export diversification requires sound exchange rate policies, limited production (not input) subsidies, access to foreign markets and other supportive policies. In the case of exchange rate policies, oil exporters face a particular problem, namely, the undesirable appreciation of their real exchange rate, which in turn discourages the development of a diversified and competitive export base. As mentioned earlier, governments can counter such a real exchange rate appreciation by reducing government expenditures, giving production subsidies to favor tradables and therefore exports, or an appropriate combination of the two.[5] Others argue that there are more fundamental problems than the Dutch Disease that mitigate the development of a vibrant private and export sector. Some make the case that in many oil-rich economies the oil sector overwhelms the broader economy.[6] Given the magnitude of oil wealth and its potential rewards, businessmen find it more worth their while to devote their energies to capturing even a small fraction of the oil rent as opposed to engaging in straightforward entrepreneurial activities. Some economists argue that since oil revenues are volatile, and since volatility does not lead to growth, oil therefore hampers private sector growth and diversification.[7] Others argue that a large oil sector promotes specialization in non-tradables, not because of the traditional Dutch Disease, but because of the impact of financial market imperfections on specialization.[8]

While production and export diversification away from oil are necessary, so is government revenue stabilization and diversification. In most of the oil-rich developing countries, oil (gas) exports have provided the bulk of export receipts and of government revenues and these have fluctuated considerably from year to year because of the volatility of oil prices. Relatively stable fiscal revenues are essential for stable macroeconomic management, for sustained economic growth and, as a result, for employment opportunities for citizens. Countries that achieve sustained long-term growth experience less volatility in growth on average:[9]

> Developing countries experience a year of negative per capita growth roughly once every three years—whereas in East Asia, the average is one-half that rate and, in OECD countries, one-third that rate.

To stabilize oil revenues, countries can, and have, adopted some form of oil stabilization fund. A portion of revenues are placed into the fund in a year in which oil revenues and prices are expected to be above average, and the monies can be "theoretically" drawn down when revenues and prices fall below the average. On the other hand, an oil-exporting country could hedge its exposure to oil price volatility through the futures market. While such funds and hedging may be used to stabilize available oil revenues from year to year, they do not diversify the basic source of government revenues.[10] Government revenue diversification ultimately requires a healthy and growing economy with an effective income tax system.

The notion of equity and social justice is of paramount importance for countries with large oil and gas resources. Economists have long ago addressed this issue, at least on the theoretical level:[11]

> The finite pool of resources (I have excluded full recycling) should be used up optimally according to the general rules that govern the optimal use of reproducible assets. In particular, earlier generations are entitled to draw down the pool (optimally, of course!) so long as they add (optimally, of course!) to the stock of reproducible capital.

Note that Solow concludes that exhaustible resources should be optimally drawn down and replaced by reproducible capital (for future output) optimally for future generations. What if governments cannot, or will not, optimally add to the stock of reproducible capital? The clear need is to find an alternative to Solow's prescribed optimal draw down and optimal addition to reproducible capital. A viable option is to take all oil revenues away from the government and create a fund to address issues of equity. Additionally, this may be the only way in which the interests of future generations can be preserved. For instance, if governments were to use oil revenues to build roads and bridges, it is not at all evident that future generation of citizens would receive the same benefit as current generations. Moreover, as the government spends current oil revenues, some citizens will benefit more than others. For instance, those who own construction companies and build the roads and bridges will benefit more than the rest of the populace. Possibly the only feasible way to preserve equity is to make the same (real purchasing power) direct cash transfers to all citizens, in this and future generations.

For any proposition regarding the management of exhaustible resources to be effective in Muslim countries, it must be compatible with basic Islamic teachings on the ownership and extraction of depletable resources.[12] Absolute ownership (by law) belongs to God. All members of society have an equal right to use and enjoy the advantages and benefits of communal property:

> Seek instead, by means of what God has granted thee, (the good of) the life to come, share in this world; and do good (unto others) as God has done good unto thee: and seek not to spread corruption on earth: for, verily, God does not love the spreaders of corruption.
>
> (Quran 28:77)

The matter of equality is further stressed in the context of Islamic economics, which is unique in its consideration that the distribution of resources is the main economic issue to be addressed by society. When it comes to resources below the ground, Islam is unambiguous. Anything under the ground belongs to society at large; that is, all citizens should have an equal share in the fruit of what is under the land; this incorporates both current and all future generations. Thus Solow's prescription is exactly what should be followed in these countries, with one important additional requirement. Solow's concern is intergenerational equity. In Islam, it is generational as well as intergenerational equity that matters.

The task for these governments is clear but difficult. First, governments must take control of all exhaustible deposits. Second, governments must make sure that they do not waste depleting mineral resources, because they are the birthright of all citizens and must be used productively. Third, as minerals are depleted, governments must make sure that they use their revenues in such a way that all citizens today and for all future time receive similar real benefits. Below we argue that all of this can be achieved through the creation of a "comprehensive" oil fund for all generations.

The best option: a "comprehensive intergenerational oil fund"

Citizens can be regarded as stakeholders in the collective ownership of natural resources that are governed and managed by the state. Assuming the equivalent role of depositors in a bank, each person receives a just and fair return on his deposits. As for the nature of such a return, such as dividend payments, again, each person must be treated in an equitable manner. From a contemporary perspective, whatever gains society makes as a result of expanded production base, technical change, increased exploitation of natural resources and economic growth, such gains should be evenly distributed among all members of society. Public ownership should afford every citizen of the state an equal right to benefit from public resources and ensure equity and socio-economic justice for all.

Some countries, most notably Kuwait, Qatar and the United Arab Emirates, have established significant (relative to their domestic populations) funds to provide a source of income for when oil and gas booms taper off. The problem is that these funds (commonly referred to as Sovereign Wealth Funds or SWFs) are hardly transparent; their operations and their ownership (rulers or citizens) are not clear. What we are suggesting is that SWFs should be the vehicle to manage the depletion of oil reserves in order to benefit all generations. How would this translate into policy?

Possibly the most feasible way to afford similar real benefits to all generations of citizens and be on the path of sustained and equitable development is to give an equal real payout from a well-managed SWF (financed from current and future oil and gas revenues) directly to each citizen, living today and for all time. This may sound like a difficult task technically, but it is not. All oil revenues would be put into a national SWF. The real payout could be readily calculated and updated, as a moving average, to reflect changes in the oil and gas markets and country populations. Such an approach would bypass wasteful government expenditures, be they subsidies or military expenditures. Individuals would be in a position to spend their money as they wished, thus this would be the most efficient way to transfer benefits to the citizenry. Governments would be forced to become both efficient and accountable because they would rely on taxes for revenues, as do most countries in the world.

The de-linking of oil revenues from government coffers should also reduce other problems, such as high level of military expenditures, which in turn could be associated with civil wars and conflicts. Conflicts in turn lead to higher military expenditures, capital flight, loss of social capital, slower economic growth, more poverty and refugees, an almost impenetrable vicious circle. This approach would also reduce corruption and result in more equitable societies. We believe that a fund that in time takes all revenues away from the government should be an integral and primary component of any template to manage natural resource depletion. The management of such funds must be transparent and outside of the personal control of rulers, and each country must design a carefully tailored system that affords appropriate incentives to individuals to live productive lives and to contribute to national economic and social prosperity.

Conclusion

In the major oil-exporting countries of the Persian Gulf, economic and social policies have been largely designed to support the ruling families (Kuwait, Qatar, Saudi Arabia, the United Arab Emirates) or groups (Iran, Iraq) in power. Corruption and state-sanctioned withdrawals from the treasury benefit those in power. Viable institutions have not been nurtured because effective institutions would reduce the role and importance of ruling families and illegitimate governments and prevent them from capturing the oil rent that rightfully belongs to the citizenry. Ruling families and powerful groups prefer individuals, usually relatives or associates, to be the source and basis of continuity. At the same time, the ruling élites in the West have followed their own personal and corporate financial interests and supported these families and groups, nurturing their dependency on Western support.

There can be little doubt that to varying degrees all of the major oil-exporting countries, besides the USA, Norway and Canada, have failed or have not come even close to their potential economically and socially. While oil has supported government revenues, economic and social injustice have become all-pervasive, corruption and waste have permeated the fabric of society, hard work has been disdained and military expenditures, conflicts and wars have robbed the region of the hope of a better future. Change needs to come while oil and gas reserves last.

In the aftermath of the widespread protests across the Middle East and North Africa, change is more likely than ever before. Citizens have been protesting for representative rule, economic and social justice, economic prosperity and better employment opportunities for all. Rulers will have to listen or they risk being swept aside.

What we propose is a fund that takes oil revenues away from the state and invests them on behalf of all generations of citizens. As our proposed fund takes the "easy" money of oil revenues away from the hands of governments and rulers, waste and corruption will by definition be reduced, there will be a better chance of adopting and implementing rational economic policies, and equity across generations will become a reality. Hope will slowly be restored to the masses in these countries. In this quest, the meddling of major powers must be reduced and the United Nations must deter regional aggressors to reduce conflicts and wars that in the end are motivated by endowments of oil and natural gas.

The rulers and élites in all oil-rich countries will of course condemn what is proposed here and the major global powers, whatever their public stance, are unlikely to abandon their favorite dictators and support such a proposal unless rulers also support it. This proposal will see the light of day only if it is supported by international agencies, NGOs and academics, and if it is given international recognition by the media.

Notes

1. Hossein Askari is the Iran Professor of International Business and International Affairs at the George Washington University.
2. See Askari, Hossein, Amin Mohseni and Shahrzad Daneshvar, *Militarization and Economic Development: A Case Study of the Persian Gulf Region*, Edward Elgar, December 2009.
3. Askari, Hossein, *Middle East Oil Exporters: What Happened to Economic Development?* Edward Elgar, 2006, pp. 296–98.

4 International Energy Agency, *World Energy Outlook 2009*, November 10, 2009. (www.worldenergyoutlook.org/)
5 Input subsidies, such as subsidized fuels, electricity and water must be avoided as they encourage overuse and waste of the subsidized resource. Output subsidies do not encourage waste of inputs.
6 See Hausmann, Ricardo and Roberto Rigobon, "An Alternative Interpretation of the 'Resource Curse': Theory and Policy Implications," in *Fiscal Policy Formulation and Implementation in Oil-Producing Countries*, J.M. Davis, R. Ossowski, and A. Fedelino (editors), International Monetary Fund, Washington DC, 2003.
7 Ibid.
8 This is the central theme of the Hausmann and Rigobon paper.
9 Zagha, Roberto, Gobind Nankani and Indermit Gill, "Rethinking Growth," *Finance and Development*, International Monetary Fund, March 2006, Washington DC, p. 8.
10 The exception are countries that are so rich that they can invest a large portion of current oil revenues in diversified assets (abroad) to give the government all the revenues it needs in the future without having to resort to taxation.
11 Solow, Robert M., "Intergenerational Equity and Exhaustible Resources," *The Review of Economic Studies*, Volume 41, Symposium on the Economics of Exhaustible Resources, 1974, p. 41.
12 Again for more details on Islamic economic principles, see Abbas Mirakhor and Hossein Askari, *Islam and the Path to Human and Economic Development*, Palgrave Macmillan, 2010, and Hossein Askari and Roshank Taghavi, "The Principal Foundations of an Islamic Economy," *Banca Nazionale Del Lavoro Quarterly Review*, Vol. LVIII, No. 235, December 2005.

References

Askari, Hossein, Amin Mohseni and Shahrzad Daneshvar, *Militarization and Economic Development: A Case Study of the Persian Gulf Region*, North Hampton, MA, Edward Elgar, December 2009.
Askari, Hossein, *Middle East Oil Exporters: What Happened to Economic Development?* North Hampton, MA, Edward Elgar, 2006, pp. 296–98.
Askari Hossein and Roshank Taghavi, "The Principal Foundations of an Islamic Economy," *Banca Nazionale Del Lavoro Quarterly Review*, Vol. LVIII, No. 235, December 2005.
Hausmann, Ricardo and Roberto Rigobon, "An Alternative Interpretation of the 'Resource Curse': Theory and Policy Implications," in *Fiscal Policy Formulation and Implementation in Oil-Producing Countries*, J.M. Davis, R. Ossowski, and A. Fedelino (editors), International Monetary Fund, Washington DC, 2003.
International Energy Agency, *World Energy Outlook 2009*, November 10, 2009. (http://www.worldenergyoutlook.org/)
Mirakhor, Abbas and Hossein Askari, *Islam and the Path to Human and Economic Development*, New York NY, Palgrave Macmillan, August 2010.
Solow, Robert M., "Intergenerational Equity and Exhaustible Resources," *The Review of Economic Studies*, Volume 41, Symposium on the Economics of Exhaustible Resources, 1974.
Zagha, Roberto, Gobind Nankani and Indermit Gill, "Rethinking Growth," *Finance and Development*, International Monetary Fund, March 2006, Washington DC.

15
Oil and Power in the Caspian Region

Richard Pomfret

Before 1990 the Caspian Basin was not an important oil-producing region and the Caspian Sea was divided between the Soviet Union and Iran. In 1991 that all changed. The modern Caspian oil industry dates from the Tengiz agreement signed between Chevron and the USSR in 1990, the largest foreign investment deal in Soviet history. Before the oilfield could be exploited, the Soviet Union was dissolved in December 1991 and the project was inherited by the new independent state of Kazakhstan. At the same time there was growing interest in the possibility of rich offshore oilfields under the Caspian Sea, but the delimitation of the Caspian among Iran and the four littoral Soviet successor states was in dispute.

During the 1990s domestic priorities in Azerbaijan, Kazakhstan and Turkmenistan drove their differing eagerness to explore and exploit offshore oilfields. The technologically challenging fields would require participation by foreign companies with the expertise to find and recover the oil, but the leadership in the three countries differed in keenness to make deals with transnational corporations.

In Azerbaijan, independence was dominated by a disastrous war with Armenia, followed by a coup which brought to power former Soviet strongman Heidar Aliyev. Aliyev saw rapid realization of oil revenues as the key to his political survival and his country's recovery. The "Deal of the Century" was signed in 1994 with a consortium led by BP. Exploitation of Azeri offshore oilfields coincided with the rise in oil prices which began in 1998 and accelerated in the early 2000s (Table 15.1).

President Nazarbayev of Kazakhstan was under less time pressure and much of the 1990s was spent in non-transparent negotiations with oil companies. The Tengiz agreement had already been signed, but through the 1990s there was continuous bargaining over the composition of the consortium, as the president played off foreign companies seeking a larger share; production did not begin to increase until 1999 (Table 15.1). Kazakhstan is fortunate in that the largest offshore oilfield, Kashagan, lies in its undisputed territory, but negotiating delays and perhaps a poor selection of lead companies meant that the oil did not flow before the oil boom ended in 2008. Nevertheless, Kazakhstan's oil production based on Tengiz and several smaller oilfields did increase rapidly in the 2000s, and Kazakhstan became a significant oil producer, while its proven reserves far exceed those of Azerbaijan.

President Niyazov of Turkmenistan was least concerned about increasing oil production. Turkmenistan has substantial onshore natural gas reserves which had been developed in the 1980s,

Table 15.1 Production of crude oil and natural gas, Azerbaijan, Kazakhstan, Turkmenistan and Uzbekistan, 1985–2009

a Oil 1985–99

Oil	1985	1986	1987	1988	1989	1990	1991	1992	1993	1994	1995	1996	1997	1998	1999
Azerbaijan	13.2	13.1	13.9	13.7	13.2	12.5	11.8	11.2	10.3	9.6	9.2	9.1	9.0	11.4	13.9
Kazakhstan	22.7	23.3	24.1	25.0	25.4	25.8	26.6	25.8	23.0	20.3	20.6	23.0	25.8	25.9	30.1
Turkmenistan	6.8	6.6	6.5	5.7	5.8	5.7	5.4	5.2	4.4	4.2	4.1	4.4	5.4	6.4	7.1
Uzbekistan	2.3	2.5	2.7	2.4	2.7	2.8	2.8	3.3	4.0	5.5	7.6	7.6	7.9	8.2	8.1

b Oil 2000–9

Oil	2000	2001	2002	2003	2004	2005	2006	2007	2008	2009
Azerbaijan	14.1	15.0	15.4	15.5	15.6	22.4	32.5	42.8	44.7	50.6
Kazakhstan	35.3	40.1	48.2	52.4	60.6	62.6	66.1	68.4	72.0	78.0
Turkmenistan	7.2	8.0	9.0	10.0	9.6	9.5	9.2	9.8	10.2	10.2
Uzbekistan	7.5	7.2	7.2	7.1	6.6	5.4	5.4	4.9	4.8	4.5

c Gas 1985–99

Gas	1985	1986	1987	1988	1989	1990	1991	1992	1993	1994	1995	1996	1997	1998	1999
Azerbaijan	12.7	12.3	11.3	10.8	10.0	9.0	7.8	7.1	6.2	5.8	6.0	5.7	5.4	5.1	5.4
Kazakhstan	4.9	5.2	5.7	6.4	6.1	6.4	7.1	7.3	6.1	4.1	5.3	5.9	7.3	7.2	9.0
Turkmenistan	75.3	76.7	79.7	79.9	81.4	79.5	76.3	54.4	59.1	32.3	29.2	31.9	15.7	12.0	20.6
Uzbekistan	31.3	34.9	36.0	36.1	37.2	36.9	37.9	38.7	40.8	42.7	43.9	44.3	46.4	49.6	50.3

d Gas 2000–9

Gas	2000	2001	2002	2003	2004	2005	2006	2007	2008	2009
Azerbaijan	5.1	5.0	4.7	4.6	4.5	5.2	6.1	9.8	14.8	14.8
Kazakhstan	10.4	10.5	10.2	12.6	20.0	22.6	23.9	26.8	29.8	32.2
Turkmenistan	42.5	46.4	48.4	53.5	52.8	57.0	60.4	65.4	66.1	36.4
Uzbekistan	51.1	52.0	51.9	52.0	54.2	54.0	54.5	59.1	62.2	64.4

Source: BP Statistical Review of World Energy www.bp.com/productlanding.do?categoryId=6929&contentId=7044622.

and hence were reasonably modern facilities at the time of independence. Turkmenistan was also the world's sixth-largest cotton producer in the early 1990s. After independence, President Niyazov was happy to live off the rents from cotton and gas, which funded populist policies and grandiose construction projects in support of an extreme personality cult. Just as those rents appeared to be declining due to poor maintenance of the irrigation channels essential for cotton and poor payment records of post-Soviet customers for gas, the increase in oil prices shifted the balance of economic power from gas consumers to gas producers and Niyazov (or Turkmenbashi the Great as he preferred to be known by then) enjoyed an increasing revenue stream until his death in December 2006.

These differing experiences were related to domestic power, primarily in terms of cementing the position of the incumbent. They have also dramatically changed the balance of power among the countries of Central Asia and the Caucasus, and affected their relations with countries outside the region. In Central Asia the 1990s witnessed a struggle for regional hegemony between Uzbekistan, the country with the largest population and a central location, and Kazakhstan, the country with the highest per capita incomes (Table 15.2). In the 1990s this

Table 15.2 Demographic data, output and income, 1990–1 and 2007

	1991				2007			
	Population (million)	GDP (USD billion)	GNI per capita (PPP in current international $)	Life expectancy (years – 1991)	Adult literacy (percent 1991)	Population (million)	GDP (USD billion)	GNI per capita (PPP in current I$)	Trade/GDP (per cent)
Azerbaijan	7.3	8.8	2,100**	65	97	8.6	33.0	6,630	97
Kazakhstan	16.5	24.9	4,680	68	98	15.5	104.9	9,520	92
Turkmenistan	3.8	3.2	2,200**	63	98	5.0	9.5	5,510	153
Uzbekistan	21.0	13.8	1,290*	69	97	26.9	22.3	2,430	71

Notes: * 1992, ** 1993.
Source: World Bank World Development Indicators at www.worldbank.org.

contest went Uzbekistan's way as it weathered the end of central planning and dissolution of the USSR better than any post-Soviet state, but with the rise of oil prices Kazakhstan has become the dominant economy in Central Asia.[1] Uzbekistan does, however, also play a role in energy trade; as a substantial gas producer and minor oil producer it has been more or less energy self-sufficient, but as it starts to export gas its interests are becoming aligned with those of Turkmenistan and Kazakhstan, a pattern reflected in co-operation over the construction of a pipeline from Turkmenistan through Uzbekistan and Kazakhstan to western China which was completed in December 2009. The extremely rapid oil-powered growth of Azerbaijan after 1998 has substantially tilted the economic balance of power in the Caucasus, with implications for the frozen conflict with Armenia over Nagorno Karabagh, and for relations with other neighbouring states.

The next three sections of this chapter will analyse the domestic interaction of oil and power in Azerbaijan, Kazakhstan and Turkmenistan. This will be followed by analysis of the changing roles of the oil producers within their region, with countries beyond the region, and in the global economic and political system.

Azerbaijan

Azerbaijan was once the centre of the world oil industry. In 1901 the Baku oilfield produced 11m. metric tons, one-half of world output (Dorian and Mangera, 1995, 3). In the second half of the twentieth century output stagnated as Soviet oil investment focused on Siberia, and Azerbaijan's facilities were in dilapidated state when the country became independent.[2] For Azerbaijan dissolution of the Soviet Union was followed by a disastrous war with Armenia in 1992–93 over the disputed territory of Nagorno-Karabakh. Military failure contributed to the overthrow of the Popular Front government in June 1993 and election of Heydar Aliyev as president in October 1993.[3] Aliyev negotiated a ceasefire in May 1994, and set about kick-starting the economy through the speedy increase in oil production, which by 1994 only just covered domestic demand (Dorian and Mangera, 1995, 8).[4]

The 'Deal of the Century' was signed 20 September 1994 with a consortium of foreign oil companies (BP, Amoco, McDermott, Pennzoil, Exxon, Statoil, Ramco, TPAO, and LUKoil), who committed to invest US$7.4bn in three major offshore oil fields over 30 years. Foreign investment, which was almost entirely oil-related, increased in the second half of the 1990s (Table 15.3). Oil production rose rapidly in the late 1990s and early 2000s (Table 15.1), with oil accounting for almost 90% of exports by 2002. The Baku-Tbilisi-Ceyhan pipeline through Georgia and Turkey to the Mediterranean Sea was completed in 2005, providing an outlet independent of the Russian pipeline system.

In 2003 the terminally ill Heidar Aliyev named as temporary president his son, Ilham, who then won a controversial election in October 2003. Ilham Aliyev had close connections to the oil sector, having been vice-president of the state oil company, SOCAR, since 1994, participating in the Deal of the Century negotiations. SOCAR has a minority stake in all 13 Production Sharing Agreements (PSAs) currently operational in Azerbaijan, including the 2003 PSA for the Caspian Sea's largest gas field, Shah Deniz, in which SOCAR is a partner with BP, Statoil, TotalFinaElf, LukAgip, OEIC and TPAO. The handover of power coincided with recognition that, apart from the oilfields covered by the Deal of the Century, Azerbaijan's offshore energy wealth was likely to lie in gas rather than oil. A gas pipeline to link with the Turkish network at Erzurum was completed in 2006.

With increasing output of oil and gas and rapidly rising energy prices SOCAR's financial position strengthened after 2003, as did the assets of the State Oil Fund (SOFAZ).[5] The nature of SOCAR's activities began to change around 2005 from resource-rent management to a more

Table 15.3 Inward foreign direct investment, 1992–2008 (US$ m.)

	1992	1993	1994	1995	1996	1997	1998	1999	2000	2001	2002	2003	2004	2005	2006	2007	2008
Azerbaijan	0	0	22	155	591	1,051	948	355	30	220	1,393	3,227	3,535	1,679	-601	-4,817	11
Kazakhstan	100	1,271	660	964	1,137	1,321	1,151	1,472	1,283	2,835	2,590	2,092	4,157	1,971	6,278	11,126	14,543
Turkmenistan	na	79	103	233	108	108	62	125	131	70	276	226	354	418	731	804	820
Uzbekistan	9	48	73	-24	90	167	140	121	75	83	65	70	187	88	195	739	918

Source: UNCTAD *World Investment Review 2009* at http://stats.unctad.org/FDI/TableViewer/tableView.aspx.

proactive role in knowledge transfer and geopolitics. Ilham Aliyev appointed a younger cohort of senior officials, and oversaw a closer integration of state company and government, including use of SOCAR to promote foreign policy goals. The rising importance of gas after the Shah Deniz PSA and the limited flexibility of gas delivery modes contributed to the shift, for example, decisions to exclude Turkmen gas from Azerbaijan's pipeline plans and to route pipelines through Georgia were politically driven. In 2007–8 SOCAR initiated international expansion, beginning with the acquisition and renovation of Georgia's Kulevi oil terminal on the Black Sea, followed by the opening of offices in the United Kingdom, Romania, Switzerland and Turkey and plans to open 20 petrol stations in Georgia.

In the use of oil revenues, SOCAR's role goes beyond that of a commercial company, being expected to make expenditures on hospitals, schools and other social welfare areas, which are usually made by the state rather than an employer. Oil revenues accruing to SOFAZ have also been used to support social welfare spending; in 2003 SOFAZ was used to finance resettlement and other assistance to people displaced by the Nagorno Karabakh conflict. By 2006 expenditures from SOFAZ amounted to $357m., including $40m. for housing of refugees and internally displaced persons (Lücke and Trofimenko, 2008). In consequence, Azerbaijan had by 2008 saved less than one-tenth of its oil windfall.[6]

In summary, the combination of pressing political and social demands and the geography of its oil deposits (the large field exploited by the Deal of the Century was known but no other major offshore oilfield has been discovered) contributed to a strategy of rapid exploitation and current use of revenues. Azerbaijan's energy future will be more closely related to gas markets, which have a different structure in terms of pricing and delivery modes, which will be discussed in the section on Turkmenistan.

Kazakhstan

Kazakhstan has the Caspian Sea region's largest recoverable crude oil reserves, and accounts for over half of the oil currently produced in the region (Table 15.1). During the 1990s, exploitation of the Tengiz oilfield and exploration for other potentially abundant oilfields was hampered by lack of technical expertise, lengthy negotiations with potential foreign partners, and Russian control over pipeline routes. These obstacles had been more or less overcome by the early 2000s, coinciding with the start of the rapid rise in oil prices. Kazakhstan's oil exports drove growth rates of over 9% per year 2000–2007 (Table 15.4).

The 1990s in Kazakhstan were characterized by a series of deals between the President and the oil majors to revise the shareholdings in Tengiz and for the development of other large energy projects such as the Kashagan offshore oilfield and the Karachaganak gasfield. The process was extremely opaque, leading to drawn-out legal proceedings in New York and elsewhere (dubbed *Kazakhgate* by the media) and the imprisonment in the USA of a Mobil vice-president for failing to declare a 'commission' in his tax return (Hersh, 2001). Despite the corruption, Kazakhstan succeeded in involving foreign companies and developing energy resources, but the process was slower and less transparent than in Azerbaijan.[7] Foreign participation also helped to ensure construction of new pipelines which reduced dependence on the Russian pipeline company, Transneft; the private CPC pipeline to the Black Sea opened in 2001 and the Baku-Tbilisi-Ceyhan pipeline to the Mediterranean opened in 2005.

Since 1997 there has been concern in Kazakhstan that Production Sharing Agreements (PSAs) gave too much to foreign partners at the expense of Kazakhstan. When such concerns were first voiced, and explained by the inexperience of Kazakh lawyers in the early post-independence years, foreign investors protested strongly and President Nazarbayev guaranteed that no existing

Table 15.4 Growth in real GDP 1989–2008 (%)

	1990	1991	1992	1993	1994	1995	1996	1997	1998	1999	1999; 1989=100	1998	1999	2000	2001	2002	2003	2004	2005	2006	2007	2008
Azerbaijan		-1	-23	-23	-20	-12	1	6	10	10	45	10	11	11	10	11	11	10	24	31	23	11
Kazakhstan	0	-13	-3	-9	-13	-8	1	2	-2	2	63	-2	3	10	14	10	9	9	10	11	9	3
Turkmenistan	2	-5	-5	-10	-17	-7	-7	-11	5	16	64	7	17	19	20	16	17	17	10	11	12	10
Uzbekistan	2	-1	-11	-2	-4	-1	2	3	4	4	94	4	4	4	4	4	4	8	7	7	10	9

Source: European Bank for Reconstruction and Development Transition Report Update, April 2001, 15; European Bank for Reconstruction and Development data at www.ebrd.com.

PSAs would be amended without consensus. In 1999 amendments to the Oil and Gas Law strengthened local content requirements, and subsequent PSAs specified local sourcing elements. There has been a growing tendency to favour domestic partners, and the 2005 PSA Law mandated a minimum 50% participation of KazMunaiGas.

KazMunaiGas (KMG) was created in November 2002 by merging state corporations with a variety of oil and gas operations to form a 100% state-owned, vertically-integrated company, whose operations include exploration and production, transportation, oil refining, petrochemicals and marketing of oil and gas. Reflecting its close connection to government and role in policy implementation KMG is the government's negotiating arm in PSA contracts, and is required to supply subsidised fuel to domestic markets and to provide some social services. KMG's role also includes increasing rent extraction for the government. In this aggressive intent KMG has some resemblance to Russian state-owned energy companies, Gazprom and Rosneft, although unlike the latter KMG has acquired larger shares of energy projects in a straightforward and transparent manner by purchase or the transfer of state-held licences.[8] By 2009 KMG owned about 30% of oil production and 40% of proved reserves in Kazakhstan (Kennedy and Nurmakov, 2010, 10). The government is promoting KMG as a national champion which will become a major international company in the mould of Statoil or CNPC (Olcott, 2007; Domjan and Stone, 2010).[9]

In 2004 Kazakhstan began to revise the tax and other laws pertaining to PSAs more actively. Legislation tightened the definition by which development costs are covered by PSAs.[10] The government also introduced a rent tax on oil exports in 2004 and increased royalty payments on oil and gas in 2005. In 2009 royalties were replaced by a natural resources extraction tax as part of a major tax reform aimed at easing the burden on small and medium-sized enterprises and on the non-extractive sector while increasing revenues from extractive industries (Kennedy and Nurmakov, 2010, 7).

The larger share for KMG in energy projects and deteriorating conditions for PSA partners built up tension between Kazakhstan and western energy companies. A flashpoint arose in 2007 when the development of the Kashagan megafield ran into technical difficulties, cost overruns and revised projections of when oil exports would begin. The lead operator, Italian company Eni, announced that the costs of first-stage development had increased from $10 to $19bn, and production would be delayed from 2008 to 2010 with peak output being reached in 2019 instead of 2016.[11] In January 2008 the foreign participants (Eni, Shell, Total, ExxonMobil, ConocoPhillips and Inpex) agreed to reduce their shares in order to permit KMG to increase its share to 16.8%.[12] Meanwhile, adding to the pressure on the foreign companies, in September 2007 Kazakhstan's parliament passed a law giving the government the power to renegotiate contracts deemed a threat to national security, although political leaders made clear that they were not intending to nationalize resources (as had happened in Venezuela, Bolivia and Russia).

Kazakhstan has also increased pressure on western participants in its energy sector by accepting Chinese participation. PetroKazakhstan, a Canadian company which in the 1990s had developed the second-largest oil and gas output after Tengiz, came into conflict with the government in 2005, including a fine for anti-competitive behaviour and protests against its environmental and labour record; in August 2005 China's state energy company, China National Petroleum Corporation (CNPC), bought PetroKazakhstan for $4.18bn, and subsequently offered KMG a share in Petro-Kazakhstan. In 2009 China was allowed to significantly increase its interests in return for providing nearly $13bn in credits and loans to help Kazakhstan weather its financial crisis; CNPC bought the Kazakh oil producer MangistauMunaiGaz (MMG) in a joint deal with KMG worth $2.6bn,[13] and China Investment Corp purchased 11% of the KMG Exploration and Production company for $939m. In June 2010 energy minister Sauat Mynbayev reported that China held a 50–100% stake in fifteen companies working in Kazakhstan's energy sector, and that out of 80m.

tons of crude oil which Kazakhstan was expected to produce in 2010, some 26m. would go to China. The Kazakh-China oil pipeline, partly owned by CNPC and the first direct oil pipeline from Central Asia to China, grew an additional 762 kilometres from Kazakhstan's Caspian Sea oilfields to western China's in 2009. The Chinese and Kazakh presidents, together with their Turkmen and Uzbek counterparts, opened a gas pipeline in December 2009. Agreements have also been reached on joint uranium production, and Kazakhstan's biggest copper mining company, Kazakhmys, and China's Jinchuan Group created a joint venture to develop a major copper project at Aktogay.

Kazakhstan established in August 2000 the National Fund for the Republic of Kazakhstan (NFRK), into which extra revenues from oil, gas, copper, lead, zinc and chrome are transferred when world prices exceed reference prices. In late 2008 the government launched an anti-crisis plan for which $10bn or 9.5% of GDP, largely from the NFRK, was pledged. The plan focused on capital injections in four major banks (through the government holding company Samruk-Kazyna), support for construction and the real estate market, assistance to small and medium-sized enterprises and agriculture, and public investment in industry. At the end of 2009 the government announced that the need for crisis measures was past and tasked Samruk-Kazyna with promoting diversification and greater economic efficiency in firms; the future relationship between the NFRK and the funding of Samruk-Kazyna is unclear, but it will impact on KMG which is owned by Samruk-Kazyna.

The energy sector and its role in the national economy has evolved over the two decades since independence. Kazakhstan was fortunate to inherit the Tengiz project and to have the world's largest oil discovery in the 1990s, Kashgaran. President Nazarbayev faced difficult issues of nation-building and the transition from central planning, while cementing his own hold on power. Oil provided the lubrication for achieving all of these goals. In the 1990s the emphasis was on presidential control over potential rents associated with alienation of rights to develop the resources, and this led to lengthy and non-transparent negotiations and large-scale corruption. After the turn of the century, as the economic situation turned around and the country enjoyed a massive oil-led boom, the President pursued a more far-sighted strategy of increasing national control over the revenue streams and using oil revenues in support of better economic policies, albeit without any loosening of his hold on power.

Turkmenistan

The other major energy producer, Turkmenistan, was less eager to negotiate contracts with foreign energy companies. At independence the country's resource base was cotton and a recently developed natural gas sector, neither of which was in urgent need of foreign expertise. President Niyazov relied on resource rents to fund populist policies and grandiose buildings (Pomfret, 2006, 89–103). Cotton provided the revenues in the mid-1990s, but the government offered little incentive to farmers and by the end of the decade the sector was languishing. As rents from cotton exports declined, revenues from gas exports began to increase after 2000, largely due to improved export market conditions; the volume of gas produced was lower in the 2000s than it had been in 1990 (Table 15.1).[14] Despite mismanagement of resources and failure to develop new exports, the revenues continued to be sufficient for the President's needs.

President Niyazov showed little interest in discovering and exploiting new sources of oil or gas, even though onshore and offshore reserves in western Turkmenistan were believed to be substantial. Initial involvement by large western firms gradually faded; Mobil and Monument cut their activities by half in the late 1990s due to high costs of extraction and transportation and to dissatisfaction with the tax regime (Lubin, 1999, 65).[15] In mid-2000 Burren took over the interests of Monument, and ExxonMobil pulled out of Turkmenistan in 2002. After the turn of the century PSAs involved smaller companies such as Burren Energy, Dragon Oil and

Petronas, and in other oilfields small foreign companies (such as, Pado Oil and Chemical of Austria) became non-operating partners in joint ventures with TurkmenNeft. Schlumberger, the only foreign service company operating at oilfields in western Turkmenistan, helped oil production by servicing the fields' wells and providing necessary equipment under a five-year contract, signed in February 1998, but Schlumberger's work was hindered by government interference and TurkmenNeft failed to pay the company on time. The target for the Turkmen companies to raise their oil production to 10m. tons by 2000 was not reached; actual output of just over 7m. tons in 2000 was not much higher than in 1985 (Table 15.1), and less than the 1975 peak.

By the mid-2000s it was becoming clear that Turkmenistan needed foreign capital and know-how, if it were to increase oil and gas output.[16] Only in the last year of his life, however, did Turkmenbashi become seriously concerned about increasing revenue, and in 2006 he made a trip to Beijing whose purpose was to involve China in Turkmenistan's gas sector. This strategy was followed by his successor, Gurbanguly Berdymukhammedov, and culminated in the opening of a Turkmenistan-China gas pipeline through Uzbekistan and Kazakhstan in December 2009, breaking Russia's quasi-monopoly on gas exports. The China deals improved Turkmenistan's bargaining position relative to Russia, as did the opening in January 2010 of a pipeline to Iran. Russia and Turkmenistan remained mired in a price dispute for most of 2009, but President Berdymukhamedov seemed unwilling to antagonize Russia by bringing in western oil firms; despite strong lobbying by western majors, contracts worth $9.7bn to develop the South Yolotan gasfield were awarded in December 2009 to firms from China, South Korea and the United Arab Emirates.[17]

In summary, under President Niyazov, Turkmenistan did not create a positive environment for foreign investors in oil and gas. Rents on existing exports were sufficient to finance the president's spending plans, and he was unwilling to allow foreign companies a significant role in the economy. Only when energy prices were well into the spectacular increase in the early 2000s did he turn to China for assistance in exploiting the country's energy resources and reducing Russia's monopoly over transit routes. Since Turkmenbashi's death in December 2006, the signals are mixed: increased Chinese activity, ongoing tensions with Russia, and involvement of international oil companies limited to foreign investors from less powerful partner countries.

International relations

With the huge increase in energy prices between 1998 and 2008 Azerbaijan, Kazakhstan and Turkmenistan all assumed a higher profile on the world stage. Kazakhstan with the largest GDP (Table 15.2) has been the most ambitious, while Azerbaijan has geographically more limited perspectives focused on its immediate neighbourhood, and Turkmenistan remains largely trapped in its isolationist position of positive neutrality.

Since the dissolution of the Soviet Union, President Nazarbayev has assumed the position of international statesman. In December 1991 he played a crucial intermediary role in ensuring that plans to dissolve the USSR by the leaders of Russia, Ukraine and Belarus did not ignore the interests of the other non-Baltic Soviet republics. Kazakhstan had no history as an independent nation and in 1992 Kazakhs only accounted for two-fifths of the population, with Russians accounting for a similar proportion. President Nazarbayev had to tread a careful path of building a Kazakhstan nation while not providing incentives for the Russians, who were concentrated in the north, to secede or turn to Russia for support. In negotiations over oil contracts he appears to have been torn between maximizing revenues for the state (and for offshore accounts under his control) and ensuring financing for nation-building projects such as construction of a new capital located in the centre of the country. Within the Commonwealth of Independent States Kazakhstan remained aligned with Russia in the various arrangements that culminated in the Eurasian Economic Community.

Increasing oil revenues allowed a more assertive international stance in the 2000s, although Nazarbayev remains careful to retain good relations with Russia. Concern about the country's international image was stimulated by the 2006 'mockumentary' film *Borat: Cultural Learnings of America for Make Benefit Glorious Nation of Kazakhstan*, at which the leadership initially took offence (even though the film was not shot in Kazakhstan and its barbs were targeted more at the USA). Nazarbayev positioned his country as a hinge of Eurasia, but European rather than Asian.[18] A highlight of this diplomacy was being Chair of the OSCE in 2010. In the same year Team Astana won the Tour de France, sporting jerseys in the distinctive pale blue and yellow national colours (although it is doubtful that many western European cycling enthusiasts understood the association).

Azerbaijan's leaders have had narrower goals, centred on resolution of the conflict with Armenia. In 1992–93 Azerbaijan suffered decisive military defeats by Armenia, which was supported by both Russia and the USA, and the May 1994 ceasefire left Armenia in control not only of the disputed territory of Nagorno Karabagh but also a large swathe of undisputed Azeri territory linking the enclave to Armenia proper.[19] In 1995 President Heidar Aliyev proposed to his Armenian counterpart that Azerbaijani oil exports to Armenia be linked to withdrawal from the occupied territories, and the USA offered support for a peace pipeline from Azerbaijan through Nagorno Karabagh and Armenia to Turkey; nothing resulted, and when the BTC pipeline to Turkey was built in the early 2000s it passed through Georgia, bypassing Armenia. The international oil companies' insistence on delinking the pipeline route from resolution of the Nagorno Karabagh conflict was a signal to Azerbaijan that it had to use the oil card in a different way, but completion of the BTC pipeline also signalled the increasing importance of Azerbaijan's oil for US companies and for a major US ally, Turkey. The shifting weight of the Armenian and oil lobbies on US policy towards Azerbaijan after the turn of the century was reflected in the substantial softening of Section 907 of the Freedom Support Act under which sanctions had been imposed on Azerbaijan.[20]

Since assuming the presidency in 2003, Ilham Aliyev has consistently strengthened SOCAR's position in the oil and gas sector making it a more focused instrument of state policy. After 2007 SOCAR's investments concentrated on Georgia and Turkey, making it by 2010 the largest energy actor in Georgia and a significant player in Turkey. EU concerns about energy security and dependence on Russian gas supplies also provided Azerbaijan with leverage, as the feasibility of any southern pipeline routes bringing Caspian or Central Asian gas to the EU depend critically on Azerbaijani participation. In 2009–10, when the USA supported a Turkey-Armenia rapprochement, Azerbaijani opposition led to a passive EU position. Only after the rapprochement collapsed did Azerbaijan sign a new gas transit agreement with Turkey.[21] By becoming a shareholder in Georgia's North-South pipeline, which links Russia and Armenia, SOCAR has influence over Armenia's only remaining energy link.[22]

Under Turkmenbashi, increasing energy-driven wealth had minimal impact on Turkmenistan's international relations. The counterpart to the autocratic President's complete autonomy in domestic policymaking was a foreign policy of neutrality, based on aversion to any foreign interference. However, as the economy became more and more dependent on revenues from gas exports, Turkmenbashi's prized neutrality in effect left the country dependent on Russia which controlled all the country's important transport and pipeline outlets (Anceschi, 2009; Pomfret, 2011). Only in the last year of his life did he make any effort to use Turkmenistan's potential energy wealth to diversify markets and external relations with his trip to Beijing.

Turkmenbashi's successor, President Berdymukhamedov, brought the China initiative to fruition. He has cautiously opened up energy exploitation to foreign companies, but avoided upsetting Russia by only involving non-western companies. Nevertheless, Turkmenistan's small shift to greater engagement had a regional implication insofar as co-operation with Uzbekistan and

Kazakhstan was required for a pipeline to China to be built. The pipeline project engendered sufficient trust among previously frosty partners that in 2009 the Presidents of Turkmenistan, Kazakhstan and Uzbekistan for the first time jointly negotiated with Russia prices for future gas deliveries.

In the Turkmenbashi era, relations between Turkmenistan and Azerbaijan were soured by disputes over demarcation of the southern Caspian, which at times led to shooting incidents, and over debts arising from gas shipped from Turkmenistan to Azerbaijan as far back as 1991. Turkmenistan's Embassy in Baku was closed in 2001. Under President Berdymukhamedov, relations warmed as Turkmenistan reopened its embassy, and in June 2007 proposals were announced for joint exploration of the Serdar/Kapaz field under the South Caspian Sea. The debt dispute was settled in March 2008 when a high-level delegation from Turkmenistan visited Baku.[23] The rapprochement clears the way for future construction of a Trans-Caspian pipeline through which Turkmen gas could be supplied to Europe.[24]

Conclusions

For Azerbaijan, Kazakhstan and Turkmenistan exploitation of oil and gas reserves and the contrast between stagnant world prices in the 1990s and the boom of 1999–2008 have been determining forces in their post-independence history. The speed and nature of energy development have been primarily determined by domestic political considerations (primarily regime survival), as well as by resource endowments (oil versus gas and onshore versus offshore). For all three countries, being energy-rich has had important consequences for national power and foreign policy.[25]

Kazakhstan has assumed a higher profile position as an emerging market economy, to the extent that commentators have discussed whether it should be linked with Brazil, Russia, India and China as the BRICKs (Olcott, 2008). More concretely Kazakhstan has sought to establish itself as a significant player in Eurasia, as its position of regional hegemon in Central Asia has become incontrovertible. Azerbaijan has had more limited international aspirations, using its newfound economic strength to influence relevant outside powers' positions on the frozen conflict with Armenia. Reflecting the extreme policies of Turkmenbashi's idiosyncratic dictatorship, Turkmenistan has been least active in international relations, but this is changing under President Berdymukhamedov.

For all three countries, increasing export revenues and economic power have been intimately connected to the energy boom in the first decade of the twenty-first century, and the future oil-and-power nexus will depend critically on global energy market trends. Azerbaijan's position is the most vulnerable, insofar as its oil reserves are limited; it has committed itself to rapid exploitation of known reserves and time will tell whether that was a serendipitous choice if prices never regain their 2008 high or whether it was over-hasty depreciation of natural capital. In the second decade of the twenty-first century Azerbaijan will come to rely increasingly on gas rather than oil. Both Azerbaijan and Turkmenistan could be crucial players in alleviating EU concerns about access to gas supplies, or they could be sidelined by a shift to LNG which will favour suppliers such as Qatar and Australia with ocean ports. Kazakhstan's future energy revenues appear most secure, with large proven oil and gas reserves and a variety of available export routes.

In all three countries, the political system concentrates power in the hands of the president. Both the strength of the leader's position and the weak pressures for greater democracy are intrinsically related to energy abundance, which provided resources to ensure the incumbent's position and also freed the leader from any need to seek the population's acquiescence in how the state raises revenue. Autocracies are the norm, but not universal, in oil-exporting countries, so there is little reason to expect imminent regime change, but the dependence of economic and political decisions on the wisdom and health of the leader may be a source of future instability.

Notes

1 On the economies of Central Asia, see Pomfret (1995; 2006) and Gleason (2003). Uzbekistan, like Turkmenistan, has been reluctant to involve foreign firms in its resource sectors, but the economy is better managed than that of Turkmenistan and cotton remains a major export. Uzbekistan's second largest export is gold, in whose production foreign partners have played a role, but the arrangements and gold output are not publicized by the government.
2 Azerbaijan's crude oil production declined from just under 15m. metric tons in 1980 to 11m. in 1992 (IMF *Economic Survey Azerbaijan*, April 1993, 53), i.e. back to 1901 output levels. Kalyuzhnova (2008, 77–78) provides an eyewitness account of the dilapidated state of some oil facilities over a decade after independence.
3 Aliyev had been appointed First Secretary of the Azerbaijan Soviet Socialist Republic by Brezhnev in 1969 and promoted to the Soviet Politburo in 1982 by Andropov, but was forced to resign by Gorbachev in 1987. He became leader of the Nakhchivan Autonomous Republic (a non-contiguous part of Azerbaijan), where he reinvented himself as an Azeri nationalist while avoiding association with the political disarray and military disasters of the early 1990s.
4 Since the ceasefire Armenia has occupied both the disputed territory and 9% of Azerbaijan's territory lying between Nagorno Karabakh and the Armenian border. Economic support for the 600,000 internally displaced Azeris placed a large burden on the state budget.
5 SOFAZ was established in 1999, and became operational in 2001. SOFAZ transfers a portion to the government budget and invests the remainder overseas to mitigate Dutch Disease effects, but from the start disputes arose over the use of funds. In 2002 SOFAZ, contrary to its statutes, supported a commercial venture, the Baku-Tbilisi-Ceyhan pipeline. There was also debate over the extent to which the fund should support social welfare spending.
6 CASE (2008, 121) contrasts this with Kazakhstan and Russia, which both saved over half of their 2003–7 windfall in their oil funds. However, SOFAZ assets increased significantly in 2008 due partly to the oil price peak, but more to PSAs reaching the point where the operators had recouped up-front costs and a larger share of revenues accrued to the host country.
7 In contrast to Azerbaijan, whose main PSAs have been published, Kazakhstan's remain secret, although according to Muttitt (2007) the terms are known to all major oil producers.
8 However, the use of environmental regulations to push out PetroKazakhstan's Canadian owner was reminiscent of Russian policy in Sakhalin, and the disposal of MMG had echoes of the Yukos affair (see below). Karachaganak is the only major energy project in which KMG does not have a share; a government threat to halt production if increased export duties are not paid (putting pressure on the existing partners British Gas, Eni, Chevron and Lukoil to give a share to KMG) is under arbitration.
9 KMG's substantial 2006–8 investments in Georgia were negatively affected by the August 2008 Russia-Georgia war. KMG has also invested in Romania, buying the country's second largest oil company, Rompetrol, for $3.6bn in 2007.
10 PSAs acknowledge a potential time inconsistency problem (Pomfret, 2011). Foreign partners have the technology to explore and exploit natural resources, and they incur large development costs in doing so, but their presence is less essential once production is under way, and the foreign companies then face a threat of expropriation. Under a PSA the foreign companies take a larger share of the revenue stream until their upfront costs have been covered; the precise shares and definition of development costs required are PSA-specific.
11 The exceptionally large cost over-runs threatened to reduce Kazakhstan's state revenues by as much as $20bn over the decade 2007–17 (Kennedy and Nurmakov, 2010, 5–6). The dispute was sufficiently serious that successive Italian prime ministers, Prodi and Berlusconi, flew to Astana to negotiate with President Nazarbayev.
12 It was also reported that Eni and its partners would make an additional payment to Kazakhstan of $5bn in compensation for lost revenue due to the delays.
13 The MMG case was complicated by the involvement in MMG of President Nazarbayev's estranged son-in-law, who was under investigation for criminal activities. Domjan and Stone (2010) liken the case to that of Yukos in Russia, where a previously powerful oligarch was displaced after falling out of political favour, but the MMG takeover was conducted by a more accepted legal process and did not result in a simple state takeover (although KMG's share of the deal was 51% and CNPC's 49%).

14 The exceptionally low output in 1997 and 1998 was due to Turkmenistan cutting supplies to Ukraine in a dispute over unpaid bills.
15 Investor confidence was not helped by doubts over the government's commitment to contractual obligations, which were highlighted when a transAfghanistan pipeline contract with Bridas was terminated in favour of one with Unocal. Bridas initiated proceedings in international courts, and Turkmenistan gained nothing as anticipated US support for a Unocal-led pipeline was withdrawn in 1997 when US relations with the Taliban government deteriorated.
16 In 2003 Turkmenbashi signalled an intention to sign a PSA with a consortium of Russian companies, Zarit, to exploit offshore oil and gas fields, but did not finalize the deal. Kalyuzhnova (2008, 83–86) emphasises lack of technical skills after the departure of Soviet specialists as the cause of falling revenues per cubic metre of gas exports (e.g. due to poorly maintained pipelines), and highlights how much time in exploring offshore oil reserves (as of 2007) had been wasted due to lack of technical expertise.
17 Eni purchased Burren Energy in late 2007, but this may have been primarily to acquire Burren's African interests. The Turkmen government was annoyed that it had not been involved in the negotiations and in 2008 refused to issue visas to Eni personnel. The bad blood reportedly also reflected information-sharing between Kazakhstan and Turkmenistan, with Kazakhstan voicing disappointment with Eni's performance as lead operator of Kashagan.
18 In international soccer, the most popular sport in Central Asia, Kazakhstan plays in European tournaments, whereas the other Central Asian countries play in the Asian region. Kazakhstan does, however, keep a foot, or a skate, in both continents, e.g. hosting the Asian Winter Games in January-February 2011.
19 In 1992 under Section 907 of the Freedom Support Act the USA denied economic and humanitarian aid, including most-favoured nation treatment, to Azerbaijan, alone among all Soviet successor states. The measure, ostensibly in response to Azerbaijan cutting the rail link to Armenia, reflected the strength of the influential Armenian lobby in the USA and, ironically, was implemented when Azerbaijan had one of the most democratic governments in the former Soviet Union. Azerbaijan's sole ally, Turkey, provided little support beyond blockading the Armenian border. Armenia still has land routes through Iran and Georgia.
20 After 11 September 2001 the US Executive pushed strongly for a Section 907 waiver, which it linked to Azerbaijan's cooperation in the war on terror. Congress granted annual waivers, which were bitterly opposed by the Armenian National Committee of America and were supported by the oil lobby.
21 Lussac (2010) analyses this episode. By increasing contracted gas sales to Russia for 2011 Azerbaijan signalled to the EU that it had alternative gas markets, and by pushing ahead with studies of the Azerbaijan-Georgia-Romania Interconnector (AGRI) project Azerbaijan indicated to Turkey that alternative transit routes to Europe were possible.
22 At the time of writing it is difficult to predict where this pressure will lead. Increased isolation and desperation for an Armenia that considers itself still militarily superior to Azerbaijan, but facing a deteriorating bilateral balance of power, is a combustible situation, and it is not helped by uncertainty over how far Russia or the USA would go in support of Armenia. Hopes that a peaceful solution might be found during Kazakhstan's OSCE chairmanship were shattered by the failure of a June 2010 peace conference in Almaty.
23 Although both countries acknowledged the debts incurred in 1991–93, at that time they both still used the rouble, whose hard-currency value was disputed; Turkmenistan sought $56m. while Azerbaijan offered $18m. Under the March 2008 agreement, Azerbaijan agreed to pay $44.8m.
24 This would require still closer co-operation between Azerbaijan and Turkmenistan, as well as expansion of Turkmenistan's production capacity. Long-term commitments to Russia, China and Iran exceed current capacity, but Turkmenistan's untapped reserves are considered to be large. EU demand for Turkmen gas depends upon relations between Russia and the EU, and related concerns about EU energy security, as well as on the viability of other options for the EU such as delivery of liquefied natural gas (LNG) by sea. Despite the uncertainties, Berdymukhamedov has signalled to the EU and to Russia and China that western pipeline routes have not been ruled out.
25 This view is not universally shared. In a recent collection of articles by international relations and security specialists (Kavalski, 2010), oil is just one among several major interests (geographical proximity to many important powers, the threat of Islamic terrorism, and energy and other raw material resources) that external actors have in Central Asia, while for the Central Asian leaders internal stability is considered to be the all-consuming concern.

References

Anceschi, L. (2009): *Turkmenistan's Foreign Policy: Positive Neutrality and the Consolidation of the Turkmen Regime* (London, Routledge).

CASE (2008): The Economic Aspects of the Energy Sector in CIS Countries, *European Commission Economic Papers 327*, Warsaw.

Domjan, P. and M. Stone (2010): A Comparative Study of Resource Nationalism in Russia and Kazakhstan, 2004–8, *Europe-Asia Studies* 62, 35–62.

Dorian, J. and F. Mangera (1995): Oil and War: Impacts on Azerbaijan and Armenia, *East-West Center Working Papers No.22*, Honolulu.

Franke, A., A. Gawrich and G. Alakbarov (2009): Kazakhstan and Azerbaijan as Post-Soviet Rentier States: Resource incomes and autocracy as a double "çurse" in post-Soviet regimes, *Europe-Asia Studies* 61: 109–40.

Gleason, G. (2003): *Markets and Politics in Central Asia* (London, Routledge).

Hersh, S. (2001): The Price of Oil; What was Mobil up to in Kazakhstan and Russia? *New Yorker*, 9th. July, pp. 48–65.

Islamov, B. (2001): *The Central Asian States Ten Years After: How to Overcome Traps of Development, Transformation and Globalisation?* (Tokyo: Maruzen).

Jones Luong, P. and E. Weinthal (2010): *Oil Is Not a Curse: Ownership Structure and Institutions in Soviet Successor States* (New York, Cambridge University Press).

Kalyuzhnova, Y. (2008): *Economics of the Caspian Oil and Gas Wealth: Companies, governments, policies* (Basingstoke UK, Palgrave Macmillan).

Kavalski, E. ed. (2010): *The New Central Asia: The regional impact of international actors* (World Scientific; Singapore).

Kennedy, R. and A. Nurmakov (2010): Resource Nationalism Trends in Kazakhstan, 2004–9, *Working paper of RUSSCASP*, the Fridtjof Nansen Institute, the Norwegian Institute of International Affairs and Econ Pöyry.

Lubin, N. (1999): Energy Wealth, Development, and Stability in Turkmenistan, *NBR Analysis* 10, 61–78.

Lücke, M. and N. Trofimenko (2008): Whither Oil Money? Redistribution of oil revenue in Azerbaijan, in B. Najman, R. Pomfret and G. Raballand, eds. *The Economics and Politics of Oil in the Caspian Basin: The redistribution of oil revenues in Azerbaijan and Central Asia* (London, Routledge), 132–56.

Lussac, S. (2010): Will Gas Help Resolve the NagornoKarabakh Conflict? *CACI Analyst* (Johns Hopkins University Central Asia – Caucasus Institute), 17 September – at http://cacianalyst.org/?q=node/5406.

Muttitt, G. (2007): *Hellfire Economics: Multinational companies and the contract dispute over Kashagan, the world's largest undeveloped oilfield*, PLATFORM: London.

Olcott, M. (2007): *Kazmunaigaz: Kazakhstan's National Oil and Gas Company* (Houston, James Baker III Institute for Public Policy, Rice University).

——(2008): Kazakhstan: Will "BRIC" be spelled with a K? *China and Eurasia Forum Quarterly 6(2)*, 41–53.

Ostrowski, W. (2010): *Politics and Oil in Kazakhstan* (London, Routledge).

Pomfret, R. (1995): *The Economies of Central Asia* (Princeton NJ: Princeton University Press).

——(2006): *The Central Asian Economies since Independence* (Princeton NJ: Princeton University Press).

——(2011): Turkmenistan after Turkmenbashi, in J. Ahrens and H. Hoen (eds) *Institutional Reform in Central Asia* (London, Routledge).

——(forthcoming): Exploiting Energy and Mineral Resources in Central Asia, Azerbaijan and Mongolia, *Comparative Economic Systems*.

16
Oil and Politics in Southeast Asia[1]

Benjamin Smith

Introduction

Most of the oil exporting regions of the world have remained fairly stable over the last two decades in terms of their populations of producers. Southeast Asia is one of three regions, however, that stand out as having undergone substantial change, along with South America and Western Africa. The latter two regions have seen a proliferation of new exporters. Southeast Asia, however, has seen perhaps the most change of any region in the world, with "old" exporters departing that group and with "new" exporters bringing export revenues on line under very different political and economic circumstances.

One thing of note about Southeast Asia is the large number of states that sit well "off the line" in terms of broad trends in oil and politics. Malaysia's relatively capable state, Indonesia's thriving democracy, and Brunei's closer resemblance to Gulf monarchies than to its neighbors all pose interesting questions for those of us concerned with how oil wealth and politics "normally" interact. As I discuss below, Southeast Asia nicely illustrates how conditional the effects of resource wealth can be. With that in mind, this essay looks at three oil-shaped dynamics: the trajectories of older exporters like Brunei, Indonesia and Malaysia, broad regional trends since 1990, and the emergence of three new exporters (Cambodia, Timor-Leste and Vietnam) since 2000. What these empirical explorations reveal is a strikingly broad set of oil-influenced political trajectories that suggests we rethink blunt assessments that assume uniform relationships. Taking a close look at the politics of oil wealth through these three lenses provides insight into a growing consensus in scholarly and policy circles that the effects of resource export dependence are strongly conditional and depend on a multitude of antecedent conditions.

The new political economy of resource wealth

The first generation of studies focused on oil and politics tended to take a mono-causal approach, assigning more or less the same (negative) effects to resource wealth across the board. From Mahdavy's (1970) original statement of the rentier state phenomenon of overspending and political overexuberance, Beblawi and Luciani (1987) elaborated a theory of the rentier state floating on oil revenues high above and apart from its citizens, able to sustain a no taxation, no representation political economy. This dynamic took further pride of place in Skocpol's (1982) refinement of her structural model of revolution. A later round of case-driven studies by Vandewalle (1998) and Karl (1997) focused on the economic development-stunting effects of oil-driven economies. Collier and Hoeffler's (1998) early work on resources and conflict and Ross's (2001) demonstration of the negative oil-democracy correlation cemented a conventional theoretical wisdom by the early 21st century holding that oil had systematic (and damaging) effects. Notably, Southeast Asian cases were missing from these early studies of oil and politics, except inasmuch as Karl (1997) referred to the "Indonesian exception."

Valuable as these studies were in getting scholars to examine the negative repercussions of commodity endowments—contradicting a generation of development economists focused on comparative advantage—they tended to focus the lens of inquiry away from contrast cases and toward those that confirmed the initial theoretical hunches. Oil politics, as a result, became the study of Algeria, Nigeria, Iran, and other large and politically troubled countries. What went missing were cases like Indonesia and Malaysia—in which oil went hand in hand, not with trouble-free political economies, but frequently with positive outcomes in at least some areas.

What has emerged over the last decade as a result is a consensus, strongly supported by increasingly sophisticated econometric and comparative historical analyses, that the effects of oil wealth are frequently conditional and therefore dependent on antecedent conditions. Moving away from his earlier, more mono-causal studies, Paul Collier and his co-authors have found increasingly clear conditional and timing-sensitive effects in the relationship between resource booms and downstream economic impact (Collier 2010; Collier and Goderis 2007a, 2007b; Chauvet and Collier 2006). Ross (2004) uncovered a more complex set of mechanisms, and a less certain linear relationship, between resource wealth and civil war. I have argued that oil's impact on long-term regime durability depended strongly on antecedent conditions surrounding the onset of state-driven economic development (Smith 2004, 2007). Dunning (2008) has demonstrated that variation in economic inequality strongly conditions the effect of oil wealth on the prospects for durable democracy, strengthening those prospects in unequal Latin America while undermining them elsewhere. Lowi (2009) has illustrated the centrality of leaders' choices at key moments in setting countries down particular trajectories of oil. In short, the new conventional wisdom is that oil's effects are embedded in and shaped by the political economies of which they become a part. This new, conditional approach to theorizing the "resource curse" is a much more appropriate analytic lens through which to look at Southeast Asia, which contains some curious outliers for any one-size-fits-all theory of oil politics. Take Malaysia: highly dependent on oil exports for much of the late 20th century, and for decades before that on other commodity exports, the country stands out both for its fairly capable state and for its successful technological export-driven manufacturing sector. It is now one of the world's leading manufacturers of computer chips. Or Indonesia: a large, relatively poor, oil-exporting Muslim country that in 2010 was judged by Freedom House (2010) to be the only fully free polity in all of Southeast Asia. How did Malaysia overcome its oil exports to develop its economy so successfully, and how did Indonesia overcome its own resource curse to establish a durable democracy? In the next section I turn to these two cases and to a third, Brunei, which in many ways can be analytically grouped with the small oil monarchies of the Persian Gulf.

"Old" oil exporters: Brunei, Indonesia and Malaysia

The oil industries in Southeast Asia's original exporters, Brunei, Indonesia and Malaysia, all had their origins under colonial rule. Following independence, oil has continued to play an important role in the export sectors of all three countries and to varying degrees in their politics.

Brunei

In many ways Brunei resembles the small Gulf monarchies Qatar, Bahrain, Oman and the United Arab Emirates more than the larger oil exporters that surround it. Brunei's small population (392,000 in 2008; World Bank 2009) and its economy truly dominated by oil[2] mark it off in important ways from Indonesia and Malaysia. Its chronological trajectory from British protectorate status tracks closely with the Gulf monarchies as well. Whereas Brunei's neighbors became independent in the 1940s and 1950s, it did so only in 1984, just 13 years after Bahrain and the Emirates emerged from the same status. Moreover, it did so hesitantly and not entirely voluntarily: an earlier rebellion supported by Indonesia raised concerns about the sultanate's capacity to sustain its own internal security.

Since then, Brunei's politics and economy have been mundane by regional standards. The regime's ability to provide cradle-to-grave welfare using oil proceeds (pejoratively termed "Shellfare" by its citizens) and to make the civil service a two-thirds' share of the labor market have guaranteed a generally smooth ride, even through the oil bust of the late 1980s and early 1990s. The events that have made other Southeast Asian countries so visible in the last two decades—the 1997–99 financial crisis, Indonesia's democratic transition in 1999—left Brunei largely unchanged politically and economically. Brunei is the purest rentier state in the region and, along with the Persian Gulf monarchies, one of the purest ideal type oil polities in the world.

Indonesia

The late 1960s and 1970s were the heyday boom years in Indonesia's oil industry, but they did not come without a cost. In 1974, for example, Ibnu Sutowo was fired from his position as head of Pertamina (Indonesia's national oil company) after the scope of the company's overstretching into shipbuilding and other sectors became apparent. The Indonesian treasury had to nearly bankrupt itself in order to make good on Pertamina's debts (Winters 1996). Nonetheless, the boom years were economically positive ones in Indonesia, albeit in the context of increasingly established authoritarian rule. Economic development that was in no small way catalyzed by oil revenues lifted millions of Indonesian citizens out of poverty and boosted the country's per capita wealth substantially while reducing social inequality.

As in nearly all exporting countries, the oil price crash of the mid-1980s forced a series of tough policy choices on the New Order government. As Winters (1996) notes, this period corresponded with a longer-term pattern in Indonesian political economy: granting more autonomy to economic officials when oil revenues were scarce. As a result, Indonesia underwent what would generally be considered a surprisingly smooth transition to export-oriented manufacturing focus during the late 1980s and early 1990s. The simultaneous decline in Indonesia's oil production and in global oil prices meant that, by 1995, oil revenues as a share of the country's GDP had dropped from a high in 1974 of 21% to just 6%.[3] This decline, coupled with the country's increasing domestic fuel consumption, moved Indonesia out of the population of serious exporters, a fact reflected in Indonesia's departure from OPEC in 2008.

What did not (and generally does not) vanish overnight were the long-term political and economic ramifications of Indonesia's decades of serious oil export dependence. Like Mexico, Indonesia's declining oil production probably made democratic transition more likely by shrinking the autonomous patronage resources available to rulers. And the increasingly integrated nature of Indonesia's relationship to the global economy left less room for Suharto to manipulate economics in order to stay in power. Finally, it is the case that the ossified political structures in place in 1998 took shape during the 1970s, and were therefore in part a product of oil-funded institutions. Still, what has happened since about 1985 is remarkable. In the context of prevalent scholarship on oil and politics, it is surprising both that Indonesia was able to make the transition from oil-led to export-led manufacturing growth in the late 1980s and that a decade later it underwent a transition to democracy that by nearly all accounts looks durable and meaningful.

Malaysia

Malaysia has been one of the post-colonial world's relatively few development success stories among oil exporters (see Luong and Weinthal 2006, Carneiro 2007). Despite substantial reliance on oil revenues—and before that tin and rubber revenues—Malaysia has moved up the development ladder of Asian industrial states. What is perhaps most interesting about economic development in Malaysia is that its transition out of import-substitution industrialization (ISI) and into export-led growth took place precisely as it became a substantial oil exporter: during the oil boom years of the 1970s (Salleh and Meyanathan 1993, 5). The political fallout of the 1969 race riots, which catalyzed assertive government response to the violent expression of Malay hostility toward ethnic Chinese economic dominance, and then the oil boom, created both a powerful incentive and an opportunity to use oil income to restructure Malaysia's economy. Here, as with Indonesia, political crisis led to an uncommon use of oil revenues, in the case of Malaysia to boost export competitiveness and to achieve greater economic equity between the country's ethnic groups.

Indonesia and to a greater degree Malaysia have sidestepped many of the common pitfalls associated with oil wealth. They have poverty rates well below those of most exporters (Carneiro 2007, 121) and Malaysia in particular has achieved a level of industrial transformation and technological prowess that is fairly remarkable for a country that in 1985 depended on oil exports for 25% of government revenues. Indonesia, on the other hand, has overcome its own legacy of oil export dependence to accomplish a transition to export-led growth economically and to stable democracy politically.[4] These two long-time oil states in Southeast Asia pose interesting puzzles for scholars of oil wealth: how do oil exporters successfully transform their economies or democratize?

Current trends: oil and politics in Southeast Asia

In this section I explore the general effects of oil export dependence in the region, using cross-national time series data from Southeast Asian countries for the last two decades. Since at least the publication of Ross's "Does Oil Hinder Democracy?" we have had a general understanding that, *ceteris paribus*, countries that depend on oil exports are more often authoritarian. And since then evidence has mounted that oil-rich countries are generally more prone to civil conflict, lower rates of growth, and have less effective states than others. However, as I discussed above there are some variations in this generally gloomy outlook: all else equal oil-rich countries suffer fewer regime breakdowns (Smith 2004) and under some conditions are more likely to become and to remain democratic (Dunning 2008). Moreover, as mentioned above two Southeast Asian oil exporting countries in particular—Indonesia and Malaysia—have in a number of studies been characterized as "success stories" in either successful democratization or development, respectively (on Indonesia, see Smith 2007 and Lewis 2007; on Malaysia, see Luong and Weinthal 2006 and Carneiro 2007). With these regularities and exceptions both in mind, in this section I present both data from the countries of the region and some cross-national trends for oil politics in Southeast Asia. The data I analyze here are drawn from the 12 countries of Southeast Asia, from

1990 to 2008, with the exception of Timor-Leste, for which data are available only from 1999 (the year in which United Nations supervision of the transition to full independence in 2002 began).[5] The time period allows for maximally complete data coverage and also covers two important and distinct periods in terms of the global oil market: the pre-1999 years, during which oil was at a low dating to the 1986 price crash, and the post-1999 years, during which oil prices reached their highest absolute price ever. Before presenting the results of some quantitative analyses of data from the region, I describe the measures I use and present some descriptive statistics.

Measuring oil export dependence: oil income per capita

For more than 10 years now scholars seeking to study the resource curse have employed different indicators for a common concept: the effective "rent" capacity that oil revenues make possible in different countries. A decade ago—when the econometric study of oil politics was fairly new—the standard measure was oil export revenues as numerator with GDP as denominator (see for example Ross 2001; Smith 2004). Despite its general utility (and fairly strong correlation with better ones) there are a number of analytical problems with this measure. First, it tells us little about the size of the country's population. A hypothetical country with 10,000 people and a US$10,000 economy, 40% of which came from oil exports would look the same as a country of 1,000,000 people, also with a $10,000 economy, 40% of which came from oil. The problem here is that the effective usability of oil revenues is masked by the lack of knowledge about population size, which is important if one is interested in how many oil dollars a regime can direct at each citizen, for public goods, patronage or coercion. Another problem is that the measure tells us nothing about oil that is consumed domestically.[6] That may have been less important 15 or 20 years ago, when oil wealth and industrialization were not so often coincidental. However, the transformation of large oil-rich economies in Russia, Brazil, Indonesia (three of the four large and emerging "BRIC" economies), and in Southeast Asia also Vietnam, points to serious problems. These are all exporters whose own growing industrial and manufacturing sectors use increasingly large shares of their production.

Here I use a fairly new measure, one that is becoming standard: *oil and gas income per capita*. By calculating the value in US dollars of oil and natural gas production in each year, and dividing it by the population of each country that year, one derives a measure of oil/gas income per capita—the amount a resource industry-owning government can effectively allocate per citizen based on oil and gas income.[7] This measure is about as close as we can come to capturing what is theoretically meaningful about oil and politics—what rulers can spend to keep themselves in office, either by co-opting, rewarding or coercing their citizens. The variation, even among the exporters, is dramatic. Even at its highest during this time period, no Indonesian government has ever enjoyed more than US$300 per citizen: the Sultanate of Brunei, by contrast, has never enjoyed *less* than $6,800. In the last five years, Vietnam's oil discoveries and first exports have not amounted to more than $165 per citizen. This is simply to say that other than in Brunei oil revenues, while important, do not constitute the massive rent boon for Southeast Asian political leaders that absolute export revenues might suggest.

Oil and political outcomes

Democracy

I employ here the index of democratic freedoms produced by Freedom House. I have inverted its measure to make it more intuitive: subsequently "7" is a fully free polity, "1" a fully closed one.

In 2008 Southeast Asia had only one fully free regime as coded by Freedom House: Indonesia, one of the original exporting countries of the region and until 2008 a member of the Organization of Petroleum Exporting Countries (OPEC). Indonesia is also the world's largest Muslim-majority country. Those two facts make Indonesia something of a statistical outlier. Brunei and Singapore are outliers of a different sort. As countries whose per head GDP numbers put them in the category of "developed" countries, but whose polities rank as "not free" and "partly free" according to Freedom House, they too sit well "off the line" of findings on the determinants of regime type. Singapore in particular—resource poor—stands out from international trends as rich and stably non-democratic. As I discuss below, however, neither Singapore nor Brunei pull the regional trends in any disproportionate way. With one-quarter of its countries qualifying as outliers, one might expect data from the countries of Southeast Asia not to confirm results that are robust in global quantitative studies (see for example Ross 2001, 2009). The main hypothesis here, in line with the extant literature, is that the more oil income that accrues to each citizen, the less democratic the polity is likely to be. I discuss the results below.

Conflict

Another increasingly common finding in econometric studies of resource politics is that, all else being equal, oil-rich countries are more prone to internal conflicts than oil-poor ones. Civil wars, coups d'etat, separatist conflicts and the like have all been found more likely the more oil income a country receives (Collier and Hoeffler 1998; Ross 2004). And Southeast Asia has seen its fair share of such internal conflicts: ongoing ethno-regional rebellions in Myanmar, the Moro Islamic Liberation Front's rebellion in the Philippines, a recently resolved 30-year war waged by the Aceh Independence Movement and the ongoing Papuan separatist movement in Indonesia, and others. Here I employ a measure of violent internal conflict from the Armed Conflict Data project at the Peace Research Institute of Oslo. The benchmark for coding a country year as having experienced a conflict is that at least 25 people must have been killed in battle between a non-state group and the central government. Any country-year with a conflict so measured is coded "1" and all others "0."

How does the region stack up in terms of the prevalence of internal conflict? In fact, Southeast Asia has a particularly high average rate of violent domestic conflicts in the last two decades. On average, in any given year in Southeast Asia there has been a 35% chance of internal conflict. That aggregate probability figure, of course, is heavily skewed by Myanmar, the Philippines and Indonesia, which between them were the sites of more than one-half of the conflict years between 1990 and 2008.[8] Nonetheless, it is an open question whether oil influences the likelihood of conflict in the Southeast Asian context the way it appears to do globally. Taking a cue from broad cross-national studies, I expect that oil income in Southeast Asia will correlate positively with conflict.

Governance

Another common finding in the resource curse literature is that oil-rich countries tend to have weaker state institutions and more corruption. Among recent data collection projects is that undertaken by the World Bank's Governance Indicators economists. I employ two of their measures here in order to chart broad governance trends in Southeast Asia: Control of Corruption and Government Effectiveness.[9] Both range from –2.5 to 2.5, with higher scores indicating better control of corruption and more effective government, respectively. Because data are only available from 1996, and only in even years until 2000, the results presented here are based on substantially fewer country-year observations than the democracy and conflict models. In line with the cross-national literature, my expectation is that Southeast Asia's oil exporting countries will score lower on both governance indicators.

Models and methods

Because this is a fairly small sample, and because I am most interested here in teasing out the impact of oil income on politics rather than on specifying a maximally complete set of models, I include a small but important set of controls for income (GDP per capita, taken as natural logarithm), growth (annual GDP per capita growth), land area (taken as natural logarithm), population share living in urban areas, and telephone lines per 100 people. The telephone lines measure is commonly used as a proxy for both income and for state capacity (i.e. state infrastructure) and more data are available for this than for another common proxy—road kilometers per 100 people. I experimented with some common sociocultural controls—whether a country's population was predominantly Muslim and a measure of ethnic fragmentation—in early analyses but omit them here because under no model specifications were they significant.

The methods I use here are a function of the data structure, the form of the dependent variables in question, and current standards in quantitative political economy research. For the models estimating the oil-democracy and oil-governance relationships, I employ fixed-effects generalized least squares regression. In exploring the oil-conflict linkage, I employ logistic regression with robust standard errors clustered on country. In the conflict model I also include a set of time-sensitivity variables recommended by Beck, Katz and Tucker (1998): three cubic splines and a variable that counts the number of years since the last conflict.

Results: oil and politics in Southeast Asia

In Table 16.1 are 2008 scores for the 12 countries of Southeast Asia on government effectiveness and political freedom. They come, respectively, from the World Bank's Governance dataset and from Freedom House. The statistical analyses discussed below reflect a somewhat curious observation: that two of the three most capable states in the region (Malaysia and Brunei) are oil exporters and one of the least capable (East Timor, just above Myanmar) has not really begun yet to exploit its oil and gas reserves.

Table 16.1 Governance and political freedom scores, 2008

	Government Effectiveness		Political Freedom
Myanmar	−1.6757594	7	Not free
Timor-Leste	−0.9984696	3.5	Partly free
Lao PDR	−0.8447597	6.5	Not free
Cambodia	−0.8050606	5.5	Not free
Papua New Guinea	−0.7980104	3.5	Partly free
Vietnam	−0.3134849	6	Not free
Indonesia	−0.2908707	2.5	Free
Philippines	0.0005807	3.5	Partly Free
Thailand	0.1097701	4.5	Partly Free
Brunei Darussalam	0.8901698	5.5	Not Free
Malaysia	1.12793	4	Partly Free
Singapore	2.5312514	4.5	Partly Free

Table 16.2 Oil and politics in Southeast Asia, 1990–2008

Independent Variable	Outcome Variable:		
	Democracy	Conflict§	Governance
Oil income per capita	−.088	−.323	.0366
	(.035)*	(.217)	(.014)*
GDP per capita$_{(ln)}$	.794	.116	
	(.265)**	(.497)	
Annual growth in GDP per capita	–	–	.012
			(.005)*
Urban population share	–	–	−1.506
			(.713)*
Land area$_{(ln)}$	–	.896	–
		(.288)**	
Democracy†	–	.452	–
		(.203)*	
Peace Years	–	1.863	–
		(.366)***	
Constant	3.983	11.656	.414
	(2.163)	(5.937)*	(.300)
Observations	196	196	115

Notes:
* $p < .05$
** $p < .01$
*** $p < .001$

† Freedom House score (1–7), reversed so that higher scores denote a more open polity.

§Analysis is by logistic regression. Robust standard errors in parentheses. Cubic splines included but coefficients not reported.

Table 16.2 presents the results of three models, each of which explores the relationship between oil wealth in Southeast Asia and a different outcome. As mentioned above, a different set of control variables are included alongside oil income: I have drawn deductively from current research in specifying the models—i.e. including at first variables that have consistently been important in other studies—and inductively by including here only those variables that were stably significant in this regional sample.

For democracy and governance models, analysis is by generalized least squares (GLS) regression. Fixed effects specified.

Column 1 in Table 16.2 presents the results of a regression model estimating the effect that oil income has on regime type across Southeast Asia. Included in this model is a control variable for per capita income, taken as the natural logarithm of GDP per capita in constant 2005 US dollars. This is the least surprising of the three models, as it confirms in a regional setting the long-standing finding (Ross 2001, 2009) that, *ceteris paribus*, the more oil income a country receives the less democratic it is likely to be. This result is not sensitive to outliers: excluding Brunei, for example, which is the country in the region most often characterized as highly shaped by oil wealth, does not change the relationship at all. But it clearly does not mean that autocracies today are what they are simply *because* of oil wealth. On the contrary, long-lived non-democracies such as Burma or semi-democracies, as Malaysia and Singapore are sometimes called, are durable for a host of reasons, of which oil wealth may be one. Malaysia's New

Economic Program, initiated in the early 1970s to ameliorate the economic causes of the 1969 race riots, was made possible in part by the country's oil export income and has contributed substantially to ethnic peace since. And oil revenues undoubtedly helped Suharto's New Order regime to placate some social groups and to control others. In short, oil income in Southeast Asia appears to have the same broad relationship to regime type that it does elsewhere.

Column 2 in Table 16.2 presents the results of a logistic regression estimating the likelihood of internal conflict as a function of oil income and an array of commonly employed control variables: wealth, land area and regime type. In Southeast Asia, interestingly, neither oil wealth nor per capita wealth are significantly related to the onset of violent internal conflicts. There are specific conflicts, of course, in which oil has been directly implicated such as Aceh (Ross 2005; Aspinall 2007). But so too are there examples of remarkably peaceful oil-rich cases such as Brunei, which in the context of a more conflict-prone region than average is surprising.

Column 3, finally, presents the results of a GLS model estimating the relationship between oil income and governance in Southeast Asia. Here the results are surprising: all else equal, during the last two decades the region's oil exporters have been ranked as having more capable states than oil-poor states. Based on recent research it is at least plausible that this trend (captured in Figure 16.1) is a result of another set of conditional effects in which oil income has been channeled into state building projects following acute political crises. I have argued that Indonesia's state actually grew in capacity during the 1970s as a result of political crisis, which spurred its leaders to use the oil windfalls to invest in the state apparatus (Smith 2007). But a look at Malaysia suggests something else: rulers built the Malaysian state on the foundation of British colonial administration in response to political challenges as well (Doner et al. 2005). On the other hand, it may also be the case that some of the region's least capable states—in Laos, Cambodia and Myanmar—are "dragging" the effect simply because they are both weak and oil-

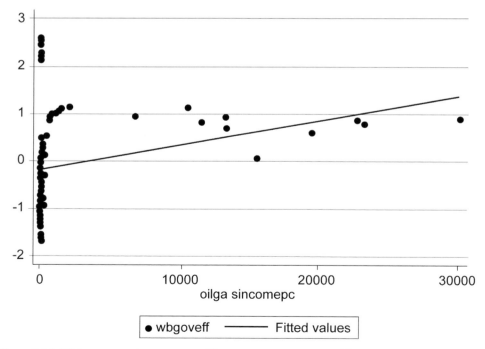

Figure 16.1 Oil income and governance (Governance score on y axis)

poor. To my mind, this last finding suggests some support for the conditional influence of oil wealth, especially as a function of past political challenges. Southeast Asia, full as it was of both ideological conflicts (communist vs. anti-communist) and ethnic ones during the early post-colonial years, provided a set of crucial tests to rulers that were arguably among the toughest to confront any developing country regimes.

New exporters: Cambodia, Timor-Leste and Vietnam

The region's broad trends—oil coinciding more often than not with authoritarianism but also with more capable state institutions—are clear. But what might we expect in the group of new regional oil producers? In Southeast Asia, there are some very poorly functioning states (and some now oil-wealthy) but in which weak states preceded oil discoveries. Oil is likely to become a defining influence in the political economies of both Cambodia and Timor-Leste. In contrast, Vietnam's relatively strong state and its diverse and large economy are fairly unlikely to be affected very much by its oil wealth. However, the region's two other new oil exporters—Cambodia and Timor-Leste—are both plagued by weak state institutions as a result of war and underdevelopment. And, as particularly poor countries, they are additionally likely to suffer resource economy problems simply because oil and gas income will dwarf the rest of their economies. Cambodia, for instance, is estimated by some to be looking at a doubling of GDP once oil and gas production is fully on line.

Cambodia

Oil exploration in Cambodia began first in 1969 when the monarchy granted a French company, Elf, a concession. That effort ended with the ascent to power of the Khmer Rouge and it was not until 2005 that it re-emerged. Since the discovery of offshore reserves that year, production has yet to commence, but estimates are that the total value of Cambodia's reserves is approximately 3–5 trillion cubic meters of natural gas and 400m. barrels of oil (*New York Times* 2007). That would represent a total value of about US$11bn. The World Bank concluded in 2006 that "Depending on the world price of oil, Cambodian reserves may be contributing annual revenues of $2bn, several times the current level of domestic revenues and ODA (overseas development aid) combined—within perhaps five to ten years" (World Bank 2006, 140).

The problems are clear across all three political outcome areas addressed here. First, increasing evidence that the Cambodian People's Party has undermined electoral and political freedom to retain power suggests that oil and gas income will augment that increasingly autocratic project. Second, the incomplete nature of the post-conflict reconstruction process means that perceived inequities in the allocation of new oil income are likely to make renewed conflict more likely. Finally, Cambodia by most accounts has one of the region's least capable states. It is rare that oil income exerts a positive influence on the quality of government, and the combination of an incomplete recovery from civil war, endemic underdevelopment, political corruption and authoritarian tendencies makes that trajectory less likely still.

Timor-Leste

Just after Timor-Leste gained independence following a 1999 referendum on leaving Indonesia and three years of UN trusteeship, expectations about the country's future potential as an oil and gas exporter ran optimistic: "oil is the potential savior of the nation's economy" (*New York Times* 2000). Some 10 years later, only a fraction of potential oil production has yet to come on line. The delay is the result of ongoing disputes with Australia over the boundary between the two countries' deposits, where to send the oil for refining, and other issues.

As the smallest and one of the poorest countries in Southeast Asia, with a population of just 600,000 and a per capita GDP of US$2,400, the country has been heavily dependent on agriculture, especially coffee, and 90% of the population works in the agricultural sector. This is unlikely to change even as Timor-Leste fully harnesses its production, in substantial part because the country has insufficient technological resources to refine oil and gas is shipped to Australia.

There are two bright spots to Timorese oil production that mitigate some common concerns. One major potential problem for countries with non-oil export sectors such as Timor-Leste—the likelihood that growing oil and gas revenues would distort the country's currency exchange rate and thereby make its other major export (in this case coffee) less competitive—is effectively sanitized by Timor's use of the US dollar as official currency. Another—the misuse of oil revenues by politicians with short time horizons—has been allayed by the establishment in 2005 of an oil fund that constitutionally insulates the country's oil revenues for investment.[10]

What it is not insulated from are the political effects that resource wealth can induce in settings plagued by weak institutions. Collier (2010) has noted the conditional effects of oil wealth and the propensity to magnify preexisting institutional trends in terms of governance. In 2006 disputes within the armed forces over wages due soldiers erupted into a violent conflict that then spread to a broader communally driven one. Since 2007 the situation has remained fairly stable, and economic growth has recovered, but as Timor-Leste's economy grows more dependent on the oil/gas sector so will the prospect of price-driven fluctuations. In short, the same problems of poor governance and infrastructure and unresolved sociopolitical cleavages are likely to be amplified by an oil-driven economy in the future.

Vietnam

While oil exploration in Vietnam began as early as the 1960s with Soviet assistance, no production took place until 1986, and it was not until the late 1990s that substantial production came on line (CCOP-EPF 2010). In 1999 production rose above 275,000 barrels per day for the first time and peaked in 2004 at 400,000. This is substantial in terms of regional producers, but again the size of Vietnam's economy and population is large enough that the political and institutional effect of oil income is likely to be modest. This is more likely to be the case given the steadily high rates of growth in Vietnam over the last decade: the country is likely to consume increasing shares of the oil it produces, lessening somewhat the foreign earnings forecast and therefore the non-domestic implications of oil revenues.

It is also the case that Vietnam has been durably and fairly stably authoritarian since the consolidation of Communist Party rule over the south in 1975. In this case, therefore, any modest effect of oil income simply will reinforce what has been in place for more than 30 years. Unlike the Cambodian People's Party, less institutionalized and more likely to evolve as a function of new oil income, the Communist Party of Vietnam emerged as a result of a decades-long fight for political primacy. Comparative perspective on such single-party projects suggests that the lessons and legacies of those battles for power are durable and can often survive for decades after the conflicts themselves.

Conclusion

Scholars of Southeast Asian politics have noted that about every decade a luminary member of their group writes a state-of-the-field essay making the case again for viewing the region as a coherent entity, much the same as the Ottoman and Islamic imperial legacies tie together the Middle East and as the Hispano-Iberian and Catholic legacies hold together Latin America. Southeast Asia, lacking a common religious, linguistic, colonial or ethnic denominator is a bit harder to hold together in this way, and oil politics is no exception. What the countries of the region do provide, however, is a number of theoretically coherent looks at the various trajectories that scholars have developed to help us understand the political economy of oil. From Brunei's archetypical oil monarchy to Indonesia's uneasy transition out of major exporter status, to Malaysia's surprising economic transformation, oil wealth in Southeast Asia has been put to nearly as many political uses as we have yet theorized. And the region's new group of exporters illustrates both how potentially transformative and how modest a sizeable oil sector can be.

Appendix: Descriptive Statistics

Variable	Obs	Mean	Std.Dev.	Min	Max
Oil/gas income per capita	219	1322.792	4267.355	0	30186.41
Oil/gas income$_{(ln)}$	219	3.083	3.662	−10.204	10.315
Urban population share	219	.415	.2566	.13	1
Annual gdp pc growth	211	3.555	4.567	−14	15
GDPpc(PPP)	196	10551.89	15782.78	648	50499
GDPpc$_{(ln)}$	196	8.313	1.318	6.474	10.830
Freedom House score	219	2.114	1.570	0	4.5
Conflict	231	.3506494	.4782095	0	1
Government effectiveness	118	−.0991044	1.00597	−1.675759	2.59764

Notes

1 I would like to thank Burcu Kanyilmaz for outstanding research assistance. I am also grateful to Thomas Smith for help in calculating the gas income per capita conversion equations used in this chapter.
2 In 2006 oil exports comprised 96% of Brunei's exports.
3 This figure climbed after the 1999 increase in oil prices, but never above 9%.
4 The puzzle is not that after its oil income decline Indonesia democratized: it is that the country was both able to make the transition to export-led development in an institutional setting heavily shaped by an oil economy and subsequently to become durably democratic.
5 Data for Brunei, Indonesia, Malaysia, Thailand and Vietnam come from BP, *Statistical Review of Energy 2010*. www.bp.com/productlanding.do?categoryId=6929&contentId=7044622. Accessed December 6, 2010. Data for Timor-Leste come from US Energy Information Administration: http://tonto.eia.doe.gov/country/country_energy_data.cfm?fips=TT. Accessed December 10, 2010. Data for Cambodia, Laos, Myanmar, Papua New Guinea, the Philippines, and Singapore come from US Geological Survey, various years. http://minerals.usgs.gov/minerals/pubs/country/index.html#pubs. Accessed December 6, 2010.
6 It is worth further consideration whether exported oil—which generates foreign currency income—might still create different political opportunities for political leaders than domestically sold oil.
7 Thanks to Michael Ross for his helpful advice on constructing this measure, and thanks to Thomas Smith for help in constructing the precise equation to convert natural gas BTUs into billion cubic feet and then into income.
8 Brunei and Singapore—neither of which have had an internal conflict in the last twenty years—do not disproportionately "pull" the data in the other direction, although without their years included the risk of internal conflict rises somewhat to 41%.

9 Because the results for government effectiveness and control of corruption were substantively very close, I report only those for government effectiveness.
10 The fund is similar to those in Norway and Alaska. I participated in a 2004 workshop coordinated by USAID for parliamentarians, NGO workers, and journalists in Dili and one of the central issues was the feasibility of creating such a fund.

References

Aspinall, Edward. 2007. "The Construction of Grievance: Natural resources and identity in a separatist conflict." *Journal of Conflict Resolution* 61, 6: 950–72.

Beblawi, Hazen and Giacomo Luciani. 1987. *The Rentier State*. London: Croom Helm.

Carneiro, Francisco G. 2007. "Development Challenges of Resource-Rich Countries: the Case of Oil Exporters." Paper presented at the VI International Colloquium, Macrodynamic Capabilities and Economic Development, University of Brasilia, March 23, 2007, Brasilia, Brazil.

Collier, Paul. 2010. *The Plundered Planet: Why We Must—and How We Can—Manage Nature for Global Prosperity*. Oxford: Oxford University Press.

Collier, Paul and Benedikt Goderis. 2007a. "Prospects for Commodity Exporters: Hunky Dory or Humpty Dumpty?" Working Paper, Center for the Study of African Economies, Oxford University.

——. 2007b. "Commodity Prices, Growth, and the Natural Resource Curse: Reconciling a Conundrum." Working Paper 274, Center for the Study of African Economies, Oxford University.

Collier, Paul and Anke Hoeffler. 1998. "On Economic Causes of Civil Wars." *Oxford Economic Papers* 50: 563–73.

Deininger, Klaus and Lyn Squire. 1996. "A New Data Set Measuring Income Inequality," *The World Bank Economic Review*, 10(3): 565–91.

Freedom House. 2010. *Freedom in the World*. www.freedomhouse.org. Accessed September 10, 2010.

Karl, Terry. 1997. *The Paradox of Plenty: Oil Booms and Petro-States*. Berkeley: University of California Press.

Lewis, Peter. 2007. *Growing Apart*. New York: Cambridge University Press.

Lowi, Miriam. 2009. *Oil Wealth and the Poverty of Politics: Algeria Compared*. New York: Cambridge University Press.

Luong, Pauline Jones and Erika Weinthal. 2006. "Combating the Resource Curse: An Alternative Solution to Managing Mineral Wealth." *Perspectives on Politics* 4, 1: 35–53.

Mahdavy, Hossein. 1970. "The Patterns and Problems of Economic Development in Rentier States: The Case of Iran." In *Studies in the Economic History of the Middle East* ed. M.A. Cook. London: Oxford University Press.

Ross, Michael. 2001. "Does Oil Hinder Democracy?" *World Politics* 53, 3: 325–61.

——. 2004. "How Do Natural Resources Influence Civil War? Evidence from 13 Cases." *International Organization* 58 (Winter): 35–67.

Salleh, Ismail Muhd and Saha Dhevan Meyanathan. 1993. *The Lessons of East Asia. Malaysia: Growth, Equity and Structural Transformation*. Washington DC: The World Bank.

Skocpol, Theda. 1982. "Rentier State and Shi'a Islam in the Iranian Revolution." *Theory and Society* 11: 265–83.

Smith, Benjamin. 2004. "Oil Wealth and Regime Survival in the Developing World, 1960–99." *American Journal of Political Science* 48, 2: 232–48.

——. 2007. *Hard Times in the Lands of Plenty: Oil Politics in Iran and Indonesia*. Ithaca: Cornell University Press.

World Bank. 2006. *Cambodia: Halving Poverty by 2015?*, Washington: World Bank, 2006.

Part IV
Country Case Studies

17

United States

The Politics of Alternative Energy

Alan Reynolds

Proponents of two quite different policy goals – reduced oil imports (energy independence) and reduced greenhouse gas emissions (climate stability) – appear to share a common presumption that US passenger cars and the fuels they use are the single most important key to solving both problems. As a result, actual and proposed energy or climate policy legislation typically puts extraordinary emphasis on tax exemptions, subsidies, and mandates for alternative fuels (94% of which is corn ethanol) and flexible fuel vehicles (95% of which use gasoline), as well as low-interest loans for manufacturers of electric vehicles, tax credits or rebates for buying electric vehicles, grants to state and local governments for related infrastructure, as well as research grants to encourage the production and purchase of new vehicles primarily fueled by ethanol, methanol, compressed natural gas, hydrogen fuel cells, and/or lithium ion batteries.

The US government is eager to give a US$7,500 tax credit or rebate to those who can afford to buy a battery-powered $33,600 Nissan Leaf. The amount of that subsidy would be almost enough to buy the slightly smaller $9,900 Nissan Versa, one of the best-rated cars at greencars.org. But people who buy a new Versa (or, more often, cheaper used cars) cannot afford the Leaf. For those who can afford a $41,000 Chevy Volt, the government will happily help with a *de facto* check for $7,500. That $7,500 would go a long way toward buying the similar gas-powered $16,995 Chevy Cruze, but the US government does not favor inexpensive cars that use little fuel. On the other hand, Uncle Sam will kick in $7,500 toward the purchase of an $87,400 Fisker Karma or $109,000 Tesla roadster. There was a big public protest in India when their government proposed similar regressive hand-outs to affluent buyers of such pricey high-tech cars. American taxpayers appear more generous, or more docile.

Unlike painful policy proposals that might seriously reduce greenhouse gas emissions (such as a carbon tax or cap and trade rationing plan) or painful schemes to slash oil imports (such as a tariff or quota on imported oil), the *political* campaign to subsidize alternative vehicles and fuels has been enormously successful.

The American Recovery and Reinvestment Act of 2009 (ARRA) was the third law in five years to raise subsidies for alternative fuels and vehicles. At least $90bn in federal "stimulus" funds were devoted to what was described as energy technology innovation, green jobs and low-income energy efficiency assistance programs. Some $6.1bn was devoted to electric cars, batteries and alternative fuels, and funds to electrify federal and state fleets. Senate majority leader

Harry Reid credited the Apollo Alliance for promoting this grab bag, which the organization described as a down payment on the $500bn they had lobbied for.[1]

That 2009 stimulus to energy interests followed the Energy Independence and Security Act of 2007 (EISA) which required fuel suppliers to blend increasing quantities of biofuels into gasoline, some 15bn gallons of corn-based ethanol by 2015. That was a big increase from the Energy Policy Act of 2005 which initiated mandates for the use of 7.5bn gallons of biofuels by 2012.

In his 2007 State of the Union Address, President Bush called for mandating 35bn gallons of biofuels by 2017, an incredible target equal to one-quarter of all gasoline consumed in the USA in 2006.[2] Not to be outdone, President Obama said during the presidential campaign that he favors a 60bn gallon-a-year target.[3]

The 2007 law instead mandated 36bn gallons of biofuels by 2022 – less than President Bush and Obama would like to promise (to farmers), yet nearly five times as much as the 8bn produced in 2008. Congress waved a magic wand to require some 16bn gallons of nonexistent "cellulosic" ethanol (from, switchgrass, poplar, algae or whatever). Yet the Energy Information Agency can only imagine 5bn gallons of (heavily-subsidized) cellulosic ethanol might be available by then, and that is just an optimistic guess. This whole exercise illustrates the increasing absurdity of mandates from Congress and the Environmental Protection Agency. The 2007 biofuel mandate is not just bad policy. It is impossible, bizarre policy.

With the current mandate that 10% ethanol be added to gasoline, the country will not be able to use much more than 14bn gallons in the foreseeable future even if electric cars prove to be a total flop. The Energy Information Agency predicts that fuel consumption of light vehicles in 2035 will be only 15% higher than it was in 2009 (though consumption of heavy vehicles, mostly diesels, will rise by 47%). That means US ethanol consumption could not possibly rise by much more than 15% so long as oil companies are required to add only 10% or even 15% ethanol to gasoline. It also means cars and light trucks are projected to account for only 16% of energy-related carbon emissions by 2035, down from 20% in 2009. The overall US share of worldwide energy use (and carbon emissions) is likewise projected to drop from 20% to 16% by 2035, with no change in policy.[4]

To somehow compel motorists to purchase the required 36bn gallons of ethanol in 2022 the government would have to mandate, as Brazil does, that 25% ethanol be added to gasoline. Brazil's tropical climate can produce relatively efficient ethanol cheaply from sugarcane, but the US produces inefficient ethanol (and sweetener) from corn. If raising the mandated share of ethanol to 25% is any politician's secret plan, nobody has dared to admit it. After all, the average US car is more than 10 years old, and most pre-2007 cars cannot handle more than 10% ethanol without damage. Besides, ethanol is a third less efficient than gasoline, so adding more ethanol reduces mileage-per-gallon. Raising the ethanol content of gasoline would anger many drivers, who are also voters, and the resulting drop in mileage would make it even more difficult for car companies to comply with fuel economy standards.

The politically convenient thing about setting grandiose (though contradictory) targets for how little fuel cars are expected to sip in 2016 and how many billions more gallons of ethanol motorists are nonetheless required to buy in 2022 is that those making such grand legislative gestures will be out of office when the time comes and few voters are apt to remember.

By 2010, the mandate that nearly 14bn gallons of ethanol be added to gasoline had already made that year's $5.4bn in ethanol subsidies totally superfluous. Yet the money kept flowing anyway. With farmers, ethanol producers and oil companies all sharing the bounty, using subsidies and mandates to pour ever-increasing amounts of ethanol into motorists' gas tanks has been win-win for politicians and lose-lose for consumers and taxpayers.

The 2007 energy law also raised corporate average fuel economy (CAFE) standards to 35 miles per gallon by 2030, which the Environmental Protection Agency subsequently pushed up to 35.5 miles per gallon in 2016. That rushed deadline is widely considered a *de facto* mandate to produce more electric cars or plug-in hybrids (sold with a fat tax credit or rebate) in order to counterbalance sales of powerful sports cars, trucks and sport utility vehicles (SUVs).

The 2005 law also added special tax breaks for alternative fuels and vehicles worth over $14bn between 2005 and 2015.[5] Yet "when the 1,724 page bill final passed," the *Washington Post* reported, "it wasn't everything that energy interest groups wanted."[6]

Bootleggers and Baptists; greens and geo-greens

Public choice theory (the application of economic analysis to political behavior) views the political marketplace as a place where favors are bought and sold. Because politicians have found energy/environmental issues an expedient device for handing out favors, affected private agents have incentives to allocate more scarce resources toward political (rather than economic) activities in order to maximize their wealth.

Those who stand to benefit from energy-related subsidies, cheap loans, tax credits or mandates share an intense interest in making investments in politics. The potential gains make energy interest groups easy to organize for political action – campaign contributions, lobbying and public education (propaganda). Taxpayers are too broad and diverse a group to stand up to such organized interests, particularly if they can be persuaded (for example, by sponsored studies, TV ads and op eds) that some "crisis" requires taxpayer assistance. As public choice economist Richard Wagner put it, "the creation and operation of public programs is guided less by wishes and high motives than by interests and strong motives."[7]

There are two distinct groups making distinctly different arguments for subsidizing alternative fuels (ethanol, electricity and compressed natural gas), and alternative vehicles (flexible-fuel vehicles, electric vehicles and plug-in hybrids).

The first group consists of a sub-set of environmental activists ("greens") who are almost exclusively concerned with climate change, as opposed to those more focused on air and water quality, food safety, or preservation of endangered species or scenic areas. Many of these greens display a singular fascination with redesigning cars and fuels, even though this paper demonstrates that US light vehicles unquestionably account for a surprisingly small and declining share of global greenhouse emissions.

The second group consists of what *New York Times* columnist Thomas Friedman calls "geo-greens." The geo-greens are individuals and organizations who argue that subsidies and mandates for ethanol (or methanol), plus subsidies and mandates for plug-in flexible-fuel vehicles, will improve US economic security by (1) reducing US vulnerability to spikes in the world price of oil, and by (2) depressing the world price of oil and thus inflicting financial discomfort on autocratic, middle-eastern oil producing countries thought to be indirect sponsors of Islamic extremism and terrorism.[8]

The alliance between greens and geo-greens has been convenient, but somewhat unnatural. Greens worry about *all* fossil fuels, not just petroleum. Yet geo-greens are enthusiastic about producing domestic auto fuel (methanol) from natural gas or coal, and for plug-in hybrids that will rely on fossil fuels for 69% of their electric power in 2035 (according to the 2011 Energy Information Agency projections). "Shifting the way we produce electricity ... has essentially nothing to do with oil dependence," explains geo-green spokesman R. James Woolsey.[9]

So far, however, greens and geo-greens have been able to combine with politically-connected business leaders and venture capitalists to form politically potent coalitions on behalf of lucrative subsidies.

The way this process works was best explained by Clemson University economist Bruce Yandle's telling metaphor of "bootleggers and Baptists" – both of whom actually lobbied for Southern laws to ban the legal sale of alcoholic beverages on Sundays, but for entirely different reasons. Bootleggers saw an opportunity to sell more liquor at premium prices. Baptists saw themselves as taking the moral high ground. Yet the Baptist's moralistic arguments provided a handy diversionary cover for politicians, and that made it cheaper (in terms of campaign support) for bootleggers to gain monopoly profits by selling moonshine on Sundays.

In the case of subsidies and tax breaks (euphemistically called "incentives") for alternative fuels and vehicles, and related grants (called "resources"), the equivalent of the Baptists' moralistic arguments are conveniently provided by greens and geo-greens. Regardless of the merit or sincerity of such arguments, there are huge sums of money at stake. Tens of billions of dollars have already been received in tax credits, federally-subsidized loans, mandated purchases, research grants, and more. It does not require undue cynicism to suspect that strong financial interests may hide behind the veil of seemingly high-toned arguments for such federal favors.

This paper reviews arguments and evidence deployed on behalf of spending billions more tax dollars on changing the cars we drive and the fuels we use. Finding those arguments unpersuasive, we uncover some evidence suggesting that the actual purpose of the proliferating subsidies and mandates for alternative fuels and vehicles is simply "rent-seeking," that is, the use of political influence-peddling, lobbying, campaign contributions and TV advertising campaigns to extract funds and favors from the government.

Social costs and subsidies

In the case of nearly every product *except* ethanol and electric cars, the prudent presumption would be that if some new technology is viable then it does not require subsidies and mandates, and if it requires subsidies then it is not viable.

If the future price of petroleum becomes persistently higher than the cost of producing ethanol, methanol or biodiesel, then the demand for such alternative fuels will soar and suppliers will respond by making more.

If the total cost of driving light vehicles powered by gasoline or diesel fuel (including purchase price) becomes persistently higher than the cost of driving vehicles powered by electricity or natural gas or hydrogen fuel cells, then the demand for alternative vehicles will soar and producers will respond by making more.

To argue that lavish subsidies are needed to provide alternatives in these markets alone, unlike others, requires talents in high demand. But such arguments turn out to require such self-serving reasoning and imaginative forecasting that taxpayers should be wary.

Arguments for subsidizing or mandating the use of otherwise unsaleable cars and fuels rely on claims of "externalities" (social costs) associated with conventional motor fuels. One such externality is the emission of carbon dioxide from passenger vehicles and its major impact on the global climate. Another is the perceived threat to economic stability or security said to be uniquely associated with US "dependence" or imported oil (unlike US dependence on imported lithium and rare earths needed to produce electric cars, or imported uranium needed to fuel nuclear power plants, or imported copper, etc.).

To assert the existence of social costs associated with automobiles is an insufficient justification for preferential subsidies and mandates, however, because subsidies and mandates also impose undesirable social costs, namely, higher energy prices, higher vehicle prices and higher taxes.

This paper suggests the real reason such auto-related subsidies and mandates are so politically popular is not because they are cost-effective ways of solving real problems, but because (1) the benefits to powerful political constituents are evident to those receiving federal tax breaks, grants and loan guarantees, while (2) the costs to consumers and taxpayers appear relatively obscure, and easy to conceal or delay.

Handing out special tax breaks, rebates, loans and mandates to grateful interest groups creates the illusion of "doing something" without most taxpayers noticing who must pay the bills. Talking about something while doing nothing is even better, because talk is cheap. Announcing magnificent objectives for the share of electricity supposedly available from renewables in the distant future, for example, is obviously much easier than proposing to raise taxes on carbon (or even on gasoline), or imposing binding caps on fossil fuel use.

A group of business leaders attempted to make a "social cost" case for their own preferred energy subsidies on two grounds: "First, innovations in energy technology can generate significant, quantifiable public benefits that are not reflected in the market price of energy. These benefits include cleaner air and improved public health, enhanced national security and international diplomacy, reduced risk of dangerous climate change, and protection from energy price shocks and related economic disruptions. ... Second, the energy business requires investments of capital at a scale that is beyond the risk threshold of most private-sector investors."[10]

The second argument that taxpayers can and should bear risks that no sensible business leader would accept is just special-interest pleading.

The first point, on the other hand, is an argument that the market price of energy is too low, and needs to be increased by taxes or by mandates such as "renewable performance standards" (which the group lauds) requiring electric utilities to use more nuclear, biomass, wind or solar power regardless of cost. If energy prices were raised by such mandates, as this group advises, then their argument that the market has mispriced energy cannot simultaneously be used to excuse the research and development (R&D) subsidies they seek. An argument for higher energy prices is not an argument for subsidies. Indeed, advocates of costly subsidies and mandates commonly claim their policies would lower the cost of driving (eventually, after many years of subsidies). There may be no more overused argument for subsidizing ethanol and hybrid cars than to claim the gifts are justified as a way to avoid $4 gasoline.

There are many possible ways to discourage industrial, commercial, residential and transportation activities that produce greenhouses gases, although some would impose *national* costs that far exceed the promised *international* benefits. Among such proposals are auction-based cap and trade schemes (as opposed to political allocation of emission rights), carbon taxes, heavy-handed "renewable performance standards" compelling electric utilities to use energy sources that could not otherwise compete. The list could even include efforts to convert consumers to a vegan diet (thus reducing methane from cattle).

Using subsidies and mandates to redesign new cars and the fuel they use has been much more politically popular than any comprehensive, economy-wide approach because it promises to both "save the planet" and achieve "energy independence" in ways that seem painless to most American voters, while making some (those first to buy a subsidized Chevy Volt from a bailed-out GM) feel morally superior to neighbors who paid for the subsidies.

The political obsession with miles-per-gallon seems to forget that reducing the user cost of driving encourages more driving. A car that averages 15 miles per gallon for 5,000 miles a year obviously uses no more fuel than one that gets 30 miles per gallon but is driven 10,000 miles a year. Why should anyone want to bias consumer choices between driving a 300-horsepower convertible for 5,000 miles a year rather than driving a 100-horsepower subcompact for 15,000 miles a year? Using mandates and subsidies in the hope of reducing some future average fuel consumption per vehicle among new cars (rather than current yearly fuel use of all vehicles) is an autocratic and impractical crusade. Yet the idea has proven politically seductive and, in many cases, economically profitable.

US passenger cars and global greenhouse gas

There are at least two big problems with the green argument that the perceived social cost of global warming justifies most or all of the political favors granted to ethanol, electric cars, and other alternatives to conventional gasoline and (especially) diesel passenger vehicles. The first problem is that US passenger vehicles do not account for nearly as large a percentage of global greenhouse gas emissions as the apologists for subsidies and mandates imply. No more than 3%, in fact.

The second problem is that the subsidies and mandates (including CAFE standards and ethanol mandates) are an extremely roundabout, costly and ineffective means of accomplishing the stated goal.

The overemphasis on passenger cars invariably begins with what we could call the "transportation fallacy." The transportation fallacy assumes that (1) passenger cars account for the vast bulk of energy used in the transportation sector, and that (2) petroleum is the main source of anthropogenic (man-made) greenhouse gases.

A lengthy *New York Times* article subtitled "A Thirst for Oil Comes Back to Haunt a Nation of Gas Guzzlers" provides an example of the transportation fallacy: "Nearly 70% of the 21m. barrels of oil the United States consumes every day goes for transportation," said the article, "with the bulk of that burned by individual drivers, according to the National Commission on Energy Policy, a bipartisan research group that advises Congress. So ... no one differs on what's really responsible for all that underlying demand here for black gold: the automobile."[11] Anyone reading that passage would surely think "the bulk" of oil is burned by individual drivers. But that is not really what it says (if anyone could navigate through all the circuitous verbiage between oil, transportation and individual drivers).

Here is another example of the transportation fallacy from a panel plugging plug-in vehicles: "The transportation sector of the US economy is a focal point for policymakers because it accounts for 27% of US greenhouse gas emissions (the gases linked to global climate change) and 70% of US petroleum consumption. A majority of the oil in the transport sector is used to power light-duty vehicles such as cars, sport-utility vehicles, vans, and pickup trucks."[12]

Anyone reading that would surely think light-duty vehicles are a major source of greenhouse gases and account for a majority of petroleum consumption. Read carefully, however, and that is not really what it says.

These convoluted ways of equating oil with transportation and transportation with individual drivers are extremely misleading. Light vehicles used 61.3% of the 26,822.6 trillion British thermal units (BTUs) used by the transportation sector in 2008, according to the *Transportation Energy Data Book*. Transportation accounts for a larger share of petroleum use (70%) but why ignore the other 30%? Besides, transportation obviously includes freight trucks, railroads, airplanes, ships, barges and buses, so why neglect their use of oil, natural gas and coal-fired electricity?

Light duty vehicles (under 8500 pounds, and subject to fuel economy standards) accounted for only 8.8mbpd of the 14.6m. barrels of oil used in 2007, or 60.3%. Nearly as many barrels (some 6.2mbpd) were used in commerce and industry, including petrochemicals. In short, light duty vehicles accounted for only 42.5% of the 20.7m. barrels of oil used in 2007.[13]

The USA used 8,997,000 barrels per day of gasoline in 2009, yet all uses of gasoline (for everything from boats to chain saws) accounted for 47.9% of total petroleum demand of 18,771,000 barrels per day.[14] The USA imported 9,013,000 barrels per day of oil and products, more than the total amount of gasoline used by passenger cars, boats, lawnmowers, snowmobiles, motorcycles and similar. Putting aside the impossibility of an economy without cars for commuting and shopping, the USA would have imported oil even if there were literally no cars, SUVs, light pickups or minivans at all. And the USA would have imported oil even if not one drop had been used for gasoline.

What about greenhouse gases? After all, that is supposed to be the reason why green groups have been pushing so hard for mandating and subsidizing alternative fuels and vehicles that promise to reduce carbon emissions. Yet the share of global greenhouse emission attributable to US passenger cars seems an unwelcome fact in all these frantic efforts to save the planet by redesigning US cars and fuels.

Petroleum used for transportation accounted for 33.5% of all carbon dioxide emissions from burning fuel in 2008, or 1,810m. metric tons, according to the Energy Information Agency. But that was only 25.6% of the 7,049m. tons of total anthropogenic greenhouse gas emissions, which include methane, nitrous oxide, hydrocarbons and sulfur hexafluoride.[15]

Since petroleum accounts for 25.6% of man-made greenhouse emissions, and passenger cars account for 42.5% of US petroleum consumption, it follows that US passenger cars account for 10.9% of US man-made greenhouse gases.

The USA, in turn, accounted for 20% of global carbon dioxide emissions during the cyclical peak of 2007, or 6bn tons of a world total of 29.9bn.[16] The US share of all greenhouses gases is also about 20%, which is impressive evidence of energy-efficiency since the US produces an estimated 26.7% of world GDP.[17]

Since light vehicles account for 10.9% of US greenhouse gas emissions and the US accounts for about 20% of global greenhouse emissions, it follows that the passenger cars in the US account for about 2.2% of global greenhouse emissions.

A different estimating technique yields only a slightly larger figure of 3.4%. Transportation accounted for 33.1% of the energy-related share of carbon dioxide emissions in 2008, and carbon dioxide accounted for 82.8% of anthropogenic greenhouses gases. That suggests that transportation of all sorts accounted for 27.4% of greenhouse gases, with light-duty vehicles accounting for 61.3% of that.[18] By that calculation, light vehicles account for 16.8% of US greenhouse gas emissions and almost 3.4% of global greenhouse gas emissions.

Minuscule as it is, the role of US passenger cars in global greenhouse emissions will be getting smaller and smaller in the years ahead because of soaring energy use in emerging economies.

The International Energy Agency expects growth of energy demand to be ten times faster in emerging economies than in the USA or Europe, with China and India accounting for a third of global energy use by 2030, when China's carbon emissions are expected to double those of the USA.[19] China alone accounted for 45% of the growth in world oil demand from 2000 to 2010.[20] But that is nothing compared to China's planned use of coal. *The Economist* reports: "The IEA estimates that China, which generates more than 70% of its energy with coal, will build 600 gigawatts (GW) of coal-fired power capacity in the next quarter century – as much as is currently generated with coal in America, Japan and the European Union put together."[21]

US utilities are already switching from coal to natural gas where possible because the price of surprisingly abundant gas from US shale (reserves have tripled in recent years) is now competitive. But there is an ironic twist to that development. Australia's Ambre Energy intends to build a terminal in Washington state to export 5.7m. tons of coal each year to China, enough to produce the carbon equivalent of about 2m. US cars.[22] There are other plans in the works to export US coal to China, as well as liquefied US natural gas.

How could adding one or 2m. electric cars in the USA, or adding more food to our fuel, make any difference to *global* greenhouse emissions in a world bent on using so much coal?

Blaming cars

Since US passenger cars account for no more than 3.4% of man-made global greenhouse gas emissions, how could anyone possibly believe that switching from one sort of car to another, or from one fuel source to another, is going to make any difference in the average temperature of the entire planet? The whole idea becomes chimerical when individual states such as California and Iowa waste time and money pretending to "change the planet" by attempting to micro-manage the types of cars and fuels their residents use.

Despite the evident futility of such efforts, the alleged purpose of subsidies and mandates ostensibly aimed at reducing fossil fuel use (greens) or petroleum imports (geo-greens) has nonetheless been very heavily focused on changing the design of new passenger cars and light trucks. The political overemphasis on new light vehicles should have raised more suspicions than it has. A quarter of a million light-duty US vehicles (those subject to CAFE standards) account for no more than 3.4% of the man-made portion of global greenhouse gases (the highest of our two estimates), and that figure will automatically shrink to 2.7% by 2035 simply because the US share of world energy use is falling. And new vehicles account for no more than 6% of such small shares in any given year, which is truly trivial.

Because time and money are limited, placing so much political emphasis on recreating new passenger vehicles means neglecting actual sources of about 97% of man-made greenhouse gases. This makes no budgetary or economic sense, because scarce resources are poorly targeted, and it makes no environmental sense. It can make political sense, however, because it is politically much easier to make symbolic gestures toward redesigning future autos and fuels (such as legislating high "average" mileage standards for cars to be produced in the distant future) than to, for example, raise everyone's electricity bills by sternly rationing or taxing power plants' use of coal and natural gas. As always, there are powerful and vocal interest groups involved. As usual, it is instructive to follow the money.

Venture capitalists, political networking and the R&D lobby

In September 2010, seven business leaders, founders of the American Energy Innovation Council, delivered "A Business Plan for America's Energy Future." The group included two prominent advisers to President Obama, Jeff Immelt, the CEO of General Electric, and John Doerr, who heads the multi-billion-dollar venture capital firm Kleiner Perkins Caufield and Byers (commonly abbreviated as "Kleiner Perkins" or KPCB). The group also included Microsoft founder Bill Gates and the CEOs of Cummins, Xerox, Bank of America and Lockheed Martin. The main message of this "business plan" was to advocate $16bn a year in annual federal subsidies for research and development on alternative energy.

The first sentence of the report said, "It may seem surprising that a group of business leaders who are not primarily in the energy field would make a strong statement on energy innovation and the need for a more vigorous public commitment."[23] On the contrary, it should not seem surprising. These business leaders represent firms which stand to receive sizeable federal grants for energy-related R&D and others that would likely benefit through related financial deals or technology.

Commenting on Jeffrey Immelt's lobbying efforts on behalf of subsidies for renewable energy, for example, *Bloomberg Businessweek* noticed that, "For GE, that could boost sales of products like low-emission turbines, devices to recharge electric vehicles, solar panels, and 'smart' electric meters."[24] They might have added that GE is also a leading producer of nuclear power plants, the one "renewable" that might (at great expense) make a serious dent in the share of electricity now coming from fossil fuels.

Venture capitalist John Doerr served on President Obama's Economic Recovery Advisory Board with Jeffrey Immelt. As *Time* magazine explained, "In the past few years, however, Doerr's interests in Beltway policies deepened, as he bet hundreds of millions of dollars in private capital on green-energy start-ups, many of which were seeking federal subsidies and regulatory aid."[25] Doerr and his wife had donated about $800,000 to Democrats since 2000, the article noted, and his firm had donated even more. But influencing policy (subsidies) in Washington D.C. requires more than money. It also requires people with connections.

Former Vice-President Gore is a partner of Kleiner Perkins.[26] Former Secretary of State Colin Powell is a strategic limited partner.

Former CIA Director R. James Woolsey (co-founder of the geo-green advocacy group "Set America Free") is a partner in Vantage Point Venture Partners, a rival of Kleiner Perkins with a billion dollars at stake in green technology investments (including Tesla Motors). Along with former CIA Director George Tenet, Woolsey is also an adviser to GridPoint, which markets services and products relating to solar power and smart grid technology.

No political bootlegger would ever admit there is any self-interest involved. "My lesson about policy is not to argue about your self-interest," advises John Doerr of Kleiner Perkins. "Make an argument that is bigger, about jobs or competitiveness, and you're going to change some minds."[27]

Despite all the selfless arguments, campaign contributions, lobbying and famous-but-costly political allies surrounding Kleiner Perkins, investing in green tech subsidies has been a dubious strategy. Kleiner-Perkins's investments ultimately have to reward the firm's big investors, which consist of university endowments, philanthropic foundations and public pension funds. After shifting investments toward information technology in 2010, Fortune wrote that "Kleiner is back from irrelevance" because new investments in information technology "outweighed some of Kleiner's clean-tech clunkers."[28]

When it comes to alternative fuels, flexible fuel vehicles, and electric cars and plug-in hybrids, Woolsey of Vantage Point represents the "geo-green" arguments for subsidies. Vice-President Gore of Kleiner Perkins represents the "green" arguments for subsidies. Vantage Point invested in electric cars from Tesla Motors, while Kleiner Perkins invested in plug-in hybrids from Fisker. The US Energy Department invested in both, handing $465m. in low-interest loans to Tesla in 2010 and $529m. to Fisker.

Famous individuals have also invested in electric car producers, which can be useful to lure other investors. Such investments would not look so tempting, however, were it not for the $7,500 per car US subsidy. Hank Paulson, former Treasury Secretary and Goldman Sachs CEO, invested in Coda Automotive, a Chinese maker of electric cars. Warren Buffett bought 10% of BYD, a Chinese maker of electric cars to be first sold in California. Google founders Sergey Brin and Larry Page invested in Tesla Motors (full disclosure: this author held 5,924 shares of Tesla Motors at the end of 2010).[29]

Messrs. Gore, Powell and Woolsey are not, of course, the only former government officials involved in alternative fuels or electric vehicles for fun or profit.

"As we've all heard before, it's often 'who you know,' instead of 'what you know,' when it comes to the world of business," notes gigaom.com; "And that's even more true for the greentech industry, which became the leading venture capital investment sector in the third quarter of 2009 largely based on investments from the US government's stimulus package. While greentech investors readily backed President Obama during his political campaign, former cabinet members all the way back to the Reagan Administration have joined the boards of greentech start-ups in droves in recent years, particularly former Department of Energy Secretaries."[30]

Former Energy Secretary, James Schlesinger, is on the advisory board of GeoSynFuels, a start-up experimenting with cellulosic ethanol. Former General Wesley Clark is co-chairman of the Board of Growth Energy, an ethanol producers trade group pushing for increasing the percentage of ethanol in gasoline.

Former Energy Secretary John Herrington and former OMB Director Jim Miller are on the Board of Directors of Clean Energy Fuels, the leading provider of compressed and liquefied natural gas for trucks, buses and taxis.

When it comes to political influence-peddling (or attracting investors), big names are worth big money. A 2011 study of lobbyist activity from 1999 to 2008 found that, "lobbyists that have issue expertise earn a premium, but we uncover that such a premium for lobbyists that have connections to many politicians and Members of Congress is considerably larger."[31]

When pleading for subsidies, low-interest loans and mandates from Congress, it is not just what you know but also who you know.

Political Trading in "Cap and Trade"

The 2010 "Business Plan For America's Energy Future" was certainly not the first time a group of politically influential CEOs had issued a report calling for more subsidies and grants for what is labeled "green energy" (a label not always warranted, as this paper demonstrates). It may seem surprising, but 2010 was also not the first time the General Electric CEO Jeffrey Immelt has taken the lead in forming such a supposedly disinterested group to influence US energy policy.

In 2006 Fred Krupp of the Environmental Defense Fund and Jonathan Lash of the World Resources Institute recruited Mr. Immelt to form The US Climate Action Partnership along with well-funded Pew Center on Global Climate Change. Immelt, in turn, helped recruit CEOs of other major corporations including oil producer BP, and such big industrial energy users as Alcoa, DuPont and Caterpillar.

Where federal money is at stake there will be financiers at the table, and this was no exception. One founding member was Lehman Brothers, the ill-fated investment bank which had made the big mistake of being a "big financier of wind power."[32]

The partnership's report, *A Call for Action*, largely consisted of a call for "incentives for technology research, development, and deployment." It argued for "policies to promote significant research, development and deployment of hyper-efficient end use technologies; low- or zero-GHG emitting technologies; and cost-effective carbon capture and storage." The report endorsed a mild cap and trade plan if it included selective loopholes and favoritism. Because "coal supplies over 50% of our current electricity generation and will play a continuing role in our energy future," the report advised that "a significant portion of allowances should be initially distributed free to capped entities and to economic sectors particularly disadvantaged by the secondary price effects of a cap."

All but one of the electric utilities who eventually joined the Climate Action Partnership (such as Entergy, NextEra, NRG Energy, AES and Exelon) would appear to gain market share under a cap and trade system that burdened rivals using fossil fuels but favored and often subsidized wind, solar, or nuclear power. One of them, Entergy, is the nation's second-largest nuclear generator.

Industrial companies in the Climate Action Partnership had even more obvious interests in the proposed policies. *Climate War* author Eric Pooley noted that, "The companies had compelling reasons for backing carbon regulation. GE, the biggest wind turbine maker in the USA, was developing carbon-capture technology. A single wind turbine included 14 products made by DuPont. That made their participation logical, and diluted its impact. The coalition needed someone with plenty at stake."[33] That someone turned out to be Jim Rogers of Duke Energy. Rogers seized on the report's helpful insistence that "a significant portion of allowances should be initially distributed free" (perhaps to Duke Energy, DuPont or Alcoa?), in marked contrast to President Obama, who had wanted to auction such allowances.

US legislative efforts to enact the Kerry-Lieberman cap and trade bill in 2009 soon degenerated into a political game of dispensing valuable emission permits to favored companies and industries. "Cap and trade, with hand-outs and loopholes" was *The Economist*'s apt headline (May 23, 2009). The word "trade" in cap and trade had come to mean trading political favors, not trading in the marketplace.

The surviving caps on carbon emissions in the failed cap and trade bill would have been disproportionately borne by the automotive industry, which was expecting different favors for electric cars and flexible fuel vehicles. In the end, however, potential cap-and-trade winners in groups like the Climate Action Partnership were thwarted in the Senate by such obvious losers as coal mining, coal-fired power plants and related heavy industry.

A lesson from the House-Senate tussle over cap-and-trade loopholes is that cap-and-trade may have a political advantage over a simple tax on carbon emissions. The steep costs to the general public of cap and trade are easily postponed and obscured, while the benefits (free permits) can be dispensed to organizations of companies expected to provide financial and media support to politicians who take good care of them.

A recent survey of the economic research on climate mitigation policy notes that, "Emissions taxes … appear to be highly unpopular, while cap and trade systems are popular among environmental advocates … and they also have active supporters in the financial sector, who see them as opportunities to make money."[34] That combination of those who see opportunities to make money from "cap, trade, permit and subsidize" forming convenient coalitions with environmental activists is a real world illustration of Yandel's model of bootleggers and Baptists.

Ethanol and flexible fuel vehicles that shun it

Calling something "alternative" or "renewable" does not mean burning "biomass" emits no carbon dioxide or methane, or that electric cars can be powered by fairy dust.

In 2008 renewable energy sources (not counting nuclear) accounted for 8% of all energy consumption. Biofuels (94% being corn ethanol) constitute only one-fifth of the 8% of US energy accounted for by renewables. That means ethanol and biodiesel cover just 1.6% of US energy consumption (20% of 8%).[35]

Heavily-subsidized wind power accounted for only 9% of the 8% of energy from renewables, or just 0.7 of 1% of energy use. Solar accounted for 1% of the 8%, which is barely worth mentioning. In 1979, President Carter had promised that 20% of our energy would come from solar power by 2000.[36] Talk is cheap, solar power is very expensive.

The largest source of renewable energy by far is hydroelectric power (35% of the total) and the second largest is wood (24%), an un-exotic form of "biomass" commonly burned to produce electricity (notably in New England).

Energy from biomass includes biofuels (corn ethanol), wood, and the not-so-clean burning of municipal solid waste. Amazingly, global climate-watchers who estimate carbon emissions arbitrarily exclude biomass when estimating carbon emissions and US officials follow that dubious convention. Since half of US renewable energy consists of biomass (mainly burning wood and garbage) ignoring biomass-related greenhouse gas emissions makes renewable energy look much "cleaner" than it really is in terms of carbon emissions (not to mention possibly hazardous ash). As in the case of growing corn to produce ethanol, growing trees to feed power plants is not as innocuous as the rigged statistics suggest. As the Energy Information Agency notes, "Energy inputs are required in order to grow, fertilize, and harvest the feedstock and to produce and process the biomass into fuels."[37] Lumber trucks, for example, are not zero-emissions vehicles.

Hydroelectric power and geothermal are renewable, but not easily available in many places. Nuclear power is sometimes wrongly counted as "renewable" (we cannot grow uranium) and emits no carbon, but capital costs of building nuclear plants are very high and regulatory obstacles formidable.

In the case of distilling corn into alcohol, considerable fossil fuel is used in fertilizing and harvesting the crop, distilling it and transporting it by truck, rail or barge. There is also a lot of water involved, and land that might otherwise have been left as carbon-absorbing forest or grassland.

A summary of two influential 2008 studies, one by Timothy Searchinger at Princeton University and the other by Joseph Fargione of the Nature Conservancy, found that "almost all biofuels used today cause more greenhouse gas emissions than conventional fuels if the full emissions costs of producing these 'green' fuels (including land use) are taken into account."[38] The Environmental Protection Agency has additional concerns about the impact on water quality and endangered species of devoting increasing amounts of land and fertilizer to producing crops for fuel.[39]

A 2010 study by economists Michael J. Roberts of Carolina State University and Wolfram Schlenker of Columbia University found that the 2009 Renewable Fuel Standard was equivalent to mandating that roughly one-third of US corn production in 2007 (equivalent to about 5% of total worldwide caloric production of corn, wheat, rice, and soybeans) be used to produce fuel rather than food. The authors estimate that the ethanol mandate increased world food prices by about 30%.[40]

As a result of widespread criticism of US energy policies that raise world hunger with little or no environmental benefit, former Vice-President Al Gore now agrees that massive subsidies to corn-based ethanol have not been good policy. He had previously supported those subsidies as a Senator to help his state's corn farmers, he acknowledged, and "I had a certain fondness for the farmers in the state of Iowa because I was about to run for President." The trouble, Gore added, is that "it's hard once such a program is put in place to deal with the lobbies that keep it going."[41]

Corn ethanol is subsidized by Congressional mandates requiring its addition to gasoline, by a tariff of 54 cents a gallon on imported (sugar-based) ethanol, by agricultural subsidies to corn farmers, and by a tax credit to blenders of 45 cents a gallon that is equivalent to 73 cents a gallon on a BTU-equivalent basis with gasoline. The Congressional Budget Office (CBO) notes that, "The corresponding amounts for biodiesel and cellulosic ethanol, calculated on the basis of the tax credits in place as of December 2009, are significantly higher—$1.08 and $1.62, respectively."[42] Despite those huge taxpayer subsidies to biodiesel and cellulosic ethanol, biodiesel nonetheless accounts for only about 6% of all biofuels, and cellulosic ethanol for zero. About 11.3bn gallons of biofuels were produced in the USA in 2009, according to the CBO, 10.8bn of which was ethanol and essentially all of that ethanol was made from corn.

The CBO report noted that the greenhouse gas benefits from corn ethanol (in the USA) come at a cost of $750 per metric ton of carbon dioxide emissions, which greentech investor Vinod Khosla calls "a mindboggling amount that is not scalable." The cost is huge, the benefit trivial. Khosla, a former partner of Kleiner Perkins, spun off his own firm to invest in such things as cellulosic ethanol, which means investing in subsidies. By the end of 2010, he finally came out against subsidies for corn ethanol (in which he is not invested), suggesting "the same money could be more effectively spent on emerging cellulosic … biofuel" (in which he is heavily invested).[43] He uses an "infant industry" argument that "mandates are valuable when they create new (hopefully short-to-medium-term) protected markets" for new technology that can't compete. Such protected firms should also get "tax credits or cash grants," Khosla argues, but (hopefully) for only 5–7 years.

The trouble with advice about subsidies and mandates from such green investors is that no matter how polished their green credentials may truly be, investors are still investors. More objective observers find the odds quite poor that any of the experimental sources of ethanol that Mr. Khosla is promoting will become commercially viable for mass production within seven years (2017), even with all the research grants and subsidies that amount to a dollar a gallon.[44]

Hopes of using any sort of ethanol to displace significant amounts of gasoline and diesel fuel were always arithmetically implausible, given the incredibly large amount of land, water and fossil fuels required. Even tax-free ethanol cannot generally compete with relatively high-taxed gasoline and diesel fuel because vehicles using 85% ethanol (E85) get 25–30% fewer miles per gallon than cars using gasoline, while vehicles using diesel get 25–30% *more* miles per gallon than those using gasoline (diesel miles per gallon ratings are at least 50% better than E85).

Consumer Reports noticed that "The FFV (flexible fuel vehicle) surge is being motivated by generous fuel credits automakers get for every FFV vehicle they build, even if it never runs on E85. This allows automakers to build more large vehicles with poor fuel economy than they could otherwise." As a result, GM, Ford and Chrysler became allies of the ethanol lobby, along with corn farmers and ethanol producers, because the FFV loophole in federal mileage standards has been helpful to the "Big Three" truck sales regardless of its obvious ineffectiveness.

Consumer Reports tested a Chevy Tahoe using E85 and found "the fuel economy of the Tahoe dropped 27% when running on E85 compared with gasoline, with highway mileage decreasing from 21 to 15 miles per gallon, and city mileage dropping from 9 to 7 miles per gallon … The range per tank of fuel declined significantly on E85."

To compete with gasoline, E85 would have to be about 27% cheaper, but it never is. On February 1, 2011, for example, the average US price of regular gas was $3.10 per gallon, while the price of E85 was equivalent to $3.53.[45]

Detroit's Big Three have been bootleggers selling FFV moonshine, with ample help from subsidized ethanol companies and farmers. But the self-interest is so transparent that all these bootleggers needed a few Baptists to convert a conspicuously futile push for flexible fuel vehicles into some sort of moralistic crusade. If moralists crusading for FFV could appear to include both liberals and conservatives, so much the better.

Several groups, common interests

In January 2004, a new group called the Apollo Alliance began an election-year lobbying effort on behalf of $300bn in federal subsidies and "investments," a target hiked to $500bn four years later. The 2004 report, "New Energy for America," said "research indicates the marginal cost for building a highly efficient auto fleet is $102bn over 20 years." What research? Most endnotes just say, "derived through aggregating findings from secondary research and expert opinion."

The Apollo report promised that with "a 10-year package of aggressive investment tax incentives … over 11m. advanced-technology cars could be sold each year by 2015." Most of that "aggressive investment" was earmarked for retooling at GM, Ford and Chrysler. But policy tools that could supplement a manufacturing focused strategy include consumer tax credits."

To those picking winners in 2004 "advanced technology" did not include plug-in cars. It meant conventional hybrids and, amazingly, cars that would supposedly run on fuel cells and tanks of compressed hydrogen. "A substantial federal investment … could ultimately place 100,000 fuel cell vehicles on the road by 2010. It could annually place 2,500,000 vehicles on the road by 2020. … Fuel cell vehicles operating on hydrogen stored on-board the vehicle can produce zero pollution if run on hydrogen derived from non-emitting energy sources." Unfortunately, making hydrogen (usually from natural gas or coal) can use up more fuel than it produces, and compressed hydrogen is so corrosive and explosive that only a very brave driver would want a tank of it on board.[46]

With visions of hundreds of billions of hypothetical federal money to dispense, Apollo Alliance offered free money for everyone, including farmers: "Tripling US biomass consumption [for electricity as well as fuel] would create $20bn dollars in new farm income … and create demand for 42m. acres of new energy crops like switch grass."

Money frequently trumps ideology, though ideological semantics can be useful to discourage citizens from simply "following the money."

A 2006 article in *The Nation*, "Green Grows the Grassroots," Mark Hertsgaard, explained how the chairman of the board of the National Wildlife Federation, Jerome Ringo, planned to "build a broader and more powerful green movement. His chosen vehicle, besides the NWF, is the Apollo Alliance, a coalition of labor unions, environmental groups, business leaders and elected officials that advocates a massive green jobs and development program for the USA. Apollo proposes investing $300bn (since raised to $500bn) of public funds in green energy technologies over the next 10 years. This investment would create 3m. new jobs and countless business opportunities, Apollo claims, while also fighting climate change and cutting US dependence on foreign oil. The benefits to poor and working-class Americans of such an economic stimulus program are clear, but the idea is also business-friendly enough to have attracted support from prominent Democratic moderates and other centrists, including the group Republicans for Environmental Protection."[47]

Is it really any surprise that such a well-funded quasi-ideological campaign focused on "countless business opportunities" from "investing $300bn of public funds" easily attracted the support of 58 business leaders and several business-friendly interest groups? Yet the author naively depicts this high-stakes lobbying effort as part of an effort to "return environmentalism to the American mainstream, where it belongs."

If anyone were looking for bootleggers hiding behind all these preachy Baptists, it might help to discover that Apollo Alliance is a "Tides Center Project" and the Tides Center is an arm of the Tides Foundation. The foundation is a 501(c)3 non-profit, which simply means contributions (largely from other foundations) are tax-deductible. The Apollo Alliance itself has no such "non-partisan" camouflage, and (like the Tides Center) is commonly considered allied with the left-wing of the Democratic Party. That is of interest because the Apollo Alliance has long been linked to another energy policy advocacy organization, "Set America Free," which is presumed to be allied with the hawkish, neoconservative wing of the Republican Party.

Set America Free (SAF) was assembled in 2004, with Apollo Alliance as a key member, to promote the idea expressed on their website that, "to achieve this goal of oil independence,

Congress should establish an open fuel standard that all new cars sold in the America be able to run on any mix of alcohol-based fuels—ethanol or methanol." Interestingly, the Kerry presidential campaign endorsed the idea as a way to "help farmers and coal miners."

Max Boot, an admirer of Set America Free, described the group as "national security hawks."[48] To be more specific, most members can be easily identified as strongly pro-Israel neoconservative national security hawks. For public relations purposes, however, Set America Free prefers Woolsey's more benign description as, "A coalition of tree huggers, do-gooders, sodbusters, cheap hawks and evangelicals."

A *Washington Post* story about Set America Free was aptly titled, "An Unlikely Meeting of the Minds: For Very Different Reasons, Groups Agree on Gas Alternatives."[49] But recall that for very different reasons, bootleggers and Southern Baptists likewise agreed to lobby for laws banning liquor sales.

The *Washington Post* seemed surprised that "a who's who of right-leaning military hawks, including former CIA director R. James Woolsey and Iraq war advocate Frank J. Gaffney Jr., has joined with environmental advocates such as the Natural Resources Defense Council to lobby Congress to spend $12bn to cut oil use in half by 2025." What could these geo-green military hawks and green environmental advocates possibly have in common? Well, it turns out that they share a common link. The National Resources Defense Council is another Tides Center Project, just like the Apollo Alliance, and the Apollo Alliance (being well-funded by Tides) is an influential member of Set America Free.

Writing in *The Nation*, William Greider praised Set America Free as a "conservative" coalition "with reform ideas that parallel the Apollo Alliance."[50] He thought "the two efforts demonstrate the potential for new alliances that leap across the usual barriers of party and ideology." In reality, the two efforts (Apollo Alliance and Set America Free) have been allied for years, which more likely demonstrates the potential for bootleggers and Baptists to form mutually advantageous alliances.

A third of the masthead of Set America Free consists of directors and advisors to the Institute for Analysis of Global Security (IAGS), although only two are identified as such. IAGS's directors and advisors have included an executive director of the International LNG Alliance, the vice-chairman of the International Committee on Coal Research, an executive director of the Gas Technology Institute, a founder of DCH Technology Inc. (a fuel-cell company), a founder of Global Energy Investors LLC, and a principal of Energy and Communications Solutions LLC. Set America Free itself includes a founder and member of a lithium industry group, whose success is clearly tied to electric cars.

Set America Free's main mission has long been to mandate "flexible fuel vehicles" (later upgraded to plug-in flexible fuel vehicles) which could run on 85% ethanol (E85) or methanol (made from coal or natural gas) as a way of supposedly smashing OPEC and thus making oil cheap. Senator Lieberman, a point man for repeatedly introducing unsuccessful bills to require that all cars be able to run on very high percentages of ethanol, said that he preferred to call the 2006 version the "Set America Free" bill. The 2007 version, for which SAF spokesman Frank Gaffney claimed due credit, was actually called The DRIVE Act (Dependence Reduction Through Innovation in Vehicles and Energy), introduced in January 2007 by 25 Senators, led by Lieberman, Bayh, Brownback and Coleman.[51] The bill had 55 sponsors in the House, but died in committee.

More than 99% of the US ethanol sold is *not* chosen by motorists but forced on them by federal mandates that require adding 10% ethanol to gasoline.[52] The ethanol lobby is pushing to have gas stations mandated or subsidized to install pumps with 15% ethanol, because cars newer than 2007 can use that much ethanol without being damaged. If that happened, however, those

E15 pumps would be rarely used. Scarcely anyone (aside from a dwindling number of innocents duped by ethanol's "green" hype) would voluntarily pick blends with a higher ethanol content because the higher the ethanol content the fewer miles can be driven on a gallon.

If the actual objective of the FFV lobbyists was to "reduce dependence on oil imports" by raising the mileage per gallon of cars and trucks, the simplest and quickest solution would be to do that the way European consumers voluntarily chose to save fuel (Europe has no fuel economy standards). About 55% of European cars have diesel engines compared with fewer than 5% in the USA.[53]

It did not help that since 1984 the USA has imposed a federal excise tax on diesel fuel that is 6 cents a gallon higher than the tax on gasoline. Unlike Europe, the USA imposes the highest tax on the most efficient fuel (diesel) and the lowest tax on the least efficient fuel (ethanol). To impose the same federal excise tax on ethanol and gasoline that we do on diesel fuel would cause some people to adjust by driving fewer miles, and others to adjust by buying cars that go further on a gallon (such as diesels and subcompacts). Subsidizing alternative fuels and vehicles, by contrast, will have ambiguous effects on total fuel consumed per vehicle or per year.

Recall, if you can, all the excitement in the old days, before 2011, when we were all expected to save the planet and defeat OPEC by buying gas-electric hybrids, albeit with tax deductions or credits. If price is no object, that would have worked out better than it did. After a decade, conventional gas-electric hybrids accounted for about 3% of new cars and less than 1% of all the light vehicles on the road. To make matters worse, most hybrids (some of them twice the size of a Prius) did not save nearly enough gas to justify their high prices.

The *Consumer Reports Buying Guide 2011* found it could take more than eight years for half of the hybrids they tested to justify their premium prices over comparable gasoline-powered cars, unless gas prices reached $5–10 per gallon. Yet they also found that, "two diesels can save you money no matter what fuel costs" (partly because of high resale value). The VW Jetta TDI, for example, averaged 35 miles per gallon in combined city and highway driving – a 52% improvement over the 23 miles per gallon for the Jetta's gasoline version. Such impressive mileage of diesels surely deserved more attention from the Apollo Alliance and "Set America Free" geo-greens whose stated goal is to reduce petroleum imports, but whose public relations campaign on behalf for flexible-fuel vehicles has had the opposite effect.

One of the biggest reasons US carmakers have not been motivated to offer fuel-efficient diesel engines (aside from the higher federal tax on diesel fuel) is the "Set America Free" flexible fuel charade. The only discernible effect of adding more than 7m. FFVs to US roads has been to invite Detroit automakers to sell more big trucks with big engines without paying fines (as German automakers do) for violating CAFE standards. But flexible fuel vehicles cannot use diesel fuel or biodiesel (which contains 9% less energy than petroleum diesel, but has other virtues). So the bootlegger-Baptist alliance promotion of FFVs has discouraged the use of diesel engines which (unlike FFVs) could actually have reduced US petroleum use. The doubly-elusive promise of a diesel hybrid running on biodiesel would be doubly-cursed in terms of price (because diesels and hybrids are both more expensive than conventional cars), but it would come closest to the geo-green dream of driving without oil (even electric cars in Hawaii and New York are likely to be using fuel oil indirectly). Ironically, the US automakers' vested interest in the flexible fuel sham, aided and abetted by geo-greens, pushes in the opposite direction.

Electric cars: plugging-in to the US Treasury

When it comes to picking winners for future motorists, the government has increasingly expensive tastes. Diesels are too mundane and sensible to generate much buzz. The recently-favored gas-electric hybrids were inherently expensive because they had both gasoline and electric power, and expensive nickel-metal-hydride batteries. Adding plug-in capability to a hybrid adds hundreds of pounds more weight and some very expensive lithium-ion batteries whose reliability and safety (they get hot) is unknown. The Chevy Volt's batteries are estimated to cost $8,000, according to *Consumer Reports*, and the Nissan's Leaf's about $18,000.

Daniel Kammen, The World Bank Group's Chief Technical Specialist for Renewable Energy and Energy Efficiency, co-authored a study which found that while previous studies found fuel costs of plug-in electric hybrids (PHEVs) to be cheaper than that of conventional hybrids "the opposite may turn out to be true because of the extra weight of the PHEV's batteries." That same study also found that "PHEVs are not currently a cost-effective means of mitigating GHGs" (greenhouse gases).[54]

There will doubtless be a niche market for several thousand plug-in cars, particularly among early adopters who like being first. But these cars are inherently very costly, because of very expensive batteries and (in the case of PHEVs) dual power sources. Although "money is no object" might be an appropriate slogan for the US Treasury, it does not apply to most consumers.

If US and/or foreign producers were willing and able to put as many electric cars up for sales as US politicians want, what happens if only a fraction can be sold at a price that comes anywhere near covering their costs? Who is supposed to make up the difference and why?

Perpetual fat subsidies to electrical cars cannot be defended because of any supposed impact on the global climate because (1) electric cars cannot possibly account for even as much as 1% of all light vehicles within the foreseeable future, and (2) US passenger cars account for no more than 3% of global greenhouse gas emissions today and that fraction will rapidly decline as China ramps up more and more coal-fired power plants.

US taxpayers are now expected to underwrite $7,500 of the cost of plug-in hybrids and electric cars, and Congress is seriously considering extending those subsidies much longer than first planned. It is true that federal and state governments are pledging to buy hundreds of electric cars (as are some affected companies such as GE). But the high cost of adding plug-in vehicles to federal and state fleets is just another way to bail out manufacturers at the expense of taxpayers. There is no assurance that current subsidies will suffice to avoid a future glut of electric cars, nor much chance that financially-strapped governments could repeatedly buy a large enough number of such vehicles to make a meaningful difference.

Hybrid hype

Before the plug-in craze, past efforts to redesign US cars in Washington, with incentives, had included the vociferous "flexible fuel vehicle" lobby, the rich and powerful ethanol lobby, the conventional hybrid lobby, and even a hydrogen fuel cell lobby (such as the Apollo Alliance).

Honorable mention is also due to the intense ad campaign on behalf of natural gas vehicles, with millions of dollars spent on TV advertisements featuring T. Boone Pickens and the equally charming Aubrey McClendon, CEO of Chesapeake Energy. Both gentlemen are victims of the sudden, unanticipated success in producing US natural gas from shale.[55] Natural gas became quite abundant and cheap, giving Pickens and others a strong incentive to lobby for government subsidies to boost demand by converting more vehicles to natural gas and providing more filling stations.

The federal government has offered a $4,000 tax credit for buying the one mass-produced car that runs on compressed natural gas, the venerable Honda Civic GX. Unfortunately, the

$25,960 price is $10,000 higher than a gasoline-powered Civic, horsepower is 20% lower, and the big CNG fuel tank uses up most of the car's trunk yet gets you half as far as a tank of gasoline. Natural gas can, however, be a competitive fuel for vehicles that stay near a central refueling location, such as city buses, garbage trucks and taxis. For short trips, natural gas vehicles could be a sensible alternative to battery electric vehicles which share their limited range but enjoy even larger federal subsidies.

While the chattering class never doubted the impulse to subsidize some kind of different auto technology, pundits and politicians can be fickle about the tech *du jour*. Gas-electric hybrids were all the rage before the enthusiasm for granting subsidies and tax credits hurriedly switched toward plug-in hybrids and pure electric cars. People came to associate hybrid technology with excellent city fuel economy because the first hybrids from Toyota and Honda used electric motors in subcompacts with tiny 4-cylinder engines. Today, by contrast, Infiniti is planning a hybrid M35h with 360 horsepower, and a hybrid option raises the Lotus Elan's horsepower from 444 horsepower to 500. Adding electric motors is not always about saving gas.

Until the end of 2010, big federal tax breaks were offered for buying even thirsty hybrids with powerful gas engines, such as the Cadillac Escalade, Dodge Durango, Lexus GS450H and Porsche Cayenne Hybrid. Several states granted such hybrids special stickers allowing access to HOV lanes with only one driver. Before 2011, California granted such badges of honor to owners of hybrid Cadillac Escalades or Chevy Suburbans with 6.6 liter V8 engines, but not to those who drive a 1-liter Smart for Two. There were also special tax credits for buying diesel cars until 2011, which was ironic given the federal government's extra 6-cent penalty tax on diesel fuel.

By 2011 the hybrid electric vehicles (HEVs) which had only recently been the darlings of government officials who deem themselves qualified to pick winners and losers suddenly seemed as politically passé as the Apollo Alliance's 2004 drive "invest" billions in hydrogen fuel cell cars. Hybrids have even been losing their special tax breaks and access to HOV lanes. The latest push is now for massive subsidies to producers and consumers of battery electric vehicles (BEVs) or plug-in hybrid electric vehicles (PHEVs).

The emphasis that greens and geo-greens have continually placed on getting federal subsidies for these different sorts of new cars is curious in several respects. First of all, even if annual US sales of new light vehicles rise to 14m., that would amount to only 5.6% of the more than 250m. already on the road (and growing). At that rate, it would take decades for a different mix of new cars to have a significant effect on the average mileage of all cars, old and new.

Second, there is no logical "green" reason to prefer higher miles-per-gallon to driving fewer miles. It uses much less fuel to drive 5,000 miles a year in a car that gets 20 miles per gallon than it does to drive 15,000 miles a year in a car that gets 40 miles per gallon. Because cars with high miles per gallon reduce the cost of driving, they also encourage people to drive more miles (for the same reason that cheap gas encourages more driving). Yet prevailing federal and state policies have been entirely devoted to trying to improve the mileage of new cars rather than, say, designing tolls, parking fees and fuel taxes to discourage traffic congestion among all cars, old and new.

Third, there is also no coherent "green" reason to be concerned with each automaker's average fuel economy, since such averages have no impact on which new or used cars or trucks US consumers choose to buy. Setting corporate average fuel economy (CAFE) standards simply means no automaker is allowed to specialize in either larger or small vehicles: Selling BMW Minis keeps that company's average mileage down. Selling Minis allows BMW to sell a 555-horsepower X5-M. Those buying an X5-M face no "gas guzzler tax" because such SUVs (and pickups) are exempt. Similarly, Mercedes sells Smart cars to keep its fleet average down, and Chrysler will sell the Fiat 500.

Regardless whether or not future CAFE standards can or will be enforced, hoards of baby boomers reaching retirement age can easily shun expensive hybrid or plug-in subcompacts by keeping more powerful and comfortable older cars for many years. Younger Americans may opt to buy a used 565-horsepower Cadillac or Camaro with low miles, or a luxury import from German companies that can easily afford to pay US fines, or one of the big-engined SUVs and pickup trucks that are exempt from gas guzzler taxes.

Amazingly, politicians keep getting away with the pretence that some combination of CAFE standards and subsidies for ethanol and electric cars can be the centerpiece of an effective "energy policy" or "climate policy." Blaming US motorists allows them to pretend they are "doing something" about some ill-defined endless "crisis" while being politically rewarded by dispensing valuable favors to interest groups.

In the case of corn ethanol, however, the politically-useful coalition of greens and geo-greens appears to breaking apart. The belated disenchantment with corn ethanol, on the part of Al Gore and other prominent environmentalists, seems to have diverted the never-ending quest for federal subsidies toward the production and purchase of electric cars (Tesla, Coda, Wheego, Ford Fusion and Nissan Leaf) and plug-in hybrids (such as the Chevy Volt and Fisker Karma). There is now a huge $7,500 tax credit for buying such electric or quasi-electric cars, which President Obama's 2012 Budget proposes to convert to a quick $7,500 rebate, like the infamous "cash for clunkers" hand-outs.

The proposed rebate is described by the Administration as "making electric vehicles more affordable." But paying for anything with tax dollars does not make it cheaper; it is simply a transfer payment to car buyers from taxpayers. Much of that subsidy actually goes to *producers* of BEVs and PHEVs, since it allows them to charge a higher price than they could get away with in the absence of the $7,500 tax credit or rebate.

In addition to the tax credit or rebate, the Energy Department has been busily handing out $25bn of low-interest loans to Tesla, Fisker, Nissan, GM and others. Such preferential loans misallocate capital while the implicit federal guarantee also shifts default risk from borrowers to taxpayers (such as, the bail-out of Fannie Mae and Freddie Mac).

In his 2011 State of the Union address, President Obama said, "With more research and incentives, we can break our dependence on oil with biofuels and become the first country to have a million electric vehicles on the road in 2015."

The quaint promise of biofuels replacing a huge amount of oil is still as unlikely as it was on November 7, 1973 when President Richard Nixon vowed that, "by the end of the decade we will have developed the potential to meet our own energy needs without depending on any foreign energy source."[56] Nixon said, "I have ordered funding of this effort to achieve self-sufficiency far in excess of the funds that were expended on the Manhattan Project." Echoing Nixon's expensively impossible promises, the Carter Administration sunk many more billions into energy research and such failed ventures as The Synthetic Fuels Corporation established in 1980 to produce fuel from coal (as geo-greens still advocate but greens cannot).

Today, as in the 1970s, it still remains a futuristic fantasy that biofuels could replace more than a tiny fraction of our oil imports at a cost that taxpayers and consumers would be willing to pay. For one thing, most oil does *not* go into passenger cars. For another, it would take too much land and water.

President Obama's second idea of using debt-financed "incentives" to put a million electric cars on the road by 2015 is also virtually impossible, according to experts involved with the industry.[57] Besides, using costly incentives to add a million electric cars would be both wasteful and useless.

Washington Post editorial writer Charles Lane impolitely pointed out that a million electric vehicles on the road in 2015 "would represent 0.4% of the US automotive fleet, yielding no substantial reduction in carbon emissions or US dependence on foreign oil for the government's multibillion dollar investment."[58]

By 2030, the Energy Information Agency estimates that 3.3 m. PHEVs may have been sold (with $7,500 rebates), or about 1% of all light vehicles on the road by then. We could reach 3.5m. by 2020, according to the University of Michigan Transportation Research Institute, if the government merely raised the PHEV subsidy to $13,500 per car (nearly one-half of which would go directly to manufacturers). That would still be a trivial change in the US car fleet, achieved at a ridiculously high cost to taxpayers.[59]

Nobody expects these numbers to be significantly increased by battery-electric vehicles (BEVs), except perhaps to retirees in warm climates. Electric cars can travel only very short distances in cold weather because batteries lose power in the cold and heating an electric car uses a lot of electricity.

Even if the numbers of subsidized PHEV and BEV cars were eventually much larger than the experts think likely, the effect on emissions (and on potential blackouts) depends on when and where they are plugged in. Plugging an electric car into a coal power plant is not exactly carbon-free. Even states with sizeable nuclear or hydroelectric power commonly burn natural gas, wood or residual fuel oil for incremental power to handle peak demand (for example, summer cooling).

The Energy Information Agency projects that 69% of US electricity will come from fossil fuels in 2035, changed imperceptibly from 70% in 2009. A slight rise in the share from renewables (from 10% to 14%) is expected to be offset by a decline in the share from nuclear power (from 20% to 17%).[60]

A 2008 study by the Oak Ridge National Laboratory compared the emissions of carbon dioxide (CO_2), nitrous oxide and sulfur dioxide between a plug-in hybrid (PHEV) and a gasoline-powered subcompact or conventional hybrid (HEV) that get 40 miles per gallon, with both vehicles driving 20 miles a day. The result varies by region, but for the country as a whole the study found, "CO_2 emissions are slightly higher with PHEVs than gas-fueled HEVs in most scenarios because of the more carbon-intensive coal and oil (than gasoline), and/or the use of less efficient gas turbines and gas-fired steam turbines to meet the added generation needs. The NO_x and SO_2 emissions are much higher" with plug-in hybrids.[61]

The Oak Ridge scientists also found that if electric cars prove as popular as their advocates imagine, that would strain the electric grid in most regions, requiring extra capacity to avoid blackouts even under the optimistic assumptions that PHEV and EV drivers plug in at night. As the authors point out, however, "drivers will control the timing of recharging, and their inclination will be to plug in when convenient, rather than when utilities would prefer."

Al Gore and other PHEV supporters claim the batteries in these cars could be charged at night at a discount (using "smart grid" devices) then used to add power to the grid during periods of peak demand in the daytime, while many drivers would be at work. But the Oak Ridge study warns that, "further analysis is needed of this strategy's costs and benefits to consumers, the electric provider, and the environment. Additional circuitry would be required in vehicles, interconnection issues would add complications, battery life may be affected, and the pollution impact of the vehicles on air quality would have to be addressed. It may be that operating the vehicles to provide electricity to the grid may be more expensive and dirtier than building additional power plants."

A similar article appeared in *Scientific American*, July 2010, called "The Dirty Truth About Plug-in Hybrids." It estimated that in the New York region switching from a high-mileage gas-powered car to a pure electric car like the Nissan Leaf would raise carbon emissions by 4.3% while switching to a plug-in hybrid would raise them by 19%. For the southeast, the comparable increases in carbon dioxide would be 2.4% and 14.4%, respectively. Electrics and plug-in hybrids *would* cut carbon emissions in California, because that state gets nearly as much power from nuclear (14.9% in 2008) as it does from coal, plus 10% from hydro (dams) and nearly 47% from natural gas.

For the nation as a whole, the Oak Ridge Lab report indicates that carbon emissions would be higher with heavily-subsidized electric or plug-in electric cars than with unsubsidized gasoline-powered subcompacts or compact hybrids.

In the heyday of hybrid hype, it was commonplace to hear claims that the savings in gasoline would more than justify the higher price paid for the dual-powered cars. We now know this is often untrue.

The same claims are now made for electric vehicles and plug-in hybrids, but the calculations commonly assume a low price for electricity (much lower than in New York City) and a rising price for gasoline. When greens claim that electric cars offer "the equivalent of dollar-a-gallon gasoline," as Al Gore put it, such dubious claims are inconsistent with their efforts to enact cap-and-trade plans, carbon taxes and renewable mandates. The intent and effect of those policies is to push electricity prices much higher by requiring utilities to switch from cheaper to more expensive energy sources.

At a federally-sponsored GovEnergy.gov conference in Dallas, August 2010, Christopher Abbuehl of Constellation Energy and Jeffrey Dominick of Johnson Controls estimated the relative costs of renewable energy technologies, taking account of "incentives" for renewable sources.[62] They *assume a carbon tax* on emissions from coal and natural gas of $30 per ton of carbon dioxide by 2015, higher than the $25 proposed by Princeton economist Alan Blinder for that year, although he like all carbon tax enthusiasts wants that tax (and the price of electricity) to be raised much higher over time.[63]

Such a carbon tax (or an equivalent cap and trade plan) would raise the price of electricity by 3.6 cents per kilowatt hour. Those who claim electric cars would be cheap to charge usually assume an average cost of electricity of about 8 cents per kilowatt hour, so this relatively small carbon tax would lift that by 4.5%.

Abbuehl and Dominick estimate that energy from Solar PV (photovoltaic) power systems would still cost twice as much as energy from natural gas or coal in 2015 even after assuming the latter are burdened by the $30 carbon tax. Nuclear power would be a penny cheaper than coal and gas, thanks to its exemption from the carbon tax, but capital costs are very high for adding nuclear or solar power. Energy from all but the largest wind projects would also be more costly than energy from fossil fuels, despite the assumed carbon tax on natural gas and coal and huge subsidies for wind power.

If efforts of the greens succeed in their goal of raising the price of US electricity, by taxing, rationing or banning electric power from fossil fuels, that would make it far less likely that future operating costs of electric vehicles will justify their high prices. Yet organizations spinning arguments for subsidizing electric cars consist of (1) greens who are simultaneously lobbying for using taxes and regulations to greatly increase the price of US electricity and (2) geo-greens who believe that plug-in cars fueled by ethanol could greatly reduce the world price of oil.

Green plans for deliberately raising electricity prices could not make plug-in cars more attractive, and neither could geo-green dreams of driving-down the world/OPEC price of oil (which is much easier said than done).

Geo-green economics

The geo-green rationale for paying more (directly and through subsidies) for plug-in hybrid cars that run on E85 or M85 (methanol) rests in part on allegations of benefits to US employment or economic security which will be discussed shortly.

However, the geo-green rationale also rests on alleged national security benefits of waging a roundabout form of economic warfare on oil exporting countries. As *New York Times* columnist Thomas Friedman put it, "we are financing the jihadists – and the Saudi, Sudanese and Iranian mosques and charities that support them – through our gasoline purchases."[64] In January 2005, Friedman claimed that "if we put all our focus on reducing the price of oil – by conservation, by developing renewable and alternative energies and by expanding nuclear power – we will force more reform [of Middle Eastern politics] than by any other strategy."

Even if world oil did fall back to $18 per barrel, which Friedman thought low enough to bring down the regime in Iran, there would then be no incentive for Asia or Europe to economize on oil use, nor for anyone to develop alternatives. Besides, the price of oil was below $18 nearly all the time from February 1986 to June 1999 – falling as low as $11 at the end of 1998 and remaining below $20 through the end of 2001. Yet cheap oil did nothing to promote economic or political liberty in Algeria, Iran, or anywhere else. This theory has been tested and it failed completely.

Gar Luft, a leading member of Set America Free, writes that "petrodollars earned by countries like Saudi Arabia, Iran and Libya have been used to sponsor terrorism, produce weapons of mass destruction and build schools preaching hatred of America and its values."[65]

Iran has been on the State Department's list of state sponsors of terrorism since 1984 but Libya is no longer on that list and on February 7, 2011 Reuters reported that the State Department was about to remove Sudan as well. Libya and Sudan were never significant sources of US oil in any case. And although Friedman and Luft (and their ally R. James Woolsey) blame American drivers for helping Iran, the USA has boycotted Iranian oil for many years. That leaves only Saudi Arabia. Friedman and Luft are, in effect, making a plea to use bribes (subsidies) or raw force (mandates) to US households to drive different cars and use different fuel than they would otherwise choose in order to compel Saudi Arabia to sell more of its oil to other countries, such as China.

Table 17.1 US crude oil imports (millions of barrels per day)

	US Imports of Crude Oil (mbpd)	Percent from Persian Gulf	Percent from OPEC
1973	6.26	13.6	47.8
1977	8.81	27.8	70.3
1985	5.07	6.1	36.1
1990	8.02	24.5	53.6
2000	11.46	21.7	45.4
2005	13.71	17.0	40.7
2006	13.71	16.1	40.2
2007	13.47	16.1	44.4
2008	12.92	18.4	46.1
2009	11.69	14.4	40.9

(in billions of constant 2000 dollars)

United States: The Politics of Alternative Energy

Table 17.2 OPEC's real oil export revenues

	1975	1980	1985	1990	1995	2000	2005	2009
Algeria	17.2	30.5	15.7	12.9	9.1	15	36.1	37.9
Angola	NA	NA	NA	NA	4.8	8.1	22.4	37.7
Ecuador	NA	NA	NA	NA	2.1	3	5.8	5.2
Iran	81	30.1	24.5	22.9	19.1	27.1	47.3	47.8
Iraq	35.7	64.3	20.4	13.8	0.8	21.9	23.4	33.8
Kuwait	33	42.9	15.5	8.7	14.5	20.3	40.6	40.2
Libya	26.1	50.7	16.6	15.6	9.8	14.7	27.6	30.6
Nigeria	31.5	58.7	23.1	20.3	13.6	22.3	46.3	41.3
Qatar	7.4	13.5	4.9	4.3	3.5	9	19	21.4
Saudi Arabia	116.6	264.7	43.1	61.5	59.9	85	157.9	137.1
UAE	28.7	49.4	18	21.9	16.4	25.2	47.5	47.1
Venezuela	28.7	45.3	19.9	18.1	15.6	28.3	36.7	29.7
OPEC Total	405.9	647.2	199.7	198.6	169.4	279.7	510.7	509.7

Source: www.eia.doe.gov/cabs/OPEC_Revenues/images/real.csv

Before we examine the logic of such geo-green proposals, it may help to look at some statistics about US imports from Persian Gulf countries in question, and from the much larger Organization of Petroleum Exporting Countries (OPEC).

The first column of Table 17.1 shows some key ups and downs of US oil imports, in millions of barrels per day, starting with the Arab Oil embargo of 1973–74. Nine Arab countries within OPEC stopped sending oil to the USA and (more importantly) reduced production, so Persian Gulf countries accounted for only 13.6% of US oil imports in 1973. But other OPEC countries picked up some of the slack (and other countries surely shipped Arab oil to the USA), so OPEC as a whole accounted for nearly half of US imports during the "embargo."

The Persian Gulf countries succumbed to greed and by 1977 accounted for a record 27.3% of US imports. In an ultimately unsuccessful effort to lift oil prices, Saudi Arabia cut oil production by 75% through 1985, which resulted in Persian Gulf countries supplying only 6.1% of US imports. Imports of oil by the USA more than doubled during the 1985–2000 period of strong US economic growth, but the Persian Gulf share declined after 1990 and was not significantly higher in 2009 than it had been during the embargo of 1973.

Table 17.2 shows real, inflation adjusted revenues that major OPEC oil producers earned at five-year intervals from 1975 to 2009. For OPEC as a whole, real revenues fell by 73.8% between 1980 and 1995, which does not suggest an omnipotent cartel. When Saudi Arabia did try cutting production after 1977, their revenues fell by 83.7% in real terms from 1980 to 1985. Collapsing revenue did not topple the Saudi regime, contrary to geo-green claims, nor have oil prices as low as $11 per barrel.

Table 17.3 compares the relatively unchanged level of US oil imports from 2000 to 2009 with the dramatic ups and down in the average price of a barrel of imported crude oil (touching $145 briefly in 2008). To imagine that the world price of oil changes because of changes in US imports, as geo-greens suggest, is to forget that prices are set at the margin. The USA has not been the world's marginal oil buyer in a long time. That honor goes to Asia in general and China in particular.

With that factual history in mind, consider the Set America Free proposal to use alternative vehicles and fuels to battle OPEC's supposedly awesome power to push oil prices as high or

Table 17.3 US crude oil imports (millions of barrels per day) an average price per barrel of imported crude oil

	Import Volume million barrels per day	Import Price $ per barrel
2000	9.97	27.72
2001	9.33	21.99
2002	9.14	23.71
2003	10.00	27.73
2004	10.08	35.89
2005	10.13	48.89
2006	10.12	59.05
2007	10.03	67.19
2008	9.78	92.57
2009	9.01	59.04

Source: U.S. Energy Information Agency

low as they like (the latter sounds as odd as it is, but is depicted as a sporadic effort to thwart competition from the likes of ethanol and methanol).

Set America Free proposals can be viewed as an indiscriminate, limited, and unilateral form of trade sanctions which allows other oil-importing countries such as China, India, Japan and Europe to be free riders. It is, first, indiscriminate because the aim is to reduce oil imports in general (through alternative vehicles and fuels) regardless where the oil imports come from. Even if forcing or bribing everyone into plug-in hybrids fueled by 85% methanol could one day result in deep cuts in US oil imports, those cuts would be most damaging to Canada and Mexico and not to Iran, whose oil we boycott. Second, the plan is severely limited because nearly 58% of US petroleum does not go into cars and would be unaffected by the geo-greens plans, and because those efforts would necessarily take decades and would doubtless face consumer and taxpayer resistance. Third, the geo-green plan is unilateral, unlike international trade sanctions against specific countries, which means all other oil-importing countries would get a free ride from any effect the bullying of US motorists might have in making petroleum cheaper and more abundant for other countries.

One argument against buying oil from countries that "don't like us" is that some or all of those countries might one day refuse to sell oil to the USA so we should supposedly pre-empt that alleged risk by refusing to buy oil from them. In other words, the USA should impose an oil embargo on itself. But any oil the USA refused to buy would obviously just flow to China, India, Europe, etc.

The risk of disruptions to world oil supplies (such as Iraq's invasion of Kuwait or the 1973 oil embargo) is an argument constantly used to rationalize ethanol mandates and subsidies, and subsidies for plug-in hybrids. We set up a huge Strategic Petroleum Reserve to take care of emergencies, and it is being expanded to 1bn barrels under the 2005 Energy Policy Act. But politicians and technocrats are timid by nature, and never tap it when they should. As oil approached $145 per barrel, the President was reluctant to stop adding more oil to the reserve, much less doing the right thing by selling future contracts against the reserve. The Energy Department rightly says "the SPR provides the President with a powerful response option should a disruption in commercial oil supplies threaten the US economy."[66] But that decision should be made by a committee or a computer, or the reserve should be privatized (investors know to buy low and sell high).

The whole idea that our "addiction" to foreign oil makes the US economy more vulnerable to sudden spikes in the price of oil is fundamentally muddled economics. Earlier in this paper, we showed that even if US passenger cars used no gasoline at all, the country would still not have enough domestic petroleum to supply other transportation, commerce and industry required. But even if the USA were entirely self-sufficient in oil, that would not insulate us from the ups and down of world oil prices. In oil exporting countries such as the United Kingdom, Canada and Mexico, motorists and energy-intensive industries suffer greatly during sudden spikes in the price of oil, and their economies commonly fall into recession at such times. When the world oil prices go up, so do domestic oil prices. Arbitrage likewise ensures that the price of ethanol, coal and other tradable fuels which may substitute for oil also track the price of oil very closely.

US dependence on imported oil is not fundamentally different from US dependence on imported lithium from Bolivia and rare earths from China needed to produce electric cars. In fact, China is becoming ominously restrictive about rare earth exports, which could give Chinese carmakers a big leg up in the subsidized US market for electric cars. Dependence on oil imports is also not fundamentally different from US dependence on imported uranium needed to fuel nuclear power plants, or imported copper needed in most green technology, and so on.

Gar Luft claims, "requiring [all] new vehicles to be flex-fuel-capable. ... would put a virtual cap on the price of oil. Consumers would opt for the most economic fuel on a per-mile cost basis and thus shift to substitute fuels the next time OPEC allows the price of oil to exceed a certain threshold." But there is no evidence that more than a miniscule fraction of the 7.1m. owners of US flexible fuel vehicles have exercised such a choice. One reason is that the price of ethanol rises and falls in lock step with the price of gasoline, which is the expected effect of arbitrage between two close substitutes. Ethanol is also an energy-intensive product whose price could not be unaffected by higher world oil prices.

Even if draconian belt-tightening by US motorists could significantly reduce the world price of oil (which is highly doubtful), the benefits of cheaper oil would by definition accrue to other countries. If the US allowed its own industries and consumers to benefit from the supposed drop in world oil prices (as a result of breaking the oil cartel), that would undo the effort to cut imports. Most petroleum consumed in the USA is not used by passenger cars and demand for petroleum among commercial, industrial and non-auto transportation sectors would rise if any induced reduction in the world oil price was allowed to be matched by a lower domestic oil price (rather than being offset by taxes or rationing).

Consider the protectionists' old idea that money spent on buying something useful from another country is just lost to the US economy, so we would be much better off buying everything close to home (regardless what it costs, though they never say that).

Attempting to defend ethanol subsidies and mandates, for example, former Speaker of the House Newt Gingrich wrote, "It is in this country's long-term best interest to stop the flow of $1bn a day overseas. ... Think of what $1bn a day kept in the US economy creating jobs, especially energy jobs which cannot be outsourced, could do."[67] That is, of course, a totally false choice. Apologists for subsidies and mandates are not proposing to pay the same price for domestic fuel as we could otherwise pay for an energy-equivalent amount of imported oil – replacing $1bn of imported fuel with $1bn of domestic fuel. They are talking about paying much more for domestic fuel than we pay for imported oil. Why else would they be asking for subsidies, tariffs and mandates?

Paying much more for something as important as energy, whether directly or through taxes, makes an economy poorer, and being poorer is no way to create "green jobs." Money wasted on something like ethanol, which politicians favor, is money that could otherwise have been spent on something else that consumers favor.

A central fallacy in the notion of "green jobs" is the idea that using more labor to produce something of less value is a net gain to the economy. Citing the California Public Interest Research Group, the Apollo Alliance's 2004 report said, "Renewable Energy generates four times as many jobs per MW of installed capacity as natural gas.". To any economist, that statement says labor productivity in renewable energy industries is only one-quarter of the level of the natural gas industry. Low productivity means consumers pay more for less. My neighborhood pays to have snow removed from our street and driveways. It would surely "create more jobs" to remove the snow with a dozen shovels, rather than one plow on a truck. But then we could either not afford snow removal, or we would have to cut back on some other expenditure. Getting more value with less work (higher productivity) is why people in affluent countries live better than poor countries.

Even a country as large as the USA cannot have any significant impact on worldwide oil demand by simply adding a few million electric cars to a fleet that is already 250m. and rising. And the huge amount of ethanol the Congress has mandated to be produced by 2022 is very unlikely to materialize. Geo-green claims that doubling down on such costly bets could crush OPEC, dismantle autocratic Islamic regimes and drive down the world price of oil are as contradictory as they are implausible.

Conclusion

We are now in a better position to ask a question that was implicit in the introduction to this chapter: Why was the campaign to mandate and subsidize ethanol and also to subsidize both producers and buyers of hybrid and/or electric cars so politically successful in 2005–9?

It is quite unlikely that these policies were chosen primarily on their merit. For reasons this paper discusses, the proliferating subsidies and mandates could not have been expected to be cost-effective means of dealing with global warming or even with supposedly excessive use of imported oil. US passenger cars account for no more than 3.4% of global greenhouse emissions and that figure will fall because of rapid increases in the use of coal and oil in China, India and other emerging economies. For similar reasons, US passenger cars also account for a relatively small and dwindling percentage of world oil demand.

A more candid explanation of recent US energy policy is that subsidies and mandates for alternative fuels and vehicles have been designed by and for energy interest groups to reward politically-influential coalitions of industrial, financial and ideological interests. In other words, realists would be well advised not to view valuable subsidies and mandates for alternative fuels and vehicles as a means to an end, but rather as the end itself.

Notes

1 Keith Schneider, "Clean Energy Is Foundation of Proposed Stimulus," January 15, 2009, and "Recovery Bill is Breakthrough on Clean Energy, Good Jobs," February 17, 2009, apolloalliance.org.
2 Laura Vanderkam, "Biofuels or Bio-fools?" *The American*, May-June 2007.
3 Steven Mufson, "Ethanol Producers Press for Higher Limits," *The Washington Post*, March 5, 2007.
4 Richard Newell, "Annual Energy Outlook 2011: Reference Case," December 10, 2010. www.eia.doe.gov/neic/speeches/newell_12162010.pdf
5 Gilbert E. Metcalf, "Federal Tax Policy Towards Energy," MIT Joint Program on the Science and Policy of Global Change, Report No. 142, January 2007.
6 Steven Mufson, "High Oil Prices Spout Gusher of Proposals," *The Washington Post*, May 20, 2006.
7 Richard E. Wagner, *To Promote the General Welfare: Market Processes vs. Political Transfers*, San Francisco, Pacific Research Institute, 1989, p. 17.
8 Thomas L. Friedman, "Geo-Greening by Example," *The New York Times*, March 27, 2005.

9 R. James Woolsey, "How to End America's Addiction to Oil," *The Wall Street Journal*, April 15, 2010.
10 American Energy Innovation Council, *A Business Plan for America's Energy Future*, 2010.
11 Nelson D. Schwartz, "American Energy Policy, Asleep at the Spigot," *The New York Times*, July 6, 2008.
12 Plug-in Electric Vehicles: A Practical Plan for Progress, The Report of an Expert Panel, School of Public and Environmental Affairs at Indiana University, February 2011.
13 David B. Sandlow, ed., *Plug-in Electrical Vehicles: What Role for Washington?* D.C., The Brookings Institution, 2009, Table 2–1, p. 24.
14 US Energy Information Agency, Petroleum Statistics. www.eia.gov/energyexplained/index.cfm?page=oil_home#tab2.
15 US Energy Information Agency, *Annual Energy Review 2009*, Tables 12.1, 12.2 & 12.3, pp. 345–51. www.eia.gov/aer.
16 Ibid., Table 11.19.
17 Mark J. Perry, "U.S. Share of World GDP Remarkably Constant," Carpe Diem blog, November 19, 2009.
18 U.S. Department of Energy, *Transportation Energy Data Book: Edition 29*, June 30, 2010, Ch. 11, Table 11.5 http://cta.ornl.gov/data/index.shtml
19 "Primary Energy" *The Economist*, November 14, 2009.
20 "China's Thirst for Oil Could Come Up Short," *The Wall Street Journal*, June 1, 2010.
21 "The Coal Boom: Burning ambitions," *The Economist*, January 29, 2011.
22 "All Fired Up Over Coal Exports to Asia," *Bloomberg Businessweek*, February 13, 2011.
23 American Energy Innovation Council, op. cit.
24 Diane Brady and Rachel Layne, "Good for GE, Good for America? The Interests of Obama and Immelt—The GE chief and new jobs adviser—increasingly overlap," *Bloomberg Businessweek*, January 27, 2011.
25 Michael Sherer, "A Green Seat at the Table," *Time magazine*, March 15, 2010.
26 Mr Gore is chairman of Generation Investment Management, which runs a $5bn fund of investments mostly held by foreign institutional investors. *The New York Times* reported that one of the fund's three biggest investments in 2008 was "Johnson Controls, the largest maker of automotive seats and batteries." "Al Gore's fund to close after attracting $5bn," *The New York Times*, March 11, 2008.
27 Michael Sherer, op. cit.
28 Adam Lashinsky, "Kleiner Perkins gets its digital groove back on," *Fortune*, November 29, 2010.
29 Mark Lemos Stein, "Are You Plugged In?" *The Wall Street Journal*, February 22, 2010.
30 Katie Fehrenbacker, "10 Political Connections in Greentech," Gigacom.com January 4, 2010. http://gigaom.com/cleantech/10-former-politicians-that-jumped-into-greentech/
31 Marianne Bertrand, Matilde Bombardini, Francesco Trebbi, "Is It Whom You Know or What You Know? An Empirical Assessment of the Lobbying Process." National Bureau of Economic Research Working Paper 16765, February 2011.
32 "Green Energy: Wild is the Wind" *The Economist*, September 25, 2010.
33 Eric Pooley, "The Smooth-Talking King of Coal – and Climate Change," *BusinessWeek*, June 3, 2010.
34 Joseph E. Aldy, et al., "Designing Climate Mitigation Policy," *Journal of Economic Literature*, Vol. XLVII, No. 4, December 2010, p. 928.
35 *Annual Energy Review*, op cit., Figure 10.1 p. 282.
36 "Captains of Subsidy," a *Wall Street Journal* editorial, June 16, 2010.
37 "According to current international convention … carbon released through biomass combustion is excluded from reported energy-related emissions. The release of carbon from biomass combustion is assumed to be balanced by the uptake of carbon when the feedstock is grown, resulting in zero net emissions over some period of time. (This is not to say that biomass energy is carbon-neutral. *Energy inputs are required in order to grow, fertilize, and harvest the feedstock and to produce and process the biomass into fuels*)." – *Annual Energy Review*, op. cit., p. 364 [emphasis added].
38 Elizabeth Rosenthal, "Biofuels Deemed a Greenhouse Threat," *The New York Times*, February 8, 2008.
39 Ben German, "Draft EPA report: Biofuels threaten habitat, water quality" *The Hill*, January 28, 2011.
40 Michael J. Roberts and Wolfram Schlenker, "Identifying Supply and Demand Elasticities of Agricultural Commodities: Implications for the U.S. Ethanol Mandate," National Bureau of Economic Research Working Paper 15921, April 2010.
41 "Al Gore's Ethanol Ephipany," *The Wall Street Journal*, November 27, 2010.

42 Congressional Budget Office, "Using Biofuel Tax Credits to Achieve Energy and Environmental Policy Goals," July 2010.
43 "Vinod Khosla on Corn Ethanol: Time to move on," greentechmedia, December 3, 2010.
44 Robert Bryce provides a properly skeptical review of the hype and reality behind cellulosic ethanol in *Power Hungry*, Public Affairs, 2010, Ch. 18.
45 http://fuelgaugereport.aaa.com/
46 Don Lancaster, "The Hydrogen Scene: It's a Gas" *Nuts & Bolts Magazine*, May 1999 www.tinaja.com/glib/resbn88.pdf
47 Mark Hertsgaard, "Green Grows the Grassroots," *The Nation*, July 31, 2006.
48 Max Boot, "The 500-Mile-Per-Gallon Solution," *The Los Angeles Times*, March 24, 2005.
49 Greg Schneider, "An Unlikely Meeting of the Minds: For Very Different Reasons, Groups Agree on Gas Alternatives" *The Washington Post*, March 31, 2005.
50 William Greider, "Apollo Now," *The Nation*, January 2, 2006.
51 Frank Gaffney, "Impending Energy Threat" *The Washington Times*, January 16, 2007.
52 *Transportation Energy Data Book*, op. cit., Table 6.1
53 Christopher Rauwald, "Fuel Prices Hamper Diesel-Cars Push," *The Wall Street Journal*, July 28, 2009.
54 David B. Sandlow, op. cit., pp. 172–73.
55 Holman W. Jenkins, Jr., "Listening to the Shale Revolution," *The Wall Street Journal*, February 5, 2011.
56 Richard M. Nixon, "Address to the Nation About Policies to Deal with the Energy Shortages," November 7, 1973.
57 Peter Whoriskey, "Plug-in cars not on a fast track," *The Washington Post*, February 2, 2011.
58 Charles Lane, "Cold truths on electric avenue," *The Washington Post*, January 28, 2011.
59 American Council for an Energy Efficient Economy, "Plug-in Electric Vehicles: Penetration and Grid Impacts," 2010. www.aceee.org/files/pdf/PHEVfactsheet.pdf
60 *Annual Energy Outlook 2011* early release overview. www.eia.doe.gov/forecasts/aeo/executive_summary.cfm
61 Stanton W. Hadley and Alexandra Tsvetkova, *Potential Impacts of Plug-in Hybrid Electric Vehicles on Regional Power Generation*, Oak Ridge National Laboratory, January 2008.
62 Christopher Abbuehl and Jeffrey Dominick, "Turning Green into Gold: The Economics of Renewable Projects," presented to govenergy.gov conference "Blazing Trails to Energy Solutions" Dallas, August 15–18, 2010.
63 Alan Blinder, "The Carbon Tax Miracle Cure," *The Wall Street Journal*, January 31, 2011.
64 Thomas Friedman, op. cit. See also R. James Woolsey, op cit.
65 Gar Luft, "How to Ruin OPEC's birthday," *The Near East Report*, October 20, 2003.
66 US Department of Energy, Petroleum Reserves. www.fossil.energy.gov/programs/reserves/
67 Newt Gingrich, "I've Always Supported an 'All the Above' Energy Policy," letter to *The Wall Street Journal*, February 3, 2011.

18

Beyond the Oil Curse

Iraq's Wealthy State and Poor Society

Abbas Kadhim

Introduction

The current Iraqi economy is almost entirely dependent on oil revenues. According to the official figures presented by the Iraqi Ministry of Finance, oil exports provided 91% of the country's revenue in 2010. Various taxes and tariffs constituted the other 9%. The figures show an increase of oil dependence in comparison with the 2009 revenue, of which 85% was made by oil exports.[1]

However, the country's oil industry is in a state of general devastation. The lack of security in several parts of the country is very prohibitive to foreign investment and it continues to hinder the patterns of production as the industry's infrastructure continue to be a target for the various terrorist groups in various parts of the country. Similarly, corruption in the Ministry of Oil and the Government of Iraq in general contributes to significant losses in revenue and provides inefficient management of the industry. As in the rest of governmental entities, loyalty to certain political parties and groups is considered before competence and expertise in the hiring of personnel at all levels of the oil industry. Furthermore, numerous militias and well-connected criminal organizations continue to smuggle Iraqi oil and cost Iraq billions of dollars each year in lost revenue.[2] That is, of course, in addition to the depletion of infrastructure that was caused by decades of war and sanctions.

This chapter will examine Iraqi's efforts to restore its capacity to produce and export its petroleum products and the challenges that hinder these efforts and delay the country's ambitions to become the world's first, or second, oil producer. The chapter will also shed light on the political and ideological debates among Iraqis concerning the control of oil production and sales, the role of foreign oil corporations and the distribution of revenues. But first, an historical background of the economic and political developments in Iraq's oil industry is essential.

Iraqi oil industry under the monarchy: 1925–58

Iraq became a nation-state following the collapse of the Ottoman Empire in 1918. Responding to the Ottoman attack on Russian ports on the Black Sea on 29 October 1914, France and Britain joined a Russian declaration of war against the Ottomans. British troops stationed in Bahrain attacked the southern part of Basra to begin the gradual occupation of the three Ottoman provinces that would form modern Iraq.³ Having occupied Basra in 1914, British forces faced several military setbacks, mostly because of the unanticipated tribal and religious resistance to their forces; but they were finally able to capture Baghdad in 1917 and Mosul in 1918, merely a few days after concluding a ceasefire treaty with the Ottomans.

As declared by British Prime Minister Asquith on 2 November 1915, protecting the oil fields was one of the main reasons behind sending a force to Iraq (or Mesopotamia, as it was known in British parlance).⁴ By oil fields, Mr. Asquith referred to the Persian oil fields and the operations of the Anglo-Persian Oil Company, which was at a very short, and dangerous, distance from the Ottoman-controlled Basra. At stake was an oil operation that cost the British empire £2.5m. that was paid at the advice of Winston Churchill, then the First Lord of the Admiralty, who told the House of Commons that the best policy concerning oil was for the British government to "become the owners or at any rate the controllers at the source, of at least a proportion of the oil which the navy required."⁵

Following the San Remo Conference, held in April 1920, the British were granted a mandate to shape the political future of the three former Ottoman provinces: Baghdad, Mosul and Basra. Under the pressure of Iraqi resistance, which was ultimately manifested in the 1920 Revolution, the British decided to form the modern Iraqi state and install an Arab king, the choice fell on Faysal, the son of Sharif Husayn of Makka, who was aided by a pro-British council of ministers that consisted of Iraqi urban notables.

In 1925, the British-controlled Iraqi government agreed to award a concession to explore and eventually produce oil, which covered most of Iraq's territory, to the Iraqi Petroleum Company (IPC), of which Iraq owned nothing except the name; the full ownership was "by five multinational oil companies (British Petroleum, Exxon, Mobil, Shell, and Compagnie Française des Pétroles)." Other areas not covered by the said concession were covered by other concessions to two IPC subsidiaries: Basra Petroleum Company (BPC) and Mosul Petroleum Company (MPC).⁶ These concessions were very far-reaching, both economically and politically, as well as in terms of their duration, that was to last for three-quarters of a century, until 2000. Under the concession, the companies were "to determine the output, price and export levels,"⁷ effectively placing the political and economic destiny of the country in the hands of a few foreign multinational companies with very strong ties to Western countries. In return, Iraq was to receive 24 cents for every barrel produced from "its" oil fields. The concession was so controversial that the Ministers of Education and Justice, Muhammad Ridha al-Shabibi and Rashid Ali al-Gaylani, respectively, resigned over this decision which, in the words of al-Shabibi, "squandered Iraq's rights."⁸ Or as George W. Stocking aptly put it: "Never in modern times have governments granted so much, to so few for so long."⁹

The work of these multinational companies was successful in discovering oil in Kirkuk, northern Iraq, in 1927. However, instead of developing this field and producing oil in commercial quantities, the IPC wasted much valuable time, 18 months to be exact, in searching for other potential areas in order to secure the best areas of concession for itself, before other competitors have the chance to bid for further concessions, according to the agreements. This practice delayed the construction of pipelines and the production of Iraqi oil in commercial quantities until 1932 and regular oil production until 1935.¹⁰

Iraq's dependence on oil revenues began immediately after the start of regular oil exports and continued to grow concomitantly with the increase of such revenues one decade after another throughout the monarchy era. The proceeds from oil increased from just above £1m. in 1935 to £6.8m. in 1950.¹¹ Two events in the surrounding Middle East region brought the profit sharing between Iraq and the IPC into question and started a new round of Iraqi demands: the first was the announcement, in 1950, of an agreement between the government of Saudi Arabia and Aramco, the company producing Saudi oil, on a 50:50 sharing of profit, and the second event was the nationalization of the oil industry in Iran in 1951 during the premiership of Dr Muhammad Mossadeq.[12] Coupled with the rise of Iraqi nationalism and general anti-British sentiments in Iraq following the failed 1948 Anglo-Iraq Treaty (Portsmouth Treaty), a national debate about the exploitation of Iraqi resources, mainly oil, by multinational companies, began to reach critical levels. Even though the Iraqi government was strongly pro-West, the pressure was very high and the exploitation of Iraqi resources was indeed indefensible. To preempt the possibility of Iraq's nationalists succeeding in forcing nationalization measures similar to the Iranian model, the IPC settled for a lesser concession, the Saudi model of 50–50 profit sharing. The agreement had a significant positive impact on Iraq's economy. Iraq's share of oil proceeds increased from just under £7m. in 1950 to £40.7m. in 1952 and jumped significantly every subsequent year to reach £84.6m. during 1958, the year of Iraq's transition from a monarchy to a republic.[13]

Oil and the rise of nationalism: 1958–79

The dawn of 14 July 1958 was meant to be a new dawn for Iraq, the beginning on an era without foreign manipulation of Iraqi politics and economy. A group of Iraqi officers took matters into their own hands and toppled one of the most pro-West governments in the region, ending years of political preparations to link Iraq to major regional and international powers through political and defence alliances, including the ill-fated Baghdad Pact, a NATO-like anti-Communist defence alliance that included Iran, Pakistan, Turkey, Britain, in addition to Iraq, whose capital was chosen to host the organization's headquarters.

What began as a typical military coup soon developed to become a political and social revolution that changed not just the Iraqi regime, but all aspects of Iraqi life as well. The change included land tenure and ownership, the social status of workers and peasants, the laws of personal status and women's rights, party politics and political associations, and a plethora of other and political and social settings. It was a new beginning of hope and high aspirations that were not seen in Iraq for a very long time.

In the period between 1958 and 1963, Iraqi oil output increased by 60%, but the revenue did not increase at the same rate, mainly because of the decline in prices.[14] This situation resurrected the question of Iraq's fair share in its oil resources. A new round of negotiations started over several issues, including: oil prices, Iraqi portion of equity in the IPC and the Iraqi control over the "unexplored portions of the concession area." The negotiations were conducted amidst an era of heightened sense of nationalism and sharp criticism of what the Iraqi government considered unfair distribution of benefits between the IPC and Iraqi government and the hegemony of the IPC over the operation of the Iraqi oil industry.[15] IPC failure to satisfy the Iraqi side was met by two significant acts of retaliation. In July 1960 Iraqi Prime Minister Abd al-Karim Qasim raised the transit rates in Basra to be 1,200% of their prior levels. He followed this measure with the passing of Law 80 in December 1961. According to Law 80, Iraq repossessed all unexplored areas of the IPC concession, leaving the IPC with 0.5% of the original concession.[16]

Although the Iraqi government did not develop the possessed areas (it lacked the capability to do so) Law 80 was praised as the prelude for the nationalization of Iraq's oil industry in the early 1970s. It seems that the decision of the IPC not to escalate the confrontation with the Iraqi government, which could perhaps be done by manipulating prices or output, was a conscious decision similar to that of 1952, when it agreed to the 50:50 profit sharing. Once again, the IPC preempted a possible government move to nationalize the oil industry by simply complying with the measure of Law 80, in spite of contending that it was in violation of the various previous concession agreements.

Although Iraq established its own Iraqi National Oil Company (INOC) in 1964, the company remained inactive and the IPC continued as the only oil producing company for the following eight years "providing an average of 80.4% of total government revenue between 1959 and 1970."[17] However, Iraq signed an agreement with the Soviet Union, in the summer of 1969, which included US$140 million as a Soviet assistance to Iraq to develop the unexplored areas of the oil concession which were repossessed from the IPC and to turn the INOC into a real oil-producing company.[18] The money was used to develop the North Rumayla oil field, near the southern city of Basra. The INOC began its production in mid-April 1972, preceded by an Iraqi-Soviet oil trade deal and a number of similar trade deals with several countries (Brazil, Italy, the USSR and the GDR).[19]

On 14 May 1972 the government presented an ultimatum to the IPC to agree to the following demands in order to avoid the nationalization of its assets:

1. 20% Iraqi participation in the IPC's assets.
2. A payment of I.D.81.4m. for back royalties the IPC owed the government owing to supposed misrepresentation.
3. Effective Iraqi participation on the IPC's board of directors.
4. IPC recognition of Law 8o's validity.
5. Relocation of the IPC's headquarters in Baghdad.
6. An IPC-Iraqi production level agreement providing for a minimum production increase per year.
7. Continuous Iraqi audit of IPC accounts.[20]

The two parties, the IPC and the Iraqi government, failed to reach a mutual agreement and, having secured alternative revenue sources and oil markets, Iraq announced the nationalization of the IPC on 1 June 1972. As the Slugletts noted, in order to insure further financial security, Iraq refrained from nationalizing the two subsidiaries of the IPC, the MPC and the BPC, which produced 25% of Iraq's oil at the time. The Iraqi government also practised its own divide-and-conquer policy by offering the Compagnie Française des Pétroles, one of the companies that participated in the IPC, "special treatment."[21] Having overcome the consequences of the first act of nationalization, Iraq nationalized the MPC and the BPC in the wake of the October 1973 war between Israel and several Arab countries, including Iraq. The 5% share of Gulbenkian was nationalized shortly thereafter.[22]

Oil, war and sanctions: the Saddam Hussein era, 1979–2003

On 17 July 1979 Saddam Hussein, then the Vice-President of Iraq and the second man in the Ba'th Party, eliminated President Ahmad Hassan al-Bakr and began his quest for controlling all the levers of power in the country, with the help of a few family members, loyal and opportunistic subordinates and a few dispensable bureaucrats.[23] The era of Saddam Hussein was marked by some unique characteristics, unlike any in the history of modern Iraq. Among these were the following: (1) the narrowing of the power base to include only Saddam and his family; those members of his family who constituted a threat to the dictator were swiftly eliminated, as in the case of his cousin and brother-in-law, defence minister Adnan Khairallah and his two sons-in-law; (2) the militarization of Iraqi society and the state, as Iraqis lived in an era of perpetual war; (3) the complete lack of human rights of Iraqis, who saw their freedom of expression, religious and political rights wither away under the increasing aggression of the police state; and (4) the gradual reversal of the economic progress that was accomplished with the help of increasing oil revenues in the post-nationalization years. The first three points are out of the scope of this paper, but the relevance of the last one warrants some further discussion.

The years from 1973 to 1979 marked an era of significant improvement in the Iraqi infrastructure and great progress in healthcare, education, family income and government services. But this progress was accompanied by a gradual decrease of individual rights and an increase in state oppression whose security forces were among the largest and the most sophisticated in the region. In 1978 the only two ministries that employed more than 10% of the total workers in the public sector were the Ministry of Industry and Minerals (14.2%) and the Ministry of the Interior (22.8%).[24]

When Saddam Hussein became President, economic prosperity and state oppression were no longer going in the same direction, the former sharply plummeted as the latter continued to rise. He also took the country to a destructive war with Iran that lasted for eight years and claimed lives by the hundreds of thousands and cost Iraq approximately $453bn, including the loss of oil revenue.[25] Only six days before marking the second anniversary of the end of the Iran-Iraq War, Saddam Hussein invaded Kuwait on 2 August 1990, dragging Iraq into a shorter, but more lethal and more destructive war with a coalition of thirty countries which was led by the USA. This time, Iraq suffered some 10,000 military and civilian deaths and about 300,000 wounded, and the economic cost was estimated at $170bn. Additionally, Iraq was forced, according to United Nations resolutions, to pay Kuwait some $60bn for the destruction of its infrastructure and the torching of the Kuwaiti oil fields.[26] So far, Iraq paid $27bn to Kuwait and is asked to pay $25bn more. Some 5% of Iraq's oil revenue is automatically deducted for this compensation until the amount is fully paid.

In addition to the losses caused by Saddam Hussein's misadventure in Kuwait, Iraq had to endure, between 1990 and 2003, the strongest economic sanctions the United Nations ever imposed on any nation in the organization's history. Initially imposed for the purpose of forcing Iraq to withdraw its forces from Kuwait, the sanctions outlived their first purpose and continued to be imposed for whatever demands were presented to Iraq by some of the permanent members of the UN Security Council (UNSC), namely: the USA and the United Kingdom. The sanctions were also a convenient vehicle for a worldwide network of corruption, the scope of which is yet to be fully determined. Corruption allegedly involved some UN personnel, businessmen, politicians, journalists, corporations and just about anybody with access to UN decision making in regards to the control of Iraq's ability to import the necessities of life.

The sanctions were exceptionally devastating to the economy of Iraq, which was almost totally dependent on oil exports. Following the Iraqi invasion of Kuwait, the UN Security Council adopted a series of resolutions for the purpose of forcing Iraq to withdraw from Kuwait. According to UNSC Res. 661, adopted on 6 August 1990, Iraqi assets in foreign countries were frozen and the country was not allowed to export anything and it was only allowed to import foodstuffs and materials strictly intended for medical purposes.[27] In order to ensure the strict enforcement of Res. 661, the UNSC adopted Res. 665, which resolved that Iraq was still in violation of UNSC Res. 660, 661, 662 and 664 and the Iraqi government was "using Iraqi flag vessels to export oil." The resolution then called "upon those Member States … which are deploying maritime forces to the area to use such measures … as may be necessary under the authority of the Security Council to halt all inward and outward maritime shipping, in order to inspect and verify their cargoes and destinations … " and called on other states to co-operate in this effort. In order to further tighten the blockade on Iraq, the UNSC adopted Res. 670, on 25 September 1990, which extended the inspection to aircraft carrying cargo to Iraq and required member states to deny permission to any aircraft carrying cargo to Iraq, except those allowed under previous UNSC resolutions. It also banned any aircraft flying to and from Iraq for other purposes.

Having failed to force, or convince, the Iraqi regime to withdraw from Kuwait, the UNSC adopted two final measures: UNSC Res. 674, on 29 October 1990, and UNSC Res. 678, on 29 November 1990. The former resolution "remind[ed] Iraq that under international law it [was] liable for any loss, damage or injury arising in regard to Kuwait and third States, their nationals and corporations, as a result of the invasion and illegal occupation of Kuwait by Iraq." It also invited all concerned states to begin gathering information about their loss and the loss of their nationals and corporations and submit them in support of their claims of restitution. The latter resolution set a deadline for Iraq to leave Kuwait and comply with all previous UNSC resolutions by 15 January 1991. In case of Iraq's failure to meet the deadline, the UNSC authorized "Member States co-operating with the Government of Kuwait ... to use all necessary means to uphold and implement resolution 660 (1990)." This was, in essence, an authorization for the US-led coalition, whose forces were already assembled at the borders of Kuwait, to go to war against Iraq any time after the 15 January 1991 deadline. On 16 January 1991, a wave of air bombing began, the like of which Iraq had not seen in its entire history. Other than the religious sites, nothing in Iraq seemed to be off the target list. The oil industry, including refineries, was heavily targeted and damaged.

On 3 April 1991, a month after the end of the war to expel the Iraqi forces from Kuwait, the UNSC adopted UNSC Res. 687, which, according to the UN Secretary-General, "represents one of the most complex and far-reaching sets of decisions ever taken by the Council [and] the longest text ever adopted by the council."[28] The resolution essentially put the UNSC in charge of the micromanagement of Iraq's domestic and international relations.

Although the war was over and Iraq was out of Kuwait, the sanctions on the country that were adopted for that purpose were not lifted. Indeed, according to UNSC Res 687 and subsequent resolutions, they became stronger and more far-reaching; they also were aiming at an ever evolving set of goals and conditions on the Iraqi regime: disarmament, compliance with nuclear non-proliferation protocols, dismantling of existing and "suspected" biological and chemical weapons, reducing the military arsenal and personnel, and the list goes on. In all of these cases, the burden of proof was completely on Iraq to satisfy an increasingly sceptical world community, or those parts of it who were leading the UNSC. Meanwhile, the worsening humanitarian conditions in Iraq were rising to catastrophic levels.

Although Res. 687 lifted the embargo and the blockade on Iraq's ability to import foodstuffs and other humanitarian necessities, Iraq had no ability to benefit from this decision, because the embargo on Iraqi oil exports continued. It was not until 15 August 1991 that the UNSC authorized Iraq to export $1.6bn of oil over a period of six months to import food and other civilian necessities, which will be merely $934m. after a number of deductions that included 30% to be used for the compensations of the loss and damages caused by the invasion and occupation of Kuwait. Compared with Iraq's spending of $3bn on food and civilian necessities just prior to the war, this permission, granted in UNSC Res. 706 and Res. 712, would barely allow Iraq to cover one-third of its pre-war needs.[29]

The Iraqi government refused to take advantage of the two UNSC resolutions, arguing that Iraq had complied with the demands of the international community and that there was no rationale for maintaining the sanctions. The government of Iraq was also using several tactics to accomplish its goals. Iraqi diplomacy appealed to many governments in the world that had good relations with Iraq, or had interests in the country, as well as those governments that politically opposed the USA, to press for lifting the sanctions. Given the determination of the USA to keep the sanctions on, no such efforts were fruitful. At the same time, the Iraqi government invited the international media, humanitarian organizations and activists to see the human catastrophe caused by the sanctions and their toll on the society, especially on Iraqi children. Again, the US official answer to the international outcry was simple, banal and as callous as could ever be. Responding to the following "60 Minutes" question: "We've heard that a half a million children have died ... that's more children than died in Hiroshima ... is the price worth it?" Madeline Albright, then the US Secretary of State, said: "I think this is a very hard choice, but the price, we think the price is worth it." This statement was seconded by Bill Richardson, the Governor of New Mexico, who was the US Ambassador to the UN while the sanctions were being enforced. Governor Richardson, when asked about former Secretary Albright's statement and whether he believed that "the price was worth it," he answered "I believe our policy was correct; yes."

The other factor the government of Iraq was counting on was the cost placed on the UN by the mandates from the various UNSC resolutions. As long as Iraq had no revenues, the UN could not ask Iraq to pay for the elaborate system of committees and task forces that were created to ensure Iraq's compliance with these far-reaching resolutions. The Iraqi government seemed to hope that the UN will end this system to save the costs or allow Iraq to sell oil on terms favourable to the government of Iraq. The hopes of Iraq's government were at least partially granted. The UN, after its failure to raise the funds from other means, decided to give the Iraqis a slightly better deal. On 14 April 1995, the UNSC adopted Res. 986, authorizing member states "to permit the import of petroleum and petroleum products originating in Iraq, including financial and other transactions directly related thereto, sufficient to produce a sum not exceeding a total of US$1bn every 90 days," to provide the foodstuffs, medical materials and other "humanitarian needs of the Iraqi people." The Iraqi government was very disappointed at the concession, because it added less than $1bn per year to the original offer. Having rejected this resolution, Iraq continued to test the will of the UNSC, as the Iraqi people were facing ever-increasing deterioration in humanitarian conditions. It was not until the end of 1996 that the UN and Iraq agreed to begin the implementation of UNSC Res. 986, without any significant modifications. "United Nations Secretary-General Kofi Annan has praised the Oil-for-Food Programme for accomplishing one of the largest, most complex and unusual tasks ever entrusted to the Secretariat."[30]

However, the Independent Inquiry Committee into the UN Oil-for-Food Programme found some of the most disturbing instances of corruption associated with the programme, including corrupt practices by the top-level UN officials and their close relatives;[31] the amounts of money involved in the various corruption schemes were in the billions of US dollars. The Committee reported that "specific illicit payments [were] made in connection with oil and humanitarian contracts under the Programme. Oil surcharges were paid in connection with the contracts of 139 companies, and humanitarian kickbacks were paid in connection with the contracts of 2,253 companies."[32]

The programme was terminated on 21 November 2003. Between 1996 and 2003, Iraq exported $64bn worth of petroleum and petroleum products, but only $37bn of these proceeds returned to Iraq in the form of food and humanitarian necessities.[33]

The dreams and the realities of the post-Saddam era

In the months leading to the US invasion of Iraq, as well as shortly after the invasion, it was assumed that Iraq was going to restore its oil production to levels that would generate enough revenues for sustaining the post-war economy and help reconstruct the country. Testifying before the US House of Representatives panel on 27 March 2003, then Undersecretary Paul Wolfowitz said, "The oil revenue of that country could bring between $50 and 100bn over the course of the next two or three years. We're dealing with a country that could really finance its own reconstruction, and relatively soon."[34] As it turned out, Iraq's total oil exports for the abovementioned period were much lower that what was estimated. The oil industry's infrastructure was falling to pieces, because of the sanctions and the past regime's neglect. The UN officials often denied Iraqi requests to fund the importing of materials and equipments for maintaining the infrastructure out of fear that such imports might be used for banned military activities.

To rectify the situation, the US government appropriated more than $4bn to help repair the oil fields, including $2.5bn as a contract awarded to Kellog, Brown and Root (KBR).[35] These efforts managed to bring the oil production to levels just below their pre-invasion average of 2.5mbpd, of which only 1.5mbpd were available to export. However, the insurgency that spread throughout major parts of the country brought the total oil production to fall below 2mbpd in 2005. This production level continued in the first half of 2006, and reached 2.5mbpd in mid-June, 2006, to fall again to 2.23mbpd two weeks later. This temporary rise notwithstanding, exports always held constant at between 1.6 and 1.67mbpd.[36]

These figures, of course, remain suspect because Iraq continued to lack a reliable metering system at the Basra Oil Terminal accurately to report the true levels of production. The quarterly report submitted by the Special Inspector General for Iraq Reconstruction (SIGIR) in July 2006 stated that "the [Basra Oil Terminal] metering system project, which was reported to be 30% complete last quarter, made little progress this quarter because the sub-contractor was delayed in mobilizing … The lack of progress implementing this metering system undermines the effort to combat corruption and smuggling in this economically crucial sector."[37] The metering system continues to be a point of dispute and remains persistently behind schedule. Four years later (by the end of 2010), the government of Iraq reported to the UNSC that 51% of the meters were installed. It is yet to finish the work on the remaining 49%, about 1,150 meters, which were planned to be installed by November 2010. Then there will be the goal to accomplish the whole metering mission, which includes a total of 4,898 meters.[38]

Throughout the post-invasion years, insurgents targeted oil pipes, refineries, power supply and workers, hindering any reconstruction efforts to increase production levels beyond the pre-war period. Furthermore, various militias, often backed by certain major Iraqi political players, established their freelance petroleum cartel, smuggling oil in defiance of the Iraqi authorities and the coalition forces, if not taking advantage of their pragmatic apathy. Meanwhile, 20% of Iraqis, who were surveyed in 10 major cities, said they paid bribes to buy gasoline.[39] The SIGIR quarterly report in July 2006 concluded that corruption in the oil sector, "threatens not only Iraq's capacity to fund new capital investment, but also its ability to sustain and increase production."[40]

Four years later, the SIGIR Report of January 2011 indicates that oil production in Iraq still lingers at 2.4mbpd, slightly higher than its level in mid-2010, but it decreased by 1% from the end of 2009. However, the Ministry of Oil, according to the report, expected to increase the production to 3.26mbpd by the end of 2011 and it has put together a plan to reach the very "ambitious goal of producing 12mbpd by 2017."[41] However, the report reminds the reader that Iraq has to overcome many technical, political and logistical challenges, not to mention the need to invest some $150bn in order to achieve this level of production. Contrary to this ambitious, and optimistic, six-year plan of the Iraqi government, the International Energy Agency (IEA) expects that Iraq may achieve the ability to produce 6.1mbpd in 2035 and it will not reach 3mbpd before 2020.[42]

In order to achieve its goal, the government of Iraq took some serious steps to encourage foreign investment, solicit technical help from various international oil companies and passed some important laws to regulate the terms and conditions of allowing foreign oil companies to invest and operate in Iraq. The Iraqi government had to choose between two different models: "production sharing agreements" or "development and service contracts." Given their injurious past with the multinational corporation that secured exploitive concessions during the era of colonization, Iraqis of various backgrounds, especially Iraq's oil experts, rejected the first model, which is not different from the infamous concessions of the past, because it places the full control of the fields in the hands of foreign oil corporations for many decades and it allows them access to a great percentage of the revenue. Opponents of this scheme argued, perhaps rightfully so, that Iraq could do better. This kind of agreement also touched on a raw nerve for the Iraqis, most of whom now hate everything from the Ba'th era, but all of whom consider the nationalization of oil a truly patriotic act. The second plan allows the government to enter into service contracts with oil companies for a fixed amount of money for every barrel produced. Interested companies were asked to present their bids in a competitive process and the government would choose the best offer according the lowest fee per barrel, after qualifying the competing companies on the basis of their reputation regarding professionalism and their environmental record. The government signed a number of contracts with remuneration fees ranging from $1.15 to $2 per barrel in most regions, as well as some higher ones in Badra, Qaiyarah and Najma, where the projected quantities are lower and the cost of production is higher; the remuneration fees for these were between $5 and $6 per barrel.[43]

The different Iraqi factions had failed time and again to reach a consensus on the final national policy regarding oil production and distribution. Although the Iraqi Constitution states that "Oil and Gas are owned by all the people of Iraq in all the regions and governorates," Iraqi parliamentarians and party leaders had a hard time in reaching agreement on what this statement means, because the Constitution also differentiates between the "present fields," which were already producing oil during the ratification of the Constitution and those that were not yet developed. The central government shares control of the first category of oil fields with the government of the producing region, whereas the government of the producing region or governorate has exclusive control over non-developed and future oil fields. This constitutional debate led to disputes between the central government and two local governments so far, the Kurdistan Regional Government (KRG) and the government of Basra.

Holding the largest portion of Iraq's oil reserves, the city of Basra has been funding more than two-thirds of Iraq's budget for many decades.[44] However, Basra has been one of the most neglected Iraqi cities in Iraq's modern history and one of the worst in services. Basra local politicians and sympathetic experts correctly note that this city can be more prosperous than any of its neighbouring Gulf States if it controls its resources. Instead, the Iraqi government allocated less than $300m. for the city in 2010.[45] In response to what Basrans perceive as persistent negligence of their city and the unfair allocation of funds, they called for forming a region (*iqleem*) for Basra alone and asked that it is treated the same way as the KRG. However, fearing that this could lead to the rise of separatist movements, strong pressures from the other parts of Iraq, especially the religious leadership in Najaf caused the proposal to collapse.[46] But, as long as the central government continues to treat Basra in the same way, the calls for forming a region will be resurrected sooner or later.

The KRG and the central government in Baghdad have not made a secret of their disputes about controlling the oil in the northern region. For instance, in August 2010, the KRG entered into a contract with the German company RWE AG, which allows RWE to develop the gas infrastructure to make it possible to link the gas produced in the Kurdish region with the Nabucco pipeline, that is intended to enable the transportation of gas produced in the Caspian region, through Turkey and Eastern Europe and ultimately to various consuming markets in Western Europe. The Nabucco consortium announced in early August that "it has shelved plans to source gas from Iran due to the further escalation of the dispute between the international community and Iran over the latter's alleged nuclear weapons program."[47] This would make the gas from northern Iraq a valuable source to compensate for the Iranian gas. The contract triggered a statement from the Iraqi Ministry of Oil affirming "that Iraq is exporting crude oil and gas through the Iraqi oil marketing company exclusively and there is no other party authorized to sign contracts with international or local companies in this regard … any contracts or agreements that do not match the official marketing company, [the State Oil Marketing Organization (SOMO)], laws are considered invalid and illegal."[48]

It is difficult to predict the outcome of the oil dispute between the KRG and the central government, because both sides have used this, and many other issues, in their political negotiations and alliance-building. The Kurds have always skillfully managed to exploit the sectarian division among their Arab counterparts, whose Sunni-Shi'a affiliations prevented them from standing united in opposing the often over-reaching Kurdish economic and political demands. Furthermore, the central government has no effective coercive means to stop the Kurds from acting in defiance of the political regime in Baghdad.

Finally, there is the ideological dispute among Iraqis, concerning the future status of the most important, indeed the only, source of the country's economy at the present time, and maybe for many years to come. The lack of trust in the integrity, and competence, of their politicians, combined with the past history of the oil corporations has caused many Iraqis to suspect the motives and the utility of the contracts between the government of Iraq and the multinational corporations. To be sure, some of the suspicions are very reasonable because, after all, the contracts are signed by multinational corporations that are treated, in many parts of the world, as guilty until proven innocent, and an Iraqi regime that has been ranked as the fourth most corrupt government in the world. However, sometimes, the suspicions border on true paranoia. No example illustrates this pathological suspicion better than the reactions Iraq's government received following an agreement with Royal Dutch Shell Group to develop the necessary infrastructure of capturing and marketing a "huge amount of gas from super-giant oil fields in the southern governorate" of Basra. The joint project will involve a $10bn to $20bn investment and it will be owned at 51% by the Iraqi South Gas Company, 44% by Royal Dutch Shell and 5% by Mitsubishi.[49]

The criticism of the deal, raised by Iraqi nationalists, political activists and oil experts, seems to be out of touch with reality, given the past practice of all previous Iraqi governments. Since the beginning of producing oil, the gas that accompanied the production was flared. The current plan will turn the 700m. cubic feet of gas, which is being flared everyday into cash-generating commodity, improve the environment and "the construction of liquefied natural gas facilities," reducing Iraq's imports of natural gas.[50] For decades, the various Iraqi governments prior to 2003 used to proudly refer to the flames of this wasteful process and "The Eternal Fire" (al-Nar al-Azaliyya).

Conclusion

Iraq has emerged from a very dark era that depleted the country's infrastructure, exhausted its human capital and retarded its economic potential through wars, political oppression and deliberate prohibition of modern technology and the flow of information. This has been mostly caused by the regime in order to minimize potential threats to its rule, but it was also due to the contribution of one of the most comprehensive and far-reaching systems of sanctions. The years following 2003 were supposed to deliver Iraq from the past. This has happened in many ways, but the new challenges that arose from the mismanagement of the post-invasion political and economic programmes kept Iraq far away from achieving its potential and lowered the expectations regarding the road to recovery.

However, many Iraqi politicians and technocrats are struggling to meet the demands of the society, if not for righteous reasons then for their own political and professional survival. Security challenges, financial and administrative corruption, lack of access to modern technology and knowledge, as well as the state of devastation in the country's infrastructure continue to be insurmountable challenges ahead of any meaningful progress. However, the situation has improved significantly from their state in 2003 to 2007. In a country that is almost entirely dependent on the oil revenues, the pressing needs for survival will supersede all other motives to slow the progress and enable the implementation of recovery plans, as long as they are not made in defiance of reality.

The Iraqi government has expressed its plan to become one of the leading oil producers worldwide in the next five years. Although this is seen as an over-reaching ambition, from an objective scientific perspective, it is possible that Iraq will achieve significant progress by trying to meet this goal, even if the level of production falls below the target quantities. As discussed above, the pessimistic forecast of the IEA, that Iraq's production will be 6mbpd by 2035 seems to be disappointing as compared with the optimistic Iraqi plan to produce 12mbpd by 2017. However, there are positive aspects to the IEA's forecast: first, there is an anticipated gradual increase in oil production over the next two decades; second, the slow increase of oil production will motivate the Iraqis to improve their performance on other economic sectors to augment the revenues and achieve greater economic prosperity; and third, the amount of Iraqi resources that will be exploited in this era of lingering financial corruption will be significantly smaller, because the level of economic prosperity and the speed of reconstruction will not only rest on how much money is available for the Iraqi government, but also how wisely and honestly this money is spent.

Therefore, Iraqis must work simultaneously on the improvement of their oil industry infrastructure and the progress in their governance, in order to balance their increased oil production with their ability to use the increased revenues in the best manner to compensate for the missed opportunities of the past. The building of effective political institutions will ensure political and economic accountability, which is almost non-existent in Iraq until this time. This is why Iraq is currently ranked among the top 50 nations in the level of budget expenditures in 2010, yet, Iraqis were among the least served, the least secure and the least prosperous worldwide.

Notes

1 Iraqi Ministry of Finance, Budget Office, "The 2010 Budget," p. 24.
2 James Glanz and Robert F. Worth, "Attacks on Iraq oil industry aid vast smuggling scheme," *The New York Times* (4 June 2006).
3 Henry A. Foster, *The Making of Modern Iraq*, New York: Russell & Russell, 1972 (1935), p. 37.
4 Ibid.
5 Quoted in ibid., p. 129. See also p. 36.
6 Abbas Alnasrawi, *Iraq's Burdens: Oil Sanctions and Underdevelopment*, Westport, Connecticut & London: Greenwood Press, 2002, p. 19.
7 Ibid., p. 20.
8 Abd al-Razzaq al-Hasani, *Tarikh al-Wazarat al-Iraqiyya* (The History of Iraqi Cabinets), Sidon, Lebanon, 1935, vol. 1, pp. 204–12. The concession was signed by Muzahim al-Pachachi, a pro-British minister at the time.

9. Quoted by Alnasrawi, p. 3. For a detailed account on the negotiation process and the changes to the concessions after Iraq's 1932 independence, see Zuhayr Mikdashi, *A Financial Analysis of Middle Eastern Concessions: 1901–65*, New York: Frederick A. Prager Publishers, 1966, pp. 65–73.
10. Mikdashi, p. 105.
11. Ibid., p. 106.
12. On the shift to 50–50 profit sharing, see Mikdashi, pp. 135ff.
13. Mikdashi, p. 196. The only exception was 1957. Iraq's revenue was £51.523m., more than £18m. down from the previous year, because of the change of payment method, following an Iraqi objection to the cost production figures presented by the IPC, which led to arbitration in order to settle the dispute and a change of payment method while the matter was in arbitration.
14. Marion Farouk-Sluglett and Peter Sluglett, *Iraq Since 1958: From Revolution to Dictatorship*, London: I. B. Tauris, 2001 (1987), p. 78.
15. Michael E. Brown, "The Nationalization of the Iraqi Petroleum Company," *International Journal of Middle East Studies*, vol. 10, no. 1 (Feb. 1979), p. 108.
16. Ibid., p. 109. See also, Farouk-Sluglett and Sluglett, p. 78.
17. Farouk-Sluglett and Sluglett, p. 145.
18. Brown, p. 110.
19. Farouk-Sluglett and Sluglett, pp. 145–47.
20. Brown, p. 111.
21. Farouk-Sluglett and Sluglett, p. 154.
22. Calouste Gulbenkian (1869–1955) was an Armenian businessman whose role in facilitating the negotiations over the concessions of oil operations in Iraq earned him 5% of the profits. In fairness to the man, he used a lot of the money he generated from the deal to fund public projects in Iraq and elsewhere. Among the main projects in Iraq by the Gulbenkian Foundation was the construction of the People's International Stadium, the only accredited soccer stadium in Iraq since 1966. Iraqis often say, jokingly, that Iraqi infrastructure would have been better if Gulbenkian got 50% and the Iraqi government got the 5%.
23. In addition to the few hand-picked associates of Saddam Hussein, like Izzat Ibrahim, Tariq Aziz and Taha Yasin Ramadhan, who served for three decades, most of the high level officials were eliminated physically or politically some time following their initial hiring to prevent any of them from becoming a threat to the regime. For an incomplete list of those eliminated by the regime, see Ali Karim Sa'id, *The Iraq of 8 February 1963: from the dialogue of concepts to the dialogue of blood*, Beirut: Dar al-Konoz al-Adabiah, 1999, pp. 391–402. The author lists 114 names of the major participants in the 1963 coup, who disappeared, died mysteriously or were tortured, and/or killed. Only a few names died in exile. The complete list of such high-level associates of the regime would extend to the thousands; all of them faced similar treatment.
24. Farouk-Sluglett and Sluglett, p. 249. Their 1978 figures do not include the Ministry of Defense, whose professional and conscript personnel exceeded those of the Ministry of Interior by 50,000 in the previous year. Given the record of the regime's use of its military to keep the people under control, the argument made here is not weakened when the Ministry of Interior takes the second place after the Ministry of Defense.
25. Ibid., p. 271.
26. Ibid., p. 288.
27. The text of all UNSC Resolutions is available at the United Nations (www.un.org).
28. Quoted by Alnasrawi, p. 79.
29. Alnasrawi, pp. 83–84.
30. Office of the Iraq Programme, Oil-for-Food (www.un.org/Depts/oip/); accessed on 6 February 2011.
31. For the names, positions and type of misconduct by various officials, companies, representatives of companies and relatives of prominent officials see the various Committee reports (www.iic-offp.org/documents.htm). The reports also detail the various schemes of the Iraqi government to defraud the programme.
32. See Committee's "Report on Programme Manipulation," issued on 27 October 2005, p. 1.
33. The Independent Inquiry Committee into the United Nations Oil-for-Food Programme; see the Committee's report on the "Management of the Oil-for-Food Programme," issued on 27 October 2005, p. 18.
34. Paul Blustein, "Wolfowitz Strives to Quell Criticism," *The Washington Post*, (21 March 2005), p. A01.

35 Anthony H. Cordesman and Khalid R. Al-Rodhan, *The Changing Dynamics of Energy in the Middle East*, Westport, Connecticut: Praeger Security International, 2006, p. 222.
36 Quarterly Report from the Office of the Special Inspector General for Iraq Reconstruction (SIGIR), July 2006, p. 29.
37 Ibid., p. 30.
38 Quarterly and Report from the Office of the Special Inspector General for Iraq Reconstruction (SIGIR), January 2011, p. 86.
39 Quarterly Report from the Office of the Special Inspector General for Iraq Reconstruction (SIGIR), July 2006, p. 37.
40 Ibid., p. 29.
41 Quarterly Report from the Office of the Special Inspector General for Iraq Reconstruction (SIGIR), January 2011, pp. 84–85.
42 The IEA, *International Energy Outlook 2010*, Appendix G; also see Ibid., pp. 85.
43 Iraqi Ministry of Oil, "General Information for Service Contracts," (www.oil.gov.iq); accessed on 5 February 2011.
44 For instance, the average of oil exports from Basra fields in 2010 was 44.94m. barrels per month, while the average exports from Kirkuk for the same period was 12.55m. barrels per month, according to official Iraqi Ministry of Oil records (www.oil.gov.iq).
45 Iraqi Ministry of Finance (www.mof.gov.iq). This amount does not include the money which is spent by the federal government in the city. However, all of the money allocated to Basra pales when compared with the $13bn the government gives to the Kurdistan Regional Government, most of which is taken from the Basra oil.
46 During a conversation I had, in December 2010, with Sayyid Muhammad Ridha al-Sistani, son of Ayatullah Ali al-Sistani and the head of his Najaf office, he said that the Sistani-led religious institution in Najaf took a leading role in stopping the formation of a federal region (*iqleem*) in Basra.
47 "RWE Signs Gas Partnership with Iraq's Kurdistan Region," *The Wall Street Journal* (10 August 2010); article is posted on the web-site of the Kurdistan Regional Government (KRG): www.krg.org; accessed on 5 February 2011.
48 Iraqi Ministry of Oil, "Ministry of Oil: Illegal Contracts Are Prohibited," (www.oil.gov.iq); accessed on 5 February 2011.
49 Hassan Hafidh, "Iraq Cabinet Approves Shell Gas Deal in [South] Iraq," *The Wall Street Journal* (29 June 2010).
50 Sinan Salaheddin, "Iraq, Royal Dutch Shell to ink gas deal," *USA Today* (21 September 2008).

19
Government Policy and Evolution of the Iranian Oil Industry

Farrokh Najmabadi

In 2008 Iran celebrated the centennial of the first discovery of oil at Masjed-e-Suleiman situated in the southwestern foothills of the Zagros Mountains. The 100-year old history of the Iranian oil industry has been extensively chronicled by many authors[1] and it is a fascinating tale of a nation struggling initially to obtain its rightful and contractual royalty and share of the income from a concessionary regime, and later, to win control of an industry that is the lifeblood of its economy. It, therefore, twists and turns through the cancellation of the concession agreement with the Anglo-Persian Oil Company in 1933, enters into another agreement with the same concessionaire on different terms and, eventually opts for nationalization in 1951 when a wave of nationalistic sentiments demands it and at a time when the concessionaire fails to offer Iran terms that had become the norm in the industry.

Once the dust settled, Iran found itself forced by events to agree to another quasi-concession type contract that left all controls in the hands of the Consortium—a group consisting of all major international oil companies and several independents. Never forgetting the dream, it set itself the task of learning by practice the intricacies of the industry with the hope of one day managing all its facets. And so in the process, it pioneered the so-called 75/25 joint-venture type agreements and then moved to Agency and later Risk Service Contracts. And eventually, in an opportune moment, it wrested control and management of its major oil operations from the Consortium. By 1974, the process is completed when the decision-making power, especially in setting production levels and prices, shifted completely from the international oil companies to the members of the Organization of Petroleum Exporting Countries (OPEC).

A pre-revolutionary snapshot of the Iranian petroleum industry

The revolutionary turmoil that started in mid-1978 had a paralyzing effect on the oil and gas industry of Iran, especially during the fourth quarter. Strikes by the employees of the industry brought the production of crude oil and all refining operations to a standstill, thus interrupting supplies of products to the domestic market and all export operations. These stoppages also affected the export of natural gas to the former Soviet Union and the fledgling domestic gas industry.

Table 19.1 Iranian oil and gas statistics (1973–78)

	1973	1974	1975	1976	1977	1978
Proven Oil Reserves (billion barrels)	58	60	62	63	63	60
Proven Gas Reserves (billion cubic metres) (bcm)	7,647	9,346	9,332	9,346	14,160	14,160
Crude Oil Production (thousand barrels per day) (kb/d)	5,861	6,022	5,350	5,883	5,663	5,242
Export of Crude Oil (kb/d)	5,277	5,369	4,671	5,214	4,867	4,447
Cumulative Production of Crude Oil (billion barrels)	18.0	20.2	22.1	24.3	26.4	28.3
Gas Production (bcm)	48.2	50.0	45.4	50.7	56.7	55.1
Gas Imports (bcm)	–	–	–	–	–	–
Gas Exports (bcm)	8,7	9.1	9.6	9.3	9.3	7.2
Gas Reinjection (bcm)	–	–	–	1.0	9.4	9.9
Flared (bcm)	28.4	27.7	23.6	27.9	26.4	25.8
Domestic Consumption (bcm)	11.0	13.2	12.7	12.6	11.7	12.2
Active Rigs	26	34	45	45	46	50
Wells Completed	74	94	153	146	165	140
Producing Wells	378	380	395	500	533	551
Refining Capacity (thousand barrels per day) (kb/d)	660	690	810	810	1,050	1,080
Product Output (kb/d)	555	592	644	652	725	670
Domestic Consumption (kb/d)	259	296	352	431	511	517
Export of Products (kb/d)	295	295	313	216	208	188

Sources: OPEC Statistical Bulletins, 1978, 1993, 1996, 1999, 2003, 2008, 2009.

A picture of the Iranian oil and gas industry during the period 1973–78 can be gleaned from the data shown in Table 19.1. Throughout this period, close to 90% of total crude oil output came from onshore fields under the management of National Iranian Oil Company (NIOC) and the remaining 10% was produced by four joint venture companies operating in the offshore region of the Persian Gulf.[2]

Onshore crude oil production came mainly from four giant oilfields (Aghajari, Gachsaran, Ahwaz and Marun) which accounted for a combined output of around 4mbpd. A second tier group of four large fields (Bibi Hakimeh, Karanj, Parsi and Rag-e-Sefid) produced nearly 1mbpd combined and the other 20 or so oilfields produced the remaining 0.5mbpd. Declining reservoir pressure, especially in the older fields such as Aghajari and Gachsaran, had made it necessary to constantly add replacement capacity through drilling new producing wells; though work-over wells, desalting facilities and secondary recovery (artificial lift systems, water and gas injection) projects also provided significant volumes. In the offshore region of the Persian Gulf, crude oil production had begun an upward trend and was planned to reach some 0.8mbpd by the end of the decade through the expansion of IPAC's output and the start of production at SIRRI C and D oilfields.

Prior to 1970, gas consumption in Iran was limited to some small usages in the southern oilfields and further quantities that were pipelined to the city of Shiraz for a fertilizer plant and other industrial units. After 1970, however, many factors contributed to the rapid entry of gas into the energy consumption picture. To begin with, the export trunkline to the former Soviet Union had a built-in excess capacity of 7bn cubic metres (bcm) for domestic market and once that pipeline became operational distribution also started in the cities along the route of the pipeline, notably in Tehran. In addition, the discovery of gas resources at Khangiran, a field located in north eastern border areas with Turkmenistan, made it possible to supply gas to the city of Mashhad while more of the associated gas and gas liquids in the southern oilfields were being supplied to the fertilizer and petrochemical industries and the Abadan refinery. More importantly, starting at the end of 1976, nearly 10bcm of gas was being re-injected annually into three oilfields (Haftkel, Gachsaran and Lab-e-Sefid).

Planning and policy in the pre-revolutionary years

The Iranian pre-revolution Fifth Economic and Social Development Plan (1973–78) was prepared at a time when the world's petroleum consumption was rising at an average annual rate of 7% and OPEC members had already won a significant victory in February of 1971 whereby the two sides had signed a 5-year agreement for an immediate increase of around 21% in the posted price of Persian Gulf crude oils, and other annual increases thereafter including one to compensate for inflation and the fall in the purchasing power of the Dollar.[3] The overarching policy in the Plan aimed at speeding up exploration programmes in order to replace reserves that were being depleted at a rate in excess of 2bn barrels per year and using secondary recovery and conservation techniques to enhance ultimate recovery from the Iranian reservoirs. Furthermore, the Plan called on NIOC to penetrate the international markets directly by selling its share of crude oil from the joint venture operations and by participating in refining, marketing, distribution and sales operations abroad. The National Iranian Gas Company (NIGC) was also called on to enter into contracts with international firms for the export of LNG to supplement export of piped gas to the former Soviet Union. There were, of course, the customary boilerplate objectives of supplying the domestic needs of a fast growing economy with petroleum products and enhancing the refining sector economics through substitution of natural gas for middle distillate products. Policy, therefore, called for the rapid expansion of natural gas network domestically.[4]

The year 1971 proved to be a pivotal one in the relationship between the international oil companies and the producing countries. A few months after the signing of the Tehran Agreement, OPEC passed its 135th Resolution to the effect that "member countries shall take immediate steps towards the effective implementation of the principle of Participation in the existing oil concessions." This started a flurry of negotiations that, in short order, resulted in the transfer of control to the producing countries by the end of 1973. This was achieved through nationalization in Libya, Algeria and Iraq; participation in all Arab countries of the Middle East and by simple abrogation of some of the companies' key contractual rights elsewhere.[5]

In Iran, however, since the oil industry had already been nationalized in 1951, the passing of control meant the wholesale replacement of the Consortium Agreement by a new contract entitled the Sale and Purchase Agreement for a duration of 20 years. The agreement provided for NIOC to exercise the right of full and complete ownership, operation management and control in respect of all hydrocarbon resources, assets and administration of petroleum industry in the Agreement Area. Other clauses provided for the complete transfer of Abadan Refinery management to NIOC and the formation of a non-profit service company by the Consortium, incorporated in Iran and named Oil Services Company of Iran (OSCO) to carry out services as assigned to it by NIOC in the southern oilfields. Furthermore, NIOC accepted to shoulder the investment required for the expansion of production (with special arrangements for the first five years) and committed itself to take stated quantities of crude oil each year for export starting at 200,000 barrels per day in 1973 and increasing to 1.5mbpd by 1981. The agreement also provided for a new regime for gas utilization whereby NIOC's requirements for reinjection, internal consumption and pipeline exports were given preferential status with the remaining available for sale to the Consortium.

With the operational management and control secured, NIOC did not waste any time in embarking on a set of comprehensive and far-reaching policies which had not, hitherto, received the enthusiastic support of the Consortium, though they were strongly recommended by the Plan such as enhanced exploration and drilling activities for the discovery and delineation of crude oil and gas reserves in the Agreement area; and implementation of a comprehensive scheme for conservation and gas reinjection into the oilfield for enhanced recovery. Thus, based on the prevailing forecast for global demand, NIOC directed OSCO to aim at reaching a production capacity of some 7.5mbpd by 1975, thereby increasing the combined onshore and offshore capacity to around 8mbpd. In the process, the flaring of associated gas was also expected to stop by 1978.

In practice, as OPEC production stagnated at about the 1973 level of 30.6mbpd, the average annual demand for Iranian crude oil from the Southern Agreement Area never exceeded 5.6mbpd and the crude oil capacity never went much beyond 6mbpd. The intensive exploratory and drilling activities, however, resulted in some two dozen new oil and gas field discoveries, a few of which such as Dehluran and Chillingar were quickly brought on stream.

By 1978 the overambitious plans of the early 1970s had somewhat been tempered by the escalation of costs, the changes in the global energy picture and the demand for OPEC oil. While the emphasis remained on resource development, conservation and enhanced recovery, the production capacity target was reduced to a plateau of 7mbpd—onshore 6.25mbpd and offshore 0.75mbpd—to be maintained for an extended period through additional drilling and recovery techniques and gas reinjection. Thus the Plan for the following five years (1979–83) called for the drilling of some 280 oil, gas, and reinjection wells; and the injection of gas into some 14 large and medium-sized oilfields (Bibi-Hakimeh, Binak, Dehluran, Gachsaran, Haftkel, Karanj, Kuh-e-kaki, Kupal, Lab-e-Sefid, Marun, Parsi, Qaleh Nar, Ramshir and Sarkan) at a rate of 33bcm in 1979 and building up to 66.5bcm in 1983 (Table 19.2). This reinjection plan was to be expanded to Ahwaz, Aghajari and Rag-e-Sefid in later years for a total annual injection rate of 92bcm. NIOC's brief also included the expansion of its own crude oil marketing already at a level of 1.5mbpd, and participation in upstream and downstream activities throughout the world beyond its joint exploration activity with BP in the North Sea and its shareholdings in India's Madras, South Africa's Sasolberg, South Korea's Kipco and Senegal refineries. The domestic refining industry was also to expand to meet the internal demand as well as the policy of maintaining Iran's position in the international markets. NIGC was not

Table 19.2 Gas Reinjection Programme in bcm/year

Injection Field	Commissioning Date	1979	1980	1981	1982	1983
Bibi Hakimeh	3rd quarter 1980		2.6	2.3	4.5	4.5
Gachsaran	2nd quarter 1977	17.9	18.2	18.5	17.0	17.4
Karanj	2nd quarter 1980		2.2	5.0	5.0	5.0
Marun	3rd quarter 1979	13.0	13.0	26.0	26.0	26.0
Parsi	1st quarter 1982			4.5	4.5	4.5
All Others	Various Dates	2.3	1.8	4.1	9.2	9.1
Total		33.2	37.8	60.4	66.2	66.5

Source: NIOC internal memos 1978.

only required to develop and expand distribution of gas throughout the country, it was specifically directed to go beyond the export of gas to the Soviet Union via a second Trunkline (under construction) and enter the LNG market through the implementation of the Kalingas project to Japan and the Columbia Gas project to USA. All this was to be complemented with the expansion of domestic transportation facilities via pipelines as well as maritime tanker capacity.

The early post-revolutionary period until the end of the Iran-Iraq war

Almost immediately after the take-over and long before the ratification of the New Constitution, the Revolutionary Government cancelled the oil exploration and production agreements ostensibly on the grounds that they did not sufficiently safeguard the interests of Iran and were imposed by the West and placed a ceiling of 4mbpd on the production of crude oil. At a later date, a dispute with the Soviet Union on the price of gas led to the annulment of the IGAT1 and IGAT2 agreements. Iran also withdrew its shareholding in the Korean, South African and Senegalese refineries. Meanwhile, articles 43 and 44 of the Constitution which was ratified in mid-1979 forbade the government to enter into agreements that led to the "foreign domination of the country's economy" and provided for all the large enterprises (commanding heights) to remain in the hands of the government.

The events of the first two years after the revolution (the hostage crisis and the start of war with Iraq) conspired to keep the Iranian production below the announced ceiling at 3.2mbpd and 1.6mbpd in 1979 and 1980, respectively. Subsequently, the damage sustained by all the oil industry facilities onshore and offshore such as oilfields, pipelines, refineries, export terminals, etc., resulted in crude oil production remaining between 2 and 2.4mbpd throughout the eight year period before the cease-fire in 1988 (Table 19.3).

It will be remembered that during this period the price of Persian Gulf crudes initially almost tripled to US$36 per barrel ushering in several years of diminishing demand for OPEC oil and the start of pro-rationing by OPEC. Initially Saudi Arabia chose the role of the swing producer, but as discipline could not be maintained among the others and demand for OPEC oil sank to around 15mbpd and prices collapsed in 1985/86 Saudi Arabia decided to relinquish that role and opted for netback pricing forcing other members of OPEC to discard their adherence to the posted price regime and accept a policy of regaining market share.

Although the OPEC quota did not allow Iran to produce above 2.4mbpd during the period 1983 to 1988, the producing capacity at some point had, according to the NIOC's Director of Production, dropped to a low of between 2.19mbpd and 2.15mbpd onshore and 36,000 barrels per day offshore.[6] Undoubtedly, the eight-year war had inflicted serious damage on the oil facilities and much of the country's revenue was reallocated to support the war efforts and the maintenance of capital stocks was deferred. But some of the damage to the oil producing capacity can also be traced to the period of turmoil and neglect between the Revolution in early 1979 and the start of hostilities with Iraq in September 1980. The cancellation of Consortium and other joint-venture agreements had resulted in the rapid exit of the expatriate technical specialists, the departure of many Iranian high and middle managers and the non-availability of high quality foreign technical services. The situation was exacerbated by the managerial appointments that were based on ideological and Islamic credentials rather than technical and operational knowledge with the result that much of the capacity maintenance activities such as new development drilling, work-over wells and secondary recovery projects had been all but stopped. These difficulties were compounded during the war years by the paucity of investment funds, the dearth of the national technical talent and the reluctance to

Table 19.3 Iranian oil and gas statistics (1980–88)

	1980	1981	1982	1983	1984	1985	1986	1987	1988
Proven Oil Reserves (billion barrels)	58.0	57.0	56.1	55.2	58.8	59.0	92.8	92.8	92.8
Proven Gas Reserves (billion cubic metres) (bcm)	14101	14085	14069	14045	14016	13986	13955	13922	14280
Crude Oil Production (thousand barrels per day) (kb/d)	1817	1565	2421	2442	2032	2192	2037	2298	2478
Export of Crude Oil (kb/d)	797	715	1623	1719	1522	1568	1454	1710	2095
Cumulative Production of Crude Oil (billion barrels)	30.0	30.4	31.3	32.2	32.9	33.7	34.4	35.3	36.2
Gas Production (bcm)	20.1	16.8	24.5	29.2	30.5	31.6	33.3	36.7	40.5
Gas Imports (bcm)	–	–	–	–	–	–	–	–	–
Gas Exports (bcm)	0.22	0.25	–	–	–	–	–	–	–
Gas Reinjection (bcm)	2.3	1.9	2.7	8.5	70.0	11.0	12.2	15.0	15.0
Flared (bcm)	10.6	8.4	14.5	9.7	7.0	6.0	5.9	5.7	5.5
Domestic Consumption (bcm)	7.1	5.7	7.2	11.0	13.5	14.6	15.2	16.0	20.0
Active Rigs	NA	NA	11	14	16	18	17	18	18
Wells Completed	25	NA	NA	15	28	50	48	29	23
Producing Wells	NA	NA	530	NA	230	237	361	650	645
Refining Capacity (thousand barrels per day) (kb/d)	1320	670	670	670	615	615	615	615	615
Product Output (kb/d)	582	627	659	624	618	647	558	541	614
Domestic Consumption (kb/d)	562	568	578	678	789	812	851	579	882

Sources: OPEC Statistical Bulletins, 1978, 1993, 1996, 1999, 2003, 2008, 2009.

engage expatriate experts or to contract for up-to-date technical consultancy. Given Iranian reservoirs' natural annual depletion rate of 5–7% and the reduced level of activity throughout the period up to 1988, it is not surprising that Iran's production capacity had sunk to around 2.2mbpd at some point during the mid-1980s. As a further example of this situation, the reinjection facilities that were completed and ready for the start of gas injection into the Marun reservoir in early 1979 also remained unutilized until the end of the 1990s. Nonetheless, in 1987, NIOC increased its estimate of proven crude oil reserves to 92.85bn barrels which included some 3.26bn barrels of condensate.[7]

Abadan refinery also became an early casualty of the war. The largest refinery in the world with a distillation capacity in excess of 700,000 barrels per day, it was bombarded at the beginning of the war and was shut down until the end. Thus the total refining capacity dropped to around 600,000 barrels per day in 1981, which was insufficient to satisfy the domestic demand especially for the middle distillate products. Consequently, as demand for petroleum products outpaced refinery outputs, import of middle distillates, kerosene and gasoil, and later gasoline and LPG rose to around 180,000 barrels per day by 1988.[8] However, NIGC managed to expand its distribution network in the country's northern cities and domestic gas consumption rose to 16bcm by the end of the war.

Policy in the Islamic Republic's first Five Year Plan (1989–93)

The war with Iraq had wreaked havoc with the Iranian economy. With destruction and devastation in many parts of the country, GDP per capita had fallen to around 60% of its level before the Revolution. To reach a more perfect, just Islamic society, the planners emphasized two imperatives: first, the need to implement a family planning scheme to slow the growth rate of the population, which had exploded from 35.4m. in 1978 to 52.8m. in 1988; and, second, the need to grow the economy as fast as possible by putting to work the excess capacity made idle during the war years while carrying out, in line with the recommendations of the IMF and the World Bank, a policy of structural adjustment. The cornerstone of the Plan was a 55% increase in oil exports from around 1.5mbpd in 1988 to 2.3mbpd in 1993 (corresponding to a production of nearly 3.8mbpd) resulting in a total of some $82bn income from the export of crude oil, petroleum products, gas liquids and natural gas during the five years. The Plan also envisaged the rehabilitation of the Abadan refinery, the construction of a refinery at Arak with a capacity of 135,000 barrels per day and a rapid expansion of the gas distribution network in the country. Recognizing the subsidies embedded in the price of all energy products, the Plan prescribed long-term marginal cost pricing for most goods and services by the Government, so that the related enterprises would be capable of raising funds from their own cash flow for investment.[9] The Plan Act provided for a total investment of around $27bn in the oil and gas industry.

Having secured support and financing, NIOC embarked immediately on a programme of expanded rehabilitation and reconstruction of the damaged facilities using its own equipment and technical resources together with turn-key contracts with foreign firms for drilling and other technical and engineering services, especially in the case of offshore platforms and loading terminals. This resulted in a gradual increase in the production capacity from both onshore and offshore fields. This period also coincided with a resurgence in the demand for OPEC oil from 18.8mbpd in 1988 to 24.2mbpd in 1993, along with a firming of crude oil prices which made it possible for all OPEC member countries to receive enhanced production allocations. However, since the end of the hostilities, Iraq had insisted on quota parity with Iran and by July 1990 both countries had an allocation of 3.14mbpd, while Saudi Arabia's quota had risen to 5.38mbpd. Under the prevailing circumstances and given its limited producing capacity, Iran could do little to rebuff this challenge to its traditional ranking within OPEC. The inability to quickly ramp up production became more agonizing for Iran when, in the wake of Iraq's invasion of Kuwait and the virtual stoppage of export from both countries, Saudi Arabia received the lion's share of the quota reallocation in April 1991. In the event, while Saudi Arabia's quota had increased from 5.38 to 8.03mbpd, Iran had only received a puny increase of 80,000 barrels per day raising its quota to 3.22mbpd which was commensurate with its production capability. While the Iraqi challenge had at least disappeared for a time, the reality was not lost on the Iranians that their position within OPEC and their general clout in the Middle East were being seriously threatened for as long as Iran's producing capacity remained around 3 to 3.5mbpd or even the 4mbpd adopted as the ceiling just after the Revolution. It was, therefore, at this juncture that they changed course and decided to aim at a total capacity of 5mbpd by 1993, thereby making it possible to have a sustained production level of between 4 and 4.5mbpd from the onshore and 0.5mbpd from the offshore fields. This decision was made at a time of financial and budgetary crisis in the country and the situation forced the Ministry of Petroleum to seek parliamentary approval to attract foreign financing and technical assistance both of which were badly needed if the country was serious in developing its oil and gas resources on a sound basis. Nonetheless, NIOC claimed at the time that its resources were adequate to take care of the onshore development and flatly rejected rumours that the international oil companies (IOCs) would be invited to explore and develop onshore oilfields.[10]

Discussions had, however, started with the international oil companies (IOCs) for the rehabilitation of some of the fields already in production and the development of offshore producing and discovered oil and gas fields. These fields consisted of those already producing: Soroush, Nowruz and Bahregansar; those discovered but not yet developed: Sirri-E, Sirri-A, Balal and Hormuz structures; and the North and the South Pars gas fields. Out of these discussions gradually emerged the contours of a service type agreement called "buy-back," which ostensibly satisfied the constitutional and ideological strictures of the Islamic Republic. This type of contract was similar in many respects to the Risk Service Agreements implemented by NIOC before the Revolution. Thus, for example, the developed field would be handed over to NIOC for operation and the foreign entity would be remunerated for the exploration and development expenditures out of the production of the field in question. But in many other respects NIOC's financial take was inferior: for example, there was no signature bonus, the rates of return on investment were very generous, there were no real oversight by NIOC on the expenditure and the NIOC was obligated to reimburse the foreign company for exploration expenditures even if the exploratory activities did not result in commercial discoveries. NIOC had foregone all these advantages for not allowing the foreign entity to purchase a part of the output of the field in question for a maximum period of 15 years and replacing it with a commitment to reimburse the investment including a high rate of return and fees with the sale of the output for a period of 3 to 5 years and, in any case, until all its financial obligations were repaid.

There were other problems with the buy-back agreements. The IOCs found a clause that provided for a separation between the exploration and development phases of the contract particularly objectionable, because according to this clause, the foreign entity would, in the event of an oil or gas field discovery, have to compete with others that NIOC invited to bid for the development phase. NIOC, too, had denied itself an ongoing relationship that would ensure access to the latest technology during the production period, a need that it had admitted to, albeit grudgingly. Given the inherent complications of the buy-back type agreement and even though none of the fields under negotiations required any exploratory investments, no contract had been concluded by the end of the First Plan in 1993. NIOC had, however, issued a letter of intent in September 1992 to a consortium led by TPL (Technologie Progetti Lavori) and Saipem of Italy in co-operation with Mitsubishi Corporation of Japan and Machinoimport of Russia in respect of a $1.7bn contract for the development of the first phase of the South Pars gas and condensate field (this field is a shared reservoir straddling the median line and called the North Dome in Qatar).

Since the end of the war, further drilling and reinjection activities had allowed NIOC to reach a production capacity in excess of its OPEC quota. Although Iran no longer feared a challenge to its position from Iraq, at least for a few years, after the first Gulf War, it was intent on avoiding a repeat of what had happened at the early 1991 Conference. The petroleum minister, therefore, ordered NIOC to increase production to an average of 3.8mbpd during the whole month of October 1992. He then invited several petroleum industry reporters to Iran and presented them with the test results which were duly advertised. The minister argued that a sustained production level of 3.8mbpd signified a production capacity of some 4.2mbpd and claimed that the capacity was slated to reach 5mbpd by March of 1993.[11] "These tactics went a long way to strengthen Iran's claim to a higher production quota and, consequently, Iran received an increase of 300,000 barrels per day compared to Saudi Arabia's 500,000 barrels per day at the next OPEC Meeting. In practice, however, the limitations on Iran's production capacity kept actual production well in line with the OPEC allocations, making a virtue out of necessity.

During the Plan, NIOC succeeded in constructing a 135,000 barrels per day refinery at Arak along with the rehabilitation of the Abadan refinery to a capacity of 230,000 barrels per day. These refineries helped supply the needs of the country for petroleum products which grew at an average annual rate of around 6%. With more gas replacing middle distillates, imports of these products and gasoline dropped to 124,000 barrels per day by the end of the Plan. The commissioning of a gas treatment plant at Pazanan oil and gas field, which was ready to go on stream in 1979, made more gas available for reinjection, albeit at a rate far below that envisaged in the original reinjection plans. As for the projected gradual increase in petroleum product prices for domestic consumption, little was achieved. Despite repeated attempts by the Government to increase prices annually at the time of budget debate, the price of gasoline remained untouched and there was only one increase in the price of the other major products in the third year of the Plan.

Petroleum policy during the second Five Year Plan (1994–99)

Having run into a serious financial crisis towards the end of the first Plan, the Iranian government opted for a more measured average annual GDP growth of 6% during the second Plan, along with a set of policies aimed at reducing the economic imbalances and at increasing efficiency. This was particularly relevant to the energy sector in that the government, for the first time, recognized the comparatively high energy-intensive nature of the economy the subsidies that were at the heart of that problem. There was also an explicit acknowledgement to the effect that, left unchecked, this profligacy could reduce Iran's petroleum export capability with its attendant problems. The Plan, therefore, recommended a set of policies which addressed all the issues in the oil and gas industry in a comprehensive manner and included:

1. the maintenance of Iran's position in the global oil markets through the diversification of energy supply to the domestic economy by expansion of the natural gas network and development of nuclear, renewable and hydroelectric power sources;
2. the reduction in the annual rate of growth of energy consumption to that of GDP through reform in energy pricing;
3. the conservation of petroleum resources through expanded injection of gas into oilfields and reduction of gas flaring;
4. the exploitation of the oil and gas fields located on Iran's territorial and offshore boundaries shared with neighbouring countries and rapid development of offshore fields;
5. the construction of new gas treatment plants, commensurate with the production of associate and dome gas, and rehabilitation of refineries with the latest technologies to reduce loss and in-plant fuel consumption;
6. the construction of a new refinery at Bandar Abbas with a capacity of 230,000 barrels per day;
7. the expansion of exploration activities with the objective of discovering new oil and gas resources;
8. studying the advisability of natural gas exports given Iran's medium- and long-term need for gas as a source of energy and a base for energy-intensive industries; and,
9. to be mindful of environmental issues in all such developments.[12]

The Plan envisaged a constant level of oil production at 4.5mbpd throughout the period with around 1.4mbpd dedicated for domestic consumption and 3.1mbpd destined for exports. To sustain crude production at this level, NIOC aimed at investing $20.4bn from the Government budget allocations and $9bn from foreign resources in the oil and gas sectors. This targeted production level was obviously unrealistic given the actual production of around 3.4mbpd in 1993 and a projected two to three year period of stagnant demand for OPEC oil.

Prior to the beginning of the second Plan, the Iranian government had already accepted the need for financial and technical assistance from foreign companies in the development of its oil and gas resources both in the onshore and offshore regions of the country, though priority was given initially to the offshore. By the beginning of 1994 it was becoming clear that reaching buy-back agreements with IOCs on the terms offered by Iran had proved very difficult. Thus, in January 1994, NIOC formally cancelled the letter of intent that it had issued two years earlier to a consortium led by TPL of Italy for the development of the first phase of South Pars gas field, because the foreign entities involved in those negotiations failed to agree to a suitable financial package. Unable to find any other interested foreign company, the project was later entrusted to Petroleum Engineering and Development Company (PEDEC), a subsidiary of NIOC. In the same month, the managing director of the Iranian Offshore Oil Company (IOOC) speaking at the second Middle East Petroleum and Gas Conference at Bahrain announced that, despite some western countries' efforts aimed at isolating Iran and blocking finance, NIOC was currently continuing its negotiations with the IOCs in respect of Sirri A, Sirri E, Balal, Hengam, North Pars and South Pars projects. He further indicated that according to a recently enacted law, work representing at least 30% of the value of major contracts such as those related to the development of the South Pars gas field should be awarded to Iranian sub-contractors.[13]

Throughout 1994, NIOC strived to keep its sustainable capacity at around 3.8mbpd without much help from foreign partners. This meant an onshore sustainable rate of 3.35mbpd together with an offshore rate of 0.45mbpd. The buy-back contract negotiations, however, continued as Iran reluctantly decided to partially overcome the unwillingness of the IOCs by offering them an acceptable return on investment. One such deal came to fruition with Conoco in March 1995 for the development of the two Sirri oil fields. This project was particularly attractive to Conoco because, in addition to producing 120,000 barrels per day of oil, it would also produce a substantial volume of gas which had a ready market in the neighbouring Emirate of Dubai for an enhanced recovery injection scheme that was being operated by Conoco. A week later, Conoco was forced to withdraw from this contract when the US President issued an executive order banning investment in Iran's energy sector. This order was followed two months later by another banning US trade and investment in Iran.

Immediately after the issue of the Second Executive Order, the Iranian petroleum minister again ordered NIOC to run a week-long test of Iran's sustainable oil production capacity at 4.1mbpd. This coincided with a field trip by an invited group of journalists. Then, in a wide-ranging interview with the journalists, while regretting the break-up of the Conoco deal, he went on to emphasize: a) that "technically speaking, NIOC did not have any problem in respect of its various operations" and "did not need foreign companies to develop its oilfields"; b) that negotiations about the development of the Sirri oilfields were continuing with other IOCs and the results would be announced shortly; c) that Iran would obviously insist on a higher quota allocation from OPEC at the next occasion; and, d) that other OPEC members were on notice not to take advantage of Iran's predicament in respect of US sanctions on oil purchases by American companies.[14] In discussing the sustainable producing capacity, the minister admitted that productivity of certain fields such as Parsi and Karanj had dropped precipitously and that continued production without gas injection might cause irreparable damage.

Hardly two months had passed when in July 1995 a buy-back contract was accorded by NIOC to France's Total for the development of the two Sirri fields for a combined total production of 120,000 barrels per day to come on stream within less than three years. A month later, NIOC received approval from the Parliament to announce a tender for 10 projects: four for development of offshore oil and gas production (Soroush, Balal, South Pars phase 2 and Khuff gas reservoir in the Salman field); two for refinery construction and expansion (a condensate refinery and expansion of Shiraz refinery); and, four for gas gathering and treatment plants. This announcement, coming on the heels of the buy-back contract with Total set in motion a flurry of activities in the US Congress which resulted in the passage of the Iran-Libya Sanctions Act (ILSA) signed into law on 5 August 1996. This law required the President of the USA to impose at least two out of a menu of six sanctions on foreign companies that made an investment of more than $20m. in one year in Iran's energy sector. With US pressure mounting, the initial somewhat enthusiastic response to the 10-project tender began to wane throughout 1996 and, despite NIOC's efforts in improving the financial terms of the buy-back model contracts, no new agreements were reached for nearly two years, although the negotiations were not completely broken off.

In June 1997, with the election of Mohammad Khatami as President, a new administration came into office in Iran on a platform of economic reform and the rule of law. Three months later, in a clear rebuff to the US extraterritoriality sanctions for a second time, France's Total signed a ground-breaking contract with NIOC for the development of phases 2 and 3 of the huge South Pars gas field. According to the information published in petroleum journals, the total capital investment amounted to $2bn to be expended in five years building a facility, offshore and onshore, capable of producing and treating 20bcm of gas and 80,000 barrels per day of condensate. Partial production of the system was to start in mid-2001 with full capacity reached a year later. Total would be compensated for its financial commitments and services by a remuneration fee of $1.4bn in addition to the associated interest charges estimated at $600m. The contract envisaged a seven-year repayment period for the investment and interest charges and five-and-a-half years for the remuneration fee. In trying to clinch this deal, NIOC had introduced two new features that were outside the initial buy-back model: 1) it agreed to maintain the level of remuneration fee if the project were completed under budget; and, 2) it agreed to tap into alternative oil sources should the quantity of condensate be insufficient to support the repayment schedule. In defending this bold move, the head of Total explained that, as a major entity on the international petroleum scene, Total needed to sustain its portfolio through involvement in Iran, a world player possessing some 10% of global oil reserves and 20% of the global gas reserves. This contract was immediately farmed out to Russia's Gazprom and Malaysia's Petronas, each receiving 30% of the shareholding.[15]

Encouraged by the momentum created as the result of the Total contract, the petroleum minister embarked on a revision of policy and new course of action. By November 1997, he announced that not only would foreign companies soon be invited to participate in the onshore oilfield remedial and enhanced recovery projects, but that onshore areas would also be opened for exploration and development to foreign participants.[16] Furthermore, NIOC indicated that the enhanced features of the buy-back contract signed with Total would henceforth become an integral part of the future contracts. These policy changes were hastened by the deterioration in the international oil market and the rapid decline of prices, following an erroneous decision by OPEC to increase output by 10% at the time of the Asian financial crisis.

Suddenly, Iran's ability to finance oil industry projects was curtailed as the specter of US sanctions and the unfavourable international atmosphere still loomed large. Facing strong opposition to its unilateral and extraterritorial action, the US government found it necessary to waive ILSA sanctions on European companies in May 1998. Two months later, NIOC offered 42 projects (16 onshore and offshore exploration and development; 15 onshore rehabilitation, enhanced oil recovery and new oil and gas field development; 7 offshore oil and gas fields; and, 4 to upgrade and expand the Abadan refinery) for international bidding which was received with enthusiasm by many foreign firms.[17]

It took another year before three buy-back contracts were signed by NIOC in quick succession. Thus, in March 1999, France's ELF joined forces with ENI of Italy on a 55%:45% shareholding basis to sign a contract with NIOC for the enhanced recovery and rehabilitation of the Doroud field, a reservoir situated under Kharg island in the Persian Gulf. This project that required an investment of $540m. would increase production of oil from 150,000 to 220,000 barrels per day through the drilling of more wells and the injection of gas and water into the reservoir. The investors were to be repaid a total of $1bn during a period of 9 years from the start of additional production. The second contract was signed for the development of the Balal field with the Canadian Bow Valley and France's ELF in April 1999. This was a fairly small discovered but undeveloped oilfield near Lavan Island requiring around $169m. for a production of 40,000 barrels per day by the year 2002. In November 1999, Shell became the signatory to a third agreement for an enhanced recovery scheme in the Souroush and Nowruz fields, in order to increase production from 50,000 barrels per day to a combined 190,000 barrels per day through the drilling of new wells and gas and water injection. The investment was estimated at $800m. and Shell would be compensated for a total of $1,455m. through off-take of oil for a period of 10 years from the start of additional production.

The lack of success in finalizing many buy-back contracts dealing with rehabilitation and enhanced oil recovery until 1999, coupled with little advance in gas injection quantities and the shortages in investment funds resulting from the oil price collapse to around $11 per barrel in 1998 hindered Iran in reaching its objective of producing an average of 4.5mbpd and reaching a capacity of 5mbpd. Nonetheless, Iran managed to maintain its capacity at around 4mbpd, to produce an average of nearly 3.6mbpd and to export 2.5mbpd during the Plan, very much in line with Iran's OPEC quota. On other issues, however, Iran managed to put in place many of its policies in the oil and gas sectors and realize much of its objectives during the second Plan. To begin with, consistent and bold increases in the price of petroleum and other energy products (both in nominal and real terms) along with a rapid increase in natural gas distribution, dampened demand for petroleum products keeping its annual rate of growth to around 1–2%. The completion of the Bandar Abbas refinery and its coming on stream in mid-1997 combined with the expansion of Abadan refinery's capacity to 350,000 barrels per day resulted in a sharp drop in import of white products to 33,000 barrels per day by 1999 while exports of petroleum products, mainly fuel oil and some middle distillates had risen to 376,000 barrels per day. As noted earlier, average annual gas consumption increased sharply from 37bcm in 1994 to 57bcm in 1999, though the annual rate of gas injection into the oilfields rose only marginally, from 15bcm to 18bcm during the same period.

The second post-revolutionary, socio-economic plan of the Islamic Republic coincided with the adoption of a serious containment policy by the USA vis à vis Iran, including the passage of the ILSA. Opposition was voiced to any talk of the Iranian territory being used for the pipeline transit of oil or gas from the Central Asian Republics or Azerbaijan. Despite political pressures on the countries of the region, Iran and Kazakhstan agreed on a swap arrangement whereby Kazakh oil would be delivered to an Iranian port on the Caspian Sea to be used in internal refineries for a similar quantity exported from the southern terminals for Kazakh accounts. This arrangement was later joined by Turkmenistan. In addition, Iran started importing Turkmen gas to supplement its gas distribution to the northeastern provinces as from 1997. Towards the end of this decade, while sanctions and political pressures remained intact, a certain change of tone and rhetoric by the US Administration became discernible when import restrictions on some Iranian traditional exports to the USA were lifted and a halting dialogue started through the back channels.

Petroleum policies during the third Five Year Plan (2000–2005)

Iran entered the 21st century on a wave of optimism. Demand for OPEC oil was on the rise and oil prices had rebounded from their lows during 1998. It seemed that, despite its drawbacks, the buy-back model was receiving grudging acceptance by the IOCs. Amongst the four major petroleum exporters of the Middle East (Iran, Saudi Arabia, Kuwait and Iraq) Iran was the only country offering acreages for exploration and development that made it possible for the IOCs to have a semblance of access to some quantities of crude oil or condensate and gas. Since 1998 ILSA had become ineffectual, at least for the European companies as Iran's international isolation appeared to be on the mend. The third Five Year Plan document attested to a realism hitherto absent from the Islamic Republic's pronouncements. None other than the President of the Republic himself was on record to say that "the economy was sick."[18] The Plan had set out to reduce the size and increase the efficiency of the bloated government through wholesale reforms. It called for the adoption of policies in order to provide incentives for the private sector to reengage with the economic activities of the country. It also called for measures to rout our monopolies and to increase competition through extensive privatization of state entities and considerably increased foreign investment. In the oil and gas sector, it prescribed not only more reliance on foreign financial and technical assistance in all phases, but permitted both Iranian and foreign private sectors to enter into down-stream operations such as refining and product distribution while calling for measures that would help rationalize the excessive energy consumption through demand management policies including better energy pricing.[19] This optimism turned into euphoria when early in 2000 a majority of reformers were elected to the Iranian parliament, allegedly providing support for the government's reform programme.

Reflecting this new mood, Iranian Petroleum Industry representatives expounded on their plans at the Iranian Oil, Gas and Petrochemical Forum held in London in July 2000. The Forum was told that given the forecast for OPEC's production in 2020, Iran expects to have to build its capacity to around 7.3mbpd if it wished to maintain its historical share at about 13 to 14%. In any case, Iran intended to raise its oil producing capacity to 5mbpd in the next five years and that would require the serious involvement of international oil companies in investment and technology transfer. Such assistance would be needed especially in exploration of new areas in order to add to the oil and gas reserve base of the country as well as the implementation of development and enhanced recovery projects in the existing producing fields. At that time NIOC had already awarded an exploration and development buy-back contract for Anaran Block, situated on the Iraqi border areas, to Norway's Norsk Hydro and other buy-back contracts in advanced negotiations were: phases 4 and 5 of the South Pars gas field; development of Bangestan reservoirs in the Ahwaz, Ab Teimur and Mansouri fields; and, the development of Azadegan, Darquain and Cheshmeh Khosh oilfields. As for the refining sector, with capacity standing at around 1.34mbpd no new capacity was needed until 2005 except for some upgrading and debottlenecking, especially in the Abadan refinery.[20]

Shortly after this forum NIOC awarded the development of phases 4 and 5 of the South Pars gas field to ENI of Italy in participation with Iranian Petropars on a 60:40 basis. The project was for an annual gas production of 20bcm together with 80,000 barrels per day of condensate. The total cost of investment plus interest and remuneration was estimated at $3.8bn to be recovered during a period of 7 to 10 years. The gas from this project which was expected to flow in 54 months was earmarked for internal consumption with nothing planned for reinjection.[21] With no interest shown by the IOCs in the Salman field rehabilitation, NIOC decided to finance that project from its own resources and carry it out on engineering, procurement and construction (EPC) basis.

Just when some momentum was building for the conclusion of new buy-back contracts as referred to previously, a controversy erupted in the Iranian Parliament by the conservative members who claimed such contracts enabled international companies to have too much control of Iranian assets. Following this debate, the Guardian Council which has oversight power over legislation had advocated a freeze on buy-back contracts pending further deliberations. Upon referral, the Expediency Council which acts as Iran's highest legislative court of appeal had voted in favour of continuing with the current model, effectively removing a potentially debilitating and serious obstacle, at least for a while. Around this time NIOC awarded two onshore blocks for exploration to: a) Italy's Edison Gas for the Munir tract, which lies east-southeast of the Gachsaran oilfield; and, b) China's SINOPEC for the Zavareh-Kashan area. These two exploration contracts were followed by a third in April 2001 with Austria's OMV for the Mehr block which lies northwest of Ahwaz oilfield close to the Iran/Iraq border.

By mid-year, not only was the buy-back debate raging again in the Iranian Parliament, the ILSA was also well on its way to being tightened and extended. At the same time, NIOC had introduced a revision of the buy-back terms especially for the post-development operational period. It insisted that NIOC should be solely in charge of field operations once development is completed, meaning that the revenues of the IOCs would be entirely dependent on NIOC's performance without having any chance of even recommending improvement for field management. Sensing renewed reluctance on the part of IOCs to vigorously pursue negotiations and in order to placate the critics in the Parliament, NIOC decided not to wait any longer and to develop 16 oilfields including eight buy-back projects that had been rejected by foreign companies, under standard engineering, procurement and construction (EPC) contracts, using its own resources. Shortly after this decision, NIOC finally signed an agreement with Italy's ENI for the development of the Darquain oilfield with ENI acting as the operator in a 60:40 partnership with NIOC's marketing subsidiary Naftiran Intertrade Company (NICO). This agreement which was for a total investment of $550m. in two phases would increase capacity initially to 50,000 barrels per day and later to 160,000 barrels per day in five years. It caused some consternation in the international petroleum community as it appeared that ENI had accepted NIOC's new terms regarding the operational phase. The irony of this solitary act was not lost on the observers who remembered the signing of an agreement by the late Enrico Mattei with NIOC on a 75:25 basis some five decades earlier in the face of fierce opposition by the Seven Sisters.

The recurrent buy-back debate in the parliament was joined in July 2001 by the Iranian judiciary investigating allegations of corruption in allocation of buy-back contracts to IOCs by Petropars, a subsidiary of NIOC entrusted with the development of the giant South Pars gas field. Ironically, just at a time when NIOC had announced that oil producing capacity was diminishing by 300,000 barrels per day each year, and that Iran's existing technology was inadequate to maintain the country's current capacity at 4mbpd and, therefore, it had invited

Table 19.4 Productivity of major Iranian oil fields ('000 barrels per day)

	1978	1992	1995	2006
Aghajari	634	278	270	200
Ahwaz Asmari	1087	847	850	700
Ahwaz Bangestan	37	132	180	155
Bibi Hakimeh	220	149	150	130
Gachsaran	743	579	650	560
Karanj	252	196	225	150
Marun	1288	560	600	520
Parsi	241	80	200	100
Rag-e Sefid	149	165	160	190

Source: Internal NIOC memos; Production tests as reported in Middle East Economic Survey.

bids from international and local consultants or joint ventures to provide management services to its Oil Production Capacity Enhancement Plan, a parliamentary commission was hard at work trying to determine whether or not the buy-back deals served the national interests and whether the job entrusted to the foreign firms could not be done by the Iranian experts.[22] It should be noted that the productivity of the Iranian oilfields had already diminished considerably because the enhanced recovery plans had not been fully implemented (Table 19.4).

The landslide re-election of President Khatami did not seem to have any effect on the opposition to his reform agenda by a strong group of conservative members of the Iranian Parliament. However, following the 11 September attacks in the USA and the Iranian government's helpfulness in Afghanistan, hopes were raised, at least for a short while, that relations between the two countries might be on a conciliatory course. Any such hopes were soon dashed when the US President took the rostrum on 29 January 2002 and stated that Iran was part of an "Axis of Evil" in his State of the Union message. The effect of this statement, though potentially devastating, was slow to come. Throughout 2002 and before the invasion of Iraq, Iran still managed to reach buy-back agreements with a few European and Asian companies which could not turn away from the lucrative business with Iran. Thus, Norway's Statoil replaced Britain's Enterprise Oil in negotiating for the development of phases 6, 7 and 8 of the South Pars gas field; Korea's Lucky Goldstar (LG) joined POGC for the development of phases 9 and 10 of the South Pars gas field; rehabilitation of Masjed-e-Suleyman was awarded to Canada's Sheer Energy Company; exploration of Farsi Block in the Persian was given to a group of Indian companies; and, development and rehabilitation of Forouzan and Esfadiar oil fields were entrusted to Petro Iran Development Company (PEDCO).

In the aftermath of Iraq's invasion, Iran became progressively embroiled, on the one hand, with the insurgency and other events in Iraq, and on the other, with the IAEA and the major western countries on its nuclear programme and proliferation issues. The referral of Iran to the UN Security Council over its nuclear programme created serious doubts for the international companies in respect of their continued involvement in Iran. The spectre of confrontation with the USA and talk of military strikes were received with trepidation in the IOCs' boardrooms. Consequently, even a last ditch effort by the NIOC to offer revised buy-back terms at a tender conference held in the Hague in early 2004 for 16 exploration and development licences did little to entice the international companies that were most in demand by NIOC for their up-to-date technology. These revisions were both a reversal of the previous demands as well as the giving-in to the IOCs' demands. They included the bundling of the exploration and development phases under the same contract, the extension of the licence terms to as much as 25 years and the inclusion of the IOCs in the decision-making process during the operational phase.[23]

Just as Iran's access to international finance and technology was slipping away the market for OPEC oil and crude oil prices were firming up. Already Iran's revenue from the export of petroleum had increased from around $19bn in 2002 to more than $26bn in 2003 making it relatively easier for NIOC to finance some projects from its own resources. There were also talks of allocating far larger funds in the order of $100bn for the petroleum sector in the next five year plan, starting in 2005.[24] In January 2004 NIOC broke off negotiations with Spain's Cepsa and Austria's OMV and decided to assign its subsidiary, Iranian Central Oil Fields Company (ICOFC), to undertake the Cheshmeh Khosh gas injection project. NIOC then set up a consortium of companies, consisting of BP, Statoil, Petronas, Norsk Hydro and Total, to study improved oil recovery (IOR) prospects of Iranian oilfields. As oil revenue topped $34bn in 2004 NIOC moved farther away from the European IOCs and opted for implementing projects through its own subsidiaries or awarding buy-back deals to the national firms and Asian petroleum companies. Thus, in March of 2005 (just before the end of the Iranian budget year), NIOC announced the award of buy-back contracts for three oilfield development projects to Iranian companies: Ahwaz Bangestan gas reinjection and South Pars oil layer projects went to PetroIran Development Company (PEDCO); and, Rag-e-Sefid production expansion project was contracted to Qeshm Oil and Energy Industries Development Company. This was followed shortly by two exploration buy-back awards: Saveh block to Thailand's PTT; and, Kuhdasht to China's CNPC. This latter had taken over the operation of the Masjed-e Suleyman oilfield redevelopment from Canada's Sheer Energy.

Policy during the fourth Five Year Plan and the 20-year perspective

When the fourth Plan was being drafted, the burning issue was no longer the revision of buy-back terms to make that type of contract more palatable to the IOCs because the stand-off with the West had already driven the international companies away from the Iranian scene. Rather, it was the run-away consumption of energy products caused by low prices and highly energy inefficient capital and transportation stocks that received a good deal of attention. Of particular significance was the galloping imports of gasoline which was running at around 150,000 barrels per day, weighing heavily on the resources of the Treasury. The Plan, therefore, recommended the aligning of petroleum product prices with Persian Gulf wholesale export prices on the condition that the government would compensate the low income and vulnerable groups with direct assistance. The Plan also directed the government to adopt many energy saving measures such as expansion of public transportation, introduction of more energy efficient building codes, regulations requiring the manufacture of more fuel-efficient and gas-consuming vehicles, etc. The Plan further emphasized the need for privatization of downstream petroleum activities, as well as the attraction of foreign investment and technology in the oil and gas industry, including buy-back contracts.[25]

The period leading up to the 2005 presidential elections brought renewed tension for the oil industry. In February the parliament ratified a bill calling for a probe into the operations of the Ministry of Petroleum. The inquiry was supposed to gauge the ministry's performance, especially its handling of the buy-back contracts between NIOC and IOCs. This was merely the continuation of the previous debate about the validity of such contracts, hampering the ministry and elevating the political risk of doing business in Iran. The election of a self-described fundamentalist was most probably the result of the people's disillusionment with the reformist government that had failed to implement any serious reforms and had retreated under pressure from the religious leadership and the conservatives. Mr Ahmadinejad had promised the reform of the petroleum sector, the resolution of the differences between the ministry and the Guardian Council, and "cutting off the hands of the mafias which have a grasp on our oil. ... people must see their share of oil money in their daily lives." While supporting foreign investment in Iran, he had added that he was not in agreement with the policies of privatization by selling state enterprises to reduce the budget deficit, rather he believed that privatization must aim at giving people shares and profits. He was also very clear that the development of the petroleum industry should make full use of domestic manpower, contracting and technical capabilities.

With parliament rejecting the President's first nominee for petroleum minister, a protracted search started, during which the Parliament made it clear that in the future it expected a good deal more co-operation and transparency from the ministry and NIOC. Once the Cabinet was fully approved, the new Minister of Petroleum announced a reshuffle of the senior positions of oil, gas and petrochemical companies in January 2006.[25] These appointments and the briefs of the respective managing directors clearly indicated that the overstretched National Iranian Oil Refining and Distribution Company (NIORDC) was to receive as much attention as NIOC and NIGC. In short, the brief for NIOC remained in improving oil and gas recovery, accelerating development of fields shared with the neighbouring countries, boosting exploration, expanding oil and gas producing capacity, and, increasing petroleum and gas exports. NIGC's focus was to remain on expansion of urban and rural gas supply and rapid increase in the use of gas domestically in the place of liquid fuels. The brief for NIORDC, however, consisted of solving the problem of petroleum products, notably gasoline-importation by adding 1mbpd throughput capacity to the existing 1.5mbpd by expanding and optimizing existing refineries and building two new condensate and heavy crude refineries. As a step towards reconciliation with parliament and more transparency, a Petroleum Council was formed, which would be chaired by the President, and whose duties included the assessment, review and supervision of the new petroleum contracts. The minister also pledged a review of the unpopular buy-back contract model in order to safeguard the national interests while reviving interest among the IOCs in investing in the Iranian oil and gas sectors.

While the reinvigorated refining programme received considerable funding and was quickly put in motion, the possibility of enticing European or even Japanese IOCs to participate in the development of Iranian oil and gas prospects almost vanished as Iran was handed several sanctions by the UN Security Council. Towards the end of the decade, the European Union added its own sanctions to those of the USA and the Security Council. The result was that, despite its keen interest in the development of the Azadegan field, the Japanese INPEX eventually bowed out in 2006. ENI refused to continue development of the Darquain oilfield once the first phase was completed. Even Norsk Hydro (now Statoil/Hydro) which was successful in discovering two fields (Azar and Changuleh) in the Anaran block discontinued any further activities on this block in 2009. Moreover, many years of negotiations with European IOCs were aborted and the development of the giant Yadavaran field went to China's SINOPEC in association with India's ONGC.

In the meantime, NIOC has had somewhat more success in attracting interest in its buy-back exploration tenders. In 2006 Garmsar and Khorramabad blocks went to SINOPEC and Norsk Hydro, respectively. Later in 2008, the onshore Danan block was awarded to Petrvietnam and Italy's Edison Gas received the exploration and development contract for the offshore Dayyer block. By NIOC's tally, 16 new oilfields and 14 new gasfields had been discovered between 1997 and 2006 adding 12bn barrels of oil and 3 trillion cubic metres of gas to Iran's total reserves.[26] Since that date many other fields such as Farzad on Farsi block explored by India's ONGC, Kuhdasht studied by China's CNPC, Tusan explored by Petrobras, Arvand near Abadan, and several other smaller gas and oilfields have been discovered by NIOC and its subsidiaries in the Khuzestan, Fars and western provinces.

As the Western European international companies discontinued their further involvement in Iran, especially in the development and rehabilitation of oil and gas fields, the Russian, Chinese and other East and South Asian companies moved in. Thus, the North and South Azadegan developments were eventually entrusted to China's CNPC, after NIOC had already developed South Azadegan on an early production programme to 25,000 barrels per day by 2008. This involved a total investment of around $6bn to increase production from the two parts to nearly 420,000 barrels per day. Russia's Gasprom took over development of the Azar oilfield in the Anaran block discovered previously by Stat/Hydro. All other oil and gas field developments, enhanced oil recovery projects, exploration activities, reinjection schemes, oil and gas pipeline constructions, refinery construction and expansion/revamping projects were carried out mostly through EPC contracts with Iranian or expatriate contractors.

The gasoline crisis

Even before the end of Khatami's presidential term in mid-2005, the conservative parliament had stymied attempts to raise fuel prices with the result that the gains of the previous Plan period were reversed. This situation was exacerbated due to the loose fiscal and monetary policies of the populist Ahmadinejad administration which were openly criticized by most Iranian economists. By the beginning of 2007, with none of the refinery expansion/revamping still in sight, petroleum product imports were running at around 220,000 barrels per day with gasoline alone accounting for 170,000 barrels per day (Table 19.5).

Apart from being a heavy burden on the Treasury in the time of rising international prices, the country found its dependence on this magnitude of imports a strategic liability, especially since suggestions were being made in the anti-Iran circles that sanctions on the supply of gasoline to Iran should become a part and parcel of any new endeavours. Finally parliament agreed on a rationing scheme whereby the price of gasoline was raised by 25% and different groups of users were allocated different monthly entitlements according to the type of vehicle. The monthly quota for a car was, for example, set at 100 litres, with more allowed for taxis and other modes of transportation and freight carrying vehicles. These measures were implemented

Table 19.5 Petroleum Product Consumption (2001–09)

	2001	2002	2003	2004	2005	2006	2007	2008	2009
Product Output (kb/d)	1437	1440	1345	1437	1440	1448	1498	1387	1726
Domestic Consumption (kb/d)	1220	1258	1329	1415	1479	1599	1680	1776	1795
Gasoline	257	298	336	375	371	383	389	414	423
Kerosene	186	175	200	215	143	142	148	159	159
Gasoil	414	430	425	433	484	513	534	552	560
Fuel oil	219	190	171	181	233	296	337	369	370
Others	144	165	196	210	248	263	272	282	283
Imports of Gasoline	49	65	95	142	156	173	120	130	138

Source: OPEC Statistical Bulletin 2005, 2009 (NIORDC website).

at the end of June 2007 with the clear understanding that the government would later propose a comprehensive set of policies for dealing with the fuel subsidies that are currently estimated by the IEA at upward of $65bn.[27] These reforms consisting of raising fuel prices and compensating the low income and vulnerable groups of people earning below a specified monthly figure by direct cash are being implemented on an experimental basis in four governorates with the hope that once the system is streamlined and refined, it would be implemented throughout the country.

Concluding remarks

With total hydrocarbon recoverable reserves standing at upward of 300bn barrels of oil equivalent, Iran possesses one of the largest hydrocarbon endowments in the world and has so far played an important role in supplying the global needs for energy products. Even in the last 30 years, during which the country has seemed to be stuck in a time warp, Iran has remained an active player on the international energy scene, although its enormous income of nearly $800bn from the export of hydrocarbon products since the Islamic Revolution appears to have done little in elevating its per capita income. Its nuclear research and development policies, harsh theocratic rules and human rights violations have kept it at loggerheads with many countries in the rest of the world, threatening it with further isolation and uncertainty. Iran's petroleum sector cannot remain immune to the national and international political forces and it cannot stand as an island of good management in a sea of gross economic mismanagement. Above all, it is a forlorn hope that the Iranian hydrocarbon industry can remain independent from political influence and be run on purely commercial bases. In Iran hydrocarbon resources are nationalized and belong to the people, the income from them forms the lifeblood of the country's economy and Iran is a steadfast member of an association of exporters bent on creating stability in the market of a substance that is historically notorious for its wild price fluctuations.

The history of planning since the Revolution, and the policy choices recommended by each Plan, attests to a keen understanding of the issues facing the energy sector and the dangers of inaction. But the regime has been incapable of facing these issues because of a tension that exists between a socially responsible economic management and a utopian view of Islamic justice. After all, it was none other than the Ayatollah Khomeini himself who, from his residence in Paris, promised the Iran nation very cheap and even free goods and services as a small token of imminent Islamic social justice. In those heady days some innocent souls were even convinced that they would soon be receiving their oil income share at the time calculated at $50 per person per month in an envelope via the mail. It, therefore, remains to be seen if the current reforms of replacing fuel subsidies with direct cash payments will eventually stick or it becomes a further populist redistribution adding to the economic woes of the country.

Making prognostications about the future of Iran's petroleum sector is a perilous exercise. It is, however, less difficult to sketch the broad outlines of the Islamic Republic's attitude towards the sector and the issues facing its future:

a) Iran considers its hydrocarbon exports strategic and intertwined with its national security;
b) Iran is supportive of OPEC and remains very jealous of its share of the quotas and its ranking within the organization;
c) income from the export of hydrocarbons will remain the linchpin of the Iranian economic development for decades to come and any talk of an oil-free economy can be safely dismissed;

d) theoretically, Iran is aware of the enormous wastefulness in its energy economy and would like to rationalize it, if at all possible;
e) natural gas is likely to play the dominant role in supplying the energy needs of the country in the foreseeable future, although some nuclear power and renewables will gradually enter the mix, because of global concern about climate change;
f) LNG projects appear to be a less attractive export option for Iran under the present international political circumstances. Gas availability is likely to limit pipeline exports if wasteful and escalating gas consumption is not checked.

The experience of the last thirty years, especially the post-Iran/Iraq war period tells us unmistakably that Iran's quest to attain a sustainable production capacity of 5mbpd has been an utter failure, though the achievement of this target has been just around the corner since the beginning of the 1990s. In fact as late as the mid-1990s, the Minister of Petroleum still boasted that: " … technically speaking, NIOC does not have any problems in respect of its various operations." But only a few years later this façade could no longer be maintained and the authorities started bemoaning the shortage of skilled manpower and technology. In a speech given at the Economics Department of the University of Tehran, a frustrated Minister of Petroleum had, with uncharacteristic candour, the following to say: "We only have 150 oil engineers in the country and we have shortcomings in science and technical fields."[28] More recently, the deputy managing Director of Exploration at the NIOC warned in an interview that: "presently a large percentage of the oil industry workforce at senior levels is in the process of retirement or leaving the industry … More than 70% of exploration management, however, are about 30 years old … these are also the same people who are mostly leaving the industry, which means the oil industry has been unable to keep its best or newest expert workforce".[29] Even if the international climate became somehow less hostile to Iran and sanctions are lifted, this shortage of skilled and experienced scientists, engineers and technical manpower constitutes the greatest obstacle to Iran's quest for higher oil producing capacity. The acknowledgment of this problem, though a step in the right direction, does not offer any solution for as long as senior and middle management assignments are made on ideological credentials and technical decisions are subservient to political considerations.

Another important issue in the Iranian petroleum sector is the raging debate as to the advisability of allocating some quantities for long-term exports in the face of the country's own need for gas, not only as an energy resource, but also for reinjection into oilfields, conversion to light and middle distillate petroleum products and as a base for high value-added industrial products such as petrochemicals and steel. However, there seems to be a consensus that beyond domestic gas distribution for energy consumption, gas reinjection into oilfields has the highest economic return.[30] And this is where the industry's performance has been dismal. Recalling the studies of the mid-1970s which recommended an annual injection rate of 92bcm and given the present condition of many Iranian oil reservoirs and the current rate of only 40bcm per year, it is essential that focus remain on supplying the reinjection requirements from the future South Pars streams until such time that the whole scheme is fully operational. The magnitude of Iran's natural gas reserves is such that its presence in the international markets would not seriously diminish its resources domestic consumption and it now appears that the authorities have chosen to export via pipelines rather than through LNG.

With oil producing capacity currently standing at around 4mbpd and declining naturally at an annual rate of 300,000 barrels per day; and given the severity of other interconnected issues referred to previously such as the shortage of technical manpower and the slow rate of gas reinjection, a Herculean effort is needed to increase sustainable capacity to 5.6mbpd (the level at which it was planned to breach at the end of the fourth Plan by 2010) in five years or 7mbpd by 2025. Iran can only hope to reach its objective of remaining an important player in the international energy scene if it succeeds in devising a suitable and inviting framework for attracting domestic and foreign investment and technology. Owing to government policy in the last 30 years, some technical, engineering, manufacturing and contracting capabilities have been created domestically in the public and private sectors, however, this resource needs to be employed effectively in order to achieve progress in projects whose delay is causing financial and economic loss. In the absence of less political and ideological interference in what is, in essence, a technical and commercial operation, and without more accountability and transparency Iran's oil and gas sector is likely to, at best, muddle through.

Notes

1 *The Prize*, Daniel Yergin, 1991: *The History of British Petroleum Company, Vol. II, The Anglo-Iranian Years, 1928–54*, James Bamberg, 1994; *Oil Politics*, Francisco Parra, 2004; *Fifty Years of Oil*, Mostafa Fateh, 1955 (in Persian); *Oil, Power, and Principle*, Mostafa Elm, 1994; *The Petroleum Nightmare*, Mohammad Ali Movahed, 1999 (in Persian).
2 SIRIP, IPAC, LAPCO, and IMINOCO.
3 *Oil Politics*, Francisco Parra, 2004, p. 131.
4 Iran's Fifth Pre-Revolution Development Plan, 1973–78, Plan and Budget Organization, June 1973.
5 *Oil Politics*, Francisco Parra, 2004, pp. 146–64, Struggle for Control.
6 *Middle East Economic Survey*, 31 January, 1994.
7 The World Bank, Iran Reconstruction and Economic Growth, Report No. 9072 IRN, July 30, 1991.
8 The National Iranian Oil Refining and Distribution Company (NIORDC) website.
9 The Islamic Republic of Iran's First Economic, Social and Cultural Plan, Legal Department, The Islamic Iran Parliament, 1989 (in Persian).
10 Middle East Economic Survey, 26 October 1992, Interview with Gholamreza Aghazadeh, the Iranian Minister of Petroleum, p. A2.
11 Ibid., p. a10.
12 Islamic Iranian Republic's Second Economic, Social and Cultural Plan, Approved by the Economic Council, 1994 (in Persian).
13 Middle East Economic Survey, 31 January 1994, Interview with Mostafa Khoee, p. A1.
14 Middle East Economic Survey, 22 May 1995, Interview with Gholamreza Aghazadeh, the Iranian Minister of Petroleum, p. A3.
15 Middle East Economic Survey, 6 October 1997, Total's South Pars Deal Breaks New Ground, p. A1.
16 Middle East Economic Survey, 27 October 1997, NIOC May Offer Out Offshore Exploration Acreage In Upcoming Buy-Back Round, p. A11.
17 Middle East Economic Digest, 17 July 1998, Investors Lap up Iranian Oil Offers by Vahe Petrossian, p. 4.
18 Jomhoori Eslami, 15 March 1998, Statement by the Iranian President Mohammad Khatami on Economic Issues (in Persian).
19 Islamic Iranian Republic's Third Economic, Social and Cultural Plan, Public Gazette, April 2000.
20 Middle East Economic Survey, 24 July 2000, Iran's ambitious Oil, Gas and Petrochemical Expansion Plans, p. A3.
21 Middle East Economic Survey, 31 July 2000, Iran Awards $3.8 Billion South Pars Phases 4 and 5 Development Project To ENI and Petropars, p. A5.
22 Islamic Republic News Agency (IRNA), 18 July 2001.
23 Middle East Economic Survey, 2 February 2004, NIOC Improves Buyback Terms for Tender of 16 Exploration and Development Licenses, p. A5.
24 Middle East Economic Survey, 5 January 2004, Iran Earmarks $90–104 billion For Petroleum Industry Under Fourth Plan, p. A10.
25 Middle East Economic Survey, 2/9 January 2006, Petroleum Ministry Reshuffle.
26 Middle East Economic Survey, 8 October 2007, Mohaddes Says NIOC Discovered 16 Oilfields, 14 Gas fields in 1997–2006.

27 International Energy Agency, World Energy Outlook 2010, 9 November 2010.
28 Middle East Economic Survey, 13 August 2001, Zangeneh Outlines NIOC Challenges, p. A15.
29 Mehr News Agency, 23 January 2010, The Deputy Managing Director for Exploration of the NIOC, Mohsen Amirian Warns of Skill Shortage in Iran Oil Industry.
30 Middle East Economic Survey, 26 November 2001, Paper presented by Narsi Ghorban at the "Middle East Gas Resources and Opportunities" Conference.

20
The Enduring Saudi Oil Power

Joseph A. Kéchichian

The strategic importance of the Arabian Peninsula and the Persian Gulf area seldom waned for Western as well as Asian Powers throughout the centuries. In fact, the region has been an ideal crossroads for trade among countries of the Mediterranean basin and Asia for several millennia. From the Greek navigator Hippalus, who first developed a direct sea route from Arabia to India during the first century B.C., to the lucrative commercial relations established with China under the 'Ummayads' (661–750 A.D.), the Persian Gulf region gained importance in trade and commerce.[1]

Geopolitical considerations took on an air of importance with the discovery of petroleum in the Gulf at the turn of the 20th century, which tied the region's fate to that of the oil-thirsty and rapidly expanding economic powers in Europe, as well as the Americas. In fact, developments in world energy markets after 1971 indicated that the Persian Gulf area was certain to command a major share of international attention well into the next century, which proved to be accurate even if highly contentious. The USA and the Soviet Union as well as a myriad of other states, both industrialized and less developed, considered the Persian Gulf's natural resources indispensable to their economic well-being, and in some instances their survival. After 1973, the region's strategic importance increased sharply, following serious disruptions that resulted in price increases levied by the Organization of the Petroleum Exporting Countries (OPEC) and the oil embargo imposed by the Organization of the Arab Petroleum Exporting Countries (OAPEC) in October of that year. Consequently, the world trade in petroleum was subjected to periodic fluctuations, as the Gulf recorded the 1979 Islamic Revolution in Iran, the 1980–88 Iran-Iraq war, the 1990 Iraqi invasion and occupation of Kuwait, the 1991 US-led, UN-sanctioned liberation of the Shaykhdom, the decade-long UN-imposed economic embargo on Iraq, the 2001 US war for Afghanistan and the 2003 US war for Iraq. Although a variety of reasons caused these conflicts that, in turn, generated undeniable consequences, oil was the single most important constant that motivated actions and reactions.

Saudi Arabia stood steadfast throughout the decades as it shepherded periodic price increases, particularly those of 1973, 1979, and 2001, which temporarily stabilized energy markets and momentarily strengthened OPEC's bargaining posture. As oil producing countries experienced major swings ranging from the 1982 oil glut that mired the oil industry in a deep crisis, to more recent price increases that altered the oil balance of power, Saudi Arabia remained the critical anchor that stabilized markets. By virtue of its immense holdings and an unparalleled capability to increase production at will, the Kingdom of Saudi Arabia earned its unique and privileged position as a stable energy producer, a trend destined to endure for the foreseeable future.

OAPEC and the 1973 oil revolution

From 1 January 1973 to 31 December 1974 a total of 17 oil price increases were recorded as the price of Arabian light marker crude jumped from $2.00 a barrel to $10.46.[2] These successive increases brought about a worldwide reduction in petroleum consumption resulting in a leveling out of Middle East oil production in 1974 and an actual decrease in 1975. Between 1975 and 1977, several OPEC member-states, led by Iran, pressed for higher prices, citing deteriorating revenues due to worldwide inflation. At the height of extensive debates, Saudi Arabia and the United Arab Emirates (UAE) led the more moderate position that called for lower future increases, which proved a failed attempt. A compromise solution was adopted at the 1976 OPEC meeting in Doha, Qatar, where a two-tier pricing system was adopted, whereby Saudi Arabia and the UAE agreed to raise their prices by 5% on 1 January 1977, whereas the other 11 OPEC member states planned to raise theirs by about 10%.[3] This was one of the most contentious OPEC gatherings in the organization's history, as major differences on pricing and production were aired, both in private debates as well as public prognostications. It was after this controversial convention that Saudi Arabia, for example, decided to abandon its self-imposed 8.5mbpd limit on production and decided to produce at maximum capacity—approximately 10mbpd—as a countermove to the more adamant positions.[4]

At the time, other OPEC producers threatened to further raise the price of their crude production, although an agreement was reached to adopt a price adjustment with Saudi Arabia and the UAE standing firm to a 5% increase. In the event, the Doha meeting demonstrated that Saudi Arabia was ready and willing to forego certain organizational principles to protect its perceived long-term interests, including favored relationships with key consuming states. Still, notwithstanding these political manoeuvres, actual oil prices declined between 1974 and 1978, when measured in constant dollars, something that concerned decision-makers in the kingdom.[5]

Even if OPEC member states unilaterally assumed control of their natural resources, which marked the beginning of a consolidation process that continued to unfold ever since, the 1973 "oil revolution" empowered Saudi Arabia more than any other oil producer. Riyadh was giddy but cautious for despite the legal restoration of hydrocarbon resources to exporting states, which stood as a major historical change between industrialized and developing countries, the process fell far short of providing economic security to producers. Saudi Arabia was aware that its bargaining power was systematically curtailed by a myriad of political forces that harbored little more than perpetual control. Riyadh's long-sought economic security was rejected as long as Saudi Arabia remained a mere residual supplier of a "single" raw material, dependent on importing refined products ranging from food to gasoline, all of which planted the seeds for diversification in the petrochemical industries.

Indeed, the one-way dependence was unacceptable to Saudi Arabia, where decision-makers quickly assessed their dire situation. Consequently, and much like the industrialized countries a century earlier, Riyadh opted to go "downstream" and embarked on the refining, marketing, transportation, and distribution of petroleum sectors. A rapid pace was adopted for the construction of refineries within the kingdom, which were quickly supplemented by petrochemical, gas, and fertilizer plants, certainly all novelties for the period. While industrial development slowed down in 1983 after world oil price drops, the long-term outlook for "downstream" industries in the Gulf remained promising. It was important, however, to note that these advances were not accomplished without sacrifice, and that many of the technical advances registered in the area were due to OAPEC's concerted efforts to promote industrialization. OAPEC drew worldwide recognition after the 1973 oil embargo and its contribution to the economic development of the region was not unnoticed.[6] Indeed, OAPEC's economic policies after 1968, and its political decisions in 1973, were responsible for the coming of age of the oil producers, particularly those in the swing group (Bahrain, Kuwait, Qatar, Saudi Arabia, and the United Arab Emirates), which represented a major change in the power relationship between consuming and producing countries. By most accounts, oil-exporting countries headed by Saudi Arabia, earned the reputation for being "regarded as major independent actors in world affairs by all the industrialized nations, including the United States."[7] This recent phenomenon, when contrasted with the relationship existing between 1908 and 1973, clearly indicated that the power and responsibility of the oil producers improved dramatically. Simultaneously, decisions and actions adopted in the 1970s demonstrated how fragile the world economy was, and highlighted OAPEC's vulnerability to outside pressures, particularly when the results of the oil embargo were taken into account. Indeed, it may be accurate to conclude that the impact of the embargo was certainly felt in industrialized countries, without, however, altering the political balance in the Middle East. With long-term commitments to Israel's security, the USA did not alter its policies even if logic dictated that Washington make necessary adjustments. That is not to say that a certain impact was not recorded for enough evidence emerged over the years that the oil embargo, and the simultaneous price increases, permanently altered global financial markets that resulted in the largest transfer of financial resources in recorded history. Under the circumstances, and to better understand the nascent oil power of Saudi Arabia, it was critical to ask what were the effects of the oil crunch on industrialized countries and how existing economic relationships between producers and consumers developed in the interim.

Supply and demand concerns

Throughout the 1970s and 1980s, Western economies experienced sharp economic slow-downs, which resulted in steady declines in the demand for petroleum products. Reduced oil consumption in industrialized countries was amplified by constant conservation measures, as well as a partial shifting to alternative energy sources. These developments left a significant impact on OPEC in general and Persian Gulf producers in particular. With low Iranian and Iraqi production levels necessitated by the 1980–88 Iran-Iraq war, Saudi Arabia agreed to play what eventually became known as the role of a swing producer, adapting its production ceilings to market conditions. Thus, while in 1973 petroleum consumption for major non-Communist industrialized countries totaled 36.4bbpd, consumption in 1975 decreased to 33bbpd, only to jump back up to an all-time record of 37bbpd in 1979 following the short-lived yet strong worldwide economic recovery. Since 1979 and until the end of the century, worldwide consumption declined steadily and stabilized around the 31–32mbpd figure. According to the US Energy Information Administration, Organization for Economic Co-operation and Development (OECD) countries accounted for nearly two-thirds of worldwide daily oil consumption, whereas "oil demand in the OECD grew by some 11% over the 1991–97 period." Demand "outside the OECD (excluding the former Soviet Union) grew by 35%," with a critical caveat on the former Soviet Union as the collapse of the Russian economy led to a sharp decline in oil consumption of more than 50% over the 1991–98 period.[8] World crude oil production between 2000 and 2009 oscillated between 76.0mbpd and 79.9mbpd, with a peak figure of 82mbpd in 2008, which was truly significant.[9]

Demand for petroleum produced by OPEC was sharply reduced in 1979 following the major increases in the price of a barrel of crude oil from $13.4 on 1 January 1979 to $26.00 on 1 January 1980.[10] Although successive price hikes severely shocked the world economy in 1979 and 1980, when consumption in non-communist industrialized countries was only 31mbpd, events in and around the Persian Gulf—the Iranian Revolution, the Makkah uprising, the Iran-Iraq War—underscored the vulnerability of the area. While Saudi Arabia's critical role as the world's premier oil producer was well established by the early 1980s, these crises heightened its value and, more important, alerted everyone to existing vulnerabilities. With the world's largest deposits located in the Middle East, which possessed approximately 43% of the world's proven oil reserves in 1984—a percentage that crossed the 52% mark in 2009—Saudi Arabia, as the undisputed leader in the pack with one-quarter of global reserves, occupied a privileged position.[11] In 2009 Saudi Arabia alone held 264bn barrels of proven oil reserves, which represented approximately 25% of the world's total reserves, and 205 trillion cubic feet of proven gas reserves (4% of world gas holdings).

Still, while Gulf petroleum production accounted for one-quarter of the world's total, local consumption was approximately 5.0% of world demand in 1983, and less than 10% in 2009. The Kingdom of Saudi Arabia alone produced 10.8mbpd of which only 2.4 were used locally. An estimated 8.4mbpd were exported each day in 2009.[12] Moreover, and as various statistical databases confirmed, the bulk of OPEC consumption continued to be in the Gulf region where rapid industrialization was under way. Despite this rising trend, nevertheless, local consumption of petroleum products in oil-producing states, including Saudi Arabia, remained limited especially when compared with consumption in the rest of the world. Overall OPEC consumption increased from 374,500 barrels per day to 2,889,600 barrels per day between 1963 and 1983.[13] By 2008 OPEC states' total consumption rates reached 8mbpd, of which Saudi Arabia was the largest end user at 2.3–2.4mbpd.[14]

Beyond these issues, economic recovery throughout the world increased demand for oil, with Mexico, the United Kingdom and Canada providing additional supplies. Indeed, non-industrialized non-OPEC production rose sharply from the mid-1980s until 2008. For all these additional resources, Mexican oil production, which with an estimated 200bn barrels in proven reserves was once hailed as a panacea for the USA, turned out to be excessively optimistic. While earlier projections for large Mexican reserves may yet materialize, it was critical to note that Mexico's oil policies throughout the 1980s and 1990s were very conservative, with exports seldom exceeding internal consumption.[15] In fact, Mexican internal consumption grew at the rate of 7–8% per year throughout this period, which required a large share of domestic production to be diverted for internal needs. OTA estimated that Mexican production would remain in the 3.5–5.5mbpd range in the year 2000, subject to government policy changes, which was spot on.[16] Similarly, while North Sea oil production rose from 1.1mbpd in 1977 to 2.9mbpd in 1983, it peaked in 1999.[17] Without denying the proven facts that Mexican and North Sea oil fields added significant resources to global supplies, accelerated production in Canada and, in the aftermath of the nascent Central Asia Republics that embarked on massive searches for black gold, they did not, individually or collectively, duplicate the Middle East in general and Saudi Arabia in particular. Simply stated, the only promising areas for large new discoveries outside the Middle East were located in remote regions of the globe such as the Arctic, or in areas involving territorial disputes, such as the Malvinas basin off the Falkland Islands, and the South China Sea. Production costs in remote regions of the world remained uneconomical but may be necessary in the not too distant future. What was certain in 2010 was that significant oil resources would still be harvested in the Gulf region, especially in Saudi Arabia.

Saudi Arabia's oil policy

Saudi Arabia's oil policy rested first on the kingdom's "ability to vary rates of oil production from a low of about 5mbpd to 6mbpd, to a maximum of over 10mbpd."[18] In addition, while production levels were not permitted to dip too far below the 5mbpd figure for development needs, Saudi Arabia retained the flexibility to meet short-term revenue requirements by drawing on its large financial reserves, estimated to be over $1 trillion. In 1983 and 1984, however, Saudi production was reduced to approximately 2.5mbpd in an effort to support the $27 bench-mark agreed to by OPEC. Needless to say, this created a serious economic dilemma for the ruling Al Sa'ud family, whose major expenditures could only be met through large borrowings from domestic banks. Throughout the 1980s, Riyadh ran significant budgetary deficits, which necessitated severe austerity measures.[19]

At the time, and as global prices collapsed, Riyadh agreed to reduce its output simply to maintain its political position within the oil organization, even though it was highly doubtful whether it would acquiesce to this role in the future. In fact, sacrificing for the sake of the organization's long-term interests created serious problems as long as all OPEC producers, led by Iran, cheated on their agreed quotas.

The second leg of Saudi oil policy was its pricing strategy, which was to pursue gradual increases pacing world inflation rates. This professed option, however, was not implemented successfully, particularly in 1979 when OPEC pricing strategies were imposed on all member states.

The third and final leg of Saudi oil policy was its readiness to extend financial assistance to developing countries that dramatically improved its political outlook. Saudi development assistance in real dollar amounts was second only to that of the USA. Between 1975 and 1982, for example, over $34bn were transferred to developing countries, averaging 5.61% of the kingdom's annual GNPs. During the same period, the USA transferred $44.67bn, averaging 0.24% of US annual GNP.[20] In the 1990s, that is between 1990 and 1999, Riyadh allocated $206bn for official development assistance (ODA). An additional $132bn was disbursed between 2000 and 2006.[21] ODA loans are often made on concessional terms but an added feature of Saudi assistance was the policy under which transfers were and are still made. For the most part, assistance tended to be either concessional or interest-free, reflecting very liberal terms. In fact, between 1975 and 1981 some 46% of the Saudi Fund's assistance was on a grant basis, although some of these terms changed more recently.[22] It was clear that Saudi Arabia's motives for providing economic assistance to developing countries, both Arab or Islamic and non-Arab non-Islamic states, were and are based on the awareness that Less-Developed Countries suffered from colonialism, poverty, and illiteracy among other deprivations, and that the kingdom had a responsibility to assist these states. Naturally, Saudi Arabia hoped that in exchange, these developing countries would support the Arab position in various Middle East crises although this was never a condition.[23]

Long before Saudi Arabia reached the $500bn annual GDP figure in 2010, which transformed this formerly desert outpost into a G-20 member, few appreciated its potential wealth. Indeed, it may still be difficult to grasp the kingdom's overall affluence, which now included a vibrant private sector that may be responsible for an estimated 40% of GDP. The kingdom's petroleum reserves were the largest anywhere in the world, with considerable potential additions yet to come, especially in the largely unexplored Rub' al-Khali Desert along the Omani and Emirati borders. Less than a few decades ago, the country was relatively poor, and its population living in dire conditions. While pockets of poverty persisted in 2010, a large portion of the population was doing well, with steady income returns at all levels. As oil prices increased, the kingdom and its population changed dramatically too, since Riyadh was thrust into the international energy arena. Indeed, Saudi Arabia's unprecedented wealth and economic growth brought massive responsibilities and a range of regional and international problems, all of which were tackled with utmost care.

Oil was discovered faster than it was being extracted in Saudi Arabia despite large daily production levels. In 2010 production hovered around the 10mbpd figure, roughly the same level as the 9.5mbpd ceiling extracted in 1979. Although capacity estimates varied, the figure of 14mbpd was often mentioned as a potential level that Riyadh aimed at, with Western experts generally in agreement that such a maximum was certainly possible to reach once current infrastructure investments were completed.[24]

Interestingly, while the bulk of Saudi oil was sold to Asian countries in the mid-1980s, the majority of the estimated 8.4mbpd in 2008 went to Japan, South Korea, China, and India. In fact, these four countries received nearly 50% of Saudi Arabia's crude oil exports in 2010, a trend expected to continue for the foreseeable future. Moreover, the bulk of all refined petroleum products and Natural Liquified Gas exports were allocated to the same customers. Japan was then as now the single largest importer of Saudi crude in Asia. In the mid-1980s, Japan purchased over 1mbpd, whereas in 2008, the daily figure stood at 1.25mbpd.[25] South Korea's imports from Saudi Arabia increased significantly too, going from less than 100,000 barrels per day to approximately 875,000 barrels per day. If 1985 exports to the USA did not exceed 400,000 barrels per day, by 2008, Saudi Arabia exported an average of 1 to 1.5mbpd of petroleum liquids to its American customers, which accounted for approximately 12% of total US petroleum imports. In fact, in recent years, Saudi Arabia ranked second after Canada as a petroleum exporter to the USA.[26]

During most of 1980 and 1981, Saudi Arabia's oil production remained close to the 10mbpd rate offsetting the losses of Iranian and Iraqi productions that were removed from the markets at the height of their war. As a result, OPEC price increases were moderate, with the $34 per barrel price agreed to by OPEC in 1981 sticking. A downturn in the world economy sharply reduced the demand for OPEC oil production that meant the $34 price could not be supported. Consequently, Riyadh reduced its output from 10mbpd to 5.6mbpd in 1982 to maintain the OPEC price, and continued to exercise some leverage on other producing states. In 1983 the kingdom supported a $5 cut in the price of a barrel to $29 and in 1984 the official OPEC price was further reduced to $27. At the time, analysts were predicting that "oil prices [would] drop to as little as $20 per barrel, producers would be hurt, the banking system would be strained, and consumers would be helped."[27] Certain OPEC producers, like Nigeria, Iran, and Iraq, were indeed hurt by these lower prices and production quotas imposed by the organization. The $27 price held for a while because Saudi production was cut in half to a low of 3.7mbpd in 1983, effectively removing from the market 5 to 8mbpd of crude oil. Still, it was clear that no other oil producer in the non-Communist world could produce at 2.5mbpd for a long period of time without feeling serious economic consequences. "It is this ability to adjust production levels over such a broad range," opined one observer, that gave "Saudi Arabia its potential market power and [made] both producers and consumers of oil look to Riyadh and its oil policies with concern."[28] This ability to vary production rates with limited technical or financial consequences for Riyadh transformed the Kingdom into the main unofficial regulator of the oil industry. Accordingly, both OPEC and OAPEC sought the Saudi imprimatur in reaching common decisions. It was thus possible to speculate that Saudi Arabia's capacity to influence world petroleum policies extended to the petrochemical industries, as Riyadh's massive production of manufactured commodities reached world markets. Therefore, while consuming countries looked to the kingdom as a stabilizing force in world energy forums, producing states perceived Riyadh's policies with ambivalence. Moderation on prices and production rates were professed to be damaging factors in the policy formulations of the so-called militant states (Algeria, Iran and others). Conversely, Arab Gulf states with similar long-term interests sought Riyadh's guidance in the turbulence of the international economic and political arenas, which underscored the kingdom's power. However, since Saudi Arabia exercised a proportionately higher degree of control over the decision-making process in both OPEC and OAPEC, "militant" members opposed the kingdom's middle-of-the-road approach. The question then arose as to whether Saudi Arabia would allow its policies to be influenced by other OPEC or OAPEC members. In the event, and after a decade of rapid expansion, Saudi Arabia's oil policy aimed at consolidating its industrial potential. To achieve that goal, the kingdom pursued a moderate approach, permitting it to maintain a stable pricing structure and ensuring its customers in the industrialized world with adequate supplies.[29] As William B. Quandt determined, "the overall picture [of Saudi Arabia was] not that of a country aggressively bent on wielding the oil weapon to extort profits and political payoffs from the industrialized West."[30] On the contrary, Saudi policies, with respect to production and pricing, aimed at selling sufficient quantities of oil on the world market to generate enough revenues for the kingdom's socio-economic endeavors. If the best means to achieve these two goals was to operate within the OPEC and OAPEC forums, then there was little expectation that the Saudis would deviate from these paths. If, on the other hand, Saudis perceived that their goals were hampered by organizational constraints, chances were excellent that they would break away from the two bodies. OPEC and OAPEC members thus evaluated whether Saudi Arabia would voluntarily withdraw. Such options were very much on the table in 1983 as an oil crisis threatened to split OPEC in two camps.

After the mid-1980s, Arab Gulf producers perceived any destabilizing elements in the oil market as a threat to their long-term interests and, to prevent further crises, embarked on joint policies within the nascent Gulf Cooperation Council. Their common policies did not translate into unified negotiations with oil-importing states but allowed each country to defend its long-term financial interests without challenging those of their neighbors.

Quest for a common Gulf oil policy

Over the past few decades, OPEC and OAPEC were the main organizations through which Middle Eastern and especially Persian Gulf oil exporting countries exerted collective influence on world energy markets. Unlike OPEC's activities, OAPEC historically concentrated on technical operations and though it demonstrated a flair for industrial and commercial affairs, it also maintained a strong line in production and pricing of oil. As such, OAPEC set an example of cooperation for the GCC and, as the GCC co-ordinated economic integration, it was clear that with respect to petroleum it intended to unify its member-states' oil policies including those pertaining to "production, pricing, prospecting, gas exploitation, petrochemical industries, and downstream activities."[31] Still, the organization did not fully succeed in formulating a common multilateral policy capable of unifying different national political and economic interests although Riyadh insisted that such an initiative was critical. What prevented such an adoption were the significant influences exercised by major oil companies that preferred to deal with oil producing countries on a bilateral basis. GCC producers were challenged time and again as their dependence on a single source of income continued. It was only in the late 1990s and early 2000s that a more sustained diversification of resources added income to various treasuries. Saudi Arabia, in particular, managed to diversify its income and, starting in 2002, saw an estimated 40% of its GDP originating from non-petroleum sources.

An industrial power

A relatively complex economic structure emerged with the construction of major infrastructure systems starting in the late 1970s, when an industrial boom both private and public accelerated investments. Saudi Arabia's rush to development transformed in less than a decade a desert monarchy into a regional industrial power.[32] Two new industrial complexes, at Yanbu on the Red Sea and at Jubail on the Gulf, literally emerged from the sand.[33]

Yanbu, which was built with the partnership of the Mobil Oil Corporation, became an export center from where refined products were shipped overseas. Jubail produced petrochemicals ranging from methanol to ethane. In addition, Jubail was the site of a large steel mill and an aluminum plant. Remarkably, a two-pipeline system carrying oil and gas from the Eastern Province to Yanbu (1,250 kilometers) linked the two cities, supplying the Western complex with its needed industrial fuel. Whereas petrochemical production stood around 2m. tons in 1970, Yanbu and Jubail set the trend for steady growth, which meant that by 2010, the country was producing close to 60m. tons. These two examples of industrial projects illustrated how far the Saudi economy came in recent years. Several other projects, including the development of mineral resources—gold, copper, lead, zinc, silver and iron—all of which were readily and abundantly available in the kingdom, saw light. While the government encouraged private enterprise participation in developing new industries, Riyadh stressed the need to diversify its development aims, and seemed cognizant of the fact that only it, as the central authority, could implement such large-scale projects without necessarily limiting them to industry. Still, these preferences evolved over the years, as the Saudi government increasingly relied on the private sector. Even agriculture, a particularly sensitive area because of its reliance on scarce water supplies, witnessed dramatic changes. Riyadh's early appetite to produce wheat and other cash crops were gradually abandoned when it became clear that water must be preserved. Simply stated, there was not enough oil in Saudi Arabia to justify wasting a single drop of truly scarce water. Only the Asir Province received any rainfall and practically all of the kingdom's needs in water were met by its three dozen desalination plants.

Saudi Arabia's goal focused on the creation of jobs and increased economic activity to serve its young and growing population. No longer satisfied to simply export its petroleum resources, Riyadh aimed to transform hydrocarbon reserves into petrochemicals such as ethylene, which can earn higher returns. In 2010 Saudi Arabia was ranked tenth in terms of the production of petroleum derivatives, and seventh in terms of basic petrochemicals. By 2015 over 80 projects either in place or under development would, according to Minister of Petroleum and Mineral Resources Ali Al-Naimi, alter these rankings, making the kingdom the world's third-largest petrochemical producer.[34] By 2015 the kingdom was expected to hit the 100m. ton mark for petrochemical production, which would represent about 8% of global production. Riyadh maintained steady investments in this vital sector, which grew from a mere $500m. in the early 1980s, to an estimated $20bn in 2000, according to Al-Naimi.[35]

Jubail and Yanbu industrial cities proved to be resounding successes and established a range of support industries and infrastructure. Consequently, primary and secondary industries were created around them, which attracted international joint venture companies from America, Europe and Asia. It was as a direct result of these types of positive developments that Riyadh initiated work on Jubail Industrial City II (Jubail II), situated about three kilometers west of the existing city, and which will be developed over four stages with the Royal Commission assuming all costs for new infrastructure, including roads, utilities, gas, electricity, seawater cooling, potable water, waste water treatment, feedstock and a product pipeline corridor to King Fahd Industrial

Port. Even the port was under expansion, better to accommodate an expanded Saudi Aramco pipeline corridor that will link oilfields from Kuwait to Ras Tanura (KRT). There were many projects either under construction or planned for Jubail II, including the recently inaugurated Yanbu National Petrochemicals Co. (Yansab) with an annual production capacity of 4m. tons of petrochemicals, as well as new Saudi Arabian Basic Industries Corporation (SABIC) expansion projects to generate 500 megawatts of power, among others.

Conclusion

The Persian Gulf region is estimated to contain between 65 and 70% of the world's oil reserves, of which large chunks are in Saudi Arabia. Likewise, the area is home to significant gas deposits, with entire sections of the desert still unexplored. Equally important, demand for oil and gas resources is slated to increase over the coming years, because of the massive expansion of Chinese, Indian and other emerging economies, with steady consumption in industrialized countries. Clearly, China and India are poised to embark on massive industrialization schemes, which will require additional energy supplies. Needless to say, most of this capacity will only be met by Gulf producers, especially those in the Kingdom of Saudi Arabia, which are unique because of the sheer volume of proven reserves.[36] Major powers with deep-water exploration capabilities are already investing in the Arctic although costs are still prohibitive. For the foreseeable future, therefore, few alternatives to the Arab Gulf producers, especially Saudi Arabia, exist.

Notes

1 For a discussion on the early history of the Persian Gulf region, see Roger M. Savory, "The Ancient Period," in Alvin J. Cottrell, ed., *The Persian Gulf States: A General Survey*, Baltimore: The Johns Hopkins University Press, 1980, pp. 3–13.
2 Public Affairs Department, *Middle East Oil, A Background Paper*, 2nd ed., New York: Exxon Corporation, September 1980, p. 26.
3 William B. Quandt, *Saudi Arabia's Oil Policy*, Washington, D.C.: The Brookings Institution, 1982, p. 15.
4 Ibid., p. 16.
5 Ibid., p. 15; the price increase agreed to by Saudi Arabia and the UAE in fact limited the total increase to 10% instead of the 15% advocated by other OPEC members. See also Nawaf E. Obaid, *The Oil Kingdom at 100: Petroleum Policymaking in Saudi Arabia*, Washington, D.C.: The Washington Institute for Near East Policy, 2000.
6 OAPEC, which is often confused with OPEC, was established on 9 January 1968 in Beirut, Lebanon by three Arab countries: Saudi Arabia, Kuwait, and Libya. According to the 1968 founding charter, OAPEC's principle objective was to facilitate the closest cooperation among member states, particularly within the petroleum industry (Article 2). This objective emanated from a desire to "depoliticize" the oil industry within OPEC, and especially the League of Arab States, which were highly mobilized at the time. While OAPEC welcomed several new members after 1970, often with incompatible political and economic systems, it could not completely divorce its proceedings from regional political tensions. This was best illustrated by its devastating actions in 1973. For a complete discussion, see Abdelkader Maachou, *L'OPAEP et le Pétrole Arabe: Organisation Internationale de Coopération Économique et Instrument d'Intégration Régionale*, Paris: Berger-Levrault, 1982. For a discussion on the use of oil as a political weapon, see William R. Brown, "The Oil Weapon," *The Middle East Journal* 36:3, Summer 1982, pp. 301–18.
7 Peter Mansfield, *The New Arabians*, Chicago: Ferguson Publishing Company, 1981, p. 193. See also, *Saudi Arabia and the United States: The New Context in an Evolving "Special Relationship,"* A Report prepared for the Subcommittee on Europe and the Middle East of the Committee on Foreign Affairs, US House of Representatives, 97th Congress, 1st Session, Washington, D.C.: August 1981, pp. 26–33.

8 "Global Oil Consumption," US Energy Information Administration, at http://www.eia.doe.gov/pub/oil_gas/petroleum/analysis_publications/oil_market_basics/demand_text.htm.
9 *BP Statistical Review of World Energy 2010*, at www.bp.com/productlanding.do?categoryId=6929&contentId = 7044622.
10 Walter J. Levy, "Oil and the Decline of the West," *Foreign Affairs* 58:5, Summer 1980, pp. 999–1015. See also Arthur Ross, "OPEC's Challenge to the West," *The Washington Quarterly* 3:1, Winter 1980, pp. 50–57.
11 For the 1984 data, see "Despite Capacity Surplus, World Oil Flow, Reserves Climb; Refining Capacity Drops," *Oil and Gas Journal* 85:52, 31 December 1984, pp. 77–114. For the 2009 figure, see the BP Statistical Review of World Energy 2010, op. cit., at www.bp.com/sectiongenericarticle.do?categoryId=9023769& contentId = 7044915. It may be useful to note that BP estimated the 2009 oil reserves at 1333.1bn barrels for its overall global proven oil reserves, with specific increases in Brazil, Denmark, Saudi Arabia, Egypt, and Indonesia that outpaced declines in Mexico, Russia, Norway, and Vietnam.
12 "Saudi Arabia," US Energy Information Administration, November 2009, at www.eia.doe.gov/cabs/Saudi_Arabia/Profile.html.
13 In 1983, demand for refined products within OPEC countries stood at a mere 2.8 mbpd, "World Consumption of Refined Products by Regions," 1963–83, *Annual Statistical Bulletin-1983*, Vienna, Austria: OPEC, 1984, pp. 14–23.
14 *World Oil Outlook 2009*, Vienna, Austria: OPEC, 2010, p. 51.
15 Office of Technology Assessment, *World Petroleum Availability, 1980–2000: A Technical Memorandum*, Washington, D.C.: US Congress, October 1980, p. 57.
16 David Luhnow, "Mexico Tries to Save a Big, Fading Oil Field: Cantarell's Drop-Off Faster Than Expected; Turning to Technology," *The Wall Street Journal*, 5 April 2007, at http://online.wsj.com/article/SB117570687954959825.html?mod=hps_us_pageone. In 2008 Mexican daily production stood at 3.71mbpd.
17 "Is the North Sea Oil Production Bonanza Approaching Twilight" 24 February 2010, http://oilprice.com/Energy/Crude-Oil/Is-the-North-Sea-Oil-Production-Bonanza-Approaching-Twilight.html.
18 Quandt, op. cit., p. 1.
19 Obaid, op. cit., pp. 50–65. See also Anthony H. Cordesman, *Saudi Arabia Enters the 21st Century: The Political, Foreign Policy, Economic and Energy Dimensions*, Westport, Connecticut: Praeger, 2003, pp. 400–410.
20 *World Development Report 1983*, Washington, D.C.: The World Bank, 1984, p. 152. The 1976 and 1977 figures are from the Report's 1982 and 1983 editions.
21 "Saudi Arabia," *World Development Indicators*, Washington, D.C.: The World Bank, September 2010, at http://data.worldbank.org/data-catalog/world-development-indicators?cid=GPD_WDI.
22 Arab Institutions Provide Development Finance; Supplement Capital Flows to Developing Nations, *IMF Survey* 12:6, March 21, 1983, pp. 85–87.
23 Ragaei El-Mallakh, *Saudi Arabia: Rush to Development*, Baltimore: The Johns Hopkins University Press, 1982, pp. 367–402.
24 Jad Mouawad, "Plan Would Lift Saudi Oil Output," *The New York Times*, 14 June 2008, at www.nytimes.com/2008/06/14/business/14oil.html.
25 Japan's daily imports of oil stood at 4.2mbpd, of which over 30% originated in Saudi Arabia. See Japan Finance Corporation, "Most Resources Consumed in Japan are Coming from Overseas," Tokyo: Japan Bank for International Cooperation, accessed on 23 October 2010, at www.jbic.go.jp/en/special/resource/001/index.html.
26 "Saudi Arabia: Oil Exports and Shipping," US Energy Information Administration, November 2009, at www.eia.doe.gov/cabs/Saudi_Arabia/OilExports.html.
27 David K. Willis, "Developing Oil Prices: Who Wins, Who Loses in World Economies," *The Christian Science Monitor*, 9 March 1983, p. 3; see also "And Now—$29 per Barrel" (editorial), *The Christian Science Monitor*, 15 March 1983, p. 24.
28 Quandt, op. cit., p. 4.
29 Zubair Iqbal, "Saudi Policy Aims at Consolidating After a Decade of Rapid Expansion," *IMF Survey* 12:22, 21 November 1983, pp. 357, 366–68.
30 Quandt, op. cit., p. 1.
31 "Gulf Council Oil Ministers Meeting in Riyadh," *FBIS-V-MEA—82–021*, 1 February 1982, p. C1.
32 Robert E. Looney, *Saudi Arabia's Development Potential*, Lexington, Massachusetts: Lexington Books, 1982.

33 El Mallakh, op. cit., pp. 129–36. The construction of Yanbu and Jubail came under severe criticisms at the time when Western analysts labeled the projects as being "economically unjustifiable." Somehow, Saudi Arabia would be wasting its resources by investing at home, advice that was routinely ignored. For a good illustration of this point, see Claude Feuillet, *Le Système Saoud: Après l'Iran, l'Arabie?* Lausanne, Switzerland: Editions Pierre-Marcel Favre, 1983, pp. 9–14. Needless to say, Riyadh accelerated its investments manyfold and embarked on the construction of industrial power plants, research universities and critical pipeline systems—all well protected—to further enhance its economic might.

34 Siraj Wahad, "Saudi Goal: To be a Leading Petrochemical Producer", *Arab News*, 10 October, 2010 at http://arabnews.com/economy/article157802.ece.

35 Ibid.

36 Siraj Wahab, "Demand for Oil Will Only Grow, Say Experts," *Arab News*, 10 October 2010, at http://arabnews.com/economy/article158407.ece.

21

Gas and Oil in Egypt's Development

Robert Springborg

Egypt's economy is not typically described as being driven, or even heavily influenced, by hydrocarbons. This is due in part to the hydrocarbon-rich company Egypt keeps in the MENA (Middle East and North Africa), a region in which fully three-quarters of merchandise exports in 2007 were comprised of oil or gas.[1] That is five times the average for lower-middle income countries globally, and seven and a half times the global average of 10%.[2] In that year, Egypt's exports of oil and gas comprised 52% of the country's total merchandise exports, thus placing it much closer to the MENA average than to that for lower middle income countries as a whole. Moreover, Egypt's export dependence on oil and gas has increased more rapidly than has the MENA's or that for lower and middle income countries globally. Between 1995 and 2007 the share of oil and gas in Egypt's total merchandise trade rose from 37% to 52%, whereas that for the MENA rose by only 3 percentage points and that for lower and middle income countries just four. For the two decades ending in 2006, hydrocarbon exports have contributed between one-fifth and one-quarter of total government revenue, either through tax payments or direct non-tax transfers.[3] Egypt, in sum, is by world standards heavily and increasingly dependent upon hydrocarbons as the dominant source of export earnings and government revenues.

The Egyptian economy's direct reliance on oil and gas constitutes, moreover, only part of its hydrocarbon dependence. Indirect economic impacts through its various relationships with other MENA hydrocarbon exporters, especially those in the Gulf, provide the second of the twin pillars of the economy. Travel and transport in 2007 constituted almost 83% of trade in services, which in turn made up more than one-quarter of GDP. Virtually the entirety of travel income was derived from tourism, to which visitors from the Gulf contributed approximately one-half. Suez Canal earnings, based primarily on shipment of oil from and goods into the Gulf, makes up the vast bulk of transport income. The $7.7bn of workers' remittances contributed almost 6% of GDP in 2007 and again, those earnings are predominantly generated from the Gulf. Direct and indirect contributions of hydrocarbons to Egypt's GDP thus dwarf all other sources. One-sixth, or some 17% of GDP is derived from oil and gas exports; another 15 to 20% from hydrocarbon related services; and say 5% from Gulf sourced remittances, taking the total to around 40% of GDP. In addition, foreign direct investment (FDI) in Egypt rose in tandem with the Third Great Oil Boom of 2003–8, ballooning in that period from $200m. to $11.2bn, with the Gulf's contribution generally estimated to be about one-half. Taken together, these direct and indirect hydrocarbon earnings render the Egyptian economy's dependence on oil and gas something like one-half to two-thirds of that of the major MENA oil exporters, where oil and gas account for some 90% of export earnings and 80% of government revenues. But Egypt's hydrocarbon dependence, as a result of both production and price increases, is much above the level of most lower-middle income countries.

Just as the general importance of hydrocarbons, including the impacts of those exported by other MENA producers, has been given insufficient attention in analyses of the Egyptian economy,[4] so has the rising importance of the production and export of natural gas. Gas production expanded from 14bn cubic meters (bcm) in 1998 to 55bcm in 2007. It is anticipated that it will reach 80bcm in 2011.[5] Egypt contributed 8.8% of the MENA's gas production in 2006, a ratio expected to rise to almost 10% in 2011.[6] By 2008 its share of world's gas production was 1.9%.[7] Its domestic consumption increased 10.8% annually after 2000, the fastest growth rate in the MENA region.[8] A year earlier, when LNG export complexes on the country's Mediterranean coast had become fully operational, Egypt had become the world's sixth-largest exporter of that commodity, placing it above such petro-states as Oman and the United Arab Emirates and at almost two-thirds the level of exports of gas-rich Algeria.[9] Three years before that, in July 2003, Egypt's pipeline to the Levant, at that time terminating in Jordan, had become operational, thereby making Egypt a major supplier to rapidly growing MENA markets. Egypt, in other words, is a player in the world's big league of gas producers and exporters.

The rapid expansion of the gas industry was fortuitous, for it substituted for the decline in oil output that was occurring as energy consumption escalated. From a high of 922,000 barrels per day production in 1996, oil production has slid to some 700,000 barrels per day and is anticipated to fall to some 600,000 barrels per day by 2011 and remain at that level through 2018, despite a recent small increase from 3.7 to 4.1bn barrels of proven reserves.[10] According to a leading source on hydrocarbons, Egypt's prospects for oil production growth are the least favorable in the MENA region.[11] Domestic energy demand has been increasing at some 8% per annum since 1998. Consumption of oil products increased by almost 600% between 1971 and 2006, resulting in domestic demand for oil outstripping supply, with a tripling (from 5 to 15%) from 2001 to 2007 in the share of oil imports of the total of merchandise imports.[12] Egypt's total energy production, however, thanks to the rapid increase in the gas sector, remained more or less flat at some 60 kt of oil equivalent from 1992/93 through 2001, when it commenced a rise to almost 80 kilotons by 2006.[13]

Given these dramatic increases in gas production and export, combined with Egypt's increasing integration not only into the MENA energy economy, but also into the region's distribution and export systems, it should come as no surprise that "Egypt is repositioning itself to be one of the biggest energy hubs in the world."[14] The physical bases that would constitute that hub are the Suez Canal, whose already important role in oil transport will be augmented by its growing importance in LNG shipments; the Sumed (Suez-Mediterranean) pipeline; pipelines linking Egypt to Israel and Jordan and through the latter, Syria, Lebanon and possibly on to Europe; integration of Egypt's electrical grid, which is already connected to Syria and Jordan, with those of the Gulf and North and even East Africa; and finally, gas shipments to Europe, North America and ultimately maybe other markets from Egypt's existing LNG trains in Damietta, Idku and Port Said, and possibly a fourth at some later date. Dreams of becoming an "energy superpower" have been encouraged by statements of the former Minister of Petroleum and Mineral Resources, Samih Fahmi.[15] He estimated in 2007 that Egypt's oil and gas sector would attract $20bn in foreign investment by 2012 and that the country's proven and probable reserves of gas are 70 trillion cubic feet (tcf), with another 100–120 tcf of unproven reserves.[16]

Fahmi was a strong proponent of expansion of the gas industry downstream into petrochemicals. His response in early 2010 to a parliamentary committee that expressed concerns about gas supply shortages was to say that his ministry is studying importing gas from "neighboring countries."[17] Egypt, in sum, appears to have great hopes that energy, both that produced in the country and that transported to and through it, will serve as the principal engine of growth for its economy. Whether this is a realistic and appropriate ambition is a matter that will be taken up after first assessing the present impacts of the energy sector, and especially gas, on the country's economy and politics.

Economic Impacts

Hydrocarbons have been both an economic blessing and curse for Egypt. The oil and gas industries attracted $9.5bn of FDI between 2000 and 2005, a figure that was predicted to more than double in the following five years, although that rosy forecast is unlikely to be realized.[18] The rapid development of the gas industry made possible by that investment underpinned the growth of overall energy production from some 10 kilotons (kt of oil equivalent) to almost 80kt by 2006.[19] This growth in turn made possible extensive downstream development. A national gas grid is nearing completion, contributing substantially to one of the world's higher rates of growth of energy use, which rose from less than 10kt of oil equivalent in 1971 to over 60kt in 2006 and on a per capita basis from 200 kilograms of oil equivalent to 800 over the same period.[20] Both the aggregate and per capita growth rates are well above those in OECD countries and about at the level of China. Since 2000 Egypt has had the fastest rate of growth of demand for gas in the MENA at almost 11% per annum, although consumption per head remains low by MENA standards, being about one-fifth of that in Saudi Arabia and one-half of that in Iran.[21] Rapid growth of energy consumption has been associated with a steady, steep rise in electricity generation as new gas fired plants have been brought on-stream. Three-quarters of the country's electricity needs are now met by gas-fired stations, compared to about one-quarter in the USA.[22] The combination of a countrywide gas distribution network and expansion of electricity generation underpins the anticipated doubling of domestic gas consumption from 26.2 to 53.3m. cubic meters between 2004 and 2013.[23] Availability of energy, in sum, has increasingly been shaping the Egyptian economy, including strategic investment choices.

Downstream there are numerous signs of expanding value added production. In 2007 the government announced its master plan for the petrochemical industry, which called for 20 major facilities by 2022.[24] The first phase of multi-tiered vertical integration of that industry was scheduled to be completed in 2010, with the construction of a polystyrene plant that will receive styrene feedstocks from the Sidi Khreir Company's plant on the Mediterranean coast.[25] By 2004 chemicals and "other manufactures," the great majority of which were of an energy intensive nature, accounted for more than 60% of total manufactures, as the share of food and beverages, clothing and textiles, and machinery and transport equipment continued to fall, as they have done since that time. Iron and steel exports, heavily dependent upon inexpensive energy, quadrupled from 2003 to 2007. Since 2000 petrochemicals and fertilizer have been the two fastest growing components of the manufacturing sector. Cement exports grew by 237% in the first five years of the 21st century.[26] In sum, Egyptian industry is increasingly reliant on downstream hydrocarbon processing and on manufactures, such as iron and steel, fertilizer, cement and ceramics, for which energy is a or the major input cost.

The prospects of success for gas-fired development depend on the upstream and downstream components of the gas industry, its impacts on macroeconomic policy, and its relationships with other sectors of the national economy. The most vital issues in the assessment of the gas industry itself are the quantity of the resource that can be recovered and the international price for it. On both these measures there are causes for concern about possible Egyptian over-reliance on gas to drive its development. Proven reserves were estimated in 2008 to be almost 73 trillion cubic feet (tcf), with the government claiming an additional 100–120 tcf of "unproven reserves."[27] This claim, in addition to the government's official reckoning that another 30tcf of proven and probable reserves will be added by the end of 2011, raises eyebrows in the gas industry.[28] In addition to doubts about the claimed magnitude of reserves, oil professionals point out that more than three-quarters of Egypt's gas is located under the Mediterranean, much at considerable depth, thereby incurring high extraction costs.[29] Some analysts, including those in major international companies, believe that Egypt will not be able to meet rising domestic demand and service existing export contracts.[30]

Increasing concern about the magnitude of gas reserves, their utilization, and the rubbery nature of relevant government data is manifested by independent Egyptian analysts. Among the apparent contradictions frequently noted is that between the stated government policy of allocating a third for local consumption, a third for export and a third for "future generations," on the one hand, and the fact that some 60% of gas produced is consumed domestically for electricity generation. Much of that gas has to be purchased from the international companies whose exploration and development of Egypt's gas on the basis of production sharing agreements has entitled them to about one-half of total production and a similar claim on reserves, thereby reducing reserves "owned" by Egypt to not more than 35–40tcf.[31] Since Egypt purchases its extra requirements directly from the producing foreign companies, these amounts do not show up as imports on national accounts. Egypt's actual energy balance is thus considerably less favorable than those accounts suggest.[32] As for the government's contention that one-third of reserves is being allocated to future generations, independent Egyptian commentators see no evidence of this.[33] In sum, Egypt has gambled on its gas reserves being sufficient to sustain its domestic development of both petrochemical and energy intensive industries; to service rapidly rising domestic consumer energy demand; to pay-off its foreign exploration and development partner companies; and to export gas on its own account. This last need is particularly vital for balance of payment support and provision of government revenues in the face of persisting budgetary deficits, which have driven public debt to more than 70% of GDP. It is safe to say that very few independent analysts believe there are sufficient gas reserves to meet these competing demands. Shortages are already manifest, thus requiring a governmental juggling act which may account for the general lack of transparency that surrounds information on the production and utilization of gas and oil.

The supply challenge is paralleled by price-related issues, including national price setting and potential long-term price stagnation as global gas production soars, delinking its price from that of oil.[34] The Egyptian government, faced with a variety of competing interests, has encountered difficulty in balancing them when setting gas prices. Its desire to attract foreign financial and operational partners into upstream development requires prices at international levels, whereas its needs for domestic consumption, exacerbated by subsidies, push its price interests in the opposite direction. As the supply squeeze has intensified and as the cumbersome price setting mechanism has not responded sufficiently rapidly to fluctuating international price levels, Egypt has alienated in various degrees international companies on which its upstream development depends. Some have responded by delaying investments and operations.[35] Alleged inefficiencies of the upstream sector and the comparatively limited number of companies involved in it are commonly attributed to price policy problems.[36] Of great political sensitivity has been the price for gas delivered to Israel since the opening of the pipeline in 2008, with critics arguing that it has been too low. The Ministry of Petroleum was dragged into court over the issue.

Hanging over these competing demands is the long-term price for gas, which since 2008 has been on a downward trajectory relative to oil and even other commodities.[37] If this trend continues, it would relieve some budgetary pressure as a result of subsidization of domestic gas consumption, but would also reduce government export revenues while undermining the competitiveness of gas dependent exports, such as petrochemicals, fertilizer, cement, and iron and steel. If in the wake of the global recession gas prices fail to appreciate in tandem with prices for other goods and services, Egypt's gas-fired development strategy will encounter major challenges.

Negative macroeconomic consequences and deleterious cross-sectoral impacts of gas-fired development include manifestations of the Dutch Disease, distortions caused by subsidies, and inadequate employment generation. Of these problems, the Dutch Disease is the most problematical. Its presence is attested to by the correlation between the value of the currency, on the one hand, and hydrocarbon production and exports, on the other. Pressure on the fixed rate Egyptian Pound in the late 1990s ultimately led to a devaluation of almost 50% and a partial float in 2001–2. The black market rate for the pound had reached almost eight to the dollar. Interestingly, 2001 was precisely the year in which total energy production, which had been more or less stable since 1991 as oil production deteriorated and gas production began to accelerate, started to rapidly escalate, going from 50,000 kilotons of oil equivalent (ktoe) to almost 80,000ktoe by 2006.[38] The currency, after sagging in the wake of the partial float, began to appreciate virtually in lock step with the expansion of the hydrocarbon sector from 2003. From around 6 to the dollar in 2004 and 2005, it then began to steadily outperform the dollar, rising to some 5.4 to the dollar by early 2010, by which time the dollar had already regained much of its lost ground against the Euro and other currencies. In sum, Egypt's currency was one of the world's better performers in the first decade of the 21st century, causing an IMF official to observe that "real appreciation pressures … may be costly in terms of growth."[39]

The resulting price inflation of Egypt's own tradable goods contributed to the deterioration of the quantity and quality of its manufactured exports during this period. As a percentage of exports they fell from an average of 38.5% between 1997 and 2001, to 18.6% in 2007, which is just slightly more than one-half of the 20-year average 1987–2006.[40] Manufactured goods' contribution to exports, in short, was almost halved in the last two decades. Egypt's merchandise trade as a percentage of GDP fell from 36.8% in 1990 to 33.2% in 2007.[41] As for tradable goods in general, between 1995 and 2007 food fell from 8 to 6% of exports, agricultural raw materials from 6 to 2%, ores and metals from 6 to 3%, and manufactures from 40 to 19%. The only category of exports that increased its share was fuels, which rose from 37 to 52%.[42] By comparison, lower-middle income countries in that same period on average increased the share of manufactures in their exports from 66 to 68%.[43]

Manufacturing for domestic consumption has probably also been affected by the Dutch Disease. Although manufacturing value added per capita rose from $265 to $281 between 2000 and 2006, that was the slowest rate of increase across a range of comparator countries used by UNIDO, including Turkey, Indonesia, India, Peru, the Philippines and Latvia.[44] Manufacturing's share of GDP fell by 1%, from 17 to 16%, from 1995 to 2007.[45] As for the composition of manufactured goods, the percentage of manufactured exports comprised by high-technology products, as reported by the World Bank, which had reached a historic high of 0.8% in 2002, low even by MENA standards, began a decline in that year that reduced it to 0.2% in 2007.[46] According to UNCTAD, which uses a different definition of high technology goods, exports of them rose from 0.3% of total exports in 1985 to 1.3% in 2005, the lowest overall percentage and the smallest rate of increase among all comparator countries, including Turkey, Morocco, Jordan and Tunisia, which by 2005 achieved an average rate of high-tech manufactures comprising some 14% of their total exports.⁴⁷ According to an IMF report, "Egypt's revealed comparative advantage remains 'stuck' with resource-based (textile and clothing, agro processing, and petro-based) rather than skill-intensive or innovation-intensive products."⁴⁸

Yet other symptoms of Dutch Disease have been the prevailing, overall inflation rate and the rapid rise of asset values, especially real estate. The consumer price index, which revealed an inflation rate of around 2% from the late 1990s until the onset of the "gas boom" in 2003, escalated first to 4.5% and finally to over 18% in 2008. By comparison, hydrocarbon-poor Tunisia's inflation rate averaged over that whole period around 3% and never exceeded 5%.⁴⁹ Prices for real estate, both urban and rural, rose yet more rapidly than the consumer price index.

In sum, gas-fired growth has brought on at least a moderate case of Dutch Disease, with its usual negative consequences for the production and export of tradable goods, and for inflation. Egypt's decreasing economic competitiveness as reflected by its ranking on the World Economic Forum's Global Competitiveness Index, which fell from 50 in 2005/06 to 70 in 2009/10, also results in part from side effects of the Dutch Disease.⁵⁰ The overall measure of the country's economic health, which is the rate of growth of GDP per capita, certainly suggests the presence of a malady. Real per capita GDP grew at an annual rate of only 1.7% between 2001 and 2005, compared to a developing country average of 5.1%. In the MENA during the period, Turkey's real per capita GDP grew by 2.9% annually, Morocco's by 3%, Tunisia's by 3.3% and Jordan's by 3.5%.⁵¹

Energy subsidies, which result in energy prices being "among the lowest in the world,"⁵² in addition to having negative budgetary consequences and causing inefficient energy use, have distorted patterns of productive investments. The magnitude of price distortion for energy resulting from government subsidies is suggested by the per liter price for gasoline and diesel fuel, the former of which remained constant at $0.30 from 1991 to 2006 before rising to $0.50 in 2007/08. The latter followed the same trajectory over that period, rising finally in 2007/08 to $0.20 per liter compared to the $0.10 it had been for the previous 16 years.⁵³ In 2005/06 energy subsidies already totaled $7bn, but they continued their upward climb from that lofty height, reaching $11.6bn in 2007/08, or a staggering 7.2% of GDP.⁵⁴ The government's announcement of reductions in energy subsidies in the spring of 2008 was met with howls of protest, with the voices of energy intensive manufacturers apparently being the most effective. Within weeks the declared price increases were rescinded. Subsidies and transfers, which had consumed 6% of the central government's budget in 1995, accounted for 39% of expenditures by 2007, as compared to 32% for the subsidy-rich MENA as a whole.⁵⁵ Of this 39%, almost three-quarters is attributed to energy subsidies, excluding electricity, which is also heavily subsidized.⁵⁶ The inexorable and steeply rising upward trend of subsidies and transfers is revealed yet more starkly if counted in Egyptian Pounds, as they rose from some 3.25bn in 1991, to 24.5bn in 2002, to 39bn in 2005 before blowing out to a huge 86bn in the following two years.⁵⁷ As just stated, the overwhelming share of these subsidies and transfers is comprised of energy subsidies, which alone consume almost one-quarter of government expenditures. Not surprising then is the fact that fuel subsidies as a percentage of GDP are higher than in all World Bank comparator countries, which include, among others, Jordan, Yemen, Indonesia, and Nigeria.⁵⁸

Since energy is so cheap, its use in production is comparatively inefficient. By the standard measure of oil intensity in production, which is defined as the number of barrels of oil required to produce $1,000 of GDP, Egypt is about one-third as efficient as Indonesia and about one-half as efficient as Brazil, Nigeria, India, China or South Korea.⁵⁹ Moreover, Egypt's energy efficiency is in decline. Based on the World Bank's measure of GDP produced in constant 2005 dollars of purchasing power parity for every kilogram of oil equivalent used, GDP output fell from almost $7 in 1980 to some $5.50 in 2006.[60] As a consequence of energy subsidies, rising energy prices, inefficient energy utilization and capacity limits on Egyptian energy production, especially of oil, Egypt has to import steadily more fuel. Its fuel imports as a percentage of merchandise imports rose from around 2% in the mid 1990s to an average of 15% in 2006 and 2007.[61] It is thus paradoxical, although not unique among energy exporters, including Iran, that Egypt's gas-fired development is associated with it having to allocate an ever greater share of its import budget to energy.

Also related to the strategy of gas-fired development is Egypt's chronic unemployment problem, which abated somewhat during the Third Great Oil Boom (2003–8), dropping officially to some 10%, a figure probably 50% below the actual rate.[62] Precise figures of those employed in the gas industry are unavailable. Since it is a newer and yet more capital intensive industry than oil, and one in which international companies play a still greater role, the number of those employed in the gas industry is probably less than that in its oil equivalent. In 2004 the upstream oil industry employed 33,000 Egyptians, the downstream an additional 30,000.[63] At that time Egypt's labor force was some 19m. strong, suggesting that the oil and gas industries combined, employing probably a few more than 100,000, did not account for more than half of one percent of the labor force. Of course employment growth has occurred further downstream, especially in energy intensive industries, such as in cement, iron and steel, fertilizer and ceramics, but even those industries are considerably less labor intensive than more sophisticated manufacturing, such as electronics, and are far less labor intensive than the garment and textile industry, which virtually throughout the Mubarak era has been estimated to employ some 1m. workers. But that industry's share of value added in manufacturing is low and declining, having fallen from 16% in 1998 to 10% in 2002, sliding slowly further downward since then.[64] Its failure to grow is due in considerable measure to the fact that it remains the most tariff protected industry in Egypt, so remains remarkably inward looking, hence non-competitive in European and North American markets, even when compared to MENA countries such as Morocco, Tunisia and Jordan, to say nothing of league leading China. But tariff protection and general lack of focus on the traditional garment and textile industry, including inadequate capital investment, is due in some measure to the relative attraction of alternatives made possible by the gas-fired development model. Moreover, the Dutch Disease has contributed substantially to price non-competitiveness of Egyptian garments and textiles, even in the protected domestic market.

The oil and gas industries, in sum, are not significant employers in their own right, but do generate employment in energy intensive industries. Against those gains, however, actual losses and opportunity costs for employment in other industries, especially garments and textiles, have to be offset. Labor force statistics reveal that the leading growth sectors are construction, tourism and services more generally, with some two-thirds of new jobs being created in the informal sector.[65] This, in turn, suggests that the gas-fired development model is not propelling the economy so that it is generating large numbers of increasingly productive, remunerative jobs, as is suggested by both low labor productivity and total factor productivity. In the MENA region only Yemen and Syria have lower labor productivity than Egypt, whose score on that measure is less than 30% of Brazil's and only some three-quarters of the MENA labor productivity average.[66] Egypt's total factor productivity (TFP)—the measure of its capacity to manage the factors of production—closely parallels the low rate of growth and absolute level of labor productivity. Its TFP is less than 40% of Brazil's and is only some four-fifths of the MENA average. And again, the only MENA countries that perform less well on this measure are Yemen and Syria.[67] GDP growth in the boom years 2003–8, which peaked at almost 8% in 2007, resulted from increased capital and labor inputs, not from improved productivity. Such factor-driven growth is particularly precarious, dependent as it is on investment capital, which in turn must be provided primarily by external sources given the low rates of domestic savings resulting in part from low labor productivity and low TFP. Continuation of the Great Recession that commenced in 2008, which has substantially reduced both FDI and portfolio investment into Egypt, thus poses a major challenge to employment and growth.

One of the arguments put forward in support of capital intensive, energy led development, is that its overall management enhances general governmental capabilities, while the hydrocarbon industries themselves create models of management and capital use efficiency that can be generalized to other sectors. One of the cases cited in support of this contention is that of the Saudi government and Saudi Aramco, the former of which has recently been compared to "developmental" states of East Asia, and the latter of which is not only one of the world's most efficient national oil companies, but one whose management and organization has had spillover effects on the Saudi economy.[68] In Egypt, however, there is little evidence of such beneficial impacts. If anything, the record suggests flawed governmental management of the sector and a comparatively poor record of development of capacities of public and private sector firms within it.

Overall management of the hydrocarbon sector suffers from lack of transparency, which in turn undermines governmental credibility both domestically and internationally. Claims for gas reserves that appear to be unduly optimistic, such as that by then petroleum minister Fahmy for 100–120 tcf of "unproven reserves," are greeted with skepticism. One authoritative source notes that "there are concerns about what the numbers actually represent," and that "inflated reserve figures do nothing to solve the problem of the imbalance between gas supply and demand in the country."[69] Even production figures are ambiguous. Ramadan Abul Ela, professor of petroleum engineering at Alexandria University and a former member of the lower house of parliament, finds that "the volume of Egypt's production of natural gas is a mystery. No one knows for sure the volume of that production."[70] Officially proclaimed ambitions of the 20-year, three-phase petrochemical master-plan that by 2022 is to attract $10bn in investment and result in 24 petrochemical plants in 14 industrial complexes, are greeted with considerable doubt.[71] "The case for Egypt as a significant petrochemicals player has yet to be made convincingly," according to international authorities on the subject.[72]

Skepticism about both gas reserves and the pace of development of downstream industries has intermittently been reinforced by events that have proved embarrassing to the government. Postponement of a planned additional LNG train by potential investors due to concerns about supply, triggered in part by chronic undersupply to one of the existing trains, was one such event.[73] So, too, was the admission in January 2010 by then minister Fahmy that no more export contracts could be concluded before 2011 because there was insufficient gas to cover needs in the domestic market.[74] Shortly thereafter he revealed that the Energy Committee of the ruling National Democratic Party had suggested that he investigate importing gas from neighboring countries.[75] The entire downstream development plan was placed in limbo in 2008 as a result of a decision to cease construction of the $1.4bn petrochemical plant at Ras al Barr, which was then more than 40% complete with more than $500m. having been invested.[76]

Lack of predictability, flexibility and transparency with regard to pricing has also marred the government's reputation for management of the gas sector with both international and domestic audiences. Unwillingness to raise prices for the government's share of gas produced on the basis of production sharing agreements as international prices skyrocketed after 2003 caused several international oil companies to delay initial or additional investments.[77] A new 20% tax on companies in free zones caused a proposed Kuwaiti-Egyptian joint venture $2.2bn petrochemical plant at Ain al Sukhna to be abandoned.[78] Much more controversial was the 2006 decision to export gas to Israel for 15 years via an Egyptian–Israeli public/private consortium at an apparent price of $2.75 per million British thermal units. Within months of gas exports commencing an Egyptian court ruled in 2008 that exports be stopped pending clarification of pricing issues, a decision which the government of Egypt ignored.[79] The issue became a cause célèbre in Egypt not only because gas exports were continued during Israel's "Operation Cast Lead" in Gaza in December–January 2009, but because in the following winter the country was stricken with a shortage of butane cylinders upon which consumers without piped gas rely. Investigations by various sources, including Amr Hamouda of the Fustat Studies Center, revealed that Egypt was paying more for imports to produce the butane than it was receiving from Israel for the gas it was exporting.[80] Ibrahim Zahran, former chairman of Khalda Petroleum Company, asked rhetorically, "What is the exact price for selling gas to Israel? How much profit does Egypt make out of it? Unless the petroleum sector is transparent about these issues we will continue to believe that their talk is for media consumption."[81] Following the "January 25 revolution" of 2011, the gas pipeline through the Sinai linking Egypt and Israel was blown up four times.

If management of the capital intensive hydrocarbon sector were to have favorably impacted governance capacities generally, it might be reflected in relevant measures of that concept. There is limited evidence that this could be the case. Despite a steady decline along the World Bank's dimension of Voice and Accountability from 1998 to 2008, Egypt did improve its ranking on government effectiveness and regulatory quality and by 2008 was slightly outperforming the average for lower middle income countries.[82] On the other hand, there was no change in the rule of law dimension over that period, while the control of corruption declined from a percentile ranking of almost 50 to one below 30.[83] On this corruption measure Egypt by 2008 was substantially below the average for lower middle income countries. As for the broader measure of ease of doing business, Egypt demonstrated some improvement in the twenty-first century, but by 2008 its score was still less than half the MENA average and well below that for even Iran and Syria.[84] On the critical measure of ease of enforcing contracts, Egypt in 2009 ranked 148th, with only Syria in the MENA ranking lower.[85]

Governance in Egypt, in sum, as measured by the relatively narrow effectiveness and regulatory dimensions, has improved, a result which might be partially attributable to coping with the complexities and international requirements of the hydrocarbon industry. But so, too, the perceived increase in corruption and declining accountability of government are also frequently associated with hydrocarbon rents. And the government has clearly not succeeded in transforming the business environment, so on balance the case for improved governance resulting at least in part from managing the hydrocarbon sector does not seem to hold. Possibly reflecting the failure to improve the business environment is Egypt's relatively low ranking on private investment as a share of GDP. The MENA in 2005–7 was the world's lowest ranking region on this measure and Egypt within that region was only underperformed by Iran.[86]

As for the efficiency of public and private Egyptian companies in the hydrocarbon sector, the evidence does not support an argument of substantial improvement nor of competitive advantage. The key state-owned entity managing the upstream end of the gas industry, Egypt Natural Gas (EGAS), is criticized within the industry for "the length of time it takes to award contracts."[87] There are indications that political involvement in this and other key public companies are a prime cause of inefficiency. As noted by one well informed international hydrocarbon industry expert, "When it comes to agreements, everyone in Egypt, up to Mubarak is involved."[88] As for the internal workings of both public and mixed sector companies in the industry, one insider laments that while all managing positions are occupied by Egyptians, they have "expat mirror images," but "unlike Oman, where they are trying to go for a

303

knowledge transfer, here they are just creating jobs without the transfer."[89] A survey of experts in international oil companies of the level of national technological development in the hydrocarbon sector rated Egypt a low two on a five point scale.[90]

Underlying the apparent failure to upgrade capacities of public and mixed sector oil and gas companies is the fact that they are used extensively for patronage purposes. The case of former Minister of Housing and New Communities, Muhammad Ibrahim Suliman, is illustrative. While engaged in a long running legal battle against charges of having allocated prime real estate to family members and friends during his twelve years as minister, he was appointed in June 2009 chairman of the state-owned Maritime Petroleum Services Company by Minister of Petroleum Fahmy. Some months later opposition members of parliament began a campaign against Suliman on the grounds that as a serving MP he was prohibited from holding a public sector post. In January the *Maglis al Dawla* (State Council) ruled against Suliman, who immediately resigned his parliamentary seat of Gammaliya, paradoxically one of the poorest districts in Cairo. He was ordered to pay back all monies received from the company since his July appointment. The Ministry of Petroleum subsequently announced that it had received LE348,600 from him, thus suggesting a monthly salary of some LE50,000, or about $9,500. Opposition MP Gamal Zahran, a professor of economics at Suez University, responded by claiming he had evidence that Suliman had in fact been paid LE9m. by the company during the less than eight months he was in its employ, or some $1.7m.[91] Suliman was reported by the authorities to be under investigation for corruption and banned from leaving Egypt in February 2011.

Possibly not coincidentally, then minister Fahmy, presumably sensitive about allegations of corruption in his domain, announced during the parliamentary struggle over Suliman that the ministry was considering floating some publicly-owned hydrocarbon companies on the Cairo stock exchange. Two years previously a similar announcement had led to speculation that one of the leading candidates was Tharwa Petroleum Company, whose ownership reveals the various tentacles of the state extending into operational areas. Its joint owners are the 100% government-owned Egyptian General Petroleum Corporation, the Egyptian Gas Company, and the Ganub al Wadi Petroleum Company, as well as the Ministry of Finance and the National Investment Bank. Tharwa in turn owns three companies involved in manufacturing and assembly of drilling rigs and other upstream operations, including several with the Chinese giant SINOPEC.[92] In short, the hydrocarbon sector provided a vital source of patronage for the Mubarak government. Utilization of the sector to that end undermined its efficiency and deterred the government from privatizing major parts of it, just as it shied away from privatizing publicly-owned banks, also instrumental in the generation and allocation of patronage. The degree of private participation in the gas industry, which is "a mere 15% of the industry's output," suggests how reluctant the government was to give away the goose that laid such golden eggs.[93]

Political impacts

The political impacts of gas fired development appear to be more negative than positive. On the latter side of the ledger, the engagement of Egypt in regional and global hydrocarbon networks and markets may have beneficial effects. If indeed Egypt does become a significant energy hub at the intersection of West Asia, Africa and Europe, it will further globalize the country's political economy, thereby likely enhancing Egyptian governance both narrowly and broadly defined, while possibly also contributing to better inter-state relations across these three continents. As far as domestic politics is concerned, the post-2003 hydrocarbon boom initially bought considerable legitimacy for the Nazif government installed in July 2004, thereby rendering its task of undertaking neo-liberal economic reforms easier. But those reforms exacerbated inequality and failed to stimulate sufficiently rapid economic growth to support political liberalization.

On the negative side of the political ledger the immediate impact of the hydrocarbon boom was to increase rents accruing to an economically and politically embattled authoritarian regime, thereby enabling it to reel in political liberalization. The strong, inverse correlation between Egypt's hydrocarbon rents and its score on the World Bank Voice and Accountability measure are reflective of the broader relationship. Empowered by having a substantial new source of rents to buy off specific constituencies while expanding employment and consumption in general, the regime concluded it could again close the political safety valve which it had previously cautiously opened. So what specific form did those vital rents take and how were they politically invested?

International sales of gas rose to some $2bn during the great gas boom, accounting in 2007 for more than 23% of total government revenues, which is somewhat more both in total and in percentage of governmental revenues than Syria, a country sometimes described as being hydrocarbon dependent, derives from its oil exports.[94] It may not be coincidence that at that time subsidies also constituted just more than 23% of total budget expenditures, of which energy subsidies comprised 74%.[95] The gas rent thus came to underpin the budget in general and its politically vital, broad subsidy component in particular. A closely related rent is generated from the state's almost total control of upstream and the immediate downstream commercial operations in the gas industry. As mentioned above, less than 15% of those operations are privately owned. Control of this profitable sector not only generates additional government revenue, but also provides opportunities for the selective distribution of patronage to favored clienteles, as the case of Muhammad Ibrahim Suliman exemplified. Both of these rents are traditional in nature, in that they flow from the government's direct control of the commodity and the industry extracting and marketing it. Gas rents of this nature are thus equivalent to rents generated by the oil industry during its boom period for some two decades after 1973.

But the gas industry has also generated a new, third source of rents, which were shared between the regime and the crony capitalists it tethered to itself by virtue of those rents. This source consists primarily of further downstream gas processing and energy intensive industries rendered competitive by access to subsidized inputs, including electricity, gas and gas derivatives. In these capital intensive undertakings the private sector dominates, with the captains of these industries, such as Ahmad 'Izz (iron and steel), the Sawiris family (cement), and Muhammad Abu al 'Inayn (ceramics), being the wealthiest men in Egypt at the twilight of the Mubarak era. A tight circle of investors at one remove from these titans extracted what might be thought of as secondary rents from these downstream industries by placing their ample funds in investment companies, such as Citadel Capital, that with governmental approval and even outright facilitations took equity positions in various of the companies.[96] The gas industry thus created a new class of super cronies, who in turn rewarded the regime through direct payments to or on behalf of its leading members. Ahmad 'Izz, for example, was a principal financier behind the Gamal Mubarak campaign for the presidency.

These rents are costs to the nation's economy, in that they are generated as a result of subsidized inputs, which might otherwise be exported on the country's account at prevailing, higher international prices. Recent research conducted under the auspices of the Egyptian Center for Economic Studies has documented the magnitude of these subsidies and their impacts on specific industries and enterprises.[97] The domestic prices for natural gas, diesel fuel and gasoline were in 2008 approximately 55%, 36% and 37%, respectively, of the actual cost of production. As a percentage of world prices, diesel fuel and gasoline were 23% and 30%, respectively, while gas was supplied domestically at 23% of its international price.[98] Electricity generation accounts for some 64% of natural gas consumed locally.[99] If all domestic energy prices were raised to the cost of production, they would cause the consumer price index to jump by between 35% and 40%.[100] Fuel subsidies as a percentage of GDP, at 4.6%, were by 2005 already higher in Egypt than in all comparator countries, including such oil producers as Nigeria (3.5%), Indonesia (3%) and Bolivia (2.2%).[101] Three years later Egypt's subsidy bill as a percentage of GDP had risen another 50%. Egypt is one of the few countries in the world in which the oil intensity of production has increased rather than fallen over the past decade.[102]

The largest single beneficiary of these energy subsidies is the manufacturing sector, which consumes 30% of petroleum products, 26% of natural gas and 38% of electricity, generation of which consumes about two-thirds of all domestically-utilized gas, thereby redoubling the subsidy passed on to electricity consumers. By comparison, transportation accounts for 42% of petroleum products, but virtually none of natural gas or electricity. Households consume slightly less electricity than does manufacturing.[103] Within the manufacturing sector the fertilizer and cement industries account for 8.8% and 7.4% of all natural gas consumed domestically. Other industries, chief of which are iron and steel and aluminum, utilize 10.5% of all natural gas, 15.8% of diesel fuel and 45.0% of fuel oil.[104]

How vital are these subsidized inputs to the manufacturing sector? For fertilizer, steel and aluminum production, fuel and electricity constitute almost one-third of total production costs, whereas for cement they are some 28%.[105] The importance of subsidized energy to the profitability of these industries is reflected in calculations of the impact on their profits were subsidies to be reduced or removed. The profit ratio per ton for domestic sales in the nitrogenous fertilizer industry, for example, would decrease from the existing 23% to 7.8% were energy prices to rise by 60%. They would become negative with a doubling of energy prices, which it should be noted would still leave energy prices well below prevailing international levels.[106] But since the domestic price for nitrogenous fertilizer is about one-half of the international price, the figures are quite different for export sales. The profit ratio for those sales is currently over 40% and would fall to 21.5% were energy prices to be doubled.[107] In the other energy intensive industries domestic and export price differentials are minimal. Prevailing profit ratios in the cement, aluminum and steel industries, for example, are 40%, 29% and 14% per ton, respectively.[108] Were energy subsidies halved, profitability would drop to 29%, 26% and 12%, respectively.[109] These profit ratios, even with a reduction in subsidies, are higher than prevailing ratios for Europe, North America and the Pacific, but similar to those in GCC countries. By way of comparison, in the United Kingdom 46 fertilizer companies have an average profit margin of 2%, compared to 21% in Egypt.[110] Leading Egyptian cement companies have profit ratios in excess of 40%,[111] presumably the key attraction to foreign interests that have invested heavily over the past several years in that industry. For example, Lafarge, the French cement giant, paid Orascom Construction Industries, a Sawiris family holding company, some 10bn euros in December 2007 for its stake in the Egyptian cement industry.

The remaining question is what are the patterns of ownership of these energy intensive industries? In a word, each is an oligopoly or, in the cases of iron and steel and aluminum, virtual monopolies. Two companies, for example, control more than three-quarters of production of nitrogenous fertilizers.[112] Along with another firm, more than 92% of production is accounted for by these three firms. A total of 11 firms constitute the cement industry, but three account for some 70% of total production. The iron and steel industry is yet more concentrated, where two of the 20 producers account for two-thirds of output. Most concentrated of all is the aluminum industry, in which Misr Aluminum Company accounts for virtually all production.[113] The principal owners of these leading firms constitute the dominant segment of the business elite, with many of them also having played prominent political roles in Mubarak's Egypt. The energy intensive industries they control are the largest beneficiaries in the country of subsidies for oil products, gas and electricity, which reached some $11bn in 2008/09. They also benefit substantially from hidden subsidies as Egypt has had to turn increasingly to international markets to purchase hydrocarbon products, transactions that in many instances do not appear on national accounts, hence are not counted as subsidies. Nor, for example, is the provision of domestically-produced oil to refineries virtually free of charge recorded as a subsidy.[114] A rough estimate would suggest then that annual rents from energy subsidies captured by the crony capitalists who controlled the commanding heights of the fertilizer, cement, iron and steel, ceramics and aluminum industries, reached $5bn. The side payments they presumably made to political elites thus compensate for the decline in patronage resulting from privatization of government owned economic assets. The upstream and immediate downstream energy sectors, however, remaining overwhelmingly under government control, directly contribute major shares to government revenues. Hydrocarbons, in sum, whether upstream or downstream, generate the predominant share of rents upon which the regime relied for patronage and upon which its private sector clients relied for their profits.

Assessment of the gas fired strategy

Egypt's heavy and increasing reliance on hydrocarbons, especially gas, is detrimental to its prospects for both economic and political development. As for the former, the country is not using resources wisely, as attested to by its low and declining efficiency of energy use. Falling oil production and poor prospects for future discoveries present worrying possible parallels for the gas industry. Governmental management of the hydrocarbon sector has not resulted in islands of efficiency that might then be generalized throughout the public service and public sector. Nor have the hydrocarbon upstream or downstream sectors served as incubators for competitive, globalized private firms. Energy-intensive industrialization has depended on subsidies for its success, meaning that its profits derive from rents, thus entail substantial opportunity costs. Moreover, such industrialization is not sustainable in the face of ever increasing competition for Egypt's limited gas and oil reserves.

Indeed, the hydrocarbon based development strategy as a whole is not sustainable, nor is it laying foundations for an alternative model. If anything it is undermining such potential foundations. Stagnating productivity of labor and management results in part from distortions resulting from the Dutch Disease, key to which is the undermining of competitiveness of non-energy intensive tradable goods. Egypt's basket of exports is diversifying comparatively slowly and its comparative advantage, outside the subsidized energy intensive sectors, is increasingly restricted to low wage, low technology production processes.[115] Maintenance of the bloated civil service and public sector, which militates against productivity growth, is also a side effect of hydrocarbon generated revenues. In the absence of productivity and export growth, jobs are increasingly dependent on factor inputs, chief of which is capital. As FDI and portfolio investment continue to decline from their peak in 2007, unemployment has escalated. Hydrocarbon based and related industries, even if successful, cannot absorb a substantial percentage of the more than three-quarters of a million youths hopeful of entering the labor market every year. The switch from oil to gas as the fuel to drive economic growth has thus not served Egypt well. It has perpetuated conditions that militate against making the economy more competitive. Because hydrocarbon dependent development in countries with limited reserves is not sustainable, Egypt is wasting both scarce resources and valuable time while pursuing this strategy.

The political consequences of gas fired growth have also been negative. Direct hydrocarbon rents have sustained authoritarianism. Rental income has been diversified and enhanced by the establishment of downstream energy-intensive industries, whose beneficiaries could not provide material bases for autonomous political organization without risking their share of rents. Thus, authoritarianism, once associated with state capitalism, was reinvented within what was nominally a privatizing economy, but which in reality was an economy whose commanding heights were controlled by regime cronies. Such an economy was one that exacerbated inequalities, as attested to by the persisting two-fifths of the population living on less than $2 per day, despite GDP growth that at its peak reached almost 8% annually. The anomaly is explained in part by the growing number of multimillionaires and even billionaires, although it is fair to say that expansion of the middle class also occurred. But that class has not grown as rapidly as in comparable countries and it in any case remained sandwiched between the poor, on the one hand, and the regime and its wealthy cronies, on the other. Gas has, in sum, perpetuated and intensified the hydrocarbon curse for Egypt's political economy. One of the greatest challenges facing the new government will be to convert that curse into a blessing.

Notes

1 World Development Indicators, 2009 (hereafter, WDI), CD-Rom, World Bank.
2 Ibid.
3 Central Bank of Egypt annual reports, cited by Amr Adly, *The Political Economy of Trade and Industrialization: Turkey and Egypt in the post-liberalization Era*, unpublished PhD thesis, Florence, European University Institute, no pagination.
4 Hydrocarbon dependence is essentially ignored, for example, in the otherwise useful assessment of the Egyptian economy by Paul Rivlin, *Arab Economies in the Twenty-First Century,* Cambridge: Cambridge University Press, 2009.
5 *Egypt Oil and Gas Report*, quarter 1, 2008, Business Monitor International, p. 22.
6 Ibid., p. 22.
7 *BP Statistical Review of World Energy 2009*, London: BP, 2009, p. 24.
8 Karin Maree, "Cairo Heads Downstream," *Middle East Economic Digest*, 51, 40 (2007), pp. 54–56.
9 "Egypt: Energy Report," Economist Intelligence Unity (January 2009), pp. 10–20; and R. Blackburn, "Energy: A Natural Gas Cartel," *Stratfor* (December 9, 2009), www.stratfor.com/print/150295
10 "Egypt: Energy Report," p. 13; and *Egypt Oil and Gas Report*, quarter 4, 2009, Business Monitor International, p. 85.
11 *Business Environment Ranking, Middle East/North Africa Region*, Business Monitor International, quarter 2, 2008, p. 27.
12 WDI; and "Consumption of Oil Products, Egypt," IEA http://www.iea.org/statis/index.html
13 WDI.
14 A.F. Alhajji, "Oil and Gas in the Capitals," *World Oil*, 228, 12 (December 2007), p. 40.
15 Ibid.
16 Karin Maree, "Cairo Heads Downstream," *Middle East Economic Digest*, 51, 40 (2007), pp. 54–56.
17 Sherine Nasr, "Under Pressure," *al Ahram Weekly* (14–20 January 2010) http://weekly.ahram.org.eg/2010/981/economy
18 "Reformers Dash for Gas," *Petroleum Economist* (October 2005), p. 1.
19 WDI 2009.
20 WDI 2009.
21 "Egypt: Energy Report," p. 11; and Maree, p. 55.
22 "Egypt: Energy Report," p. 19.
23 Ibid., p. 12.
24 Maree, p. 54.
25 "Cairo Starts on Masterplan," *Middle East Economic* Digest, 51, 32 (August 10, 2007), p. 14.

26 WDI and Clement M. Henry and Robert Springborg, *Globalization and the Politics of Development in the Middle East*, second edition, Cambridge: Cambridge University Press, 2010.
27 "Egypt: Energy Report," p. 14.
28 Richard Nield, "Turning Potential into Fact," *Middle East Economic Digest*, 51, 23 (June 8, 2007), pp. 63–67; and Maree.
29 Perry Williams, "Cairo Improves Pricing for Energy Firms," *Middle East Economic Digest*, 52, 35 (August 29, 2008), p. 9.
30 Nield, p. 67; Maree.
31 Nasr, "Under Pressure."
32 Soheir Abouleinein, Heba El-Laithy and Hanaa Kheir-El-Din, "The Impact of Phasing out Subsidies of Petroleum Energy Products in Egypt," Working Paper no. 145, Egyptian Center for Economic Studies (April 2009), p. 9.
33 Nasr.
34 See for example Christof Ruhl, "Global Energy after the Crisis," *Foreign Affairs* (March/April 2010), pp. 63–75; Blackburn; and Flynt Leverett and Hillary Mann Leverett, "Debating the Strategic Significance of Iran's Natural Gas," www.raceforiran.com/debating-the-strategic-significance-of-irans-natural-gas
35 "Egypt: Energy Report," p. 16.
36 Maree, pp. 55–56; Nield, pp. 63–64.
37 Blackburn.
38 IEA Energy Statistics, www.iea.org/statist/index.htm
39 Klaus Enders, "Egypt—Searching for Binding Constraints on Growth," IMF *Working Paper*, WP/07/57 (March 2007), p. 3.
40 WDI.
41 *Pocket World in Figures,* Economist Intelligence Unit, 2009, p. 74.
42 Ibid., p. 216; and WDI.
43 WDI.
44 UNIDO, www.unido.org/index as cited in Adly.
45 WDI.
46 Ibid.
47 UNCTAD COMTRADE (WITS Database), cited in Klaus Enders, "Egypt—Searching for Binding Constraints on Growth," IMF *Working Paper*, WP/07/57 (March 2007), p. 21.
48 Enders, pp. 20–21.
49 WDI.
50 www.weforum.org/en/initiatives/gcp/Global%20Competitiveness%20Report/index.htm
51 Enders, p. 3.
52 Enders, p. 27.
53 WDI.
54 "Egypt: Energy Report," p. 12.
55 WDI.
56 Abdallah Shehata Khattab, "The Impact of Reducing Energy Subsidies on Energy Intensive Industries in Egypt," Working Paper 124, Egyptian Center for Economic Studies (May 2007), p. 2.
57 WDI.
58 Figures cited in Khattab, p. 9.
59 Ibid., p. 10.
60 WDI.
61 WDI.
62 Tarek H. Selim, "On Efficient Utilization of Egypt's Energy Resources: Oil and Gas," Egyptian Center for Economic Studies, Working Paper 117 (December 2006), p. 18.
63 Ibid., p. 20.
64 WDI.
65 Ragui Assaad, "Labor Supply, Employment and Unemployment in the Egyptian Economy, 1988–2006," in Ragui Assaad, *The Egyptian Labor Market Revisited*, Cairo: American University In Cairo Press, 2009, pp. 1–52.
66 *Mena Development Report: From Privilege to Competition: Unlocking Private-Led Growth in the Middle East and North Africa.* World Bank, 2009, p. 66.
67 Ibid., p. 65.

68 On the Saudi government as potential "developmental state," see Tim Niblock with Mona Malik, *The Political Economy of Saudi Arabia*, London: Routledge. On Aramco see Valerie Marcel, *Oil Titans: National Oil Companies in the Middle East*, Washington, D.C.: Brookings Institution, 2006.
69 Cited in Maree, p. 56.
70 Nasr, "Under Pressure."
71 See for example Nield, pp. 63–67; and "Reformers Dash for Gas."
72 "Reformers Dash for Gas."
73 *Egypt: Energy Report*, p. 16.
74 Sherine Nasr, "Gas Saga Drags On," *al Ahram Weekly* (January 21–27, 2010), http://weekly.ahram.org.eg/2010/982/ec2.htm
75 Nasr, "Under Pressure."
76 Maree, "Dispute Tarnishes Cairo's Image," *Middle East Economic Digest*, 52, 32 (August 8, 2008), pp. 18–19.
77 Perry Williams, "Cairo Improves Pricing for Energy Firms," *Middle East Economic Digest*, 52, 35 (August 29, 2008), p. 9.
78 Ibid.
79 *Egypt: Energy Report*, p. 15.
80 Lina Attalah, "Bad Planning, Gas to Israel, Butane Shortages," *al Masry al Youm* (February 2, 2010) http://www.almasryalyoum.com/node/15231
81 Nasr, "Gas Saga Drags On."
82 WDI.
83 Ibid.
84 Compiled from Doing Business database, IMF, WTO, UNCTAD and World Development Indicators and cited in Henry and Springborg, p. 170.
85 Ease of Doing Business Database, World Bank, 2010, www.doingbusiness.org/EconomyRankings/
86 *From Privilege to Competition*, p. 53, http://siteresources.worldbank.org/INTMENA/Resources/Privilege_complete_final.pdf
87 "Reformers Dash for Gas."
88 Adal Mirza, "Egypt General Petroleum Corporation," *Middle East Economic Digest* 53, 25 (June 19, 2009), p. 32.
89 Ibid.
90 Ibid.
91 Gamal Essam El Din, "The Woes of Suleiman," *al Ahram Weekly* (February 4–10, 2010), http://weekly.ahram.org.eg/2010/984/eg2.htm; and Gamal Essam El Din, "New Take on Parliamentary Business," *al Ahram Weekly* (February 11–17, 2010), http://weekly.ahram.org.eg/2010/985/eg4.htm
92 "Oil Shares for Sale," *al Ahram Weekly* (February 4–10, 2010), http://weekly.ahram.org.eg/2010/984/eg2.htm; and Gamal Essam El Din, "New Take on Parliamentary Business," *al Ahram Weekly* (February 11–17, 2010), http://weekly.ahram.org.eg/2010/985/eg4.htm
93 Randa Alami, *Oil in Egypt, Oman, and Syria: Some Macroeconomic Implications*, Oxford Institute for Energy Studies (October 2006), p. 17.
94 Compiled from IMF Article IV publications and World Development Indicators, 2009, and cited in Henry and Springborg, p. 177.
95 Khattab, p. 2.
96 Interview with Hisham El-Khazindar, Citadel Capital, 22 June 2008.
97 Khattab; and Abouleinein, El-Laithy and Kheir-El-Din.
98 Abouleinein, El-Laithy and Kheir-El-Din, p. 11.
99 Abouleinein, El-Laithy and Kheir-el-Din, p. 14.
100 Ibid., p. 18.
101 Khattab, p. 9.
102 Ibid., p. 10.
103 Ibid., p. 19.
104 Ibid., p. 20.
105 Ibid., p. 22.
106 Ibid., pp. 22–23.
107 Ibid., 24.
108 Ibid., 24.
109 Ibid., p. 24.

110 Ibid., p. 25.
111 Ibid., p. 25.
112 Ibid., p. 22.
113 Ibid., p. 27.
114 Aboulenein, El-Laithy and Kheir-El-Din, pp. 9–10.
115 Enders, p. 21; and *From Privilege to Competition*, pp. 60–65.

22
Oil and the Russian Economy

Philip Hanson

If Russia is a petro-state, it is a rather unusual one. It exports metals, nuclear reactors, weapons systems and, in most recent years, grain, as well as hydrocarbons. Its economy is, despite its leaders' current insistence on the need to modernize, moderately developed and diverse. It is, furthermore, an exception among major oil exporters in that most (about 60%) of its oil production is by private firms; a monopoly national oil company has not been created.

At the same time, it does have several of the traits of a petro-state. Figures for the first half of 2010 show exports of crude oil, oil products and natural gas making up 64.9% of its total merchandise exports; identified state revenues from oil and gas make up 48% of the federal budget revenue planned for 2010; in 2009 exports of oil and gas were equivalent to 15% of GDP.[1] And if private enterprise still bulks large in Russia's oil industry, the political leaders exert plenty of influence on those private Russian oil companies, and the presence of international oil companies is restricted.

In this chapter we will consider how this semi-petro-state operates: what the role of oil and gas in the economy is, how sustainable present arrangements are, and what state policies on the hydrocarbons sector, including "modernization" plans for the whole economy, amount to.

The role of oil and gas in the Russian economy

It is commonly said that Russia's recent growth has been driven by rising oil prices. This is true, but it is useful to explore the connection a little further. A rise in the oil price or any other price obviously cannot raise real (that is, inflation-adjusted) output levels in any direct way. What an oil-price rise does do for an oil-exporting nation is (other things equal) improve its terms of trade, giving its government, firms and households greater purchasing power over imports; it also tends to raise real incomes, so long as not all the increased hydrocarbon revenue is "sterilized" by being taxed and diverted to a sovereign wealth fund. In the absence of total sterilization domestic demand is raised, pulling in more imports but also increasing demand for domestic production. Provided the domestic economy is capable of increasing supply, domestic production will rise.

This is what happened in Russia for most of the inter-crisis period, 1998–2008. Growing capital and labour inputs and rising productivity were an important part of the story, but rising

Oil and the Russian Economy

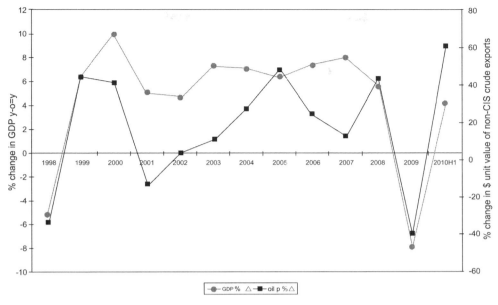

Figure 22.1 Russia: GDP and the oil price 1998–2010
Sources: Average unit value of crude oil exports outside the CIS from the Central Bank of Russia.

oil prices provided the stimulus on the demand side. The connection between changes in the oil price and changes in GDP was modified from 2004, when the government stabilization fund was set up, but it was by no means eliminated. The annual data in Figure 22.1 illustrate this link.

So far as Russia's macro-economic dynamics are concerned, oil is the key fuel. It provides far more export revenue than does gas; and Russia's gas export prices are (with some recent modifications, to be discussed later) based on the prices of oil products, under the terms of long-term gas supply contracts. In 2009 Russia was the world's largest producer of oil and the second largest producer of natural gas. At just over 10mbpd it accounted for a little over one-eighth of world output of crude oil. Its gas output of 527.5bn cubic metres (bcm) amounted to 17.6% of the global total, just behind the USA's 20.1%.[2] In tons of oil equivalent, Russian oil and gas production levels are closely similar. But Russia utilised nearly three-quarters of its gas production domestically and only one-quarter of its oil output.[3] In 2009 gas accounted for 55% of Russia's domestic energy usage, compared with just under 20% for oil.[4] One reason for this is that gas is the leading fuel for Russian power stations. Far more oil than gas, accordingly, goes to export. The gap between oil production and consumption is illustrated in Figure 22.2.

In recent times Russia's foreign earnings from oil have been of the order of four times those from gas. It is the non-fungible nature of gas supplied through pipelines, not the scale of Russian gas exports, which makes Russian gas a far more sensitive energy security issue than Russian oil (see Chapter 25).

It can be seen that the output of oil grew more rapidly in 1999–2004 than subsequently. In the earlier period a number of businessmen from the financial sector moved into the oil industry, taking over assets and establishing particularly dynamic oil firms: Yukos, Sibneft and TNK. They brought in western oil-services companies as contractors to boost extraction rates, rationalized their businesses and secured an acceleration of petroleum output. Surgutneftegaz

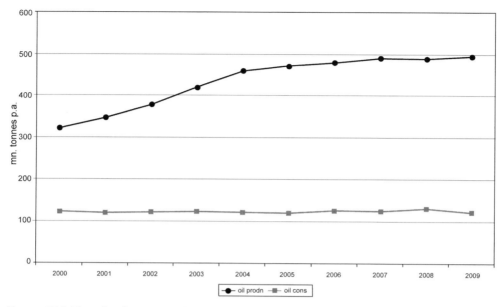

Figure 22.2 The development of Russian production and domestic consumption of oil, 2000–2009

and Lukoil, also private but still run by Soviet-era managers and former officials, exhibited less dynamism but, in the case of Lukoil, a greater propensity to invest long-term in exploration and the development of new fields.

This rapid growth was short-lived. The subsequent slowdown was brought about by a number of developments: the arrest of Mikhail Khodorkovskii, the main owner of Yukos, and the subsequent acquisition of most Yukos assets by the state-controlled oil firm, Rosneft; Gazprom's acquisition of Sibneft; an increase in taxes on the industry, and perhaps also some diminution of the scope for rapid output increases from established fields. Incentives to boost production were certainly weakened. That includes the incentive to invest long-term, since the Yukos affair damaged the already-weak confidence in property rights. Subsequently, there is some evidence that the rules of the game may have stabilized, but politicians' leverage over private oil companies is a fact of Russian business life.[5]

The sensitivity of Russian GDP to world oil prices probably reflects more than a narrow price-income-demand-production set of links. The year-on-year decline in GDP in 2009 was substantially greater for Russia than for other oil producers (see Figure 22.3). Yet the fall in oil prices was, for practical purposes, the same for all of them. One hypothesis is that Russian and foreign businesspeople, aware of the weakness of property rights in Russia and of the unusual scope for political interference in business, have an asymmetric perception of Russian country risk: they attach a low weight to it when the oil price is rising and a suddenly much higher weight when the oil price falls. Thus the oil-price signal is, in the case of Russia, unusually amplified. There is some evidence for this in the scale and timing of capital outflows and the unusually large role of inventory declines in Russia's recession.

One other feature of the Russian hydrocarbon economy is the divorce between export and domestic prices. This has considerable consequences. Both oil and gas are exported at prices well above the domestic price, with export duties forming a wedge between the two price levels. The export of both fuels is in the hands of state monopolies: Transneft for oil and

Oil and the Russian Economy

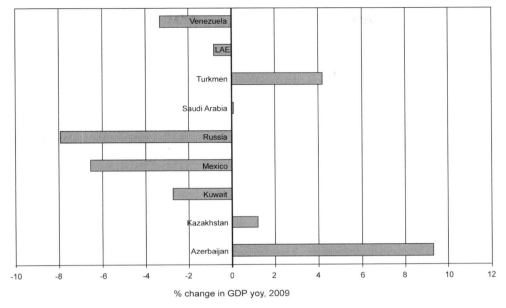

Figure 22.3 The effects of a falling oil price? % change, year-on-year, 2009, Russia and other major oil-exporting nations

Gazprom for gas. In principle, the volumes of hydrocarbons exports could be stepped up considerably, because domestic energy usage is highly inefficient.

Figure 22.4 shows Russia's energy efficiency alongside that of a number of other countries, including other oil exporters (Saudi Arabia and Venezuela), another ex-communist country (the Czech Republic), another northerly country (Canada), a highly intensive user of motor vehicles (the USA) and the United Kingdom. The comparison suggests, quite simply, that Russia uses energy in an exceptionally inefficient fashion. A substantial rise in the domestic prices of oil, gas and electricity would, on the face of it, stimulate major reductions in domestic energy usage; at all events, the scope for such reductions is enormous. Therefore, given time for adjustment, Russia has the potential to export substantially more oil and gas even if its output of hydrocarbons were to stagnate.

The sustainability of Russia's 'energy power'

Russia derives considerable influence in the world from its role as a major energy supplier. That influence is likely to remain strong for the foreseeable future. The influence is regional, not global: the bulk of Russia's oil and gas exports go to Europe. It is derived from gas rather than oil, despite the much greater scale of oil exports. This is because oil is fungible: supplies from any one source can readily be substituted by supplies from other sources; in contrast, most gas trading in Europe is by pipelines whose sources and destinations are fixed, and is based on long-term, 'take or pay' contracts.

Over the next decade or so, hydrocarbon prices are widely expected to remain high by historical standards, in both a real (that is, relative to other goods) and a nominal sense. There are good reasons for this prognosis. The international oil companies now have only limited access to reserves and have been opting to boost dividends rather than long-term investment. Many of

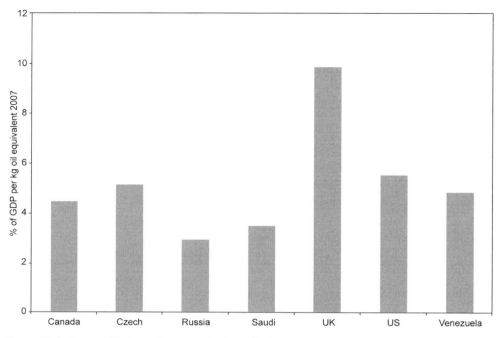

Figure 22.4 Energy efficiency: Russia and selected other nations, 2007

the national oil companies are inclined to regard oil and gas underground as sound, appreciating assets, and are in no rush to raise rates of exploitation. Offshore, including Arctic, hydrocarbon deposits are there to be developed but will be relatively costly and, in the Arctic, politically contentious. Alternative energy sources will not play a large role for some time.

To that extent, external conditions are likely to favour a continuation of Russian energy power. At the same time there are a number of influences or potential influences that could tend to erode it.

Slow growth in Europe means a correspondingly modest growth in energy demand, so far as Russia is concerned. Asian markets are in better shape and offer faster growth, but re-adjusting Russia's energy system to serve them is a slow process. In the summer of 2010 the Russian section of the East Siberia-Pacific (VSTO in its Russian acronym) oil pipeline was completed. That brings a capacity to deliver about 600,000 barrels of oil per day to the Chinese border, or somewhat under a quarter of expected Russian deliveries to Europe in 2010.[6] Gas supplies eastwards are also being developed, but not rapidly. The Shell-Mitsui-Mitsubishi project on Sakhalin, Sakhalin 2, is delivering liquefied natural gas (LNG) to Japan and Mexico.[7] Negotiations over energy supplies to China have been prolonged and difficult. China seems determined to avoid having Russia as a supplier on a scale that would yield influence.[8] So far as gas is concerned, Gazprom has postponed the development of the Kovykta field, which might have been a major source of supply to China; priority is now being given by the Ministry of Energy to building the Altai gas pipeline, which would supply 30bcm per year to China from West Siberian fields from some point between 2015 and 2018. But Turkmenistan already has an agreement to supply a larger amount to China, perhaps from as early as 2011.[9] Russia looks to be stuck with Europe as its main energy market for some time to come.

Meanwhile there are developments in the gas market globally that Gazprom and, presumably, the Russian leadership do not welcome. One is the development of LNG, which can lend itself rather better than pipeline delivery to the creation of spot markets in gas. As liquefaction plants and terminals are put in place, Europe has become more open to competition between alternative sources of supply of gas. In 2010 this forced Gazprom to accept changes in its contracts; these allowed customers to obtain somewhat lower prices for Russian gas than would have followed from the price formulae in the original long-run supply contracts. Russia has been slow to develop LNG. It owes its only established LNG capacities entirely to projects financed and managed by foreign companies (Sakhalin 2). In 2009 its LNG exports were 3.6% of its total gas exports, while for the world as a whole the figure was 27.7%.[10]

Another development involves shale and other 'unconventional' gas. Shale gas production has developed fast in North America, transforming gas markets there and pushing some third-party supplies towards Europe. It remains to be seen whether there will be further rapid growth of shale gas production in the USA and Canada, and whether there can be similar rapid growth in some parts of Europe. Meanwhile, developments so far have not suited Russian interests.

Sustainability in the ultimate sense of the preservation of available reserves is barely an issue so far as Russian policy is concerned. Hydrocarbon reserves in Eastern Siberia and offshore are not fully explored but are certainly large. Their development may be costly, but they are comfortingly there. A major expansion of nuclear power is planned: its timescale is over-ambitious but there is no reason to think that it will not be completed eventually. And there is another reserve still to be tapped, in the extravagantly wasteful domestic usage of energy. The partial privatization of the electricity supply industry has created pressure for higher electricity prices as foreign firms with generating assets in Russia and contractual undertakings to expand and update their capacity seek to secure a return on their investments.

Sustainability in another sense is more of an issue. Can Russia continue to thrive economically while remaining so dependent on oil and gas exports? It is to this question and the policy issues connected with it that the next section is devoted.

Russian policies and policy options

Liberal critics of the present Russian economic order, from the late Yegor Gaidar to Andrei Illarionov, have argued that high oil prices damage Russia in the long term by reducing the incentive to reform. The Russian government understandably prefers to have its cake and eat it, too: it plans for 'modernization' in the sense of economic diversification into high-tech activities from IT to pharmaceuticals; it also plans for the further long-term expansion of the hydrocarbons sector. Radical economic liberalization, let alone political liberalization, is not on its agenda.

In the medium term Russia obviously benefits from its oil and gas export earnings, for reasons set out above. In the long run, however, the disadvantages could outweigh the gains. Russia appears to cope particularly badly with the volatility of raw material prices, as we have noted. Whether Russia has been significantly affected by 'Dutch Disease' is disputed.[11] There is some evidence that it has.[12] However, it can be argued that much, perhaps even most, of the real appreciation of the rouble can be accounted for by the Balassa-Samuelson effect, in which any emerging economy is likely to experience a convergence of its exchange rate from below purchasing power parity towards that parity, that is, for its currency to become less undervalued over time.

Most Russian liberal critics see Russia's natural-resource dependence as damaging for other reasons: chiefly, because swelling oil and gas revenues make the status quo comfortable and reduce the pressure on the political leadership to change anything. This is plausible.

Two American economists, Clifford Gaddy and Barry Ickes, argue that Russia's problem with natural resources is not dependence; specializing in oil, gas and metals exports could work out well for the Russian population even in the long term. The problem, rather, is that the Russian political and economic system is addicted to the wasteful use of natural-resource rents.[13] This wasteful use includes higher-than-necessary extraction costs, subsidized domestic energy prices, corrupt side-payments and tax revenues that are inefficiently used. This misuse of energy rents, Gaddy and Ickes argue, props up a 'legacy' sector of inefficient, Soviet-era enterprises.

This interpretation is compatible with the more general liberal contention that plentiful oil-and-gas revenues stave off reform. It is perhaps too focused on the notion that propping up dinosaur enterprises is the key weakness of Russia's political economy. All producers, whether they have their origins in the Soviet era or are *de novo* or restructured businesses, receive energy subsidies; excessive extraction cost is not a benefit to other sectors; budget spending on industrial support is modest, and the weakness of competition in the Russian economy is to do above all with cronyism and the ability of incumbent firms to call in political favours in order to undermine rivals. Meanwhile the structure of the Russian economy has, after all, altered substantially since the fall of communism; inefficient, Soviet-era enterprises have closed or shrunk, even if they could have shrunk faster. And it is not clear how the Gaddy and Ickes 'addiction', whatever its dimensions, would be cured short of a comprehensive liberalization of the Russian economy and polity.

The general point remains: a large, inefficient but highly prosperous hydrocarbons sector probably is not a helpful ingredient in Russia's long-term development. Current Russian policy, however, assumes that the future will be much like the present, without any major increase in either economic or political competition, but with a programme of state-led, top-down diversification added.

Russia's long-term plans for the energy sector

In November 2009 the Russian government approved an energy strategy to the year 2030.[14] It replaces an earlier document covering the period to 2020, and is comprehensive in its coverage.

The broad outlines of the strategy are summarized in Table 22.1. Output of oil is projected to grow very slowly indeed, output of gas a little faster. Coal, a lesser but significant contributor to Russian energy supply, grows more briskly than either oil and gas, while other energy sources, projected to grow at 2.9% per year over the 22-year period, exhibit the most rapid expansion. This last projection is based mainly on an ambitious nuclear programme, in which nuclear generating capacity more than doubles over the period.[15]

Consumption of the main fuels is also projected to rise at modest rates: slightly more slowly than production in the case of gas and more rapidly in the case of oil. Imports, hitherto chiefly of gas from Central Asia, rise a little, and the net effect is that exports (including re-exports) of gas are expected to grow rather modestly and, on this author's interpolation of data, to decline very slightly in the case of oil. Total energy exports, consisting of crude oil, oil products, natural gas, coal and (on a very small scale) electricity, are projected as growing at less than half a percentage point a year over 22 years.

The predictive value of projections such as these is low. What they reveal is not the future but the attitudes and assumptions of the state's officials. Clearly, those officials do not see Russia getting out of the energy export business. They anticipate considerable energy saving over time in domestic consumption. They count on a modest increase in gas imports from Central Asia; and they expect East Siberian gas development to roar ahead: from an output of 4 bcm in 2008 to 45–65 bcm annually by about 2030, together with an almost equally rapid expansion in the Russian Far East.[16]

Table 22.1 Russian government projections of production, domestic consumption, import and export of main fuels, annual totals in mn tons of standard fuel, 2008 actual and 2030 projected

Sources & uses of main fuels		RF Energy Strategy to 2030			implied % change
		2008A	2030 low	2030 high	p.a. 2008 to 2030 high
Prodn	Oil	694	758	765	0.4
	Gas	761	1018	1081	1.6
	Coal	222	282	381	2.5
	non–fuel	126	219	236	2.9
	Total	1803	2276	2456	1.4
to reserves		−10	−3	−3	
Imports		83	86	87	
total supply		1876	2359	2540	
dom cons		991	1375	1565	2.1
o/w	Gas	526	656	696	1.3
	Oil	187	309	343	2.8
Exports	Total	883	985	974	0.4
o/w	Gas	281	423	401	1.6
	Oil	482*	415**	456**	−0.2

Notes: high output projection less high consumption projection can lead to lower export projections;
* derived from www.customs.ru;
** interpolated from the strategy document on assumption of zero imports; *Conversion rates to standard fuel (sf)*: 1 ton oil = 1.43 t sf; 1000 cm gas = 1.15 t sf; 1 t coal = 0.65 t sf. Non–fuel = Nuc + Hydro + Other.
Source: derived from *EnergeticheskayastrategiyaRossiina period do 2030 goda*, 2009; World Bank (http://data.worldbank.org/indicator/EG.GDP.PUSE.KO.PP.KD, accessed 13 September 2010).

The capital cost of these plans is high. In US dollars at 2007 prices, the investment estimated for the extraction, transportation and storage of gas over the whole period 2009–30 is $565–90bn, and the corresponding figure for oil is $609–25bn.[17] The hydrocarbons investment total happens to be approximately equal to Russia's GDP in 2009, so one can envisage the oil and gas investment required, in very round numbers, as of the order of 4% of base-year GDP in each of 21 years. This is not an outrageous or manifestly unachievable investment programme but it does suggest two things: that there is a strong commitment to remaining an 'energy power', and that there will be powerful incentives to try to attract serious amounts of inward foreign direct investment as part of the sector's development.

Inward foreign direct investment (IFDI), excluding mergers and acquisitions which create no additional capital, is currently about one-sixth of Russian capital formation, as Table 22.2 illustrates. The share of that IFDI going into all extractive industries, when Russian-controlled funds from tax havens are excluded, is about one-eighth, as the calculations in Table 22.3 show. The implication is that foreign investment currently plays a modest role in the hydrocarbons sector. If the ambitious oil and gas investment programme foreseen for the next two decades is to be implemented, there is likely to be pressure on Russian policy-makers to reduce the restrictions, impediments and disincentives that limit foreign involvement in the sector at present. The pressure will be all the greater because there will be a need for leading-edge (mostly foreign) technology to develop offshore deposits.

Table 22.2 Scale of Russia's total fixed Investment, equipment investment, equipment imports, and IFDI creating new capital, 2008, US$ billion[a]

Category	Value
Total fixed investment	385.4
Equipment investment	138.4
Equipment imports	106.2
IFDI New capital formation	59.7

[a]Ruble figures converted at annual average exchange rate of R24.9 = $1. Equipment imports exclude cars but not trucks; adjusted IFDI excludes mergers and acquisitions and 'other capital.'
Sources: Compiled by the author from European Commission, website, n.d. [http://ec.europa.eu?economy_finances/en/forecasts/20010_spring/non_russia_en.pdf], last accessed 25 August, 2010.
Russian Customs Service, 2009 [www.customs.ru/ru/stats/arhiv-stats-new/trfgoods/popup.php?id286=509], last accessed 25 August, 2010; and Central Bank of Russia.

Table 22.3 Sectoral composition of Russia's IFDI, 2009, percent[a]

Sector	All countries	Cyprus	Netherlands
Agriculture	0.1		
Extractive industries	20	3.9	3.7
Manufacturing and electrical	27		
Construction	4.7		
Transport and communications	3		
Services[b]	44	12.9	
Other	0.7		

[a]With some notes on selective countries of origin.
[b]Services here include financial and property.
Source: Rosstat and author calculations.

Diversifying the economy

I observed at the beginning of this chapter that Russia is a good deal more than a hole-in-the-ground economy. Still, the political leaders have been insisting with some vehemence lately that the economy must be 'modernized'. Complaining about Russia's 'de-industrialization' and its becoming a 'raw materials appendage of the West' has been a staple part of Russian political rhetoric for several years. It is part nostalgia for the might of the Soviet past and part resentment at what is perceived as a role suitable only for a backward country. The fact is that even under the old order Soviet manufacturers were never able to sell anything much on competitive markets beyond weapons systems. That is routinely overlooked.

On the other hand, if there is after all something in the view that reliance on oil and gas exports will not serve Russia well in the long term, then diversification should be beneficial. The question is whether the present Russian economic order is favourable to diversifying and 'modernizing' the economy.

Modernizing, in the sense in which President Medvedev and Prime Minister Putin use the term, means moving to a position where Russia is a substantial net exporter of high-tech products and its reliance on oil and gas is reduced. There are three reasons why this will be extremely difficult to bring about in the foreseeable future.

The first is that Russian science is in poor shape. Its status has declined as funding and relative pay have fallen. Many scientists have left the country and there is a shortage of young recruits to research in the hard sciences. In the five years 2005–9 inclusive, the origins of the global total of scientific papers were: Brazil 2.1%, Russia 2.6%, India 8.4% and China 2.9%.[18] In the *Times Higher Education* 2010–11 ranking of the world's top 200 universities there is no Russian institution included, yet China has five in the list, not counting Hong Kong institutions, Egypt has one and Turkey has two. Moscow University is said to be just outside the top 200, but the same applies to three Brazilian universities.[19] Of the total of patent applications filed outside the country of residence of the first-listed applicant in 2007, Russia was responsible for 0.14%. This is marginally better than Brazil's 0.13% but below India's 0.48% or China's 0.90%.[20]

The second reason is that the structure of the Russian economy makes a leap to high technology difficult. One way of looking at economic development is to track a nation's journey through 'product space'. Global commodity trade, classified into 775 products at the 4-digit level of the commodity classification, can be mapped according to the 'proximity' between pairs of products. Proximity between products A and B is a measure of the likelihood that a country that is a net exporter of A will also be a net exporter of B. When this is done, the 'forest' of products is seen as an expanse of more or less dense clusters with gaps between them. Historically, it appears, countries develop their net exports by moving through the product space from one cluster of products to another cluster that is close by. Oil and gas appear as a cluster that is associated with high per capita GDP but is comparatively remote from the densely-connected cluster of highly sophisticated goods.[21]

Another way of looking at this question of structure is less abstract. The leading branches of Russian industry are not, broadly speaking, the kinds of industries that have a high demand for research and development (R & D). Anatolii Chubais, the head of the state corporation for nanotechnology, Rosnanotekh, pointed this out to President Medvedev in February 2010, at a meeting of the presidential Commission on Modernization and Technical Development. Russian R & D spending by companies, he said, had barely increased since the mid-1990s, and was well below that seen in China. Of total Russian R & D spending, around 70% was from the state budget.[22] This is an unhealthy situation. Companies are more strongly motivated than the state to turn research into commercially successful innovation. And the Russian state is particularly corrupt and ineffective.

The third reason for scepticism about rapid diversification into 'advanced' lines of production is the character of the Russian business environment. In the 2010 World Bank ranking of 183 countries for 'ease of doing business', covering 2008–9, Russia came 120th.[23] Studies of Russian productivity levels repeatedly draw attention to the weakness of competition as a malign influence on progress.[24] We shall come back to this subject in the concluding section.

Much of the debate in Russia about modernization is political. Liberal critics of the Putin regime assert that only a free market, providing scope and incentives for firms to adopt new products and processes, can generate a process of genuine modernization, and that in turn requires political liberalization. Defenders of the regime deploy arguments about Russia's lack of readiness for competitive politics[25] and examples of state-led modernizing that range from South Korea in the 1960s to the contribution of US defence research spending to the creation of the internet.

Modernization strategies are formulated by both a presidential (Medvedev) and governmental (Putin) commission. The former is behind plans to create a research and innovation enclave at Skolkovo, near Moscow, referred to as Russia's Silicon Valley. Anatolii Chubais, the head of Rosnanotekh, is a leading architect of the scheme. It is a public-private joint venture. Viktor Veksel'berg, the boss and main owner of the Renova group, has taken on a coordinating role. Foreign investors, including US venture capital funds, have been wooed. Cisco Systems, Siemens and some other foreign companies have pledged funds to the project. Renova has recently gained control of two Swiss high-tech firms, Oerlikon and Sulzer, and that provides one channel by which technology can be transferred from West to East. It is therefore inaccurate to caricature the project as akin to Soviet-era science cities such as Akademgorodok. It is state-led but with considerable scope for private initiative.

The problem remains that unpredictable state interference, insecure property rights and corrupt links between state and business bedevil any attempt to improve Russian economic performance. That includes state-led campaigns to 'modernize' or diversify the economy.

Conclusions: oil, politics and the Putinist system

I observed at the beginning of this chapter that Russia, unlike other major oil-exporters, has not brought all oil production under a single national oil company, and indeed has a majority of its oil production coming from the private sector. This contrasts not only with Middle Eastern oil exporters like Saudi Arabia but also with such developed-country exporters of hydrocarbons as Norway. Given Russian and Soviet history, this is remarkable.

There is a line of argument about state control of oil and gas production that runs, in brief summary, as follows. The extraction and processing of oil and natural gas is an activity with great economies of scale, so that oil companies are likely to be large and, in any one country, few in number. Their market power, together with the widespread notion of subsoil resources as in some sense 'national', calls for state regulation in some shape or form. Regulation in a state with strong and reasonably sophisticated institutions could be conducted at arm's length with private oil companies as the subjects of regulation. In states with a weak rule of law and a poorly-functioning state administrative machine, the risk of collusion and state capture by the private oil firms is high, and direct state ownership may be more effective. That, at least, provides one rationale for the establishment of national-monopoly state oil companies.

After the Russian state's attack on Yukos, it was reasonable enough to suppose that the Russian state would, step by step, take over the whole industry. When Gazprom acquired Sibneft, that conjecture looked all the more plausible. However, the process has stopped there. Gazprom continues to control some 85% of natural gas production, plus all gas export pipelines and all gas storage, while the state-controlled Rosneft is the largest single Russian oil company, thanks to its acquisition of Yukos assets. But Lukoil, TNK-BP and Surgutneftegaz remain the next largest oil producers; together with other private firms they account for around three-fifths of oil production. This has seemed, over the past four years, to be a tolerably stable situation.

It is my contention, elaborated more fully elsewhere,[26] that the informal, often corrupt, links between political power and private business in Russia allow leading politicians to derive personal wealth and/or economic influence in their dealings with private oil companies just as readily as they could through state entities. They have no particular incentive to nationalize the whole industry.

The owners of private Russian oil companies typically are individuals or a very small group of co-owners, operating through offshore holding companies and needing at all times to keep on the right side of the political leadership. It is as though the state remains the real owner while the ostensible owners are mere tenants who could be evicted from their property at any time.

Occasionally, tensions arising from this awkward relationship become manifest. German Gref, a former minister of the economy and latterly the chief executive of Sberbank and, among other things a member of the board of Lukoil, said at Davos in 2010 that since the Yukos affair, 'the main issue on Lukoil's agenda has been not development but self-preservation.'[27] The second-rank oil company Russneft was subjected in 2007 to the standard array of administrative pressures: new claims of back-tax due, accusations of breaches of environmental regulations, threats of the withdrawal of operating licences, until its owner, Mikhail Gutseriev, sold up and fled to London. In 2010 he returned to Russia and resumed partial control of Russneft.[28]

Speculation over just who was aiming to do just what in this saga has been endless. The bottom line is that the owner of an oil company had that company first separated from him and then in part returned to him by a variety of state actions whose rationale and ultimate objective remain obscure.

The oil business in Russia is *sui generis*. It is mainly private and has made fortunes for a number of tycoons. As an industry it boomed in the early 2000s but is now expected to grow only slowly in the next two decades. The state's involvement is often opaque and informal. International oil companies have been kept at arm's length, with BP's 50:50 TNK-BP joint venture a special case. The state envisages both heavy, continuing investment in oil and gas in the future and at the same time a programme of diversification. The prospects for the latter are not good. At the same time requirements of both finance and technology create strong pressures for a more co-operative relationship with international oil companies in the future.

Notes

1 These numbers are derived as follows: trade data from the Central Bank of Russia (www.cbr.ru); budget data from the Ministry of Finance's Economic Expert Group *Ekonomicheskii obzor* (www.eeg.ru); GDP from Rosstat (www.gks.ru), all accessed 13 September 2010. Total state revenue includes sub-national budgets as well as the federal budget, so the share in all public revenue of taxes and duties on oil and gas is less than 48%. On the other hand, profits taxes on oil firms are not included in the total.
2 *BP Statistical Review of World Energy*, London: BP, 2010.
3 Ibid. The fact that Russia also imports and re-exports substantial amounts of Central Asian gas complicates the picture a little.
4 BP, op. cit. These are shares of a total that excludes wood, peat, wind, geothermal and solar energy sources.
5 See Philip Hanson, 'The Resistible Rise of State Control in the Russian Oil Industry,' *Eurasian Geography and Economics*, 50: 1 (2009): 14–28.
6 *Oxford Analytica Daily Brief*, 30 August 2010. Deliveries were scheduled, at the time of writing, to start in November 2010 (Natal'ya Kostenko, 'Rossiya podklyuchit Kitayu neft' i gaz,' *Vedomosti*, 27 September 2010).
7 Routine and shameless use of state administrative power has enabled Gazprom to install itself as a controlling stakeholder in Sakhalin 2, but the project was implemented by Shell and its Japanese partners.
8 For more on this see chapter 8 of Bobo Lo's *Axis of Convenience. Moscow, Beijing and the New Geopolitics*, London: Chatham House and Washington, DC: Brookings Institution, 2008.
9 *Oxford Analytica Daily Brief*, 24 August 2010. On 23 September Gazprom agreed with China's CNPC a set of conditions for future gas supply, but the price issue was still unresolved; at best, a contract could be signed in mid-2011 and gas deliveries could flow from 2015 (Kostenko, op. cit.).
10 Derived from *BP Statistical Review of World Energy 2010*, London: BP, 2010.
11 Dutch Disease, a term coined by *The Economist* in 1977, refers to exchange-rate effects from an increase in price or quantity of a nation's oil and gas (and, in principle, other staple natural-resource exports) that strengthens the exchange rate of its currency to the point where the international competitiveness of its other industries is damaged.
12 Simon-Erik Ollus and Stephen Barisitz, *The Russian Non-fuel Sector: Signs of Dutch Disease? Evidence from EU-25 Import Competition*, BOFIT Online no. 2, Helsinki: Bank of Finland, 2007.
13 Clifford G. Gaddy and Barry W. Ickes, 'Russia after the Global Economic Crisis,' *Eurasian Geography and Economics*, 51: 3 (2010): 281–312.
14 *Energeticheskaya strategiya Rossii na period do 2030 goda*, approved by government directive 1715-r on 13 November 2009, at http://energystrategy.ru/projects/docs/ES-2030_(utv.N1715-p_ 13.11.09).doc, last accessed 27 September 2010. Henceforth *ES-2030*.

15 *ES-2030*, annex 4, p. 6.
16 *ES-2030*, annex 3, pp. 3–5.
17 *ES-2030*, annex 4, pp. 5–6.
18 Michael Banks, 'Russian science in a state of decline,' www.Physicsworld.com of 26 January 2010, citing Thomson Reuters Web of Science database.
19 www.timeshighereducation.co.uk/world-university-rankings/2010–11/top-200.html#orderBy-Country accessed 29 September 2010.
20 www.wipo.int/ipstats/en/statistics/patents/ accessed 12 February 2010.
21 C.A. Hidalgo, B. Klinger, A.L. Barabási, R. Hausmann, 'The Product Space Conditions the Development of nations,' *Science*, 317 (27 July 2007): 482–87.
22 www.rosnano.ru/Post.aspx/Show/25035, accessed 10 March 2010.
23 www.doingbusiness.org/economyrankings/
24 See, for example, McKinsey Global Institute, *Lean Russia. Sustaining economic growth through improved productivity*, McKinsey, 2009; *OECD Economic Surveys. Russian Federation*, vol. 2009/6, Paris: OECD, 2009.
25 Vladislav Surkov, a deputy head of the Presidential Administration and one of the cleverest defenders of Putinism, has said that social and political liberalization is indeed desirable but must be gradual; for the time being, Russia needs a 'consolidated state', Maksim Glikin and Natal'ya Kostenko, '< <Chudo vozmozhno > > – Vladislav Surkov, perviy zamrukovoditel'ya administratsii prezidenta, zampredsedatel'ya kommissii po modernizatsii', *Vedomosti*, 15 February 2010. On the *Grani.ru* website on the same day, Yevgenii Yasin, the doyen of Russian liberal economists, was quoted as saying that a 'consolidated state' reminded him of Mussolini and Franco. That exchange captures the flavour of the debate.
26 Hanson, 'The Resistible Rise … ', op. cit., 2009.
27 www.moneycontrol.com/news/business/davos-fear-uncertainty-casts-pall-over-russian-business_439096.html, posted 1 February 2010. The fact is that Lukoil *has* developed new fields, so the claim is exaggerated; but it is not without foundation.
28 Anastasiya Kornya, 'Delo Gutserieva zakryto,' *Vedomosti*, 23 April 2010.

23
An Oil Giant From the Emerging World
Petrobras

Flavia Carvalho

Introduction

The oil industry is traditionally one of the most internationalized in terms of trade and in foreign investments flows (Goldstein, 2010), in a market historically dominated by a few giant companies from developed countries. In the last half of the 20th century, however, companies originated from developing countries, operating predominantly through state ownership, started taking an important share in the sector, in an attempt to grant access to one of the main fuels of economic development.

Oil is a unique commodity in terms of strategic importance – it is the main source of energy and an essential input to industrial production. It is also strategic because of a remarkable North-South divide: more than 80 percent of world oil production takes place in developing countries, while OECD countries consume around 54% of the total produced (Aykut and Goldstein, 2009).

Foreign investments in the oil sector are driven by the usual motivations: access to resources, markets or strategic assets. In the case of the oil industry, resource-seeking purposes have a special role on the internationalization of firms, for they have to chase the oil reserves where these are available. Oil companies from emerging markets are driven by the strong purpose of securing access to such strategic resources; technology, nevertheless, also plays a strong role in the internationalization process, though differently for each country.

This chapter presents the case of Brazilian state-owned oil company Petrobras, discussing its creation, the strategic and political motivations of setting up a strong national oil industry. More important, we discuss how the company developed and accumulated technological capabilities that enabled its placement among the leading oil and energy players in the world. We also emphasize how the company's recent reserve discoveries and its investments in alternative energy sources are reshaping the energetic matrix in Brazil.

The chapter is divided in three sections, besides this introduction. The next section presents the trajectory of Petrobras, from its creation to the achievement of fourth largest oil company worldwide. Section 3 discusses the role of technological development and strong R and D efforts placing Petrobras in a distinguished position among the world oil industry. Section 4 considers the impact of state ownership in the trajectory of the company. Section 5 contains the concluding remarks.

The making of a national oil giant

Petrobras was established in 1954 by President Vargas under the Import Substitution Industrialization programme, which aimed to make the Brazilian economy more independent from international ups and downs. The state-owned company was granted exclusive rights over exploitation and production (E and P) in the domestic territory, a monopoly broken only in the late 1990s, when the country's economy adopted a more liberal positioning in terms of trade and investments with the rest of the world. It is currently the largest Brazilian company in terms of assets and revenues, being also the top Brazilian exporting company (Revista Exame, 2010). In 2009 the company had around US$103bn in revenues, and net profits of over $16bn (Table 23.1). In 2009 Petrobras rose to the fourth place among the world's largest energy companies, with a market value of US $199.2 bn (in 2008 Petrobras was ranked ninth) (PFC Energy, 2010). Petrobras is also one of the largest multinationals from Brazil, with external revenues of over US$5bn (Chevarria, 2006).

The foundation of Petrobras, along with other state-owned enterprises in basic industries (such as Vale in iron ore and CSN in steel), was one of the cornerstones of the import substitution industrialization strategy carried out in Brazil, with the aim of enabling the country to reduce its external dependence in basic industries. Oil has always been a political matter, which legitimized the need of a strong, state-controlled enterprise to manage the country's resources. The 1970s oil crises gave new dimension to the political side of the oil question, also revealing that the Brazilian energy policy had failed until then to make the country independent from foreign oil sources. In this context Petrobras increased its strategic importance and focused on: a) the development of specific technological capabilities for prospecting oil in deep waters (owing to the particular location of most Brazilian reserves); b) the search for alternative energy sources. The international expansion started in 1972, with the creation of Braspetro. At the time oil imports accounted for 80% of domestic demand. Its international branch was, at that time, concerned primarily with assuring domestic supply. The national production in those years supplied only 17% of the internal demand, equivalent to 184,000 barrels per day (bpd) (Chevarria, 2006).

The initial expansion focused on Latin American countries, followed by Africa (Angola in 1979, where similar exploration conditions existed) and the Gulf of Mexico. Keeping pace with the technological developments of the leading oil firms in the 1970s and the development of its own technology for deep-water extraction have been the cornerstone of Petrobras' international expansion. Nowadays, the company holds more than 100 production platforms and 16

Table 23.1 Petrobras – corporate information, 2009

Assets (US millions)	184,197
Revenues	102,830
EBITDA	25,593
Production	
Oil (bpd)	1,791
Biodiesel (m3)	326,000
Natural Gas production (m3/day), millions	57,6
Ethanol production (m3)	330,000
Oil proved reserves (BOE), billions	12.08
NG proved reserves (BOE), billions	2.11

Source: elaborated by the author with data from Revista Exame, 2010; Petrobras, 2010.

An Oil Giant From the Emerging World: Petrobras

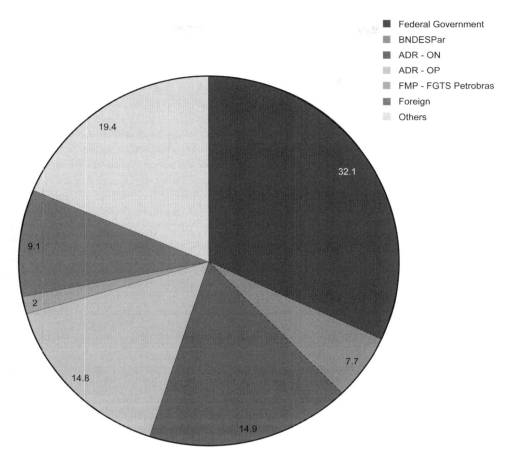

Figure 23.1 Petrobras: social capital composition, 2009
Source: elaborated by the author with data from Petrobras, 2010.

refineries (in Brazil, Argentina, the USA and Japan), being directly present in 27 countries (Petrobras, 2010). The core operations remain in Latin America, mainly Argentina, where the company invests in search for synergies (scale and scope economies) with its operations in Brazil (Chevarria, 2006; Dalla Costa and Pessali, 2007).

After a long time monitoring and limiting the operations of foreign firms in their national reserves, governments were pressed by technological and fiscal requirements to open up the sector to foreign direct investment (FDI) (Aikut and Goldstein, 2009). The same happened in Brazil under the Cardoso government (Carvalho and Goldstein, 2009). Since then, around 50 new companies have established operations in Brazil; among them, a series of small enterprises started operating in the sector, in the field of onshore exploration (Estado de Sao Paulo, 2007). Regulatory controls regarding exploration and production licences are since then implemented by ANP (National Petroleum Agency), an institution under autarchic management. The role of Government has been reshaped, from production and promotion of the sector to regulation and surveillance. Concession rounds are now on their ninth phase, and today there are 71 concessionaires operating in Brazil (35 of which are foreign investors). Production reached 1.97m bpd, a rise of 6% compared to the previous year (Petrobras, 2010).

Today the government is the major owner of the company with 32.1% of the social capital, and 57.8% of voting shares. The company has recently made a public offering of shares, in order to capture funds for further investments in the pre-salt exploration. Over 2bn shares were put in the market and the company capitalized around US$70bn.

The recent discoveries of oil in the pre-salt layers have shifted the focus of Petrobras expansion towards a domestic challenge, to develop technology to make such reserves profitable (Economist, 2010). In these new discovered sources, Petrobras has operated long-term tests (LTDs) in consortiums with foreign oil companies, such as BG Group and Repsol in the Santos basin, BG Group and Petrogal in the Tupi basin. The LTDs have already reached an average of 20,000 barrels per day. In 2010 new pre-salt reserves were announced in the Brazilian coast.

The focus on the pre-salt exploitation, however, did not extinguish investments overseas. In 2009 the company started refining operations in Japan, where it will provide gas for a compound with 3% of ethanol to be consumed in that country. In Portugal Petrobras established an office to be run alongside its exploration activities in the Portuguese coast. In total, Petrobras invested over US$174bn in 2009, mostly in the E and P segment (Petrobras, 2010).

The next section will present the technological achievements of Petrobras over the years, and how they contributed to the expansion of its businesses to foreign markets. We also stress the technological challenges posed by biofuel production and the exploration of the recent pre-salt reserves.

Technological capabilities and international expansion – the path to the top

The reason why Petrobras achieved such remarkable position among the leading world oil producers derives from the successful development of a state-of-the-art set of techniques to explore specific features of Brazilian reserves. Thanks to intensive R and D efforts, the accumulation of technological capabilities evolved from an initial set of incremental innovations from imported technologies to the development of its own set of techniques, the result of intensive R and D efforts (Neto and Dalla Costa, 2006).

Throughout its history, Petrobras accumulated strong capabilities in deep-water extraction, for which it has received several industry awards (Dalla Costa and Pessali, 2008). Its technological accumulation derived from the fact that oil reserves in Brazil are in deep and ultra-deep waters, which from the start required special extracting expertise.

Petrobras started its technological shift when it decided to focus on upstream activities specially in offshore locations. It took place in the early 1980s, when offshore exploration was at the technological frontier of the oil industry. The choice to prioritize this source of oil led the company to develop much more significant technological efforts than hither to (Furtado, 1997).

The accumulation of technological capabilities in the 1980s is an 'innovation jump'; in fact, Petrobras jumped from the absorption and reproduction of external technologies already in use to the development of production systems in deep waters, prompted by discoveries of massive oil deposits at depths from 400 to 2000 metres (Furtado, 1997).

The company made extensive investments in R and D in order to develop its own technology in the deep-water field, and innovation was incrementally implemented through the process. It was financial restriction, rather than a simple choice, to work upon the production system already developed and employed, the floating production system (SPF in Portuguese), primarily developed to operate in marginal fields.

Such an achievement was possible due to extensive research efforts carried out in co-operation with institutes and universities in Brazil and abroad. Those foreign partnerships evolved from a co-sponsorship to Petrobras establishing itself as leading articulator of the innovation process (Furtado and Freitas, 2000). The strategy of focusing on offshore-drilling technologies has yielded benefits: while in 1987 only 1.7% of production came from the sea, in 2000 this amounted to 55% (Bruni, 2002).

The accumulation of technological capabilities took place due to a series of research centres created by Petrobras, many of them operating in close co-operation with renowned Brazilian universities. CENPES is one of the most important ones, where the company carries out R and D activities in association with UFRJ (Federal University of Rio de Janeiro). Set up in the state of RJ in the 1960s, CENPES helped the transition of experimental technologies to industrial applicability, specially the development of the floating production system applied for increasingly deep-water extraction (Furtado, 1997; Furtado and Freitas, 2000). In 2009 the institute received US$872m. for technological development projects (Petrobras, 2010). As do most R and D projects, uncertainty in the development of appropriate technologies for deepwater prospection is diminished through joint projects with other firms, the strategy used by the company especially in the 1980s, when technologies were starting to reach a breakthrough (Furtado and Freitas, 2000).

Brazilian universities have been important providers of high quality human resources to the industry. Results from R and D projects have been quite impressive. In terms of expenditure on R and D, Petrobras is ranked as the fifth world oil company (DTI, 2006), with over US$1bn spent in R and D activities in 2009 (a 7 % increase in relation to the year before) (DTI, 2009). In terms of R and D output, Petrobras is similarly impressive. It has more patent applications, and has also had more patents granted in the US Patents Office (USPTO) than any other Brazilian enterprise. Until 2005 the company also held the largest number of patents from the Brazilian Patent's Office (INPI) (222 in the period 1990–2001). On average, Petrobras files 80 patent claims per year and the company has already reached the 1,000th patent filed.

Whereas the company's initial expansion in foreign markets was markedly driven by the technological expertise in deep water drilling, recent movements have different objectives. The emphasis now is towards business expansion and conquering new markets; diversifying in the downstream segments is a new directive of the company's international strategy. This goes in line with its aim to become a global, integrated company in the energy sector as a whole. The expansion of downstream investments also has the purpose of exploring and expanding the brand of Petrobras petrol throughout the world. The acquisition of refineries in the USA and Japan has this specific goal. Petrobras is searching for large profits from refining its excess capacity and operating in the downstream segment.

The rise of foreign investments from Petrobras in the 2000s reflects a new moment in the history of the company and a change in trends in the oil market in Brazil. First, the end of the monopoly in oil exploration in 1997 and the openness to foreign investors put the firm in a new, competitive market. Since then its executives face the expansion overseas as a source of growth to the firm (Chevarria, 2006). Second, the country's achievement of self-sufficiency in oil supply, following the opening of another platform for deep water exploration in April 2006 at the Bay of Campos (Rio de Janeiro), has expanded investment strategy beyond the search for resources into establishing new markets for distribution of by-products, refining and logistics (downstream activities).

The international efforts are proving to be positive: while in 2000 there were still no refining activities abroad, in 2002 the refining capacity was of 100,000 barrels per day; in 2009, it reached 140,700 barrels per day (Petrobras, 2002; 2010). The refining capacity is concentrated in the Southern Cone of America, one of the strategic areas of action by the company.

Recently, Petrobras is aiming to increase its production capacity in ethanol and biodiesel, making vigorous efforts in research of alternative energy sources. Ethanol production and exports had its kick start in December 2009 with the acquisition of 40% shares in a sugarcane powerplant in the state of Minas Gerais (Petrobras, 2010). A big challenge lies ahead for Brazil to conquer technological supremacy and establish itself as a major producer of this biofuel in the global market. The company aims to expand its capacity in ethanol production by 45.5% a year, reaching exports of 4,759,000 cubic feet by 2012.

The efforts in ethanol production are part of a new strategy followed by the company to become a major energy player. As oil reserves have a deadline, conflicts among producers are always a threat, and environmental pressures demand urgent search for alternative energy sources, Petrobras is now redefining its business. Nowadays the company has operations in hydroelectrical energy and biodiesel, besides its traditional business in oil, natural gas and diesel (Petrobras, 2010).

Technological prowess has rendered the company a valuable brand both domestically and internationally. It is among the top 10 most valuable brands in Brazil, and is the only Brazilian brand to show in the Millward Brown Optimor report of most prominent brand names of the world (Economist, 2010a).

Petrobras is an exemplar emerging company that has established its international position owing to the accumulation of technological capabilities. Such technological capabilities evolved through what became the strategic plan of the company. As Dantas and Bell (2006) stress, "[the company's capabilities] evolved from those of an imitative technology-user to those of a leading player at the international innovation frontier" (2006: 9). Moreover, a change in the Brazilian regulatory scenario for oil investments has fostered a further internationalization strategy, in order to strengthen its competitive position. The accumulation of technological capabilities by Petrobras was the factor enabling the company's international expansion. The move towards the Gulf of Mexico (where the company owns more than 170 deepwater blocs) and the western shore of Africa are an evidence of the exploration of offshore technologies, since these sites are at the frontier of deep shore exploration in the world (Chevarria, 2006).

The national relevance of Petrobras has taken a new dimension since the announcement that the country became self-sufficient in oil supply in 2006, after the inauguration of deepwater exploration in the Campos basin. Since then, and added to the discoveries of pre-salt reserves in the Brazilian coast, the country is building potential to become a major oil producer. Whereas the Tupi field discovered in 2007 will add between 5 and 7bn barrels of crude oil and natural gas production (Carvalho and Goldstein, 2009), the pre-salt reserves might add over 1m. barrels per day by 2017 (Petrobras, 2010).

Today the biggest challenge for Petrobras is the development of groundbreaking technology for the exploration of the pre-salt reserves. Making the activity profitable will also take extra innovative efforts, and demand great numbers of highly skilled workers; it will also be imperative to prove that the accomplishments in the new reserves are environmentally sustainable (Economist, 2010b). So far, the company's directors and the Brazilian government have been optimistic with the promises of abundant sources for the future. Several partnerships with universities, research institutes and other companies in related industries are under way, looking for solutions in drilling wells, storage and transportation – a CENPES initiative denominated Prosal (Technological Programme of the pre-salt) (Gouveia, 2010; Petrobras, 2010). Investments related to the pre-salt discovery are projected to be of around US$28bn per year, at least until 2014 (Época Negócios, 2010).

The visible hand: the role of policies and state ownership in oil companies

The oil sector is not neutral to government decision-making, for the very reason that oil is a key, strategic asset, upon which the economic prosperity of most nations depend. The national ownership of oil firms, mostly observed in developing and emerging economies, has also shaped their influence in the national economy. In this section we will approach the role of the government in the performance of Petrobras, both as an energy company and as a Brazilian multinational. Such a role is rooted in the import substitution regime, which earmarked basic industries as the drivers of economic growth and kept them safely in the hands of the state. Technological capabilities were developed in accordance with this strategic valuing of the industry, and were central to the establishment of the company as a global energy player.

The prominence of Brazilian firms, and of Petrobras specifically, in the energy sector worldwide is partly a result of an increasing process of internationalization that took off in the 2000s, with important acquisitions of firms from developed countries. In the specific case of Petrobras, another side of this matter relies on the redesign of policies in the energy sectors (Sennes and Narciso, 2009). Since the 1990s, Brazil has moved from a self-sufficiency policy towards an integrated, energy security approach as its central strategy, which took shape through the government's designs for Petrobras. In line with this changing perspective, internationalization, verticalization and investments in finding better energy sources have come to the heart of the company's strategic plans.

The role of the government in the development of the Petrobras of today has several facets. To begin with, the choice of oil and energy as a key driver of the country's economic industrialization, during the import substitution industrialization process carried out the 1950s was crucial for the pursuit of technological development required in order to access the domestic oil reserves. In this sense, it is hard to detach the presence of the government from the impressive technological trajectory of the company, which was also developed through consistent partnerships with public universities and research institutes.

The internationalization of Petrobras was also a strategic political decision, which aimed to keep the country safe from the economic imbalances originating from international oil crises. In terms of internationalization, the role of the government is restricted to the strategic search for oil sources at the early global expansion of Petrobras. Policies to foster internationalization of Brazilian firms have only recently entered the government's agenda, as part of a strong policy aimed at boosting export performance and improving competitiveness through investment in R and D towards new strategic sectors (Almeida, 2009). Until then, in Brazil the predominant vision among the government was that foreign investments by domestic companies represented a crowding out of capital, investments and employment, and therefore were very harmful to the domestic economy. This view has been subverted by evidence, not only in Brazil but also throughout the world, that internationalized firms perform better and possess better technologies and human resources, and their exports achieve a better profitability (De Negri et al., 2005).

In summary, Petrobras became a national global player owing to its reliance on a strong competitive asset: its deepwater exploration technologies, which have been developed from the specific circumstances present in the Brazilian oil reserves. The role of the government in the process was in picking the oil sector as strategic for industrial development and providing means for the building of a scientific and technological network to enable the development of the required capabilities. There were no direct incentives in internationalization apart from the strategic and political purposes of reaching key oil sources.

It is useful to counterbalance the case of Petrobras with that of the state oil companies of China. In the latter case, the government had a major role in creating big global companies from the start, since the country lacked both oil reserves in sufficient amounts for its demand and the technological capacity necessary to explore the sources that they own (Carvalho and Goldstein, 2009). In this sense, Petrobras' international expansion is highly technology-driven by nature, whereas the Chinese expansion has a strong technology-seeking purpose.

Petrobras is of crucial importance in the Brazilian political scenario and is often the reason for political distress. With a budget bigger than most ministries, the company accounts for a third of all investments foreseen by the Growth Acceleration Plan (PAC), an equivalent of over US$80bn (Revista Exame, 2010b). For that reason, every little movement in the company's administration is followed, and investment plans, governance structure and indebtedness levels are subject to public scrutiny.

Concluding remarks

This chapter presented the trajectory of a Brazilian state-owned company, and also one of the largest multinationals originated from an emerging country. It has achieved a remarkable technological trajectory, becoming a world leader in the field of deepwater oil extraction. Such a feat is by no means ordinary, let alone for a firm in a developing country where financial and technological resources are scarce by nature.

The oil industry has a series of specific features that are not easily shared by many other sectors; the fact that Petrobras is a state-owned company from an emerging country adds some idiosyncrasies to its trajectory. We tried to highlight the role of the government in providing the company with the assets it holds today and that enabled it to become a major oil producer and a technological reference for deepwater drilling. In our view, the government played one major role: choosing oil as a strategic industry to be developed and controlled by the state, given its crucial role for the consolidation of an industrial basis within the country. This one decision has given rise to and shaped the opportunities for technological development and also for international expansion (a feature common in the oil industry trajectory).

State ownership has granted Petrobras the resources necessary to foster technological excellence, and here once more the strategic choice for keeping the sector in state command was crucial for the achievements that the company accomplished over its history.

Pressures from the market have driven changes in the legislation regarding oil concessions in the national territory, and nowadays several other oil companies explore oil fields in Brazil. Petrobras' expertise in offshore, deepwater exploration makes it a partner for those companies, rather than a regular competitor.

It is therefore because of its technological development that Petrobras became one of the most important oil companies in the world, and also one of the most important Brazilian businesses both domestically and overseas. Much of the prosperity expected for the Brazilian economy in the forthcoming years lies with the success of Petrobras. The future of alternative energy sources and the possibility of the country becoming a world leader in ethanol production and exports is also in the company's hands.

References

Amann, E. (2009), "Technology, Public Policy, and the Emergence of Brazilian Multinationals", in Brainard, L. and Martinez-Diaz, L. (eds.), *Brazil as an Economic Superpower? Understanding Brazil's Changing Role in the Global Economy*, Washington, D.C.: Brookings Institution Press.

Aykut, D. and Goldstein, A. (2009), *FDI in the Oil Sector*. Mimeo, DECPG-International Finance Team, The World Bank and OECD Development Centre.

Carvalho, F. and Goldstein. A. (2009), The 'making of' national giants: the inter-national expansion of oil companies from Brazil and China, in Dolfsma, Duysters, and Costa (eds.), *Multinationals and Emerging Economies: The Quest for Innovation and Sustainability*, Cheltenham, Edward Elgar.

Economist, (2010a), Making a name for themselves: emerging markets are now creating highly valuable brands. April 28th, 2010.

———(2010b), Over a Barrel – Brazil's oil giant may be paying too much to pump the stuff. September 2nd, 2010.

Época Negócios (2010), *Os negócios do pré-sal*. Ano 4, n. 43, September 2010. Editora Globo.

Furtado, A. (1997), A trajetória tecnológica da Petrobras na produção *offshore*. Unicamp, Departamento de Política Científica e Tecnológica, *Textos para discussão* n. 18.

Furtado, A. and Freitas, A. (2000), The Catch-up strategy of Petrobras through cooperative R&D. *Journal of Technology Transfer*, 25, pp. 23–36.

Goldstein, A. (2009), New Multinationals from Emerging Asia: the case of National Oil Companies. *Asia Development Review*, Vol. 26 n. 2, pp. 26–56.

———, (2010), The emergence of Multilatinas: the Petrobras experience. *Universia Business Review*, primer cuatrimestre 2010, pp. 98–111.

Gouveia, F. (2010), Tecnologia nacional para extrair petroleo e gás do pré-sal. *Conhecimento & Inovação*, ano 6, n.1, pp. 30–36.

Petrobras S.A. (2010), *Relatório de Sustentabilidade 2009*. Available at: www.petrobras.com.br. Accessed in October 2010.

Revista Exame (2010a), *Melhores e Maiores*. São Paulo, Editora Abril, edição 2010.

———(2010b), *O poder da SuperPetrobras*. Ed. 976, year 44, n. 17, pp. 26–39.

Sennes, R., and Narciso, T. (2009), "Brazil as an International Energy Player", in Brainard, L. and Martinez-Diaz, L. (eds.), *Brazil as an Economic Super-power? Understanding Brazil's Changing Role in the Global Economy*, Washington, D.C.: Brookings Institution Press.

Part V
Key Issues for the Future

24
The Oil Curse
Causes, Consequences, and Policy Implications

Richard Auty

The context

A study of resource-driven development from 1960 to 1997 reveals scant evidence of a resource curse in the 1960s when the income per head of the resource-rich economies remained on average 50% above those of the resource-poor economies (Auty 2001, 5). However, when commodity price volatility increased during 1974–85 growth collapses proliferated, especially among resource-rich economies. Thereafter, during 1985–97 both large and small resource-rich economies grew slower than the resource-poor economies, whose mean income per head surpassed that of the resource-rich economies. Among the resource-rich economies the mineral economies had the highest resource rent but the slowest growth, with oil exporters having the highest rent and weakest growth of all (Table 24.1).

The absence of evidence of the effects of a resource curse in the 1960s suggests the curse is not an inevitable outcome. Moreover, economists predict that a high rent/GDP ratio facilitates economic development if it is efficiently deployed to boost capital formation and expand the capacity to import the capital goods required to build a modern economy. However, high rent also creates contests for its capture and if this causes political objectives to override economic ones then the resulting rent deployment distorts the economy. This paper argues, first, that the oil-rich economies were especially vulnerable to the policy failure that triggered growth collapses among resource-rich economies through the 1970s and 1980s and, second, that policy failure confers scope for a policy learning curve.

This perspective helps explain why 15 years of statistical research have failed to provide a definitive explanation for the resource curse and its existence remains contested (Lederman and Maloney 2007). Although patronage-driven rent cycling adversely impacted economic growth through the 1970s and 1980s, IFI-backed reforms subsequently reduced its incidence. Yet statistical analysis has neglected this policy improvement (Sachs and Warner 1995; Brunnschweiler 2008). In addition, statistical analysis neglects the fact that resource curse is part of a broader rent curse that can be caused by geopolitical rent (foreign aid) and regulatory rent (that governments create by changing relative prices (Tollison 1982)), as well as by natural resource rent (Auty 2010).[1] Focusing on natural resource rent underestimates the total rent cycled by governments.

Table 24.1 Share of rents in GDP 1994 and GDP growth 1985–97, by country natural resource endowment

Resource Endowment	PCGDP growth 1985-97 (%)	Total rent (% GDP)	Pasture and cropland rent (% GDP)	Mineral rent (% GDP)
Resource Poor[1,2]				
Large	4.7	10.56	7.34	3.22
Small	2.4	9.86	5.41	4.45
Resource Rich				
Large	1.9	12.65	5.83	6.86
Small, non-mineral	0.9	15.42	12.89	2.53
Small, hard mineral	−0.4	17.51	9.62	7.89
Small, oil exporter	−0.7	21.22	2.18	19.04
All Countries		15.03	8.78	6.25

[1] Resource-poor = 1970 cropland/head < 0.3 hectares
[2] Large = 1970 GDP > $7 billion
Source: Derived from World Bank (2010).

Foreign aid shared the unearned or 'windfall' characteristic of resource rent until donors became more discriminating regarding its application in the 1990s (Collier 2006). Regulatory rent tends to expand with rising levels of state intervention and decreasing trade openness. Each rent source can comprise 10–20% of GDP or more (World Bank 2006; Svenssen 2000 and Krueger 1992), potentially taking the total rent within the economy to one-fifth to one-third of GDP or more.

This paper argues that the oil curse is an extreme manifestation of a broader rent curse that is rooted in policy failure. It draws on the emerging theory of rent cycling, which posits that rent systematically shapes elite incentives, thereby moulding policy, which in turn drives the economic trajectory (Auty 2010). The next section (2) of the paper relates rent cycling theory to the resource curse literature. Section 3 explains why oil-driven economies were particularly vulnerable to the post-1960s manifestation of the resource curse and identifies economic policies for effective rent deployment. Section 4 evaluates the evidence for a policy learning curve from the oil exporters' deployment of the windfall rent from the 2003–8 oil boom. Section 5 proposes a dual track strategy for economic reform that can circumvent the political constraints on such reform.

The literature

Academic speculation about the existence of a resource curse was fuelled by case study analysis of the deployment of the 1974–78 and 1979–81 oil windfalls (Gelb 1988, Karl 1997), which revealed mostly disappointing outcomes. Sachs and Warner (1995 and 1999, 23) triggered a series of systematic statistical analyses. They identified Dutch disease effects as the driver of the curse whereby the booming commodity revenue stream strengthens the real exchange rate, which causes the non-booming tradable sectors (agriculture and manufacturing) to contract so that when commodity prices eventually fall the economy may be less prosperous than it was before the boom occurred. Sachs and Warner also find that most natural resource-rich governments close their trade policy as their dependence on primary product exports increases in order to counter the employment-diminishing effects of Dutch disease.

Interestingly, the trade policy/resource export dependence curve traces an inverted U-shape because at very high levels of resource dependence trade policy re-opens. This reflects the responses of the oil-rich Gulf monarchies, whose unusually high rent per head supplied sufficient revenue to subsidize the livelihoods of nationals, including providing public sector employment that permitted governments to ignore employment destruction by imports. But a more common response among commodity exporters, including other oil exporters, was to protect manufacturing and channel some rent into state-led industrialization, much of which was inefficiently executed and unprofitable (Auty 1990). Lal and Myint (1996) show that protective policies repress markets, thereby distorting the economy and causing growth to collapse.

Subsequently, Acemoglu et al. (2001, 2002) argued that the quality of institutions is more important than natural resources *per se* in determining whether resources are a blessing or a curse. In particular, they identify as detrimental to economic growth those extractive colonial institutions associated with colonies that were too unhealthy for significant European settlement. Yet Glaeser et al. (2004) relegate institutions to secondary status: they find that institutions improve as a consequence of rising incomes but do not cause that rise, which is explained by human capital and policy choice. Moreover, Khan (2000) notes that the political rationale for choosing policies that are economically sub-optimal is often compelling: governments in many newly independent countries find it necessary to deploy rents to secure political cohesion without which economic activity struggles. North et al. (2009) model the resulting rent-driven outcome as Limited Access Order societies wherein rent is deployed primarily to limit potential violence by co-opting into the elite those deemed capable of wielding violence.

It therefore seems that in low-income economies, institutions bend to accommodate political incentives rather than mould those incentives. For example, Schlumberger (2008) associates a patrimonial form of capitalism with oil exporting countries in which informal rules override formal institutional rules because that benefits élite rent recipients. It also gives the élite an interest in resisting economic reform (World Bank 2009). More recent work by Acemoglu and Robinson (2008) backtracks on their earlier findings and recognizes the ability of the elite to manipulate institutions. This shift is consistent with the central role that rent cycling theory assigns to élite incentives.

Rent cycling theory identifies two basic development trajectories, namely low-rent competitive industrialisation and the high-rent staple trap. The high-rent staple trap trajectory describes the development of most oil-rich economies but the low-rent competitive industrialization trajectory furnishes an instructive counterfactual. More specifically, low rent creates incentives for the élites to create wealth efficiently since economic growth expands tax revenue, which in the presence of low rent is the principal source of discretionary expenditure, and one that the élite in low rent economies frequently benefit from disproportionately. Such wealth creation requires the provision of public goods and maintenance of efficiency incentives, which align the economy with its comparative advantage that in low-rent economies lies in the early export of labour-intensive manufactures.

The resulting low-rent trajectory triggers three virtuous circuits (Figure 24.1). First, competitive manufacturing rapidly absorbs surplus rural labour so that rising wages automatically drive diversification into productivity-boosting, skill-intensive and capital-intensive sectors. Second, the associated early urbanization accelerates the demographic cycle to reduce the dependant/worker ratio, which raises the share of investment in GDP and accelerates the GDP growth rate per head (Bloom and Williamson 1998). Third, the rapid structural change engendered by competitive industrialization proliferates social groups that impede policy capture by any one group and drive incremental democratization as three sanctions against anti-social governance strengthen. Specifically: private firms protect their investment by lobbying for property rights and the rule of law (Li et al. 2001); unsubsidized urbanization strengthens self-help civic voice (Isham et al. 2005); and government reliance on taxing income, profits and expenditure (forced by the absence of rent from commodity trade) spurs demand for accountable public finances (Ross 2001).

In contrast, the high rent that is characteristic of oil-driven economies elicits political contests for its capture that deflect élite incentives into cycling rent to boost patronage that offers larger and more immediate (often personal) rewards than the long haul of economic growth. Consequently, rent

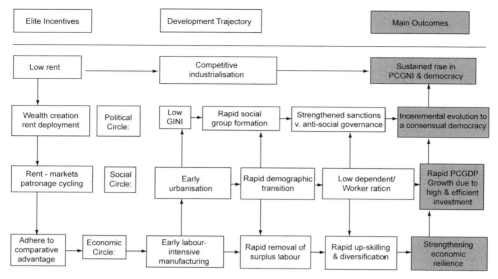

Figure 24.1 Low Rent Competitive Industrialization Development Model

flows through patronage networks at the expense of markets, which shifts the high-rent economy away from its comparative advantage and lowers investment efficiency. This locks the economy into a staple trap of decelerating growth and over-reliance on a weakening primary sector.

The high rent trajectory represses all three virtuous circuits that drive the low rent trajectory (Figure 24.2). First, in the absence of competitive industrialization, surplus labour persists so that income inequality rises, which puts pressures on élites to deploy rent to grow the bureaucracy and expand employment in protected industries that markets would not support. Second, the burgeoning demand for transfers from the subsidized sector eventually outstrips the rent, either through structural change or falling commodity prices, so governments extract returns to capital

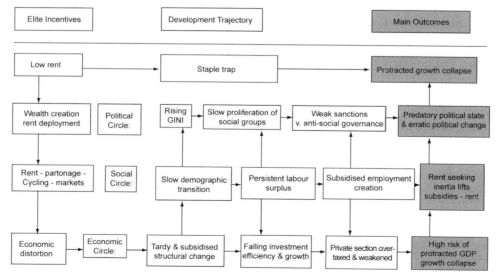

Figure 24.2 High Rent Competitive Industrialization Development Model

Table 24.2 GDP growth per head, MENA and other developing regions, 1961–2008

	1961–70	1971–80	1981–90	1991–2000	2001–08
Middle East and North Africa	3.9	3.0	–1.3	1.1	2.7
MENA oil exporting economies	5.8	–0.2	–1.6	–5.9	3.4
East Asia and Pacific	4.3	3.6	2.5	6.4	8.0
Latin America and Caribbean	2.7	2.3	0.5	1.7	1.5
Sub-Saharan Africa	1.8	1.6	0.2	–0.4	2.5
South Asia	2.0	0.7	3.2	2.7	5.4
World	3.1	2.5	1.0	1.3	1.7

Source: World Bank (2010).

and labour in the primary sector to augment the rent. The transfers impede competitive structural change and increase reliance on a primary sector that is weakening. Third, sanctions against anti-social governance atrophy as: businesses benefit more from lobbying politicians than from productive investment; social capital is subservient, reflecting dependence on government largesse; and government reliance on revenue from rent streams rather than direct and indirect taxation eases public pressure for financial accountability. Since rent recipients resist market reform because it shrinks their rent, growth eventually collapses and recovery is protracted.

These two basic rent-driven models explain the intensifying post-war divergence of global rent-driven development trajectories (Auty 2001, 5). Although growth rates show little evidence of a resource curse in the 1960s, case studies reveal that the statist policies favoured in the post-war decades were already cumulatively distorting high-rent economies, as the staple trap model explains, a process that persisted into the 1970s. The commodity price shocks of 1974–85 hit the weakened high-rent economies and triggered growth collapses, first in the late 1970s in the least credit-worthy states, namely many sub-Saharan African (SSA) oil-importers; then spreading in the early 1980s to economies in receipt of recycled petrodollars in SSA and in Latin America; before hitting the oil-exporters in the mid-1980s when the oil price abruptly plummeted. Despite initial resistance to international financial institutions (IFI)-backed reforms by rent recipients, many developing country governments, but not all, subsequently pursued a policy learning curve that eventually raised growth rates through the 1990s and 2000s (Table 24.2).

Finally, rent cycling theory recognizes that the adverse impacts of high rent are exacerbated (and therefore more intractable) in the presence of four factors. First, statist policies (Van der Walle 1999; Ndulu et al. 2008) expand scope for rent-seeking that few governments are able to resist. Second, concentrated commodity linkages (as in mining) boost such opportunities by concentrating rent on governments rather than spreading it across many economic agents (Baldwin 1956). Third, ethnic tension feeds competition for patronage rent cycling (Montalvo and Reynal-Querol 2005, 294). Fourth, parliamentary parties target expenditure at swing voters via projects rather than at universal programmes that benefit the broader electorate (Collier and Hoeffler 2006). This is especially so in young democracies that lack voter credibility (Keefer 2007). The first two augmenting factors (statist policies and concentrated linkages) interact, and when combined with oil's typical high rent/GDP ratio help to explain the intensity of the oil curse.

The oil curse

Rent cycling theory identifies three key reasons why the mineral economies and especially the oil-exporting economies have proved so vulnerable to the rent curse. First, oil rent tends to be unusually high relative to GDP so that governments that tax the rent away increase the impact of public expenditure on the economy, for better or for worse, and risk intensifying the Dutch disease effects. Within the non-mining tradable sector, Dutch disease effects tend to be stronger for agriculture than manufacturing because manufacturers have proved more effective at lobbying for protection against cheaper imports than farmers have. The resulting pro-industry policy bias represses the strong contribution that agriculture can make to the early stages of development, not least as a source of labour-intensive employment and transmitter of basic business skills, but also by supplying inputs for further domestic processing, expanding the home market for basic, locally-made manufactured goods and diversifying export revenue and taxation (Mellor 1976 and 1995; Timmer 2007). Unfortunately, protected industry usually has had little incentive to mature and compete because it invariably functions primarily to accommodate rent seeking. It has also been capital-intensive and created few jobs so governments compensate by over-expanding public sector employment.

However, compared with soft commodities oil revenue streams tend to be not only large relative to GDP but also volatile (Cashin et al. 2000; Cashin and McDermott 2002; van der Ploeg and Poelhekke 2009), so that they severely test macro-economic management, not least by unleashing intense political pressure to spend during booms and vociferous opposition to cut-backs during downswings (Gelb 1988). The volatility of oil prices is rooted in the unusual capital intensity of hydrocarbon extraction, which results in long lead-times between the decision to invest and the start-up of production. Project lead times of four to seven years and more render it difficult to match supply and demand so that productive capacity either lags demand or runs ahead of it, which amplifies booms and busts (Auty 1987).

The second key reason why oil exporting economies under-perform also reflects the exceptionally capital-intensive production function of oil extraction, which concentrates rent on very few economic actors, notably the government. Expressed in terms of the four domestic economic linkages of the oil sector: backward and forward production linkages (for locally-sourced inputs and further processing, respectively) tend to be limited since mining inputs are often imported due to their sophistication, which benefits from scale economies, whereas downstream products incur higher freight costs than upstream products and tend to locate at major markets. Moreover, the small albeit well-paid oil sector labour force and frequent foreign ownership of capital limit second round expenditure (final demand linkage) within the host economy. This leaves fiscal linkage, or taxation, as the dominant contribution to domestic economic growth, which is concentrated on the government and elicits political contests for its capture. Governments tend to react to windfalls as if they represent permanent changes in income (Gelb 1988). Private economic agents are more cautious and tend to save more and to seek more efficient returns on their investments. Consequently, rent tends to be deployed less effectively when it is concentrated on governments than when the linkages disperse rent across many economic agents, as with peasant agriculture (Bevan et al. 1999).

The singular economic linkages from hydrocarbon extraction trigger the third factor behind the oil curse, namely over-ambitious state intervention within the economy. Several oil-rich governments used their windfalls to intensify state-led heavy industry drives in the mid-1970s (Auty 1990), including Venezuela, Trinidad and Tobago, Algeria, Iran and Indonesia while Malaysia, Mexico and Nigeria did so in response to the 1979–81 boom. In addition, most oil-rich governments expanded social entitlements that were most generous in the Gulf monarchies, which incurred levels of public expenditure that proved both difficult to sustain and to reduce when the oil price softened in the mid-1980s. Many oil-exporting governments augmented their rent with foreign borrowing during the booms, which they could not service when oil prices fell. Even those that accumulated financial reserves during the boom, quickly depleted them in the downswing: Saudi Arabia struggled towards the close of the initial decade of lower oil prices (Auty 2001, 193–207). Where reserves were limited and IFI-backed stabilization proved difficult to sustain, the political system was destabilized, notably in Algeria

(Chemingui and El-Said 2007), Nigeria (Sala-y-Martin and Subramanian 2003), Russia (Gaddy and Ickes 2010) and Venezuela (Hausmann 2003).

It may be recalled that rent cycling theory notes that the risks of rent misallocation are still further heightened for oil-rich economies in the presence of high ethnic diversity and youthful democracies. These characteristics imply that newly independent and ethnically fractured oil-exporting democracies like Nigeria and Trinidad and Tobago were especially vulnerable. Their 1974–78 and 1979–81 oil booms conferred rent windfalls equivalent to an extra 20% (Nigeria) and 35% (Trinidad and Tobago) of non-oil GDP annually (Gelb 1988).

Yet the policies required to manage commodity windfall rents were known (Gelb 1988), although environmental accounting has since supplied the basic rationale for effective rent deployment. Environmental accounting demonstrates that part of the revenue from the depletion of the hydrocarbon assets should be transformed into infrastructure and human capital in support of non-oil productive capacity to sustain productivity increases and drive the economy when the oil is exhausted (World Bank 2006). The two critical requirements for achieving this are to match the rate of domestic rent absorption to absorptive capacity and to expand competitive employment in activity that does not depend on rent transfers to sustain it. Typically, this requires the public sector to expand basic infrastructure and promote competitive markets to stimulate private investment in economic diversification. The Permanent Income Hypothesis provides a guide for managing the public finances (Segura 2006). It converts the projected hydrocarbon income stream into a stock of capital and calls for the maintenance of the non-oil fiscal deficit at a level that can be sustained indefinitely by the income stream from the hydrocarbon stock of capital. These objectives are achieved by sterilizing a fraction of the windfall revenue in diversified offshore accounts.

Unfortunately, the economic policy prescriptions say little about managing the political pressures that accompany windfall revenues. Governments have invariably made over-optimistic assumptions about both the scale of the future income stream and their capacity to control the rate of domestic absorption to ensure efficient rent deployment. Most governments absorbed their 1974–81 oil rent windfalls too rapidly, which triggered Dutch disease effects that weakened the non-mining tradables sector and established social entitlements that proved difficult to scale back when oil prices sagged, perpetuating fiscal deficits and inflation. However, despite cycling some rent for political patronage, the two most successful oil exporters, Indonesia and Malaysia, ensured that rent cycled into their large but lagging rural economies by taking advantage of green revolution farming techniques efficiently to boost farm incomes and productivity. This objective also demanded cautious macropolicy. Crucially, they also established competitive manufacturing sectors. Their success confirms that the oil curse is policy-induced and not a deterministic law.

More specifically, both Malaysia and Indonesia established state-owned white elephant projects for political reasons (Auty 1990) but Malaysia deliberately compensated with the expansion of competitive manufacturing, while Indonesia did so more by accident. Malaysia recognized early the inefficiency of infant industry policies and established export-processing zones from 1971, which expanded to a sufficient scale so that when oil prices collapsed in the mid-1980s the zones' activity sustained economic growth (Saleh and Meyanathan 1993). This outcome appears rooted in a tacit compact between the majority Malays and the more prosperous large Chinese minority to tolerate patronage rent cycling (to Malays) provided it did not undermine incentives for efficient (Chinese) investment. In Indonesia a relatively small number of important Chinese entrepreneurs took advantage of protective tariffs to earn high profits that they re-invested in efficient activity, rather than subsidizing inefficient plants as occurred in the state sector (Flatters and Jenkins 1986). When oil prices weakened in the mid-1980s, Indonesia's competitive manufacturers performed a similar role to Malaysia's export processing zones and expanded exports on a sufficient scale to sustain rapid economic growth.

The 2004–8 oil boom: meagre evidence of a policy learning curve

Most resource-rich economies struggled to recover from their 1980s growth collapses owing to opposition from entrenched rent seeking constituencies. Their governments reluctantly embraced IFI-backed reforms in exchange for help with debt service but then struggled with reform implementation in the face of intense opposition. Eventually, the combination of shrinking rent per head and increasingly conditional IFI-backed assistance elicited improvements in economic performance. Table 24.2 traces the growth collapses within resource-rich Latin America, sub-Saharan Africa and Middle East and North Africa (MENA) and identifies the onset of recovery in Latin America through the 1990s with sub-Saharan Africa and MENA picking up during the 2000s.

However, the unexpected oil boom of the mid-2000s sharply expanded resource rent streams, which reduced the urgency of sustaining economic reform and stoked political expectations for immediate distribution of the benefits. Villafuerte and Lopez-Murphy (2010) show the overall public expenditure of the oil exporting economies was pro-cyclical. It widened the non-oil fiscal deficits through the boom before sharply shrinking them during 2009. But variations occurred in the overall policy response that reflect differences between capital-surplus economies (with high oil reserves per head) and capital-scarce/labour-surplus economies (Nankani 1979). Whereas the capital-surplus oil exporters increased savings and also domestic investment (thereby boosting potential long-term growth prospects), most labour-surplus economies expanded consumption.

Many capital surplus MENA oil-exporters deployed their rent more shrewdly than in previous booms: oil industry estimates indicate that Saudi Arabia, Libya, Kuwait and the United Arab Emirates saved 65–80% of their increased revenue 2004–7 whereas regional labour-surplus economies like Algeria saved 40% and Iran ran deficits. Comparable saving rates for Angola, Nigeria and Venezuela are 30%, 28% and 18%, respectively. Regrettably, however, few of the capital-surplus governments took advantage of the oil boom to accelerate labour market reforms designed to shift nationals from oil-dependent state sector jobs to the private sector, which in the Gulf monarchies predominantly relies on immigrant labour. Even for capital-surplus oil-exporters the post-1980s policy learning curve is incomplete.

A second index of policy learning is provided by estimates of the oil price required to balance national budgets. In 2007–8, the price of oil required to sustain expenditure on social entitlements ranged from $18 to $100 per barrel. The estimated oil price required to balance the budget among capital-surplus oil exporters ranged downwards from $42 for Saudi Arabia. Qatar and Libya each required $39, Kuwait $29 and the United Arab Emirates required $18 per barrel. Elsewhere, large labour-surplus economies like Venezuela required $100 per barrel to balance its budget, Iran and Russia $80 while Nigeria required $70, rates of domestic absorption that the 2008–9 price collapse rendered unsustainable.[2] Algeria, however, required just $45 per barrel.

Far less progress along the policy learning curve occurred in the established hydrocarbon producers in South America, a group that excludes emerging Brazil. Their growth collapses exacerbated deep-seated social tensions, whether racial (Bolivia), regional (Ecuador) or class (Venezuela) that empowered populist regimes that implemented three flawed policies. First, mining contracts were repudiated, deterring the foreign investment required to sustain exploration and maintain production. Second, reliance on national oil companies increased, which lowered hydrocarbon extractive efficiency as state firms struggled to execute political favours while also pursuing their commercial mandate. PDVSA underwent a spectacular dilution of corporate autonomy as it boosted expenditure on populist programmes. Third, public consumption was boosted in ways that resemble the populist booms that damaged Latin American growth in the 1960s and 1970s. Sachs (1989) identifies a populist cycle that undermines long-term wealth generation. It begins with an initial surge in public expenditure and real wages that triggers rapid economic growth as spare capacity is employed. However, the expenditure outstrips supply and widens the trade deficit as some exports are diverted to the domestic market and imports fill the gap. Inflation also accelerates and expands the fiscal deficit, denting business confidence and triggering capital flight. The initial growth spurt therefore proves unsustainable and within four years of the launch of the boom (longer during an oil boom), emergency stabilization causes real incomes to collapse to levels below those when the populist boom was launched.

The sub-Saharan African oil exporters fared no better: despite high levels of poverty the windfalls continued to benefit the élite disproportionately. Nigerian hydrocarbon production faltered in the face of civil unrest in the Delta producing region that has its roots in the steady shrinkage of local revenue retention as ethnic groups elsewhere demanded, and achieved, statehood in order to expand their ethnic group's share of the rent (Ejobowah 2000). Even so, the rent accrued to the ethnic élites rather than the majority. Angola extracts rent more efficiently than Nigeria but deploys it inefficiently from a development perspective. Over-rapid domestic rent absorption has tripled Angola's real exchange rate compared with the early 1990s when agriculture was last internationally competitive (World Bank 2007, 103–20). This cheapens imports and feeds a consumer boom among the urban middle class. But as war-torn transport infrastructure is repaired the 80% of the population reliant on farming, which struggles to re-establish itself after three decades of civil war, is exposed to low-cost imported food. Finally, in Chad, a flagship World Bank experiment to direct rent flows into development expenditure collapsed when a rigid spending agreement encountered the unexpected and massive surge in rent through 2003–8 (Frynas and Paolo 2007).

Dual track reform for oil-exporting economies

This paper has argued that the oil curse is an intense form of a broader rent curse that reflects the unusual capital intensity of hydrocarbon production. Most oil exporters mismanaged their 1974–81 oil windfalls, but since rent shapes élite incentives that mould the policies that in turn drive the development trajectory, the rent squeeze associated with a growth collapse allows for a policy learning curve. Although most capital-surplus MENA oil exporters achieved partial policy improvement through the 2003–8 oil windfalls, the labour-surplus MENA oil exporters along with the emerging producers in sub-Saharan Africa and established Latin American oil exporters lag behind.

The inertia of rent-seeking interests explains the lagged learning curve and suggests that effective economic reform requires a complementary political strategy to circumvent policy capture by self-serving élites. Successful economic reformers that include resource-poor China and Mauritius as well as oil-rich Indonesia and Malaysia, suggest that a dual track reform strategy can achieve this (Lau et al. 2000). The strategy builds a dynamic market economy within special geographical areas (Track One) that function as early reform zones (ERZs). ERZs provide immediately 'post-reform' conditions, namely: world class infrastructure; competitive incentives (not subsidies); and enabling (uncorrupted) public services and legal safeguards (Auty 2006). The ERZs postpone reform of the rent-distorted economy (Track Two), which lowers the threat to reforming governments from antagonized rent recipients.

Track One rapidly expands non-oil employment, foreign exchange and taxes to reach a size that can absorb workers and capital from the distorted sector in Track Two, which undergoes a relative decline. Crucially, Track One also builds a pro-growth political constituency that becomes sufficiently powerful to neutralize rent recipients. The experience of the successful economic reformers suggests ERZ-based activity requires 15 to 20 years to become large enough to drive the economy and also permit the gainers from reform in Track One to compensate losers in the rent-distorted sector. Such a strategy for managing political opposition to economic reform appears critical to avoiding the rent curse.

One further feature of dual track reform with important implications for development economics is that it accelerates structural change, in marked contrast to the ossified social relationships of the staple trap development trajectory that is caused by maladroit oil rent deployment. Such structural change spawns the social groups that can prevent policy capture by one group and, in the terminology of North et al. (2007), propel 'Limited Access Societies' across the threshold into 'Open Access Societies'.

Notes

1 Crowson (personal communication) helpfully points out that these 'rent' streams may be more accurately identified as 'supernumerary government revenue'.
2 Oil producers reportedly consider $80 per barrel as a realistic oil price and they attribute previous prices above that level to market speculators. There is some support for this contention about the role of speculation in boosting prices from the positive link between the prices of oil and gold, which is a well-recognized speculative commodity (IMF 2008, 27–28).

References

Acemoglu, D., Johnson, S. and Robinson, J. (2001) The colonial origins of comparative development: An empirical investigation, *American Economic Review*, 91(1), 1369–1401.
——(2002) Reversal of fortune: Geography and institutions the making of the modern world income distribution, *Quarterly Journal of Economics*, 117, 1231–94.
Acemoglu, D. and Robinson, J. (2008) Persistence of power, elites and institutions, *American Economic Review*, 98(1), 267–93.
Auty, R.M. (1987) Producer homogeneity, heightened uncertainty and minerals market rigidity, *Resources Policy*, 13, 189–206.
——(1990) *Sowing the Oil: Resource-Based Industrialisation in Eight Developing Countries*, Oxford: Clarendon Press.
——(2001) *Resource Abundance and Economic Development*, Oxford: Clarendon Press.
——(2006) From mining enclave to economic catalyst: Large mineral projects in developing countries, *Brown Journal of World Affairs*, 13(1), 135–45.
——(2010) Elites, rent cycling and development: Adjustment to land scarcity in Mauritius, Kenya and Cote d'Ivoire, *Development Policy Review* 28(4), 411–33.
Bevan, D., Collier. P. and Gunning, J.W. (1987) Consequences of a commodity boom in a controlled economy: Accumulation and redistribution in Kenya, *World Bank Economic Review* 1, 489–513.
Bloom, D.E. and Williamson, J. G. (1998) Demographic transitions and economic miracles in emerging Asia, *The World Bank Economic Review* 12, 419–55.
Brunnschweiler, C.N. (2008) Cursing the blessings? Natural resource abundance, institutions and economic growth, *World Development* 36 93, 399–49.
Cashin, P., Liang, H. and McDermott, C.J. (2000) How persistent are shocks to world commodity prices? *IMF Staff Papers*, 47, 177–217.
Cashin, P. and McDermott, C.J. (2002),The long-run behaviour of commodity prices: Small trends and big variability, *IMF Staff Papers*, 49(2), 175–98.
Chemingui, M.A. and El-Said, M.M. (2007) Algeria's macroeconomic performances from 1962–2000, In: Nugent, J. and Pesaran, H. (eds.) *Explaining Growth in the Middle East*, Elsevier: Amsterdam, 335–58.
Cho, Y.J. (1996) Government intervention, rent distribution and economic development in Korea, In: Aoki, M., Kim, H. and Okuno-Fujiwara, M. (eds.) *The Role of Government in East Asian Economic Development*, Oxford: Clarendon Press, 208–32.
Collier, P. (2006) Is aid oil? An analysis of whether Africa can absorb more aid, *World Development* 34(9), 1482–97.
Collier, P. and Hoeffler, A. (2009) Testing the Neo-con agenda: Democracy in resource-rich societies, *European Economic Review* 53, 293–308.
Ejobowah, J.B. (2000) Who owns the oil? The politics of ethnicity in the Niger Delta of Nigeria, *Africa Today* 47 (1), 29–47.
Flatters, F. and Jenkins, G. (1986) 'Trade policy in Indonesia', Cambridge MA: HIID.

Frynas, A and Paolo, M. (2007) New Scramble for African Oil? Historical, Political, and Business Perspectives, *African Affairs* 106, 229–51.

Gaddy, C.G. and Ickes, B.W. (2010) 'Russia after the global financial crisis', *Eurasian Geography and Economics*, 51(3), 281–311.

Gelb, A.H., and Associates (1988) *Oil Windfalls: Blessing or Curse?* NewYork: Oxford University Press.

Glaeser, E.L., La Porta, R., Lopes-de-Silanes, F. and Shleifer, A. (2004) *Journal of Economic Growth* 9(3), 271–303.

Hausmann, R. (2003) Venezuela's growth implosion: A Neo-classical story? In: Rodrik, D. (ed.) *In Search of Prosperity: Analytic Narratives of Economic Growth*, Princeton NJ: Princeton University Press, 244–70.

Isham, J., L. Pritchett, M. Woolcock, and G. Busby (2005) The varieties of resource experience: How natural resource export structures affect the political economy of economic growth, *World Bank Economic Review* 19 (1), 141–64.

Karl, T.L. (1997) *The Paradox of Plenty: Oil Booms and Petro-States*, Berkeley: University of California Press.

Keefer, P. (2007) Clientelism, credibility and policy choices of young democracies, *American Journal of Political Science* 51(4), 804–21.

Khan, M. (2000) Rent-seeking as process, In, Khan, M. H. and Jomo, K.S. (eds.) *Rents, Rent-seeking and Economic Development: Theory and Evidence in Asia*, Cambridge: Cambridge University Press, 70–144.

Krueger, A.O. (1992) *Political Economy of Agricultural Pricing Policies*, Johns Hopkins University Press, Baltimore MD.

Lederman, D. and Maloney, W.F. (2007) *Natural Resources: Neither Curse nor Blessing*, Palo Alto CA: Stanford University Press.

Lau, L.J., Y. Qian and G. Roland (2000) Reform without losers: An interpretation of China's dual-track approach to transition, *Journal of Political Economy* 108, 120–43.

Li, S., Li, S. and Zhang, W. (2000) The road to capitalism: Competition and institutional change in China, *Journal of Comparative Economics* 28, 269–92.

Macintyre, A. (2000) Funny money in Indonesia, In: Khan, M.H and Jomo, K.S. (eds.) *Rents, Rent-Seeking and Economic Development*, Cambridge: Cambridge University Press, 248–73.

Mellor, J.W. (1976) *The New Economics of Growth: A Strategy for India and the Developing World*, Ithaca NY: Cornell University Press.

——(1995) *Agriculture on the Road to Industrialization*, Baltimore MD: Johns Hopkins University Press.

Montalvo, J.G. and Reynal-Querol, M. (2005), Ethnic diversity and economic development, *Journal of Development Economics* 76, 293–323.

Nankani, G.T. (1979) Development problems of mineral-exporting countries, *World Bank Staff Working Paper* 354, Washington DC: World Bank.

Ndulu, B.J., O'Connell, S.A., Azam, J-P, Bates, R.H., Fosu, A.K., Gunning, J.W. and Njinkeu, D. (2008) *The Political Economy of Economic Growth in Africa 1960–2000*, Cambridge: Cambridge University Press.

North, D., Wallis, J., Webb, S. and Weingast, B. (2009) *Violence and Social Orders: A Conceptual Framework for Interpreting Recorded Human History*, Cambridge: Cambridge University Press.

Ross, M. (2001) Does oil hinder democracy? *World Politics* 53/3, 325–61.

Sachs, J. D. (1989) Social conflict and populist policies in Latin America, *NBER Working Paper* 2897, Cambridge MA: National Bureau of Economic Research.

Sachs, J.D. and Warner, A.M., (1995) Economic reform and the process of global integration, *Brookings Papers on Economic Activity* 1, pp. 1–118.

Sachs, J.D. and Warner, A. (1999) Natural resource intensity and economic growth, In: Mayer, J., Chambers, B. and Farooq, A. (eds.) *Development Policies in Natural Resource Economies*, Cheltenham: Edward Elgar, 13–38.

Sala-y-Martin, X. and Subramanian, A. (2003) Addressing the natural resource curse: An illustration from Nigeria, *IMF Working Paper* 03/109, Washington DC: IMF.

Salleh, I.M. and Meyanathan, S.D. (1993) *The Lessons of Asia: Malaysia Growth, Equity and Structural Transformation*, World Bank, Washington DC.

Schlumberger, O. (2008) Structural reform, economic order and development: patrimonial capitalism, *Review of International Political Economy*, 15(4) 622–49.

Segura, A. (2006) Management of oil wealth under the permanent income hypothesis: The case of Sao Tome and Principe, *IMF Working Paper* 06/103, Washington DC: IMF.

Svensson, J. (2000) Foreign aid and rent seeking, *Journal of International Economics* 51, 437–61.

Timmer, C.P. (2007) How Indonesia connected the poor to rapid economic growth, In: Besley, T. and Cord, L. J. (eds.) *Delivering on the Promise of Pro-Poor Growth*, Washington DC: World Bank, 29–57.

Tollison, R.D. (1982) Rent-seeking: A survey, *Kyklos* 35/4, 575–602.

van der Ploeg, F. and Poelhekke, S. (2009) Volatility and the natural resource curse, *Oxford Economic Papers* 61(4), 727–60.
van de Walle N. (1999) *African Economies and the Politics of Permanent Crisis 1979–99*, Cambridge: Cambridge University Press.
Villafuerte, M. and Lopez-Murphy, P. (2010) Fiscal policy in oil producing countries during the recent oil price cycle, *IMF Working Paper* 10/28, Washington DC: IMF.
World Bank (2006) *Where is the Wealth of Nations?* Washington DC: World Bank.
——(2007) *Angola: Oil-Based Growth and Equity*, Washington DC: World Bank.
——(2009) *From Privilege to Competition: Unlocking Private-Led Growth in MENA*, Washington DC: World Bank.
——(2010) *World Development Indicators 2010*, Washington DC: World Bank.

25
Challenges in Global Oil Governance

Andreas Goldthau[1]

Introduction

Oil politics is about a large variety of intertwined global policy challenges, relating to the fact that oil is a global commodity; that it is produced and traded across time and geographical space; and that actions by governments, subnational actors or transnational companies create costs or benefits for third parties. In this, oil politics is about addressing challenges arising in a highly interdependent sector and policy field, in which actions by one party inevitably have repercussions on second or third actors. These interdependencies are obvious. Domestic turmoil in, say, Nigeria, may trigger a rise in oil prices on a global level; energy choices of the Chinese government are decisive for upstream investments made by multinational drilling consortia in Central Asia; and the speculative behaviour of financial market actors may put a premium on forward prices, altering price levels independent from changes in actual supply and demand balances. As argued more extensively elsewhere, current debates on oil politics tend to fall short on properly conceptualizing this interdependence. They tend to centre on states as units of analysis, to ignore global externalities and to frame energy in terms of zero sum games rather than accounting for possible win-win situations (Smith 2010; Bahgat 2003; Barnes and Jaffe 2006; Klare 2008). Evidently, however, 'oil politics' is no longer, and in fact has never been, a matter of national governments or nation states alone. Rather, it is about the actions of a myriad of agents involved in financing, producing, trading or consuming oil and about the incentives and constraints they face with regards to the institutional structures they are embedded in, on a national, international or global level. Such a setting can best be grasped by a governance framework. A global governance perspective on oil stresses the importance of policy actors beyond the state, acknowledges the existence of externalities of transnational scope, and conceptualizes oil politics as subject to various levels of policy making. In light of this, the key goal of this chapter is to frame pressing issues in oil as global policy challenges, requiring policy answers in the absence of a global energy authority and rendering oil politics a global governance challenge. The main argument this chapter advances is that challenges in global oil can be dealt with through the market as a key governance mechanism in global oil, flanked by institutional arrangements accounting for shortcomings the market may exhibit in delivering security of supply or demand.

In more general terms, what does a global governance framework add to our thinking about oil politics? First, it allows accounting for involved key actors and their incentive structures beyond the state, and hence goes beyond a reductionist security lens. Second, it enables us to think about pressing issues in global oil in terms of governance challenges necessitating public policy answers, rather than in terms of peace or war. In this sense, the notion of governance as used in this chapter is a teleological, purpose driven one. Rather than aimed at describing a certain state of affairs it is instrumental in assessing the call on re-regulating interaction between involved state and non-state actors on a given problem – supply security, investment or energy transition. Third, it allows thinking about the drivers and policy answers to oil related challenges on various levels, from nation state to transnational and global.

The remaining parts of the chapter are organized as follows. The second section sets out a governance perspective on global oil. It argues that the existing global oil system is best described as being 'polycentric' and that the predominant mechanism governing it is the market. The third section discusses (institutional) challenges to the global oil market arising from changes in demand and supply patterns, from changes in the global business structure and from the implications of a looming transition towards a low carbon energy future. It also discusses consequences for prices and investment in global oil. The fourth section discusses implications for global oil governance.

Global oil as a governance issue

Oil has become a global commodity. It is produced and exchanged across time and geographic space while energy actors create and are subject to interdependencies and externalities of a global scope. Oil therefore is a case in which, according to standard IR theory, scholars would expect the emergence of an international institution aimed at enhancing expectations among involved actors, enabling them to overcome adverse incentives, information asymmetries and the like (Keohane 1984; Axelrod 1984).[2] Such an institution, however, is clearly missing in energy. Standard references to the United Nations system as a classic example of international governance through international institutions obviously miss the target, as the UN is not an organization designed to specifically address energy issues. In fact, and despite attempts to pool competences in 'UN-Energy', the UN has so far not reached the stage of a veritable 'energy player' (Karlsson-Vinkhuyzen 2010). Other international bodies such as the World Trade Organization, by contrast, created to provide for a clear regulatory framework for globally exchanged commodities, have been ill designed to comprise trade in oil. WTO rules are primarily preoccupied with granting access to markets, not with addressing export restrictions, a key problem in oil trade and investment (Desta 2003). In other words: global oil is left without a global institution governing it. This very simple but important finding constitutes the starting point to frame oil (politics) in terms of global governance.

Actors in global oil

Global governance commonly refers to the regulation of interdependent relations in the absence of an overarching political authority.[3] In essence, this means that pressing global policy problems need to be addressed without having a proper structure in place that would provide for hard incentives or constraints for involved actors. Translated to the sphere of oil, global governance would therefore refer to systems of rules or institutions structuring the interaction of key actors in the provision or consumption of the 'black gold'. Since there is no global energy organization able to structure this very interaction and exert power over the system's participants, the global oil system and its actors essentially need to work without a last resort authority. Admittedly, international and state-sponsored organizations exist to govern the oil industry. Yet, rather than governing the system as a whole, they tend to organize interests among certain segments of the oil value chain. Most importantly, these institutions comprise the Organization of Petroleum Exporting Countries (OPEC) and the International Energy Agency (IEA). OPEC, a club of oil producer countries formed in 1960, organizes the interests of nations controlling some 77% of the world's oil reserves and currently 41% of oil production (BP 2010). OPEC's creation was partly a response to the fact that a buyers' cartel of international oil companies (the Seven Sisters) controlled global oil trade in the first half of the 20th century, leaving reserve holding countries with only minority shares of the accrued oil rents. Setting up a producer organization was, however, also a means to overcome the adverse incentives individual oil-rich nations faced when striking deals and negotiating with international oil companies (IOCs). In a similar vein, the International Energy Agency (IEA) was created in 1974 to pool the consumer power of then 71% of world oil demand vis-à-vis the producer cartel that first showed its teeth during the 1973 oil crisis (BP 2010). To the same extent, however, the IEA was a means to overcome collective action problems among consumer countries related to oil stocks and usage, the lynchpin of their emergency response system set up after the oil shock.

Pooling producer and consumer power, OPEC and the IEA are important elements of global oil governance. Yet, the latter goes far beyond formal multilateral institutions. Key actors in a system of global oil governance centrally also comprise non-state actors. At that point, and this is where a governance approach deviates from 'classic' IR/security perspectives on supply security, resource access or climate diplomacy, states no longer are the only 'game in town'. In other words: global oil governance is not confined to inter-state relations alone. Rather, it is also traders, private investors, and not the least oil companies, state-owned or private, that drive energy agendas and create the very 'rules of the game' according to which energy actors play (North 1990). As a matter of fact, and while writings on oil politics have very much focused on state-to-state relations, the way oil is exchanged and traded today has been as much driven by companies as it has been by governmental policies. Following the forced break-up of vertically integrated companies in the context of key producer countries nationalizing their oil assets, for instance, businesses had to find new ways to price oil and hedge their risks.[4] This process led to the development of spot and forward markets, key elements in the global oil system as we know it today. In a similar vein, technological progress such as the development of very large crude carriers (VLCCs) enabled companies to bring down transport costs of oil and to physically integrate formerly regional markets in Europe, the USA and elsewhere. Business and private innovation were therefore as much the drivers of making oil a global commodity as were governmental actions or their (often unintended) consequences. In fact, global energy and global oil relations, for that matter, know numerous incidents in which states are by and large on the backburner. Cases in point are the various mechanisms and instruments for mediation, dispute settlement and resolution used in the oil sector, both between private companies and between states and (foreign) corporations.[5] Furthermore, business consortia consisting of private and state-owned companies regulate their interaction through Production Sharing Agreements (PSA) or Joint Ventures which, private in nature, stipulate procedures of co-operation, split costs and revenues, and specify liabilities. Finally, these multi-stakeholder consortia may use the financial market to hedge their risks surrounding large scale exploration and production (E & P) projects and hence collectively become subject to regulatory arrangements even outside the core energy business. In all of these incidents, states tend to play a minor role while, important as rule setters, rule enforcers, facilitators or preventers of producing and trading oil, they are complemented by companies and other non-state actors in negotiating energy contracts, in implementing upstream projects and in setting rules, at least for the scope of the energy project in question.

Market as prevalent governance mechanism in global oil

To date, and in contrast to the various stages of the oil age predating 1960,[6] oil is global, decentralized and integrated. In fact, and without aiming at stretching this analogy too far, the global oil system is probably best described as being 'polycentric' (Scholte 2004). It is characterized by various 'nodes', which are manifold and highly diverse in nature and function. These nodes comprise clubs of states (such as OPEC, or rather its biannual meetings), influential business associations (such as the American Petroleum Institute), key physical hubs (such as Cushing, Oklahoma, the price settlement point for West Texas Intermediate) or virtual trading places such as London's ICE or New York's Mercantile Exchange (NYMEX). As a key feature of today's system of global oil, and despite ever re-surfacing talks about 'oil weapons' or other attempts to use crude for foreign policy purposes, none of its participants is able to 'control' the entire system or exert power over the entirety of its participating members. The global oil system comprises far too many agents and has come to be too deeply integrated to be utilized by one single actor or to cater to individual agendas.[7]

So what is the mechanism that governs this 'polycentric system' and makes it deliver? In short, this central mechanism is: the market. To date, oil is traded and priced in a highly efficient global marketplace, characterized by a large number of buyers and sellers and by a fungible commodity that is priced on a global supply and demand balance. The market is an organizing principle that translates actors' preferences into universal signals for other system participants (through the price), and produces strong incentives and constraints for them (by providing for alternatives regarding costs and prices) to respond to these signals. The market as a system of oil governance proves to be by-and-large effective. It delivers a high value commodity, crude oil or its products, from producers to consumers; it does so over large geographical distances and long periods of time; it makes the global balance adjust to significant changes in consumption and production, now supplying the world with some 84mbpd, up from 65mbpd just 30 years ago (IEA 2010); and, despite longstanding debates about 'peak oil', it still tends to add more new oil to the global reserve balance than gets consumed.

Signals provided by the 'market governance system' can certainly be ignored. Some participants (or members of the global oil system, for that matter) may choose to leave the system or try to at least shield themselves against the incentives and constraints the system sets. This, however, is either costly or may simply come to nothing. At least it is not very effective. Given the law of one price, consumers in Iran, for instance, are subject to the same oil price levels as are consumers in, say, Western Europe. Shielding Iranian consumers for political reasons against price increases therefore requires state subsidies, which is a reason why Tehran ends up spending some estimated US$66bn or 20% of the country's GDP in energy subsidies to keep prices low and people happy (IEA 2010). Furthermore, given that significant refinery capacity for heavy, sulphur-rich oil sits in the USA, Venezuela is forced to export more than 60% of its crude to the very country whose regional dominance it tries to challenge politically by forming the energy club of PetroCaribe (EIA 2010). And given the globally integrated nature of the market, politically motivated suggestions to 'drill one's way into energy independence', a phrase that has regained popularity during the 2008–9 presidential elections in the USA, would simply translate into improving the global oil balance, not the national one. Finally, and for quite similar reasons, 'energy diplomacy' pursued by oil consuming nations to secure their supplies is by and large in vain. Oil brought onstream through, for instance, much discussed bilateral deals struck by Chinese national oil companies (NOCs) in Africa or elsewhere either ends up on the global market, improving the global supply side; or it is shipped back home to China, thus taking pressure off global demand. As further elaborated below, upstream investments in regions 'opened up' by diplomatic means also tend to come with an economic premium. As a consequence, aims at circumventing the market may easily translate into burning money rather than improving energy security.

Despite its strong 'track record' in governing investment, trade, production and consumption in global oil, the market is all but a perfect mechanism. First, while the market provides for the common grounds all players act on, the existing system of global energy governance is anything but coherent and well designed. As outlined elsewhere, it is rather fragmented, characterized by overlapping institutions and nested regimes (Goldthau and Witte 2009). More importantly, however, it can fail in governing global oil effectively. As some would argue, a wide range of market failures indeed characterize global oil. These comprise inefficiencies in pricing due to incomplete information, externalities such as Greenhouse Gas (GHG) emissions, or Cobweb cycle investment problems. Most obviously probably, the sheer existence of strategic petroleum reserves (SPRs) and the very fact that they are created by government decree not upon private initiative points to potential shortcomings that the market obviously exhibits in dealing with unexpected supply shocks. Moreover, just as the market can fail, it also is far from being the answer to everything. As the history of oil reveals, existing governance systems have changed, been abandoned or replaced by alternative ones over time. In fact, the market has come to govern global oil only since the mid-1970s. Previously, and while spot markets already existed, bilateralized energy relations prevailed, leaving oil pricing to complex formulae that did not necessarily reflect supply and demand patterns, nor (market) expectations on their future development. Price transparency was extremely poor while oil markets remained by and large regionalized. The governance mechanism underpinning interactions in that system was vertical integration. In order to hedge risks and ensure profits, companies remained in control of the entire oil value chain until the 1950s and 1960s. The global market, whose development was eventually fostered by nationalization policies in key oil producer countries, replaced bilateral arrangements and gave way to the decentralized, market-based governance system known today. The latter enabled now-disintegrated companies to interact with other actors over time and space.

Challenges to the market as the prevalent global oil governance arrangement may emerge along a number of fronts. Challenges can occur in the context of rapidly changing external conditions, notably a shift in the global structure of producers and consumers, putting in question the effectiveness of the institutional arrangements created to foster the latter's needs or stabilize the market. Some of the institutions that have been created to shape the supply side (OPEC) or pool consumer power (IEA) in fact exhibit their own internal, complex and dynamic governance structures. As we will outline in more detail later in this chapter, both of these organizations are now facing their own challenges in a changing global energy world, which requires adjusting the way they function. Challenges can emerge from actors which have to respond to non-market based incentives, notably NOCs. Enjoying increasing prominence, those actors by no means leave the system as such; yet, the fact that they are charged with political agendas or may be able to tap on soft loans may lead to a suboptimal allocation of capital, putting in question the effectiveness of the system as a whole. Challenges can, finally also stem from spillovers from one policy area to another, notably from emerging climate regimes (or the lack thereof) to the oil market. It is particularly in the context of the looming energy transition towards low carbon that such issues may emerge and lead to uncertainty and friction among participating parties. Based on these few principal premises, the next section proceeds by exploring further the challenges that may be looming to the existing system of global oil governance.

Challenges to oil market governance

The existing governance mechanism in global oil (the market) faces severe challenges against the backdrop of major trends that currently reshape the global energy landscape. These include a fundamental shift in consumption, away from traditional OECD energy consumers towards Asia but also the Middle East, coinciding with plateauing OECD production; a change in the global business structure in oil; and a looming transition towards a low carbon energy future. As a consequence, uncertainty may rise on future prices while oil price volatility may increase, putting in question necessary investments.

Changes in global consumption and production patterns

According to all forecasts, OECD consumption in oil has peaked. Future increments in global demand will exclusively stem from non-OECD, notably Asian countries. As the IEA projects, a fall in OECD demand by some 6mbpd until 2035 will be offset by an increase in non-OECD demand more than three times that volume. China alone is expected to account for 57% of the global demand increment. Even in what the IEA calls the 'New Policy Scenario', which accounts for already planned but not yet implemented climate policies, China's consumption is projected to almost double between 2009 and 2035, to more than 15mbpd. Exhibiting even higher annual growth rates, India's oil consumption is set to more than double in the same period of time, from 3.0mbpd to 7.5mbpd (IEA 2010, 105). In addition, Middle Eastern countries enter the global energy balance as an increasingly important demand side factor, as their domestic energy consumption tends to be heavily subsidized. Coinciding with a growing domestic population and oil being used as a carrier for electricity production, oil demand is set to rise by almost a third in this region.[8] In all, global oil consumption will shift eastwards, with Asia gaining significance and Europe, the USA and the remaining OECD countries losing shares.

Where do these new supplies come from? As the IEA projects, the bulk of additional supplies will originate from Saudi Arabia, Iraq, Brazil and Canada (IEA 2010, 114). Output in the OECD world, by contrast has clearly plateaued and will fall in the near future. Since most of the production increment is projected to occur in Saudi Arabia and Iraq, OPEC's market share will rise from 41% in 2010 to 52% by 2035, pushing the cartel into the prominent position it last had in the 1970s (IEA 2010, 133). Obviously, the price is a crucial component in this scenario, as oil production in Canada and Brazil is economic at oil price levels close to those in 2010 rather than those at the end of 2008. Canadian tar sand production in fact recently fell due to oil prices scratching the $30 mark at that point in time, a price level at which tar sands are not produced at economic costs. Likewise, and despite promising signals stemming from the recent capital increase carried out by Petrobras, the Brazilian oil company, Brazilian deepwater reserves are costly and difficult to extract, requiring competitive oil price levels. National politics will play a role, too. Owing to ongoing domestic turmoil, a stalemate in federal level politics and the absence of a national hydrocarbon law, Iraq is far from coming close to its production and export potential. However, despite some uncertainty, the supply side is likely to change in reaction to both increasing non-OECD demand and plateauing OECD production.

These changes in consumption and production trigger a variety of challenges, first and foremost with regards to existing international institutions of global oil governance, notably IEA and OPEC. With regards to the IEA, the OECD's energy watchdog, the problem obviously lies in the effectiveness of its emergency supply mechanisms. Put simply: once the share of OECD demand drops, so does the share of the market 'covered' and 'hedged' by the IEA's strategic supply stocks. In turn, newly emerging consumers, notably China and India, are not organized within IEA. Hence, they are not part of the organization's emergency response mechanisms to a price shock, or more specifically to the joint rules on the mandatory volume of Strategic Petroleum Reserves (SPR) among IEA member countries, and on the mechanism to release them. A straightforward policy answer to this governance problem would be to integrate China and India into the IEA. As participation in the IEA is linked to OECD membership, emerging consumers such as India and China are currently excluded from this system for formal reasons, as accession countries need to live up to standards the OECD regards as at the core of its existence, essentially market economic principles and democratic rule. Yet, besides these formal obstacles, there is a more pertinent and fundamental problem: none of the non-members should have any interest in joining in the first place. The reason for this lies in a fundamental free rider problem, as non-IEA members can profit from oil stocks held and paid for by OECD countries. Both China and India have recently begun building up strategic petroleum reserves. Yet, in total, Chinese crude reserves account for only some 30-days' worth of current net imports, whereas India's stock is equal to approximately three weeks of its current net oil imports (Colgan 2009). In that, China and India not only fall short on the IEA's 90-day stock holding requirement; they also constitute an increasingly pressing problem to the security of all global oil consumers, as a price shock would entail severe economic implications for all import-dependent countries, particularly countries characterized by high oil intensity, that is developing nations.

OPEC, while it will grow in terms of significance on the oil market, will see challenges of a different kind, although also related to its membership structure. In the years to come, the organization will see the return of a real oil heavyweight: Iraq. As indicated above, the world's third largest reserve holder in conventional oil reserves, is preparing its comeback on the world oil market. As a corollary, it will be back in OPEC, where the Iraqi seat has been dormant following the 1991 Gulf War. This may come with costs for OPEC's internal coherence. OPEC members in the Middle East have traditionally been locked into a continuous battle over regional primacy (Ahrari 1986, Claes 2001). Particularly Riyadh and Baghdad have been long term contenders for regional dominance in the Middle East, a fact that has significantly impacted OPEC decision making in past decades. In fact, Saudi Arabia has been a key beneficiary of Iraq effectively leaving OPEC, acting as the unrivalled leader of the organization since then. A re-emerging Iraq will likely lead to resurfacing quarrels about quotas, prices and internal dominance, which may eventually translate into difficulty for OPEC members to find common ground. For the oil market, this is not likely to be a positive development. Besides all the criticism that has been expressed about OPEC, the organization in fact plays a crucial role in stabilizing the supply and demand balance in oil. Less coherent OPEC policies towards output price targets may leave traders, investors and consumers with increased uncertainty on developments regarding half of the global crude output.

Changes in global business structure

The rise of new, mostly Asian, oil consumers comes with another trend that confronts the existing oil governance structure with an equally challenging problem: the emergence of new, state-controlled business heavyweights. During the last decade or two, NOCs have become important vehicles for governments in Beijing, India and elsewhere in securing their countries' oil supplies, in fostering domestic development agendas, and in gaining influence in the global oil business.[9] To date, NOCs populate seven out of the first 20 places in Platts' annual survey 'Top 250 Global Energy Company Rankings'. Among them, PetroChina was ranked seventh, whereas India's OVL ranked 18th in 2010.[10] NOCs are well known players in the oil market since OPEC members renationalized their resource assets. Yet, throughout the last 30 years, they predominantly existed in producer countries and their actions have by and large remained restricted to the development and exploitation of national reserves.[11] NOCs of the kind of PetroChina or OVL, however, 'go out'. Activities of Chinese companies in Africa have come to be widely perceived as a symbol of the country's rise as an economic and political world power. Some of their actions, such as Chinese National Petroleum Corporation's (CNPC) engagement in Pariah state Sudan, CNPC's ignorance of environmental standards in Gabun or a general 'non-interference attitude' towards repressive African regimes hosting Chinese companies extracting oil have sparked international criticism. In addition, the Chinese government has been accused of giving its NOCs a competitive edge in bidding processes, flanking the latter with favourable 'no strings attached' loans, comprehensive aid packages including infrastructure as well as political support, notably in the UN Security Council.[12] Activities of Indian oil companies abroad have attracted less public interest, yet they are increasing in scale. As in the Chinese case, they are flanked by the occasional economic assistance Delhi grants to governments in energy-rich countries, particularly in Africa (e.g. Sudan and Nigeria) but also Central Asia (Madan 2008). Some observers suggest that India has even engaged in military assistance to certain countries such as Myanmar in which its oil corporations hold interests and assets (Kugelman 2008, 11f).

Yet, and counter to widespread debates about whether these new corporate heavyweights 'take over', the main challenge for the oil market does not stem from the fact that the deals struck by Asian consumer NOCs in Africa, the 'Stans' or elsewhere are bilateral in nature.[13] As pointed out earlier, the oil brought on-stream either ends up being sold on the global market, strengthening the global supply side; or it is transported back to the home market, thus taking pressure off global demand. It also does not make a difference whether crude is extracted by a state-owned or a private business, so long as it becomes part of the global supply and demand balance. The real problem in fact is a rather different one: this crude is no longer made 'visible'. NOCs tend to be opaquely governed, they are not obliged to report on a quarterly basis, and their main stakeholders (governments) often treat activities of 'their' companies as subject to the national security realm. As a consequence of both, access to important information such as E & P costs, investment volumes, crude oil output or the projects' financial fundamentals is restricted and market transparency suffers.

When opening doors for their NOCs through diplomacy, development or financial assistance, governments in addition risk blurring signals the market sends on the prospects and economic viability of upstream projects. Put differently, if projects are selected on political opportunity rather than on economic fundamentals, investment location and volume may not be 'optimal'. As some observers note, Chinese investments in Africa tend to focus on assets of little interest to international oil companies (IOCs) due to comparatively small size and minor business prospects (Downs 2007). Generating a comparatively smaller equity oil output and yielding a comparatively smaller return on investment, these upstream investments may well end up with higher costs for the barrel produced. This, in other words, means burning money, compared to a situation in which the market would drive investment decisions and allocate capital effectively. Further, if financial state backing in its various formats is available as a default option for upstream investments, capital markets may no longer be a primary source of acquiring funds for large scale upstream projects. This, in turn, further decreases transparency regarding not only the volume of investment but also the business fundamentals of the projects.

Energy transition and low carbon

Finally, challenges to the market governance system may stem from spillovers from one policy area to another. In the case of oil, these spillovers may primarily come from climate change policies.[14] GHG emissions undoubtedly are a key externality of burning fossil fuels, notably oil. Climate change now is widely accepted as being anthropogenic, and global warming has come to be regarded as the key challenge for mankind during this and probably the coming centuries. To date, a 450 'parts-per-million CO_2-equivalent' (ppm CO_2e) scenario is the politically targeted means to curb global warming at 2 degrees Celsius and to stabilize the climate.[15] Yet, policies addressing this market failure, aiming at internalizing these externalities into the price for oil (and other fossils), may have severe side effects if ill designed or flawed. In this case, regulatory failure may simply provide for adverse incentives for the oil market rather than solving the climate problem. Cases in point are ongoing efforts to establish carbon cap and trade (C&T) mechanisms and to put a price on carbon. Attempts in Copenhagen in 2009 to set a binding CO_2 emissions reduction target and to transit the global carbon regime into a Post-Kyoto arrangement have failed. While endorsing the 2 degree climate goal, the non-binding character of the final declaration fell short on establishing a global framework to achieve that target. The 2010 Cancun Agreement, while generally regarded as a modest step in the right direction, does not stipulate binding reduction targets on a country level, either. Regional C&T systems, by contrast, remain in their infancy. The EU's Emissions Trading System (ETS), for instance, while widely regarded as a role model and front runner in C&T does not even cover half the EU's CO_2 emissions. The system has also been plagued with overallocation of emission rights and a carbon market collapsing in 2006 (Ellermann 2007). In the USA, by contrast, an initiative to establish a similar system got abandoned owing to a lack of support in the Senate. In addition to that, it may prove difficult to link regional systems once established, given their politico-economic incompatibility (Witte 2007).[16] Depending on the success of emerging regional carbon regimes and the degree to which they are effectively linked to each other, the price of carbon will vary, as will the price of oil with it. This will impact on investment needs and timelines of planned upstream projects. Yet, instead of a global level playing field on carbon pricing, regionalized patchworks are likely to prevail, which may lead to uncertainty among business on how future carbon policies will affect their costs. Since it is uncertain at what pace the necessary energy transition occurs, and to what extent climate policies affect the oil price, the oil sector will be faced with uncertainty on future price levels of their core products. This situation also implies uncertainty for low carbon energy business and the renewables industry, in term of whether their products are cost-competitive.

Consequences for price signals and investment

The trends discussed above have significant consequences for the core mechanisms the market relies on: information and the price translating them into incentive and constraint for energy actors. As discussed, the rise of new Asian energy consumers might put in question the IEA's existing emergency supply mechanisms, decreasing the market's belief in their effectiveness and hence leading to an overshooting price in case of supply problems.[17] OPEC, in turn, may see internal cohesion problems due to resurging Iraqi production, challenging Saudi leadership in the organization. This may increase uncertainty about OPEC behaviour and hence the credibility its announcements enjoy on output policies, targeted price bands and production levels. Furthermore, the emergence of NOCs on the consumer side and the state backing they enjoy in upstream projects exacerbate an existing transparency problem in the global oil market. Consequently, oil price formation becomes even more determined by the educated guesses of traders who, short on real market fundamentals, may need to find the price based on assumption and secondary data. As a consequence of both, oil price volatility may increase.[18] Oil volatility has indeed become more pronounced in the last two decades, with the most massive swings so far occurring in 2008. After reaching an all-time high of almost $150 per barrel in July 2008, prices dipped to close to $30 by the end of the same year, and shot up again above $100 since early 2010.[19] Since then, prices have hovered around this level. Price volatility, however, has a major drawback: it disincentivizes investment into costly upstream projects (Hunt 2004, 10). Since the oil price tells little about future price levels and hence future revenues during periods of high volatility, companies will not put billions of dollars into developing new, crucial reserves. As a consequence, and while there is widespread agreement on oil demand increasing in the future, the question hence becomes whether oil can in fact find the money.

Adding to this, patchwork-like, ill-designed or even merely pending carbon policies will lower incentives for investments in oil to be made in a timely and sufficient manner. As the IEA estimates, $8 trillion need to be spent in global oil infrastructure between 2010 and 2035, mostly in upstream, and mostly in non-OECD countries (IEA 2010, 139f). Yet, since most of the major reserve holders tend to be one-sector economies relying almost exclusively on oil revenues, and given lead times of several years, these nations might not be ready to invest the necessary sums into finding new resources if future prospects on prices, and hence demand patterns, are uncertain. In turn, for a transition towards low carbon and for the necessary technologies to be put in place, a reliable price environment for oil is essential (Blyth 2010). Uncertainty and increased volatility may harm oil supply investment to much the same extent as it puts in question a timely transition towards a low carbon economy.

Conclusion: implications for global oil governance

Adopting a governance perspective, this chapter has touched upon selected crucial aspects of oil politics, including security of supply, environmental and climate concerns, or regional dimensions of oil, some of which have also been dealt with separately in previous chapters of this volume. It argued that global oil is best described as a polycentric system, governed by the market. The market exerts incentives and constraints on actors, whether on state, substate or transnational level, making the system as a whole 'work' and deliver crude over time and space effectively. The chapter has then focused on emerging challenges to the market governance system relating to a significant shift in global demand trends in oil away from OECD towards Asian consumers, and a coinciding plateau in OECD oil production; to the resurgence of National Oil Companies in the global market, particularly originating from Asian consumer countries; and to spillovers from climate policies to the oil market. It has been argued, finally, that the market may be challenged with regards to the degree to which it is able to efficiently and effectively translate emerging trends into price signals and steer investment decisions. Crucial issues in this regard comprise uncertainty and a lack of transparency.

What are the implications for global oil governance? The market as a governance mechanism can certainly continue to work under the changed conditions and adjust to them. New nodes will probably emerge and the system will certainly look different from the existing one. What's for sure is that it will be more 'Asian'. Yet, and crucial for a successful adjustment, the market needs to be able to translate the new trends into signals that all participating parties understand. In other words, the market needs to find ways to effectively 'price in' low carbon policies, to translate changing global consumption patterns into investment decisions and to accommodate new players, particularly consumer NOCs. For this, information is key. To be sure, the market will continue to send signals and to provide for incentives (or constraints) for companies, households, traders, investors or finance ministers, also under increasingly incomplete information. Yet, these signals will inevitably be blurred. The main and most visible instrument of the market is the price. If the price is distorted, cannot be formed effectively or reflects false assumptions, then the system as such is endangered. Adjustments will then involve abrupt changes in price. Strengthening effective global governance in oil should therefore focus on strengthening measures that support transparent and efficient price formation. This is essential to provide for planning security for producers, investors and consumers alike to provide for effective pricing signals and to channel sufficient investment into energy supplies and services. Public policies should support this on all levels, from global to regional and national. From a governance perspective, these policies will need to be as decentralized as the system is. Yet, they need to be concerted in order to be effective.

On an international level, it is obviously key to enhance producer-consumer co-operation, particularly within the International Energy Forum (IEF). The IEF, an emerging platform for producer-consumer-business talks is an example of a platform that includes both states as key members and non-state actors such as energy companies in its IEF Business Forum. This platform is likely to help tackling problems related to a notoriously intransparent oil market. The IEF's Joint Oil Data Initiative (JODI) promises to emerge as an important element in this regard, and in relation to the reporting problems related to NOCs as discussed earlier (Harks 2010). In more general terms, platforms such as the IEF will have a crucial role to play with regards to moderating change in global energy landscape and to managing or mitigating inevitable frictions. They will be instrumental in helping the 'newcomers' (consumer countries and their NOCs) to find their place in the system, that is, accommodating them in the market rather than making them circumvent it. The IEA but also OPEC will need to contribute to this important goal, too, by accommodating new consumer heavyweights and, respectively, by findings way to overcome internal quarrels.

With regards to planning security relating to carbon pricing, regional solutions will likely be most crucial. Solutions will inevitably need to be tailored to regional contexts and hence take on different forms. In light of this, it will be particularly important to find ways to align emerging regional carbon pricing regimes and make them contribute to a clearly defined global GHG emissions trajectory, as already sketched out modestly in Cancun. National level policies will be crucial to flank all of the above.

Global oil governance obviously comprises a much larger set of facets than discussed in this chapter. Some important aspects have been treated more extensively elsewhere in this volume, among them resource transparency and climate change. Successfully addressing these issues will help to enhance security of supply, calming down oil price volatility and enhancing a smooth and predictable transition towards a low carbon future. Policies addressing these issues are by definition a very political exercise and nothing that the market would achieve per se. Again, as historic evidence reveals, a different future, one without the market, is certainly possible. But since transition periods are bumpy processes creating great adjustment costs, it may be worth spending time, effort and political capital to preserve the existing one and adjust it to the new circumstances.

Notes

1. Contact: goldthaua@ceu-budapest.edu
2. The terms institution and organization are use interchangeably here.
3. In this, this chapter subscribes to the definition put forward by Rosenau (1999).
4. See Yergin (1991) and Maugeri (2006) for a historical assessment of oil market developments.
5. See Thomas Waelde's various works on this topic, among others Waelde (2003).
6. In 1960 oil producers organized themselves within OPEC, eventually marking the end of the system of the Seven Sisters.
7. On this point see also Noel (2008).
8. See also Mitchell and Stevens (2008) for a discussion of these countries' export capacities.

9 For a comprehensive empirical study see the Baker Institute's 2007 report on the emerging role of NOCs on the global oil market (Baker 2007).
10 www.platts.com/Top250Home, accessed 10 December 2010.
11 There are obvious exceptions to this rule. Norwegian Statoil, for instance, is active on a global level. It is also noteworthy that OECD countries had their own NOCs, e.g. British Petroleum, privatized in the 1980s.
12 On this debate see Alden (2005), Downs (2007), Zweig (2005) and Taylor (2006).
13 This sections draws on Goldthau (2010).
14 This point is admittedly ironic as spillovers, i.e. externalities are usually discussed as occurring in the oil market and creating costs for third parties through Greenhouse Gas emissions and climate change.
15 See http://unfccc.int/2860.php, accessed 10 December 2010. Note, however, that scientists surrounding the IPCC as well as the Stern Report advocate 350 ppm as the maximum level. IPCC (2007), Stern (2007).
16 See also Flachsland (2009) and Edenhofer (2009) for a comprehensive discussion.
17 OPEC members, notably Saudi Arabia, would likely be able to respond to a price shock by ramping up production in order to stabilize the market; yet, it is certainly questionable at what price levels this would occur.
18 Some observers in fact regard a lack of market fundamentals as causal for oil price volatility. See Tempest (2001).
19 For recent empirical assessments of the drivers behind the 2008 oil price hike see Kaufmann (2011) and Pirrong (2010).

Disclaimer: Parts of this chapter draw from results of larger research projects, published in A. Goldthau and J. M. Witte (eds) 2010. *Global Energy Governance: The new rules of the game*. Washington, DC: Brookings Press, and a contribution forthcoming in International Studies Perspectives.

Bibliography

Ahrari, M. E. 1986.*OPEC: The Failing Giant*. University Press of Kentucky.
Alden, C., D. Large, and R. Soares de Oliveira. 2007. *China Returns to Africa: A Rising Power and a Continent Embrace*. London: C. Hurst.
Arnold, S., and A. Hunt. 2009. National and EU-Level Estimates of Energy Supply Externalities. *CEPS Policy Brief* 186.
Axelrod, R. 1984. *The Evolution of Cooperation*, New York: Basic Books.
Bahgat, G. 2003. Pipeline Diplomacy: The Geopolitics of the Caspian Sea Region. *International Studies Perspectives* 3:310–327.
Barnes, J., and A. M. Jaffe 2006. The Persian Gulf and the Geopolitics of Oil. *Survival*, 48:143–62.
Blyth, W. 2010. How do carbon markets influence energy sector investments. In *Global Energy Governance. The new rules of the game*, edited by A. Goldthau and J. M. Witte. Washington DC: Brookings Press.
BP, *Statistical Review of World Energy* (London: British Petroleum, 2010).
Claes, D. H. 2001. *The Politics of Oil-Producer Cooperation*. Boulder CO: Westview Press.
Colgan, J. 2009. The International Energy Agency. Challenges for the 21st Century. *GPPi Energy Policy Paper* 6.
Desta, M. G. 2003. The GATT/WTO System and International Trade in Petroleum: An Overview. *Journal of Energy and Natural Resources Law* 24/4 384–398.
Deutch, J. M., J. R. Schlesinger, and D. G. Victor 2006. *National Security Consequences of U.S. Oil Dependency: Report of an Independent Task Force*. New York: Council on Foreign Relations.
Downs, E. 2007. The Fact and Fiction of Sino-African Energy Relations. *China Security* 3, no. 3.
Edenhofer, O., C. Carraro, J.-C. Hourcade, K. Neuhoff, G. Luderer, C. Flachsland, M. Jakob, A. Popp, J. Steckel, J. Strohschein, N. Bauer, S. Brunner, M. Leimbach, H. Lotze-Campen, V. Bosetti, E. de Cian, M. Tavoni, O. Sassi, H. Waisman, R. Crassous-Dorfler, S. Monjon, S. Dröge, H. van Essen, P. del Rio and A. Türk 2009. RECIPE – 'The Economics of Decarbonization'. Synthesis Report.
EIA 2010. 'Country Analysis Brief: Venezuela'. US Department of Energy. Accessible online at http://www.eia.doe.gov/cabs/venezuela/pdf.pdf

Ellerman, A.D. and B.K. Buchner 2007. The European Union Emissions Trading Scheme: Origins, Allocation, and Early Results. *Review of Environmental Economics and Policy* 1 (1).

Flachsland, C., R. Marschinski and O. Edenhofer. 2009a. Global Trading versus Linking. Architectures for International Emissions Trading. *Energy Policy* 37, 1637–47.

Goldthau, A. 2010. Energy Diplomacy in trade and investment of oil and gas. In *Global Energy Governance. The new rules of the game*, edited by A. Goldthau and J. M. Witte. Washington DC: Brookings Press.

Goldthau, A., and J. M. Witte. 2009. Back to the future or forward to the past? Strengthening markets and rules for effective global energy governance. *International Affairs* 85 (2):373–90.

Harks, E. 2010. 'The International Energy Forum and the mitigation of oil market risks'. In *Global Energy Governance. The new rules of the game*, edited by A. Goldthau and J. M. Witte. Washington DC: Brookings Press, 250.

IEA, 2010. *World Energy Outlook 2010*. Paris.

IPCC. 2007. 'Fourth Assessment Report': Climate Change.

James A. Baker III Institute for Public Policy. 2005. Baker Institute *Policy* Report 35 on National Oil Companies.

Kaufmann, R. K. 2011. The role of market fundamentals and speculation in recent price changes for crude oil. *Energy Policy* 39 (1), 105–115.

Madan, T. 2008. India's Global Search for Energy. In Kugelman, Michael (ed). Foreign Addiction: Assessing India's Energy Security Strategy. Asia Program Special Report 142, Woodrow Wilson Center, October, 6–17.

Maugeri, L. 2006. *Age of Oil. The Mythology History and Future of the Worlds Most Controversial Resource*, Westpoint, CT: Praeger Publishers.

Mitchell, J. V., and P. Stevens. 2008. Ending Dependence: Hard Choices for Oil-Exporting States. *Chatham House Report*.

Noel, P. (n.d.) The future world oil market: state of nature or social contract?, comments on article by M. A. Tétreault, Institute for Energy Economics and Policy, University of Grenoble, p. 3. Accessible at http:// web.upmf-grenoble.fr/iepe/textes/pn9912.pdf, accessed 15 December 2010, p. 5.

North, D. 1990. *Institutions, Institutional Change, and Economic Performance*. New York: Cambridge University Press.

Karlsson-Vinkhuyzen, S. I. 2010. The United Nations and global energy governance: past challenges, future choices. *Global Change, Peace & Security* 22:175–95.

Keohane, R. 1984. *After Hegemony*, Princeton: Princeton University Press.

Klare, M. 2008. *Rising Powers, Shrinking Planet: The New Geopolitics of Energy*. New York: Metropolitan Books.

Kugelman, M. (ed). 2008. Foreign Addiction: Assessing India's Energy Security Strategy. Asia Program Special Report 142, Woodrow Wilson Center, October.

Pirrong, C. 2010. An Evaluation of the Performance of Oil Price Benchmarks during the Financial Crisis. C.T. Bauer College of Business, University of Houston.

Scholte, J. A. 2004. Globalization and Governance: From Statism to Polycentrism. CSGR Working Paper No. 130/04.

Smith, K. 2010. *Managing the Challenge of Russian Energy Policies. Recommendations for U.S. and EU Energy Leadership*. CSIS Report, December.

Stern, N. 2007. *The Economics of Climate Change: the Stern Review*. Cambridge: Cambridge University Press.

Taylor, I. 2006. China's Oil Diplomacy in Africa. *International Affairs* 82, no. 5.

Tempest, P. 2001. Distortion, Illusion, and Confusion: How to Improve Global Oil Market Data. *Energy Policy* 29, no. 5.

Waelde, T. 2003. Mediation/Alternative Dispute Resolution in the Oil, Gas and Energy Transactions: Superior to Arbitration/ Litigation from a Commercial and Management Perspective. *Oil, Gas and Energy Law* (2).

Witte, J. M., T. Behr, W. Hoxtell, and J. Manzer. 2009. Towards a Global Carbon Market? The Potential and Limits of Carbon Market Integration. *GPPi Policy Paper* 7.

Yergin, D. 1991. *The Prize: The Epic Quest for Oil, Money, and Power*. New York: Simon and Schuster.

Zweig, D. and B. Jianhai. 2005. China's Global Hunt for Energy. *Foreign Affairs*. 84 (5).

26
Sovereign Wealth Funds in the Gulf: Opportunities and Challenges

Gawdat Bahgat

From the early 2000s to mid-2008 oil prices witnessed an unprecedented surge, reaching a peak of US$147 per barrel before collapsing by the end of the year and later stabilizing around $80 by early 2010. Most oil exporting countries, particularly the Gulf Co-operation Council (GCC) states (Bahrain, Kuwait, Oman, Qatar, Saudi Arabia, and the United Arab Emirates) continue to be heavily dependent on oil revenues as their main source of income. Thus, the rise in oil prices provided crude exporters with massive accumulation of wealth. The relative small size of their economies and the concern about fuelling inflation meant that their ability to absorb these oil revenues domestically was, and still is, limited. Thus, a large proportion of these revenues had to be invested abroad. A number of sovereign wealth funds (SWFs) were founded to initiate and manage these investments. It is important to point out that other fast-growing economies, particularly China and Singapore, have witnessed a similar development, accumulated massive current account surpluses, and created their own SWFs. The focus of this paper is on the oil funds created by the GCC states.

This is not the first time a set of SWFs had been created. A similar wave had occurred in the 1970s following the jump in oil and gas prices. The newly-established funds, however, have substantially expanded the number and size of SWFs. The overall volume of assets under management by SWFs is still relatively small in comparison with total global financial assets. However, these assets are significant relative to hedge funds or private equity (Santiso, 2008, p. 2). Furthermore, their assets are projected to substantially increase over the next few years. Deutsche Bank predicts that SWF holdings will rise from $3.6 trillion in 2008 to $10 trillion by 2015 (Deutsche Bank, 2008, p. 6) and JP Morgan researchers make a similar prediction stating that SWFs' assets are likely to double from 2009 to 2015 (JP Morgan, 2009, p. 4). In short, one important element in the changing global economy is the increasing prominence of SWFs from a wide range of home countries.

This increasing prominence of SWFs and the emergence of oil exporting countries as major creditors to the world and to industrialized countries in particular have highlighted two fundamental changes in the international financial system. First, the progressive running of large current account surpluses in oil exporting countries had been in parallel to current account deficits built by major industrial countries in Europe and the USA. Indeed, it can be argued that without the contribution of oil funds in bailing out major international financial institutions the global recession would have been deeper and would have lasted longer. In short, oil exporting countries have increasingly resumed a prominent role as major creditors. Second, these oil funds are owned by their home governments and are largely controlled by the state. This framework is at variance with the traditional private-sector, market-oriented approach, dominant in most western countries (Truman, 2008, p. 3)

The rapid expansion of petro-dollar investments has fuelled anxiety regarding these new dynamics in the global financial system. Principally, most countries welcome foreign investments. However, when the money is owned and controlled by foreign governments, suspicion arises. Policy-makers in receiving markets are concerned about possible political objectives behind these SWF investments. Following their capital injections into European and US banks that suffered big losses from the subprime mortgage crisis, oil funds have attracted heightened attention from policymakers, national legislatures and the media in the USA and several European countries. Meanwhile, these capital injections have been welcomed by the International Monetary Fund (IMF) and others because they have helped to stabilize markets.

This heightened attention and the lack of consensus on the role of SWFs underscore the fact that the structure, objectives and investment strategies of SWFs in general and those in the Gulf region in particular are poorly understood. This study seeks to contribute to the growing systematic academic research of oil funds. In the next section I discuss the different definitions of the concept and highlight the points of differences and similarities between them. This will be followed by a close examination of two main funds created and owned by the Gulf states, the oldest fund (Kuwait Investment Authority) and the wealthiest fund (Abu Dhabi Investment Authority). In the concluding section I summarize the main findings of the study.

Sovereign wealth fund – definition

Sovereign wealth funds have been around for more than half a century. The proliferation of SWFs since the early 2000s, however, has stimulated academic and political curiosity to define what SWFs are and how to distinguish them from other investment vehicles. Analysts at the IMF have provided a number of similar definitions. Davis, Ossowski, Daniel, and Barnett define a SWF as a mechanism designed to reduce the impact of volatile revenue on the government and the economy. Its objectives may also include supporting fiscal discipline and providing greater transparency in the spending of revenue (Davis, Ossowski, Daniel, and Barnett, 2001, p. 8). Allen and Caruana see SWFs as government-owned funds, set up for a variety of macroeconomic purposes. They are commonly funded by the transfer of foreign exchange assets that are invested long term, overseas. They allow for a greater portfolio diversification and focus on return than traditionally is the case for central-bank-managed reserve assets (Allen and Caruana, 2008, p. 4). Sun and Hesse state that SWFs are special-purpose investment funds owned by the general government. They are often established out of balance of payments surpluses, official foreign currency operations, proceeds of privatization, fiscal surpluses, or receipts resulting from commodity exports (Sun and Hesse, 2009, p. 4). Finally, Das, Lu, Mulder, and Sy argue that SWFs hold, manage, or administer financial assets to achieve financial objectives, and employ a set of investment strategies which include investing in foreign financial assets (Das, Lu, Mulder, and Sy, 2009, p. 5).

The US government's definition focuses on the degree of risk-tolerance: SWF managers typically have a higher risk tolerance and higher expected return than traditional official reserve managers (U.S. Department of Treasury, 2007, p. 1). The European Commission's definition concentrates on the source of funding – the distinguishing feature of SWFs from other investment vehicles is that they are state-funded (European Commission, 2008, p. 4). The Monitor

Group, a financial consulting firm, identifies five qualifying characters: owned directly by a sovereign government; managed independently of other state financial institutions; does not have predominant explicit pension obligations; invests in diverse asset classes in search of commercial return; and has made a significant proportion of its publicly-reported investments internationally (Barbary and Chin, 2009, p. 17).

These definitions suggest a number of common characters of SWFs. First, the underlying characteristic of SWFs that distinguishes them from other investment vehicles is that they involve a dramatic increase in the role of governments in the ownership and management of international assets. Second, SWFs are commonly established out of balance of payment surpluses. In the case of oil exporting countries, high oil prices for a prolonged period of time provide such surpluses. Third, there is a general preference to place SWFs' assets abroad, mainly to allay fears about appreciation of the domestic currency (Ter-Minassian, 2007, p. 15). Fourth, SWFs holdings do not include foreign currency reserve assets held by monetary authorities for the traditional balance of payments or monetary policy purposes; operations of state-owned enterprises in the traditional sense; government-employee pension funds; or assets managed for the benefit of individuals.

Fifth, typically, SWFs have a diversified investment strategy, with a higher level of risk accepted in search of higher returns. Sixth, the various objectives of SWFs imply different investment horizons and risk/return trade-offs, which lead to different approaches in managing these funds. SWFs usually pursue multiple objectives. Seventh, generally SWFs can be divided into two categories based on the source of their assets. Commodity funds receive most of their holdings from exporting one or a few commodities that are largely owned by the government (for example, oil funds). Non-commodity SWFs are usually established through transfers of assets from official foreign exchange reserves (some Asian SWFs such as those of China and Singapore). The goal of such transfers is to pursue higher returns. Eighth, two broad types of SWFs can be identified based on their main objectives: (a) stabilization funds, where the primary objective is to insulate the economy against commodity price swings; and (b) savings funds for future generations, which aim to share wealth with upcoming generations.

To sum up, SWFs are a heterogeneous group. They take many forms, pursue different strategies, and establish a variety of legal, institutional and governance structures.

Investment portfolios

SWFs from the Gulf region employ a wide range of investment strategies that seek to strike a balance between safe assets and high returns. Given these broad objectives, Gulf SWFs have allocated their holdings in a variety of investment vehicles including conservative (relatively safe with low returns) ones such as debt and equity securities to riskier investments with potential for higher returns such as private equity, real estate, and hedge funds. By their nature, SWFs are expected to invest in more diversified portfolios and riskier assets than traditional reserve holdings.

The older Gulf SWFs such as the Kuwait Investment Authority (KIA), Abu Dhabi Investment Authority (ADIA), and Oman's State General Reserve Fund tend to be cautious, discreet, and conservative investors. Meanwhile, the "younger" funds (those founded since the early 2000s) tend to be more aggressive investors, reflecting the financial confidence of high oil prices in most of the decade. Many of them have pursued attractive opportunities in all sectors all over the world. Some of these newly-created funds borrowed to invest in high-profile assets, instead of relying on their own capital accumulations. The collapse of oil prices in mid-2008 and the end of the era of cheap and easy credit have underscored the shortfalls of such a strategy.

The investment portfolios of the Gulf SWFs are not different from their counterparts in other countries. According to researchers at the Organization for Economic Cooperation and Development (OECD) SWFs invest on average 38% in the financial sector, 14% in the communication and transportation sectors and 6% in the energy sector. Other sectors, with allocations below 5% each, are consumer durables and non-durables, utilities, and technology services (Avendano and Santiso, 2009, p. 20). Other analysts (Bortolotti, Fotak, Megginson, and Miracky, 2009, p. 18) give similar trends. From 1986 to 2008, 30.9% of all SWF investments' deals by number and 54.6% of the value of all acquisitions were in the financial sector. Other targets were real estate (11.9% of deals, 15.3% of value), information technology (7.5% of deals, 7.7% of value), industrials (9.1% of deals and 5.3% of value), and infrastructure (11.9% of deals, and 15.3% of value).

Investments by Gulf SWFs have established similar portfolios, with even more concentration on the financial and energy sectors. Other sectors include real estate, industrial, aerospace, healthcare, and transportation. A close examination of the Gulf SWFs' portfolios shows that they have disproportionately favoured financial companies, particularly since the early 2000s. At least two factors had contributed to this concentration. First, large banks continued to be regarded as having substantial growth and profitability potential in the medium and long terms. Second, investing in the US and European financial institutions has improved SWFs' image. Shortly before the eruption of the sub-prime crisis and broad economic recession, many American and European policymakers and media outlets were suspicious of SWFs' motives and goals. Following their investments in the financial institutions (at a time when some banks were facing serious problems regarding their capitalization) SWFs have experienced a more benign reception and an appreciation of the helpful role they played in a critical phase of market developments (Deutsche Bank, 2008, p. 10).

Another large and growing target of SWF investments is the nascent market for Islamic finance, or investment products that comply with the Islamic law (Sharia). From profit-sharing accounts and crude products, Islamic finance spans derivatives, bonds, fund management, credit cards, and car loans, all of which often use complex structures to circumvent the Islamic ban on interest.

Sharia forbids interest, on the grounds that money alone should not create profit. Thus, the challenge is how to replace conventional financial practices (deemed to be usury-based) with Islamic alternatives (a profit-and-loss sharing partnership).

In recent history, an attempt to reconcile Sharia and modern financial practices was made by the Ottomans in the late 19th century when they introduced western-style banking to the Islamic world to finance their expenditures. While some (fakaha) jurists approved it, others considered them in violation of Islamic prohibition of riba (usury). This lack of consensus lasted through the European colonial period. With the rise of Islamic revival in the 20th century, many Muslim intellectuals have sought to reform Islamic economic systems to adapt to the fast-developing international regimes and norms.

The rise of Islamic finance in the second half of the 20th century coincided with the two oil shocks (1973–74 and 1979–80), which created an immense amount of wealth. Since then there has been a rapid growth in Islamic financial institutions and diversification of available products that comply with Sharia. The goal is to appeal to a growing rich population, particularly in the Gulf region. Some of the earliest Islamic banks of the modern era include Dubai Islamic Bank, Faisal Islamic Bank, Al-Baraka Groups, Kuwait Finance House, and Bahrain's First Islamic Investment Bank, among others (El-Gamal, 2006, p. 9).

To sum up, SWF portfolios typically involve more diversified asset allocations than traditional reserves holdings, with considerable stakes in equities and a wide geographical dispersion.

Historically, Gulf SWF favoured investments in Western markets. Traditionally European and American capital markets offer the widest selection of investments and a high level of liquidity and are thus able to absorb the large volumes institutional investors typically seek to allocate. Within the OECD, most SWF investments have gone to just two countries, the USA and the United Kingdom. Gulf SWFs make more cross-border investments in US-headquartered companies than in any other country. These heavy Gulf investments in the USA simultaneously reflect and cement the strategic relations between the two sides.

Meanwhile, SWF investments in the United Kingdom have their roots in the establishment of the Kuwait Investment Office in London in the early 1950s. Since then the ups and downs of the British economy have not deterred Gulf SWF investments from coming to London. These strong financial ties are driven by two fundamental dynamics. First, long-standing political and economic relations have served as the glue in strengthening the partnership between Britain and the Gulf states. Second, London enjoys special characteristics which make it a leading global financial services hub, attracting businesses and traders not only from the Gulf region, but from all over the world. These include a legacy of internationalism, tradition of economic opening and stability, and broad and liquid market.

Despite these strong financial ties to Western markets, Gulf SWF have shown great interest in investing in emerging markets in Asia particularly China, Hong Kong, India, Indonesia, Malaysia, Singapore, Taiwan, and Thailand. The underlying reason for investing in Asian markets is their miraculous economic performance over the last few decades. This astonishing performance means that SWF investments in Asia can earn much higher profit rate than in OECD countries.

Finally, the global economic recession of the late 2000s prompted Gulf SWF to invest a large proportion of their assets in their own home countries and the broad Middle East. Gulf states, like the rest of the world, could not escape the severe economic and financial crisis. They called on their SWFs to help addressing challenges such as low financial liquidity, high unemployment and overall stagnated economic systems. They also sought to play a role in helping overcoming the economic crisis in the broad Middle East. As a leading Bahraini banker put it, "True security comes with the stability of one's neighbors." (Kerr, 2008).

Gulf SWFs

The Gulf Co-operation Council (GCC) was established in 1981 by Bahrain, Kuwait, Oman, Qatar, Saudi Arabia, and the United Arab Emirates to enhance their economic and financial integration. Its total population (including expatriates) is estimated at 38m., with a GDP of $1.1 trillion in 2008. The six GCC countries possess 40% of the world's proven oil reserves and provide 23% of global production. The figures for natural gas are 25% of proven reserves and 24% of global production (British Petroleum, 2010, pp. 6 and 22). Their spare oil production capacity accounts for the bulk of the world's total. All these figures illustrate the leading role the region plays in global energy markets. On the other hand, despite persistent efforts to diversify their economies and reduce their heavy dependency on hydrocarbon resources, the GCC states are still deeply dependent on oil revenues. Oil accounts for about 50% of the region's GDP and 80% of fiscal and export revenues (Khamis and Senhadji, 2010, p. 1).

The GCC states are home to some of the largest and oldest SWFs, with estimated assets between $600bn and $1 trillion at the end of 2008 (Friedman and Meakin, 2009, p. 65). The main impetus for the growth of these SWFs comes from high oil prices up to 2008. Thus, through most of the 2000s, the GCC states became the largest source of net global capital flows in the world, rivalling China as a "new financial superpower" (Economist, 2008, p. 2).

Countries such as the GCC states that rely on oil and other non-renewable resources for a substantial share of their revenue face two key problems: the revenue stream is uncertain and volatile, and the supply of the resource is exhaustible. Stated differently, government revenue derived from the exploitation of non-renewable resources differs from other revenue in that it partly represents a depletion of wealth. This suggests that some of this wealth should be saved, both to help stabilize the financial market and for intergenerational equity (Davis, Ossowski, Daniel, and Barnett, 2001, p. 4). These two objectives, stabilization and saving, are further reinforced by the fact that most oil-producing countries cannot absorb the amount of wealth they are generating.

The combination of all these factors was the main drive for the creation and growth of a large number of SWFs in the Gulf region. Indeed, each jump in oil and gas prices has increased the number and size of SWFs in the region. Thus, it is not a coincidence that the majority of Gulf SWFs were founded in the 2000s, when oil prices started their inexorable climb to their peak of July 2008, reflecting the confidence of a Gulf flooded with cash. Little wonder, the region represents the highest concentration of SWF assets worldwide. In 2008 analysts at the Deutsche Bank estimate assets under management by Gulf SWFs at $1.6 trillion, representing 46% of total SWF assets worldwide (Deutsche Bank 2008, p. 4). Other analysts raise the share to 60% (Friedman and Meakin, 2009, p. 6). This disparity is due to the fact that most SWFs in the Gulf and elsewhere do not publish official figures of their assets.

The availability of substantial financial resources proved crucial in both the ability of the Gulf SWFs to play a significant role in overcoming the global financial crisis of late 2000s in their own home countries and in continuing their investments, albeit at much lower levels, in troubled Western banks and corporations. According to one source, the market value of the Gulf's foreign portfolio fell by an estimated $350bn over the course of 2008 (Setser, 2009, p. 1). Another source estimated that the Gulf SWFs lost on average between 20 and 25% of the value of their known equity portfolios (Barbary and Chin, 2009, p. 4). The IMF estimates that the GCC states' combined current account surplus fell to $53bn in 2009, after having risen more than tenfold in the previous decade to $362bn in 2008. (IMF, 2010, p. 1). Thus, as the global financial crisis deepened, the demand for oil, and consequently the prices, declined. As a result, the stock and real estate markets plunged and external funding for the financial and corporate sectors tightened. Despite these huge losses, Gulf SWFs have managed to maintain their financial leverage. This relative success is due to the execution of comprehensive economic strategies prior to the global financial crisis. The GCC states grew on average by a robust 5.75% per year between 2005 and 2008 (IMF, 2009, p. 6). They launched huge investment projects to pursue economic diversification and human capital development through investments in oil and gas and infrastructure, as well as in petrochemicals, tourism, financial services, and education. In addition, they saved and invested a significant portion of their oil revenues.

This strong economic base has enabled the GCC states to address the severe global financial crisis from a relatively better stance than most other countries. Governments used their strong international reserve positions to maintain high spending and introduce exceptional financial measures. Saudi Arabia adopted a $400bn public investment package (equivalent to 110% of its annual GDP, which was the largest fiscal stimulus package relative to GDP among the G20 nations for 2009–10) to be implemented over five years. The increased spending on social sectors and infrastructure in 2009 cushioned the downturn. Countercyclical fiscal policy in the United Arab Emirates also played a key role in avoiding a major disruption in economic activity. Abu Dhabi's support of Dubai on the debt crisis has limited contagion to the rest of the economy and the banking system not only in the United Arab Emirates, but in the rest of the Gulf region. In Qatar, the government's pre-emptive intervention in the banking sector was equivalent to 6.6% of GDP, mainly in the form of equity injections and asset purchases by the Qatar Investment Authority (QIA). The Kuwaiti authorities' response to the financial crisis was complicated by prolonged negotiations between the government and the parliament. In early 2010 the parliament approved a four-year $105bn spending package (equivalent to 95% of GDP). The Omani and Bahraini authorities introduced liquidity and prudential measures that helped to mitigate the adverse effects of the crisis, particularly on the banking system (Institute of International Finance, 2010, p. 5).

In short, the GCC authorities' response to the global financial crisis focused on restoring liquidity by providing capital injections into the banking system, supplemented by deposits from government institutions. To shore up investor confidence, Kuwait, Saudi Arabia, and the United Arab Emirates provided guarantees for deposits at commercial banks and asked SWFs to support domestic asset prices and to provide capital injections for banks. SWF resources in Bahrain, Kuwait, Oman, and Qatar were used to set up funds investing in local equity markets. Furthermore, the KIA and QIA bought domestic bank shares to help boost bank capitalization and confidence. Thus, the experience of late 2000s demonstrates that in the times of financial stress, SWF domestic investments may temporarily deviate from pure profit maximization to support broader macroeconomic and financial stabilization objectives.

The role Gulf SWFs have played in addressing and mitigating the impact of the global financial crisis in their home countries was crucial. On the other hand with regard to foreign markets, on the whole, the Gulf SWFs have weathered the financial storm fairly well, outperforming their Asian counterparts in some cases. Generally, older funds with large and diversified portfolios were somewhat protected from critical damage, while younger funds that pursued aggressive investment strategies fared much worse. For example, after buying stocks in Western banks at the height of the global financial crisis, the KIA sold a large portion of its stakes in Citigroup and the ADIA and the QIA did the same with their portions of the British bank Barclays PLC. The three Gulf SWFs made huge profits in these transactions.

The experience of the last several years has contributed to the formulation of the Gulf SWF response to the criticism and reservations expressed by some Western policymakers and media outlets. Indeed, as their profile has risen in recent years, Gulf SWFs were ill-prepared to counter the negative coverage they received in some European countries and the USA. Officials from the Gulf SWFs have repeatedly argued that their record shows that their investment decisions are driven exclusively by economic and financial interests and that they do not have any political agenda. They rightly challenge politicians in the USA and Europe to name a single Gulf investment that was made for political rather than commercial reasons (Khalaf, 2008).

Gulf investors accept the need for increased scrutiny from recipient countries when the investments have potential national security implication, so long as the process is clear, fair, and timely. In return, they call for a reciprocal responsibility meaning that the entire world community (SWF home and recipient countries) has a shared interest in ensuring that financial markets remain open and that investors (private or government) playing by the rules are not discriminated against, and that the regulatory process remain transparent and predictable (Al-Otaiba, 2008).

Gulf investors also argue that Western suspicions of their SWFs are grossly inflated. The efforts to regulate SWF investment operations are unjustified given that there are no similar guidelines for private-equity or hedge funds and therefore, it is unfair to single out SWFs. They assert that SWFs tend to be passive rather than active investors. On average, a SWF takes less than 5% of the shares outstanding in a company, not a controlling stake. With such a small share, SWFs can hardly be viewed as possessing control over companies (Avendano and Santiso, 2009 p. 12). Furthermore, the majority of the Gulf SWFs use external managers, partly to fill the skill gap and their relative shortage of indigenous professional financial experts.

Two conclusions can be drawn from this discussion of the Gulf SWFs. First, while the GCC states' short-term economic outlook is clouded by the global economic slowdown and by the credit crisis in Dubai, the region's medium-term outlook seems broadly positive. This projection is based on the substantial investments in both economic and human infrastructures. All over the region new cities have been built, economic projects and financial centres have opened, and new schools and universities have been established. In short, it can be argued that the Gulf governments have managed their massive petrodollars in the 2000s better and wiser than they did in the 1970s (following the jump in oil prices). Not surprisingly, analysts at the McKinsey Global Institute conclude that petrodollar investors are "poised for future growth in almost any scenario. Their foreign assets reach nearly $9 trillion by 2013 in our base case, and more than $13 trillion if the economy recovers more quickly" (Roxburgh, Lund, Lippert, White, and Zhao, 2009, p. 12).

Second, it is true that the GCC states have amassed immense financial reserves and accordingly managed to weather the global economic crisis much better than many other regions and their outlook in the medium and long terms looks promising. But, their prosperity is still largely linked to oil prices. The efforts to diversify the region's economies away from oil and create other sources of national income have achieved a modest success.

Kuwait Investment Authority and Abu Dhabi Investment Authority

This broad generalization about the GCC economies and SWFs should not give the wrong impression that they are identical. Gulf SWFs differ in their age, size, and investment strategies. They have also adopted diverse stances on transparency, governance, and other issues. A close examination of the region's oldest and wealthiest SWFs underscores the similarities and differences between these state-controlled funds.

Kuwait Investment Authority (KIA): Kuwait was the first oil producing country to establish a SWF, namely the KIA. Sheikh Abdullah al-Salem al-Sabah, the ruler of Kuwait from 1950–65 decided in 1953 to establish the Kuwait Investment Board (KIB) with the aim of investing the surplus oil revenue in order to provide a fund for the future and reduce reliance on a single finite resource. The Kuwait Investment Office in London (KIO) was set up to pursue these objectives. Preparing for independence from the United Kingdom, the Kuwaiti government established the General Reserve Fund (GRF) in 1960. The GRF is the main treasurer for the government and receives all revenues (including all oil revenues) from which all state budgetary expenditures are paid. It also holds all government assets.

In 1976 Jaber al-Ahmed al-Jaber al-Sabah, Deputy Emir of Kuwait and Crown Prince, issued Law No. 106, under which the Future Generations Fund (FGF) was established. Article 1 stated: "An amount of 10% shall be allocated from the state's general revenues every year." Article 2 stated: "A special account shall be opened for creating a reserve that would act as an alternative to oil wealth. An amount of 50% of the available state's GRF is to be added to this account." Finally, the law stipulated that the Ministry of Finance shall employ these funds into investments, and the profits accruing from them shall go into this account (KIA 2009A).

Finally, in 1982 Jaber al-Ahmed al-Sabah, Emir of Kuwait issued Law No.47, establishing the Public Investment Authority, now known as the KIA. The law stated that the objective of the KIA is to "undertake the management of the GRF, the monies allocated to the FGF, as well as such other monies that the Minister of Finance may entrust the KIA with its management" (KIA 2008). The KIA's mission is to achieve a long-term investment return on financial reserves, providing an alternative to oil reserves. In 1986 the KIA's revenues from investments exceeded revenue from exporting oil.

The degree of transparency of the KIA cannot be understood in isolation of the broader socio-economic and political system in Kuwait. Many Kuwaitis take pride in the fact that in 1962 their country was the first Gulf state to adopt a parliamentary democracy and a constitution. For many years the Kuwaiti press was among the most open in the Gulf region and the broader Middle East. Furthermore, the Kuwaiti General Assembly (parliament) has enjoyed real power in supervising public policy. This parliamentary power was clearly demonstrated in 2006 when a succession crisis erupted and the parliament members voted Sheikh Sa'ad al-Abdullah al-Sabah, the then Emir, out of office on health grounds.

Members of the Board of Directors and the employees of the KIA are banned from disclosing data or information about their work or the position of invested assets, without a written permission from the chairman of the Board of Directors. Meanwhile, the KIA's activities are reviewed by both external and internal auditors. The Board of Directors appoints an external auditor, who reviews the FGF and GRF as well as the funds managed by the KIA. The KIA has an independent Audit Department that reports to the chairman of the board. In addition, the State Audit Bureau has on-site personnel to monitor KIA's activities on an ongoing basis. Finally, the KIA makes annual closed-door presentations on the full details of all funds under its management, including its strategic asset allocation, benchmarks and rates of return, to the Council of Ministers and to the National Assembly (KIA 2009B).

Like many other SWFs, the KIA does not disclose information on its assets, rates of return, and allocations of its investments. However, in the last few years some data became available. In 2007 the Kuwaiti finance minister Bader Mishari al-Humaidhi announced that the KIA's assets had reached $213bn, the largest in the country's history. Due to the global financial crisis, the KIA, like other SWFs, lost a proportion of its assets.

Investment guidelines prohibit the KIA from investing in the following: a) share ownership in companies whose principal business involves gambling, alcoholic beverages or adult entertainment; b) private placements and venture capitalization; and c) investing in single issuer/issues in excess of 5% of the portfolio at the time of the purchase (KIA, 2009C). Historically, the KIA pursued a conservative investment strategy aimed at preserving capital. Accordingly, the bulk of the KIA's assets were invested in US Treasury. With a new management since the mid-2000s, the KIA has moved away from safe but low-return bonds and started to invest in alternative assets, such as private equity, real estate, hedge funds and commodities. Like other Gulf SWFs, the KIA has targeted Islamic finance and purchased stakes in Islamic financial institutions and the securities they issued. Other major investments were allocated to Daimler AG, the owner of Mercedes-Benz, and British Petroleum (BP).

In addition to these changes in the KIA portfolio, the fund has sought to diversify its investments across various geographic locations. Owing to historical and strategic strong ties with Europe and the USA, KIA's holdings in these two markets are significantly high. This geographical allocation has witnessed fundamental changes in recent years. The KIA management has expressed strong interest in investing in emerging markets in Asia. The drive behind this shift is commercial. As Bader al-Sa'ad, managing director of the KIA argued, "Why invest in 2% growth economies when you can invest in 8% growth economies" (Sender 2007).

Finally, at the peak of the global financial crisis many Kuwaitis and the parliament called for the government to spend more of its wealth at home to stabilize the country's economy. The KIA pumped $418m. into Gulf Bank, Kuwait's fourth-largest traded lender, after it suffered heavy derivatives-trading losses. The KIA also invested $5.2bn as part of a government fund to stabilize the stock market. Despite this scale back on investments overseas and focus on local economy, the KIA managers have been aware of the fact that the global economic crisis offers some investment opportunities and have sought to take advantage of such "bargains."

Sovereign Wealth Funds in the Gulf: Opportunities and Challenges

Abu Dhabi Investment Authority (ADIA): The ADIA is one of the wealthiest and oldest SWFs. It was established in 1976 by Sheikh Zayed bin Sultan al-Nahyan, the founder of the United Arab Emirates. The ADIA replaced the Financial Investment Board, created in 1967 as part of the Abu Dhabi Ministry of Finance. ADIA's current constitutive document is Law No. (5) of 1981, which provides separation of roles and responsibilities among the Abu Dhabi government and the ADIA management. The main objective behind the creation of ADIA is to invest funds on behalf of the government of the Emirate of Abu Dhabi to make available the necessary financial resources and maintain the future welfare of the Emirate (ADIA, 2010A).

The ADIA is not the only SWF in Abu Dhabi and the United Arab Emirates. Since the early 2000s a number of SWFs have been established. The creation of several funds reflects the accumulation of massive wealth due to the rise of oil prices up to July 2008 and the interest in pursuing several financial strategies. Some analysts also suggest that these funds illustrate the influence of various members of the royal family. For example, Sheikh Khalifa bin Zayed al-Nahyan, President of the United Arab Emirates and ruler of Abu Dhabi, is the Chairman of the Board of Directors of the ADIA. Crown Prince Sheikh Mohamed bin Zayed al-Nahyan is the chairman of Mubadala. His full brother Sheikh Mansour bin Zayed al-Nahyan is the chairman of the International Petroleum Investment Company (England and Khalaf, 2009). Still the ADIA is the largest SWF in Abu Dhabi and the United Arab Emirates.

ADIA's Board of Directors comprises a chairman, managing director, who along with other Board members, are appointed by a decree of the Ruler of Abu Dhabi. The Board holds primary responsibility for implementation of ADIA's strategy. It also oversees ADIA's financial performance and the activities of management. The Board does not involve itself in ADIA's investment and operational decisions, for which the managing director is responsible. Several

Table 26.1 Portfolio Overview by Asset Class

	Minimum	Maximum
Developed Equities	35%	45%
Emerging Market Equities	10%	20%
Small Cap Equities	1%	5%
Government Bonds	10%	20%
Credit	5%	10%
Alternative	5%	10%
Real Estate	5%	10%
Private Equity	2%	8%
Infrastructure	1%	5%
Cash	0%	10%

Table 26.2 Portfolio Overview by Region

	Minimum	Maximum
North America	35%	50%
Europe	25%	35%
Developed Asia	10%	20%
Emerging Asia	15%	25%

Source: ADIA, Portfolio Overview, available at www.adia.ae/En/Investment/Portfolio.aspx. Accessed 31 May, 2010.

committees provide assistance to the Board of Directors including Investment, Strategy and Guideline Committees as well as Evaluation and Follow up Department (ADIA 2010B). The ADIA management depends heavily on foreign experts. United Arab Emirates nationals make up around 30% of the total analysts (ADIA 2010 C).

Until the late 1980s, ADIA invested in mostly low-profile, conservative havens like US Treasury securities and government bonds. However, in recent years it has altered its asset allocation substantially and became a more risk-tolerating investor. ADIA has always sought to have a diversified portfolio, both across regions and asset classes, as Tables 26.1 and 26.2 illustrate.

ADIA usually does not invest in the United Arab Emirates or in the Gulf region, except in instances where such investments constitute part of an index. Like other Gulf SWFs, ADIA has recently taken a closer interest in emerging markets, particularly China and India. ADIA has pursued investment opportunities in insurance, financial, infrastructure, and energy sectors.

In March 2010 ADIA published its first annual review, marking the first performance disclosure of any sort since the fund was established in 1976. The review states ADIA's 20-year and 30-year annualized rate of return to the end of 2009 was 6.5% and 8%, respectively. The fund, however, declined to divulge its total assets. Whatever these assets are, it is likely ADIA, like other SWFs, has suffered significant losses as a result of the global financial crisis.

Conclusion

The global financial crisis in the late 2000s and the constructive role Gulf SWFs have played in the efforts to overcome the challenges and provide liquidity have partly reduced the intensity surrounding SWFs. It is uncertain what direction the controversy might take in coming years. Will sceptics in the USA and Europe accept these government-controlled investment vehicles? Or will they seek more regulations? The experience of the last several years suggests a few lessons. First, the financial muscles and leverage Gulf SWFs might have in coming years will largely depend on the future oil prices and the scale of their domestic spending. The higher the price and less domestic spending, the more assets they have to invest overseas.

Second, while some information on Gulf SWF assets, strategies, management, and governance is available, there is no uniform public disclosure. As the KIA's and the ADIA's experiences suggest, a number of SWFs have come to accept the need for transparency and accountability in recent years. This acceptance might be driven by pressure from domestic public opinion or the desire to adhere to Santiago Principles. Still, there is much to be desired. Third, both SWF host and recipient countries share a mutual interest in maintaining an open international investment climate in which all participants have confidence. A sensible management of oil-producing countries' petroleum wealth in well-functioning financial markets is in everyone's interest.

Fourth, the record of Gulf SWFs and indeed most SWFs demonstrates that they are generally passive investors with no desire to impact company decisions by actively using their voting rights, purchasing controlling shares, replacing old management, or any other means. Furthermore, there is no evidence that these SWF investments are motivated and driven by political objectives. Like other investors, Gulf SWFs seek to maximize their profit.

Finally, in the last several years there have been many political and academic arguments put forth regarding the potential positive and negative effects of SWFs on global financial markets. Despite the hyper-ventilation surrounding SWFs, a close examination suggests these funds are not threatening to the established financial system. Rather, the evidence suggests that they can be, and have been, a stabilizing force.

References

Abu Dhabi Investment Authority (2010 A) 'Mission', available at www.adia.ae/En/About/Mission.aspx. Accessed 31 May, 2010.
Abu Dhabi Investment Authority (2010 B) 'Governance', available at www.adia.ae/En/governance/governance.aspx. Accessed 31 May, 2010.
Abu Dhabi Investment Authority (2010 C) 'Portfolio', available at www.adia.ae/En/Investment/Portfolio.aspx. Accessed 31 May, 2010.
Al-Otaiba, Yousef (2008) 'Our Sovereign Wealth Plans', *Wall Street Journal*, 19 March, 2008.
Allen, Mark, and Caruana, Jaime (2008) 'Sovereign Wealth Funds – A Work Agenda'. Washington, DC: International Monetary Fund.
Avendano, Rolando, and Santiso, Javier. (2009) 'Are SWFs' Investments Politically Biased? A Comparison with Mutual Funds' OECD, available at www.oecd.org/dataoecd/43/0/44301172.pdf. Accessed 13 May, 2010.
Barbary, Victoria, and Chin, Edward (2009) 'Testing Time: Sovereign Wealth Funds in the Middle East and North Africa and the Global Financial Crisis', available at www.monitor.com/portals/0/MonitorContent/imported/MonitorUnitedStates/Articles/PDFs/Monitor_testing_time_SWF_MENA_May_2009.pdf. Accessed 11 May 2010.
Bortolotti, Bernardo, Fotak, Veljko, Megginson, William, and Miracky, William (2009) 'Sovereign Wealth Fund Investment Patterns and Performance', available at http://admin.darden.virginia.edu/emupload/uploaded2009/swf-invest-patterns-perform-nov288.pdf. Accessed 13 May, 2010.
British Petroleum (2010) 'BP Statistical Review of World Energy', London.
Das, Udaibir, Lu, Yinqiu, Mulder, Christian, and Sy, Amadou (2009) 'Setting up a Sovereign Wealth Fund: Some Policy and Operational Considerations', Washington, DC: International Monetary Fund.
Davis, Jeffrey, Ossowski, Rolando, Daniel, James, and Barnett, Steven (2001) 'Stabilization and Savings Funds for Non-renewable Resources: Experience and Fiscal Policy Implications', Washington, DC: International Monetary Fund.
Deutsche Bank (2008) 'Sovereign Wealth Funds and Foreign Investment Policies – An Update', available at www.dbresearch.com/PROD/DBR_Internet_EN-PROD/PROD0000000000232851.pdf. Accessed 8 May 2010.
Economist (2008) 'Asset-backed Insecurity,' Vol. 389, No. 8564, 27 January 2008.
El-Gamal, Mahmoud A. (2006) 'Overview of Islamic Finance, United States Department of Treasury', available at www.UStreas.gov/offices/international-affairs/occasional-paper-weries/08042006_occasionalpaper4.pdf. Accessed 13 May 2010.
England, Andrew and Khalaf, Roula (2009) 'Abu Dhabi Multiplies Investment Arms,' *Financial Times*, 5 May, 2009.
European Commission (2008) 'A Common European Approach to SWFs', available at http://ec.europa.eu/internal_market/finances/docs/sovereign_en.pdf. Accessed 9 May, 2010.
Friedman, Tim, and Meakin, Sam (2009) 'The 2009 Preqin Sovereign Wealth Fund Review', London, Preqin.
Institute of International Finance (2010) 'GCC Regional Overview', available at http://www.iif.com/press/press+146.php. Accessed 17 May, 2010.
Institute of International Finance (2009) 'Regional Economic Outlook: the Middle East and Central Asia', Washington, DC.
Institute of International Finance (2010) 'Regional Economic Outlook: The Middle East and Central Asia', Washington, DC.
International Working Group (2008 A) 'International Working Group of Sovereign Wealth Funds Meets in Singapore; Continues to Make Progress on Drafting Set of Principles and Practices'. Available at http://www.iwg-swf.org/pr.htm. Accessed 23 July, 2008.
Kerr, Simeon (2008) 'Gulf States Told to Invest Oil Wealth at Home', *Financial Times*, 2 May 2008.
Khalaf, Roula (2008) 'Transparency Is in Everyone's Interest,' *Financial Times*, 19 May, 2008.
Khamis, May, and Senhadji, Abdelhak (2010) 'Learning from the Past,' *Finance and Development*, Vol. 47, No. 1, pp. 1–4, March 2010.
Kuwait Investment Authority (2009 A) 'Overview of Funds', available at http://www.kia.gov.kw/En/About_KIA/Overview_of_Funds/Pages/default.aspx. Accessed 18 March, 2009.
Kuwait Investment Authority (2009 B) 'Governance at KIA', available at http://www.kia.gov.kw/En/About_KIA/Governance/Pages/default.aspx. Accessed 18 March, 2009.

Kuwait Investment Authority (2009 C) 'Portfolio Management', available at http://www.kia.gov.kw/En/Marketable_Securities/Portfolio_Management/Pages/default.aspx. Accessed 21 March, 2009.

Kuwait Investment Authority (2008) 'Mission and Principles', available at http://www.kia.gov.kw/NR/exeres/028BE69B-028BE69B-0BBE-449E-8FB3–0A6AD8E62639.htm. Accessed 27 January, 2008.

JP Morgan (2009) 'Sovereign Wealth Funds: A Bottom-up Primer', available at http://www.econ.puc-rio.br/mgarcia/Seminario/textos_preliminares/SWF22May09.pdf. Accessed 22 May, 2009.

Roxburgh, Charles, Lund, Susan, Lippert, Matt, White, Olivia, and Zhao, Yue (2009) 'The New Power Brokers: How Oil, Asia, Hedge Funds, and Private Equity Are Faring in the Financial Crisis', San Francisco, CA: McKinsey Global Institute.

Santiso, Javier (2008) 'Sovereign Development Funds', OECD Policy Insights No.58, available at http://www.oecd.org/dataoecd/17/57/40040692.pdf. Accessed 8 May, 2010.

Sender, Henny (2007) 'Deep Well: How a Gulf Petro-State Invests Its Oil Riches; Kuwait's Mr. Al-Sa'ad Likes Asian Real Estate but Is Cool to Treasury,' *Wall Street Journal*, 24 August, 2007.

Setser, Brad (2009) 'How Badly Were the Gulf's Sovereign Funds Hurt by the 2008 Crisis?' Council on Foreign Relations, available at http://blogs.cfr.org/setser/category/sovereign-wealth-funds. Accessed 17 January 2009.

Sun, Tao, and Hesse, Heiko (2009) 'Sovereign Wealth Funds and Financial Stability – An Event Study Analysis', Washington, DC: International Monetary Fund.

Ter-Minassian, Teresa (2007) 'The Role of Fiscal Institutions in Managing the Oil Revenue Boom', Washington DC: International Monetary Fund.

Truman, Edwin M. (2008) 'A Blueprint for SWF Best Practices, Peterson Institute', available at www.iie.com/publications/pb/pb08–3.pdf. p.3. Accessed 8 May, 2010.

United States Department of Treasury (2007) 'Semiannual Report on International Economic and Exchange Rate Policies', available at www.UStreas.gov/offices/international-affairs/economic-exchange-rates/pdf/2007_appendix-3.pdf. Accessed 9 May, 2010.

27

Oil, the Dollar, and the Stability of the International Financial System

Eckart Woertz

Introduction

Oil is fueling the wheels of globalization and is indispensable for the modern 'Hydrocarbon Man' (Daniel Yergin) who is accustomed to consuming an ever-growing amount of transport services, plastics, pesticides, fertilizers, pharmaceuticals and other petrochemical products. The important role of petrodollar recycling in financing the US trade deficit is less well known, although at times it has been crucial in ensuring the stability of the global financial system. The dollar was at the center of the international financial system when the Bretton Woods system of fixed exchange rates emerged after World War II. When growing US balance of payment problems led to the demise of this system in the early 1970s, the dollar still remained the cornerstone of the world economy in a new arrangement of floating exchange rates and US deficit financing. It has enabled consumption above one's means in the USA and export-led growth elsewhere. Financing for US deficits came from oil exporters in the 1970s. When low oil prices in the 1980s and 1990s turned oil surpluses to deficits, other creditors like Japan and Germany stepped in. Today the US current account deficit is financed by oil exporters along with China and other Asian exporter nations.

Petrodollar recycling today differs from that of the 1970s. The development of financial markets has now reached a stage that is hardly comparable to their rudimentary outlines then. The Eurodollar market, non-existent until 1958, has exploded since the 1970s. Beyond traditional commodities trading, derivatives markets were only founded in the 1970s and started to take off in the 1990s.[1] Higher yielding corporate and agency bonds, offshore accounts, hedge funds and private equity funds were still nascent during the first oil boom, if they existed at all. Today they form an important option in asset allocation considerations of oil exporters and other international investors. With the advent of the euro, the dollar is facing emerging competition as international reserve currency for the first time since it took over from the British pound in the wake of World War I. Earlier, the thinness of markets for hard currencies like the deutschmark and the yen impeded diversification away from the dollar. However, the dollar still remains the world's dominant trade currency. Diversification options are limited because of the sheer size of accumulated debt and market capitalization of dollar-denominated securities. Furthermore, the Eurozone has shown crucial weaknesses in the wake of the debt crises in its southern member states. Unlike the USA, it does not have centralized political institutions and no common fiscal policy. It is at the crossroads of oil prices and new trends in capital and currency markets that the character of a new age of petrodollar recycling is taking shape.

This chapter analyzes how oil exporters situate themselves in the international financial system and how they contribute to its stability. Firstly, it examines the emergence of a new international financial system in the 1970s and the historical development of petrodollar recycling. Secondly, it outlines how the oil price collapse in the mid-1980s put severe economic strains on the oil exporters and led to a temporary end of petrodollar recycling. Thirdly, it analyzes oil exporters' role in the overall system of global imbalances today and sheds light on differences between them. Fourthly, it discusses their asset allocation and how this relates to dollar stability and domestic development plans. Finally, it deals with some far-reaching conspiracy theories about the might of petrodollar recycling and discusses different scenarios of the future role of oil exporting countries in the global financial system.

The demise of Bretton Woods and the search for a new international financial system

After World War II, the US commanded about one-half of the world's industrial production, was its largest oil producer, held two-thirds of global gold reserves, and had a current account surplus. Naturally, the dollar was at the center of the newly-emerging international financial order of Bretton Woods: A system of fixed exchange rates with the dollar as its anchor currency, which in turn was linked to gold at a fixed price. By the 1960s, this system was in trouble as the USA faced increasing balance of payment problems, which were caused by capital exports beyond current account surpluses, not by current account deficits like nowadays. With the exception of 1959, the USA achieved current account surpluses all through from 1954 to 1970, and throughout the 1960s domestic savings exceeded domestic investments. Immediately after World War II, capital exports mainly consisted of grants, while by the 1960s private investments of US-based multinational companies were dominant. Apart from that, there were large outflows for military spending abroad, especially after the American entanglement in Vietnam from 1965 onwards.[2]

Thus, the USA functioned as the main global liquidity provider by offering maturity-transformation services to the rest of the world. While the USA exported long-term capital, foreigners reinvested the proceeds in the liquid market for US bank deposits and treasuries, leading to increased short-term liabilities for the USA. This mechanism entailed risks in case of a reversal of capital flows and it was not sustainable, as from 1959 onwards liabilities to foreigners were not fully covered by US gold reserves anymore. The bedrock of the Bretton Woods system, the dollar-gold exchange rate came under pressure and was only temporarily defended over the 1960s by administrative measures like capital controls or the Gold Pool. Foreigners started to worry about the value of their dollar holdings, and France, in particular, agitated against the 'exorbitant privilege' of the USA.[3] By issuing the reserve currency, the USA was able to live beyond its means: It could import foreign goods, acquire foreign assets at attractive prices, and undertake military adventures abroad, all at the same time. Once doubts about the value of outstanding dollar liabilities set in, there was a constant drain of gold from the USA to Europe and Japan. Eventually, the USA defaulted on its promise to pay gold for dollars and closed the gold window in 1971.

Any international financial system needs to provide three basic conditions: confidence, liquidity, and a balance of payments adjustment mechanism. Usually these conditions are guaranteed by a hegemonic power.[4] By the early 1970s, all three aspects were compromised. An untested mechanism of floating exchange rates replaced the Bretton Woods system, the confidence in the dollar was shaken and it devalued, while the erstwhile liquidity provision via US capital exports became questionable. The USA started to accumulate intermittent current account deficits in the 1970s. During the 1980s these deficits grew and became permanent, and from the mid-1990s they witnessed a virtual explosion. Fiscal deficits equally rose until they departed from the current account dynamic in the mid-1990s and moved into surplus territory for a while, only to deteriorate again during the 2000s. It is this US deficit spending that has provided global liquidity over recent decades. Issues about its sustainability have been raised, as the net international investment position of the USA compared to its GDP has declined since the early 1980s, turned negative by 1986 and has faced an accelerated deterioration since the mid-1990s. In 2010 it stands at 15% of GDP and indicates a diminished ability of the USA to serve its debt.[5] More than one-half of all outstanding US treasury bonds in 2009 were held by foreigners (57%), for all long-term US securities this number stood at 18% on average.[6] The total private and public debt in the USA has doubled in comparison to GDP since the early 1980s and stands now at about 350%.[7]

However, it was not just a free lunch for the USA; the rest of the world was content with this arrangement as well. Under the Bretton Woods system, increasing dollar liabilities were a problem, now they have become the 'solution', fuelling export-led industrialization in Asia and globalization in general. An influential working paper of the National Bureau of Economic Research in the USA has argued that today's international financial architecture constitutes an informal but sustainable 'Bretton Woods II' system with the US issuing debt titles and Asia buying them to facilitate its export-led growth.[8] In the same vein, current Fed Chairman Ben Bernanke has argued that rising US debt levels were necessary to accommodate a 'savings glut' in Asia.[9]

The global financial crisis has led to a reconsideration of such theories. The savings glut implied a 'debt glut' on the other side of the bargain, but high levels of debt are not as sustainable as it was thought and the risk assessment of markets has been inaccurate. Financial markets are in a process of reform, including reining in of shadow banking practices, regulation of OTC derivatives, and reconsideration of capital requirements and executive remunerations. On a global level, the role of emerging markets has been upgraded. In an envisaged IMF reform they are to obtain more voting rights, while the G20 has been superseding the G8 in the economic field and has been charged with co-ordinating global policies on financial reform. However, prevalent debates about the causes of the global financial crisis focus predominantly on technicalities of the financial industry without addressing the issue of global imbalances, which have been a root cause of excessive debt finance as Steven Dunaway of the Council on Foreign Relations has pointed out.[10] In a similar vein, Barry Eichengreen has argued that global imbalances are unsustainable, as export-led growth in Asia will face diminishing returns. This in turn will provide incentives to let the real exchange rate rise as future development efforts will focus more on domestic demand, the non-tradable sector, services, finance and education.[11]

Increasing US debts and the policy of quantitative easing have raised concerns among US creditors about the quality of their assets. In the yet most outspoken way Chinese President Hu Jintao has labeled the dollar-based international currency system a 'product of the past.'[12] China and Russia have suggested an alternative international reserve currency that could replace the dollar with a currency basket in the form of the Special Drawing Rights (SDR) of the IMF. Russia has also suggested that gold could be part of such a currency basket, while China has agreed to settle some bilateral trade with selected trade partners (Brazil, Russia, and Turkey) in Chinese yuan.[13] At this stage, such proposals are probably just rhetoric and intended to remind the USA of its obligation to safeguard a stable dollar. SDRs are not a traded currency, and the dollar is still without competition on the international stage. It is the major trade and reserve currency, and US deficit spending is fueling globalization and export-led growth elsewhere. Global rebalancing would require increased savings of recession-hit US consumers and an appreciation of the Chinese currency, which China has been resisting as it fears for thin profit margins of its export industries. Thus, the dollar will not be replaced easily, as too many have a stake in it and with the exception of Euroland other capital markets lack the depth and capitalization to constitute a meaningful alternative.

Politics and markets: petrodollar recycling in the 1970s

After the oil price explosion of 1973 there had to be a solution for the balance of payment problems that had been caused by the tectonic shift in the world oil market and the ensuing transfer of wealth to OPEC countries. Developing and Newly Industrialized Countries (NICs) especially were in dire straits, while industrialized countries like Japan, Germany, the United Kingdom and France were able to bring their current accounts back into surplus territory only several years after the initial shock. The USA maintained a surplus from 1973–76 and only slid into deficit territory thereafter. The problem of international imbalances was of such magnitude that many feared a repetition of the Great Depression of the 1930s should it remain unsolved. A vicious cycle of trade wars and competitive devaluations to solve balance of payments problems was looming around the corner.[14]

The conventional wisdom about petrodollar recycling in the 1970s is that markets worked. High oil prices led to surpluses in oil-exporting countries and deficits in other regions. Petrodollars were deposited with Western banks, which lent them out to developing countries to finance their deficits, which were in turn often caused by an increased bill for oil imports. Ultimately this supposedly led to the debt crisis of the 1980s, when these countries faced payment problems. David E. Spiro has pointed out several flaws in this conventional wisdom:[15]

a) Western banks were not as awash with petrodollars as the theory suggests; a lot of the petrodollars were invested directly in US treasuries. In the case of Saudi Arabia this happened at preferential rates and after political lobbying to do so. The kingdom received special tranches of treasury bonds and was exempted from the competitive auctioning process.[16] After initial resistance, the USA agreed to a Saudi seat on the board of the IMF and a 350% increase of its IMF quota. In exchange the Saudis agreed to continue pricing of oil in dollars instead of a contemplated switch to Standard Drawing Rights (SDR) of the IMF.[17] To prevent such a switch the US Treasury department had conveyed that "harm to the dollar would wipe out Saudi reserves."[18] There were also rumors within the administration that a security umbrella for the Gulf had been informally promised in exchange for Saudi treasury purchases. The initiatives to ameliorate the balance of payments situation were decidedly unilateral. A special oil facility with the IMF that could have functioned as a multilateral and supranational means of balancing current accounts did not receive comparable support. Other nations (such as France) also tried to get bilateral preferential treatment in order to deal with the balance of payment disruption, but were decidedly less successful than the US hegemonic power. The petrodollars that were deposited with Western banks only reinforced an already ongoing trend of lending to selected NICs, they did not cause it. Neither did they cause or affect the tremendous growth in Eurodollar markets in the 1970s. These were, by and large, an effect of expansive US monetary policy and had started to grow before the oil shock.[19] If growing US debts were essential for maintaining liquidity in the new international financial order, pricing of oil in dollars and saving of petro surpluses in dollars were crucially important to this system in the 1970s:

So long as OPEC oil was priced in US dollars, and so long as OPEC invested the dollars in US government instruments, the US government enjoyed a double loan. The first part of the loan was for oil. The government could print dollars to pay for oil, and the American economy did not have to produce goods and services in exchange for oil until OPEC used the dollars for goods and services. Obviously, the strategy could not work if dollars were not a means of exchange for oil. The second part of the loan was from all other economies that had to pay dollars for oil but could not print currency. Those economies had to trade their goods and services for dollars in order to pay OPEC. Again, so long as OPEC held the dollars rather than spending them the US received a loan. It was therefore important to keep OPEC oil priced in dollars at the same time the government officials continued to recruit Arab funds.[20]

b) The vast majority of developing countries did not receive any petrodollar-recycled commercial loans of Western banks. Three-quarters of these mostly state-guaranteed commercial loans went to only 14 NICs, many of them oil exporters themselves, like Mexico, Algeria and Venezuela.[21] They had not accrued their current account deficits via increased bills for oil imports but by trade deficits with the five biggest economies at that time (USA, Japan, Germany, United Kingdom and France). Thus, the debt accumulation of NICs and developing countries in the 1970s and the ensuing debt crisis of the 1980s were also a result of a new international division of labor and associated trade and debt flows. Petrodollars did not play the main role. Finally, the vast majority of developing countries had to rely on aid money, not commercial bank loans to finance their deficits, which indeed had been severely increased due to rising bills for oil imports. These aid monies were once again distributed after political negotiations, not by market mechanisms.

It is important to stress how revolutionary this new arrangement was. International capital markets were not used as a means to balance current accounts under the Bretton Woods system. Besides, the IMF used to be a mere 'fire brigade' to balance current accounts and was not meant to finance long-term structural deficits. Now its character changed to becoming a lender of last resort for the deficit-ridden developing countries and NICs. Unlike the USA they could not print the money they owed. They had to rely on the IMF's credit facilities and accept its conditionality. By setting the rules and ensuring ability to pay, the Fund has been functioning as an important facilitator of liquidity to rapidly changing financial markets.

For the oil-exporting countries, the rise in oil prices meant a steep increase in wealth. This wealth was partly squandered in misguided prestige projects and conspicuous consumption: At the height of the second oil crisis, the Mexican President remarked to the US Assistant Secretary for Economics Richard T. McCormack that the Mexican government's task was the 'distribution of abundance,'[22] and conspicuous consumption of Arab Gulf élites became legendary. Nevertheless, enough was left to be invested and provide a cushion for the richer among the oil exporters once oil prices corrected in the 1980s. In 1974, more than one-half of the revenues were set aside as bank deposits and money market instruments, and slightly less went into long-term investments like loans to national governments and international agencies, equity and property investments, and government bonds, mainly in the USA and the United Kingdom. This pattern persisted throughout the 1970s in varying magnitudes.[23]

However, skepticism about petrodollar recycling was uttered by Iran in the mid-1970s. The country was concerned about 'currency devaluation,' while 'excessive' investment in private industry would entail the risk of 'eventual nationalization.' Real estate investments on the other hand, for example in Arizona, would only bid up prices, create resentment and ultimately make future investments too costly. Beside value preservation, Iran should focus its foreign investments on industries that could benefit its economic diversification at home.[24]

The US government monitored investment patterns of oil exporters and was interested in attracting their funds. Saudi Arabia in particular was successfully wooed and a close relationship established, while other countries like Kuwait allocated a smaller share of their funds in US treasuries. On the other hand the USA was concerned that oil exporters could use their new financial might 'to bring down currencies' in case of a political crisis like the Arab oil boycott.[25] In 1974 the first annual survey of foreign holdings of US securities was undertaken by the Treasury International Capital (TIC) System, an institution within the US treasury that was originally founded in 1934 to monitor US holdings of international portfolios, not the other way around. Kuwait and Saudi Arabia, for example, faced limits in increasing their equity investments in 1977 as they were anxious not to hold more than 5% of any company's stock. They wanted to avoid the publicity and the mandatory disclosure to the US Security and Exchange Commission (SEC) that would have come with purchases beyond that threshold. At the same time their approach to invest only in a number of selected stocks via trust fund managers put a ceiling on their investment options. On the one hand, the selectivity was motivated by trust fund managers' efforts at performance improvement; on the other hand, Kuwait and Saudi Arabia shunned investments in industries they deemed 'politically sensitive' or 'religiously or culturally objectionable.' In a briefing to the White House, the CIA presented an analysis of how the Saudis and Kuwaitis could restructure their portfolios along the lines of pension and mutual funds and invest in a wider array of stocks in order to escape their self-imposed 5% limit. Kuwait in fact had already begun to invest in broader market-weighed equity portfolios.[26]

While Kuwait and Saudi Arabia were interested in increasing their equity investments in the USA, there were concerns about the stability of their investments. As Saudi Arabia produced oil well beyond its revenue needs, some Saudi officials started asking for protection of assets against inflation, exchange rate fluctuations and expropriation. Otherwise, they wondered aloud, it might be better to leave the oil in the ground instead of investing its proceeds in intangible financial assets of which Saudi Arabia had already accumulated $55 billion by the end of 1976. The State Department discussed three possible reactions to such Saudi requests. Firstly, one could merely acknowledge a connection between asset stability and oil production in bilateral talks. Secondly, one could offer special treatment for Saudi assets in return for oil production increases. As mentioned above, Saudi Arabia had already received such special treatment since 1974 with exclusive tranches of treasury bonds outside of the competitive auctioning process. The third option would have been an outright guarantee of the real value of purchased assets with a special security in return for Saudi enforcement of an oil price agreement within OPEC about limited and gradual oil price increases over a 5–6 year period.[27] Shortly after concerns mounted as the dollar's value slid. Between December 1977 and September 1978 OPEC dollar denominated assets fell by 40% on a purchasing power parity basis.[28] In late 1978 Saudi Arabia embarked on what the CIA termed 'a modest diversification program,' and other OPEC members like Kuwait also shifted out of the dollar.[29] In order to pre-empt such discussions US diplomacy went to great lengths to make further promises such as increased economic co-operation.

On another occasion the National Foreign Assessment Center analyzed how OPEC countries reacted to the freezing of Iranian assets in the USA in the wake of the Tehran hostage crisis. On November 16, 1979 the Iranian acting Foreign Minister and economic adviser Bani Sadr had announced that Iran was aiming at ending the dollar's role as an international reserve currency. Iran would henceforth only accept deutschmark, yen, French or Swiss franc as payment for its oil, and he called on other OPEC members to follow Iran's lead and additionally cut off oil supplies to the USA. Although his statement was denied by other Iranian officials, the US government was naturally concerned about possible spillover effects to other oil producers.

However, OPEC's reaction was 'judged sympathetic' as serious negative reactions within OPEC were missing, and a Libyan initiative to take reprisals against the USA was rebuffed by the Conference of Arab Foreign Ministers:

> It is highly unlikely that OPEC members would seriously entertain Iranian calls to move out of dollars. Further disturbance of already unsettled foreign exchange markets would not be in the interest of OPEC. More important, any widespread attack on the dollar would also seriously affect the assets other OPEC countries hold in dollars. Key OPEC states, like Saudi Arabia and Kuwait, have repeatedly acknowledged their responsibility to help maintain the soundness of the international monetary system.[30]

The petrodollar meltdown 1986–99

Fears in the 1970s of a continuous rise in oil prices did not materialize, on the contrary. From 1980 to 1986 non-OPEC production increased by 10mbpd; new capacity came on stream in Mexico, Alaska, the North Sea and the Soviet Union. At the same time high prices caused demand to fall from 64.1mbpd in 1979 to 57.7mbpd in 1983.[31] This unhinged the market balance in favor of consumers. After sliding since 1982 from over $35 to below $30, oil prices plummeted in 1986 within months towards $10, when Saudi Arabia decided to regain market share instead of acting as a swing producer and shutting in capacity to stabilize prices. The price for one barrel of West Texas Intermediate (WTI) at the NYMEX in New York more than halved within two months when it fell from $26 in January 1986 to $12 by March.[32] OPEC oil revenues plunged from a high of $277bn in 1980 to $65bn in 1986 and remained in a trough for two decades. It was only from 2000 onwards that a recovery set in. In inflation adjusted real terms the lofty heights of the 1970s were only reached again in 2005, and only in 2008 did real oil net export revenues of $859bn supersede the record set in 1980 when they had reached $647bn (see Figure 27.1).

Thus, petrodollar surpluses were a thing of the past, and what was left was spent by Gulf countries to finance the allied military campaign against the Iraqi occupation of Kuwait in 1991. In the 1990s, many oil exporters became net capital importers as they accumulated increasing deficits. Saudi Arabia, in particular, developed large current account deficits in comparison to GDP of 10–15% during the second half of the 1980s.[33] In the case of the Gulf countries, most of the financing was done by foreign bank loans and domestic debt issues; unlike in other emerging markets, international bonds were not issued.

Other oil producers developed serious current account deficits and balance of payment problems too. Mexico started off the Latin American debt crisis when it went into default in 1982; other countries on the continent followed and had to turn to the IMF for help, among them Venezuela. Nigeria was also part and parcel of the debt crisis in developing countries in the 1980s.[34] Thomas Friedman has argued in the *New York Times* that it was low oil prices that brought the Soviet Union down.[35] The share of oil in total exports had risen from 10–15% to 40% in the 1970s, and the economic impact of $10 oil was dramatic as the Soviet Union had to make up for revenue shortfalls by borrowing from abroad. The lack of hard currency earnings contributed to the economic and, finally, political demise of the Soviet Union. Imports of crucial technology and grains for an ambitious program of livestock breeding had been financed in the 1970s by the sale of oil, gold and other commodities. With the general decline of commodity prices in the 1980s, the possibility to raise finance via this window diminished. Only

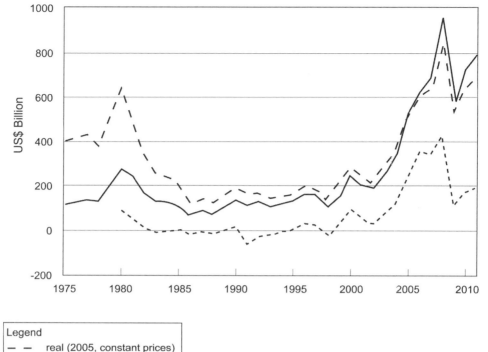

Figure 27.1 OPEC net oil export revenues
Note: OPEC: Saudi Arabia, United Arab Emirates, Islamic Republic of Iran, Kuwait, Nigeria, Venezuela, Algeria, Angola, Libya, Iraq, Qatar, Ecuador. Angola and Ecuador not included prior to 1994. 2010 and 2011 revenues are estimates. Current account data since 2009 are estimates; in the case of Iran, Iraq, Ecuador and Algeria already since 2008, Iraq data not available prior to 2005. Indonesia not included, as its OPEC membership has been suspended from 2009 on as it has ceased to be an oil exporter. Gabon not included as it terminated its OPEC membership in 1995.
Source: US Energy Information Administration (EIA), 'OPEC Revenues Fact Sheet,' September 2010, available at: www.eia.doe.gov/emeu/cabs/OPEC_Revenues/Factsheet.html (accessed 8 October, 2010); IMF, World Economic Outlook Dataset, October 2010.

Norway escaped the resource curse of excessive exposure to volatile oil revenues and non-transparent government structures. With a diversified economic structure, it had other pillars for its economy to rest on and as a latecomer, oil production only started at a time when oil prices had already corrected.

Oil exporters not only did not play a role in financing global imbalances in the 1980s and 1990s, they often had to turn to international capital markets to receive funds themselves. Other countries stepped in; Japan was a major bankroller of the US current account deficit in the 1980s and 1990s and received preferential tranches of US treasuries like Saudi Arabia earlier.[36] The NICs in Asia (Hong Kong, Taiwan, South Korea and Singapore) also accumulated substantial current account surpluses, as did Germany in the 1980s, before it turned into a deficit country for most of the 1990s as a result of German reunification and increased import needs

Oil, the Dollar, and the Stability of the International Financial System

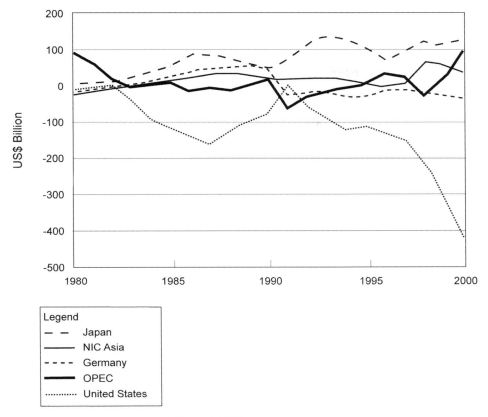

Figure 27.2 Global imbalances 1980s and 1990s
Source: IMF, World Economic Outlook Dataset, October 2010. For OPEC countries see remarks Figure 27.1
NIC Asia: Newly Industrialized Countries: Hong Kong, Taiwan, Singapore, and South Korea

(see Figure 27.2). China is strikingly absent during this time (see Table 27.4 in Appendix). However, from 1997 it started to develop significant current account surpluses, which soared from 2005 onwards. The USA, on the other hand, developed huge current account deficits during the same time period, which peaked at a record of $803bn in 2006 and dwarfed the already substantial deficits of the 1980s and 1990s (see Figure 27.3).

Back to the future? Oil and global imbalances in the 2000s

The Asian crisis in 1997/98 and oil prices below $10 from December 1998 to February 1999 marked a low point for oil exporters after two frustrating decades. However, prices staged a recovery during 1999 and after a modest current account surplus in the same year, oil exporters established themselves again as major international financiers during the 2000s. Together with Japan they were the most important surplus countries in the first half of the decade before China increasingly moved to center stage from 2005 onwards (see Figure 27.3). The NICs in Asia also had substantial surpluses, while the US current account deficit reached record levels during the decade. Even though it narrowed after 2008, it still remains very high. The European Union was

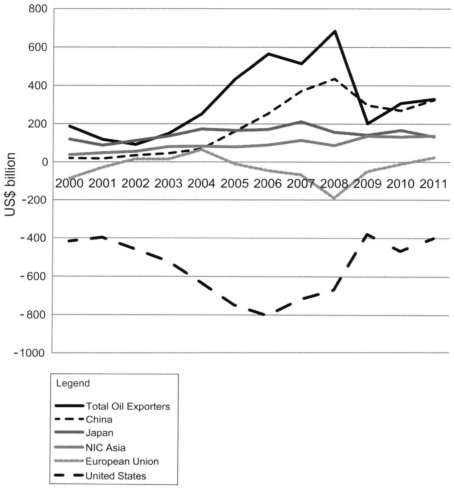

Figure 27.3 Global imbalances in the 2000s
Source: IMF, World Economic Outlook Dataset, October 2010.
Total oil exporters: OPEC plus other oil exporters. For OPEC data composition see remarks Figure 27.1. For composition of other oil exporters see Figure 27.4.
NIC Asia: Newly Industrialized Countries: Hong Kong, Taiwan, Singapore, and South Korea

on average more or less balanced; only in 2008, did it amass a large deficit. However, it showed grave internal imbalances mainly between Germany and southern member states like Greece, Spain, Portugal and Italy, which contributed to a credibility problem for the euro in the wake of the Greek debt crisis. Additionally, the countries of Central and Eastern Europe also ran up substantial current account deficits and had to finance themselves via their capital account, which increasingly became a problem as a result of the financial crisis. Other world regions have mattered less with regard to global imbalances. In the 2000s Latin America at times had a deficit and at times a surplus; so too Sub-Saharan Africa, albeit on a much smaller scale due to its limited integration into the global economy. The ASEAN-5 countries (Indonesia, Malaysia, Philippines, Thailand, and Vietnam) also achieved continuous surpluses during the 2000s, though on a lower level than their above mentioned Asian peers (see Table 27.4 in Appendix).

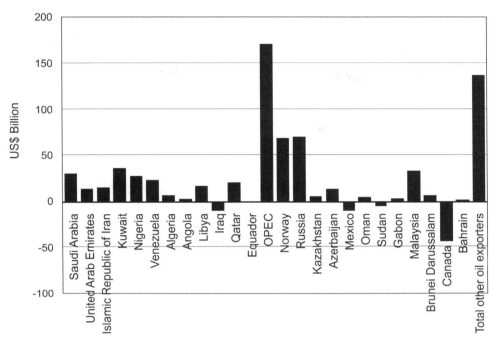

Figure 27.4 Current accounts of oil net exporters, 2010
Source: IMF, World Economic Outlook Dataset, October 2010, Numbers are estimates.

So it comes down to US deficits and surpluses in Asia and in oil-exporting countries when discussing global imbalances and their sustainability. In 2009 imbalances diminished in the wake of the global financial crisis, reduced global trade, and steep oil price corrections, but overall striking disparities remain and they have started to grow again with the tentative recovery in 2010. The IMF estimates that they will continue to do so until 2015 at least (see Table 27.4 in Appendix). The belief in a sustainable Bretton Woods II system and the 'savings glut' has only been temporarily shattered among leading decision makers and economists. On the other hand, there were increased rumblings about competitive devaluations at the end of 2010. The USA urged China to revalue its currency, which the latter steadfastly refused to do, while Japan and South Korea intervened to prevent a further appreciation of their currencies. The Brazilian Minister of Finance Guido Mantega mulled similar steps as he feared for the competitiveness of his national economy and spoke of the danger of 'international currency wars'.[37]

China has superseded oil exporters in importance, and discussions about redressing imbalances very much focused on China and a revaluation of its currency. Financially, the USA and China are in a situation of mutually assured destruction. China depends on US deficit spending for its export-led growth and has a currency reserve of about $2.6 trillion (Oct. 2010), while the USA needs China to finance its deficit and keep the US consumer afloat. Because of the overriding importance of China and the USA in international politics, Zbigniew Brzezinski has suggested an 'informal G2' in a widely noticed article.[38] However, the oil exporters commanded similar significance in the 2000s when it came to global imbalances. First, crude oil and mineral fuel imports make up a large part of the US trade deficit, nearly 40% in 2006, according to a study of McKinsey.[39] Secondly, a sale of their substantial financial assets could equally disrupt international financial markets and the value of the dollar. On the other hand, the oil exporters also stand to lose from dollar weakness and financial disintegration, as this would mean devaluation of their substantial assets, and oil demand would suffer in the wake of an economic crisis. As has been seen above, the US government was well aware of this potential counter threat during the first oil crisis. Internally, White House staff deliberated how a bankruptcy of a major economy could be instrumentalized to this end and scenarios were pondered on how to 'use the corpse of Italy to flog OPEC into being reasonable on oil prices.'[40]

There are considerable differences between the various net oil exporters in terms of current account surpluses and accumulated financial assets. Some of them actually do not run surpluses but deficits, such as Mexico, Iraq, Canada, Sudan and Ecuador (see Figure 27.4), or their surpluses and accumulated financial assets are relatively small. Therefore, crucially important are only those countries that hold substantial assets beyond reserve requirements to manage short-term liquidity like Saudi Arabia, United Arab Emirates, Kuwait, Qatar, Libya, Algeria, Russia and Norway. Accumulated assets of countries like Kazakhstan, Azerbaijan, Nigeria, Oman, Iran or Venezuela considerably fall behind this group in terms of size.

After the slump in oil prices since the summer of 2008 some of the currency reserves had also to be mobilized to defend local currency (e.g. Russia, Venezuela), shore up capital in domestic equity markets (e.g. Kuwait), bail out companies (e.g. Abu Dhabi/Dubai), pay for a high level of subsidies (e.g. Saudi Arabia, Iran), or finance anti-cyclical stimulus programs (e.g. Saudi Arabia). OPEC production cuts also led to reduced production compared to 2007/2008. It therefore remains to be seen whether current account surpluses and SWF assets in oil-exporting countries will take the steep growth trajectory forecast until summer of 2008. The projection of a McKinsey report in 2006 that oil funds would continue to grow even if oil prices corrected to $30 a barrel was incorrect.[41] In fact many oil exporting countries faced budget deficits after the steep oil price corrections in the second half of 2008 and were forced to take recourse to savings and/or debt issuance in 2009. Therefore, the threshold price for a balanced budget varied considerably from country to country. It ranged from below $40 per barrel of Brent in the case of Qatar and the United Arab Emirates, to over $90 in the case of Iran and Venezuela. Saudi Arabia and Kuwait had a more modest threshold price of around $50, while for Bahrain, Oman and Russia it hovered at and above $70.[42] This threshold has continuously moved upward in recent years and received a renewed push in 2011 when governments engaged in fiscal expansion to calm political protests.[43] Large funds are required for ambitious domestic development plans and growing import needs. Saudi Arabia repatriated about $50bn in the wake of the global financial crisis in order to finance a public spending program. From July 2009 to July 2010, Middle East oil exporters divested a total sum of $20.2bn in long-term US securities, according to monthly TIC figures, possibly to finance anticyclical spending at home.[44] Thus, the longevity of oil assets crucially depends on oil price developments and domestic spending patterns. A large part of the Oil Stabilization Fund of Iran, for example, has been loaned to domestic development projects inside the country, and Ahmadinejad's government authorized the withdrawal of about $17bn of an estimated total of $23–25bn.[45] Venezuela also has considerable financing needs because of populist spending programs at home and substantial foreign aid given to neighboring Latin American countries like Cuba, Nicaragua and Bolivia.[46]

Size and asset allocation of oil funds

The size and allocation of oil assets are often shrouded in secrecy as many of them are not managed by central banks that publish reserve figures and report to the Bank for International Settlement (BIS) but by Sovereign Wealth Funds (SWF). As investments by such funds are mostly undertaken by financial intermediaries and assets are deposited with overseas custodians, they are

Table 27.1 Total long-term and short-term US assets held by foreigners, US$ millions

	June 2009
African Oil-Exporters*	5,130
Middle East Oil-Exporters**	352,822
Russia	149,835
Norway	118,941
Venezuela	9,485
Kazakhstan	18,133
Malaysia	32,405
Brunei	1,616
Total Oil Exporters	688,367
China, Mainland	1,464,027
Hong Kong	221,578
Taiwan	194,301
Japan	1,269,291
South Korea	113,050
Singapore	145,183
Total Asian Exporter Nations	3,407,430
United Kingdom	787,887
Cayman Islands	650,094
Bermuda	199,387
Switzerland	327,860
Belgium	415,103
Luxembourg	577,877
Ireland	347,815
Total Financial Hubs	3,306,023
Rest of the World	2,289,278
Total World	9,640,560

*Algeria, Gabon, Libya, Nigeria
**Bahrain, Iran, Iraq, Kuwait, Oman, Qatar, Saudi Arabia, United Arab Emirates
Source: US Treasury Department, Treasury International Capital (TIC) System, historical annual survey data, available at: www.treas.gov/tic/shlhistdat.html (accessed 7 October 2010).

often not accurately reported in the TIC data of the US treasury about foreign holders of US securities. Still, the TIC data is the best we have, as comparable data for European countries is missing and SWFs have often scant disclosure of information. When looking at the TIC data's last published annual report with comprehensive data from June 2009,[47] it is striking that oil exporters' officially recorded US assets of $688bn are small compared to Asian countries, which hold a total of $3.4 trillion, of which $1.46 trillion is held by China. This is because the Asian assets are much better recorded as they are mainly held by central banks.[48] When a Gulf SWF buys a US treasury bond via a financial intermediary in the United Kingdom, Switzerland or Luxembourg it appears as a purchase of these respective countries in the TIC statistics and not as one of a Gulf country. Therefore, many oil assets figure among the very large assets held by financial hubs (see Table 27.1). Given the estimated sizes of assets of Libya, Nigeria, and Algeria (see Table 27.3), the numbers for African Oil Exporters in the TIC data must be deemed heavily underreported as well.

To these securitized assets, bank deposits need to be added. For June 2009 the TIC data shows substantial net liabilities of the US banking system to oil exporters and major Asian exporter nations (see Table 27.2).

Table 27.2 Net liabilities to foreigners of US banking system, June 2009, US$ billion

African Oil-Exporters	3.8
Middle East Oil-Exporters	96.4
Russia	73.7
Norway	-5.8
Venezuela	21.7
Total	189.7
China, Mainland	185.4
Hong Kong	74.7
Taiwan	32.6
Japan	15.7
South Korea	2.6
Singapore	34.2
Total	345.2

Source: Treasury International Capital (TIC) Reporting System.

Not surprisingly, estimates of some SWF assets constitute an art form rather than hard statistics. They vary greatly and usually combine accumulated current account surpluses with an estimated average return over the years. Especially the investment authorities of Abu Dhabi (ADIA), Qatar (QIA), and Libya (LIA) do not disclose the size of their assets. The Kuwait Investment Authority (KIA) at least divulges its assets under management occasionally and is deemed a relatively transparent Gulf SWF, according to a ranking by the Peterson Institute.[49] Still it is far removed from the disclosure practice of the Norwegian SWF, which publishes detailed quarterly reports on its website with size and allocation according to asset class, currency and geographic location. The official assets of Saudi Arabia are also well known as they are held by the country's central bank, the Saudi Arabian Monetary Agency (SAMA); the Russian SWF also reports the size of its assets.

These estimated funds of $2.35 trillion held by SWFs and central banks only represent one aspect of oil wealth. In the Gulf region, there are also SWFs which have a more private equity nature like the International Petroleum Investment Company (IPIC) and Mubadala in Abu Dhabi or companies that engage in foreign acquisitions be they mostly state-owned like Saudi Basic Industries Corporation (SABIC) or privately-held like Kingdom Holding in Saudi Arabia. Most importantly there is significant wealth in the hands of private individuals in the Gulf. McKinsey estimates that 40% of the oil wealth in the region is held by such high net worth individuals.[50] This would add another $550bn or so to the estimated $1.39 trillion of official Gulf assets in Table 27.3 and would bring the estimated total foreign assets of all oil exporters to around $2.9 trillion in 2009. In any case the accumulated wealth of oil exporting countries is comparable with the $2.3 trillion foreign assets of the Chinese official sector during the same period. Not surprisingly, the US Administration is once again paying attention to Middle East investors and engaging in a financial shuttle diplomacy reminiscent of the 1970s. In May 2008 then US Treasury Secretary Henry Paulson visited Saudi Arabia, the United Arab Emirates and Qatar, and in July 2009 his successor Timothy Geithner visited the former two countries. Both officials stressed the openness and reliability of the USA as an investment destination besides discussing issues like increased oil production or Iran sanctions regime.

How many of these oil assets are invested in US dollars is again a matter of approximation. Many central banks do not publish a breakdown according to currencies; this is also true for the

Table 27.3 Selected oil funds, assets, US$ billion

	Sep-2010
Abu Dhabi Investment Authority (ADIA) and ADIC	423
Kuwait Investment Authority (KIA)	272
Qatar Investment Authority (QIA)	85
Libyan Investment Authority (LIA)	68
SAMA non-reserve and pensions	463
GCC central banks	80
Total GCC	1391
Algeria Reserves	144
Norway Government Pension Fund – Global	458
Russia: Reserve Fund	39
Russia: Wealth Fund	85
Kazakstan Stabilization Fund	28
Azerbaijan State Oil Fund*	18
Iran Reserves**	84.3
Iran, Oil Stabilization Fund*	23 (possibly lower, see endnote 45)
Oman State General Reserve Fund*	8.2
Bahrain Mumtalakat*	9.1
Nigeria Reserves	34.5
Venezuela Reserves and FEM	28.6
Total	2350.7

Source: Rachel Ziemba, 'Slow Growth in MENA Sovereign Assets Ahead?', Roubini Global Economics, 30 September, 2010; SWF Institute (*); ** in 2009/2010 according to IMF; Central Banks of Nigeria and Venezuela.

Chinese Central Bank. Rachel Ziemba estimates that central banks of Middle East oil exporters hold about 75% of their assets in the dollar, while she puts this figure at 45–50% for their SWFs, which leads to an average of 55–60% dollar share in the total portfolio.[51] This is at the lower end of the global share of dollars in global currency reserves, which stood at 62.1% in September 2010 according to the IMF.[52] In an interview with German newspaper Handelsblatt, the late head of ADIA Sheikh Ahmed Bin Zayed Al Nahyan said that in geographic terms between 35% and 50% of ADIA's assets have been invested in the USA, 25–35% in Europe and around 10% to 20% in Asia.[53]

Russia has repeatedly questioned the solitary status of the dollar as a reserve currency, and in January 2009 the euro overtook the dollar in its currency reserves for the first time as it made up 47.5% vs. 41.5% for the dollar, according to a report of the Russian central bank.[54] Iran and Venezuela have agitated against the dollar in the most outspoken way. By 2008 Iran switched payment for its oil from dollar to euro and yen,[55] and in 2009 President Ahmadinejad ordered the replacement of the dollar by the euro in the country's foreign exchange accounts. This was also motivated by the severe restriction in dollar transactions that Iran faced as a result of US and UN economic sanctions. Even before that the share of dollars in the currency reserve had been below 20% only, as the Iranian Central Bank Governor announced in 2007.[56] The Iranian central bank has not released its annual economic report in the last three years and there seem to have been some institutional rivalries between the government and its statistics center.[57] Thus, data dissemination has been more limited, the IMF has estimated reserve assets in 2009/

2010 at $84.3bn after they had slightly decreased the year before by $3bn.[58] In October 2010 the central bank had to mobilize an estimated $10bn to counter a precipitate weakening of the Iranian Rial in the wake of tightened economic sanctions.[59]

Venezuela slashed the dollar share of its currency reserve from 95% to 80% in 2006 and endorsed an Iranian proposal to sell oil in euros instead of the dollar at an OPEC meeting the same year.[60] In 2009 Hugo Chávez proposed an oil-backed currency while visiting the Gulf but received little enthusiasm from his Arab hosts.[61] Like Iran, Venezuela had to intervene in its two tiered domestic currency market in 2010 to prop up the Bolivar.[62] While the Iranian and Venezuelan forays make headlines, they need to be put into perspective. The size of their assets is limited in comparison to other oil exporters and the threshold prices for oil that they require to balance their budgets are the highest among the major net oil exporters. Both have also struggled with increased domestic spending and economic problems in the wake of the global financial crisis.

Thus, the relative share of dollar assets of oil exporters is lower than China's, which Brad Setser estimates to be 70%.[63] Oil exporters also differ in terms of asset allocation. Middle East SWFs have a high equity share of up to 60% in their portfolios and also invest in alternatives like hedge funds, real estate or private equity, while Asian investors still mostly invest in fixed income instruments. There is a crucial difference in terms of the overarching development goals for which such investments are pursued. Foreign asset accumulation in China and other Asian countries is to a certain extent a function of a mercantilist, export-led growth strategy. Profit maximization is not the main goal, but undervaluation of the exchange rate and the build-up of a capital stock that comes with the export-led growth model.

Once the central bank intervenes, it buys up foreign exchange with local currency. To prevent an increase in money supply and ensuing inflation, the Chinese central bank has increasingly taken recourse to sterilization, i.e. issuance of domestic securities to mop up excess liquidity.[64] Such sterilization comes with negative side effects like an overexpansion of the export sector; for our purposes, one aspect is important: The dollar assets of the central bank have a liability in domestic currency standing against them. This results in a considerable hurdle rate as Andrew Rozanov points out.[65] To be profitable, a foreign asset held by the Chinese central bank not only needs to earn the interest rate of the domestic currency liability that is standing against it, but also a possible appreciation of this liability in case of an upward revaluation of the yuan. Between 2005 and 2008, Chinese authorities let the yuan appreciate by 21% before pegging it again to the dollar in July 2008 in order to protect domestic exporters.[66] The yuan is still regarded as undervalued by up to 40%.[67] Artificially low interest rates and wide spreads between lending and deposit rates are equally under revaluation pressure. The cost of domestic debt and an annual appreciation of the yuan of about 7% as in 2005–8 would add up to a hurdle rate of 10% or more, which is unachievable by investing in US treasury bonds.

Strictly financially the Chinese investment approach does not make sense, but possibly it does not need to. In the event of a financial meltdown, China would still have its industries, though producing then below capacity, but the oil countries would have sold their past wealth for paper. The Chinese have already got something for their dollars, i.e. industrialization and a capital stock, while the oil exporters still want to buy something with theirs. This is a crucial difference. The assets of oil SWFs mostly accrue directly to the respective governments via oil companies they own and mostly stay offshore. As these overseas assets do not have a sterilization involved, they constitute clean equity with no immediate short-term liability standing against them. However, they face an unspecified long-term liability as they are supposed to finance economic diversification and provide revenues in an after-oil age. Thus, the rationale for holding them is largely commercial and they are not subordinated to a politically wanted exchange rate undervaluation as in China. The motivation of long-term risk adjusted returns and capital preservation is therefore more important than in the case of official Asian assets.

False Conspiracies and Future Scenarios

Oil exporters have been important for the stability of the international financial system in the 1970s and the 2000s, and the USA has a vested interest in the 'exorbitant privilege' of issuing the global reserve currency. Some accounts therefore argue that oil pricing in dollars is so essential for the acceptance of the dollar as a preferred means of global payments that the USA was ready to defend it at all costs.[68] Saddam Hussein's decision in 2000 to price oil in euros is seen as a major motivation of the Iraq war in 2003, just as Iran's moves away from the dollar and its vastly overrated oil bourse on Kish island are seen as major factors in US-Iranian hostilities.[69] Oil pricing in dollars is seen as so crucial that the four-fold oil price hike in 1973–74 is not explained by a shift of the supply demand equation in favor of OPEC or the psychological impact of the Arab oil boycott, but by the engineering of the Bilderberg group at a meeting in Sweden in 1973 that aimed at ensuring sufficient demand for dollars. Such views are not confined to conspiracy buffs but have also been endorsed by Zaki Yamani, the former Saudi oil minister, who argued in an *Observer* interview in 2001 that the USA and the United Kingdom engineered the oil price hike in 1973 at the said Bilderberg meeting in order to benefit their own oil industries, which needed higher prices to be competitive.[70] As with any conspiracy theory, the public record is scant.[71] Proponents might interpret this as just another indication of the wicked shrewdness of the conspirators, but there are also some logical fallacies with these accounts.

While petrodollar recycling has been important in the 1970s and the 2000s in financing the US current account deficit, it had all but disappeared in the 1980s and 1990s; its exclusive responsibility for the maintenance of global imbalances, therefore, is questionable. The US deficit remained, but other nations took over in financing it. There is also rich archival evidence that the USA and other industrialized countries far from welcoming the oil price hikes, worked to counter them by increasing global supplies and curbing demand. After they succeeded in doing so, oil prices in fact came down in the 1980s. The Iraq war was planned at a time when the renewed petrodollar boom was only at its beginning and oil prices of $150 were inconceivable. After 2008 oil savings have taken a hit, and even before that, the role of China in financing global imbalances had moved to the center stage. The assets of oil-based SWFs have risen rapidly in the 2000s, but it has to be kept in mind that they still pale in comparison to the assets of mainly Western financial institutions such as insurance companies ($18.7 trillion), mutual funds ($18.9 trillion) and pension funds ($24 trillion).[72] Originally projected growth rates of their assets have been too high as oil prices have declined and domestic spending increased.[73]

Thus, oil exporters currently form an important part of the international financial system and are a major funder of the US current account deficit, but their importance needs to be put into perspective. This is also true for the role of oil in international trade and the demand for US currency that its pricing in dollars generates. Oil is not the only item traded in dollars, so are Barbie dolls from China, copper from Congo or cars from Korea. Global daily merchandise exports in 2009 amounted to $34.1bn, fuel exports like gasoline, diesel and LNG constituted 23% of the total ($7.8bn) and crude oil exports 12% ($4.1bn).[74] As refining is still mostly located in consumer nations, the part of global trade that is controlled by oil exporters (12%) is substantial, but not overwhelming. If daily trade in services and illegal trade in drugs are taken into consideration this share falls below 10%.[75]

Thus, petrodollar recycling undoubtedly played a crucial role for the nascent Bretton Woods II system of US deficit spending in the 1970s and the USA applied political influence to achieve desired results. However, to suggest some masterminded plan steered by an annual meeting of high ranking figures contradicts the real life experience of the inert workings of large bureaucracies and their competing interests. In this case as well the road was bumpy, the actors many and the respective diplomacy often conducted in ad-hoc fashion.[76] Nowadays trade in physical items like oil has also decreased in importance for dollar demand as the financial sector has entered an incestuous relationship with itself and supersedes physical trade turnovers many times over.

The governor of the Saudi Arabian Monetary Authority (SAMA) Muhammed Al Jasser has proposed at the Jeddah Economic Forum in February 2010 to differentiate clearly between pricing of oil, pegging of oil currencies to the dollar, and allocation of oil revenues in dollar denominated assets and securities. Each has its own dynamic and all three vary considerably with regard to their importance in stabilizing the dollar and, therefore, the international financial system at large. Pricing of oil in itself is only an accounting unit, payments can be in other currencies and even if the payment is done in dollars the proceeds can be exchanged and invested in assets with other currency denomination. The widespread usage of dollars in international trade, not only for oil, certainly leads to liquidity needs and preferences in that currency and the same is true for the dollar-pegged currencies of GCC countries, but the ultimate litmus test for dollar confidence is the investment of such trading receipts in dollar-denominated assets. Despite widespread concerns, there has been no wholehearted flight out of the dollar by most oil exporters or anybody else for that matter.

As the US deficit is flabbergasting this is hardly attributable to sound monetary policies and fiscal discipline. However, other major currencies have serious flaws as well ranging from Japan's record public debt/GDP ratio of nearly 200% to Euroland's ailing banking sector and its lack of central institutions and common fiscal policy. In the wake of the Greek debt crisis, these structural weaknesses have been exposed and have tempered the appetite for currency diversification. The Chinese yuan is not even fully convertible yet, although China has started to use it in settlement with selected bilateral trade partners like Russia, Brazil and Turkey. Finally, gold has regained some of its luster as a reserve asset of central banks, with purchases by India, China, Saudi Arabia, Iran and others. While gold has proven its value as a store of wealth and a means of diversification, a reintroduction of any sort of gold standard is unlikely due to the massive deflationary implications such a move would have.[77] Because of the centrality of US deficit spending for global growth models, it is better to think of the dollar as the currency of a system rather than of a country. Other currencies are somehow its derivatives and all nations have a stake in US deficit spending. To paraphrase John Conally, the Treasury Secretary in the Nixon Administration, the dollar is not only their problem it is their currency as well. Many emerging markets have actually issued their bonds in dollars. While everybody knows that this system of deficit spending is unsustainable, they hope that it will go on forever out of fear of the consequences.

If the biggest flaw of the dollar is too much debt, it is paradoxically also its strength. As every debt is an 'asset' on the side of the creditor, a lot of debt contributes to deep and liquid capital markets that are attractive to large investors. Financial markets in Asia still lag far behind in terms of market capitalization and could accommodate diversification only to a limited extent. Thus, the dollar is illiquid because there is so much of it. It is difficult to find sufficient assets denominated in other currencies to diversify into. At this stage the capital markets of Euroland are the only meaningful competitor to the US in terms of depth and breadth and also offer other advantages like large transaction domain, established monetary institutions, political stability, rule of law, absence of capital controls and fall-back value in the form of currency reserves.[78] Arab Gulf countries are in a politically unstable region and rely heavily on US security guarantees. This may influence their currency decisions as well, but overall it is safe to assume that dollar dominance in international trade and its use as a reserve currency do not need enforcement by military might but continue to struggle along due to customary practice, devaluation fears and lack of alternatives.

The global financial crisis has made emerging market countries more visible on the international stage. As they contribute an increasing share of global GDP, countries like China, India, Brazil and Russia have become more vocal in addressing global problems that cannot be solved without them anymore. The old G8 world is gradually fading away, and the G20 has been upgraded as the forum of choice for addressing global economic issues. G20 members have demanded a reform of the IMF, whose voting rights are still mainly distributed among OECD countries. Currently, the EU holds 32% of the voting rights and the USA 17%. The aim is to redistribute 5% of the IMF voting rights; this could also affect G20 nations that are over-represented compared to their GDP, such as Saudi Arabia or Argentina. While Saudi Arabia endorses IMF reform, it opposes any reduction of its voting rights, arguing that the transfer of voting rights would need to come from developed countries. It might be forced to compromise, however; currently it holds 3.2% of voting rights, while India and China with their much larger economies hold 1.9% and 3.7%, respectively.

The role of oil exporters on the international financial stage is essentially a function of oil prices times the amount of oil exported and subtracted by domestic import requirements. Predicting these variables is fraught with errors. Status of oil reserves, depletion rates, new discoveries, development of alternative fuels, global economic growth, OPEC quota policies and domestic energy requirements are all part of the equation. The head of Saudi Aramco, Khalid Al-Falih, warned in 2010 that even with production increases, Saudi Arabia's oil export capacity in 2028 might be reduced by 3mbpd if skyrocketing domestic energy demand is not curtailed by more efficient usage.[79] On the other hand, Iraq's ambitious plan to increase production to 10–12mbpd by 2017 might lead to supply pressures; meanwhile, OPEC aims to reintegrate Iraq into its quota system once its production moves beyond 4–5mbpd.[80] While price corrections are always possible, it seems that oil prices have undergone a paradigm shift over the 2000s and hold out fairly well in the range of $70–85 at the end of 2010. Thus, it is likely that oil exporters will continue to play a role in the international financial system at least in the middle run. However, their overall influence will be weaker than that of China and other large emerging markets.

Notes

1 The first futures contracts on non-commodity underlyings (currencies, interest rates, bonds) were established by the Chicago Mercantile Exchange in the 1970s. Futures on stocks followed suit in the 1980s, which also saw the expansion of swaps and other unregulated over the counter (OTC) derivatives. In terms of market value, skyrocketing growth of derivatives has only been taking place since the 1990s.

2 For discussions of the demise of the Bretton Woods system see Peter Garber, 'The Collapse of the Bretton Woods Fixed Exchange Rate System,' in *A Retrospective on the Bretton Woods System*, ed. Barry Eichengreen and Michael D. Bordo (Chicago, London: University of Chicago Press 1993) and Michael D. Bordo, 'The Bretton Woods International Monetary System: A Historical Overview,' also in *A Retrospective on the Bretton Woods System.*

3 The term was coined by Valéry Giscard d'Estaing who was the French Minister of Finance at that time.

4 Benjamin J. Cohen, *Organizing the World's Money: The Political Economy of International Monetary Relations*, The Political Economy of International Relations Series (New York: Basic Books, 1977).

5 Yu Yongding, 'Will US Fiscal Deficits Undermine the Role of the Dollar as Global Reserve Currency? If So Should US Fiscal Policy Be Geared to Preserving the International Role of the the Dollar?' in *The Future Global Reserve System – an Asian Perspective*, ed. Jeffrey D. Sachs, Masahiro Kawai, Jong-Wha Lee and Wing Thye Woo (Asian Development Bank, June 2010), p. 13.

6 Department of the Treasury, Federal Reserve Bank of New York, and Board of Governors of the Federal Reserve System, 'Report on Foreign Portfolio Holdings of U.S. Securities as of June 30, 2009,' (April 2010), p. 5. The corresponding numbers for agency bonds are 17%, for equities 10% and for corporate and other debt 19%.

7 See Z 1 Flow of Funds tables of the Federal Reserve, available at: http://www.federalreserve.gov/releases/z1/.
8 David Folkerts-Landau, Michael Dooley and Peter Garber, 'An Essay on the Revived Bretton Woods System,' *NBER Working Paper no. 9971* (September 2003).
9 'The Global Saving Glut and the U.S. Current Account Deficit,' Remarks by Governor Ben S. Bernanke at the Sandridge Lecture, Virginia Association of Economics, Richmond, Virginia, 10 March, 2005, available at: www.federalreserve.gov/boarddocs/speeches/2005/200503102/default.htm.
10 Steven Dunaway, 'Global Imbalances and the Financial Crisis,' in *Council Special Report No. 44* (New York: Council on Foreign Relations. Center for Geoeconomic Studies, March 2009).
11 Barry J. Eichengreen, *Global Imbalances and the Lessons of Bretton Woods*, Cairoli Lecture Series (Cambridge, Mass.: MIT Press, 2007), p. 31.
12 Andrew Browne, 'Hu Highlights Need for U.S.-China Cooperation, Questions Dollar,' *The Wall Street Journal*, 16 January, 2011.
13 Joe Parkinson, 'Turkey, China to Shun Dollar in Trade with Each Other,' *Wall Street Journal*, 8 October 2010; Artyom Danielyan and Emma O'Brien, 'Yuan Trading Against Russian Ruble Said to Start Within Weeks in Shanghai,' *Bloomberg*, 8 September 2010.
14 David E. Spiro, *The Hidden Hand of American Hegemony: Petrodollar Recycling and International Markets*, Cornell Studies in Political Economy (Ithaca, NY: Cornell University Press, 1999), pp. 55–57 and 85–91.
15 For an overview of literature in the vein of this conventional wisdom see ibid., pp. 53–55.
16 Ibid., pp. x, 109–10 and 25. This add-on arrangement was offered to central banks in other OPEC and OECD countries as well once word of its existence leaked out.
17 Ibid., p. 105.
18 Ibid., p. 124.
19 Ibid., p. 60.
20 Ibid., p. 121.
21 Ibid., p. 71.
22 Interview with Ambassador Richard T. McCormack by Charles Stuart Kennedy, The Foreign Affairs Oral History Collection of the Association for Diplomatic Studies and Training, 2 January 2002, available at: http://memory.loc.gov/ammem/collections/diplomacy/index.html.
23 IMF, *World Economic Outlook*, April 13, 2006, Chapter II: 'Oil Prices and Global Imbalances', p. 85. Richard P. Mattione, *OPEC's Investments and the International Financial System* (Washington D.C.: The Brookings Institution, 1985).
24 US Congress, 'Old Problems – New Relationships, Report of a Study Mission to the Middle East and South Asia, May 1974,' Committee on Foreign Affairs (Washington: US Gov Printing Office, 1974), p. 20; US Congress, 'The Middle East. Report by Senator Charles H. Percy to the Committee on Foreign Affairs, April 21, 1975,' (Washington D. C.: US Government Printing Office, 1975), p. 36.
25 US Congress, 'The United States Oil Shortage and the Arab-Israeli Conflict. Report of a Study Mission to the Middle East. October 22 to November 3, 1973, Pursuant to H. Res. 267,' Committee on Foreign Affairs (Washington D.C.: U.S. Government Printing Office, December 20, 1973), p. 19.
26 CIA, Economic Intelligence Weekly, Secret, Carter Library, NLC-31-76-3-4-7, 28 April 1977. The US equity investments of Kuwait at the end of 1976 were $2.2bn, and those of Saudi Arabia $1.5bn according to this report – only a minor fraction of their overall portfolio.
27 Department of State brief by Julius L. Katz, Assistant Secretary of Economic and Business Affairs to the Vice President, various Secretaries and other high ranking executives of the Carter administration. Carter Library, NLC –132-26-1-1-4, 4 March, 1977, pp. 4–8.
28 Spiro, *The Hidden Hand of American Hegemony: Petrodollar Recycling and International Markets*, p. 122.
29 Ibid., p. 123.
30 National Foreign Assessment Center, Iranian-US Economic Sanctions: Impact and Reactions, Top Secret, Carter Library, NLC-25-43-2-1-4, 29 November, 1979, p. B-2.
31 BP, *Statistical Review of World Energy 2010*, available at: www.bp.com/productlanding.do?categoryId=6929&contentId=7044622.
32 For historic weekly price data see the EIA's website: http://tonto.eia.doe.gov/dnav/pet/hist/LeafHandler.ashx?n=PET&s=rclc1&f=W
33 IMF, World Economic Outlook Dataset, October 2010.
34 Brian-Vincent Ikejiaku, 'Africa Debt Crisis and the IMF with a Case of Nigeria: Towards Theoretical Explanations,' *Journal of Politics and Law* 1, no. 4 (December 2008); Yusuf Bangura, *IMF/ World Bank*

Conditionality and Nigeria's Structural Adjustment Programme (Uppsala: Nordiska Afrikainstitutet, 1987); Bade Onimode and Institute for African Alternatives, *The IMF, the World Bank, and the African Debt*, 2 vols. (London; Atlantic Highlands, N.J., USA: Zed Books, 1989).

35 Thomas L. Friedman, 'The Oil-Addicted Ayatollahs,' *New York Times*, February 2, 2007; 'Sleepless in Teheran,' *New York Times*, October 28, 2008.
36 Spiro, *The Hidden Hand of American Hegemony: Petrodollar Recycling and International Markets*, p. 156.
37 Martin Wolf, 'Currencies Clash in New Age of Beggar-my-Neighbour,' *Financial Times*, 28 September 2010.
38 Zbigniew Brzezinski, 'The Group of Two that Could Change the World,' *Financial Times*, 13 January, 2009.
39 Diana Farrell et al., 'The US Imbalancing Act: Can the Current Account Deficit Continue?' (San Francisco: McKinsey Global Institute, June 2007), p. 18.
40 Richard T. McCormack Interview by Charles Stuart Kennedy.
41 Diana Farrell et al., 'The New Power Brokers: How Oil, Asia, Hedge Funds, and Private Equity Are Shaping Global Capital Markets,' (San Francisco: McKinsey Global Institute, October 2007), p. 12.
42 Institute of International Finance (IIF), 'Regional Report Gulf Cooperation Council Countries,' Washington D.C., 8 December, 2008.
43 After the announcement of a $125bn spending program it is estimated that Saudi Arabia now requires an oil price of $88 to balance its budget, an increase of 30% to former estimates. Other oil producers have faced similar upward pressures. Ed Morse, 'The New Geopolitics of Oil,' *Financial Times*, 6 April, 2011.
44 TIC data: Net Transactions in Long-Term Domestic and Foreign Securities. Asian Oil Exporters, available at: www.treas.gov/tic/asiaoils_46612.txt (accessed, 16 October, 2010).
45 The Iranian central bank does not disclose the size of the fund. Anna Fifield, 'Iran Feels Pinch of Oil Price Fall,' *Financial Times*, 22 October, 2008.
46 Cesar J. Alvarez, Stephanie Hanson, 'Venezuela's Oil-Based Economy,' Backgrounder, *Council on Foreign Relations*, 9 February, 2009.
47 Department of the Treasury, Federal Reserve Bank of New York, and Board of Governors of the Federal Reserve System, 'Report on Foreign Portfolio Holdings of U.S. Securities as of June 30, 2009.' For a discussion of the Treasury International Capital dataset of the US Treasury and its methodology see Carol C. Bertaut, William L. Griever and Ralph W. Tyron, 'Understanding U.S. Cross-Border Securities Data,' *Federal Reserve Bulletin* 92 (May 2006).
48 Even though there is also underreporting of reserves in China in the case of 'other foreign assets' of the central bank and on the level of state banks see Brad Setser and Arpana Pandey, 'China's $1.7 Trillion Bet. China's External Portfolio and Dollar Reserves,' (New York: Council on Foreign Relations. Center for Geoeconomic Studies, January 2009), p. 6.
49 M. Edwin, 'A Scoreboard for Sovereign Wealth Funds', *Peterson Institute for International Economies*, Washington D.C., 2007.
50 Farrell et al., 'The New Power Brokers: How Oil, Asia, Hedge Funds, and Private Equity Are Shaping Global Capital Markets,' pp. 45–60.
51 Rachel Ziemba, 'Slow Growth in Mena Sovereign Assets Ahead?' (New York, London: Roubini Global Economics, September 30, 2010).
52 'U.S. Dollar's Share of Global Reserves Expanded in 2nd Quarter, IMF Says,' *Bloomberg*, 30 September 2010. The share of the euro was 26.5%, the yen's 3.3% and the British pound's 4.2%.
53 'Scheich Ahmed Bin Zayed Al-Nahyan: Öffentliche Aufmerksamkeit gehört nicht zu unserer Strategie,' *Handelsblatt*, 11 January, 2010.
54 'Dollar Stops being Russia's Basic Reserve Currency,' *Pravda*, 19 May, 2009.
55 'Iran Conducts all Crude Trade in Euro, Yen–Agency,' *Reuters*, 30 April, 2008.
56 'Iran Is Cutting Dollar Reserves, Central Bank Says,' *Bloomberg*, 27 March, 2007.
57 Farnaz Fassihi, 'Iran's Economy Feels Sting of Economic Sanctions,' *Wall Street Journal*, 12 October, 2010.
58 IMF, 'Islamic Republic of Iran: 2009 Article IV Consultation – Staff Report,' (Washington D.C. March 2010), p. 21.
59 *Tehran Times*, 7 October, 2010.
60 'Venezuela, Oil Producers Buy Euro as Dollar, Oil Fall,' *Bloomberg*, 18 December, 2006.
61 Brian Murphy, 'Hugo Chavez Promotes a "Petro-Currency" over Dollar, but his Arab Hosts Show Little Enthusiasm,' *The Huffington Post*, 31 March, 2009.
62 'Disappearing Dollars. An Oil Producer's Strange Foreign-Exchange Squeeze,' *The Economist*, 16 September, 2010.

63 Setser and Pandey, 'China's $1.7 Trillion Bet. China's External Portfolio and Dollar Reserves,' p. 1.
64 John Greenwood, 'The Costs and Inplications of Pbc Sterilization,' *Cato Journal* 28, no. 2 (Spring/Summer 2008).
65 Andrew Rozanov, 'A Liability-Based Approach to Sovereign Wealth,' *Central Banking Journal* XVIII, no. 3 (February 2008).
66 'China CEOs Join Obama in Supporting Yuan Appreciation,' *Bloomberg*, 24 March, 2010.
67 Roya Wolverson, 'Confronting the China-U.S. Economic Imbalance,' in *Backgrounder* (New York: Council on Foreign Relations, 19 October, 2010).
68 William R. Clark, *Petrodollar Warfare: Oil, Iraq and the Future of the Dollar* (Gabriola Island, B.C.: New Society, 2005); William Engdahl, *A Century of War: Anglo-American Oil Politics and the New World Order*, Revised ed. (London; Ann Arbor, MI: Pluto Press, 2004).
69 Clark, *Petrodollar Warfare: Oil, Iraq and the Future of the Dollar*, pp. 150–57. Iran's oil bourse on Kish Island has been a major issue in the blogosphere. After several delays it opened in 2008. So far no crude oil is traded there, only petrochemical products. Due to the deficiencies of the Iranian financial sector and economic sanctions, it is not in a position to attract meaningful numbers of international traders and corresponding liquidity. Other oil exporters of the Gulf are unlikely to join. The Omani crude contract of the Dubai Mercantile Exchange is more likely to gain acceptance, although it struggles as well to attract liquidity and is not traded in euros. The information on the website of the Iran Mercantile Exchange is extremely scant thus far and does not hint to a thriving market place: www.ime.co.ir/site/487/default.aspx. See also Robert Looney, 'A Euro-Denominated Oil Bourse in Iran: Potential Major Force in the International System?' in *Gulf Papers* (Dubai: Gulf Research Center, 2006).
70 Faisal Islam and Oliver Morgan, 'Saudi Dove in the Oil Slick. Interview with Sheikh Zaki Yamani,' *Observer*, January 14 2001.
71 Engdahl bases his theory on secret minutes of the Bilderberg meeting, which he claims to have obtained from a Paris bookseller – a remarkable lapse of security in an otherwise successful conspiracy.
72 IFSL Research, *Fund Management 2009*, London, October 2009.
73 The IMF, for example, predicted that SWF assets in general would grow from $3.9 trillion to $12 trillion by 2012, and Morgan Stanley estimated that the same figure would be reached by 2015. Deloitte, 'Insurance Firms: The Missing Link in the Sovereign Wealth Fund Acquisition Spree,' Report, 2008.
74 Calculated from WTO International Trade Database, June 2010.
75 Daily trade in commercial services of 90 nations was $10.1bn on average in 2009 according to the WTO, ibid. Drug trade in 2003 was estimated at $322bn annually at the retail level by the 2005 World Drug Report of the United Nations Office on Drugs and Crime.
76 Spiro, *The Hidden Hand of American Hegemony: Petrodollar Recycling and International Markets*, p. xi.
77 For an early argument for GCC reserve diversification into gold see Eckart Woertz, 'The Role of Gold in the Unified GCC Currency,' in *Gulf Papers* (Dubai: Gulf Research Center, 2005). World Bank President Robert Zoellick raised eyebrows in 2010 when arguing that gold was an 'alternative monetary asset' that could be used as 'an international reference point of market expectations,' although he rushed to clarify that he was not advocating the reintroduction of a strict gold standard. For a discussion of proposals for currency reform see Alan Beattie, 'Currencies: Strength in Reserve,' *Financial Times*, 8 February, 2011. Recently Nasser Saidi and Fabio Scacciavillani have argued for GCC currency diversification into gold. They also proposed a new international financial architecture with a multi-currency basket at its core that should contain a 20–25% share of gold. Nasser Saidi and Fabio Scacciavillani, 'The Case for Gold as a Reserve Asset in the GCC,' in *DIFC Economic Note No. 11* (Dubai 2010); Nasser Saidi and Fabio Scacciavillani, 'The Role of Gold in the New Financial Architecture,' in *DIFC Economic Note No. 13* (Dubai 2010).
78 Robert Mundell, 'The Euro and the Stability of the International Monetary System,' Paper presented at a conference of the Luxembourg Institute for European and International Studies and the Pierre Werner Foundation on 'The euro as a stabilizer in the international economic system,' 3–4 December, 1998, January 1999, available at: www.robertmundell.net/pdf/The%20Euro%20and%20the%20Stability%20of%20the%20International%20Monetary%20System.pdf.
79 Kate Mackenzie, 'Saudi Arabia's Oil Exports Warning,' *Financial Times*, 29 April 2010.
80 David Blair, 'OPEC Says Iraq Oil Quota Unlikely Before 2013,' *Financial Times*, 15 October, 2010.

Appendix

Table 27.4 Current account balances, annual five year averages, billion US$ (rounded)

	1980–84	1985–89	1990–94	1995–99	2000–04	2005–09	2010–14	Estimates Start After
OPEC								
Saudi Arabia	11.2	−10.3	−15.4	−3.4	23.2	87.6	36.4	2009
United Arab Emirates	8.1	3.9	2.9	2.3	7.9	22	16	2009
Islamic Republic of Iran	−0.9	−2.9	−4.1	3.1	4.8	21.4	14.6	2008
Kuwait	9.3	6	−3.5	5.5	10.5	41.3	43.8	2009
Nigeria	−2.9	−1.4	−0.5	−0.9	0.2	26.7	30	2009
Venezuela	3.1	−0.9	1.5	2.5	9.8	23.7	23.7	2009
Algeria	−0.1	−0.8	0.8	0.3	8.1	23.1	7.9	2008
Angola	−0.2	−0.3	−0.3	−1.1	−0.2	5.7	1.5	2008
Libya	−0.1	−0.4	0.7	4.1	5.1	24.4	20.5	2009
Iraq	n/a	n/a	n/a	n/a	n/a	2.4	−1.2	2008
Qatar	6.3	2.3	−1	−1.5	5.2	20.1	36.1	2009
Ecuador	−0.6	−0.5	−0.6	−0.6	−0.4	0.9	−1	2008
Indonesia*	−2.4	−2.5	−3.2	−1.6	6.5	6.5	−2.9	2009
Total OPEC	30.9	−7.8	−22.6	8.7	80.6	305.7	226.4	
Other Oil Net Exporters								
Norway	1.9	−2	3.8	6.9	27.5	58.3	71.8	2008
Russia	n/a	n/a	3.1	8.5	41	81.8	51.9	2009
Kazakhstan	n/a	n/a	−1	−0.6	−0.3	−1.7	4.8	2009
Azerbaijan	n/a	n/a	−0.2	−0.8	−1.1	7.9	13.3	2009
Mexico	−4.5	−0.9	−19.9	−8.3	−12.6	−7.7	−15.2	2009
Oman	0.8	0	−0.4	−0.9	1.6	3.6	2.5	2009
Sudan	−1	−1.5	−1.8	−1	−1.4	−5.3	−5.7	2009
Gabon	0.7	−0.3	0.1	0.3	0.7	2.2	1.8	2009
Malaysia	−2.3	0.8	−3.2	0.6	10.4			2007

Table 27.4 (continued)

	1980–84	1985–89	1990–94	1995–99	2000–04	2005–09	2010–14	Estimates Start After
Brunei Darussalam	n/a	2.6	2	1.4	3	29.4	32.8	2009
Canada	-4.1	-13.4	-19.6	-3.1	16.4	6.2	5.7	2009
Bahrain	0.5	-0.1	-0.4	-0.1	0.3	4	-40.5	2009
Total other oil exporters	-8	-14	-38.3	3.1	85.4	1.9	1.6	2009
						180.4	124.8	
China	2.9	-5.3	5.5	18.6	37.6	303.8	420.8	2009
Japan	11.3	72.9	97.4	101.5	125.7	169.2	138.1	2009
NIC Asia**	-1.4	24.7	14.7	25.6	61.2	101.2	136.7	2009
ASEAN–5***	-9.1	-3.8	-16.1	-4.8	21.3	42.5	33.6	
Total Asian Exporters	3.6	88.5	101.5	140.8	245.7	616.7	729.2	
United States	-26.3	-129.3	-66.8	-178	-484.6	-663.1	-455.2	2009
European Union	-27.4	8.1	-48.8	41.1	-3.7	-72.1	17.5	2009
Germany	-0.2	41.1	-10.3	-19.4	36.5	198.8	182.4	2009
Central and eastern Europe	-9	-5.1	-4	-15.8	-29.7	-94.7	-83.8	
Latin America and the Caribbean	-24.5	-8.9	-30.2	-58	-17.6			
Sub-Saharan Africa	-9.2	-3.4	-5	-9.8	-7.1	10.2	-85.8	
						4.2	-17.8	

Notes:
* Not an oil net exporter anymore. OPEC membership suspended in 2009
**Newly Industrialized Countries, Hong Kong, Taiwan, Singapore, and South Korea

References

Bangura, Yusuf. *IMF/World Bank Conditionality and Nigeria's Structural Adjustment Programme.* Uppsala: Nordiska Afrikainstitutet, 1987.

Bertaut, Carol C., William L. Griever and Ralph W. Tyron 'Understanding U.S. Cross-Border Securities Data.' *Federal Reserve Bulletin* 92 (May 2006): A59-A75.

Bordo, Michael D. 'The Bretton Woods International Monetary System: A Historical Overview.' In *A Retrospective on the Bretton Woods System*, edited by Barry Eichengreen and Michael D. Bordo. Chicago, London: University of Chicago Press, 1993.

Clark, William R. *Petrodollar Warfare: Oil, Iraq and the Future of the Dollar.* Gabriola Island, B.C.: New Society, 2005.

Cohen, Benjamin J. *Organizing the World's Money: The Political Economy of International Monetary Relations*, The Political Economy of International Relations Series. New York: Basic Books, 1977.

Department of the Treasury, Federal Reserve Bank of New York, and Board of Governors of the Federal Reserve System. 'Report on Foreign Portfolio Holdings of U.S. Securities as of June 30, 2009.' April 2010.

Dooley, Michael, David Folkerts-Landau and Peter Garber. 'An Essay on the Revived Bretton Woods System.' *NBER Working Paper no. 9971* (September 2003).

Dunaway, Steven. 'Global Imbalances and the Financial Crisis.' In *Council Special Report No. 44*. New York: Council on Foreign Relations. Center for Geoeconomic Studies, March 2009.

Eichengreen, Barry J. *Global Imbalances and the Lessons of Bretton Woods*, Cairoli Lecture Series. Cambridge, Mass.: MIT Press, 2007.

Engdahl, William. *A Century of War: Anglo-American Oil Politics and the New World Order.* Revised ed. London; Ann Arbor, MI: Pluto Press, 2004.

Farrell, Diana, Susan Lund, Eva Gerlemann, and Peter Seeburger. 'The New Power Brokers: How Oil, Asia, Hedge Funds, and Private Equity Are Shaping Global Capital Markets.' San Francisco: McKinsey Global Institute, October 2007.

Farrell, Diana, Susan Lund, Alexander Maasry, and Sebastian Roemer. 'The US Imbalancing Act: Can the Current Account Deficit Continue?'. San Francisco: McKinsey Global Institute, June 2007.

Garber, Peter. 'The Collapse of the Bretton Woods Fixed Exchange Rate System.' In *A Retrospective on the Bretton Woods System*, edited by Barry Eichengreen and Michael D. Bordo. Chicago, London: University of Chicago Press 1993.

Greenwood, John. 'The Costs and Inplications of Pbc Sterilization.' *Cato Journal* 28, no. 2 (Spring/Summer 2008).

Ikejiaku, Brian-Vincent. 'Africa Debt Crisis and the IMF with a Case of Nigeria: Towards Theoretical Explanations.' *Journal of Politics and Law* 1, no. 4 (December 2008).

IMF. 'Islamic Republic of Iran: 2009 Article IV Consultation – Staff Report.' Washington D.C., March 2010.

Islam, Faisal and Morgan Oliver. 'Saudi Dove in the Oil Slick. Interview with Sheikh Zaki Yamani.' *Observer*, January 14 2001.

Looney, Robert. 'A Euro-Denominated Oil Bourse in Iran: Potential Major Force in the International System?' In *Gulf Papers*. Dubai: Gulf Research Center, 2006.

Onimode, Bade, and Institute for African Alternatives. *The IMF, the World Bank, and the African Debt.* 2 vols. London; Atlantic Highlands, N.J., USA: Zed Books, 1989.

Rozanov, Andrew. 'A Liability-Based Approach to Sovereign Wealth.' *Central Banking Journal* XVIII, no. 3 (February 2008).

Saidi, Nasser, and Fabio Scacciavillani. 'The Case for Gold as a Reserve Asset in the GCC.' In *DIFC Economic Note No. 11*. Dubai 2010.

———'The Role of Gold in the New Financial Architecture.' In *DIFC Economic Note No. 13*. Dubai 2010.

Setser, Brad, and Arpana Pandey. 'China's $1.7 Trillion Bet. China's External Portfolio and Dollar Reserves.' New York: Council on Foreign Relations. Center for Geoeconomic Studies, January 2009.

Spiro, David E. *The Hidden Hand of American Hegemony: Petrodollar Recycling and International Markets*, Cornell Studies in Political Economy. Ithaca, NY: Cornell University Press, 1999.

US Congress. 'The Middle East. Report by Senator Charles H. Percy to the Committee on Foreign Affairs, April 21, 1975.' Washington D.C.: US Government Printing Office, 1975.

———'Old Problems – New Relationships, Report of a Study Mission to the Middle East and South Asia, May 1974.' Committee on Foreign Affairs. Washington: US Government Printing Office, 1974.

———'The United States Oil Shortage and the Arab-Israeli Conflict. Report of a Study Mission to the Middle East. October 22 to November 3, 1973, Pursuant to H. Res. 267.' Committee on Foreign Affairs. Washington D.C.: US Government Printing Office, December 20, 1973.

Woertz, Eckart. 'The Role of Gold in the Unified GCC Currency.' In *Gulf Papers*. Dubai: Gulf Research Center, 2005.

Wolverson, Roya. 'Confronting the China-U.S. Economic Imbalance.' In *Backgrounder*. New York: Council on Foreign Relations, October 19, 2010.

Yongding, Yu. 'Will US Fiscal Deficits Undermine the Role of the Dollar as Global Reserve Currency? If So Should US Fiscal Policy Be Geared to Preserving the International Role of the the Dollar?' In *The Future Global Reserve System – an Asian Perspective*, edited by Jeffrey D. Sachs, Masahiro Kawai, Jong-Wha Lee and Wing Thye Woo. Asian Development Bank, June 2010.

Ziemba, Rachel. 'Slow Growth in Mena Sovereign Assets Ahead?'. New York, London: Roubini Global Economics, September 30, 2010.

28
China's Impact on Oil Markets

John Calabrese

China's spectacular economic growth over the past three decades has significantly altered its position in both regional and global oil markets. The International Energy Agency's (IEA) June 2010 *Oil Market Report* states that "China's urgent need for energy supply to sustain economic growth and raise the wellbeing of its people has become a global market issue."[1] In an interview reported in *The Wall Street Journal*, IEA chief economist Fatih Birol went further, contending that China's economic ascent marks the beginning of "a new age in the history of energy."[2]

This "new age" is marked partly by China's soaring demand for oil and increasing dependence on foreign sources of supply. It is not surprising that these developments have raised concerns in China about "energy insecurity." Nor is it surprising that China's expanding oil consumption requirements and efforts to secure its future energy needs have raised concerns by others about China.[3] Some contend that China's quest for overseas oil supplies is likely to lead to rivalry and discord,[4] while others believe that such risks can be mitigated.[5]

Patterns and trends in the global oil market

China's efforts to meet its growing oil consumption requirements have taken place during a period of oil price volatility and in the context of longer term structural changes in worldwide oil supply and demand. Crude oil prices have risen and fallen dramatically for most of the 2000s. The price of crude oil doubled (to $60 per barrel) between 2003 and August 2005, skyrocketed to $145 in July 2008, and then plunged to $33 six months later. These wild price fluctuations have been attributed to a complex combination of financial and supply-and-demand factors: "price fixing" by the Organization of Petroleum Exporting Countries (OPEC), i.e. setting production quotas based on assessments of the market's call on OPEC supply; the erosion of OPEC's spare capacity; the shift by international oil companies' (IOCs) to a "just-in-time" inventory management system; the increasing importance of the oil futures market in the pricing system; the poor quality of data; and the weakening of the US dollar.[6]

Meanwhile, the global oil market has been undergoing profound changes. On one side of the equation, OECD demand has leveled off and is forecast to decline, while non-OECD countries have emerged as the main demand growth centers.[7] In fact, the primary sources of projected demand growth are in Asia, chiefly China, India, and Middle Eastern countries. There have been major changes on the global supply side as well. Oil production in Organisation for Economic Co-operation and Development (OECD) countries is in decline. By 2030, production in the USA and other industrialized countries is expected to decrease from current production levels, while OPEC countries are expected to provide most of the increase in world oil output.[8]

This changing global supply-and-demand profile has been accompanied by a structural change in supply relationships. While the USA, which is still the world's leading oil consumer by far, has been shifting away from its reliance on oil from the Middle East, China and other Asian countries have become the leading customers for oil from the region. This new pattern is perhaps best illustrated by the case of Saudi Arabia. In 2009, Saudi Arabia's oil exports to the USA dropped below 1mbpd for the first time in two decades just as China's purchases climbed above that level.[9]

What are the net effects of this pattern? For one thing, unstable and high oil prices might well be here to stay. Many experts are skeptical that future demand growth needs can be met. Slack investment due to the financial crisis threatens to constrain capacity growth, which could risk a supply shortfall when demand recovers. For another, the current supplier structure is fragmented; therefore, decisions by or conditions in just one of the many producing countries tend to have a rippling effect. In addition, there are multiple sources of potential dislocation, ranging from instability in the Niger Delta to uncertainty about Iraq's ability to expand production. According to the IEA, this pattern "consolidates mutual dependence but also enhances the risk of supply interruptions, as much of the additional oil imports have to transit vulnerable maritime routes."[10]

These trends and concerns have evoked several types of behavior worldwide, including resource nationalism and resource mercantilism.[11] As will be shown, China has engaged in these, as well as in other forms of behavior.

China's energy fundamentals

Though coal is by far China's predominant energy source, oil nonetheless constitutes roughly 20% of the primary energy mix and is thus of critical importance to the economy.[12] For more than a decade, China has experienced 1) a widening gap between domestic oil production and consumption requirements, 2) an increasing dependence on foreign sources of oil, and 3) continued heavy reliance on maritime transport of the bulk of imported supply.

As recently as the 1980s, China was a net oil exporter. Most of the country's oil output at the time came from three enormous onshore fields in the northeastern part of the country: Daqing (Heilongjiang Province), Liaohe (Liaoning), and Shengli (Shandong). China became a net oil importer in 1993 due to slowly declining production and the failure to discover new fields of comparable size. Nevertheless, China is still the world's fourth-largest oil producer after Saudi Arabia, Russia, and the USA.[13] The bulk of output is obtained from onshore fields, though production from offshore fields has expanded rapidly in recent years.

Meanwhile, however, China's oil consumption requirements have risen dramatically. Since 2004, China has been the world's second-leading consumer of oil, behind the USA. China recorded its largest oil demand in June 2010 at 8.98mbpd, 10% higher than a year before, and 0.7% higher than May 2010, the previous record.[14] There are several reasons for China's surging demand for oil: urbanization, the increasing number of registered vehicles, and the use of fuel oil and diesel to generate electricity in order to overcome power shortages.

The growing gap between domestic production and consumption requirements has translated into increasing dependence on imported oil. While the largest share of Chinese oil imports comes from the Middle East, in recent years China has sought to manage risk by diversifying its foreign sources of supply. As a result, Africa's share of the oil imported by China, for example, rose from 24% in 2003 to 30% in 2008.[15] Yet, even while having succeeded in thus diversifying its sources of supply, China remains heavily dependent on Middle Eastern oil and its overall oil import requirements have continued to grow.

China is highly dependent not only on foreign sources of oil but also on the maritime transport of its oil supplies from abroad. Approximately 80% of China's imported oil is delivered by sea.[16] As will be shown, China has completed (with Kazakhstan) and is pursuing several ambitious and expensive overland pipeline projects (with Russia, Burma, and Pakistan) in order to reduce its reliance on maritime transport of oil. However, it is not clear whether or when these efforts to achieve higher overland oil deliveries will bear fruit, much less whether they will greatly enhance China's oil supply security. Indeed, some analysts believe that the country's seaborne oil imports are likely to increase.[17]

Yet another aspect of China's foreign dependence is the fact that Western oil companies (such as, British Petroleum, Chevron, ConocoPhillips, Exxon-Mobil, Royal Dutch Shell, and Total) control most of the world's high-quality oil reserves as well as substantial shares of the oil technical services market, international oil trade and investment in oil projects, and advanced technology in the oil and petrochemicals sectors.

Most analysts believe that China's oil consumption and net import needs will continue to increase. According to the IEA's 2009 Reference Scenario, China's oil consumption would more than double in the medium term, from 7.7mbpd in 2008 to 16.3mbpd in 2030. The IEA also projects that China's domestic production would drop from 3.8mbpd in 2008 to 3.2mbpd in 2030. As a result, the country's net import needs would rise from 3.9mbpd in 2008 to 13.1mbpd, making China the world's largest net importer of crude oil by 2030, slightly ahead of the USA (13.5mbpd in 2008, 12.7mbpd in 2030). Under this scenario, China's net import dependence ratio would jump from 51% in 2008 to 80% in 2030.[18] Issues related to this projected long-term dependency on foreign oil are at the core of Chinese perspectives on energy security.

Chinese perspectives on energy security

Over the past decade, Chinese perspectives on energy security have tended to reflect concerns about the extent of the country's dependence on foreign sources of oil and transport of oil supplies over maritime routes they do not control, and about the uses of American power.

As a number of observers have noted, Chinese leaders and analysts do not consider energy as a purely economic issue. Nor do they regard oil as a common commodity.[19] Some Chinese officials and experts have argued that the country's growing dependence on foreign oil supplies poses a strategic threat, while others have maintained that this reliance should be treated as a natural byproduct of its growing interdependence with the rest of the world.[20]

The 2003 Iraq War seemed to have bolstered the conviction of some in China at the time that the USA was pursuing hegemony in the Middle East and that if conflict were to erupt over Taiwan, Washington would do everything in its power to reduce China's access to imported oil.[21] The setbacks suffered by Chinese oil companies following the launching of the war appeared to have reinforced this view. In May 2003, for example, Royal Dutch Shell and five other companies used their shareholders preferential purchasing rights to block the joint offer of China National Offshore Oil Corporation (CNOOC) and Sinopec Corporation to acquire shares of an oilfield in the Caspian Sea owned by Kazakhstan. In 2005 CNOOC's bid to buy the American oil company Unocal ran up against strong US resistance. At the time, these setbacks were interpreted by some Chinese scholars (perhaps also by some officials) as part of a scheme by the West to contain China.[22]

Sandwiched between these two setbacks was the accession to power of the "Fourth Generation" Chinese leadership led by President Hu Jintao. The political transition occurred in the midst of electrical power shortages throughout China, which raised awareness of energy security as a basis for economic development and led to a call for government action. It was at this very time that the Development Research Center of the State Council assembled leading energy research institutes in China to analyze the energy situation and to recommend a comprehensive energy strategy. The team produced a summary report and 11 sub-reports, which were published in 2004 as the China National Energy and Strategy Policy (NESP). According to the NESP, oil security entails guaranteeing that the country's demand for oil is met satisfactorily in terms of quantity, quality, and price. Oil insecurity, on the other hand, refers to potential damage to the country's economy due to supply cut-offs, shortages, or price shocks.[23]

Chinese responses to energy insecurity

The NESP brought to light the energy-related challenges facing China and proposed a number of policy recommendations to address them, including:

- Using the world oil market, including the futures market, in order to obtain oil and oil products.
- Diversifying sources of oil imports and oil business activities, including exploration, development, refineries and pipelines.
- Investing more in upstream development, both domestically and internationally.
- Deepening the reform of Chinese national oil companies while continuing to transform them into powerful international companies.
- Seeking a "proper mix" of competition and alliances with regard to countries and companies.
- Establishing a strategic petroleum reserve.[24]

The actions that China has taken since the issuance of the NESP to deal with China's dependence on imported oil are consistent with many of these recommendations: pursuit of diversified import sources; investment in foreign production facilities, as well as in oil (and gas) pipelines in producing countries or from them to China; creation of a strategic oil reserve; and more receptive policies toward foreign investment in Chinese energy.

Traditionally, most of China's oil imports had been obtained by long-term supply contracts or bought on the spot market rather than derived from equity investments. The early 1990s were the exploratory phase of China's international acquisitions policy. The successful bid by China National Petroleum Corporation (CNPC) for an oilfield in Peru in March 1993 marked the entry of China's petroleum industry into the international market. This success was followed shortly thereafter by acquisitions in Canada, Thailand, Indonesia, and Sudan.

Since the early 2000s, these international acquisitions efforts have gained momentum. Outward investment by China's three main state-owned oil companies (CNPC, China National Offshore Oil Corporation (CNOOC) and the China Petroleum and Chemical Corporation (Sinopec)[25] has surged. This investment has taken several different forms, including: 1) both the acquisition of specific resource concessions or shares in resource concessions (projects) and of overseas companies (or shareholdings in companies) that hold a range of assets, and 2) a "finance-for-assured supply" model involving long-term loans from Chinese banks to support overseas oil and gas companies' efforts to develop new resources and pipelines.[26]

As reported by the IEA in its June 2010 *Oil Market Report*, between January 2009 and April 2010 alone, CNPC, Sinopec, and CNOOC spent about $29bn worldwide on acquiring oil and gas assets.[27] In the same period, Sinopec and CNPC negotiated 11 finance-for-assured supply deals with eight countries worth $77bn, and entered contracts committing them to invest at least $18bn in future exploration and development, mainly in Iraq and Iran.[28] Here, one should mention that it is not necessary to own oilfield concessions in order to import oil. In fact, most countries have neither oilfields nor oil companies. As it happens, Chinese oil companies do not operate any oilfields in Saudi Arabia, though the latter is their top supplier. Nor is all of the oil that is produced by Chinese companies overseas consumed in China. Furthermore, all three of Chinese major companies still produce most of their output within China, a fact that tends to be underreported in the Western press.

Regardless of how China acquires foreign oil contractually, there is still the issue of transporting it. In order to reduce its reliance on maritime transport of oil supplies through the Malacca Strait, China has identified several alternative strategic access routes, through Kazakhstan, Myanmar (Burma), and Russia. The Kazakhstan-China pipeline has been operational since 2006.[29] In June 2010, construction began on the China section of the Sino-Myanmar oil pipeline, which is expected to be finished in 2013.[30] September 2010 marked the completion of an oil pipeline from Russia to China.

China's impact on oil markets

What have been and could be the effects of China's growing oil demand and import dependence and expanding overseas involvement in oil markets? Let us first consider China's impact on the *global* oil market and then discuss its impact on *regional* markets.

The global market

With respect to China's impact on the global oil market, several areas deserve attention: 1) oil prices, 2) market supply, 3) commercial competition, and 4) investment. Expert opinion on the impact that China has had or might have on both the price of oil and access of oil is decidedly mixed. Here, it is useful to distinguish between the impact of Chinese demand growth and the effects of Chinese overseas activities in the oil sector.

Oil Prices: According to BP's *Statistical Review of World Energy*, Chinese oil consumption in 2009 rose by 6.7% from the previous year (to 8.6mbpd), in spite of the economic downturn.[31] The IEA reports that, "China is currently seen generating 40% of 2010 incremental demand and nearly 45% of 2010–15 growth."[32] Clearly, China's buoyant oil demand has helped sustain oil prices during the global economic recession. For suppliers, therefore, China has been a bright spot in the market. This is especially true in the case of the Gulf Co-operation Council (GCC) countries, for whom oil accounts for a substantial portion of their revenues and export earnings. These earnings are a vital source of financing for the economic programs and projects they have undertaken, and influence consumer and investment confidence.

But one must be careful about extrapolating from this experience. The fact that the Chinese have been buying oil does not necessarily mean that they have been consuming it. The Chinese oil industry is not transparent. The volume of crude oil (and refined products) that has been put in storage is unclear. It is possible that government encouragement and expectations of higher prices has spurred a storage boom. Thus the boost to the recovery of GCC economies provided by robust Chinese oil demand might be only temporary, and if so, will not necessarily recur. In addition, one must consider the possibility that China's foreign acquisitions may be primarily focused on the long-term goal of controlling oil at its source in order to influence prices as a global producer, not just as a strategic consumer.

Finally, tight spare capacity, whether due to "peak oil" or, as the IEA argues, because of underinvestment in oilfield development, is a real possibility. Tight capacity would drive oil prices higher. Under such circumstances, prices would rise even if China's consumption growth were flat; they would rise even more were China's rate of consumption to increase.

Market Supply: Some assert that China's practice of "locking up" oil supplies takes oil off the market. Others contend that Chinese oil companies are investing in the few remaining underdeveloped oil regions of the world. The latter argue that China's NOCs contribute to a better-supplied world oil market by extracting oil from countries that are off-limits to Western firms. If, for example, China seeks oil supplies from Sudan, it buys less elsewhere, thereby making more oil available to all other consumers.[33]

Commercial Competition: Chinese oil companies have become increasingly sophisticated and successful players in the international commercial arena. As such, they have become both respected competitors and valued partners of their Western counterparts.

Chinese firms are a significant force in global mergers and acquisitions (M&A) activities in a wide band of business sectors. In the oil sector, Chinese state companies have been active in acquiring entire companies, as well as stakes in smaller (and non-US) companies with overseas (oil and gas) assets. The IEA estimates that Chinese firms accounted for 13% of total acquisitions in 2009 and that they are operating in 31 countries and producing equity barrels in 20.[34]

CNPC, Sinopec, CNOOC and Sinochem are involved variously as operator, non-operator shareholder, and joint venture partner with many foreign companies. CNPC's overseas exploration and production relationships are primarily with host-country state oil companies, with CNPC serving as project operator. Sinopec, CNOOC, and Sinochem also have links through their overseas operations with Western oil companies. For example, Sinopec collaborates with Total in Yemen and Canada. CNOOC is a shareholder in the BP-operated Tangguh liquefied natural gas project and off-shore oil and gas fields in West Java, BHP Billiton-operated assets in Australia, and Total-operated assets in Nigeria. Sinochem is partnered with Sweden's Lundin in Tunisia and with Repsol in Ecuador. PetroChina teamed up with Royal Dutch Shell for a joint bid for Arrow Energy, the Australian gas company. CNOOC and Total are seeking to work with each other to develop Tullow Oil's assets in Uganda. In July 2010, CNPC and BP took over operation and management of Rumaila, Iraq's largest oilfield.[35]

The circumstances of each deal are different. In Iraq, for example, where the projects are technically straightforward but have political and security risks, having a Chinese partner provides important benefits to foreign counterparts. Samuel Ciszuk, Middle East Energy Analyst for IHS Global Insight, argues that CNPC brings political clout because it is state owned; a skilled, cheap workforce; and a willingness to invest in a low-margin project.[36] Overall, these arrangements facilitate high-level business relationships across functions and engender habits of cooperation. Furthermore, as discussed below, Western companies hope to build on their respective relationships to secure greater access to the Chinese oil market.

Investment: There are numerous reasons why Chinese oil companies have been able to compete successfully for business in the oil market, including that they have no shareholders and that they have generally been willing to accept higher political and security risks than their counterparts.[37] China's strict adherence to a policy of non-interference in the domestic affairs of other countries furnishes an additional advantage. Yet, perhaps the most important factor has been Chinese oil companies' ability to leverage their own sizable financial resources and to supplement them with state support in the form of loans and development assistance.[38]

China is not only a major source of investment in the oil sector, but also is an increasingly important destination for it. China needs several trillion dollars in energy investments. Western oil majors have become strategic investors in the internationally listed subsidiaries of China's three leading oil companies, and, as previously shown, are extensively involved with these same companies in China and elsewhere, particularly in the refinery sector.[39]

Investment in China's oil sector is also driven by the competition for market share among foreign suppliers of oil and refined products. According to Kuwait Petroleum Corporation (KPC) CEO Saad Al-Shuwaib, Kuwait is seeking to obtain the Chinese government's approval to build a 300,000 barrels per day refinery and petrochemical complex in southern China.[40]

Regional markets

Chinese oil companies have established a global presence, and they are having a significant impact on *regional* oil markets: 1) establishing new footholds, 2) emerging as major players, 3) building complex interdependent relationships, and 4) creating new and dynamic nodes of energy-led economic growth.

Establishing New Footholds: In recent years, Chinese oil companies have successfully penetrated regional markets in which they previously had had little, if any involvement. They have done this both by signing long-term supply contracts and by acquiring strategic assets.

North America is a case in point. In December 2009, CNOOC acquired a small stake in four oilfields in the Gulf of Mexico from Statoil of Norway. The same month, PetroChina obtained the Canadian government's backing to buy a stake in two Alberta oil-sands projects for about $1.9bn.[41]

In South America, CNOOC established a joint venture partnership with an Argentine firm, Bridas Energy, by acquiring a 50% share in the Bridas Corporation, one of the company's subsidiaries.[42]

Chinese oil companies have been active in the Caribbean Basin as well. In 2009, Petro China assumed Saudi Aramco's lease on the NuStar LP Statia fuel oil terminal on the Dutch Caribbean island of St Eustatius. Some observers believe that Petro China's immediate goal is to establish itself as a major player in the ship fuel trading market.[43] But the company could be positioning itself for the future, a decade or so from now, by which time it might have secured significant crude oil production (perhaps through involvement in the development of Venezuela's Orinoco Belt) and a maritime crude oil corridor to the Pacific markets resulting from the widening of the Panama Canal.[44]

Over the past decade, Chinese firms also have been very active in Africa. They have established new footholds there, as illustrated by the $23bn deal between the China State Construction Engineering Corporation Limited (CSCEC) and the Nigerian National Petroleum Corporation (NNPC) to construct four new refineries in Nigeria. CSCEC described this venture as part of an effort to "expand its presence on the African continent and establish its footprint firmly in the Nigerian oil and gas landscape."[45]

Emerging as a Major Player: China has rapidly become a major player in regional oil markets in three respects: 1) as an oil customer, 2) as an owner of strategic assets, and 3) as a source of investment.

China is the largest importer of oil from the Middle East, importing 1.94mbpd, or 14% more than the USA.[46] Within the region, China is Iran's number one oil importer, with about a 23% share.[47] In the case of Latin America, Venezuela, which supplies China with 400,000 barrels of oil per day, aims to increase this to 1m. barrels by 2013. This would put Venezuela's oil exports to China roughly on a par with its exports to the USA.[48]

China has become a major player in Central Asia as well, particularly in Kazakhstan. CNPC has a 67% stake in PetroKazakhstan. In 2009, CNPC purchased a 50% stake in MangistauMunaiGaz, giving it joint ownership of the latter's main producing assets at the Kalamkas and Zhetybay fields and of the company's other upstream assets. It is estimated that Chinese companies already control nearly one-third of Kazakhstan's oil output.[49]

China has also become a vital source of investment for some of its partners. CNPC is the largest stakeholder (with a 40% share) in the Greater Nile Petroleum Operating Company, Sudan's biggest energy consortium. In addition, CNPC is the largest equity partner in all but one of Sudan's operational oilfields. China is now the biggest single investor in Iraq's post-war oil (and gas) sector as well, giving it control of about one-fifth of the reserves that have been auctioned since 2009. In June 2009, CNPC secured the 17-billion-barrel Rumaila field, as an almost equal partner with BP. Six months later, CNPC took a 50% share as the operator of the Halfaya field (partnered with Malaysia's Petronas and France's Total). CNPC also has a stake the Al-Ahdab field, which was revived in March 2009 by China's Al-Waha Petroleum (in a joint venture with the Zhenhua Oil Company).[50] Most recently, a Chinese consortium led by CNOOC and Sinochem Corporation signed an initial agreement with Baghdad to develop the Missan oilfield complex.[51]

China has leveraged its financial power in its dealings with Russia as well. After years of negotiation and maneuvering, the two countries reached agreement in February 2009 on a $25 billion loan-for-oil deal. The pipeline carrying oil from Russia to China was completed in September 2010,[52] thereby helping to forge a major long-term supply relationship.

Building Complex Interdependence: China's long-term oil supply ties with its partners form the backbone of increasingly extensive, multifaceted economic relationships. They have laid the basis for reciprocal investment in the energy sector and the development of non-oil trade.

Over the past decade, China's non-oil trade with the Middle East especially with the Gulf Co-operation Council (GCC) countries and Iran, has climbed rapidly.[53] Three years ago, McKinsey and Company estimated that total trade flows between China and the Middle East could climb to between $350bn and $500bn by 2020.[54] In 2009 China passed the USA as the biggest exporter to the region. Today, China not only buys more oil but sells more products in the Middle East than does any other country.

Creating Growth Nodes: China's energy plans and activities could foster the development of new nodes of energy-led economic growth. It is not far-fetched, for example, to imagine the Chinese province of Xinjiang a decade or two from now having become part of a dynamic economic region binding together western China and Central Asia. After all, Xinjiang borders eight countries, including Russia, Kazakhstan, India, and Pakistan. It has an operational oil pipeline originating in Kazakhstan (and another pipeline that carries gas from Turkmenistan). The Chinese government plans to embark on a 10-year development program to elevate Xinjiang into a leading "energy center," that is, a center of oil-and-gas production, refining, petrochemical and other chemical manufacturing, oil storage, and engineering, and technology services.

The area encompassing Myanmar and Yunnan Province in southwestern China constitutes a second promising economic region-in-the-making. In June 2010, CNPC held a groundbreaking ceremony to mark the start of construction of the Sino-Myanmar oil (and gas) pipeline, which will transport crude oil sourced from the Middle East and Africa from the port of Kyaukryu on the Bay of Bengal to Runming, the capital of China's Yunnan Province.[55] The pipeline project also includes railway, road, and waterway construction, as well the upgrading of the Kyaukryu port facilities.

It is important to view these efforts within the broader framework of China's modernization plans for Yunnan. In fact, the project as a whole is subsumed in China's Western

Development Strategy. In preparation for receiving oil accessed through Myanmar, China is building three oil product pipelines in Yunnan.[56] The energy pipeline feed from Myanmar is part of a broader commercial corridor that would also include an outlet for Yunnan's industrial sector to ports that would carry its products westward to South Asia, the Middle East, and Europe.

A third such economic region could take shape in the border area between the Russian Far East (RFE) and Heilongjiang Province in northeastern China. Over the past decade, cross-border trade has been robust. There are other sinews of economic interdependence as well. Heilongjiang Province operates feed mills in Russia and has leased land across the border to grow crops.[57] Since 2004, the province also has been purchasing electricity from Russian hydroelectric plants.[58] While energy cooperation does not constitute the main strand of this web of interdependence, it is nonetheless an important element of the Northeast China Revitalization Plan, which aims to invigorate the province's industrial base. A key part of this effort has been the construction of a spur of the East Siberia-Pacific Ocean (ESPO) oil pipeline, which is expected to become fully operational in 2011, that will extend from Skovorodino in the Amur region of Russia to the city of Daqing.[59]

Changing oil markets or changing China?

How might China's involvement in oil markets change the behavior of others? And how might China's behavior, including the possible consequences of its own actions, alter Chinese perspectives on and activities in oil markets?

Playing by whose rules?

The growing involvement of Chinese companies in global and regional oil markets has prompted closer scrutiny of their business practices. Some of these practices, including the use of financing as a competitive tool (one which the Organisation for Economic Cooperation and Development (OECD) long ago agreed not to employ) have given the impression that China is determined to play by its own rules, come what may. Chinese firms also have been accused of igniting "bidding wars" to secure overseas oil contracts that could fuel geopolitical tensions.

On a number of occasions over the past decade, Chinese companies have outbid their Indian counterparts. In 2005, for example, Sinopec outbid ONGC for PetroKazakhstan and did so again one month later in buying the assets of EnCana Corporation in Ecuador.[60] Later that same year, however, CNPC and India's Oil and Gas Corporation (ONG) placed a successful joint bid for a 37% stake in the al-Furat oil and gas fields in Syria, demonstrating both that there is scope for Sino-Indian energy cooperation and that there is at least some interest in pursuing it. Mani Shankar Aiyar, then India's petroleum minister, hailed the venture as a model.[61] However, few other such initiatives have followed.

Meanwhile, the practices used by Chinese companies to secure overseas oil assets have been adopted by some of their competitors, including by Indian firms. As far back as 2005, ONGC had agreed to spend as much as $6bn on roads, ports, railways, and power plants in Nigeria in exchange for oil supplies. Since then, the government of India has authorized an increase in the amount that ONGC and some other state-owned companies may spend in order to acquire overseas assets and establish joint ventures, and the creation of a sovereign wealth fund to support overseas energy investments.[62]

In East Asia, however, the situation looks less benign, in spite of China's participation in an array of consultative arrangements. China is a member of the energy working group of the

Asia-Pacific Cooperation (APEC), the ASEAN plus China, Japan and the Republic of Korea (ASEAN +3) Energy Cooperation, the International Energy Forum, the World Energy Conference, and Asia-Pacific Partnership for Clean Development and Climate. Yet, China and its neighbors (ASEAN and Japan) remain locked in dispute over Beijing's claim to the entire South China Sea.[63]

Rigid or adaptive?

Chinese attitudes regarding energy security are not immutable. To the contrary, " … ideas about energy security are evolving from a vision of tight government control and self-reliance to a more liberal outlook that accepts market forces and diversified energy types and sources".[64] Nor are China's leaders completely indifferent to the concerns that Chinese overseas oil activities have engendered. They have emphasized the importance of international energy co-operation.[65] The 2007 White Paper on China's *Energy Conditions and Policies* states that, "To ensure world energy security, it is imperative to strengthen dialogue and co-operation between energy exporting countries and energy consuming countries, as well as between energy consuming countries".[66]

There are also signs that Chinese oil companies might not be stuck in a "proprietary" mindset. The participation of Chinese oil companies in Iraq's oil tenders, for example, signaled a possible shift away from the proprietary control of reserves toward a market-based approach and offered evidence that Chinese oil companies have become more skilled and more confident of their ability to compete and collaborate with global majors.

Unfettered or lashed to The Market?

In an effort to reduce the risks associated with its foreign oil dependence, China might well have created some problems both for itself and for others. CNOOC and its fellow energy companies have been willing to enter areas of political uncertainty, buying assets in countries that face major problems such as internal conflict, endemic corruption, huge crime rates, or ineffective governments. One possible consequence of this surge of investment is that Chinese companies might incur big financial losses. Another is that it could spur more rapid investment into countries that might once have been considered unsuitable, and by any objective standard still are. Thus due diligence will have been sacrificed in the race for assets and, as a result, Chinese companies and their rivals could end up paying premium prices for inferior assets.

In addition, whether some of China's energy partners will be able to follow through on complex oil deals is open to question. Venezuela is a case in point. Refineries have yet to be built. Agreements are non-binding. Venezuela's offshore reserves are deep beneath the surface and covered by rock and salt deposits, requiring sophisticated technology that will be very costly to mobilize. Venezuela's President Hugo Chávez has announced many deals in the past (for example, with Uruguay and Iran), but few of them have materialized.

Conclusion

The nature and extent of China's future impact on global and regional markets will depend on numerous factors. Of these, perhaps the most important is whether China's appetite for oil will continue to grow at rates similar to those experienced in recent years. This, in turn, will depend on which path the Chinese leadership will choose; a low energy future modeled on that of Japan or a high energy future resembling that of the USA? While most analysts project strong demand growth, those who take seriously Beijing's determination and ability to curb China's appetite for oil are more skeptical.[67]

A second important factor is whether China's large national oil companies (NOCs) will continue to dominate the policy process and whether corporate interests or national interests will control the energy sector and guide industry practices.

A third key factor will be how the rest of the world, particularly the USA, but also India and Japan, responds to China's increasing presence in and influence on oil markets, and indeed to its emergence as a global power.

Notes

1 International Energy Agency (IEA), *Oil Market Report* (June 2010), p. 21, http://omrpublic.iea.org/omrarchive/10jun10full.pdf.
2 Quoted in Spencer Swartz and Shai Oster, 'China Tops US in Energy Use', *The Wall Street Journal*, 18 July 2010, http://online.wsj.com/article/SB10001424052748703720504575376712353150310.html?mod=rss_whats_news_us_business#project%3DCHENERGY0719%26articleTabs%3Darticle.
3 Cherie Canning, 'Pursuit of the Pariah: Iran, Sudan and Myanmar in China's Energy Security Strategy', *Security Challenges*, Vol. 3, No. 1 (2007), p. 51; Philip Andrews-Speed, 'China's Energy Policy and its Contribution to International Stability', in Marcin Zaborowski, 'Facing China's Rise: Guidelines for an EU Strategy', *Chaillot Paper* no. 94, December 2006, p. 73; Flynt Leverett, 'The Geopolitics of Oil and America's International Standing', statement before the Committee on Energy and Natural Resources, US Senate, 10 January 2007.
4 Gal Luft, 'U.S., China Are on a Collision Course over Oil', *Los Angeles Times*, 2 February 2004; Gal Luft, 'Fuelling the Dragon: China's Race into the Oil Market', *Institute for the Analysis of Global Security*, www.iags.org/china.htm; and Peter Hatemi and Andrew Wedeman, 'Oil and Conflict in Sino-American Relations', *China Security*, Vol. 3, No. 3, 2007, p. 110.
5 Henry Lee and Dan Shalman, 'Searching for Oil: China's Oil Initiatives in the Middle East', Belfer Center for Science and International Affairs, John F. Kennedy School of Government, Harvard University (January 2007), pp. 31–32.
6 Bassam Fattouh, 'The Causes of Crude Oil Price Volatility', *Middle East Economic Survey (MEES)*, Vol. 58, No. 13 (28 March 2005).
7 Jad Mouawad, 'China's Growth Shifts the Geopolitics of Oil', *The New York Times*, 19 March 2010.
8 International Energy Agency (IEA), *World Energy Outlook 2008 Fact Sheet*, www.iea.org/weo/docs/weo2008/fact_sheets_08.pdf.
9 Gregory Meyer, 'Oil Geopolitics Shifts as China Taps Saudi Crude', *The New York Times*, 22 February 2010.
10 International Energy Agency (IEA), *World Energy Outlook 2008 Fact Sheet*, www.iea.org/weo/docs/weo2008/fact_sheets_08.pdf.
11 Resource nationalism refers to national governments making decisions about the production and marketing of the hydrocarbon reserves under their control not only on the basis of economic factors, but also on the basis of strategic and political calculations. Resource mercantilism refers to reliance of energy importing states on national energy companies to secure access to overseas oil and gas resources on more privileged bases than simple supply contracts. For a good discussion of these trends, see Flynt Leverett, 'The Geopolitics of Oil and America's International Standing', Testimony Before the Committee on Energy and Natural Resources, United States Senate, 10 January 2007.
12 US Energy Information Agency (EIA), *Country Analysis Brief—China*, www.eia.doe.gov/cabs/China/Full.html.
13 See *BP Statistical Review of World Energy* (2009), pp. 8, 9.
14 'China's Oil Demand in June Hits New High, Up 10% from Year Ago', *Platt's Report*, 21 July 2010, www.prnewswire.com/news-releases/platts-report-chinas-oil-demand-in-june-hits-new-high-up-10-from-year-ago-98919164.html.
15 Hongyi Lai, 'China Builds Bridges to Fuel Its Engine Room', *Financial Times*, 5 July 2010.
16 Andrew S. Erickson, 'Pipe Dream: China Seeks Land and Sea Energy Security', *Jane's Intelligence Review* (China Watch) Vol. 21, No. 8 (August 2009), pp. 54–55.

17 See Andrew S. Erickson and Gabriel B. Collins, 'China's Oil Security Pipe Dream: The Reality, and Strategic Consequences, of Seaborne Imports', *Naval War College Review*, Vol. 63, No. 2 (2010), pp. 89–111.
18 International Energy Agency (IEA) *World Energy Outlook 2009* (WEO-2009).
19 Joseph Y.S. Cheng, 'A Chinese View of China's Energy Security', *Journal of Contemporary China*, Vol. 17, Issue 55 (2008), p. 315.
20 Erica Downs, 'The Chinese Energy Security Debate', *The China Quarterly*, No. 177 (March 2004), pp. 21–41.
21 See, for example, Peter S. Goodman, 'Big Shifts in China's Oil Policy', *Washington Post*, 13 July 2005; Kenneth Lieberthal and Mikkal Herberg, 'China's Search for Energy Security: Implications for US Policy', National Bureau of Asian Research (April 2006), p. 16.
22 Joseph Y.S. Cheng, 'A Chinese View of China's Energy Security', *Journal of Contemporary China*, Vol. 17, Issue 55 (2008), p. 315.
23 S. Tønnesson and A. Kolås, 'Energy Security in Asia: China, India, Oil and Peace'. Report to the Norwegian Ministry of Foreign Affairs, International Peace Research Institute, Oslo (PRIO), April 2006.
24 Development Research Center of the State Council, English Summary Report, China's Oil and Gas Resources and Safety Countermeasures (2004), www.efchina.org/csepupfiles/report/2006102695218188.8060385177036.pdf/0_Main_Report.pdf.
25 In 2002, another state-owned enterprise (SOE), Sinochem, previously a trading company, diversified into upstream oil and gas operations.
26 Along with this financial assistance, the foreign company engages in a long-term contract with a Chinese state oil company to supply a guaranteed annual volume of product at prevailing market prices. Deals of this kind have been agreed with Russia's Transneft and Rosneft; another is in negotiation with Brazil's Petrobras. Under the agreed Russia deal, China Development Bank will lend $25bn over 25 years to Rosneft and Transneft, who in turn guarantee the supply of 15m. tons of crude oil annually to CNPC at market prices.
27 International Energy Agency (IEA), *Oil Market Report* (June 2010).
28 Ibid.
29 In April 2009, Transneft and Rosneft signed an agreement for a $25bn loan from China Development Bank in exchange for delivering 300,000 barrels per day of oil to China for the next twenty years and also building a 64 km spur pipeline from Skovorodino to the Chinese border. The deal is currently on track.
30 The Sino-Myanmar oil and gas pipeline starts at Kyaukryu port on the west coast of Myanmar and enters China at Yunnan's border city of Ruili. It saves about 1,200 km of shipping and reduces reliance on the Strait of Malacca. See 'China Starts Building Sino-Burma Oil-Gas Pipeline', BBC, 10 September 2010.
31 BP, *Statistical Review of World Energy* (June 2010), p. 4, www.bp.com/liveassets/bp_internet/globalbp/globalbp_uk_english/reports_and_publications/statistical_energy_review_2008/STAGING/local_assets/2010_downloads/statistical_review_of_world_energy_full_report_2010.pdf.
32 International Energy Agency (IEA), *Oil Market Report* (June 2010), http://omrpublic.iea.org/omrarchive/10jun10full.pdf.
33 Mikkal E. Herberg, statement before the US–China Economic and Security Review Commission, hearing on 'China's Energy Consumption and Opportunities for US–China Cooperation to Address the Effects of China's Energy Use', 14–15 June 2007.
34 International Energy Agency (IEA), *Oil Market Report* (June 2010), http://omrpublic.iea.org/omrarchive/10jun10full.pdf.
35 'Chinese Oil Giant and BP Start Operating Largest Iraqi Oilfield', *BBC Asia Pacific*, 12 July 2010.
36 Quoted in Ed Crooks, 'Drive to Tap into China Spurs Partnerships', *Financial Times*, 14 March 2010.
37 For example, Chinese companies profited from the fact that American and other firms turned away from Canadian tar sands oil because of its heavy carbon footprint. The Pentagon also reduced its use of tar sands oil to meet a 2007 law requiring the US government to source fuels with lower greenhouse gas emissions. Major oil companies such as Shell came under shareholder pressure to pull out of the Canadian projects. See Suzanne Goldenberg, 'Canada Looks to China to Exploit Tar Sands Rejected by US', *The Guardian*, February 14, 2010.
38 China National Petroleum Corp., parent of the state-run oil and natural gas giant PetroChina, announced that it had received a low-interest $30bn loan from the China Development Bank to

finance overseas acquisitions. Reported by Chris V. Nicholson, 'Chinese Oil Company Gets $30 Billion Loan for Acquisitions', *The New York Times*, 9 September 2009.
39 Ed Cooks, 'Drive to Tap into China Demand Spurs Partnerships', *The Financial Times*, 14 March 2010.
40 'Kuwait Becomes China's 6th Crude Supplier', Qatar News Agency, 2 March 2010.
41 There have been several other investments in the Canadian oil sector by Chinese companies in recent years, including CNOOC's investment in the Northern Lights project in 2005 and CNPC's purchase of oil sands leases that it has not yet developed. See Chris Kahn, 'Syncrude Deal Part of China's Shopping Spree', AP, 13 April 2010.
42 Jad Mouawad, 'Deal for South American Oil fields Extends China's Global Quest for Energy', *The New York Times*, 14 March 2010.
43 It is also important to note that fuel oil—burned in power plants and ships—is China's leading imported oil product. See Robert Campbell and Aizhu Chen, 'China Eyes Caribbean Fuel Oil Market Now, Crude Later', Reuters, 7 January 2010.
44 Simon Romero, 'Offer of $20 billion in Loans to Venezuela Extends Needed Cash to Chavez', *The New York Times*, 10 March 2010.
45 'Nigeria, China Sign $23bn Refinery Deal', AFP, 14 May 2010.
46 Sarah A. Topol, 'Why China Has Become the Middle East's Favorite Customer', *The Christian Science Monitor*, 13 July 2010.
47 Ibid.
48 Simon Romero, 'Offer of $20 billion in Loans to Venezuela Extends Needed Cash to Chavez', *The New York Times*, 10 March 2010, p. 11.
49 Stuart Elliott, with Naubet Bisenov, 'Chinese Expand Presence in Kazakhstan's Oil Sector', Platt's Oilgram News, November 26, 2009.
50 *Middle East Economic Digest* (MEED), 25 March 2009.
51 *Middle East Economic Digest* (MEED), 9 March 2010.
52 'China, Russia Mark Completion of Crude Oil Pipeline', *China Daily*, 27 September 2010.
53 For a discussion of China's role in the broadening and deepening of Gulf-Asia economic interdependence, see John Calabrese, 'The Consolidation of Gulf-Asia Relations: Washington Tuned In or Out of Touch?', *Middle East Institute Policy Brief* (22 June 2009), www.mei.edu/Portals/0/Publications/Consolidation-of-Gulf-Asia.pdf. See also Ben Simpfendorfer, *The New Silk Road* (New York: Palgrave Macmillan, 200); and Samir Ranjan Pradhan, 'Dubai Inc. in China: A New Vista for Gulf-Asia Relations', *China Brief*, Vol. 8, No. 9 (28 April 2008), www.jamestown.org/programs/chinabrief/single/?tx_ttnews[tt_news]=4887&tx_ttnews[backPid]=168&no_cache=1;
54 Dominic Barton and Kito de Boer, 'Tread Lightly Along the New Silk Road', *McKinsey Quarterly* (March 2007), http://mkqpreview2.qdweb.net/article_print.aspx?L2=7&L3=10&ar=1945.
55 Eric Watkins, 'CNPC Begins Work on Oil, Gas Pipelines in Myanmar', *Oil & Gas Journal*, 4 June 2010,
56 'China to Build Three Pipelines to Deliver Myanmar Oil', Reuters, 26 August 2010.
57 'Northeast China Province Leases Land, Grows Crops in Russia', *China Daily*, 29 May 2009.
58 Kyre Braeckus and Indra Overland, 'A Match made in Heaven? Strategic Convergence between China and Russia', Norwegian Institute of International Affairs Working Paper, No. 717 (2007), p. 13.
59 The project was made possible by a $25 bn Chinese loan to Rosneft and Transneft. It is important to note that Moscow's solicitation of Chinese investment represented a reversal of its policy of seeking to prevent Chinese economic penetration of the RFE and Central Asia. On this point, see Stephen Blank, 'China Quietly Reshapes Asia', *Asia Times*, 12 August 2009.
60 See for example, Keith Bradsher and Christopher Pala, 'Chinese Beat India for Kazakh Oil Fields', *The New York Times*, 23 August 2005.
61 Indrajit Basu, 'India, China Pin Down $573m Syria Deal', *Asia Times*, 22 December 2005; Richard MacGregor, 'China and India Forge Oil Alliance', *Financial Times*, 12 January 2006.
62 Rakteem Katakey and John Duce, 'India Loses to China in Africa-to-Kazakhstan-to-Venezuela Oil', Bloomberg, 29 June 2010.
63 Eric Watkins, 'China Pushes the Boundaries', *Oil & Gas Journal*, 2 August 2010.
64 China's Thirst for Oil, International Crisis Group, Asia Report No. 153, June 9, 2008, pp. 5–7, www.crisisgroup.org/~/media/Files/asia/north-east-asia/153_china_s_thirst_for_oil.ashx.
65 Hu Jintao, 'G8 Written Statement'; Hu Jintao, 'An Open Mind for Win-Win Cooperation', speech at the Asia Pacific Economic Co-operation (APEC) CEO summit, Busan, Republic of Korea, 17 November 2005; Angie Austin, *Energy and Power in China: Domestic Regulation and Foreign Policy*

(London: Foreign Policy Centre, n.d.); and Eurasia Group, 'China's Overseas Investment in Oil and Gas Production', report for the US–China Economic and Security Review Commission, 16 October 2006.
66 China State Council Information Office, *China's Energy Conditions and Policies* (2007), www.china.org.cn/english/environment/236955.htm.
67 See, for example, Fereidun Fesharaki, Chief Executive of FACTS Global Energy, 'Outlook for Global Energy Markets after the Great Recession: With Perspectives on China and Iran', presentation delivered at the Center for Strategic and International Studies (CSIS), Washington, DC, 16 September 2010.

29

The Future of Oil in a Carbon Constrained World

Daniel J. A. Johansson, Fredrik Hedenus and Thomas Sterner

Introduction

Global climate is changing. This fact is supported by robust scientific evidence, and there is no real doubt that the main reason is the increased concentration of greenhouse gases in the atmosphere caused by human activity, primarily related to the combustion of fossil fuels. Policies to handle the problems that a changing climate will bring about and what to do to limit the change in the climate are among the top issues in contemporary international politics. In connection with this, virtually all nations have ratified the UN Framework Convention on Climate Change (UNFCCC). The overarching aim of the UNFCCC is to avoid *dangerous anthropogenic interference with the climate system* (UNFCCC, 1992). Based on this the so-called 2°C target has, at least on paper, widespread political support as a target aimed at avoiding the most serious risks of climate change such as a potential dieback of the Amazon rainforest, melting of the Greenland ice sheet and increased global water stress problems (Fee et al., 2010). However, it is becoming more and more difficult to achieve this target given the difficulties in agreeing on any real international emission reductions.

Climate change policies have the potential to dictate the long-term prospects for the fossil fuel markets. Irrespective of the 2°C target it is clear that the use of fossil fuels (coal, natural gas and oil) cannot continue along historical trends. To avoid substantial climate change, the growth of anthropogenic carbon dioxide (CO_2) emissions needs to be reversed, for instance by a transition to other sources of energy complemented by technologies that capture and store CO_2 in sealed reservoirs and technologies that contribute to a more efficient use of energy. However, such a transition does not necessarily imply that the oil era is over yet.

In this chapter we outline how international climate policies to reduce emissions may affect long-term demand and supply of oil. In order to understand how the oil market will be affected we also have to understand the potential for CO_2 neutral alternatives to oil as well as how CO_2 from other fuels can be reduced. In doing this we primarily take a global perspective; climate change cannot be controlled in the long run unless the relevant policies are virtually global, or at least co-ordinated at a global level. The chapter will inevitably be somewhat speculative since it deals with the distant future, but the discussions and material presented will be based on available scientific literature. We will not cover issues related to the *impact* of climate change itself such as effects of melting arctic ice on the prospects for production or transportation of oil in that region. Such topics are outside the scope of this chapter. In section 2 we discuss some central aspects of international climate policies and in section 3 the relationship between cumulative emissions of CO_2 and the increase in global mean surface temperature. In section 4 we briefly outline the conventional view of the future of oil demand in a world where climate change is not a major issue and then analyze how it may change in response to climate policies. In section 5 we discuss alternatives to conventional oil, both fossil-based alternatives and renewable, as well as energy efficiency prospects, focusing mainly on the transport sector. In section 6 we discuss how OPEC and oil companies have approached the issue of climate change and analyse how oil producers may be affected by climate policies. Section 7 contains a final discussion on how policies in the short term may affect the oil market.

Global climate policies

The only long-term climate target that has gained some measure of universal acceptance within the international climate negotiations is the goal of stabilizing the global mean surface temperature at or below 2°C above the preindustrial level. This political target was re-emphasized in the outcome of the 16th Conference of the Parties (COP-16) meeting in Cancun 2010 (UNFCCC, 2010).

The climate problem is global; therefore, the relevant policies must be on the same geographical scale, at least in the long run. If merely a fraction of countries co-operate to reduce their emissions, the policy would be more costly and less effective. The countries outside the coalition have the opportunity to increase their consumption of relatively inexpensive fossil fuels to pick up the slack left by those within the coalition (Gerlagh & Kuik, 2007). This could become especially important in the long run if the coalition does not include a dominant share of global greenhouse gas emissions (Sterner, 2010).

Given the considerable difficulties in reaching and enforcing a global deal to reduce emissions of greenhouse gases that covers the majority of large countries, it appears improbable that a global climate regime with policies stringent enough to meet a 2°C target will come into existence sufficiently soon. It is generally accepted that limiting warming to less than 2°C reduces the risk of significant and irreversible changes in the climate system. However, this does not mean that there is any particular threshold at exactly 2°C. Significant negative impacts can occur already below 2°C, and if we were to miss the 2°C target, stabilizing the increase in the global average surface temperature at, say, 2.5 °C would still imply less severe consequences than risking an increase of 3°C (Smith et al. 2009; Harvey, 2007).

Reducing CO_2 emissions to levels discussed in this chapter will entail significant costs, although along with the benefits of increasing our chance of avoiding a range of costly climate impacts. There are considerable uncertainties but for instance the Stern Review mentions abatement costs on the order of a percentage of global GDP (Stern, 2007). In the perspective of a growing economy, this is not prohibitively costly; it does not mean that humanity cannot enjoy a good life. It does not mean that the poor cannot lift themselves out of poverty or even that the broad global middle class cannot continue to enjoy its welfare and economic standard (Azar & Schneider, 2002). However, the costs are high enough to warrant careful attention to economic efficiency in the design of climate policy. A cost-effective climate policy can never be achieved without relying heavily on an almost universal price-signal for CO_2 emissions, either generated by globally co-ordinated CO_2 taxes or a global cap-and-trade system.[1] However, such a policy is still a distant thought. Today greenhouse gas emissions are genuinely priced in only a few places, and there is little progress in international negotiations concerning climate mitigation. The reader should note that efficiency requires equalization of the marginal cost of abatement through a global CO_2 price. This does not imply that the cost of abatement should be split equally among the world's citizens. The distribution of costs can be separated completely from the efficiency issue and handled by a range of principles based on different perspectives of equity and responsibility, see Ringius et al. (2002) or Sterner (2002). The trouble is that the "scarcity rent" created by regulation of these emissions will generate very large sums of money, and there is genuine disagreement among countries how this rent should be shared. As shown by Sterner (2010), equal per capita shares would give India 16% of the global emission rights, while 'grandfathering' (emission rights based on historical emissions) would give India only 4% of total emission rights (since they currently emit about 4% of global emissions). The figures for the USA are roughly the mirror image: per capita rights would give the USA some 4% and grandfathering 16%. Naturally, when the disagreement implies such big differences in allocation, negotiations may be difficult and lengthy. The trouble is that we need a global agreement in order to make serious national policies possible, and we need it very fast if we are to reach targets such as the 2°C target.

Essential climate facts

Up to 2010 the global average surface temperature has increased by about 0.7°C above the pre-industrial level. Even if we immediately stop all greenhouse gas emissions, we would still witness an additional increase in the global average surface temperature of about 0.5° C.[2] The reasons for this increase are threefold:

The full warming effect of the greenhouse gases is masked by the cooling effect of (primarily sulphate) aerosols. The majority of these aerosols are co-emitted with CO_2 when coal and oil are burned. If we cease to burn fossil fuels, we would also cut aerosol emissions significantly (Wigley, 1991). Hence, their cooling effect would rapidly lessen, since the aerosols have a short atmospheric life time, resulting in a temperature increase.

CO_2 and some other greenhouse gases have a long atmospheric lifetime. A kg of CO_2 emitted from combustion of fossil fuel would result in an elevated atmospheric concentration of CO_2 for a very long time. About 30 to 40% of the initial effect on the CO_2 concentration would prevail after 100 years, while about 20% would remain after 1000 years (Archer et al., 2009).

The climate system responds slowly to changes in the warming generated by greenhouse gases due to the large thermal inertia of the oceans (Wigley, 2005; Johansson 2010).

The above applies to a complete and immediate cessation of fossil emissions, but that is not possible. These emissions are, in a baseline scenario, expected to grow a few percent per year. Just stabilizing emissions at the current level would require quite strong policy instruments. But this is a 'stock' problem: stabilizing *emissions* would still imply that the atmospheric stock continued to grow (although close to linearly rather than exponentially). This would still be entirely insufficient in meeting the 2°C target; it would bring us above 600 ppm CO_2 and making temperature more than 3°C warmer already this century.[3]

Even though the science of climate change itself is robust, there are large uncertainties concerning how sensitive the climate is to emissions of greenhouse gases. Climate sensitivity is a measure of the change in the global mean surface temperature that would occur if we were to double the pre-industrial level of CO_2 concentrations in the atmosphere and wait for the full temperature effect to take hold. The global mean surface temperature would in this case *likely* increase by 2–4.5°C, with a best estimate of 3°C according to Meehl et al. (2007).[4]

This uncertainty about how much a given change in the concentration of greenhouse gases affects the global mean surface temperature results in large uncertainties in how much CO_2 the world may emit and still keep the global mean surface temperature below a targeted limit. If climate sensitivity is low (i.e., ~2°C), we can emit considerably more CO_2 than if climate sensitivity is high (i.e., ~4.5°C) for any given increase in global average surface temperature.

Because emissions of CO_2 accumulate in the atmosphere, cumulative emissions are strongly correlated with the level of global warming, see Allen et al. (2009), Matthews & Caldeira (2008), Zickfeld et al. (2009) and NRC (2010). Hence, it is not of direct importance when emissions take place; what matters to the global average temperature is the cumulative amount of CO_2 (within half a millennium or so), *ceteris paribus*.

This relationship between cumulative emissions of CO_2 and temperature change can be used to assess how much fossil fuels can be used while keeping the global average surface temperature below a certain level.[5] The cumulative emissions of carbon emitted as CO_2 from 2010 and onwards that are compatible with an increase in the global mean surface temperature of 2°C and 3°C have been estimated by the use of NRC (2010), CCC (2011) and the MiMiC model (Johansson, 2010), see Figure 29.1 for results. For example, in order to keep the global average surface temperature below 2°C with a probability of about 50%, we may emit about 550 Gton[6] carbon (as CO_2) beyond 2010. For 3°C, more CO_2 may be emitted, about 1100 Gton carbon beyond 2010. However, there is a great deal of uncertainty in these numbers, beyond what the error bars in Figure 29.1 indicate. The error bars only include the uncertainty from the climate sensitivity and the carbon cycle. In addition, the cumulative carbon that may be emitted while reaching a specific temperature target also depends on how emissions of other greenhouse gases (methane, nitrous oxide, etc.) and aerosols develop. In addition, it is important to note that Figure 29.1 shows the cumulative *net* emissions of CO_2. If biomass with carbon capture and storage becomes a feasible option on a large scale, which would imply net negative emissions of CO_2, the cumulative gross emissions of CO_2 from fossil fuels could potentially be greater than those shown in Figure 29.1 (see Azar et al., 2006).

There are large uncertainties in the remaining recoverable resources of oil, natural gas, and coal.[7] So as to be able to compare recoverable resources of oil and other fossil fuels with the cumulative emissions of CO_2 that are compatible with different temperature stabilization levels, we have assessed a range of sources that provide estimates on proven reserves and recoverable resources.

The proved reserves of conventional oil amount to about 1,300bn. barrels according to BP (2010). In line with BP we include both crude oil and natural gas liquids (NGL) in the category conventional oil. Given standard conversion factors these reserves contain about 160 Gton carbon.[8] The estimated additional recoverable resources, i.e., conventional oil left in reservoirs that are yet not classified as proven reserves and that may become economical to recover in the future, are uncertain. Estimates range from close to zero to about equal to the current proven reserves or even more (IEA, 2008; Aguilera et al., 2009; USGS, 2000; Kjärstad & Johnsson, 2009; Sorrel et al., 2008). Setting aside the extreme estimates, we assume that the additional recoverable resources contain about 110 Gton carbon.

In addition to the recoverable resources of conventional oil, the recoverable resources of oil sands and heavy oil are estimated to be substantial, on the order of about 1,000 bn. barrel oil equivalent (boe) (Kjärstad & Johnsson, 2009), corresponding to about 130 Gton carbon.[9]

Proven reserves of natural gas amount to about 1,200 bn. boe (BP, 2010) and additional recoverable resources to about equally large, i.e., about 1,200 bn. boe (Aguilera, 2009; USGS, 2000), in total corresponding to about 220 Gton carbon.[10] In addition, there is a substantial amount of unconventional gas. These resources may be several times larger than the proven reserves of conventional gas. The unconventional sources include shale gas, coalbed methane, and tight formation gas. In addition, if methane hydrates stored in ocean sediments become recoverable, these could potentially add thousands of billion boe of gas, see Sims et al. (2007).[11]

The proven reserves for coal are larger (in energy terms) than those of conventional oil and natural gas, amounting to about 3,000 bn. boe and contain about 500 Gton carbon.[12] In addition, the recoverable resources of coal are likely to be considerably larger than the proven reserves, estimated up to about an order of magnitude larger than the proven reserves (Thielmann, 2007; Sims et al., 2007), although much more conservative estimates of the recoverable resources of coal are also available (Höök et al., 2010).

The estimated recoverable resources (including the proven reserves) of fossil fuel contain considerably more carbon than can be emitted as CO_2 with a maximum increase in global mean surface temperature of 2°C or any temperature level nearby, see Figure 29.1. Burning only the proven reserves of coal, oil and natural gas would foreclose the 2°C target, but would likely keep the increase in the global mean surface temperature below 3°C. However, if only the recoverable reserves of conventional oil and natural gas were used, but no other fossil fuels (i.e., no coal, oil sands, etc.), the amount of CO_2 emitted would be compatible with meeting a 2°C limit, with a probability of roughly 50%.

The latter scenario may seem far from realistic today (2011). For the last few years, coal has been the most rapidly growing source of fuel globally. However, coal is the worst of the fossil fuels from a climate perspective; per energy unit, the CO_2 emissions are higher than those of oil and natural gas.[13] For this reason and since the recoverable resources for coal are estimated to be large, it is not uncommon to see suggestions that the most important strategy to combat climate change is to control the use of coal and to develop and rapidly deploy Carbon Capture and Storage (CCS) methods to minimize CO_2 emissions from coal use (Kharecha et al., 2010).

The use of oil in a world with or without climate policies

Global demand for energy is expected to grow considerably over the coming decades. In a baseline scenario without strong climate policies, demand is expected to roughly double by 2050 (Clarke et al., 2009). Of the various energy sources oil is today the most important in energy as well as economic terms. Oil is used in virtually all sectors of the economy. The use and production of oil may grow by 1 to 2% per year in the coming decades (Dargay & Gately, 2010; EIA, 2010; IEA, 2010a). The growth will probably be strongest in rapidly industrializing countries such as China and India and for petroleum products used for transportation fuel and as feedstock for the petrochemical industry (Dargay & Gately, 2010; EIA, 2010; IEA, 2010a). For example, the consumption of light and medium distillates has grown about 8% per year in China in the past decade (BP, 2010).

In 2009, about 85m. barrels of oil were extracted per day (BP, 2010). About 60% of the global refinery output (measured in energy terms) was used within the transport sector (road, rail, aviation and shipping) and this share is expected to increase over the coming decades. Roughly 15% of the energy content of oil is used internally within the refining process; the use of crude oil directly as a fuel without any refining is rare (IEA, 2010b).

Growth of the energy system cannot be fuelled by fossil fuels if we are to avoid serious changes in the climate system. The use of fossil fuels without carbon capture and storage has to fall quite fast, and energy must be used more efficiently. In order to illustrate one possible transition path for the energy system, we use the Global Energy Transition (GET) model (Azar et al., 2003, 2006; Hedenus et al. 2010). This model makes assumptions on costs and energy conversion efficiencies for a large range of technologies, resource availabilities, and costs of extraction as

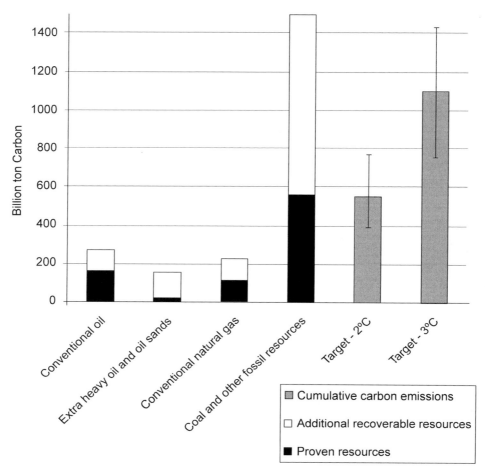

Figure 29.1 Proven reserves and estimated additional recoverable resources of different fossil fuels, compared to cumulative emissions of CO_2 compatible with climate targets of 2 or 3°C above the pre-industrial level
Note: > 3000 G ton carbon

well as constraints on how fast technologies can expand. Given these assumptions, the model minimizes the total cost of meeting energy demand. In addition, an explicit constraint is included so that cumulative emissions beyond year 2010 are kept below 550 Gton carbon. This gives the world a ~50% chance of keeping the global average surface temperature change below 2°C.

A constraint of 550 Gton carbon can be met if global emissions peak by 2020 and then decline by about 2% per year. Such a scenario requires a rapid expansion of new energy sources, new infrastructure, and new end-use systems for higher efficiency. By 2050 more than 60% of the global primary energy supply would need to come from sources with virtually zero CO_2 emissions, see Figure 29.2. This can be compared to the situation in 2005 where about 20% of the primary energy supply came from renewable fuels. Similar results to those generated by the GET model and presented here can be found in a range of studies, see for example IEA (2010a) and Clarke et al. (2009).

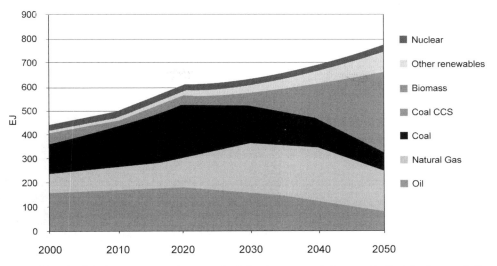

Figure 29.2 A global energy supply scenario following an emissions path that limit cumulative carbon emissions to 550Gtons (post 2010)

The feasibility of a large scale expansion of some of the new technologies necessary for an energy scenario such as described here needs to be proven and costs must come down before they will make a real dent within the energy system. For example, crucial technologies such as CCS or Biomass-to-Liquids (BTL) only exist in the demonstration phase today.

The transition of the energy system will involve major changes in all sectors of the economy. However, how much emissions will be reduced in the various economic sectors depends on both market forces and political choices. A related question is how emission of greenhouse gases should be reduced to minimize economic costs of abatement? This related question has been approached and analyzed in a number of studies; see for example Azar et al. (2003, 2006), Clarke et al. (2009) and Edenhofer et al. (2010). Although future costs and resource availability are very uncertain, some patterns emerge from such studies. It seems that reducing CO_2 emissions by reducing the use of petroleum products within the transport sector tends to be relatively costly while reducing emissions from coal tends to be relatively inexpensive. This is confirmed in Working Group 3 of the IPCC where the results of many model studies are assessed " ... *in all models, coal use is significantly reduced under the climate policy scenarios, compared to the baseline ... In 2030, oil use is only modestly reduced by climate policies ...* " (Fisher et al., 2007).

This is illustrated in Figure 29.3 where results from the GET model on the use of fossil fuels in the climate policy scenario presented above are compared with the use of fossil fuel in a baseline scenario. Coal is the fossil fuel that is reduced most. Coal is largely used for power production, for which less carbon-intensive alternatives are available, such as wind power, natural gas, or by using the coal with carbon capture and storage (Haszeldine, 2009). The substitution of natural gas for coal explains the increase in natural gas in the climate policy scenario. Oil is reduced in 2050 compared to 2030 in both the baseline scenario and the climate policy scenario due to resource depletion.[14] However, the differences are small in both 2030 and 2050, mainly due to the limited low-cost abatement options in the transportation sector. In the baseline scenario Coal-to-liquids is the main substitute to petroleum products in the transport sector, while in the climate policy scenario a range of alternatives are used, including more efficient

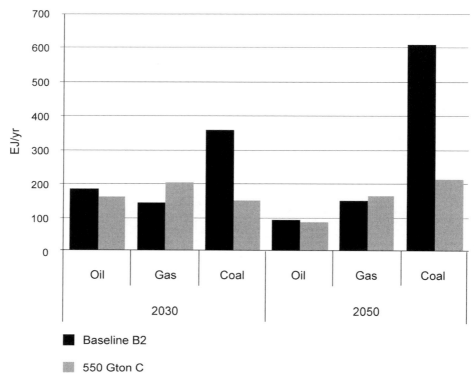

Figure 29.3 Primary fossil fuel supply in baseline scenario compared to a stabilization of 550Gtons carbon of cumulative emissions. About two-thirds of the coal use in the stabilization scenario has CCS applied in 2050

vehicles (including hybrid vehicles), biofuel and natural gas. Petroleum products are considered less costly to substitute for in heating and electricity production than in the transport sector. However, the share of petroleum products in these sectors is already small, see Dargay & Gately (2010), EIA (2010) and IEA (2010a).

Options for reducing conventional fuel use

In this section we focus our attention on alternatives to petroleum products from conventional oil, especially for the road transport sector. This sector uses close to 50% of refinery output, a share that is likely to grow. However, all large scale substitutes for oil in the transport sector that has low CO_2 emissions have important limitations, at least in the short to mid-term (less than 20 years). This explains the results in Figure 29.3, namely that there is a relatively small difference between oil use in a baseline scenario and in a climate stabilization scenario. Given stringent climate policies, the main large-scale changes in the coming decades in the transport sector are likely to be more energy-efficient and smaller vehicles and perhaps biofuels. Still, in the long run (beyond 2020–30 or so), the transport sector cannot continue to rely on fossil fuels, and the choice seems to be between biofuels, electricity, and hydrogen (Hedenus et al., 2010). We will in this section present an overview of the different options.

The Future of Oil in a Carbon Constrained World

Shifting fuel and propulsion technologies

In the transport sector, oil-based fuels have totally dominated for more than a hundred years. Still, several liquid alternatives may replace oil-based fuels when conventional oil becomes scarce, costly and/or is phased out due to policy concerns. These alternatives include fuels derived from extra heavy oils, oil sands, coal, natural gas, or from biomass. However, all liquid substitutes based on fossil alternatives have higher lifecycle CO_2-equivalent emissions than conventional oil, see Figure 29.4 and Brandt & Farrell (2007).

Other technologies may also yield important substitutes for oil in the transport sector, especially electricity in battery electric vehicles as well as hydrogen. To briefly assess these options, we describe their potentials and caveats.

Extra heavy oils and oil sands

Extra heavy oils and oil sands are extracted today in Venezuela and Canada, respectively, and are economically viable at current oil prices. Production costs are still higher than for conventional oil, around US$ 50–70 per barrel synthetic crude for oil sands, slightly lower for Venezuelan extra heavy oil, and higher for oil shale (IEA, 2010a). Moreover, the lifecycle CO_2 emissions per barrel synthetic crude are considerably higher than for conventional oil: for oil sands, 10–30 % higher (Charpentier et al., 2009) and higher yet for oil shale. In addition, there are severe environmental consequences of recovering oil sands and extra heavy oil that may prohibit larger-scale expansion of these fuels.

Coal and Coal-to-Liquids

The Coal-to-Liquids (CTL) technology was developed in the beginning of the 20th century and adopted large-scale during the Second World War in Germany and during the apartheid regime

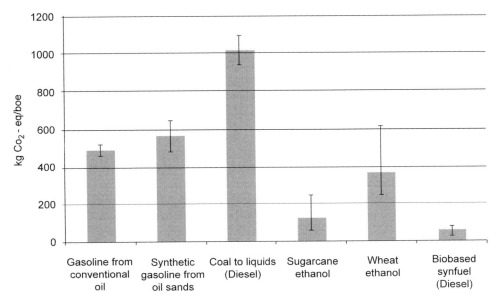

Figure 29.4 Life-cycle CO_2-equivalent emissions for different liquid fuels
Source: (Concawe, 2006; Brandt & Farrell, 2007; Charpentier et al., 2009).

in South Africa. To produce liquid fuels, coal is gasified and thereafter synthesized to synthetic fuels. Considering the widely held view that coal is very abundant, see Figure 29.1, CTL could provide a large-scale oil substitute in the future. However the CO_2 emissions are around twice those from conventional oil-based fuels. On the other hand with the use of CCS technologies, the emissions would come down to comparable levels as those for conventional oil. This would come at an increased cost of around US$10 per barrel if the CCS technology succeeds in becoming a commercial technology with safe and permanent storage sites for the captured CO_2. The oil price needs to be stable over $60 to $100 per barrel for CTL projects to be economical (IEA, 2008).

Natural gas and Gas-to-Liquids

Natural gas is sometimes mentioned as an alternative fuel to petroleum products in the transport sector. Natural gas would reduce the CO_2 emissions by about 30% if used to replace gasoline; but it would reduce CO_2 emissions by about 60% if used to replace coal in the power sector, and at a lower cost. Arguably, it is better to use the limited gas resources in the latter way, from a climate perspective.[15] Natural gas can also be used to synthesize diesel or other synthetic fuels, i.e., Gas-to-Liquids (GTL). The process is rather costly and involves energy losses on the order of 40 to 50%, which results in slightly higher CO_2 emissions compared to conventional oil (IEA, 2005).

Biofuels

There has been considerable optimism about biofuels as an alternative to petroleum products. This optimism has declined in recent years, in part due to the dubious experience of public support for cereal-based ethanol. This is a costly source of biofuel, with rather large emissions of greenhouse gases, giving small or no carbon benefits compared to gasoline or diesel, see Figure 29.4. If biofuels are to make an important contribution in the future energy system, other sources have to be used, such as sugarcane or woody biomass, as both costs and potentials for greenhouse gas reductions are more promising (Hamelinck and Faaij, 2006).

Regardless of the feedstock, the production of biomass requires land, which globally is a scarce resource. Bioproductive land is essential for providing society with food, fibres, and bioenergy, and for preserving ecosystems and biodiversity. The demand for such land is currently increasing for several reasons, and there is little reason to expect that the demand growth will level off in the foreseeable future (Smith et al., 2010).

The increased scarcity of land and expansion of bioenergy have several important implications:

An increase in land use will increase land rents, and thereby both food and biomass prices (Johansson and Azar, 2007). The high food prices in 2007/2008 are believed to at least partly have been a result of the rapid expansion of cereal-based ethanol production in the USA and the EU. Higher food prices may have adverse social effects, and the increased land rents may also undermine some of the cost-effective potential of biofuels. Bioenergy will be a scarce resource and cannot, even in the long run, be used for all energy purposes. Biomass has competing uses as a source of liquid fuel, heat, electricity, and as feedstock to the chemical industry. Where the biomass will be used will be determined by cost differentials and policy design. Assuming an equal price on CO_2 from all sources, several studies have come to the conclusion that it is more cost effective to use the limited biomass resources for residential and industrial heat or for electricity production rather than for liquid biofuels, see Azar et al. (2003) and Gul et al. (2009).

Expansion of bioenergy requires additional land use. There may be large CO_2 emissions associated with land-use conversion from pasture or forests to agricultural land, see for instance Fargione et al., 2008. However, there is also the risk of indirect land-use change. Even though bioenergy itself is not grown on former forest land, the expansion of bioenergy crops may displace food production, so that food instead is grown on former forest or pasture land (Searchinger et al., 2008). The effect of indirect land-use change could be substantial and even totally negate the greenhouse gas benefits obtained if the biofuel replaces oil.

Electric vehicles

Electricity may be used in light utility vehicles, either in Battery Electric Vehicles (BEV) or in Plug-in Hybrid Electric Vehicles (PHEV). The first BEV was developed in the 1890s, but was later out-competed by the internal combustion engine. Since the 1990s there has been a renewed interest in the electric car. However, the electric car faces several obstacles to becoming more than a marginal contributor to the transport sector. BEVs are typically more expensive than their counterpart internal combustion vehicles, with roughly the same size, top speed, range, etc. The cost (and success) of BEVs depends critically on the cost of their batteries. Today these batteries cost around 700 US$/kWh (Brooker and Thornton, 2010). To become a cost-effective option given stringent climate policies, this cost would need to be cut by 80% (Offer et al., 2011).

The energy efficiency in an electricity motor is around three times higher than in the internal combustion engine. On the other hand, there are larger losses when electricity is generated and transmitted compared to when petrol is refined from crude oil. If coal is used to produce the electricity, the carbon emissions per km driven are roughly the same for a BEV as for a conventional car (Jaramillo et al. 2009). Thus, to make the electric car a viable option in the case of climate policy, the electricity system must first be transformed, and a large share of the electricity must be produced by renewables, nuclear, and/or coal and natural gas with CCS. Finally, the limited range of a BEV constitutes an important barrier.

The PHEV has both an internal combustion engine and a large battery that can be charged from the grid. This enables the internal combustion engine to work more efficiently, as in hybrid vehicles, but also enables a larger range compared to a BEV. PHEVs do not require as large a battery, which makes them cost-effective at a higher battery cost of around 300 US$/kWh (Hedenus et al., 2010; Offer 2011), significantly higher than for the BEV.

Hydrogen

Hydrogen cars are often perceived as the sustainable solution for the transportation sector, although the technical obstacles are probably even more substantial than for electric cars. Hydrogen is produced using an energy source that determines the carbon footprint. Producing hydrogen using fossil fuels does not make sense from a climate mitigation perspective. Instead, viable energy sources are renewables such as wind and solar, nuclear energy, or fossil fuel plants with CCS. Distribution and storage of hydrogen tend to be both costly and energy-consuming, since high pressure gas tubes have to be used in order to compress the gas into a manageable volume. Hydrogen may be used in both internal combustion engines and fuel cells. Fuel cells have higher conversion efficiency, but both the cost and the limited lifespan are presently prohibitive (von Helmolt and Eberle, 2007). Even so, if batteries turn out to remain rather expensive, and biofuels are constrained by land availability, hydrogen may become an attractive alternative in the future.

Daniel J. A. Johansson, Fredrik Hedenus and Thomas Sterner

Reducing the use of liquid fuels

When the price of petroleum (products) goes up the use tends to go down (*ceteris paribus*). This reduction in demand is a result of two main factors; a decline in the use of the service the fuel provides (such as transport distance or heating) or a switch to a new technology using the fuel more efficiently. These two main factors are captured in the price elasticity of demand for liquid fuels.[16] Hence, pricing of CO_2 emissions will not only result in a shift toward other sources of energy with lower CO_2 emissions as discussed above, it will also result in a reduction of demand for liquid fuels.

The demand price of liquid fuels is in general considered to be inelastic, although this is in part a function of the time horizon studied. In the short run (about a year) the price elasticity is very low, close to zero. The options for shifting to other energy sources in the short run are limited, and the energy services provided by the fuel in general rather essential. In the long run (about 10 years) the price elasticity is considerably larger. Given time to adjust the capital stock to a new price level implies that vehicles, burners, or other equipment with a more efficient use of the fuel become profitable to invest in given that the fuel price increases. As a consequence, if CO_2 emissions are priced, the consumer price (producer price plus emissions price) of oil will increase, thus reducing demand.

Sterner (2007) reports on a number of reviews of fuel price elasticities and concludes that they are about −0.3, in the short run, and about −0.7, in the long-run. However, this is the price elasticity for engine fuel (gasoline and diesel), not oil. The fuel price includes refinery margins, insurances, transport costs, taxes, etc. Therefore, the corresponding price elasticity of oil is lower. Studies that have focused explicitly on oil price elasticities find values around 0 to −0.1 in the short run and less than −0.5 in the long run (Gately & Huntington, 2002; Dargay & Gately, 2010).

An implication of the price inelasticity of oil demand is that CO_2 prices will only have a small effect on demand for oil as illustrated in Table 29.1, which shows relative reduction in oil demand for various CO_2 price levels. These price levels can be compared with the price in the EU Emissions Trading Scheme (EU ETS) which is about US$20 per ton CO_2.

However, we need to be cautious here, the estimates of price elasticities point to the fact that the demand for liquid fuels is not very price responsive. This does not mean that the fuel could not be used much more energy efficiently. There is a large technical potential for improved energy efficiency in the transport sector, see ICCT (2011) and Bandivadekar et al. (2008). However, it is well accepted that even if many energy efficiency measures tend to appear cost-effective on paper, the potential is often not realized, for a range of reasons, see Jaffe & Stavins (1994) and Brown (2004). This difference between the cost-effective technical potential and the realized outcome is sometimes referred to as the "energy efficiency gap."[17]

Historically, engine losses, the rolling resistance of tires, and air drag have all decreased, but these efficiency gains have to a large degree been balanced by an increase in the performance and size of the vehicle. By increased performance we mean increased acceleration, larger

Table 29.1 The decline in demand for oil for three different CO_2 prices. In the calculations an untaxed world market price of oil of US$100 per barrel was assumed together with a long-run elasticity of −0.4

CO_2 price (US$/ton CO_2)	Reduction in demand
20	3 %
50	8 %
100	14 %

engine, air conditioning, increased passenger space and weight, among other changes requiring energy, see An & DiCicco (2007) and Sprei et al. (2008). If the consumer desires these, it is "costly" to reduce fuel use.

Fuel economy and/or CO_2 emissions from vehicles are regulated in the USA, the EU, China, South Korea, and Japan among other countries (ICCT, 2011). The proposed targets in these countries for the coming years would imply cuts in CO_2 (or fuel use) per kilometre in the order of several percent per year. Hence, these fuel economy standards point to the fact that much of the potential for energy efficiency improvements must be realized together with a trend toward lighter and smaller vehicles if the standards are to be met. In addition, this increase in energy efficiency cannot be counteracted by increases in vehicle performance that require additional energy, as has been common in the past, if the vehicle manufacturers are to comply with regulations. However, regulation of fuel economy is far from being an optimal instrument from the viewpoint of fuel savings. It is not likely to cut fuel use as much as fuel economy is improved since only vehicle characteristics and not usage is regulated. As the vehicle becomes more energy efficient the marginal cost of an extra mile declines which acts as an incentive to increase driving distance. This effect is commonly dubbed the "direct rebound effect." For example, Small & Van Dender (2007) estimate that 5–20% of the potential fuel savings from vehicle fuel economy improvements have been eaten up by the rebound effect. In addition, the fuel price would tend to fall if demand is reduced, encouraging all kinds of new use of fossil fuel. For these reasons we should not expect that fuel efficiency standards will cut petroleum product demand as much as fuel economy is improved.

Oil producers and climate policy

One major challenge in international climate policy negotiations has been related to the issue that energy-exporting countries, especially the OPEC member countries Saudi Arabia and Kuwait, claim that their oil resource rents will decline as a consequence of measures to reduce CO_2 emissions. The concerns are understandable since many OPEC countries and other energy-exporting countries depend heavily on energy exports for their national income. Some energy-exporting countries push the claim that they either should be compensated for lost oil export revenues or be supported in their attempt to diversify their economies to be less dependent on oil export revenues (Barnett & Dessai, 2002; Aarts & Janssen, 2003; Depledge, 2008; Loumi, 2009). In order to get the energy exporting countries as signatories to the UNFCCC and the Kyoto protocol, article 4.8 in the UNFCCC and articles 2.3 and 3.14 in the Kyoto protocol state that these energy exporting countries should (at least in part) be compensated for losses in energy export revenues or obtain assistance in diversifying their economies (UNFCCC, 1992, 1997). In the Cancun Agreement, paragraphs 88–94 consider, among other issues, the concerns among the energy-exporting countries and the impact emissions-reducing policies may have on these countries' national income (UNFCCC, 2010).

OPEC countries have in part based their concerns on energy-economic model studies that show that OPEC countries are negatively affected by measures to reduce greenhouse gas emissions. Such studies are plentiful, see for example Berg et al. (1997), Bernstein et al. (1999), Ghanem et al. (1999), McKibbin et al. (1999), Bartsch & Muller (2000), Radetzki (2002), IEA (2010a), Kitous et al. (2010) and van Vuuren et al. (2010). Briefly summarized, these studies suggest that policies and measures aimed at reducing CO_2 emissions will reduce oil consumption, and push the producer price of oil down, and that both these effects cause a decline in revenue from oil export.

Echoing the concerns expressed by the oil nations, international oil companies have worried that climate change policies will erode their business, see van den Hove et al. (2002). Some oil majors are also known for their intense lobbying campaigns against climate policies and for their support for campaigns to confuse the public about the science behind climate change, see Oreskes & Conway (2010).

Although the concerns expressed by countries rich in oil endowments and oil companies make intuitive sense, i.e., that climate policies will erode their rents and profits, many studies on climate policies point toward the fact that such policies alone may not put an end to the petroleum era, at least not in the transport sector. The reasons for this have been discussed above, but we summarize them here.

- The carbon content in the estimated recoverable resources for conventional by oil is smaller (less than half) than the cumulative emissions of CO_2 compatible with meeting long-term stabilization levels of the global average surface temperature in line with the targets discussed in international climate politics.
- Most conventional oil is inexpensive to extract, according to the EIA (2008) less than US $20 per barrel in the Middle East, and less than US$40 per barrel in other places, see also Aguilera et al. (2009) and Brandt & Farrell (2007), for studies suggesting even lower production costs for conventional oil.[18] Hence, even if the producer price of oil would drop below current levels (~US$100 per barrel) due to climate policies, most conventional oil would be used anyway, unless the CO_2 price is very high or alternative technologies inexpensive.
- Oil is superior for production of liquid fuels, which are crucial in the transport sector, with few contenders. Oil used in other sectors than transport is easier to substitute, but transport is the major sector that uses petroleum products, and the share of petroleum products used within the transport sector is expected to grow.
- The price elasticity of demand for liquid fuel has been low historically, and there is no obvious reason to believe the situation is different today or will be different in the coming decades. Recent studies have even estimated that the oil price elasticity has become even smaller over the last decade (Hamilton, 2009). Hence, an increase in the consumer price of petroleum would only imply a relatively small reduction in demand.
- The lowest-cost substitutes for conventional oil are fuels derived from unconventional oil, coal (CTL), natural gas (GTL), sugar cane (ethanol), lingo-cellulosic biomass (second generation ethanol or BTL). The fuels derived from these sources involve greater lifecycle CO_2-eq emissions, with the exception of the biomass-derived fuels. This implies that the cost of producing and using these fuels will increase more than the cost of producing and using fuels derived from conventional oil if CO_2 emissions are priced. This would increase the relative advantage of conventional oil to the other fossil alternatives. This could result in an increased producer price for conventional oil (Manne & Rutherford, 1994, Person et al., 2007, Johansson et al., 2009). However, the relative advantage for conventional oil would be small if CCS expands large-scale and is used to capture and store upstream emissions from the production of synthetic petroleum products from unconventional oils, coal, and natural gas.

Although most studies suggest that oil resource owners will see a drop in their resource rent due to climate policies, no firm conclusions can be drawn. Based on the first four arguments presented above one may suggest that it is likely that most of the conventional oil in the estimated recoverable resources will be used even if globally and stringent climate policies are in place.[19] Taking the fifth argument into account, one cannot rule out that the net present value oil rent for OPEC and other conventional oil owners may *increase* due to climate policies[20] that are stringent enough to allow the 2°C target to be met, as suggested in Persson et al. (2007) and

Johansson et al. (2009). Whether resource rent will increase or not will also depend on the pricing strategies adopted by OPEC, see Johansson et al. (2009) for an analysis of OPEC and climate policies.

Final discussion – policies in the short term

In the previous sections of this chapter we have taken a perspective that policies directed towards reducing emissions of greenhouse gases primarily have a close to global coverage and are driven by economic efficiency considerations. However, climate policies may predominantly in the short-run, take other routes. Existing and planned national policies aimed at reducing the use of petroleum are in a sense ambitious. More than 25 nations have biofuel blending mandates (REN21, 2010), and plans for fuel economy standards in the coming years are strong in many major countries (ICCT, 2011). A continuation of these policies aimed at reducing petroleum use in the transport sector is likely irrespective of the success of international climate negotiations. However, these policies are not the most cost-effective approach to cut emissions of green house gases. As we have already mentioned, they depart from the ideal of a universal price on all greenhouse gas emissions in two different ways. Such policies may put a higher burden (in the form of a higher marginal cost of abatement of CO_2) on the transport sector than on other sectors, and they are not even cost-effective for the transport sector compared to policies that increase fuel taxes (Sterner, 2002).

Putting a higher burden on the transport sector may be motivated by a series of considerations. The domestic transport sector is not subject to international competition, and there is a strong inter-relationship with energy security issues. The distributional and political effects of transport fuel taxes are not easy to deal with but may be preferred[21] to the corresponding effects related to fuels such as kerosene (used by the very poor) or fuels that are used by industry where fear of the loss of jobs is a dominant factor. Regulating and pricing greenhouse gas emissions from energy-intensive industries exposed to international competition would affect prospects negatively and lead to massive lobbying in favour of jobs. Dealing with emissions (of CO_2, nitrous oxides (N_2O), and methane (CH_4)) from soils, forests, and ecosystems may turn out to be administratively more complicated than dealing with transport fuels. Still taxing fuels is also very difficult politically (at least in some countries) and thus may increase the temptation to use other second-best policies such as fuel efficiency standards, biofuel blending mandates and subsidies for certain technologies. It is easy to see that there are powerful lobby groups in favour of these policies, but essentially no one lobbies for higher fuel taxes, see further Sterner (2002) and Anthoff & Hahn (2010).

For these reasons, the transport sector may have to undertake a larger share of mitigation than would have been the case if the policies were driven by global cost-effectiveness alone, especially as long as only a limited fraction of the world's nations have binding emissions targets. This in turn will have an impact on the oil market (including the relative demand for different petroleum products) that may go beyond what we have presented in this chapter. Hence, the effect of climate worries and policies on the oil market will not only depend on the stringency of climate policy and the alternative technology solutions available but also on the strategies chosen with respect to policy instruments used and sectors targeted.

Acknowledgements

We would like to thank EON, Formas and the Swedish Energy Agency for funding and Jessica Coria, Paulina Essunger and Jonas Nässén for their helpful comments.

Notes

1 It can be noted that cost-effectiveness of policies is stated as a principle in the UNFCCC (1992).
2 The response on the global average surface temperature due to different CO_2 emission scenarios can be tested with the simple climate model Chalmers Climate Calculator (CCC) available online via www.chalmers.se/ee/ccc.
3 Estimated with the CCC model, using best estimates such as climate sensitivity being 3°C.
4 Note that likely means the probability is 66 to 90% that climate sensitivity is in this interval (Meehl et al., 2007).
5 See also Grubb (2001).
6 G stands for Giga. It is a unit prefix indicating multiplication of a unit by 10^9 or 1,000m.
7 By recoverable resources we mean resources left to be extracted. This includes both proven reserves and additional recoverable resources that may become extractable due to reserves growth, new findings and the impact of technological progress.
8 Based on 6.1 GJ/boe and 20 kg C/GJ. We use the same factors for NGL; this will overestimate the energy content and the weight of stored carbon in the conventional reserves somewhat, but the overestimation will be small since the share of NGL to that of crude oil within the proven reserves is rather small.
9 Based on 6.1 GJ/boe, and 22 kg C/GJ.
10 Based on 6.1 GJ/boe and 15 kg C/GJ.
11 The extraction of methane hydrates would involve large climatic risks related to the danger of methane leakage during the recovery of the hydrates.
12 Based on 6.1 GJ/boe and 25 kg C/GJ.
13 The ratio of CO_2 emitted per energy unit is about 3:4:5 for gas, oil and coal, respectively.
14 In the studies discussed here the oil price assumed was in general lower than in recent years (2007–2010) and lower than current price forecasts (IEA, 2010; EIA, 2010a). For this reason, abatement options may have been underestimated. See also van Ruijven & van Vuuren (2009) for an analysis of the importance of oil price on cost effective mitigation options.
15 The leakage of natural gas in production, transmission and distribution is substantial, on average 2–3 % of the world's gas production (EPA, 2006). As natural gas to a large degree consist of methane, this leakage causes additional global warming in addition to the CO_2 emissions from combustion of natural gas. As a result, the climate benefits of switching from gasoline to natural gas are relatively smaller than the reduction in CO_2 that such a switch results in.
16 The demand price elasticity measures the percentage change in quantity demanded divided by the percentage change in price.
17 Hypotheses about why the "energy efficiency gap" exists include costs not covered in the technical cost calculation that are real for the consumer (and/or investor), the consumer (and/or investor) lacking information about benefits of energy efficiency, and that he/she may irrationally undervalue the economic benefits of energy efficiency.
18 However, ultra-deep off-shore reservoirs and oil extracted by enhanced recovery may be more costly than the suggested numbers.
19 The so-called "green paradox" (Sinn, 2007; Gerlagh, 2010) is related. This paradox suggests that policy plans aimed at reducing the demand for fossil fuels cause the suppliers of the fuel to expect that future fossil fuel prices will be eroded as a result of the planned policies and as a result the suppliers extract their resource more rapidly with an acceleration of climate change as a result.
20 Unlike a carbon tax, other climate policies such as fuel economy standards, subsidies to biofuels, or hydrogen would not contribute to an increase in the producer price of oil, they would only contribute to cutting the demand for oil and in turn also its price.
21 Distributional consequences of fuel taxation are considered in Sterner (2011).

References

Aarts P., Janssen D. (2003). 'Shades of Opinion: The oil exporting countries and international climate policies'. *The Review of International Affairs*, 3(2): 332–51.
Aguilera R.F., Eggert R.G., Lagos G., Tilton J.E. (2009). 'Depletion and the future availability of petroleum resources'. *Energy Journal* 30 (1): 161–94.
Allen, M. R., Frame, D. J., Huntingford C., Jones C. D., Lowe J. A., Meinshausen M. & Meinshausen N. (2009). 'Warming caused by cumulative carbon emissions towards the trillionth ton'. *Nature* 458: 1163–66.

An F., DeCicco J. (2007). 'Trends in Technical Efficiency Trade-Offs for the U.S. Light Vehicle Fleet'. SAE Technical Paper 2007–01-1325, SP-2089.

Anthoff D., Hahn R.W. (2010). 'Government Failure and Market Failure: On the Inefficiency of Environmental and Energy Policy'. *Oxford Review of Economic Policy* 26(2): 197–224.

Archer D., Eby M., Brovkin V., Ridgwell A., Cao L., Mikolajewicz U., Caldeira K., Matsumoto K., Munhoven G., Montenegro A., Tokos K. (2009). 'Atmospheric lifetime of fossil-fuel carbon dioxide'. *Annual Reviews of Earth and Planetary Sciences* 37:117–34.

Azar, C. and Rodhe, H. (1997) 'Targets for stabilization of atmospheric CO_2'. *Science* 276: 1818–19.

Azar C., Lindgren K., Andersson B.A. (2003). 'Global energy scenarios meeting stringent CO_2 constraints – cost-effective fuel choices in the transportation sector.' *Energy Policy* 31(10): 961–76.

Azar C., Lindgren K., Larson E., Möllersten K. (2006). 'Carbon capture and storage from fossil fuels and biomass – Costs and potential role in stabilizing the atmosphere'. *Climatic Change* 74(1–3): 47–79.

Azar, C., Schneider S. (2002). 'Are the economic costs of stabilising the atmosphere prohibitive?' *Ecological Economics*, 42: 73–80.

Bandivadekar A., Bodek K., Evans C., Groode T., Heywood J., Kasseris E., Kromer M., Weiss M. (2008). On the road in 2035 – 'Reducing Transportation's Petroleum Consumption and GHG emissions', Report No. LFEE 2008–05 RP, Laboratory for Energy and Environment, Massachusetts Institute of Technology, Cambridge, USA.

Barnett J., Dessai S. (2002). 'Articles 4.8 and 4.9 of the UNFCCC: adverse effects and the impacts of response measures.' *Climate Policy* 2(2–3): 231–39.

Bartsch U., Müller B. (2000). *Fossil fuels in a changing climate*, Oxford University Press, Oxford, U.K.

Berg E., Kverndokk S., Rosendahl K.E. (1997). 'Market power, international CO_2 taxation and oil wealth'. *Energy Journal*, 18 (4): 33–71.

Bernstein P., Montgomery D., Rutherford T., Yang G. (1999). 'Effects of restrictions on international permit trading: The MSMRT model.' *The Energy Journal* (special issue edited by Weyant, J.): 221–56.

BP, 2010, BP 'Statistical Review of World Energy 2009', downloadable via www.bp.com.

Brandt A.R., Farrell A.F. (2007). 'Scraping the Bottom of the Barrel: Greenhouse gas emissions consequences of a transition to low-quality and synthetic petroleum resources'. *Climatic Change*, 84 (3–4): 241–63.

Brooker A, Thornton M. (2010). 'Technology improvement pathways to cost-effective vehicle electrification SAE 2010 World Congress Detroit', April, 2010.

Brown M.A. (2004). 'Obstacles to Energy Efficiency', *Encyclopedia of Energy* 4: 465–75.

CCC (2011) 'Chalmers Climate Calculator', available at www.chalmers.se/ee/ccc.

Charpentier A.D., Bergerson J.A., MacLean H.L. (2009). 'Understanding the Canadian oil sands industry's greenhouse gas emissions,' Environmental Research Letter 4.

Clarke L., Edmonds J., Krey V., Richels R., Rose S., Tavoni M., 2009, 'International climate policy architectures: Overview of the EMF 22 International Scenarios', 31(Supplement 2): S64-S81.

Concawe (2006). 'Well-to-wheels analysis of future automotive fuels and power trains in the European context'. Well-to-Tank report Version 2b, May 2006.

Dargay J.M., Gately D. (2010). 'World oil demand's shift toward faster growing and less price-responsive products and regions', *Energy Policy* 38(10): 6261–77.

Depledge J. (2008). 'Striving for No: Saudi Arabia in the Climate Change Regime', *Global Environmental Politics* 8(4): 9–35.

Edenhofer, O., Knopf, B., Barker, T., Baumstark L., Belevrat E., Chateay B., Criqui P., Isaar M., Kitous A., Kypreos S., Leimback M., Lessmann K., Magné B., Scieciu S., Turton H., van Vuuren D.P. (2010). 'The Economics of Low Stabilization: Model Comparison of Mitigation Strategies and Costs'. *The Energy Journal*, 31(Special Issue), 11–48.

EIA (2010). 'International Energy Outlook (2010)'. Energy Information Administration, US Department of Energy, Washington DC.

EPA (2006). 'Global Mitigation of Non-CO_2 Greenhouse Gases', EPA Report 430-R-06–005, United States Environmental Protection Agency.

Fargione J., Hill J., Tilman D., Polasky S., Hawthorne P. (2008). 'Land Clearing and the Biofuel Carbon Debt', *Science* 319(5867): 1235–38.

Fee E., Johansson D.J.A., Lowe J., Marbaix P., Meinshausen M., Smith B. (2010). 'Scientific perspectives after Copenhagen', Report written for EG Science.

Fisher, B.S., Nakicenovic N., Alfsen K., Corfee Morlot J., de la Chesnaye F., Hourcade J.-Ch., Jiang K., Kainuma M., La Rovere E., Matysek A., Rana A., Riahi K., Richels R., Rose S., van Vuuren D., Warren R. (2007). 'Issues related to mitigation in the long term context', In *Climate Change 2007:*

Mitigation. Contribution of Working Group III to the Fourth Assessment Report of the Inter-governmental Panel on Climate Change [B. Metz, O.R. Davidson, P.R. Bosch, R. Dave, L.A. Meyer (eds)], Cambridge University Press, Cambridge, UK.

Gately D., Huntington H.G. (2002). 'The asymmetric effects of changes in price and income on energy and oil demand'. *Energy Journal* 23(1): 19–55.

Gerlagh R., (2010). 'Too Much Oil. Forthcoming in CESifo' *Economic Studies*, doi:10.1093/cesifo/ifq004.

Gerlagh R., Kuik O. (2007). 'Carbon leakage with international technology spillover', Nota di Lavoro 33.2007.

Ghanem S., Lounnas R., Rennand G. (1999). 'The impact of emissions trading on OPEC', *OPEC Review* 23: 79–112.

Grubb M. (2001). 'Who's afraid of atmospheric stabilization? Making the link between energy resources and climate change.' *Energy Policy* 29: 837–45.

Gul T., Kypreos S., Turton H., Barreto L. (2009). 'An energy-economic scenario analysis of alternative fuels for personal transport using the Global Multi-regional MARKAl model (GMM)', *Energy* 34: 1423–37.

Hamelinck C.N. Faaij A.P.C. (2006). 'Outlook for advanced biofuels.' *Energy Policy* 34(17): 3268–83.

Hamilton J.D. (2009). 'Understanding Crude Oil Prices', *The Energy Journal* 30(2): 179–206.

Harvey L.D.D. (2007). 'Dangerous anthropogenic interference, dangerous climatic change, and harmful climatic change: non-trivial distinctions with significant policy implications'. *Climatic Change*, 82(1–2): 1–25.

Haszeldine R.S. (2009). 'Carbon capture and Storage: How green can black be?' *Science* 325: 164–66.

Hedenus F., Karlsson S., Azar C., Sprei F. (2010). 'Cost-effective energy carriers for transport – The role of energy supply system in a carbon-constrained world', *International Journal of Hydrogen Energy* 35: 4638–51.

Hedenus, F. (2008). 'On the Road to Climate Neutral Freight Transportation – a scientific feasibility study.' *Vägverket Publication 2008: 92.*

Höök M., Zittel W., Schindler J., Aleklett K. (2010). 'Global coal production outlooks based on a logistic model', *Fuel* 89(11): 3546–58.

ICCT (2011). 'The regulatory Engine: How smart Policy Drives vehicle innovation,' The International Council on Clean Transportation, available via www.theicct.org.

IEA (2005). 'Resources to Reserves – Oil and Gas Technologies for the Energy Markets of the Future, International Energy Agency', IEA/OECD, Paris, France.

——(2008). 'World Energy Outlook 2008. International Energy Agency', IEA/OECD, Paris, France.

——(2010a). 'World Energy Outlook 2010. International Energy Agency', IEA/OECD, Paris, France.

——(2010b). 'Statistics & Balances, International Energy Agency', available via www.iea.org

Jaffe A.B., Stavins R.N. (1994). 'The energy-efficiency gap What does it mean?' *Energy Policy* 22(10): 804–10.

Jaramillo P., Samaras C., Wakeley H., Meisterling K. (2009). 'Greenhousegas implications of using coal for transportation: Lifecycle assessment of coal-to-liquids, plug-in hybrids, and hydrogen pathways.' *Energy Policy* 37 2689–95.

Johansson D.J.A. (2010). 'Temperature stabilization, ocean heat uptake and radiative forcing overshoot profiles.' Accepted for publication in *Climatic Change*.

Johansson D.J.A., Azar C, Lindgren K., Persson T.A. (2009) 'OPEC strategies and oil rent in climate conscious world', *The Energy Journal*, 30(3): 23–50.

Johansson D.J.A., Azar C. (2007). 'A scenario based analysis of land use competition between bioenergy and food production in the US,' *Climatic Change*, 82(3–4): 267–91.

Kharecha P.A., Kutscher C.F., Hansen J.E., Mazria E. (2010). 'Options for near-term phaseout of CO_2 emissions from coal use in the United States'. *Environmental Science and Technology*, 44, 4050–62.

Kitous A., Criqui P., Bellevrat E., Château B. (2010). 'Transformation Patterns of the Worldwide Energy System – Scenarios for the Century with the POLES Model', *The Energy Journal*, 31(Special Issue): 49–82.

Kjärstad J., Johnsson F. (2009). 'Resources and future supply of oil,' *Energy Policy* 37(2): 441–64.

Loumi M. (2009). 'Bargaining in the bazaar – Common ground for a post-2012 climate agreement?' Briefing paper 48, The Finnish Institute of International Affairs.

Manne A.S., Rutherford T.F. (1994). 'International Trade in Oil, Gas and Carbon Emissions Rights: An Intertemporal General Equilibrium Model'. *Energy Journal*, 15(1), 57–76.

Matthews H. D., Caldeira K. (2008). 'Stabilizing climate requires near-zero emissions'. *Geophysical Research Letters*, 35, L04705.

McKibbin W., Ross T., Shackleton R., Wilcoxen P. (1999). 'Emissions trading, capital flows and the Kyoto Protocol.' *The Energy Journal* (special issue edited by J. Weyant): 287–335.

Meehl G.A., Stocker T.F., Collins W.D., Friedlingstein P., Gaye A.T., Gregory J.M., Kitoh A., Knutti R., Murphy J.M., Noda A., Raper S.C.B., Watterson I.G., Weaver A.J., Zhao Z.-C. (2007). 'Global Climate Projections'. In *Climate Change 2007: Mitigation. Contribution of Working Group III to the Fourth Assessment Report of the Intergovernmental Panel on Climate Change* [B. Metz, O.R. Davidson, P.R. Bosch, R. Dave, L.A. Meyer (eds)], Cambridge University Press, Cambridge, United Kingdom and New York, NY, USA.

NRC (2010). 'Climate Stabilization Targets: Emissions, Concentrations, and Impacts over Decades to Millennia', National Research Council of the National Academies, National Academy Press, Washington DC, USA.

Offer G.J., Constestabile M., Howey D.A., Clauge R., Brandon N.P. (2011). 'Techno-economic and behavioural analysis of battery electric, hydrogen fuel cell and hybrid vehicles in a future sustainable road transport system in the UK'. *Energy Policy* [forthcoming]

Oreskes N., Conway E.M. (2010). *Merchants of Doubt – How a Handful of Scientists Obscured the Truth on Issues from Tobacco Smoke to Global Warming*, Bloomsbury Press, New York, USA.

Persson T.A, Azar C., Lindgren K., Johansson D.J.A. (2007), 'Major oil exporters may profit rather than lose, in a carbon constrained world'. *Energy Policy* 35: 6346–53.

Radetzki M. (2002). 'What will happen to the producer prices for fossil fuels if Kyoto is implemented?' *Energy Policy* 30: 357–69.

REN21, 2010, 'Renewables Global Status Report 2010', downloadable via www.ren21.net/.

Ringius L., Torvanger A., Underdal A. (2002). 'Burden Sharing and Fairness Principles in International Climate Policy', *International Environmental Agreements: Politics, Law and Economics* 2(1): 1–22.

Searchinger T., Heimlich R., Houghton R.A., Dong F., Elobeid A., Fabiosa J., Tokgoz S., Hayes D., Yu T.-H. (2008). 'Use of U.S. Croplands for Biofuels Increases Greenhouse Gases Through Emissions from Land-Use Change', *Science* 319(5867):1238–40.

Sims R.E.H., Schock R.N., Adegbululgbe A., Fenhann J., Konstantinaviciute I., Moomaw W., Nimir H. B., Schlamadinger B., Torres-Martínez J. Turner C., Uchiyama Y., Vuori S.J.V., Wamukonya N., Zhang X. (2007) 'Energy Supply', In *Climate Change 2007: Mitigation. Contribution of Working Group III to the Fourth Assessment Report of the Inter-governmental Panel on Climate Change* [B. Metz, O.R. Davidson, P.R. Bosch, R. Dave, L.A. Meyer (eds)], Cambridge University Press, Cambridge, UK.

Sinn, H.W. (2008). 'Public policies against global warming: A supply side approach', *International Tax and Public Finance*, 15, 4, 360–94.

Small K.A., Van Dender K. (2007). 'Fuel efficiency and motor vehicle travel: The declining rebound effect', *Energy Journal* 28(1): 25–51

Smith J.B., Schneider S.H., Oppenheimer M., Yohe G.W., Hare W., Mastrandrea M.D., Patwardhan A., Burton I., Corfee-Morlot J., Magadza C.H.D., Füssel H.M., Pittock A. B., Rahman A., Suarez A., van Ypersele J.-P. (2009). 'Assessing dangerous climate change through an update of the Intergovernmental Panel on Climate Change (IPCC)' "reasons for concern" *PNAS* 106(11): 4133–37.

Smith P., Gregory P.J., van Vuuren D., Obersteiner M., Havlík P., Rounsevell M., Woods J., Stehfest E., Bellarby J. (2010). 'Competition for land', *Phil. Trans. R. Soc.* B 27 365 (1554): 2941–57

Sorrell S., Speirs J., Bentley R., Brandt A., Miller R. (2009). 'An assessment of the evidence for a near-term peak in global oil production'. UK Energy Research Centre.

Sprei F., Karlsson S., Holmberg J. (2008). 'Better performance or lower fuel consumption? Technological development in the Swedish new-car fleet' 1975–2002, Transportation research part D 13: 75–85.

Stern N.H. (2007). *The Economics of Climate Change: The Stern Review*, Cambridge University Press, Cambridge, U.K.

Sterner T. (2002). 'Policy Instruments for Environmental and Natural Resource Management', RFF Press in collaboration with the World Bank and Sida, Washington DC, ISBN: 1-891853-13-9 & ISBN: 1-891853-12-0.

——(2007). 'Fuel taxes: An important instrument for climate policy', *Energy Policy* 35(6): 3194–3202.

Sterner, T. (2010). 'Voluntary Pledges and Green Growth in the Post-Copenhagen Climate', Speech to the World Bank Annual ABCDE meeting in Stockholm, June 2010.

Sterner, T. (2011). 'Fuel Taxes and the Poor: The distributional effects of gasoline taxation and their implications for climate policy', RFF Press, [Forthcoming]

Thielemann T., Schmidt S., Gerling J.P. (2007). 'Lignite and hard coal: Energy suppliers for world needs until the year 2100 – An outlook.' *International Journal of Coal Geology*, 72(1): 1–14.

UNFCCC (1992). 'United Nations Framework Convention on Climate Change'.

——(1997). 'Kyoto protocol to the United Nations Framework Convention on Climate Change'.

——(2010). 'Cancun Agreement – Outcome of the work of the Ad Hoc Working Group on long-term Cooperative Action under the Convention'.

USGS (2000). 'U.S. Geological Survey World Petroleum Assessment 2000 – Description and Results.', U.S. Geological Survey Digital Data Series – DDS-60, available via http://pubs.usgs.gov/dds/dds-060/.

van den Hove S., le Menestrel M., De Bettignies H.C. (2002). 'The oil industry and climate change: strategies and ethical dilemmas.' *Climate Policy* 2: 3–18.

van Ruijven B., van Vuuren D.P. (2009). 'Oil and natural gas prices and greenhouse gas emission mitigation', *Energy Policy* 37: 4797–4808.

van Vuuren D.P., Isaac M., den Elzen M.G.J., Stehfest E., van Vliet J. (2010). 'Low Stabilization Scenarios and Implications for Major World Regions from an Integrated Assessment Perspective', *The Energy Journal*, 31(Special Issue), 165–91.

Wigley T.M.L. (1991). 'Could reducing fossil-fuel emissions cause global warming?' *Nature* 349, 503–506.

——(2005). 'The Climate Change Commitment', *Science* 307(5716): 1766–69.

von Helmolt R., Eberle, U. (2007). 'Fuel cell vehicles: Status 2007' *Journal of Power Sources* 165 833–43.

Zickfeld K., Eby M., Matthews H.D., Weaver A.J. (2009). 'Setting cumulative emissions targets to reduce the risk of dangerous climate change', *PNAS* 106 (38) 16129–34.

Index

Bold page numbers indicate figures; italics indicate tables. Not all cited authors are listed in the index; readers requiring complete lists of cited works and authors should consult the notes and references at the end of each chapter.

1973 oil revolution, and OAPEC 285–86

Abadan refinery 267–68
abatement costs 416–17
Abbuehl, Christopher 241
aboveground factors 66, 67
Abu Dhabi 127
Abu Dhabi Investment Authority (ADIA) 371–72; portfolio overview by asset class *371*; portfolio overview by region *371*
access to energy resources 109
accountability 160
Acemoglu, D. 339
Afghanistan 33
Africa: China in 356; Chinese energy security 37; corruption 159–61; economic impacts of oil 153–55; energy crisis 152–53; foreign direct investment 153; governance 157, **158**; instability 150; natural resources and governance *159*; oil and conflict 161–63; oil and policy process 159; oil dependence *153*, 153–54; personalized rule 154; petroleum refinery output *152*; political impacts of oil 155–63; resource curse 149–50, 153; review of oil sector 150–53; security 155–56; stability 155; state building 156; summary and conclusions 163–64; top crude exporters *151* see also sub-Saharan Africa; individual countries
aid 160–61
al-Ahmed al-Jaber al-Sabah, Jaber 369
al-Ahmed al-Sabah, Jaber 369
al Naimi, Ali 50, 129
al-Salem al-Sabah, Abdullah 369
Algiers Summit 82
Aliyev, Heidar 191, 194
Aliyev, Ilham 194, 196, 201
Allen, M. 363

alternative energy 7, 15; expansion of 421
aluminium 127
American Recovery and Reinvestment Act 2009 221–22
anchors and storms 99–100
Anglo-Iraq Treaty 251
Anglo-Persian Oil Company (APOC) 31
Angola 345; conflict and instability 161–62; economic impacts of oil 154
Apollo Alliance 233–35, 246
Arab oil embargo 113–15
Aramco: flow of funds 47–48; independence 49, 50; major projects 49; management of funds 50; public relations 50–51 *see also* Saudi Arabia
Arctic: geopolitical competition 38, 40–41; technological and environmental challenges 40
Argentina 175–76; natural gas imports **176**
armed conflict *see* conflict and instability
authoritarianism: Egypt 305; Russia 8
Auty, R. 337, 338, 339, 341, 342, 343
Aykut, D. 325, 327
Azerbaijan 7, 191, 194–96, 201, 202

Baker, James A. III 136
balance of payments 381
balancing budgets 344
Barbary, V. 364, 367
barter deals 82
Basra 257
Basra Oil Terminal 256
Basra Petroleum Company (BPC) 250
battery electric vehicles (BEVs) 238, 240, 425
Beblawi, H. 206
benchmarks, reference pricing 97
Berdymukhammedov, Gurbanguly 200, 201–2
bilateral relations 82
Bilderberg meeting 391

435

Index

bin Sultan al-Nahyan, Zayed 371
biofuels 222, 232, 239, 424–25
Bolivia 172–73; natural gas exports **173**
Bongo, Omar 157
bootleggers and Baptists metaphor 224
boundary disputes, Arctic 40–41
Brazil 8–9, 173–75; internationalization 331; oil production **174** *see also* Petrobras
Brent market 96–97
Bretton Woods II 391
Bretton Woods system 375; demise 113, 376–78
Brunei 208
budgets, balancing 344
Bureau of Ocean Energy Management, Regulation and Enforcement (BOEMRE) 16
Bush, George H.W. 34, 136
Bush, George W. 34, 35–36, 222
buy-back 269, 271–73, 274, 275–76, 277, 278–79

Cambodia 215
Cancun agreement 357, 427
cap-and-trade 17, 230–31, 357, 416
capital-scarce/labour-surplus economies 344
capital-surplus economies 344
carbon emissions 357; global energy supply scenario **421**; reduction 415; regulation 427; and temperature change 418 *see also* greenhouse gases
carbon taxing 17
Carter Doctrine 33–34, 116–17; extension 35–36
Carter, Jimmy 136, 137, 239
Caruana, J. 363
Carvalho, F. 327, 330
Caspian region: context and overview 191–94; demographic data, output and income 193; foreign direct investment *195*; growth in GDP *197*; international relations 200–202; oil and gas production *192*; regional hegemony 192, 194; summary and conclusions 202
Caspian Sea: Russian energy security 38; US energy security 35
Center for International Science Information Network 127
Central Asia, Chinese energy security 37
Chad 345
champagne effect 13
Cheney, Dick 34
Chin, E. 364, 367
China 9; in Africa 356; context and overview 401; East China Sea 39–40; effect on oil markets 409–10; energy overview 402–3; energy security 403–4; geopolitical initiatives 36–38; global imbalances 391; global importance 385; in global market 405–7; and global oil governance 354–55, 356; growth nodes 408–9; interdependence 408; in international market 404; investment 390, 406–7; in Iran 274; in Kazakhstan 198–99; as major player 407–8; mixed ownership NOCs 55–56; new footholds 407; oil imports 19, 403; patterns and trends in global market 401–2; in regional markets 407–9; summary and conclusions 410–11; transport 14; and USA 385; Western Development Strategy 408–9
China National Energy and Strategy Policy (NESP) 404
China National Offshore Oil Corporation (CNOOC) 403–5, 406, 407
China National Petroleum Corporation (CNPC) 404–5, 406
China Petroleum and Chemical Corporation (Sinopec) 404–5, 406
Churchill, Winston 31
Clean Air Act (USA) 17
climate change 5, 6, 357; abatement costs 416–17; context and overview 415–16; essential facts 417–19; Global Energy Transition (GET) model 419–22; global policies 416–17; lack of effective legislation 17; oil producers and policy 427–29; possible impact 18; reducing conventional fuel use 422–27; short-term policies 429; use of oil 419–22
climate change, Middle East: context and overview 121–22; environmental stress 122–27; foreign policy implications 131–32; predicted effects 121; regional security 130–31; regional stability 128–30; vulnerability 127–28
climate sensitivity 417–18
Clinton, Bill 34, 35
Clinton, Hillary 117, 118
co-operative international storage 102, 104
coal, proved reserves 419
coal-to-liquids (CTL) 11, 421, 423–24
coastal states, offshore boundaries 39
Collective Security Treaty Organization (CSTO) 38
Collier, P. 76, 207, 211, 338
Colombia 176–77; oil production **177**
commodity windfall rents, managing 343
common oil policy, Gulf Co-operation Council (GCC) 290
company ownership 264–65
competition, China's role in 406
comprehensive intergenerational oil fund 188–89
compressed natural gas (CNG) transport 15
Conference on International Economic Co-operation (CIEC) 82
conflict and instability: Africa 150, 161–63; context and overview 73; difficulties of resolution 75–77; MENA region 184; oil wealth as trigger 74–75; Southeast Asia 211
consumer government taxation 84–85
consumer tastes 16
consumers, energy expenditure 91

consumption and production patterns 354–55
conventional fuel use, reduction 422–27
conventional oil 11, 64
cooperation, producers and consumers 4–5
corn ethanol 239
corporate average fuel economy (CAFE) standards 223, 238–39
corruption 6; Africa 150, 159–61; Iran 275–76; Iraq 253, 256; Kazakhstan 196; NOCs 56–57; Oil-for-Food Programme 255; and oil wealth 74
cotton, Turkmenistan 199
crude oil prices, structural instability 5
currency reserves 389–90; mobilization 386
current account balances *397–8*
current account deficits/surpluses 381, 386, 392

Dargay, J.M. 419, 426
Das, U. 363
Davis, J. 363, 367
de-institutionalization, Africa 155
Deal of the Century 194
deep-offshore fields, problems of 39
deep-water petroleum 65
Deepwater Horizon disaster 16–17
demand: elasticity 139; and prices 68–69, 91; projected growth 126, 227, 419
demand destruction 91
demand forecasting 91
demand security 102–3, 104
democracy, Southeast Asia 210–11
dependency, mutual 140
deprivation 6
desalination 125
development and service contracts 257
development assistance, Saudi Arabia 288
Dhawan, R. 140–41
diamonds, conflict and instability 75
disruptive technologies 16
Doerr, John 228, 229
Doha, economic development 127
dollar assets 389–90
dollar pegging 392
dollars: dominance 392; illiquidity 392; international trade 392; as pricing currency 391
Dominick, Jeffrey 241
drilling techniques 66
dual track reform 345–46
Dubai, economic development 126
Dunaway, S. 377
Dutch Disease 4, 74, 154, 183, 299–300, 317, 338, 342, 343

early reform zones (ERZs) 345
East China Sea, territorial claims 39–40
economic development, Middle East 126–27
economic growth, Middle East 126–27
economic policies, MENA region 183

Egypt 8; assessment of strategy 307–8; business efficiency 303–4; context and overview 295–97; domestic politics 304–5; economic costs of rents 305–6; economic impacts of hydrocarbons 297–304; employment 301; energy consumption 297; energy efficiency 300–301; gas dependency 297–98; governance 303; master plan 297; ownership 306–7; patronage 304; political impacts of hydrocarbons 304–7; prices 298–99, 302–3; subsidies 306; subsidies and transfers 300; total factor productivity (TFP) 301–2
Eichengreen, B. 377
elasticity of demand 139
electric cars 236–37
electric transport 14–15
electric vehicles 425
electricity production 16
embargoes, selective 137–38
emergency supply mechanisms 354–55
emissions **423**
Emissions Trading System (ETS) 357
energy demand, projected growth 61
energy-economic model studies 427
energy efficiency, comparative **316**
energy efficiency standards 17
energy expenditure, consumers 91
Energy Independence and Security Act 2007 (EISA) (USA) 222
Energy Information Agency 240
energy insecurity, responses to 113–14
Energy Intelligence Administration (US) 92, 126, 419
energy policies, USA 7
energy security 5–6; China 403–4; context and overview 109–10; defence of market 115–18; defining 109; effects of competition 111; and global markets 115; Hubbert's peak 110–12; meaning of 111–12; USA 5–6
enhanced oil recovery (EOR) 13–14, 66
environmental accounting 343
environmental adaptation 128
Environmental Protection Act (USA) 17
environmental stress, Middle East 121–22, 122–27
environmental vulnerability, Middle East 127–28, *128*
equity 187
ethanol 222, 231–33, 239, 330
Ethiopia, Italian invasion 112
EU Emissions Trading Scheme (EU ETS) 426
Eurasian Economic Community 200
European Economic Community (EEC), energy strategy 82
European Union, oil imports 19
euros, oil pricing 391
Eurozone 375–76
exhaustible resources, as state property 181

Index

export diversification 186
external financing, MENA region 185
extra-heavy oil 64–65, 423
extraction: capital-intensiveness 342; increasing level of 13–14
Extractive Industries Transparency Initiative 76

Failed States Index 157
Fargione, J. 232
Fifth Economic and Social Development Plan (Iran) 264
financial markets 375–76
financialization 97–99
fiscal discipline 74
Fischer-Tropsch process 11
flexible fuel vehicles (FFVs) 233
floating exchange rates 376
flow of funds **48**, 49–50, **51**; national oil companies (NOCs) 47–48
Ford, Gerald 137
foreign aid 160–61
foreign asset accumulation 390
foreign direct investment: Africa 153; Caspian region *195*; Iran 269, 271–73, 276–77; Iraq 257; Russia 318
foreign interests, in Kazakhstan 198–99
foreign interference, MENA region 185–86
foreign policy implications, of climate change 131–32
foreign support, MENA region 184–85
forward markets 85
fossil fuels: and climate change 415; proved reserves 418–19; reserves and estimated additional recoverable resources **420**; supply **422**
fracking 14
France, in Iran 271–73
free rider problem 355
Freedom House 157, 207, 210–11
Freitas, A. 329
Friedman, Thomas 242–46, 381
Frum, David 143
fuel cell vehicles 234
fuel economy 427
fuels, manufacture 11–12
funds: flow of 47–48, **48**, 49–50, **51**; management of 48–50
Furtado, A. 329
fusion energy 16
future demand 67

G20 393
Gabon, economic impacts of oil 153–54, 155
Gaddy, C. 317–18
gas-to-liquids (GTL) 11
Gately, D. 419, 426
GDP growth per head *341*
Geithner, Timothy 388
Gelb, A.H. 343
General Agreement on Tariffs and Trade (GATT) 82
General Reserve Fund (GRF) (Kuwait) 369
geo-green economics 242–46
geopolitics 4; Carter Doctrine 33; context and overview 30–31; inter-war 32; new arenas 38–41; origins of 31–33; Persian Gulf 33–34; summary and conclusions 41; US and Persia 33; US and Saudi Arabia 32–33; World War I 31–32; World War II 32
George, Henry 143
Ghazvinian, J. 154, 157
Gingrich, Newt 245
Giscard, D'Estaing, Valery 82
Glaeser, E.L. 339
global business structure, global oil governance 355–56
global energy dilemma 3
global energy supply scenario **421**
Global Energy Transition (GET) model 419–22
global financial crisis 393
global governance: context and overview 349–50 *see also* governance
global imbalances 377, 378, **383**, 391; 21st century 383–86, **384**; financing 382–83
global markets: Africa in 152; China in 405–7; context and overview 90–92; and energy security 115; patterns and trends 401–2; strategic advantage 112–13; vulnerability of producers 131 *see also* prices
global mean surface temperature 415, 416, 417
global oil, as governance issue 350
global oil governance 9; actors in 350–51; challenges to market 353–54; consumption and production patterns 354–55; energy transition and low carbon 356–57; global business structure 355–56; non-state actors 351; prices and investment 357–58; role of markets 352–53; summary and conclusions 358
global warming, attitudes to 17–18
goals, NOCs and IOCs 59
gold 392
Goldstein, A. 325, 327, 330
Gore, Al 229, 232, 240, 241
governance: Africa 157, **158**; Egypt 303; Middle East 116; and natural resources *159*; Southeast Asia 211–12 *see also* global governance
government-controlled reserves 69
government policy, uncertainties 16–17
government revenues, from oil products 84–85
governments, price-making power 95
green jobs 246
greenhouse gases 357; effects 417; and passenger cars 226–28; pricing 416–17; reduction 416 *see also* carbon emissions
Greenspan, Alan 135

growth nodes, China 408–9
Gulf Co-operation Council (GCC) 366; common oil policy 290; sovereign wealth funds (SWFs) *see* sovereign wealth funds (SWFs); water demand 123–26
Gulf states: ecological and carbon footprints *127*; stakeholders 130 *see also* Middle East
Gulf War (1st) 136

Hamilton, J.D. 68
heavy oils 11, 12, 64
Hesse, H. 363
high rent competitive industrialization development model 340–41
high-rent staple trap 339
Hoeffler, A. 207, 211
Hotelling, H. 67, 81
Hubbert, M. King 62, 110–11
Hubbert's peak *see* peak oil
Hulst, Noe van 83
human rights: Africa 157; Iraq 252–53
human security 109
Huntingdon, H.G. 426
Hussein, Saddam 136, 139–40, 252–55
hybrid cars 236, 237–41
hybrid electric vehicles (HEVs) 238
hydrogen 425

Ickes, B. 317–18
ideology 79–80
IEA 13
Immelt, Jeffrey 228–29, 230
import substitution 8
Import Substitution Industrialization program 326
India: and global oil governance 354–55; global oil governance 356
Indonesia 208–9, 343
instability: Africa 150; Middle East 115–18; of oil-producing countries 4, 18–19; oil transport 19–20; prices 90–91, 92–93
institutions, MENA region 180–82
insurgencies 74–75; tools for ending 75
integration, of market 115
interdependence, China 408
interest groups, USA 228–29
Intergovernmental Panel on Climate Change (IPCC) 121
International Energy Agency (IEA) 81, 227, 419; global oil governance 351, 354–55; hostility to OPEC 81; principles for energy policy 81
International Energy Forum (IEF) 83–84; Cancun Summit 86; duplication of role 87; objectives 86
International Energy Outlook 92
international financial institutions (IFIs) 344
international financial system: conspiracy theories 391–92; context and overview 375–76; current accounts of oil net exporters **385**; demise of Bretton Woods 376–78; global imbalances 377, 378, 382–83, **383**; global imbalances in 21st century 383–86, **384**; oil assets, size and allocation 386–90; petrodollar meltdown 381–83; petrodollar recycling 375, 378–81, 391; role of oil exporters 391, 393
International Monetary Fund (IMF) 377, 378–79, 393
international monetary system 9
international oil companies (IOCs) 4; and climate policy 427–28; context and overview 45–46; dependence/independence 57–58; government intervention 57; in Iran 269, 271–73, 274–75, 276–77, 278–79; nationalistic pressures 57; summary and conclusions 58–59; variations 57; working with NOCs 53–55 *see also* national oil companies (NOCs)
international pressure, limiting effects of oil curse 77–78
international relations, Caspian region 200–202
international relations (IR) theory 350, 351
international reserve currency 377
internationalization, Brazil 329, 331
investment: alternative energy 229–30; China 406–7; in future supply 68; global oil governance 357–58; lack of 49
Iran 8; agreement with Kazakhstan 273–74; agreement with Turkmenistan 274; buy-back 269, 271–73, 274, 275–76, 277, 278–79; context and overview 262; corruption 275–76; early post-revolutionary period 266–68; effects of Iran-Iraq War 268; first Five Year Plan 268–70; fourth Five Year Plan 277–79; gas consumption 263–64; gas reinjection programme *265*, 265–66; gasoline crisis 279–80; international oil companies (IOCs) 269, 271–73, 274–75, 276–77, 278–79; lack of investment 49; management of oil industry 52; nuclear capability 118, 276; oil and gas statistics *263*, *267*; oil field productivity *276*; Petroleum Council 278; petroleum product consumption *279*; pre-revolutionary oil industry 262–64; pre-revolutionary planning and policy 264–66; relations with USA 276; second Five Year Plan 270–74; summary and conclusions 280–82; third Five Year Plan 274–77; USA freezing of assets 380–81 *see also* Persia
Iran-Iraq War 34
Iran-Libya Sanctions Act (ILSA) (USA) 272, 274
Iranian Oil, Gas and Petrochemical Forum 274
Iraq 7; conflict and instability 257–58; Constitution 257; context and overview 249; corruption 253, 256; effects of re-emergence 355; effects of US invasion 142; foreign direct investment 257; ideology 258; insurgency 256; invasion 2003 118; mismanagement 49; mistrust and suspicion 258; nationalism 251–52; oil

industry 1925–58 249–51; oil industry 1958–79 251–52; oil industry 1979–2003 252–55; post-Saddam Hussein 255–58; sanctions 34, 253–55; summary and conclusions 258–59; working with IOCs 54–55
Iraqi Petroleum Company (IPC) 250, 251–52
Islam 181, 187
Islamic radicalism 118
Italy: invasion of Ethiopia 112; in Iran 274

Japan: East China Sea 39–40; US embargo 112–13
Jeske, K. 140–41
Joint Oil Data Initiative (JODI) 84, 86, 358
joint ventures 351
Jordan, fresh water availability 124
Jubail 291–92
Jubail II 291–92

Kammen, Daniel 237
Kansteiner, Walter 35
Karl, T. 207
Kashagan megafield 198
Kazakhstan 7, 191, 196–99, 200–201, 202; agreement with Iran 273–74
KazMunaiGas (KMG) 198
kerogen 11; extraction costs 12
Kerry-Lieberman cap and trade bill 231
Khan, M. 339
Khosla, Vinod 233
Kimberley Process 75
Kissinger, Henry 81, 136
Klare, M. 117
Kleiner Perkins Caufield and Byers 228–29
Kurdistan Regional Government (KRG) 257–58
Kuwait 380; invasion 83, 139, 253–54, 381; sovereign wealth funds (SWFs) 369–70
Kuwait Investment Authority (KIA) 369–70, 388
Kyoto Protocols 17, 427

Latin America 6; context and overview 168; summary and conclusions 177–78 see also individual countries
Latin American debt crisis 381
legal institutions 180
Lehman Brothers 86
Limited Access Order societies 339
liquid fuels, reducing use 426–27
liquidity 98–99
lobbying 230, 233–36
long-term equilibrium prices, attempts to define 93–94
Lopez-Murphy, P. 344
low-rent competitive industrialization trajectory 339–40, **340**
Lowi, M. 207
Luciani, G. 206
Luft, Gar 242, 245

Mabro, Robert 84
Mahdavy, H. 206
Malaysia 209, 343
Malthus, Thomas 111
management of funds 48–50
market forces 79–80
market leverage 116
market supply, China's role in 406
market tastes 16
markets: defence of 115–18; effect of China 409–10; effects of climate change planning 129–30; global see global markets; global oil governance 352–53; integration 351; restraint 126
Maugeri, L. 67
MENA region: comprehensive intergenerational oil fund 188–89; conflict and instability 184; context and overview 180; economic policies 183; external financing 185; foreign interference 185–86; foreign support 184–85; military expenditure 183–84; oil and institutions 180–82; oil curse 181–82; policy-making 182–85; protests 189; summary and conclusions 189; ways to address problems 186–88 see also Middle East
Mesopotamia, control of 31–32
Mexico 168–70, 287, 381; natural gas imports **170**; oil production **169**
Middle East 5, 6–7; agricultural development 124; aluminium 127; aquifer depletion 123; climate change see climate change, Middle East; desalination 125; economic growth 126–27; environmental vulnerability 127–28, *128*; fresh water availability *123*; instability 115–18; oil revenues 126; population *125*; water demand 123–26; water scarcity 122–26 see also Gulf states; MENA region
migration, Middle East 131
militarization, of energy ties 34–36, 37
military deployment, East China Sea 40
military expenditure, MENA region 183–84
Minerals and Mines Management Service (MMS) 16
mixed ownership NOCs 55–56
modernization, Russia 320–22
momentum trading 98
morality, international oil companies (IOCs) 46
Mosul Petroleum Company (MPC) 250
Mozambique, conflict and instability 161

National Fund for the Republic of Kazakhstan (NFRK) 199
National Iranian Gas Company (NIGC) 264, 267–68, 278
National Iranian Oil Company (NIOC) 264–65, 268–69, 271–72, 276–77, 278
National Iranian Oil Refining and Distribution Company (NIORDC) 278

Index

national oil companies (NOCs) 4, 50; context and overview 45–46; corruption 56–57; dependence/independence 47, 51–52, 56; flow of funds 47–48, **48**, 49–50, **51**; global oil governance 355–56; government interference 52–53; hybrid forms 55–56; internationalization 58; lack of investment 49; management of funds 48–50; mixed ownership 55–56; success 47; summary and conclusions 58–59; working with IOCs 53–55 *see also* international oil companies (IOCs)
nationalism, Iraq 251–52
nationalization 264
natural gas 424; East China Sea 39; proved reserves 418–19
natural gas liquids (NGL) 65
natural resources, and governance *159*
Nazarbayev, Nursultan Abishuly 191, 200–201
near oil 11
"New Energy for America" report 233–34
new political economy, resource wealth 206–7
new producers 73
Nigeria 345; Chinese energy security 37; conflict and instability 161; debt crisis 381; oil spills 17; US energy security 36
Nixon, Richard 81, 136, 239
Niyazov, Saparmurat 191–92, 199–200, 202
nonconventional resources 64–66
North, D. 339
North South Dialogue 81–82
Norway 382

Oak Ridge National Laboratory 240
Obama administration 16–17, 35, 239–40; South China Sea 40
obsolescing bargain cycle 79
offshore boundaries 39, 41
offshore extraction 66
oil and gas income per capita 209
oil assets, size and allocation 386–90
oil-based transport, demand for 14–15
oil boom 2004–8 344–45
oil companies, ownership 264–65
oil consumption 36
oil crisis, 1973–74 113–14
oil curse 4, 9, 73–74; capital-intensiveness 342; context and overview 337–38; GDP growth per head *341*; international pressure 77–78; limiting effects of 76–78; MENA region 181–82; rent cycling theory 339, 341–42; state intervention 342–43; underperformance 341–42 *see also* resource curse
oil demand, and CO_2 prices *426*
oil dependency 112
oil, dispersal of reserves 62
oil embargoes 112–15
oil exporters: international financial roles 393; investment patterns 380

Oil-for-Food Programme 255
oil funds, assets 389
oil imports 36
oil industry, fragmentation 95
oil price bubble 97
oil price explosion 1973 378
oil producers, and climate policy 427–29
oil-producing countries, instability of 4
oil rents 6, 7, 160
oil reserves 18; depletion 39; potential 20; proved reserves 418
oil resource rents, and carbon emissions 427–28
oil resources, measuring 63
oil revenue streams 342
oil revenues: de-linking 188; dependence 367; lack of transparency 76; managing flow 76–77; Middle East 126
oil sands 423
Oil Services Company of Iran (OSCO) 264–65
oil shale 11
oil shocks 114; producer/consumer relations 80–83
oil spills 17
oil stabilization funds 187, 386
oil supply, economics of reduction 138–40
oil transport 138; geopolitics 30; Russian policy 38; uncertainties 19–20
oil wealth: conflict and instability 74–75; nature of 387–89; political effects 74; and separatism 75; trading for services 77 *see also* sovereign wealth funds (SWFs)
oil weapon 112–13; bluntness 139
Oman contract 103–4
Organization of Economic Cooperation and Development (OECD) 81
Organization of Petroleum Exporting Countries (OPEC) 80; Algiers Summit 82; global oil governance 351, 355; hostility to IEA 81; net oil export revenues **382**; oil embargo 113; oil export revenues *243*; price-making power 95, 114; quota policy 90–91; response to taxation 85
Organization of the Arab Petroleum Exporting Countries (OAPEC), and 1973 oil revolution 285–86

Pahlavi, Shah Reza Mohammed 33
paper markets 85–86, 97
Parra, F. 81, 82
passenger cars: blaming 228; and greenhouse gas 226–28; natural gas 237–38; subsidies 221
patronage, Egypt 304
Paulson, Henry 388
PDVSA, management of company 52–53
peak oil 4, 13, 110–12; aboveground factors 66, 67; context and overview 60; defining 60–61; estimating oil resources 63; forecasting 62; investing in future supply 68; nonconventional

441

Index

resources 64–66; political importance 61–62; prices and demand 68–69; public perspective 110–11; reserve estimates 63–64; risk management 61; role of prices 67–68; technology 66–67; uncertainties 62–63
pegging 392
Pelletreau, Robert H. 34
Pemex 168–70
Permanent Income Hypothesis 343
Persia: US interests 33 *see also* Iran
Persian Gulf: geopolitics 33–35, 116–17; military expenditure 183–84
personalized rule 154, 157, 192
Petrobras 8–9; context and overview 325–26; corporate information *326*; establishment and development 326–28; foreign expansion 329; market share 326; R&D 329; regulation 327; role of government 330–32; social capital composition **327**; summary and conclusions 332; technological capabilities 328–29, 330 *see also* Brazil
petrodollar boom 391
petrodollar meltdown 381–83
petrodollar recycling 375, 378–81, 391
petrodollars, and terrorism 242
petroleum industry, uncertainties 3–5
physical trading 100–101
plug-in electric hybrid vehicles (PHEVs) 237, 238, 240, 425
polar oil 65
policy-making 6–7; MENA region 182–85; peak oil 61–62
policy process, Africa 159
political cycles 79
political effects, of oil wealth 74
political leadership, quality of 75
political openness 157, 160
political responses 5
politics, uncertainties of 18
polycentrism 352
Pooley, E. 231
population, Middle East *125*
Portsmouth Treaty 251
possible reserves 64
poverty, and oil funds 49–50
Powell, Colin 229
price bubbles 97, 98
price control 67–68, 140–41
price fixing 401
price-making power 94–95
price risk 85
price shocks 341
prices: 1986 collapse 85, 381; 2008 collapse 86, 386; advance notice for consumers 103; anchors and storms 99–100; Brent market 96–97; China's role in 405–6; co-operative international storage 102, 104; conflict over causes of rises 86; and cooperation 83; and data transparency 84; and demand 68–69, 91, 289; demand security/TOP contracts 102–3, 104; economic costs of production 354; effect of rises 13, 14–15; effects of fall **315**; effects of instability 92–93; Egypt 298–99, 302–3; explosion 1973 378; financialization 97–99; forecasting 91; global oil governance 357–58; instability 90–91; long-term equilibrium 93–94; and peak oil 67–68; physical trading 100–101; and recession 118; reference pricing 96; role of Gulf producers 103–4; Russia 314–15; takers and makers 94–96; taxation 84–85; two tier system 285; USA controls 137; vertical integration 101, 104; volatility 87, 342, 358, 401
pricing 392; in dollars 391
private equity 388
probable reserves 64
producer/consumer dialogue: extended agenda 84; reasons for early failures 82–83; revival of interest 83–87; theoretical approaches 79
producer/consumer relations: context and overview 79–80; early years 80; lack of realism 82; oil shocks 80–83
production and consumption patterns 354–55
production costs: regional variation 12–13; types of oil 12
production sharing agreements (PSAs) 54, 196, 198, 199–200, 257, 298, 351
prospecting 10
protests, MENA region 189
proved reserves 63–64
public choice theory 223
public relations, Aramco 50–51

Qatar 53–54
Quandt, William B. 290
quota policy 90–91, 114, 268, 270

Rapid Deployment Joint Task Force 33, 136
Reagan, Ronald 33–34
recovery and processing, advances in 66–67
reduction of supply 138–40
reference pricing 96
regime change 118
regional markets, China in 407–9
regional security, Middle East 130–31
Renewable Fuel Standard 232
rent cycling theory 339, 341–42, 343
rentier states 8, 206–7
repression, Africa 157
Republic of Congo: conflict and instability 161; economic impacts of oil 154–55
reserve currency 389–90
reserve estimates 63–64
reserves: as contested 116; government-controlled 69; production costs **93**

resilience: of modern economies 140–41; social and political 131
resonance 98
resource curse: academic literature 338–41; Africa 149–50, 153; dual track reform 345–46; oil boom 2004–8 344–45; share of rents and GDP growth *338 see also* oil curse
resource nationalism 69
resource nationalist cycle 79
resource wealth, new political economy 206–7
Ricardo, David 115
rigidity 90
rising sea levels 128
risk management, peak oil 61
risk tolerance, sovereign wealth funds (SWFs) 363–64
risks: hedging 351; from Middle East 116–18; oil supply disruptions 244; from water scarcity 123
Roberts, M.J. 232
Robinson, J. 339
Rogers, Jim 231
Roosevelt, Franklin D. 32
Ross, M. 207
rule of law 180
Russia 8; context and overview 312; economic diversification 320–22; economic roles of oil and gas 312–15; foreign direct investment 318; GDP and oil price **313**; geopolitical initiatives 38; hybrid NOCs 56; investment and imports *320*; long-term strategy 318–20, *319*; modernization 320–22; oil production and consumption **314**; policies and policy options 317–18; prices 314–15; R&D 321; sectoral composition of IFDI *320*; summary and conclusions 322–23; sustainability of energy power 315–17; as wild card 115; working with IOCs 56

Sachs, J.D. 338, 344
sales taxes 84–85
San Remo Agreement 31–32
San Remo Conference 250
sanctions: Iran investors 272; Iraq 253–55
Saudi Arabia 8; 1973 oil revolution 285–86; agricultural development 124–25; climate planning 129; context and overview 284–85; desalination 125; development 127; development assistance 288; financial structure 50; grain production **124**; industrial power 291–92; investments 380; and IOCs 50; markets 289; oil policy 288–90; oil reserves 69; price moderation 85; quota policy 114; role in pricing 100; summary and conclusions 291–92; supply and demand 286–87; Supreme Petroleum Council (SPC) 49; as swing producer 286; and USA 32–33 *see also* Aramco
Savimbi, Jonas 162

scarcity rent 417
Schlenker, W. 232
Schlesinger, James R. 136, 230
Schlumberger, O. 339
Scientific American 241
sea levels 128
Searchinger, T. 232
security, Africa 155–56
Segura, A. 343
selective embargoes 137–38
separatism, and oil wealth 75
Set America Free (SAF) 234–35, 243–44
seven sisters 94–95, 351
shale oils 11, 12, 65
Shanghai Cooperation Association 37, 38
shuttle diplomacy 81
Sinochem 406
Sinopec 55–56
Skocpol, T. 207
Smith, Adam 115
Smith, B. 207, 209
SOCAR 194, 196, 201
social costs, and subsidies 224–26
social justice 187
SOFAZ 194, 196
Solow, R.M. 187–88
South China Sea, territorial claims 39, 40
Southeast Asia 7; conflict and instability 211; context and overview 206; democracy 210–11; descriptive statistics 217; governance 211–12; governance and political freedom *212*; oil and political outcomes 210–12; oil and politics 209–10, *213*; oil export dependence 209–10; oil income and governance **214**; political economy of resource wealth 206–7; research methods 212; research results 212–15; summary and conclusions 216–17 *see also* individual countries
sovereign wealth funds (SWFs) 9, 188; Abu Dhabi Investment Authority (ADIA) 371–72; characteristics 364; context and overview 362–63; defining 363–64; disclosure 388; growth forecasts 386; Gulf Co-operation Council (GCC) 366–69; investment portfolios 364–66; investments and assets 386–88; Kuwait Investment Authority (KIA) 369–70; risk tolerance 363–64; summary and conclusions 372
Soviet Union: collapse 381; as threat to US interests 32–33
Special Drawing Rights (SDR) 377
Spiro, D.E. 378
stability, Africa 155
stagflation 140
stakeholders, Gulf states 130
standards, energy efficiency 17
state building, Africa 156
Statoil 47

443

Index

sterilization 390
Sterner, T. 426
storms and anchors 99–100
strategic advantage 112–13
Strategic Petroleum Reserve 244
strategic petroleum reserves (SPR) 354–55
structural instability, crude oil prices 5
sub-Saharan Africa 6; context and overview 149–50 *see also* Africa
subsidies 67–68, 91, 221, 224–26, 232, 238, 300, 352; Egypt 306
Sudan: Chinese energy security 37; conflict and instability 162–63
Sun, T. 363
super heavy oils 11
supply and demand 286–87; interactions 79
Supreme Petroleum Council (SPC) 49
swing producers 90–91
synthetic oil 65

take or pay (TOP) contracts 102–3, 104
tar sands 11, 64–65; production costs 12
taxation 84–85, 91, 236
technological uncertainties, extraction 13–14
technologies: changing attitudes to 3; disruptive 16; expansion of alternative technologies 421; and peak oil 66–67; relative costs of renewable energies 241; as yet unknown 111
Tehran Agreement 264
Tengiz agreement 191
terrorism 19–20, 242
test drilling 10–11
Tides Center 234–35
Timor-Leste 215–16
total factor productivity (TFP) 301–2
trade expansion, and use of force 115
transparency: Egypt 302; of information 67, 84; market 356
transport: climate change 429; compressed natural gas (CNG) 15; effects of regulation 17; electric 14–15; improving efficiency 15; reducing conventional fuel use 422–27; use of oil 14–15
transportation fallacy 226
Treasury International Capital (TIC) System (USA) 380, 387–88
Turkmenbashi 191–92, 201, 202
Turkmenistan 7, 191–92, 199–200, 201–2; agreement with Iran 274
types of oil 11; regional variation 12–13

UC Central Command (CENTCOM) 33–34
UN Conference on Trade and Development (UNCTAD) 82
UN Convention on the Law of the Sea 39
UN Framework Convention on Climate Change (UNFCCC) 415, 427

UN Security Council (UNSC) 253–55
uncertainties: climate change 18, 417–18; government policy 16–17; petroleum industry 3–5; of politics 18; summary of 20–21; technological 13–14
unconventional oil 11, 12
under-reporting, of reserves 69
United Nations, North South Dialogue 81–82
US Africa Command (AFRICOM) 35–36
US Central Command (CENTCOM) 136
US Climate Action Partnership 230–31
US current account deficit 375
US Geological Survey 40, 63, 64
USA: attracting investment 380; and China 385; corporate average fuel economy (CAFE) standards 223; crude oil imports *242*, *244*; demise of Bretton Woods 376–78; domestic politics 132; embargo on Japan 112–13; energy policies 7; energy security 5–6, 33–36; foreign-held assets *387*; foreign oil dependence 140; foreign policy 5; freezing Iranian assets 380–81; Iran-Libya Sanctions Act (ILSA) 272; lack of climate legislation 17; in MENA region 185; Middle East policy 132; net liabilities to foreigners 388; oil dependency 245; oil imports 18, 243–44; and Persia 33; Persian Gulf 116–18; policy towards Iraq 254–55; price controls 137; regulations and oversight 16–17; relations with Iran 276; and Saudi Arabia 32–33; taxation 236; threats of war for oil 136; top sources of oil imports *138*; Treasury International Capital (TIC) System 380, 387–88
USA alternative energy: biofuels 222; cap and trade 230–31; cars and greenhouse gas 226–28; context and overview 221–23; geo-green economics 242–46; greens and geogreens 223–24; implications and effects 231–33; interest groups 228–29, 233–36; investment 229–30; passenger cars, subsidies 221; social costs and subsidies 224–26; summary and conclusions 246; vehicle emissions studies 240–41
use of force, and trade expansion 115
Uzbekistan 192, 194

Venezuela 170–72, 390; oil production **171**
vertical integration 101, 104, 353
very large crude carriers (VLCCs) 351
Vietnam 216
Villafuerte, M. 344
volatility, prices 92–93

Wagner, R. 223
Walther, Arne 83
war for oil 6; arguments for 135–36; benefit to specific firms 144; cheap oil argument 142; context and overview 135; continued supply

argument 135–41; expensive oil argument 143–44; increased supply argument 141–42; threats 136
Warner, A. 338
Washington Consensus 79–80
waste-based fuels 11–12
water demand 123
water scarcity, Middle East 122–23
West Africa, US energy security 35
West Texas Intermediate (WTI) 96
Western Pacific, territorial claims 39
windfall rents, managing 343
Wolfowitz, Paul 256
Woolsey, R. James 229
World Trade Organization (WTO) 350
World War I 31–32
World War II 32
World Wildlife Foundation 127

Yanbu 291–92
Yemen, fresh water availability 123–24
Yom Kippur War 113–14
yuan 390, 392

Zhang Huachen 37–38
Ziemba, Rachel 389